## A LAWYER'S HANDBOOK FOR ENFORCING FOREIGN JUDGMENTS IN THE UNITED STATES AND ABROAD

This book assists the practitioner seeking to enforce a foreign judgment in the United States or a U.S.-rendered judgment abroad in navigating the lack of procedural uniformity that exists and in planning strategies likely to ensure effective enforcement. As a handbook, it provides the practitioner with a framework and resources with which to approach and further research the laws of the relevant state or country. In Part One, the guide takes the practitioner chronologically through the process of obtaining a U.S. court's recognition and enforcement of judgments rendered abroad. Part Two takes the practitioner through the process of obtaining an overseas jurisdiction's recognition and enforcement of judgments rendered in the United States. Part Three assesses the current trends in the United States and in the international trade environment regarding enforcement of judgments.

Robert E. Lutz is Professor of Law at Southwestern University School of Law in Los Angeles, California. He has held the Treusch and Buchalter Chairs at the law school and teaches a wide variety of public international law, international commercial law, and dispute-resolution subjects. He is a member of the American Law Institute and the Pacific Council on International Policy (affiliate of the Council on Foreign Relations), a Fellow of the American Bar Foundation, and former Chair of the American Bar Association's Section of International Law (2001–2002). He arbitrates public international and private international commercial disputes, actively serves on NAFTA binational arbitration panels, is a member of the NAFTA Advisory Committee on Private Commercial Dispute Resolution and a member of the State Department's Advisory Committee on Public International Law, and is a listed panelist for the World Trade Organization. He was the editor-in-chief of *The International Lawyer* for a number of years and has authored numerous articles, books, and legislation.

# A Lawyer's Handbook for Enforcing Foreign Judgments in the United States and Abroad

**Robert E. Lutz**
Southwestern University School of Law, Los Angeles

CAMBRIDGE
UNIVERSITY PRESS

CAMBRIDGE UNIVERSITY PRESS
Cambridge, New York, Melbourne, Madrid, Cape Town, Singapore, São Paulo

Cambridge University Press
32 Avenue of the Americas, New York, NY 10013-2473, USA

www.cambridge.org
Information on this title: www.cambridge.org/9780521858748



First published 2007

Printed in the United States of America

*A catalog record for this publication is available from the British Library.*

*Library of Congress Cataloging in Publication Data*

Lutz, Robert E.
A lawyer's handbook for enforcing foreign judgments in the United States
and abroad / Robert E. Lutz.
p. cm.
Includes bibliographic references and index.
ISBN-13: 978-0-521-85874-8 (hardback)
ISBN-10: 0-521-85874-7 (hardback)
1. Judgments, Foreign – United States. 2. Judgments, Foreign.
I. Title.
KF8729.L88 2007
347.73′77–dc22 2006051711

ISBN 978-0-521-85874-8 hardback

# Contents

# Preface

This *Handbook* has its genesis in two bibliographies I published in 1993 in *The International Lawyer* on the subject of enforcement of foreign judgments.[1] Those bibliographies were apparently useful to many, so since their publication I have received numerous inquiries from practicing lawyers about the "how to" aspects of enforcing foreign judgments here in the United States and taking U.S.-rendered judgments and having them enforced abroad. Given this interest – and, from my own experience, given that there are quite practical and tactical considerations involved – I decided to put together this *Handbook*.

Because of the press of other demands, this guide at first was just a pile of notes in a folder. Eventually, I developed the notes into a short draft, and then that draft sat gathering dust for almost a decade. Increased opportunities to consult with practitioners about enforcement issues and the added motivation of a publication contract enabled me to revisit and complete the project recently. In doing so, I tried to include the kind of legal and practical guidance that a lawyer initially confronting the prospect of enforcing a foreign judgment would need and find useful. Thus, the guide contains not only "how to" text but also bibliographies that are updated and enlarged from the ones published in 1993, useful forms, and copies of some of the legal instruments (and Web site citations to others).

As Part Three of this *Handbook* demonstrates, the law governing the enforcement of foreign judgments is in flux both in the United States and abroad. While this book attempts to guide practitioners through some of the basic and difficult aspects of inbound and outbound judgment enforcement, the law in this area is experiencing new attention as the globalization of business accelerates. Thus, it is most likely that a book written five years from now will include new issues to which practitioners should be alerted. I am confident,

[1] Robert E. Lutz, *Enforcement of Foreign Judgments, Part I: A Selected Bibliography of U.S. Enforcement of Judgments Rendered Abroad*, 27 Int'l Law. 471–93 (1993); and Robert E. Lutz, *Enforcement of Foreign Judgments, Part II: A Selected Bibliography on Enforcement of U.S. Judgments in Foreign Countries*, 27 Int'l Law. 1029–59 (1993).

however, that what is presented here will continue to describe the basic framework and considerations involved in enforcing foreign judgments.

I hope the user will find this volume helpful and will keep it near his or her desk for frequent consultation.

Los Angeles
August 2005

# Acknowledgments and Dedication

I am grateful for the assistance provided by Southwestern University School of Law, which has generously supported this project in its various iterations over the last decade. In addition to a summer stipend partially supporting the book's development, it provided research assistance. In that regard, I have been pleased to have many students assist with the development of the bibliographies. At the risk of omitting someone, I express my appreciation for the research assistance with the bibliographies to the following present and former students: Debra Belanger, Patrick Benedek, Bill Danziger, C. B. Everitt, Hamed Ghaemmaghami, Ava Sadripour, Fabienne Struell, Mark Tackitt, and Russell Trice. Several students also contributed significantly to researching substantive portions of the text. I gratefully acknowledge the research, drafting, and editing assistance of Fredrick M. Ray and Anna von Franque.

David McFadden, Southwestern's Senior Reference Librarian, has always cheerfully and ably handled all research tasks asked of him – whether simple or complex – and has contributed significantly to the accuracy of the citations of the sources herein. I thank him for his help. A special expression of appreciation is also due John Berger, Senior Editor at Cambridge University Press and a long-time friend, who encouraged me early on to write a book on the subject of enforcement of foreign judgments and patiently awaited its production over the course of a decade.

Also, I have greatly appreciated the interest in my inquiries about foreign judgment issues shown and the advice offered by the many practitioners with whom I have come into contact over the years. They have contributed greatly to my understanding of the practical and strategic aspects of this subject, whether through educational programs sponsored by the bar or via various consulting assignments in which I have been engaged.

Of course, in all respects, I am responsible for the accuracy of what follows.

Finally, I dedicate this work to my wonderful wife, Colleen, who has encouraged me throughout and without whose love and support I would not have been able to write this book.

# Introduction

As world trade steadily increases, transnational corporations proliferate and individuals transact business and personal affairs across borders with increasing frequency. Today's practitioners representing domestic civil litigants face the prospect of guarding against or satisfying judgments rendered by foreign courts. Similarly, these practitioners may seek to obtain and enforce judgments in foreign courts against their clients' foreign adversaries. Practitioners who are in specialties such as bankruptcy, family law, estate planning and probate, personal injury, products liability, intellectual property, and real estate, among others, are likely to encounter the challenge of international recognition and enforcement of judgments. As an aspect of transnational legal practice, international litigation and arbitration have become more complex since the 1960s, when the United States began to emerge from a conflicting and unpredictable common law past to embrace sophisticated uniform statutory approaches[1] to recognition and enforcement of foreign judgments.[2]

Despite these domestic law developments, the United States is one of the few major industrial nations that has not acceded to any international agreements for the recognition

[1] Although no uniform federal statute governs recognition and enforcement of judgments rendered abroad, many of the 50 states have adopted one or more uniform acts. The acts are the Uniform Foreign Money-Judgments Recognition Act, 13-II U.L.A. 39 (2002 & Supp. 2003) [hereinafter Recognition Act]; the Uniform Enforcement of Foreign Judgments Act, 13-I U.L.A. 155 (2002 & Supp. 2003) [hereinafter Enforcement Act]; and the Uniform Foreign-Money Claims Act, 13-II U.L.A. 13 (2002 & Supp. 2003) [hereinafter Claims Act]. *See* Part One, Instruments, Laws, and Other Materials texts and the Bibliography to Part One for a list of jurisdictions that have adopted each act. *Always refer to the adopting state's code for any modifications to the model acts.*

[2] To be enforceable, a foreign judgment must first be recognized. Center for International Legal Studies, International Execution Against Judgment Debtors Int-12 (Dennis Campbell & Suzanne Rodriguez eds. 2004) [hereinafter Campbell]. "Recognition" (used here interchangeably with "conversion") refers to the process whereby the petitioner brings an action, files briefs, and presents argument to persuade a court to give collateral estoppel effect to a foreign country judgment creditor's claim. "Enforcement" (used here also as a synonym for "execution") refers to the process whereby a foreign judgment creditor seeks satisfaction for the judgment debt in a foreign country, leading to satisfaction of the judgment creditor's claim by an asset transfer from the judgment debtor to the judgment creditor. The process follows the following steps: recognition/conversion; enforcement/execution; collection. For further discussion of the distinction among these terms, *see* Ronald A. Brand, *Enforcement of Foreign Money-Judgments in the United States: In Search of Uniformity and International Acceptance*, 67 Notre Dame L. Rev. 253, 278–80 (1991).

and enforcement of civil judgments.[3] Laws of the several states govern recognition and enforcement of civil judgments rendered abroad. However, unlike sister-state judgments rendered in courts in another state jurisdiction, judgments rendered abroad do not enjoy the protection of the U.S. Constitution's Full Faith and Credit Clause.[4] Conversely, absent federal statute, there is no federal preemption.[5]

This text assists the practitioner seeking to enforce a foreign judgment in the United States or a U.S.-rendered judgment abroad in navigating this lack of uniformity. Providing step-by-step instructions would be foolish and perhaps impossible, since procedures vary from state to state and country to country. Instead, this book describes the general sequence of events, some form of which will take place in a given enforcement scenario. As a "handbook," the text also provides the practitioner with a framework with which to approach and further research the laws of the relevant state or country.

Part One of this guide takes the practitioner chronologically through the process of obtaining a U.S. court's recognition and enforcement of judgments rendered abroad. Although these procedures may vary from state to state, this part of the book includes examples of the procedures common to most states. Strategic considerations are highlighted at each stage of preparation and litigation. These considerations should alert the practitioner to areas in which further state-specific research is necessary. A bibliography of statutes, cases, and commentary, and texts of relevant documents and sample forms follow the text.

Part Two takes the practitioner through the process of obtaining an overseas jurisdiction's recognition and enforcement of judgments rendered in the United States. This section of the book describes and analyzes general approaches and strategies that the practitioner might employ abroad. Although further country-specific research will be necessary, these general approaches are meant to guide the practitioner to identify key issues and potential areas of conflict. A bibliography of country laws, conventions, and commentary, and texts of relevant documents follow the text.

Part Three assesses the current trends in the United States and in the international trade environment regarding enforcement of judgments that may be made by foreign courts. A bibliography of conventions, statutes, and cases follows.

[3] American Law Institute, Restatement (Third) of Foreign Relations Law of the United States, ch. 8, Introduction note (1986).

[4] *See Jaffe v. Accredited Surety and Casualty*, 294 F.3d 584 (2002) (neither the Full Faith and Credit Clause nor the full faith and credit statute apply to judgments issued by a foreign country).

[5] Brand, *supra* note 2, at 278–80. However, once recognition of the foreign judgment has been obtained, the foreign judgment becomes subject to the Full Faith and Credit Clause and is enforced as a sister-state judgment. The manner of enforcement is not provided in this act. *Id.* at 278.

**PART ONE**

# Enforcing Foreign Country Judgments in the United States

## I. OVERVIEW

This part of the guide has two purposes: to walk the U.S. practitioner through the procedural steps and strategies for: (1) converting a foreign country judgment to a domestic civil judgment; and (2) enforcing and executing the judgment. While largely the same throughout the states, the exact procedures for conversion, enforcement, and recognition vary from state to state. The laws of California and New York serve as principal examples, but practitioners in other states should refer to their states' versions of the uniform acts, where codified.[1] In states that have not adopted and codified the uniform acts, practitioners should refer to other recognition statutes and common law.

An important distinction regarding the uniform acts must be drawn at the outset. There are three relevant uniform acts that will be discussed. The Uniform Foreign Money-Judgments Recognition Act (abbreviated as UFMJRA, but hereinafter Recognition Act) proscribes procedures through which a foreign country judgment is converted into a judgment of a U.S. court and receives the same status as a sister-state judgment, thereby becoming enforceable in other U.S. fora under the Full Faith and Credit Clause. The 1964 Uniform Enforcement of Foreign Judgments Act (abbreviated as UEFJA, hereinafter Enforcement Act) creates a registration system for the enforcement of sister-state judgments which, in conjunction with the Recognition Act, can provide for more streamlined enforcement of foreign country judgments in jurisdictions that have adopted both acts.[2]

Thus, the difference between recognition and enforcement as ways of describing stages in a larger process is not paralleled by the difference between the Recognition Act and the Enforcement Act. Finally, the Uniform Foreign-Money Claims Act (abbreviated as UFM-CA, hereinafter Claims Act) deals with the conversion of foreign country judgment amounts into U.S. dollars.

Focusing on its practical purpose, this guide discusses the historical development of the law on enforcement of foreign judgments and provides more detailed analyses of the enforcement rules only insofar as these discussions are helpful in understanding the practice of enforcement of foreign country judgments. Furthermore, not all recognition and enforcement situations may fit the procedure outlined here, depending on variations in the statutory or common law of the jurisdiction where enforcement is sought. If, however, the practitioner determines that the matter is one of first impression, citation to the uniform acts and sister-state statutory or common law is often persuasive.

Here is a simplified, chronological checklist of the steps required to obtain recognition and enforcement of a foreign judgment. A detailed discussion of each step follows.

1. **Choosing a jurisdiction**

- Have the parties **expressly agreed to a choice of forum**?
- Does **jurisdiction exist** based on other theories, such as minimum contacts, stream of commerce, *in rem* or quasi-*in rem* jurisdiction, or harmful effects?
- Are there assets of the defendant that can be located and seized?
- Should suit be brought in **federal or state court**?

[1] For the important distinction between the uniform acts and between recognition and enforcement, *see generally* Part One, Introduction, notes 1 and 2.

[2] The Recognition Act was recently revised by the National Conference of Commissioners on Uniform State Laws. *See infra* Part Three, IV.

*Consider*:

- **Diversity**
- **Amount** in controversy
- Docket **backlog**
- **Procedural** differences
- **Court's sophistication**
- **Convenience** to the parties
- **Inconvenient forum** as a possible defense

*Strategy*: If the amount in controversy and diversity apply under 28 U.S.C. §1332(a)(2)–(3), yet you bring the action in state court, the defendant may remove the action to U.S. District Court, pursuant to 28 U.S.C. § 1441(a). Note also that it might be quite common for a foreign citizen to sue a compatriot (who happens to reside in the United States), for enforcement of a foreign judgment. In such a case, only state court will have subject matter jurisdiction to entertain the suit.

If you can choose among **different forum states**, check the **statute of limitations** in each state for the more liberal statute. You may decide to bring suit in the more liberal state and then enforce the judgment as a sister-state judgment elsewhere.

*Exception*: New York, California, and Illinois do not apply the Enforcement Act to recognition of foreign judgments. In these states, you must bring an action to obtain a domestic judgment.

### 2. Authenticating the judgment

- Has the **judgment** been translated and authenticated by the **foreign court**?
- Has the judgment been authenticated by **other** necessary parties?
  - The foreign country's **embassy or consulate in the United States**, *or*
  - A U.S. diplomatic or consular official posted to the **American Embassy or Consulate in that country**, *or*
  - By filing an ***apostille***[3] if the jurisdiction where the judgment was rendered is a party to the Hague Convention on Legalization for Foreign Public Documents[4]

  *Reminder*: Be sure to check the applicable evidence code and local court rules for specific authentication requirements.[5]

  *Reminder*: Be sure that *different people* attest to authentication and issue the authenticating document, whether under chain of authentication or by *apostille*.

### 3. Determining Whether the uniform acts apply

- Has the state where you seek recognition and enforcement adopted *both*:
  - The Recognition Act, *and*
  - The Enforcement Act, *and*
  - Is *not* New York?

[3] *See infra* Part One, II.B.1.a.

[4] 527 U.N.T.S. 189, T.I.A.S. 10072, 20 I.L.M. 1405–14 (1981) [hereinafter Legalization Convention], available at http://www.travel.state.gov/family/hague_foreign_docs.html. *See* Part One, Instruments, Laws, and Other Materials.

[5] *See, e.g.*, FED. R. CIV. P. 44(A)(2); FED. R. EVID. 902(3); CAL. EVID. CODE §§ 1450–4 (West 1987).

- If so, **GO TO STEP** 6.
- Otherwise (most states), **CONTINUE TO STEP** 4.[6]

4. **Preparing and filing the complaint (MOST STATES)**

- Has the complaint been prepared and filed under the jurisdiction's **statutory or common law framework** for recognition?
- Have you included a prayer for **damages plus interest**?

  *Consider*: If the jurisdiction has adopted the Claims Act, a **foreign-money claim** may be permitted; for example, in California.[7]

5. **Anticipating defenses (MOST STATES)**

- Is your judgment a *non-conclusive, unenforceable judgment* due to any of the following?
  - No personal jurisdiction
  - No subject matter jurisdiction
  - Court rendering judgment was not impartial or due process violated.
- Could the judge choose not to recognize the judgment on a discretionary basis?
  - Insufficient notice by foreign court.
  - Judgment obtained by fraud.
  - Cause of action violates your state's public policy.
  - Judgment conflicts with another final and conclusive judgment.
  - Foreign proceeding contrary to express agreement between the parties.
  - Seriously inconvenient forum if jurisdiction based only upon personal service.
  - No final judgment rendered.
  - Parallel proceedings in other U.S. courts consolidation/transfer/removal.

6. **Moving for summary judgment (MOST STATES)**

- Can you show that a **final judgment has been obtained in a foreign court**[8] and move for summary judgment?
  - If yes, **GO TO STEP** 8.
  - If no, **CONTINUE TO STEP** 7.

  *Strategy*: Courts may deny enforcement of a foreign judgment to protect the state's interest, represented by a domestic defendant's property within the court's

[6] In California, the Recognition Act, CAL. CODE CIV. PROC. § 1713.3 (West 1987 & Supp. 2005), explicitly prohibits use of the Sister-State Money Judgments Act for registration of foreign country judgments. Instead, you must obtain recognition of the foreign judgment as a domestic judgment. For the importance of the distinction between the uniform acts and between recognition and enforcement generally, *see supra* Part One, Introduction, notes 1 and 2.

[7] CAL. CODE CIV. PROC. §§ 676–676.1 (West 1987 & Supp. 2005). For other states that have adopted the Uniform Foreign-Money Claims Act, *see* 13-II U.L.A. 13 § 4 (2002 & Supp. 2005).

[8] The summary judgment motion rests on two theories: vested rights and its derivative theory creating a legal obligation of the court of the plaintiff's forum. Concisely, the two theories seek to achieve stability and continuity by recognizing that a right declared by a foreign court should be binding in the forum court's jurisdiction. Campbell, *supra* Introduction, note 2. These theories have today generally replaced the theory of comity of nations, expressed in *Hilton v. Guyot*, 159 U.S. 113 (1895).

jurisdiction. Therefore, to persuade the court to weigh the competing domestic and foreign interests in the foreign plaintiff's favor, show any or all of the following:

- Defendant had at least minimum contact with the jurisdiction.
- Defendant had other, substantial links to the jurisdiction.
- The subject matter of the litigation centers in the jurisdiction.

7. **Litigating**

- Have you properly filed an **action for conversion** (recognition)?
- Are you prepared to plead the claim *ab initio*, including anticipating defenses, such as claim or issue preclusion?

  *Warning*: If the **statute of limitations** is about to run, you should plead the underlying cause of action alternatively to the action for conversion of the judgment.

- Have you brought a complaint for **recognition of the judgment debt** under the jurisdiction's statutory or common law framework, including a prayer for damages?

  *Note*: Generally such damages would be in U.S. currency, but the Claims Act[9] may permit prayer for damages in a foreign currency.

  *Reminder*: Be sure to include interest and reasonable attorney's fees, if appropriate.

8. **Filing and executing the judgment**

- Have you filed the judgment with the **court clerk** and paid the statutory filing fee?
- Have you waited the **statutory period** before proceeding to execution?
- Have you filed the necessary **motions to prevent removal of assets** and to **seize defendant's assets**?

  *Exception*: If defendant shows that an **appeal** from the foreign judgment is **pending** or will be taken, **enforcement may be stayed** until the appeal is concluded, the time for appeal expires, or the stay of execution expires or is vacated.

9. **Registering the judgment**

- Have you **filed** with the court clerk under Enforcement Act §§ 2–3?

  *Note*: Confirm that § 3 of the Recognition Act and common law precedent in your jurisdiction do not exclude use of the Enforcement Act as the enforcement method.

- If satisfaction is not forthcoming, have you obtained a **writ of execution** and conducted discovery, if necessary?
- Have you filed a **lien** on the judgment debtor's assets?
- Once satisfied, have you filed a **satisfaction of judgment**?

[9] 13-II U.L.A. 13 § 4 (2002 & Supp. 2005).

# II. PHASE ONE: BEFORE RECOGNITION

## A. CHOOSING A JURISDICTION/LOCATING ASSETS

### 1. Jurisdiction and Venue

First decide in which state and where in the state to bring the action. Choosing a state in which to enforce your judgment is fairly simple if both the judgment debtor and his assets are in the same state. Even if the judgment creditor does not reside in that state, an enforcement judgment from the debtor's home state will be enforceable in the creditor's home state via Full Faith and Credit. The standard governing all questions of personal jurisdiction is minimum contacts with the forum state, fair play, and substantial justice (the "minimum contacts test"). Although this standard is easily met in the above situation, issues of personal jurisdiction may complicate matters if out-of-state assets are involved.

Since *Shaffer v. Heitner*, 433 U.S. 186 (1977), the minimum contacts standard applies even in *in rem* and quasi-*in-rem* actions. Most *in rem* cases will meet this threshold, and an *in rem* judgment by a court with jurisdiction is valid in all jurisdictions, as the Supreme Court recognized in *Hilton v. Guyot*.[1] Thus, if the judgment will likely be satisfied by the seizure of real property, choose a court in the jurisdiction where the *res* is located. Quasi-*in-rem* bases of jurisdiction – for example, out of state bank accounts, real estate or pension plans – are more problematic. In order to establish personal jurisdiction in a state where such assets are located, it is necessary to establish some other ties between the debtor and the forum state. The court's inquiry into these ties will be the modern, multi-factor minimum contacts test, but it will pragmatically be focused on issues of fairness. If assets are scattered among various jurisdictions, you may now want to skip to Section IV. Phase Three: Executing a Converted Judgment in U.S. Courts and consider what assets are preferable for collection.[2]

### 2. Choice of Forum: Federal or State Court

**a. Generally:** Under the *Erie* doctrine, state common law or the Recognition Act as enacted by the state legislature applies in federal court actions for the enforcement of foreign country judgments.[3] You may decide to bring the case for enforcement in federal court after considering the following factors:

- **Diversity**
- **Amount** in controversy
- Docket **backlog**
- **Procedural** differences
- **Court's sophistication**
- Convenience to the parties
- Inconvenient forum as a possible defense

[1] 159 U.S. 113, 167 (1895).
[2] For guidance as to the law of jurisdiction in various states and in federal courts, *see* Part One, Bibliography.
[3] *See Erie Railroad Co. v. Tompkins*, 304 U.S. 64, 58 S. Ct. 817 (1938).

To do so, you must show diversity of citizenship and amount in controversy exceeding $75,000.[4]

**b. Federal or state court?**[5] The *Erie* doctrine reflects federal policy discouraging forum shopping between federal and state courts, thereby minimizing the differences between the two forums. However, differences between the courts may still influence your forum selection. Selecting federal court might favor the plaintiff's case for enforcement for two reasons: (1) federal courts have had more experience in enforcing foreign judgments; and (2) these courts benefit from informed support from research staff. Before you choose federal court, however, research case law interpretations of your state's recognition law to determine if federal or state courts more consistently favor recognition. California state courts are widely familiar with the adjudication of foreign judgments, but they tend to be more stringent in recognizing[6] and effectuating such claims.[7] Furthermore, in dealing with the Recognition Act, the California state courts account for reciprocity as a factor more so than the federal courts.[8] New York state courts, by contrast, take a more restrictive view of reciprocity as grounds for non-recognition.[9]

**c. Burden of proof:** Regardless of which forum you select, the judgment creditor has the burden of proving that the court should recognize the foreign judgment.[10] Show that the authenticated foreign judgment confirms that a foreign court had proper jurisdiction; that the judgment debtor received notice; that a final judgment issued; and that there is no public policy conflict. Also argue that reciprocity weighs in favor of recognition.[11] For example, the defendant in *Banque Libanaise Pour Le Commerce v. Khreich* argued as an affirmative defense that the recognition of foreign judgments in Abu Dhabi was done at the discretion of the trial judge, and that this was in practice quite rare.[12] Although the court explicitly rejected any notion that reciprocity was a requirement for recognition,[13] it did consider it in addition to the defendant's due process defense.[14]

**d. Defenses:** If defendant can show that the foreign court had no proper jurisdiction, that the defendant did not receive notice, that no final judgment was issued or that an appeal is pending or anticipated, or that enforcement of the judgment violates public policy,

[4] 28 U.S.C. § 1332(a).

[5] For a detailed discussion of forum selection, *see* ROBERT C. CASAD, JURISDICTION AND FORUM SELECTION, ch. 6 (1988, Supp. 1998); *see also* DAVID EPSTEIN, JEFFREY L. SNYDER & CHARLES S. BALDWIN IV, INTERNATIONAL LITIGATION: A GUIDE TO JURISDICTION, PRACTICE AND STRATEGY, ch. 6 (1998).

[6] *Julen v. Larson*, 101 Cal. Rptr. 796 (1972); *In Re Estate of O'Dea's*, 105 Cal. Rptr. 756 (1973).

[7] *Herczog v. Herczog*, 9 Cal. Rptr. 5 (1960).

[8] *In Re Estate of Kraemer*, 81 Cal. Rptr. 287 (1969).

[9] *Cowans v. Ticonderoga Pulp & Paper Co.*, 219 N.Y.S. 284, 286–7 (1927).

[10] *Hernandez v. Seventh Day Adventists*, 54 S.W.3d 335, 335 (2001) (if a foreign judgment is not facially final, the judgment creditor bears the burden of producing evidence demonstrating the judgment is final); *Shen v. Lao A. Daly*, 222 F.3d 472, 476 (2000) (burden of proof of preclusive effect is on the party seeking to have judgment recognized).

[11] The reciprocity doctrine, enunciated in *Hilton v. Guyot*, 159 U.S. 113 (1895), is not favored in most states that have adopted the Recognition Act. *See infra* Part One, III.C.8; *see also Nicol v. Tanner*, 310 Minn. 68, 68 (1976) (reciprocity not a prerequisite for enforcement of a foreign judgment if the foreign court had jurisdiction and fully adjudicated the issues).

[12] 915 F.2d 1000, 1005–6 (5th Cir. 1990).

[13] *Id.* at 1005.

[14] *Id.* at 105, n.4.

the court will likely find the Enforcement Act void on one or more of these grounds. Therefore, plaintiff will have to litigate the claim *ab initio*.

### 3. Choice of Venue: Defenses

Defendants to enforcement of foreign judgments have two major weapons in their arsenal regarding venue: *forum non conveniens*[15] and transfer between courts in the federal system, assuming no contrary agreement between the parties. Defendants can also seek to have the suit removed to state court, causing delay and expense for plaintiff.[16]

### 4. Preemption

The United States is not a party to any international agreements to enforce foreign judgments, nor are there any relevant federal statutes; therefore, state law, under the *Erie* doctrine, governs foreign country judgments in federal court, as well as state court.[17]

## B. EVIDENTIARY REQUIREMENTS: COPY OF THE JUDGMENT

### 1. Authentication

Meeting state evidence code requirements for admissibility of the foreign judgment presents one of the more procedurally complex requirements in enforcing foreign judgments.[18] Generally, federal courts presume that properly attested to foreign documents are authentic.[19] For a foreign public document to be self-authenticating, state and federal statutes require both the attestation of an official of the adjudicating country that the judgment is authentic and a final statement certifying that the signature of the foreign official is valid.[20]

**a. Simplified authentication:** If the foreign jurisdiction is a party to the Hague Convention on Legalization of Foreign Public Documents,[21] completion of a standardized

[15] Discussed *infra* Part One, III.C.2.d. *Chong v. Superior Court of Los Angeles*, 68 Cal. Rptr. 2d. 427 (1997) is an example of the court determining that Hong Kong would be a more suitable forum.

[16] *See* 28 U.S.C. § 1441, *et seq.*

[17] The argument that federal law should govern the enforcement of foreign country judgments has been unsuccessful, except as applied to the act of state doctrine. *Banco Nacional de Cuba v. Sabbatino*, 376 U.S. 398, 84 S. Ct. 923 (1964).

[18] For federal courts, refer to Fed. R. Civ. P. 44(a)(2) and Fed. R. Evid. 902(3).

[19] Fed. R. Evid. 902(3).

[20] For example, Cal. Evid. Code § 1530(3) specifies the procedure for obtaining attestation that the copy of the foreign country judgment is a correct copy of the writing or entry. The court generally requires, in addition to the attestation, a final statement certifying the genuineness of the signature. The court may, however, admit the attested copy without the final statement for good cause shown.

[21] *See* Part One, I at note 4. The Convention is *in force* for the United States and the following countries and territories: Andorra, Angola, Anguilla, Antigua and Barbuda, Argentina, Armenia, Aruba, Australia, Austria, Bahamas, Barbados, Belarus, Belgium, Belize, Bermuda, Bosnia-Herzegovina, Botswana, British Antarctic Territory, British Virgin Islands, Brunei, Bulgaria, Cayman Islands, Comoros Islands (formerly Moroni), Croatia, Cyprus, Djibouti (formerly Affars and Issas), Dominica, El Salvador, Falkland Islands, Fiji, Finland, France, French Guiana, French Polynesia, Guadeloupe, Germany, Gibraltar, Greece, Grenada, Guernsey (Bailiwick of), Hong Kong, Hungary, Isle of Man, Israel, Italy, Japan, Jersey (Bailiwick of), Kiribati (formerly

authentication form, called an *apostille*, affixed to the original document in lieu of the generally required chain of authentication, will verify the document's authenticity.[22]

**b. Procedure**

1) **Obtaining authentication:** The seeking party must ascertain whether the jurisdiction requires chain of authentication or whether apostille authentication is sufficient.[23] Be sure that different people attest to authentication and issue the final statement under the chain of authentication, or certify and issue the apostille. The Department of State issues apostilles for documents to be certified through federal agencies on a country-by-country basis. Forms can be obtained from the United States Department of State, Authentications Office, 518 23rd St., N.W., Washington, D.C. 20520 (telephone: 202-647-5002; voice mail with information options: 1-800-688-9889). For authentication of state documents, contact the specific state's Office of the Secretary of State (addresses and other information available at www.travel.state.gov/family/hague_foreign_docs.html).

2) **Seal:** The seal of the issuing country or one of its public entities must appear on the authenticating document. The seal is presumed genuine if the United States recognizes that nation.[24]

3) **Translations:** There are no "official" translations in U.S. courts; usually, a translation will be accepted as accurate. Some courts, however, have refused to accept a translation of an official document without admissible evidence that the translation is correct.[25] To avoid this problem, you can: (1) have the diplomatic official who issues the final statement attest to and certify the translation of the copy of the judgment together with the copy of the judgment and/or; (2) obtain a translation from a translator with whom the court is familiar and whom it knows to be reliable.

4) **Proof of service:** In addition to submitting proof of service of the complaint in the U.S. jurisdiction, you should also submit proof of service in the foreign jurisdiction, such as a copy of the summons and documents showing receipt (and translation, if applicable) together with a copy of the judgment and translation.[26] Note that the translation of the service of process itself may become an issue in assessing the adequacy of service. In *Jules v. Larson*, the California Court of Appeals found that the defendant had not been properly served in a Swiss lawsuit because the documents of service were in German.[27]

Gilbert Islands), Latvia, Lesotho, Liechtenstein, Luxembourg, Macao, Macedonia, Malawi, Malta, Marshall Islands, Martinique, Mauritius, Mexico, Montserrat, Mozambique, Netherlands, Netherlands Antilles (Curacao, Bonaire, St. Martin, St. Eustatius, and Saba), New Caledonia, Norway, Panama, Portugal, Reunion, Russian Federation, St. Christopher (Kitts) and Nevis, St. Georgia and South Sandwich Islands, St. Helena, St. Lucia, St. Pierre and Miquelon, St.Vincent and the Grenadines, San Marino, Seychelles, Slovenia, Solomon Islands (formerly British Solomon Islands), South Africa, Spain, Suriname, Swaziland, Switzerland, Tonga, Turkey, Turks and Caicos, Tuvalu (formerly Ellice Islands), United Kingdom, Vanuatu (formerly New Hebrides), Wallis, and Futuna.

[22] *See* Part One, Instruments, Laws, and Other Materials for the *apostille* form.

[23] *See* Bruno Ristau, International Judicial Assistance 341–45 (2000) [hereinafter Ristau]; *see generally Hernandez v. Seventh Day Adventist Corp., Ltd.*, 54 S.W.3d 335 (2001) (authentication is a prerequisite to recognition proceedings).

[24] *See, e.g.*, Cal. Evid. Code § 1452 (West 1995 & Supp. 2005).

[25] *Smith v. California Portland Cement Co.*, 134 Cal. App. 630, 632, 25 P.2d 1013, 1013 (1933).

[26] *See, e.g.*, 101 Cal. Rptr. 796 (not sufficient service if not translated); *but see Tahan v. Hodgson*, 66 F.2d 862 (1981) (service not translated but sufficient because in accordance with domestic law).

[27] 101 Cal. Rptr. 796, 797 (1972).

The court stressed that the service papers did not "give notice of the [legal] nature of the documents," were not "informative," and were therefore "ineffective."[28] In *Tahan v. Hodgon*, however, a District of Columbia Court of Appeals sustained a default Israeli judgment against a man who had been served with documents written in Hebrew.[29] Although the defendant could not read Hebrew, the court stressed that the defendant "had done business is Israel for many years" and should have been able to deduce the legal nature of the documents.[30] Moreover, the court reasoned that it would be "insulting" to require Israeli lawyers to translate such documents.[31]

[28] *Id.* at 798.

[29] 662 F.2d 862, 865 (1981).

[30] *Id.* at 865.

[31] *Id.*

## III. PHASE TWO: CONVERTING THE JUDGMENT

### A. CONVERSION METHODS UNDER THE RECOGNITION ACT

The following material explores the various methods for obtaining recognition of a foreign judgment. Inasmuch as 29 states, Washington, D.C., and the Virgin Islands have adopted the Recognition Act at this writing,[1] the Act is the principal enforcement vehicle. The discussion also explores alternative strategies for use either in the absence of or in conjunction with pleading under the Act.

#### 1. Conversion Under the Uniform Foreign Money-Judgments Recognition Act: Introduction

The Recognition Act[2] converts foreign country money judgments, excluding tax and domestic relations judgments, and penalties, into judgments entitled to the same recognition as those of sister states, under the Full Faith and Credit Clause.[3] The Recognition Act codifies common law on recognition of judgments, so the Act's elements, and their requirements and interpretation will be relevant to any pleading for recognition of a judgment rendered abroad. Note that the Recognition Act applies to judgments rendered by foreign courts outside the United States and its territories, commonwealths, districts, or other possessions.[4] However, Recognition Act § 7 does not prevent the recognition of judgments that do not fall within the Act, at the jurisdiction's discretion.[5]

#### 2. Conversion by Common Law Action

In states that have not adopted the uniform act, a plaintiff may bring an action under common law to enforce a foreign country money judgment. If the action succeeds, the court will recognize the judgment. A judgment obtained by a common law action, in which the judgment debtor receives notice and can raise grounds for non-recognition as well as all defenses, can then be enforced in other domestic jurisdictions based on extension of full faith and credit to sister-state judgments.[6]

[1] *See* Part One, Bibliography. If you seek recognition and enforcement in Puerto Rico of a judgment rendered abroad, see Part Two, Enforcing Foreign Judgments Abroad, for a discussion of the *exequatur* procedure (requiring a petition to a special court with exclusive jurisdiction of recognition proceedings); *see also* 31 P.R. Laws Ann. § 7 (2002). If you seek recognition and enforcement in Guam of a judgment rendered abroad, *see* 6 Guam Code Ann. § 4214–15 (2003).

[2] The first step in selecting a recognition strategy is to check the forum state's statute of limitations. If the statute has or will shortly run in the first choice state, you may be able to bring suit in another state with a more liberal statute. The most recent proposed revision draft of the Recognition Act contains a 15-year statute of limitation, or the time period in which the judgment is enforceable in the rendering country, whichever is earlier. You can then enforce any judgment you obtain as a sister-state judgment under the Full Faith and Credit Clause, except in New York, California, and Illinois, where you must bring an action to obtain a domestic judgment. On the other hand, if significant time remains before the statute runs, it may be wise to plead under the Recognition Act only. If only a short time remains, you should consider pleading in the alternative.

[3] Brand, *supra* Introduction, at note 2.

[4] *See* Part One, Instruments, Laws, and Other Materials.

[5] The most recent proposed revision of the Recognition Act makes clear, however, that the law is to apply to only foreign *country* judgments. National Conference of Commissioners on Uniform State Laws, Uniform Foreign Country Money Judgments Recognition Act (2005) [hereinafter Revised Recognition Act]. *See* Part One, Instruments, Laws and Other Materials.

[6] U.S. Const. art. IV, § 1; 28 U.S.C. § 1738 (1982).

A common law action is the only way to obtain recognition and to enforce a foreign country money judgment in states that have not adopted both the Recognition and Enforcement Acts. Nonetheless, in states that have adopted both Acts, a judgment creditor may still bring an action for recognition. If the judgment creditor has brought an unsuccessful summary judgment motion, the underlying cause of action will have to be litigated in order to obtain an enforceable judgment.

### 3. Conversion by Registration

In states that have adopted both the Recognition Act and the Enforcement Act,[7] simplified procedures under the Enforcement Act are available for registering a foreign judgment under the Recognition Act, § 3.[8] Generally, the Act provides for registration of a foreign country money judgment, according to the state's version of the uniform act. Registration under the Enforcement Act allows the judgment creditor to attach a specified form to the authenticated judgment and to file it with the court clerk. If a state has not adopted the Recognition Act, the only means of obtaining and enforcing a domestic judgment is by bringing a common law action for enforcement.[9]

**a. The California and New York exceptions:** California[10] (which has a statute similar to the Enforcement Act) and New York[11] have adopted non-uniform versions of the Recognition Act, which in § 3 specifically prohibit using this simplified procedure for foreign country money judgments. The California act provides that foreign country money judgments cannot be entered and enforced as sister-state judgments. Rather, a judgment creditor must bring an action in California to obtain a domestic judgment.[12] If successful, the money judgment may be entered in a foreign currency, under the Claims Act.[13]

In New York, a judgment creditor cannot apply the Enforcement Act's registration procedures to foreign-country money judgments. The judgment creditor must bring a plenary action or a motion action, even if the foreign judgment was entered on default for defendant's failure to appear.[14]

[7] At this writing, Alaska, Colorado, Connecticut, Delaware, D.C., Florida, Georgia, Hawaii, Idaho, Illinois, Iowa, Maine, Maryland, Michigan, Minnesota, Missouri, Montana, New Jersey, New Mexico, New York, North Carolina, Ohio, Oklahoma, Oregon, Pennsylvania, Texas, Virgin Islands, Virginia, and Washington.

[8] Be certain to confirm that your state's version of § 3 of the Recognition Act does not limit use of Enforcement Act procedures to sister-state judgments only, and that case law interpreting this simplified procedure has not narrowed or proscribed its use. Grounds for limiting use of the Enforcement Act registration procedure include, among others, denial of due process. *See, e.g.*, *Don Docksteader Motors, Ltd. v. Patal Enter., Ltd.*, 794 S.W.2d 760, 761 (1990). The proposed revision of the Recognition Act, however, explicitly rejects recognition by registration, stating that the policies weighing in favor of this process between sister-states are inapplicable to foreign country judgments. *See* Draft Revised Recognition Act, *supra* note 5, at Reporter's Notes for § 5.

[9] *Id.*

[10] CAL. CODE CIV. PROC. § 1713.3 (West 1987 & Supp. 2005). *See* Part One, Instruments, Laws, and Other Materials.

[11] N.Y. C.P.L.R. § 5303 (McKinney 1997 & Supp. 2005).

[12] *Supra* note 10. *See also* RICK SCHWARTZ & ALAN M. AHART, CALIFORNIA PRACTICE GUIDE: ENFORCING JUDGMENTS AND DEBTS, ch. 6 (1988, Supp. 2003) [hereinafter SCHWARTZ & AHART].

[13] CAL. CODE CIV. PROC. § 676, *et seq.* (West 1987 & Supp. 2005). *See generally* discussion at I. Overview, *supra*.

[14] N.Y. C.P.L.R. §§ 5401, 3213 (West 1997).

## B. THE COMPLAINT

In states that have not adopted any of the uniform acts, or that have adopted both, requirements for the complaint are dictated by the common law or uniform acts, respectively. In states that have adopted that Recognition Act but not the Enforcement Act (e.g., California and New York), the complaint for conversion of the foreign judgment to a domestic judgment must identify:

- Parties
- Name and place of the foreign court
- Cause of action
- Time, place, and amount of judgment
- Amount outstanding on the judgment[15]

Be sure to attach an authenticated copy of the judgment or an apostille if the country that adjudicated the underlying cause of action is a party to the Hague Legalization Convention.[16]

Once in court, plaintiff should move for summary judgment on the pleadings. If the court denies the motion, plaintiff will have to litigate it on the merits.

## C. SELECTED KEY PROVISIONS OF THE RECOGNITION ACT

### 1. Conclusiveness Requirement

**a. Plaintiff:** Under the Act,[17] the foreign judgment must be conclusive, as determined by the law of the foreign jurisdiction.[18] Therefore, plaintiff must plead and prove that the foreign judgment is entitled to recognition. A judgment creditor may satisfy this requirement simply by the judgment being facially final under the law of the foreign state, as was the case in *Hernandez v. Seventh Day Adventist Corp., Ltd.*[19] In that case, a Texas Court of Appeals held that, absent convincing evidence from the defendant as to the judgment's invalidity, the judgment was to be considered conclusive.[20] Proof of a foreign judgment's finality may also require further evidence. For example, in *Black Clawson v. Kroenert*, the Eighth Circuit recognized a German settlement agreement as a final judgment after plaintiffs presented proof of a German court's "accepting the settlement agreement and dismissing the [original German] case with prejudice."[21]

[15] *See generally* John J. Baer, *Strategies in Framing Pleadings under the Uniform Foreign Money Recognition Act*, Enforcement in California of Judgments Rendered Abroad (International Law Section, State Bar of California 1988). *See also* Uniform Foreign-Money Claims Act, *supra* Part One, Introduction, at note 1.

[16] *See supra* Part One, III.B.

[17] Recognition Act; Cal. Code Civ. Proc. § 1713 (West 1987 & Supp. 2005), *et seq.*

[18] *See Alberta Securities v. Ryckman*, 30 P.3d 121, 126 (2001) (conclusiveness is a requirement for recognition and enforcement); *Nicor International v. El Paso*, 292 F. Supp. 2d 1357, 1365 (2003) (conclusiveness is a requirement for recognition); *Gonzalez v. Lebensversicherung* A.G., 761 N.Y.S.2d2, 3 (2003) (considering the finality of a judgment under Spanish law).

[19] 54 S.W.3d 335, 337 (Tex. App. 2001).

[20] *Id.* at 337.

[21] 245 F.3d 759, 764 (8th Cir. 2001).

A foreign judgment that is final and conclusive between the parties will be enforceable even if an appeal will be taken or is pending in a foreign jurisdiction.[22] The revised Recognition Act[23] emphasizes, however, that conclusiveness, finality, and enforceability are three *separate* requirements that must be established under the laws of the foreign country.

**b. Defendant:** Defendant may have to move to stay the proceeding because an appeal will be taken or is pending in a foreign jurisdiction.[24] In doing this, the defendant should argue that the "final and conclusive" standard is set by the country whose laws categorize cases on which appeals are pending as inconclusive. The defendant in *Korea Water Resources v. Lee* argued unsuccessfully that such a Korean Civil Code standard should preclude enforcement of a Korean judgment in California until all Korean appeals were concluded.[25] In *Mayekawa v. Sasaki*, however, the Washington Court of Appeals held that a Japanese judgment that was enforceable – but still not conclusive under the Japanese Civil Code – did not meet the conclusiveness requirement, and stayed enforcement proceedings.[26]

The court has the power to stay the proceeding on these grounds until the appeal has been determined or until a sufficient amount of time to prosecute the appeal expires, provided that the delay does not prejudice plaintiff. Defendant may have to provide adequate security for payment of the judgment, should the foreign court affirm the judgment.[27] However, a judgment subject to modification by the foreign court will probably not meet the conclusiveness requirement.[28]

**c. Mandatory non-recognition:** Under the Recognition Act,[29] a U.S. court must find that a foreign country judgment is not conclusive and, therefore, not entitled to recognition, on three grounds:

> ***Firstly***, if the judgment was rendered under a system that does not provide impartial tribunals or procedures compatible with due process of law, the foreign judgment would not be conclusive and entitled to recognition.[30] In making this determination, courts will not inquire into whether specific proceedings conformed with U.S. Due Process standards, but rather into the country's judiciary system as a whole.[31] If the defendant in the foreign

[22] *But see Mayekawa v. Sasaki*, 888 P.2d 183, 186–8 (1995); 76 Wash. App. 791, 797–8 (1995) (notwithstanding that Japanese preliminary judgment on promissory notes was immediately enforceable in Japan, foreign judgment was not "final and conclusive" under Japanese civil code as required for enforcement under Recognition Act).

[23] *See supra* note 5.

[24] *Id.*

[25] 8 Cal. Rptr. 3d 853, 859 (Cal. App. 2004).

[26] 888 P.2d at 186–8.

[27] *See* Recognition Act §6. *See, e.g.*, CAL.CODE CIV. PROC. §1713 (West 1987 & Supp. 2005), *et seq.*

[28] *See generally Herczog v. Herczog*, 9 Cal. Rptr. 5 (1960).

[29] Recognition Act § 4; CAL. CODE CIV. PROC. § 1713.4 (West 1987 & Supp. 2005).

[30] *See* Jay Conison, *What Does Due Process Have to Do with Jurisdiction?* 46 RUTGERS L. REV. 1073 (1994); *see, e.g, Bank Melli Iran v. Pahlavi*, 58 F.3d 1406, 1411 (1995) (foreign default judgments against sister of former Shah of Iran would not be enforced, since she could not have obtained fair trial in courts of Iran at time of judgments); *S.C Chimexim v. Velco*, 36 F. Supp. 2d 206 (1999) (discussing impartiality of tribunal of former communist country); *Bridgeway Corp. v. Citibank*, 201 F.3d 134, 140 (2000) (voluntary participation in proceedings of foreign court does not estop the defense that the foreign court was unfair or not impartial); *Society of Lloyd's v. Ashenden*, 233 F.3d 473, 476–7 (2000) (impartiality and uniform act concept of due process are not equivalent to the U.S. concept of Due Process).

[31] *Society of Lloyds v. Mullins*, 255 F. Supp. 2d 468, 472 (2003) (Recognition Act required a "panoramic exam" of English judiciary).

action did not receive timely notice or if the judgment was obtained by extrinsic fraud, the U.S. court will find that the foreign judgment was not conclusive. For example, the defendant in *Srichanchao v. Reedstrom* made an extrinsic fraud argument claiming that "the parties Polupei counsel colluded against respondent."[32] In *de la Mata v. American Life Ins.*, the defendant successfully precluded recognition by arguing that the plaintiff's failure to tell a Bolivian court about her waiver of all claims under the insurance policy at issue in the Bolivian suit constituted extrinsic fraud.[33] However, courts will generally not inquire into fairness; rather, the defendant must raise fairness or impartiality as a defense.[34] For example, the defendant could argue that fairness does not allow *res judicata* to bar suit subsequent to a default judgment.[35]

***Secondly***, if the foreign court did not have personal jurisdiction over the defendant, the foreign judgment is not conclusive and would not be entitled to recognition and/or enforcement.[36] The Recognition Act § 5(a)[37] lists six alternative mandatory bases on which the U.S. court shall base a finding of the foreign court's personal jurisdiction:

(1) The defendant was personally served in the foreign state;

(2) The defendant voluntarily appeared and submitted to personal jurisdiction;[38]

(3) The defendant agreed to submit before the proceeding to the foreign court's jurisdiction regarding the subject matter (e.g., in a contract clause);

(4) The defendant was domiciled or was a corporate defendant incorporated or with headquarters in the jurisdiction;

(5) The defendant had a business office in the foreign state and the cause of action arose from defendant's business done through that office in the foreign state; or

(6) The defendant was operating a vehicle or airplane in the foreign jurisdiction and the cause of action arose from that operation.

***Thirdly***, if the foreign court did not have subject matter jurisdiction, the foreign judgment is not conclusive and is not entitled to recognition and/or enforcement.[39] Most courts have continued to recognize additional bases for jurisdiction. A Texas district court found subject matter jurisdiction in an English action regarding the expropriation of an American-owned oil concession in Libya based on the English court's general jurisdiction.[40] Be sure to research your jurisdiction's case law before asserting or countering any defenses.

[32] 1997 W.L. 461176 (Minn. App. 1997, *5).

[33] 771 F. Supp. 1375 (D.C. Del. 1991).

[34] Campbell, *supra* Introduction, note 2 at US-9, n.32.

[35] *Van Den Biggelaar v. Wagner*, 978 F. Supp. at 856 (D.C.N. Ind. 1997).

[36] *See, e.g., CIBC Mellon Trust v. Mora Hotel*, 762 N.Y.S.2d5, 10–11 (2003) (corporations' voluntary appearance in English court subjected them to personal jurisdiction in England); *Wimmer Canada v. Abele Tractor*, 750 N.Y.S.2d 331, 333 (2002) (Quebec court had personal jurisdiction over defendant who purposefully transacted business in Canada and there was a direct nexus between the business and the claim).

[37] *See also* CAL. CODE CIV. PROC. § 1713.5(a) (West 1987), *see* Part One, Bibliography.

[38] *See Citadel Management v. Hertzog*, 703 N.Y.S.2d 670, 671 (1999) (individual defendant's voluntary appearance in foreign proceeding constituted submission to jurisdiction and removed any jurisdictional barrier to granting recognition to foreign country judgment).

[39] However, the New York Act, codified in N.Y. C.P.L.R. § 5304(b)(1) (McKinney 1997) and the Restatement (Third) of Foreign Relations § 482 [hereinafter Restatement (Third)] list lack of subject matter jurisdiction as a permissive ground for non-recognition.

[40] *Hunt v. BP*, 492 F. Supp. 885 (D.C. Tex. 1980).

**d. Permissive non-recognition:** A U.S. court need not recognize a foreign judgment if the proceeding involved:

- Insufficient notice to defendant;[41]
- Obtaining the judgment by fraud;[42]
- A judgment repugnant to public policy in the domestic state jurisdiction;[43]
- A judgment that conflicts with another final and conclusive judgment;[44]
- A foreign court proceeding contrary to the parties' agreement to settle the dispute in question in another forum;[45] or
- A seriously inconvenient forum for the trial of the action.

## 2. Permissive Non-Recognition: Defenses and Strategies

This section offers strategies for defendants in foreign judgment recognition actions and caveats for plaintiffs, in their original foreign adjudication, for ultimately avoiding non-recognition in the domestic jurisdiction.

### a. Sufficient notice:

- A domestic court has discretion not to recognize a foreign judgment if the defendant did not receive notice of the action in the foreign forum in sufficient time to enable him to defend.[46] Note that appearance in court does not necessarily preclude this basis for non-recognition. In *Gondere v. Silberstein*, a New York District Court held that, although defendant's filing of an opposition constituted an appearance under French law, this was only one factor to consider in defendant's claim of insufficient notice, and was not a waiver of it.[47]

  *Standard*: U.S. Constitution, amendment V; federal and state rules of civil procedure.

  *General test*: How offensive to due process requirements of the U.S. Constitution were the foreign notice procedures?[48]

[41] *See Kam Tech Systems v. Yardene*, 774 A.2d 644, 653–4 (2001) (defendant's claim that he did not receive proper notice of Israeli action negated by his participation in that action).

[42] *See Society of Lloyd's v. Mullins*, 255 F. Supp. 2d 468, 473 (2003) (although defendant claimed to have been fraudulently induced to sign a contract, he provided no proof that the English judgment was obtained fraudulently, and it was therefore enforceable).

[43] *See, e.g., id.* at 475–6 (enforcement of "pay-now-sue-later" clause in English contract action not repugnant to Pennsylvania public policy); *but see Yahoo! v. La Ligue Contre Le Racisme et L'Antisemitisme*, 169 F. Supp. 2d 1181 (2001) (French judgment could not be enforced because of conflict with First Amendment guarantees).

[44] *See AAR Int'l. v. Nimelias*, 250 F.3d 510, 517–8 (2001) (under the *Colorado River* doctrine, a court must look for exceptional circumstances in deciding to abstain from exercising jurisdiction due to a pending parallel proceeding).

[45] *See The Courage Co. v. Chemshare*, 93 S.W.3d 323 (Tex. App. 2002) (judgment not recognizable under the uniform act where parties had agreed to arbitrate disputes).

[46] Recognition Act § 4(b)(1); CAL. CODE CIV. PROC. § 1713.4(b)(1) (West 1987 & Supp. 2005).

[47] 744 F. Supp. 429, 431–2 (U.S.D.C. E.D.N.Y. 1990).

[48] *But see* 233 F.3d at 476–7 (impartiality and uniform act concept of due process are not equivalent to the U.S. concept of Due Process).

*Specifically*: Defendant should receive notice

- With as much time for answering as is available in the foreign jurisdiction;
- In the language of the jurisdiction where defendant is served;[49]
- That defendant is being sued;
- Of the nature of the lawsuit and amount involved;
- Of the time and place of the hearing;
- Of the deadline for response;
- Of the consequences of not appearing.[50]

**b. Service Under the Hague Convention:** Notice in the foreign jurisdiction will be sufficient if it complied with the terms of the Hague Service Abroad Convention.[51] The Convention provides for international service of process for civil and commercial matters for parties in signatory countries. In the United States, the Federal Rules of Civil Procedure provide for service under the Convention.[52] Each country establishes a "Central Authority" that must receive service and that may send service to other Central Authorities, and provides model forms for request for service and proof of service. In the United States, the Department of Justice is the Central Authority, and you can obtain the "Request for Service Abroad of Judicial or Extrajudicial Documents" form[53] from the Offices of United States Marshals. Any sheriff, marshal, or court officer (including attorneys) may request that the Central Authority serve documents. Many countries require translation of the documents. Service may also be available under the local rules of the country of service informally, by a specified method, or by certain alternate methods.

**c. Lack of personal jurisdiction:** Lack of jurisdiction as defined by the United States Supreme Court is the most powerful weapon a defendant has against recognition, and it is the most common ground for refusal of recognition. Personal jurisdiction should be based upon residency, situs of the cause of action, or business or personal contacts consistent with the *International Shoe*[54] line of cases.[55]

[49] *But see Tahan v. Hodgson*, 662 F.2d 862, 865 (1981). [50] 101 Cal. Rptr. at 798.

[51] Convention on the Service Abroad of Judicial and Extrajudicial Documents in Civil or Commercial Matters 658 U.N.T.S. 163 (Nov. 15, 1965) [hereinafter Hague Service Convention], *supplemented by* Conclusions and Recommendations Adopted by the Special Commission on the Practical Operation of the Hague Apostille, Evidence and Service Conventions, Oct. 28–Nov. 4, 2003, *reprinted in* 2 Ristau, *supra* Part One, II, note 23, at A-11; *see also* 36 I.L.M. 516 (1997) for parties to the Convention. The United States is a party to the Hague Service Convention.

[52] Fed. R. Civ. P. 4; *see also* 28 U.S.C. §§ 1696 (service in foreign and international litigation) and 1782 (assistance to foreign and international tribunals and to litigants before such tribunals). *See* Ristau, *supra* Part One, II, note 23 at 145–232, for details of the Hague Service Convention.

[53] U.S. Department of Justice, Civil Division, Office of International Judicial Assistance, Washington, D.C. 20530. For a complete list of Central Authorities *see* Part One, Instruments, Laws, and Other Materials (also available at the Hague Conference on Private International Law Web site http://www.hcch.net/index_en.php?act=conventions.authorities&cid=17). For the "Request for Service Abroad of Judicial or Extrajudicial Documents" form (U.S. Marshals form USM-94), *see also* Part One, Instruments, Laws, and Other Materials (also available at http://www.usdoj.gov/marshals/forms/usm94.pdf).

[54] 326 U.S. 310 (1945).

[55] *But see* 202 F. Supp. 2d at 909–10 (assignee of Australian court's judgment not required to establish basis for district court's exercise of personal jurisdiction over corporation in action seeking recognition and enforcement of judgment since assignee was not seeking any new relief from corporation, and most devices for enforcement of judgment would have operated *in rem* against corporation's property). For a discussion of personal jurisdiction of the recognizing court, *see supra*, Part One, II.A.1.

Authorities disagree as to whether the enforcing court should judge personal jurisdiction in the underlying adjudication by U.S. standards or the laws of the original court's jurisdiction. In *CIBC Mellon Trust v. Mora Hotel*,[56] for example, the court held that any bases of jurisdiction recognized by internal New York law would be acceptable bases of personal jurisdiction in a foreign suit seeking enforcement in the U.S. system.[57] It perhaps is noteworthy that the court did not, however, state that such bases were the exclusive bases recognizable under the law.

Usually, the foreign forum will have personal jurisdiction over the defendant, although lack of jurisdiction issues may arise if the defendant did not appear and a default judgment was issued in the foreign forum. A U.S. enforcing court, however, is likely to be concerned if the foreign court rendering the judgment exceeded its exercise of personal jurisdiction over the defendant according to standards acceptable in the United States.[58] The Restatement (Third) § 482(1)(b) suggests that *both* U.S. and foreign forum personal jurisdiction requirements must be met. Note that the Recognition Act specifies circumstances in which personal jurisdiction cannot be found lacking and, arguably, suggests that the enforcing court should not test the rendering forum's personal jurisdiction over the defendant by its standards of jurisdiction.[59]

**d. Inconvenient forum** To defeat recognition of a foreign judgment under the Recognition Act, defendant must show that, even if jurisdiction was based on personal service, the foreign country forum was seriously inconvenient.[60] U.S. courts generally recognize personal jurisdiction based on the fact that the legal basis was fair – for example, defendant appeared and unsuccessfully challenged jurisdiction or conducted business in the forum that was the subject of the litigation.[61] In contrast, courts will scrutinize jurisdictional determination on the merits if jurisdiction rested on questions of law or law and fact.[62] However, if plaintiff can show that defendant traveled previously to the forum or could have done so with relative ease, this defense will fail.[63]

## 3. Default Judgments and Foreign Long-Arm Statutes

**a. Default judgments:** Default judgments in foreign country courts create a conversion problem for United States courts because jurisdiction over the defendant may not have

[56] 743 N.Y.S.2d 408 (N.Y. App. Div. 2002).

[57] *Id.* at 420.

[58] For example, transient or tag jurisdiction may present a problem. *See* EPSTEIN & SNYDER, *supra* Part One, II, note 5, at 6.04[3]; *see also* Eric Fastiff, Note, *The Proposed Hague Convention on the Recognition and Enforcement of Civil and Commercial Judgments: A Solution to Butch Reynolds Jurisdiction and Enforcement Problems*, 28 CORNELL INT'L L.J. 469 (1995); *but see Flores v. Melo-Palacios*, 921 S.W.2d 399, 402–3 (1996) (where other factors existed and "tag" jurisdiction did not offend due process).

[59] *See* GEORGE A. BERMANN, TRANSNATIONAL LITIGATION, 339 (2003). Interestingly, the New York Supreme Court (i.e., New York's trial court) held in *Lechyshyn v. Pelko Elec.*, 723 N.Y.S.2d. 285, 288 (S. Ct. N.Y. 2001) that personal jurisdiction over parties to a judgment in the United States was immaterial to recognition.

[60] CAL. CODE CIV. PROC. § 1713.4(b)(6) (West 1987 & Supp. 2005); N.Y. C.P.L.R. § 5304(b)(7) (McKinney 1997).

[61] *See, e.g., DSQ Property Co. v. DeLorean*, 1989 WL 161032 *11 (E.D. Mich. 1989) (rejecting defendant's argument for non-recognition of a London court's judgment because jurisdiction was not based on personal service alone, but on "actions both inside and outside the U.K.").

[62] Restatement (Third) § 482 cmt. c. (1987).

[63] *Bank of Montreal v. Kough*, 612 F.2d 467 (1980).

been proper and the jurisdictional question may not have been adjudicated.[64] A questionable jurisdictional basis coupled with a default judgment is a powerful argument against enforcement. An example is presented by the case of *Bank Melli v. Pahlavi*[65] in which an Iranian bank was unable to enforce a default judgment against the sister of the former Shah based on the additional concerns of due process in the Iranian proceeding.[66] Specifically, the defendant was unable to travel to the prior proceeding without placing herself in physical danger and the Iranian proceedings at the time were highly politicized, which was especially prejudicial to the defendant.[67] Furthermore, a U.S. court may hesitate to recognize a default judgment primarily because the underlying merits were not adjudicated.[68]

**b. Foreign long-arm or exorbitant jurisdiction statutes:** Long-arm statutes,[69] like personal jurisdiction, raise special personal jurisdiction problems. Just as the U.S Constitution defines the outer limits of personal jurisdiction in domestic cases, so does it define the outer limits of personal jurisdiction for U.S. courts that are determining whether the foreign court properly asserted personal jurisdiction. If defendant can successfully argue that a foreign court exercised exorbitant jurisdiction by U.S. standards, the U.S. court is likely to refuse recognition based on violations of due process or takings protection. In *Falcon Mfg.Ltd. v. Ames*,[70] for example, the court refused to recognize a Canadian judgment for lack of due process.[71] The applicable Canadian long-arm statute permitted the Canadian court to exercise personal jurisdiction over defendant, whose only contact with the foreign forum was a letter placing an order mailed to the Canadian plaintiff.[72]

Other plaintiffs have argued with mixed success that foreign state long-arm statutes would have permitted personal jurisdiction in the underlying adjudication. In *Siedler v.* Jacobson,[73] the defendant's purchases during a week's visit in Austria was insufficient nexus for enforcing a default judgment, although the New York long-arm statute would have permitted personal jurisdiction over the defendant in the same circumstances. In *Nippon v. Emo Tran*,[74] however, a shipping company had sufficient contacts with Japan under New York's long-arm statute where only one percent of the shippers' business was done with Japan, earning gross annual revenues of $600,000. A commentator has proffered that once a defendant has lost a personal jurisdiction challenge and proceeds to litigate on the merits, a U.S. court will likely find personal jurisdiction and recognize the foreign judgment.[75]

[64] *See Somportex, Ltd. v. Philadelphia Chewing Gum Corp.*, 453 F.2d 435 (3d Cir. 1971), *cert. denied*, 405 U.S. 1017 (1972).

[65] 58 F.3d at 1411–13 (9th Cir. 1995).

[66] *Id.* at 1411–13.

[67] *Id.* at 1411–12.

[68] *Falcon Mgf. Ltd. v. Ames*, 53 Misc.2d 332, 278 N.Y.S.2d 684 (1967). Courts in jurisdictions that have not enacted the Recognition Act have more discretion under a "comity" analysis to refuse to recognize foreign judgments; however, even under the Recognition Act, U.S. courts can summon public policy or due process violations as bases for denying recognition.

[69] *See* John Fitzpatrick, *The Lugano Convention and Western European Integration: A Comparative Analysis of Jurisdiction and Judgments in Europe and the United States*, 8 CONN. J. INT'L L. 695 (1993). See this article for a discussion of exorbitant jurisdiction ("assertions of jurisdiction that are not generally recognized by accepted principles of international law"); *id.* at 703; and a comparison between United States and European Community approaches, *Id.* at 723–7.

[70] *Falcon Mfg. Ltd. v. Ames, supra* note 68.

[71] *Id.* at 687.

[72] *Id.*

[73] 383 N.Y.S.2d 833 (1976).

[74] 744 F. Supp. 1215 (E.D.N.Y 1990).

[75] Campbell, *supra* Introduction, note 2, at US-17.

Based on the outcome of *Nippon,* a defendant who defaults by not appearing in the foreign forum may have a better chance of persuading a U.S. court to deny recognition of the foreign judgment than a defendant who unsuccessfully challenges jurisdiction and then appears to litigate. The reasoning was as follows:

> If a defendant genuinely has no significant contacts with a particular forum, then it can challenge jurisdiction there and safely default on the merits; presumably, the judgment will be meaningless in the foreign country . . . since the defendant has no assets there and such a judgment will be enforced in New York.[76]

As a federal case interpreting New York law, *Nippon* may nonetheless be of limited persuasive value in other U.S. jurisdictions.[77]

The Recognition Act also provides a discretionary basis for denying enforcement if the jurisdiction was based on transient or tag jurisdiction. The test for exorbitant jurisdiction in this case rests on whether the forum was seriously inconvenient if personal service was the only basis for jurisdiction. As noted by the New Jersey Superior Court in *El-Maksoud v. El-Maksoud,*[78] the Recognition Act allows for such jurisdiction and "any unfairness to the defendant can be addressed by the application of the doctrine of *forum non-conveniens.*"

Thus, absent case law on point, the better practice is to combine this argument with other, established defenses to jurisdiction.

### 4. Non-Judicial Dispute Resolution Clauses

A U.S. court may not recognize a foreign judgment if it was based upon breach of an agreement between the parties providing for non-judicial resolution of disputes generally, or for a particular type of dispute-resolution process regarding the dispute at issue.[79] Certainly the modern trend is for courts to honor forum-selection clauses in contracts where a U.S. court would otherwise have jurisdiction, as the U.S. Supreme Court has noted in particular with respect to international arbitration.[80] If the contract requires arbitration, the New York Convention on Recognition and Enforcement of Foreign Arbitral Awards[81] provides for enforcement of arbitration awards. Furthermore, the New York Convention and the underlying Federal Arbitration Act prohibit U.S. courts from enforcing a foreign country judgment that violates the parties' prior agreement to arbitrate.

### 5. Public Policy

**a. Generally:** A foreign country judgment may not be recognized under the Recognition Act if it is "repugnant to the public policy of this state."[82] Although public policy violations

[76] *Id.* at 1225.
[77] As of the date of this writing, there has been very little use of this case at all. *CIBC Mellon v. Mora Hotel,* 762 N.Y.S.2d 5 (2003) is the only case to discuss it in relation to this issue.
[78] 568 A.2d 140, 144 (1989).
[79] Cal. Code Civ. Proc. § 1713.4(b)(5) (West 1987 & Supp. 2005); N.Y. C.P.L.R. § 5304(b)(6) (McKinney 1997).
[80] *Scherk v. Alberto-Culver,* 417 U.S. 506 (1979); *see also The Bremen v. Zapata Off-shore Co.,* 407 U.S. 1, (1972). Many state courts have also followed this trend. *See, e.g., Smith, Valentino & Smith, Inc. v. Superior Court,* 551 P.2d 1206, (Cal. 1976).
[81] The New York Convention is codified as the Federal Arbitration Act, 9 U.S. C. § 201, *et seq.*
[82] Cal. Code Civ. Proc. § 1713.4(b)(3) (West 1987 & Supp. 2005); N.Y. C.P.L.R. § 5304(b)(4) (McKinney 1997).

are undefined in the Act or state codification, courts have generally held that differences between jurisdictions' laws or the non-existence of a cause of action in the U.S. jurisdiction[83] are not sufficient to trigger this catch-all defense.[84] The proposed revision of the Recognition Act makes clear that the substantive law on which the judgment is based must violate public policy, not the specific judgment.[85] It also emphasizes that the policy exception will apply only in a small category of cases. However, some courts have denied recognition of foreign country judgments based on unfairness to one of the parties if the judgment were held to be conclusive.[86]

The Third Circuit has held that a foreign country judgment violates a state's public policy if the judgment is injurious to public health, public morals, or public confidence "in the purity of the administration of the law" or must undermine the public's sense of security for individual rights.[87] The Texas Supreme Court has held that foreign laws violate Texas public policy if they are "inimical to good morals, natural justice, or the general interests" of the state's citizens.[88] A New York state court refused to enforce a libel judgment by a British court because it would be contrary to First Amendment protection of free speech.[89] In addition, the California Supreme Court ruled that a judgment of a foreign court could never have greater force in California than where it was pronounced.[90] Therefore, the courts will prevent foreign judgments from undermining public policy while at the same time ensuring that there are no additional incentives to enforcing such claims.

**b. Combination with other defenses:** In practice, U.S. courts find that few foreign country judgments violate state public policy as the sole grounds for refusing recognition. However, when combined with other defenses, such as jurisdiction or due process violations, courts may refuse to recognize a foreign country judgment.[91] For example, a California court refused to recognize a Mexican judgment that required spousal support payments to a divorced wife even after her remarriage because the judgment conflicted with fundamental California public policy ending such support upon a spouse's remarriage.[92]

[83] *See* Winston Anderson, *Enforcement of Foreign Judgments Founded upon a Cause of Action Unknown in the Forum*, 42 INT'L & COMP. L.Q. 697 (1993).

[84] *See Lloyd's v. Webb*, 156 F. Supp. 2d 632, 639–40 (2001) (English judgment was not unenforceable even though pretrial discovery was barred and procedures used in English courts were not identical to American procedures, as long as the proceedings of the foreign judgment were fundamentally fair); *see also Southwest Livestock v. Ramon*, 169 F.3d 317, 320–1 (1999) (underlying action of foreign judgment must violate public policy of receiving court).

[85] *See supra* note 5 at § 3 and Reporters' Notes to § 3.

[86] R. Doak Bishop & Susan Burnette, *United States Practice Concerning the Recognition of Foreign Judgments*, 16 INT'L LAW. 425 (1982).

[87] *Somportex*, *supra* note 64 at 443 (quoting *Goodyear v. Brown*, 155 Pa. 514, 518 (1893)).

[88] *Gutierrez v. Collins*, 583 S.W.2d 312, 322 (Tex. 1979).

[89] *Bachachan v. India Abroad Publications, Inc.*, 585 N.Y.S.2d 661 (1992).

[90] *In re Cleland's Estate*, 258 P.2d 1097 (1953); *accord Weiss v. La Suisse*, 161 F. Supp. 2d 305 (2001).

[91] Campbell, Introduction, *supra* note 2, at US-26. For a detailed treatment of the public policy defense, *see* Wanda Ellen Wakefield, Annotation, *Judgment of Court of Foreign Country as Entitled to Enforcement or Extraterritorial Effect in State Court*, 13 A.L.R. $4^{th}$ 1109 (1982).

[92] *Pentz v. Kuppinger*, 31 Cal. App.3d 590, 107 Cal. Rptr. 540 (1973); CAL. FAM. CODE § 4337 (West 1994).

A New York court held a Thai judgment unenforceable based on the public policy of "enforcing letters of credit agreements according to their terms."[93]

**c. Corrupt judicial system:** Under both the American Law Institute's International Juridiction and Judgments Project and the efforts to revise the Recognition Act[94] a court "*must* deny recognition to a foreign country judgment if 'the judgment was rendered under a judicial system which does not provide impartial tribunal or procedures compatible with the requirements of due process of law."[95] Thus, a defensive claim that a corrupt judicial system rendered the judgment sought to be enforced is similar to the separate defensive ground that the judgment was the result of unfair procedures, but it is different in that it requires a showing that corruption was involved in the specific litigation on which the judgment in question is based.[96]

### 6. Parallel Proceedings

**a. *Res judicata*/collateral estoppel:** A U.S. court need not recognize a foreign country judgment if it conflicts with another final and conclusive judgment[97] entitled to recognition.[98] U.S. courts will generally allow foreign default judgments to have *res judicata* effect, but a *res judicata* defense to recognition could trigger issues of the foreign court's personal jurisdiction over the defendant, as was the case at the sister-state level in *Covington Indus. v. Restinex.*[99]

The court has discretion, based on the facts, to recognize the later inconsistent judgment, the earlier inconsistent judgment, or neither. It should be noted, however, that in assessing the *res judicata* effect of a judgment, U.S. courts will not apply foreign theories of *res judicata.* For example, a Greek action involving the death of a Greek seaman did not have binding effect in subsequent U.S. litigation, despite the binding effect it would have had in Greek courts.[100]

Thus, a defendant in a foreign country action may bring suit in the United States while the foreign action is pending to block enforcement of an unfavorable judgment on *res judicata* or collateral estoppel grounds.[101] The District of Columbia Court of Appeals held, for example, that a U.S. claim could go forward despite a pending English suit brought for the sole purpose of precluding U.S. jurisdiction over the matter.[102]

[93] AG *Zurich v. Bangkok Bank,* 681 N.Y.S.2d 21, 22 (1998).

[94] *See supra* note 5 and *infra* Part Three, IV for the Proposed Revision of the Uniform Foreign Money-Judgment Recognition Act. The ALI International Jurisdiction and Judgments Project is available at http:// www.ali.org. For additional discussion of this project, *see infra* Part Three, III.

[95] *See* Revised Recognition Act, *supra* note 5, at § 3(c)(7); and ALI Project, *supra* note 94 at § 5(a)(ii). The ALI Project's language is: "A foreign judgment shall not be recognized or enforced in a court in the United States if the party resisting recognition or enforcement establishes that: ... (ii) the judgment was rendered in circumstances that raise substantial and justifiable doubt about the integrity of the rendering court with respect to the judgment in question."

[96] *See* ALI Project, *supra* note 94, at Reporters' Notes 3 to § 5.

[97] Cal. Code Civ. Proc. § 1713.4(b)(4) (West 1987 & Supp. 2005); N.Y. C.P.L.R. § 5304(b)(5) (McKinney 1997).

[98] Restatement (Third) § 482(2)(e).

[99] 629 F.2d 730 (2d Cir. 1980).

[100] *Zorgias v. SS Helenic Star,* 370 F. Supp. 591 (D.C. E.D. La. 1972).

[101] *See generally* Margarita Trevino, *Stay, Dismiss, Enjoin or Abstain?: A Survey of Foreign Parallel Litigation in the Federal Courts of the United States,* 17 B.U. Int'l. L.J. 79 (1999).

[102] *Laker Airways Ltd. v. Sabena,* 731 F.2d 909 (1984).

**b. Rules and proposed strategies:** The parallel proceeding rule in the United States allows proceedings to continue until judgment is reached in one case,[103] thereby subsequently precluding adjudication of other cases. This rule may present strategic options for defendants in major transnational litigation.

Defendant's Strategy:

- After the original suit is filed in a foreign jurisdiction, counter sue in the United States to enjoin the foreign country litigation and to seek a decision on the merits.
- If plaintiff is successful in the foreign country litigation and seeks U.S. recognition of the foreign country judgment, request a stay in the recognition proceedings or seek judicial abstention until the domestic countersuit is concluded.
- If favorable judgment in the domestic countersuit is reached first, argue *res judicata* to prevent recognition of the foreign country judgment.

Plaintiff's Strategy:

- The best defense to parallel litigation in the U.S. is to argue that comity[104] requires that the court dismiss the suit because the overseas adjudication was filed first and, furthermore, that dismissal is in the interests of judicial economy and fairness.[105]

**c. American Bar Association proposal:** The American Bar Association (ABA) proposed a Conflict of Jurisdiction Model Act as a solution to parallel proceedings problems.[106] At this writing, only Connecticut has adopted the Model Act.[107] The Act discourages parallel proceedings by requiring that a party to both proceedings apply to the court for designation of an adjudicating forum within six months of reasonable notice of the proceedings or of selection of an adjudicating forum. The adjudicating forum selection is presumed valid if the decision determining the forum evaluated the statutory factors. The judgment of the adjudicating forum is then binding on enforcement of all other judgments in the same matter, regardless of when rendered.

[103] *See* Louise E. Teitz, *Taking Multiple Bites of the Apple: A Proposal to Resolve Conflicts of Jurisdiction and Multiple Proceedings*, 26 INT'L LAW. 21 (1992) [hereinafter *Multiple Bites*]; and Louise E. Tietz, *Both Sides of the Coin: A Decade of Parallel Proceedings and Enforcement of Foreign Judgments in Transnational Litigation*, 10 ROGER WILLIAMS UNIV. L. REV. 1 (2004).

[104] The Supreme Court, in *Hilton v. Guyot, supra*, Part One, I, at note 8, defined comity as

> neither a matter of absolute obligation . . . nor of mere courtesy and good will. . . . But it is the recognition which one nation allows within its territory to the legislative, executive or judicial acts of another nation, having due regard both to international duty and convenience, and to the rights of its own citizens or of other persons who are under the protection of its laws.

[105] *See Colorado River Water Conservation Dist. v. United States*, 424 U.S. 800 (1976). This argument has been successful in inducing U.S. court abstension, for example in *Turner Enter.Co. v. Degeto Film GmB*, 25 F.3d 1512, 1518 (11th Cir. 1994), in which the Eleventh Circuit stated that "In some private international disputes the prudent and just action is to abstain from the exercise of jurisdiction." However, *Quackenbush v. Allstate*, 517 U.S. 706, 719–22, held that federal courts may not abstain in common law actions for damages. Thus, it is unclear whether a federal suit may be dismissed on the basis of comity due to pending foreign proceedings. *See also Goldhammer v. Dunkin Donuts*, 59 F. Supp. 2d 248, 252 (D. Mass. 1999).

[106] *See* Teitz, *Multiple Bites*, *supra* note 103, at 56–64.

[107] CONN. GEN. STAT. § 50a-200 (Supp. 2005), *et seq.*; *see also* articles by Tietz, *supra* note 148.

## 7. Extrinsic and Intrinsic Fraud

The Recognition Act provides that a foreign judgment need not be recognized if it was obtained by fraud, without distinguishing between extrinsic and intrinsic fraud.[108] Extrinsic fraud concerns non-litigated matters, whereas intrinsic fraud concerns the successful party's improprieties during trial, resulting in obtaining a judgment.[109] If defendant can show that plaintiff engaged in extrinsic fraud by misrepresenting or concealing a claim, thus causing defendant to default or consent to judgment, or depriving defendant from fairly or entirely presenting his case, defendant may be able to attack the foreign country judgment collaterally in an independent proceeding in a U.S. court. For example, the court in *de la Mata v. American Life Insurance*[110] the court found the plaintiff's failure to inform the Bolivian court of her waiver of all claims under the insurance policy at issue was extrinsic fraud and precluded recognition.

Intrinsic fraud, on the other hand, involving perjury in the proceedings where defendant has had an opportunity to present defenses, is not fatal to subsequent recognition. A Louisiana Federal District Court, for example, enforced an English judgment despite evidence of intrinsic fraud, stating that intrinsic fraud is "an on-the-merits defense which does not preclude the enforcement of the [foreign] . . . judgment."[111]

Be sure to check common law or state statutes barring recognition based on fraud.[112]

## 8. Reciprocity

The common law reciprocity defense may block recognition of a foreign country judgment as non-conclusive if the foreign forum does not reciprocally recognize judgments rendered in similar proceedings in U.S. courts.[113] Today, U.S. courts in states that have adopted the Recognition Act no longer follow this doctrine, although it has not been overruled.[114] Although some cases have required reciprocity and denied enforcement based on its absence, those cases usually involved other bases for non-recognition as well.[115] The Act itself has no reciprocity provision, although several states have modified the Act to include lack of reciprocity as a ground for permissive non-recognition.[116] In both California and New York, although the state Recognition Acts do not provide for a lack of

[108] The proposed revised version in the Reporter's Notes, however, confirms that only extrinsic fraud – "conduct of the prevailing party that deprived the losing party of an adequate opportunity to present his case" – is a ground for non-recognition. *See* Revised Recognition Act, *supra* note 5 at Reporter's Notes for § 4 (c)(2).

[109] *See generally Rondette v. Peterson*, 518 So.2d 1183 (1988) (intrinsic v. extrinsic fraud); 255 F. Supp. 2d 468 (extrinsic v. intrinsic fraud).

[110] 771 F. Supp. 1375 (D. De. 1991).

[111] *Standard SS Owners Protection & Indemn. Ass'n v. C&G Manne Svcs.*, 1992 WL 111186, *3 (E.D. La. 1992).

[112] CAL. CODE CIV. PROC. § 1713.4(b)(2) provides discretionary non-recognition based on extrinsic fraud. *See also Los Angeles Airways, Inc. v. Hughes Tool Co.*, 156 Cal. Rptr. 805, 808 (1979) (discussing the "extrinsic/intrinsic fraud rule"); *Fairchild, Arabatzis & Smith, Inc. v. Prometco Co., Ltd.*, 470 F. Supp 610 (S.D.N.Y. 1979). *See generally* RUSSELL J. WEINTRAUB, INTERNATIONAL LITIGATION AND ARBITRATION 217 (1994, Supp. 2003).

[113] *Hilton*, *supra*, Part One, I, note 8, at 227–8.

[114] *See, e.g., Bank of Montreal v. Kough*, 612 F.2d 467 (9th Cir. 1980); *Nicol v. Tanner*, 310 Minn.68 (1976).

[115] *See, e.g., Ogden v. Ogden*, 159 Fla. 604 (1947).

[116] Massachusetts, Georgia, Texas, Idaho, Maine, North Carolina, and Florida. Georgia lists lack of reciprocity as a mandatory basis for non-recognition. New Hampshire, which has not adopted the Act, provides reciprocity for Canadian judgments to the extent that Canada recognizes New Hampshire judgments. Campbell, *supra* Introduction, note 2, at US-9, n.23.

reciprocity defense, the common law reciprocity rule often applies if the defendant is a U.S. citizen.[117]

## D. OTHER CONVERSION METHODS

### 1. Common Law Recognition

In states that have not adopted the Recognition Act, the judgment creditor must bring an action to obtain a domestic judgment based on the state's common law. The common law rule enunciated in *Hilton v. Guyot*[118] is still good law today.[119] The rule provides that if courts in the foreign adjudicating jurisdiction give conclusive effect to U.S. judgments and the circumstances of the judgment are not offensive to the U.S. court,[120] the U.S. court will recognize the foreign country judgment.

### 2. Other Recognition Statutes

A few states that have adopted the Recognition Act nonetheless have modified their statute to incorporate unique approaches to recognizing foreign country money judgments.[121] If your state has not adopted the Recognition Act, check other statutes concerning recognition of foreign (sister-state or foreign country) judgments first before drafting a complaint based on the common law approach.

### 3. New Complaint

A complaint for recognition not based on the Recognition Act should plead and prove the underlying cause of action *ab initio*.[122] However, be aware of pitfalls in pleading the underlying cause of action: defendant can use the defense of *res judicata* or collateral estoppel, based on the foreign trial, or plaintiff might have to retry the entire case. However, if the statute of limitations will soon run, you should consider pleading the underlying cause of action alternatively in case the foreign judgment is not recognized in the conversion action, assuming there is proper jurisdiction. Alternatively, the judgment creditor may file a writ of execution of the judgment debt if the state's recognition act permits filing of the foreign country judgment to obtain recognition.[123]

[117] *Hilton*, *supra* Part One, I, note 8.

[118] *Id.*

[119] *Hilton* was a pre-*Erie* case; subsequent federal court decisions have held that the law of the state in which the federal court sits controls. *Somportex*, *supra* note 64. You should be familiar with case law precedents interpreting the law of recognition and enforcement of foreign judgments in the jurisdiction where you are seeking recognition.

[120] The reasons set forth in *Hilton* for denying recognition, which are the basis for similar provisions in the Recognition Act, are: unfairness in the underlying proceedings; the foreign court's lack of personal or subject matter jurisdiction; fraud in the proceedings; or violation of public policy.

[121] For example, New Hampshire. See *supra* note 116.

[122] For example, in a negligence cause of action, the complaint would set out the facts as they occurred in the foreign country to show duty, breach, causation, and damages. Similarly, a contract cause of action should set out facts to show an enforceable agreement between the parties, breach and damages.

[123] Campbell, *supra* Introduction, note 2, at US-33–5.

***Review***: Verify what the foreign country judgment recognition and execution procedures are in the jurisdiction where execution will occur. Determine if the jurisdiction will grant recognition based on

- filing of the authenticated foreign country judgment (if Recognition Act applies;
- complaint for conversion of the foreign country judgment (if Recognition Act does not apply); or
- complaint for the underlying cause of action, *ab initio* (if Recognition Act does not apply).

### 4. Action for Conversion in Other Jurisdictions: Strategy

If circumstances in the state where you are ultimately seeking conversion do not favor recognition, an alternative strategy to obtaining direct recognition is to seek a judgment in another state under that state's foreign country judgment recognition procedures, and then establish the recognized domestic judgment in your state as a sister-state judgment entitled to full faith and credit. In most states, enforcement of sister-state judgments falls under the Enforcement Act.[124]

## E. CURRENCY OF DAMAGES

### 1. Generally

U.S. courts usually require that judgments be rendered in U.S. currency, unless the parties agree otherwise. If the parties have not agreed to satisfy the judgment in a foreign currency, U.S. courts will follow the common law by applying either the "breach day" rule or the "judgment day" rule for converting foreign currency judgments into U.S. dollars.[125] California determines which rule to apply by determining whether the obligation or cause of action arose entirely under foreign law or American law. If the obligation or cause of action arose entirely under foreign law, California applies the judgment day rule; whereas, if the obligation or cause of action arose entirely under American law, California applies the breach day rule.[126] Additionally, if the state has adopted the Claims Act,[127] the court will follow the Act's provisions. In states that have not adopted the Claims Act, the court will also follow the common law breach day or judgment day rule. Be sure to check state common law or secondary sources to determine which rule your state applies.

[124] *See supra* Part One, Introduction, note 1. The states that *have not* adopted the Act are California, Indiana, Massachusetts, and Vermont.

[125] For a discussion of breach day and judgment day rules, *see generally Manches v. Gilbey*, 646 N.E.2d 646 (1995).

[126] *See* B. E. Witkin, California Procedure § 421A (1985, Supp. 2004) [hereinafter Witkin]. The general rule derives from *Deutsche Bank Filiale Nurnberg v. Humphrey*, 272 U.S. 517 (1926); *Pecaflor Construction, Inc. v. Landes*, 198 Cal. App.3d 342, 345–6, 243 Cal. Rptr. 605, 607 (1988).

[127] 13-II U.L.A. 13 (2002 & Supp. 2003). As of this writing, twenty-three jurisdictions have adopted the Claims Act: California, Colorado, Connecticut, D.C., Delaware, Hawaii, Idaho, Illinois, Minnesota, Montana, Nevada, New Jersey, New Mexico, North Carolina, North Dakota, Ohio, Oklahoma, Oregon, Utah, Virgin Islands, Virginia, Washington, Wisconsin. *See* Part One, Instruments, Laws, and Other Materials for the full text of the Act.

## 2. "Breach Day" and "Judgment Day" Rules

The breach day rule allows the court to convert the foreign currency at the exchange rate prevailing on the date the legal obligation arose, whereas the judgment day rule requires the court to apply the exchange rate in effect on the date the judgment was entered. New York nominally follows the breach day rule, but it converts the foreign currency at the exchange rate prevailing on the date the obligation became due, in some cases the date of entry of judgment.[128] In *Comptex v. LaBow*,[129] for example, New York law required payment of the amount specified in the U.S. enforcement judgment, not the one listed in the original English lawsuit.

California, on the other hand, applies the general rule of *Deutsche Bank Filiale Nurnberg v. Humphrey*,[130] which provides that the judgment day rule applies if the obligation arose entirely under foreign law, but that the breach day rule applies if the obligation arose under American law. This general rule neither favors judgment creditors nor judgment debtors insofar as exchange rate fluctuations might affect the value of the judgment. Both bear the risk equally under this rule.

The debate about which rule to apply has become important only since floating exchange rates replaced fixed exchange rates in the 1970s. In following the general rule, courts do not have to ascertain whether the foreign and U.S. currencies have appreciated or depreciated relative to each other, nor do they then have to balance the interests of the judgment creditor and judgment debtor to avoid unfairness.[131] Moreover, in California, this rule avoids forum-shopping.[132]

## 3. Uniform Foreign-Money Claims Act

**a. Pleadings:** California enacted the Claims Act in 1991,[133] and by its terms it applies to actions commenced on or after January 1, 1992. The Act provides that the prayer for damages may be pled in any currency according to the following criteria: (1) the money regularly used between the parties in their regular course of dealing;[134] (2) the money used at the time of the international trade transaction;[135] or (3) the money in which the loss will ultimately be felt or incurred by the claiming party.[136] The Act also adopts a third rule for converting a foreign currency judgment into U.S. dollars: the "payment day" rule. The payment day rule provides for converting the foreign currency based on the exchange rate on the date the judgment is paid.[137] In allocating the risk of exchange rate fluctuations between the judgment creditor and the judgment debtor, the Act provides that the judgment creditor is entitled to receive the amount due in his own currency or the currency in which the loss was suffered.[138] The Massachusetts Supreme Court applied this rule in *Manches v. Gilbey*[139] to the enforcement of an English judgment because

[128] Monroe Leigh, *Enforcement of Foreign Judgments*, 80 AM. J. INT'L L. 958, 959 (1986) (analyzing the court's decision in *Competex, S.A. v. LaBow*, 783 F.2d 333 (1986), to convert an English judgment on date of entry of judgment).

[129] 783 F.2d 333 (2d. Cir. 1986).

[130] *Deutsche Bank, supra* note 126.

[131] Leigh, *supra* note 128.

[132] WITKIN, *supra* note 126.

[133] CAL. CODE CIV. PROC. § 676 (West 1987), *et seq.*

[134] CAL. CODE CIV. PROC. § 676.4(b)(1) (West 1987).

[135] CAL. CODE CIV. PROC. § 676.4(b)(2) (West 1987).

[136] CAL. CODE CIV. PROC. § 676.4(b)(3) (West 1987).

[137] CAL. CODE CIV. PROC. § 676.5(a) (West 1987).

[138] WITKIN, *supra* note 126, § 423B.

[139] 646 N.E.2d 86, 87 (Mass.1995).

the plaintiff was "entitled to be restored to the position in which it would have been if the defendants had paid their obligations, but is not entitled to more." The court added that "the payment day rule achieves this result." The parties are always free, however, to agree before or after the action has commenced as to the currency that will apply in their transaction.[140]

Thus, the following are the Claims Act's major provisions:

- The Act's provisions may be varied by agreement of the parties; parties to a contract can agree on the currency of judgment if a dispute arises.
- If the plaintiff does not assert a claim in a specified foreign money, the claim will be in U.S dollars.
- The currency of the claim may be the currency of the transaction, the currency the parties usually use in their course of dealing, or the currency in which the loss was suffered.
- If the judgment debtor pays the claim in another currency, the payment day rule determines the conversion rate, as the closing exchange rate on the day before payment. The judgment debtor has the option of paying the judgment in U.S. dollars based on this conversion rate.
- Foreign-money claims must be asserted in the pleadings in the foreign currency; otherwise, claims will be in U.S. dollars. Determination of the proper currency of the claim is a question of law; defendant may allege and prove that the claim is in a different currency from that which the plaintiff alleged.
- Judgments bear interest at the rate applicable to judgments in the state where recognition is sought. Prejudgment interest is determined as a matter of law governed by state laws.

**b. Defenses:** The determination of the proper money is a threshold question, which the court determines, if contested, according to the following factors: factual issues regarding expenditures, custom, usage, or course of dealing.[141] Furthermore, if the transaction impacts more than one area, the court may render judgment in more than one currency.[142]

Under the Act, a defendant may assert and prove the following defenses:

- That all or part of the claim is in a different money than that asserted by plaintiff;
- That there is a setoff, recoupment or counterclaim in any money regardless of the money of the other claims;
- That the determination of the proper money is a question of law.

140 Claims Act § 3; CAL. CODE CIV. PROC. § 676.3 (West 1987). For in-depth background and analysis of the Act, *see* Fairfax Leary & Howard T. Rosen, *The Uniform Foreign-Money Claims Act*, 12 U. PA. J. INT'L BUS. L. 51 (1991).

141 CAL. CODE CIV. PROC. § 676.6 (West 1987).

142 WITKIN, *supra* note 126, § 423F.

## IV. PHASE THREE: EXECUTING A CONVERTED JUDGMENT IN U.S. COURTS

Once you have pursued a recalcitrant defendant halfway around the world to obtain a valid foreign judgment, you must still employ judicial means to enforce and execute the judgment. A general summary of execution procedures, which may vary from U.S. jurisdiction to U.S. jurisdiction, follows.

### A. PLAINTIFF: LOCATING AND FREEZING ASSETS

If you have followed the checklist in Part One Section I, you will have located defendant's assets in the jurisdiction that can be used to satisfy the judgment, through private investigation and judicial discovery. State procedural rules govern execution of a judgment, so you should follow the procedure for execution of civil judgments in your state. For example, in California, a judgment creditor may apply to have a judgment debtor appear before the court to provide information in executing the judgment, by obtaining from the court an order to show cause.[1] Be aware that, under The Hague Convention on Taking of Evidence Abroad in Civil or Commercial Matters,[2] if the defendant is a national of a signatory country, a U.S. court may request through letters rogatory that documents or information be provided. However, California courts may now accord less deference to the foreign defendant's special protection under the Evidence Convention, based upon a U.S. Supreme Court decision.[3] The Supreme Court held that the Convention does not provide either exclusive or mandatory procedures for obtaining documents from a foreign party located in a foreign jurisdiction. Rather, a court may choose to apply the Convention's provisions as an optional procedure. Thus, a foreign judgment debtor may be subject to the same jurisdictional reach as a domestic judgment debtor.

Importantly, the Supreme Court did not find that the language or intent of the Hague Evidence Convention preempted state law in obtaining evidence from parties under the court's personal jurisdiction. Consequently, in New York and under the Federal Rules of Civil Procedure, the judgment creditor may compel disclosure of assets from any person including the judgment debtor.[4] In fact, the court in *Societe Nationale*[5] held that discovery against a French defendant could take place according to the Federal Rules of Civil Procedure without using the Hague processes, despite a French statute weighing in favor of compliance with the Evidence Convention.

Once the court has handed down the judgment, the judgment creditor files it with the court clerk and serves the judgment debtor, the judgment creditor may want to take

[1] Cal. Code Civ. Proc. § 708.110(a) (West 1987 & Supp. 2005).

[2] 1970 Hague Convention on the Taking of Evidence Abroad in Civil and Commercial Matters, 23 UST 2555, 847 UNTS 231 [hereinafter Evidence Convention]; *see also* 28 U.S.C. § 1781 (regarding transmittal of letters rogatory or requests).

[3] Robert I. Weil & Ira A. Brown, Jr., Civil Procedure Before Trial, ch. 8:50 (1995), citing *Société Nationale Industrielle Aérospatiale v. U.S District Court for the Southern District of Iowa*, 482 U.S. 522 (1987); *see generally* Schwartz & Ahart, *supra* Part One, III, note 12; Patrick J. Borchers, *The Incredible Shrinking Hague Evidence Convention*, 38 Tex. Int'l L.J. 73 (2003).

[4] N.Y. C.P.L.R. § 5223 (McKinney 1997 & Supp. 2005); Fed. R. Civ. P. 69.

[5] *See Societe Nationale, supra* note 3 at 544 n. 29 and 544–6.

steps to restrain the judgment debtor from transferring target assets.[6] Under state law, the procedure for enforcing a money judgment is generally by writ of execution, which allows the judgment creditor to obtain discovery from any person, including the judgment debtor,[7] about the location of assets within the court's jurisdiction. This is only an intermediate step, however, which creates no interest in the frozen assets.

Thus, after ascertaining the extent and location of the judgment debtor's assets and obtaining the judgment, the judgment creditor may want to perfect a lien on the defendant's target assets, which is generally the quickest and least expensive method for obtaining an interest in the judgment debtor's assets. In California, the judgment creditor files the judgment with the court, obtains a writ of execution, and then levies on the asset, creating an execution lien whose duration is two years from the writ's issuance date, unless the judgment is satisfied sooner.[8] The judgment creditor perfects the lien by filing it with the state secretary of state and/or the county clerk where the property is located.[9] In New York, a copy of recognition of the judgment must be filed within 90 days of authentication, along with an affidavit stating the amount not yet paid.[10] This entitles the judgment to the same treatment that a New York judgment would receive.

## B. COLLECTING THE JUDGMENT

The next step is the transfer of assets from the judgment debtor to the judgment creditor. If the judgment debtor still refuses to convey the property, the judgment creditor may petition to the court to issue a writ of execution of *fieri facias*.[11] The writ of execution will levy on certain property, usually real property but also personal property, by describing the property to be seized. The court clerk forwards the writ to the sheriff, who then levies by seizing the property. The sheriff then sells the property and turns the proceeds over to the judgment creditor.

In New York, for example, the judgment creditor has an alternative to the writ of execution: the "turnover order," whereby the court will order the judgment debtor to turn over the property to the judgment creditor for satisfaction of the judgment.[12] The court may hold the judgment debtor in contempt for failure to comply with the order.

## C. FILING SATISFACTION OF JUDGMENT

Once the judgment creditor has received the entire amount of the judgment, the court may require some notice that the judgment has been satisfied. If the judgment was satisfied by writ of execution, notice will usually have been met because the court directed the sale; however, if the judgment debtor satisfied the judgment voluntarily, the judgment creditor may have to file a satisfaction of judgment with the court.[13]

[6] N.Y. C.P.L.R. § 5222 (McKinney 1997 & Supp. 2005).
[7] Fed. R. Civ. P. 69(a).
[8] Cal. Code Civ. Proc. § 697.710 (West 1987 & Supp. 2005); Witkin, *supra* Part One, III. note 126, § 247A.
[9] Editor's Notes to Cal. Code Civ. Proc. § 697.670 (West 1987 & Supp. 2005). *See generally* 9 Theodore Eisenberg, Debtor-Creditor Law, ch. 37A (1988).
[10] N.Y. CPLR §5402 (McKinney 1997 & Supp. 2005). [11] *Id.*
[12] N.Y. C.P.L.R. § 5225 (McKinney 1997 & Supp. 2005).
[13] Cal. Code Civ. Proc. § 724.010 (West 1987 & Supp. 2005), *et seq.*

## V. CONCLUSION

State law generally governs recognition, enforcement, execution, and satisfaction in the United States of a judgment rendered abroad. Many states have adopted and codified the uniform acts treating recognition, enforcement, and foreign-money claims, while others follow common law. Even among those states adopting one or more of the uniform acts, legislatures may have modified the acts' provisions to accord with state procedure or public policy. As in any other areas of practice, the transnational law practitioner must become familiar with the governing state and federal codes and rules of procedure, case law, and international agreements affecting recognition and enforcement in the United States of judgments rendered abroad. Where a jurisdiction's law is unclear, you, as a practitioner, will have the opportunity to persuade the court to follow another jurisdiction favorable to your client, thus creating new law in your jurisdiction.

# Bibliography

## INTRODUCTION

This is a selected bibliography of primary and secondary materials on the recognition and enforcement in the United States of foreign country judgments. The time span represented by the cited publications is the nineteenth century through June 2004, with an emphasis on works published in the last three decades.[1] Works regarding enforcement of money judgments handed down from courts form the core of the bibliography. Therefore, although some general and introductory materials concerning non-money judgments (such as family law matters) and arbitral awards are included, an exhaustive listing of those materials is beyond the scope of this bibliography.

Only materials published in English are included, with the exception of a few materials in German. The anticipated user of this bibliography is a legal practitioner who seeks to enforce foreign judgments in the United States.

In each section the materials are divided by type, beginning with the primary materials and followed by secondary materials. Each type of material is subdivided into topics, with general topics presented first and specific topics following. The overall organization of materials in each section, as well as the order of citations in each topic area, follows rule 1.4 of *A Uniform System of Citation*. Citation forms are, wherever possible, in *Bluebook* format with additional information provided where available, such as city and publisher.

Every effort was made to confirm sources cited. In order to provide the most complete listing, however, some citations have been taken from bibliographical listings of other materials and therefore may be subject to error from multiple transpositions. The author invites readers to bring to his attention citation errors and other useful sources.

## A. APPLICABLE LAWS AND OTHER LEGAL INSTRUMENTS

### 1. Federal Laws

#### *a. Jurisdiction*

Federal Question, 28 U.S.C. § 1331 (2000).

Diversity of Citizenship; Amount in Controversy; Costs, 28 U.S.C. § 1332(a)(2) (2000).

[1] All primary treaty materials and secondary materials are cumulative (i.e., they are listed, although they may be subsequently superseded or outdated) with the exception of those treaties that have revised editions, in which case the most recent edition found is listed. U.S. statutes and foreign statutes are those in effect in 2004.

*b. Service of Process*

Service in Foreign and International Litigation, 28 U.S.C. § 1696 (2000).

Summons; Service with Complaint; By Whom Made, FED. R. CIV. P. 4(c) (2004).

Service upon Individuals in a Foreign Country, FED. R. CIV. P. 4(F) (2004).

Service upon Foreign, State, or Local Governments, FED. R. CIV. P. 4(J) (2004).

*c. Pleadings of Special Matters*

Judgment, FED. R. CIV. P. 9(e) (2004).

*d. Judicial Procedure*

Foreign Official Documents, 28 U.S.C. § 1741 (2000).

Proof of Official Record, FED. R. CIV. P. 44 (2004).

*Full Faith and Credit*, 28 U.S.C. § 1738 (2005)

*e. Registration of Judgment*

Registration of Judgments for Enforcement in Other Districts, 28 U.S.C. § 1963 (2000).

*f. Relief from Judgment or Order*

Mistakes; Inadvertence; Excusable Neglect; Newly Discovered Evidence; Fraud; etc., FED. R. CIV. P. 60(b) (2004).

*g. Stay of Proceedings to Enforce Judgment*

Stay of Proceedings to Enforce a Judgment, FED. R. CIV. P. 62 (2004).

**2. State Laws (including District of Columbia)**[2]

| | |
|---|---|
| Alabama | Ala. Code 1975<br>§§ 6-9-230 to 6-9-238 [UEFJA] |
| Alaska | A.S.<br>09.30.100 to 09.30.180 [UFMJRA]<br>09.30.200 to 09.30.270 [UEFJA] |
| Arizona | A.R.S.<br>§§ 12-1701 to 12-1708 [UEFJA] |
| Arkansas | A.C.A.<br>§§ 16-66-601 to 16-66-608 [UEFJA] |
| California | West's Ann. Cal. C.C.P.<br>§§ 676 to 676.16 [UFM-CA]<br>§§ 1713 to 1713.8 [UFMJRA] |

[2] Abbreviations used in this subsection are as follows: Uniform Foreign Money-Judgments Recognition Act = UFMJRA; Uniform Enforcement of Foreign Money Judgments Act = UEFJA; Uniform Foreign-Money Claims Act = UFM-CA; Justice of Peace = JOP.

| | |
|---|---|
| Colorado | West's C.R.S.A.<br>§§ 13-62.1-101 to 13-62.1-118 [UFM-CA]<br>§§ 13-62-101 to 13-62-109 [UFMJRA]<br>§§ 13-53-101 to 13-53-108 [UEFJA] |
| Connecticut | C.G.S.A.<br>§§ 50a-50 to 50a-65 [UFM-CA]<br>§§ 50a-30 to 50a-38 [UFMJRA]<br>§§ 52-604 to 52-609 [UEFJA] |
| Delaware | 10 Del. C.<br>§§ 5201 to 5215 [UFM-CA]<br>§§ 4801 to 4808 [UFMJRA]<br>§§ 4781 to 4787 [UEFJA] |
| District of Columbia | D.C. Official Code, 2001 ed.<br>§§ 15-901 to 15-914 [UFM-CA]<br>§§ 15-381 to 15-388 [UFMJRA]<br>§§ 15-351 to 15-357 [UEFJA] |
| Florida | West's F.S.A.<br>§§ 55.601 to 55.607 [UFMJRA]<br>§§ 55.501 to 55.509 [UEFJA]<br>*Fla. Stat. Ann.* 55.605 (West 1994 & Supp. 2004) |
| Georgia | O.C.G.A.<br>§§ 9-12-110 to 9-12-117 [UFMJRA]<br>§§ 9-12-130 to 9-12-138 [UEFJA]<br>*Ga. Code Ann.* 9-12-114 (1993) |
| Hawaii | HRS<br>§§ 658C-1 to 658C-9 [UFMJRA]<br>§§ 658B-1 to 658B-14 [UFMCA]<br>§§ 636C-1 to 626C-8 [UEFJA] |
| Idaho | I.C.<br>§§ 10-1501 to 10-1517 [UFM-CA]<br>§§ 10-1401 to 10-1409 [UFMJRA]<br>§§ 10-1301 to 10-1308 [UEFJA]<br>*Idaho Code 10-1404* (Michie 2004) |
| Illinois | S.H.A. 735 I.L.C.S.<br>5/12-630 to 5/12-645 [UFM-CA]<br>5/12-618 to 5/12-626 [UFMJRA]<br>5/12/650 to 5/12-657 [UEFJA] |
| Iowa | I.C.A.<br>§§ 626B.1 to 626B.8 [UFMJRA]<br>§§ 626A.1 to 626A.8 [UEFJA] |
| Kansas | K.S.A.<br>§§ 60-3001 to 60-3008 [UEFJA] |
| Kentucky | K.R.S.<br>426.950 to 426.975 [UEFJA] |

| | |
|---|---|
| Louisiana | L.S.A.-R.S.<br>13:4241 to 13:4247 [UEFJA] |
| Maine | 14 M.R.S.A.<br>§§ 8501 to 8509 [UFMJRA]<br>§§ 8001 to 8008 [UEFJA]<br>*Me. Rev. Stat. Ann. tit.* 14, 8505 (West 2003) |
| Maryland | Maryland Code, Courts, and Judicial Proceedings,<br>§§ 10-701 to 10-709 [UFMJRA]<br>§§ 10-801 to 10-807 [UEFJA] |
| Massachusetts | M.G.L.A. ch. 235, § 23A [UFMJRA]<br>Mass. Gen. Laws. Ann. ch. 235, 23A (West 2000) |
| Michigan | M.C.L.A.<br>§§ 691.1171 to 691.1179 [UEFJA]<br>§§ 691.1151 to 691.1159 [UFMJRA] |
| Minnesota | M.S.A.<br>§§ 548.40 to 548.53 [UFM-CA]<br>§§ 548.35 [UFMJRA]<br>§§ 548.26 to 548.33 [UEFJA] |
| Mississippi | Miss. Code 1972<br>§§ 11-7-301 to 11-7-309 [UEFJA] |
| Missouri | V.A.M.S. §§ 511.770 to 511.787 [UFMJRA]<br>V.A.M.S. §§ 511.760 [UEFJA – 1948 Act]<br>V.A.M.R. Civ. Proc. R. 74.14 [UEFJA – 1964 Act] |
| Montana | M.C.A.<br>§§ 25-9-601 to 25-9-609 [UFMJRA]<br>§§ 25-9-701 to 25-9-715 [UFM-CA]<br>§§ 25-9-501 to 25-9-508 [UEFJA] |
| Nebraska | R.R.S. 1943<br>§§ 25-1587.01 to 25-1587.09 [UEFJA] |
| Nevada | N.R.S.<br>§§ 17.410 to 17.660 [UFM-CA]<br>§§ 17.330 to 17.400 [UEFJA] |
| New Hampshire | R.S.A.<br>524-A:1 to 524-A:8 [UEFJA] |
| New Jersey | N.J.S.A.<br>§§ 2A:49A-1 to 2A:49A-15 [UFM-CA]<br>§§ 2A:49A-16 to 2A:49A-24 [UFMJRA]<br>§§ 2A:49A-25 to 2A:49A-33 [UEFJA]<br>§§ 2A:82-4 to 2A:82-4.7 |
| New Mexico | N.M.S.A. 1978<br>§§ 39-4C-1 to 39-4C-16 [UFM-CA]<br>§§ 39-4B-1 to 39-4B-9 [UFMJRA]<br>§§ 39-4A-1 to 39-4A-6 [UEFJA] |

New York
McKinney's C.P.L.R.
5301 to 5309 [UFMJRA]
5401 to 5408 [UEFJA]

North Carolina
G.S.
§§ 1C-1820 to 1C-1834 [UFM-CA]
§§ 1C-1800 to 1C-1808 [UFMJRA]
§§ 1C-1701 to 1C-1708 [UEFJA]
*N.C. Gen. Stat. 1C-1804* (2003)

North Dakota
N.D.C.C.
32-41-01 to 32-41-13 [UFM-CA]
28-20.1-01 to 28-10.1-08 [UEFJA]
28-20.2-01 to 28-20.2-06 [UFMJRA]

Ohio
R.C.
§§ 2337.01 to 2337.15 [UFM-CA]
§§ 2329.90 to 2329.94 [UFMJRA]
§§ 2329.021 to 2329.027
*Ohio Rev. Code Ann.* 2329.92 (West 2004)

Oklahoma
12 Okl. St. Ann.
§§ 729.1 to 729.16 [UFM-CA]
§§ 710 to 718 [UFMJRA]
§§ 719 to 726 [UEFJA]

Oregon
O.R.S.
24.260 to 24.335 [UFM-CA]
24.200 to 24.255 [UFMJRA]
24.105 to 24.175 [UEFJA]

Pennsylvania
42 P.S. §§ 22001 to 22009 [UFMJRA]
42 P.A.C.S.A. §§ 4306 [UEFJA]

Rhode Island
Gen. Laws 1956, §§ 9-32-1 to 9-32-8 [UEFJA]

South Carolina
*S.C. Code Ann.* Code 1976 §15-35-900 to -960 (Law. Co-op. 1993) [UEFJA]
Code 1976 § 38-25-570 (Law. Co-op. 1993)
Code 1976 §§15-35-900 to -960 [UEFJA]
S.C. RULES OF CIVIL PROCEDURE 9 (Law. Co-op. 1994)

South Dakota
SDCL 15-16A-1 to 15-16A-10 [UEFJA]

Tennessee
T.C.A. §§ 26-6-101 to 26-6-107 [UEFJA]

Texas
V.T.C.A., Civil Practice and Remedies Code
§§ 36.001 to 36.008 [UFMJRA]
§§ 35.001 to 35.008 [UEFJA]
*Tex. Civ. Prac. & Rem. Code Ann.* 36.005 (Vernon 1997)

Utah
U.C.A. 1953
§§ 78-22b-101 to 78-22b-116 [UFM-CA]
§§ 78-22a-1 to 78-22a-8 [UEFJA]

| | |
|---|---|
| Virgin Islands | 5 V.I.C. §§551-558 [UEFJA]<br>5 V.I.C. §§561-569 [UFMJRA]<br>11 V.I.C. §§1530-1545 [UFM-CA] |
| Virginia | Code 1950<br>§§ 8.01-465.1 to 8.01-465.5 [UEFJA]<br>§§ 8.01-465.6 to 8.01-465.13 [UFMJRA]<br>§§ 8.01-465.14 to 8.01-465.25 [UFM-CA] |
| Washington | West's R.C.W.A.<br>6.44.010 to 6.44.904 [UFM-CA]<br>6.40.010 to 6.40.915 [UFMJRA]<br>6.36.010 to 6.36.910 [UEFJA] |
| West Virginia | W. Va. Code 55-14-1 to 55-14-8 [UEFJA] |
| Wisconsin | W.S.A.<br>806.30 to 806.44 [UFM-CA]<br>806.24 [UEFJA] |
| Wyoming | *Wyo. Stat. Ann.* §§ 1-17-701 to 1-17-707 [UEFJA] |

### 3. Multilateral Treaties

United Nations Convention on the Recognition and Enforcement of Foreign Arbitral Awards (New York Convention), June 10, 1958, 9 U.S.C.A. 202, available on *Westlaw*, 21 U.S.T. 2517, 330 U.N.T.S. 38 (1959), available at: http://untreaty.un.org.

Convention Abolishing the Requirement of Legalization for Foreign Public Documents

(Hague Apostille Convention), Oct. 5, 1961, 527 U.N.T.S. 189, 20 I.L.M. 1405, available at: http://untreaty.un.org.

Hague Convention on the Choice of Court, November 25, 1965, 4 I.L.M. 348, Receneil de Conventions Hague [RCH] 96.

Hague Convention on the Service Abroad of Judicial and Extrajudicial Documents in Civil and Commercial Matters, Nov. 15, 1965, 20 U.S.T. 361, 658 U.N.T.S. 163, 4 I.L.M. 341 (1965) [*supplemented by* Conclusions and Recommendations Adopted by the Special Commission on the Practical Operation of the Hague Apostille, Evidence and Service Conventions, 28 October–4 November, 2003]

Hague Convention on the Taking of Evidence Abroad in Civil or Commercial Matters, Mar. 18, 1970, 23 U.S.T. 2555, 8 I.L.M. 37 [*supplemented by* Conclusions and Recommendations Adopted by the Special Commission on the Practical Operation of the Hague Apostille, Evidence and Service Conventions, 28 October–4 November, 2003]

American Law Institute, Transnational Insolvency: Cooperation Among the NAFTA Countries, Procedural Principle 10 and Appendix B (Guidelines Applicable to Court-to-Court Communications in Cross-Border Cases).

American Law Institute, Intellectual Property: Principles Governing Jurisdiction, Choice of Law, and Judgments in Transnational Disputes – Preliminary Draft No. 3 (February 28, 2005)

### 4. Bilateral Treaties

Convention on the Reciprocal Recognition and Enforcement of Judgments in Civil Matters, October 26, 1976, U.S.–U.K., 16 I.L.M. 71; Third Consultative Paper, March 1979, reprinted in 8 N.C. J. INT'L L. COM. REG. 322 (1983)

Treaty of Friendship, Commerce, and Navigation Between the United States and the Republic of Korea, 8 U.S.T. 2217 (1957)

Treaty of Friendship, Commerce, and Navigation Between the United States and Greece, 5 U.S.T. 1829 (1954).

### 5. Uniform Laws (Generally) and Restatements

Conflict of Jurisdiction Model Act, *reprinted in* 26 INT'L. LAW. 21, 56 (1992)

Uniform Enforcement of Foreign Judgments Act, 13 U.L.A. 149 (West, WESTLAW 2004).

Uniform Foreign-Money Claims Act, 13 U.L.A. 149 (West, WESTLAW 2004).

Uniform Foreign Money-Judgments Recognition Act, 13 U.L.A. 263 (West, WESTLAW 2004).

Restatement (Second) of Conflict of Laws §§ 92–107 (West, WESTLAW 2004).

Restatement (Third) of the Foreign Relations Law of the United States §§ 481–8 (West, WESTLAW 2004).

## B. TREATISES AND BOOKS

### 1. General

AMERICAN INTERNATIONAL LAW CASES 1990–2001: THIRD SERIES (Bernard D. Reams, Jr., ed., 1998).

BARTOLUS OF SASSOTERATO, ON THE CONFLICT OF LAWS, CH. 10 (Joseph Henry Beale, tr., 2003), (1914).

GARY B. BORN, INTERNATIONAL CIVIL LITIGATION IN UNITED STATES COURTS (3rd ed. 1996).

Ronald A. Brand, *Recognition of Foreign Judgments as a Trade Law Issue: The Economics of Private International Law,* in the ECONOMIC ANALYSIS OF INTERNATIONAL LAW 592, Jagdeep Bhandari & Alan O. Sykes eds., 1998).

JAMES J. BROWN, JUDGMENT ENFORCEMENT (2nd ed., 2002).

DECLINING JURISDICTION IN PRIVATE INTERNATIONAL LAW: REPORTS TO THE XIVTH CONGRESS OF THE INTERNATIONAL ACADEMY OF COMPARATIVE LAW – ATHENS, AUGUST 1994 (J.J. Fawcett ed., 1995).

ALBERT V. DICEY & JOHN H. C. MORRIS, THE CONFLICT OF LAWS (13th ed., 2000).

GEORGES R. DELAUME, TRANSNATIONAL CONTRACTS – APPLICABLE LAW AND SETTLEMENT OF DISPUTES, CH. 9: A STUDY IN CONFLICT AVOIDANCE (1990).

EFFECTIVE DISPUTE RESOLUTION FOR THE INTERNATIONAL COMMERCIAL LAWYER 197 (Dennis Campbell & Peter Summerfield eds., 1989).

ALBERT A. EHRENZWEIG, A TREATISE ON THE CONFLICT OF LAWS §§ 45–67 (1967).

Albert Ehrenzweig & Erik Jayme, Private International Law: A Comparative Treatise on American International Conflicts Law, Including the Law of Admiralty, 20–49, 54–8 (1973).

Enforcement of Foreign Judgments (Dennis Campbell & Center for International Legal Studies, eds., 1997).

Enforcement of Money Judgments, Vol. 1–2 (Lawrence W. Newman ed., 2003).

Enforcing Foreign Judgments in the United States and United States Judgments Abroad (Ronald A. Brand ed., 1992).

David Epstein et al., International Litigation: A Guide to Jurisdiction, Practice and Strategy (3d ed., 2004).

John Fellas, International Commercial Litigation, ch. 4 & 6 (1999).

William F. Fox, Jr., International Commercial Agreements: A Primer on Drafting, Negotiating and Resolving Disputes, 165–96 (Deventer, Kluwer Law and Taxation Publishers, 1987).

Ruth B. Ginsburg, *Recognition and Execution of Foreign Civil Judgments and Arbitral Awards*, in Legal Thought in the United States of America Under Contemporary Pressures 237 (John N. Hazard & Wenceslas J. Wagner eds., 1970).

Judicial Enforcement of International Debt Obligations (David M. Sassoon & Daniel D. Bradlow eds., 1987).

Arthur K. Kuhn, Comparative Commentaries on Private International Law or Conflict of Laws, 103–14 (1937).

Andreas F. Lowenfeld, International Litigation and Arbitration, ch. 5 (1993).

Andreas F. Lowenfeld, International Litigation and the Quest for Reasonableness: Essays in Private International Law, ch. 6: Recognition and Enforcement of Judgments (1996).

Andreas F. Lowenfeld & Linda J. Silberman, *United States of America*, in Enforcement of Foreign Judgments Worldwide 259 (Charles Platto & William G. Horton, eds., 2d ed., 1993).

Joseph M. Lookofsky, Transnational Litigation and Commercial Arbitration: A Comparative Analysis of American, European and International Law, ch. 3–6 (1992).

Martindale-Hubbell Law Digest-United States Law Digests (New Providence, New Jersey, Martindale-Hubbell, 1992).

Micheal L. Morkin, United States, Enforcement of Money Judgments Abroad (Lawrence W. Newman, ed., 2003).

Ven P. Nanda & David K. Pansius, Litigation of International Disputes in Unted States Courts, ch. 12 (1986–2003).

Covey T. Oliver et. al, International Legal Systems: Cases and Materials (4th ed., 1995).

Ernst Rabel, The Conflict of Laws: A Comparative Study (2d ed., 1958).

Rudolph B. Schlesinger, Comparative Law (6th ed., 1998).

EUGENE F. SCOLES & PETER HAY, CONFLICT OF LAWS, CH. 24 (4th ed., 2004).

JOSEPH STORY, COMMENTARIES ON THE CONFLICT OF LAWS, FOREIGN AND DOMESTIC, IN REGARD TO CONTRACTS, RIGHTS AND REMEDIES, AND ESPECIALLY IN REGARD TO MARRIAGES, DIVORCES, WILLS, SUCCESSIONS, AND JUDGMENTS, CH. 15 (1972).

Robert Taylor, *The Enforcement of Foreign Judgments in the United States of America: Due Process Hurdles in Light of the Uniform Foreign Money Judgments Act*, in EFFECTIVE DISPUTE RESOLUTION FOR THE INTERNATIONAL COMMERCIAL LAWYER 197 (Dennis Campbell & Peter Summerfields eds., 1989).

LOUISE ELLEN TEITZ, TRANSNATIONAL LITIGATION, CH. 8 (1996).

RUSSELL J. WEINTRAUB, INTERNATIONAL LITIGATION AND ARBITRATION: PRACTICE AND PLANNING (2nd ed., CH. 1–3 (4th ed., 2003)).

David Westin, *Enforcing Foreign Judgments in the United States*, in INTERNATIONAL LITIGATION 473 (ABA Section of International Law and Practice, 1989).

JOHN WESTLAKE, A TREATISE ON PRIVATE INTERNATIONAL LAW WITH PRINCIPLE REFERENCE TO ITS PRACTICE IN ENGLAND AND OTHER COGNATE SYSTEMS OF JURISPRUDENCE, AND NUMEROUS REFERENCES TO AMERICAN AUTHORITIES (1986).

Arthur T. von Mehren, *Recognition and Enforcement of Foreign Judgments: Contemporary Practices and Roles of Conventions*, in PRIVATE INVESTMENT ABROAD: PROBLEMS AND SOLUTIONS IN INTERNATIONAL BUSINESS IN 1980 (M. Landwehr, ed., 1980).

BRUNO A. RISTAU, INTERNATIONAL JUDICIAL ASSISTANCE: CIVIL AND COMMERCIAL (2000).

LUTHER L. MCDOUGAL ET AL., AMERICAN CONFLICTS LAW (5th ed., 2001).

Courtland H. Peterson, *Limits on the Enforcement of Foreign Country Judgments and Choice of Law and Forum Clauses*, in LAW AND JUSTICE IN A MULTISTATE WORLD (James A. R. Nafziger & Symeon C. Symeonides eds., Transnational, 2002).

### 2. States

#### *California*

2 RICK SCHWARTZ & JUDGE ALAN M. AHART, CALIFORNIA PRACTICE GUIDE, ENFORCING JUDGMENTS AND DEBTS, CH. 6J (1988).

8 B. WITKIN, CALIFORNIA PROCEDURE, Enf. Judgm. §431, 434 (4th ed., 1997).

#### *Maryland*

STEPHEN M. GOLDBERG & GERARD R. VETTER, COLLECTING JUDGMENTS IN MARYLAND: BEYOND THE BASICS (Eau Claire, WI, National Business Institute, Inc., 1993).

THE MARYLAND GUIDE TO INTERNATIONAL TRADE (Frank, Bernstein, Conaway & Goldman eds., Baltimore, MD, Maryland International Division, 1992).

#### *Massachusetts*

RICHARD M. GELB, PRACTICAL SKILLS COURSE IN COMMERCIAL ARBITRATION: FROM DRAFTING THE INITIAL CLAUSE TO APPEALS (Boston, MA, MCLE, 1994).

*North Carolina*

The Unique Impact of North Carolina Law on International Transactions (Raleigh, NC, North Carolina Bar Association Foundation, 1993).

### 3. Specialized Areas

#### *a. Antitrust*

Alan D. Neal & Mel L. Stevens, International Business and National Jurisdiction, 151 (1988).

The Unique Impact of North Carolina Law on International Transactions (Raleigh, NC, North Carolina Bar Association Foundation, 1993).

#### *b. Arbitration Awards/New York Convention*

Gary B. Born & David Westin, International Civil Litigation in United States Courts: Commentary and Materials (2d ed., 1992).

Georges R. Delaume, Law and Practice of Transnational Contracts, chs. 9–10 (1988).

George R. Delaume, Law and Practice of Transnational Contracts Applicable Law and Settlement Disputes, ch. 13–14 (New York, Oceana Publications, 1992).

Yves Dezalay & Bryant G. Garth, Grand Old Men v. Multinationals: The Routinization of Charismatic Arbitration into Off-Shore Litigation (ABF Working Paper # 9317) (1993).

David Epstein & Jefrey L. Snyder, International Litigation: A Guide to Jurisdiction, Practice and Strategy (3d ed., 1998).

The International Arbitration Kit: A Compilation of Basic and Frequently Requested Documents (Laura Ferris Brown ed., 4th ed., 1993).

M. Sornarajah, International Commercial Arbitration: The Problem of State Contracts, ch. 7 (1990).

Joseph T. Mclaughlin, *Enforcement of Arbitral Awards Under the New York Convention: Practice in the U.S. Courts*, in 2 International Commercial Arbitration Recent Developments 275 (1988).

#### *c. Bankruptcy and Creditors' Rights*

Charles D. Booth, *Recognition of Foreign Bankruptcies in a Transnational Setting: An Analysis of the Laws of the United States*, in II The Law of Transnational Business Transactions, ch. 9 (Ved P. Nanda & Ralph B. Lake eds., 2003).

Current Developments in International and Comparative Corporate Insolvency Law (Jacob. S. Ziegel ed., with assistance of Susan I. Cantlie, 1994).

J. H. Dalhuisen, Dalhuisen on International Insolvency and Bankruptcy, §§ 1.05 to .07 (New York, Mathew Bender & Co., 1986).

Evan D. Flaschen and Ronald J. Silverman, *Maxwell Communication Corporation plc: The Importance of Comity and Co-operation in Resolving International Insolvencies*, in

CROSS-BORDER INSOLVENCY AND REORGANIZATIONS (E. Bruce Leonard and Christopher W. Besant, eds.) (IBA, 1994).

FREE TRADE WITH MEXICO AND CANADA: OVERVIEW OF BUSINESS FINANCE AND INSOLVENCY (Chicago, IL, American Bar Association, 1993).

INTERNATIONAL CRIMINAL LAW, 478, 492–6 (Gerhard O. W. Mueller and Edward M. Wise, eds., 1965).

DAVID L. SHAPIRO, PRECLUSION IN CIVIL ACTIONS, 153–67 (2001).

*d. Domestic Relations*

JUDGE WILLIAM P. HOGOBOOM & DONALD B. KING, CALIFORNIA PRACTICE GUIDE: FAMILY LAW 18 (2004).

INTERNATIONAL CHILD ABDUCTIONS: A GUIDE TO APPLYING THE HAGUE CONVENTION, WITH FORMS (Gloria F. DeHarted ed., 2d ed., 1993).

CHRISTIAN E. MARKEY JR., CALIFORNIA FAMILY LAW: PRACTICE AND PROCEDURE, §§ 52.05.06 (1987).

*e. Non-Money Judgments*

TRENDS IN THE ENFORCEMENT OF NONMONEY JUDGMENTS AND ORDERS (Ulla Jacobsson & Jack Jacobs eds., Norwell, MA, Kluwer Law and Taxation Publishers, 1988).

*f. Sovereign Immunity/U.S.-Iran Claims Tribunal*

GEORGES R. DELAUME, LAW AND PRACTICE OF TRANSNATIONAL CONTRACTS, CH. 8, 10 (1988).

GEORGES R. DELAUME, TRANSNATIONAL CONTRACTS APPLICABLE LAW AND SETTLEMENT DISPUTES: A STUDY IN CONFLICT AVOIDANCE, CH. 11–12 (1997).

JOSEPH W. DELLAPENNA, SUING FOREIGN GOVERNMENTS AND THEIR CORPORATIONS (2d ed., 2003).

M. SORNARAJAH, INTERNATIONAL COMMERCIAL ARBITRATION: THE PROBLEM OF STATE CONTRACTS (1990).

Hugh J. Turner, *Collection Procedures Against Foreign Sovereigns*, in INTERNATIONAL LITIGATION 515 (ABA Section of International Law and Practice, 1989).

PAUL H. VISHNY, GUIDE TO INTERNATIONAL COMMERCE LAW, CH. 12 (2003).

## C. JOURNALS

### 1. General

*a. Signed*

Matthew H. Adler, *If We Build It, Will They Come? – The Need for a Multilateral Convention on the Recognition and Enforcement of Civil Monetary Judgments*, 26 LAW & POL'Y INT'L BUS. 79 (1994).

Jennifer Anglim, *Crossroads in the Great Race: Moving Beyond the International Race to Judgment in Disputes over Artwork and Other Chattels*, 45 HARV. INT'L L.J. 239 (2004).

Violeta I. Balan, *Recognition and Enforcement of Foreign Judgments in the United States: The Need for Federal Legislation*, 37 J. MARSHALL L. REV. 229 (2003).

Samuel P. Baumgartner, *Is Transnational Litigation Different?*, 25 U. PA. J. INT'L ECON. L. 1297 (2004).

Crystal Beal, *Foreign Currency Judgments: A New Option for United States Courts*, 19 U. PA. J. INT'L ECON. L. 101 (1998).

Ayelet Ben-Ezer & Ariel L. Bendor, *The Constitution and Conflict-of-Laws Treaties: Upgrading the International Comity*, 29 N.C.J. INT'L LAW COM. REG. 1 (2003).

George A. Bermann, *Provisional Relief in Transnational Litigation*, 35 COLUM. J. TRANSNAT'L L. 553 (1997).

R. D. Bishop & Susan Burnette, *United States Practice Concerning the Recognition of Foreign Judgments*, 16 INT'L LAW. 425 (1982).

Ronald A. Brand, *Restructuring the U.S. Approach to Judgments on Foreign Currency Liabilities: Building on the English Experience*, 11 YALE J. INT'L L. 139 (1985).

Ronald A. Brand, *Enforcement of Foreign Money Judgments in the United States: In Search of Uniformity and International Acceptance*, 67 NOTRE DAME L. REV. 253 (1991).

Ronald A. Brand, *Exchange Loss Damages and the Uniform Foreign-Money Claims Act: The Emperor Hasn't All His Clothes*, 23 LAW & POL'Y INT'L BUS. 1 (1992).

Ronald A. Brand, *Symposium on U.S.-E.C. Legal Relations: Enforcement of Judgments in the United States and Europe*, 13 J. L. & COM. 193 (1994).

Adrian Briggs, *Which Foreign Judgments Should We Recognize Today?*, 36 INT'L & COMP. L.Q. 240 (1987).

Stephen B. Burbank, *The Bitter with the Sweet Tradition, History and Limitations on Federal Judicial Power – A Case Study*, 75 NOTRE DAME L. REV. 1291 (2000).

Stephen B. Burbank, *Jurisdictional Conflict and Jurisdictional Equilibration: Paths to a Via Media?*, 26 HOUS. J. INT'L L. 385 (2004).

Robert C. Casad, *Issue Preclusion and Foreign Country Judgments: Whose Law?*, 70 IOWA L. REV. 53 (1984).

Beverly Carl, *Suing Foreign Governments in American Courts: The United States' Foreign Sovereign Immunities Act in Practice*, 33 SW. L.J. 1009 (1979).

Cedric C. Chao & Christine S. Neuhoff, *International Law Weekend – West Symposium Issue: Enforcement and Recognition of Foreign Judgments in United States Courts: A Practical Perspective*, 29 PEPP. L. REV. 147 (2001).

Harry L. Clark, *Dealing with U.S. Extraterritorial Sanctions and Foreign Countermeasures*, 25 U. PA. J. INT'L ECON. L. 455 (2004).

Christopher D. DeCluitt, *International Patent Prosecution, Litigation and Enforcement*, 5 TULSA J. COMP. & INT'L L. 135 (1997).

Ronan E. Degnan & Mary Kay Kane, *The Exercise of Jurisdiction over and Enforcement of Judgments Against Alien Defendants*, 39 HASTINGS L. J. 799, 844–54 (1988).

Rochelle C. Dreyfuss & Jane C. Ginsburg, *Draft Convention on Jurisdiction and Recognition of Judgments in Intellectual Property Matters* (Symposium on Constructing International Intellectual Property Law: The Role of National Courts), 77 CHI.-KENT LAW REV. 1065 (2002).

Paul S. Edelman, *Enforcements of Foreign Judgments*, N.Y.L.J., MAR. 2, 1990, at 3.

John Fellas, *Lessons on Enforcing Foreign Judgments in the United States*, N.Y.L.J., Sept. 26, 2002.

Sharon E. Foster, *Does the First Amendment Restrict Recognition and Enforcement of Foreign Copyright Judgments and Arbitration Awards?*, 10 PACE INT'L L. REV. 361 (1998).

Jonathan A. Franklin & Roberta J. Morris, *International Jurisdiction and Enforcement of Judgments in the Era of Global Networks: Irrelevance of, Goals for, and Comments on the Current Proposals*, 77 CHI.-KENT L. REV. 1213 (2002).

Alan E. Golomb, *Recognition of Foreign Money Judgments: A Goal-Oriented Approach*, 43 ST. JOHN'S L. REV. 604 (1969).

Orlando A. Gonzales-Arias, *The Enforcement of United States Default Judgments*, 10 HASTINGS INT'L & COMP. L.R. 97 (1986).

Michael W. Gordon & Matthew Adler et al., *Some Post-Litigation Issues: Enforcement of a Foreign Judgment Which Includes Compensatory, Moral and/or Punitive Damages; Enforcement of Injunctive Relief and Specific Performance: Enforcement of Costs, Interest, and Attorneys' Fees, Determination of the Proper Currency in an Enforcement Proceeding*, 5 U.S.-MEX. L.J. 183 (1997).

Brett Harrison, *Enforcing U.S. Judgments: Due Process, Proper Jurisdiction*, 45 FOR THE DEFENSE 75 (2003).

J. Noelle Hicks, Andrew P. Vance Memorial Writing Competition Winner, *Facilitating International Trade: The U.S. Needs Federal Legislation Governing the Enforcement of Foreign Judgments*, 28 BROOKLYN J. INT'L L. 155 (2002).

Christopher P. Hall & David B. Gordon, *Enforcement of Foreign Judgments in the United States*, 10 INT'L LAW PRACTICUM 57 Autumn 1997, at 57.

Janet Hallahan, *Should a Foreign Nation's Jury Awards Limit American Juries?* 67 TEMPLE L. REV. 729 (1994).

Adolf Homburger, *Recognition and Enforcement of Foreign Judgments: A New Yorker Reflects on Uniform Acts*, 18 AM. J. COMP. L. 367 (1970).

William C. Honey & Marc Hall, *Bases for Recognition of Foreign Nation Money Judgments in the U.S. and Need for Federal Intervention*, 16 SUFFOLK TRANSNAT'L L. REV. 405 (1993).

Carol C. Honigsberg, *The Uniform Foreign Money-Judgments Recognition Act: A Survey of the Case Law*, 14 VAND. J. TRANSNAT'L L. 171 (1981).

Gary N. Horlick, A *Practical Guide to Service of United States Process Abroad*, 14 INT'L LAW. 637 (1980).

Charles W. Joiner, *The Recognition of Foreign Country Money Judgments by American Courts*, 34 AM. J. COMP. L. SUPP. 193 (1986).

Wei Jia Ju, *The Enforcement Clause: A New Development in the Recognition and Enforcement of Foreign Judgments*, 31 AM. JUR. COMP. L. 520 (1983).

Friedrich K. Juenger, *The Recognition of Money Judgments in Civil and Commercial Matters*, 36 AM. J. COMP. L. 1 (1988).

Barbara Kulzer, *Some Aspects of Enforceability of Foreign Judgments: A Comparative Summary*, 16 BUFF. L. REV. 84 (1967).

Fairfax Leary, Jr. & Howard T. Rosen, *The Uniform Foreign-Money Claims Act*, 12 U. PA. J. INT'L BUS. L. 51 (1991).

Arthur Lenhoff, *Reciprocity and the Law of Foreign Judgments: A Historical Critical Analysis*, 16 LA. L. REV. 465 (1956).

Peter S. Levitt, *The Extraterritorial Assertion of Long-Arm Jurisdiction and the Impact on the International Commercial Community: A Comment and Suggested Approach*, 9 U. PA. J. INT'L BUS. L. 713 (1986).

Graham C. Lily, *Jurisdiction Over Domestic and Alien Defendants*, 69 VA. L. REV. 85 (1983).

Albert A. Linder, Comment, *Judgments Rendered Abroad – State Law or Federal Law?*, 12 VILL. L. REV. 618 (1967).

Paul L. Lion III, *The Need to Retreat from Inflexible Conversion Rules – An Equitable Approach to Judgments in Foreign Currency*, 22 SANTA CLARA L. REV. 871 (1982).

Ernest G. Lorenzen, *The Enforcement of American Judgments Abroad*, 29 YALE L.J. 188 (1919).

Andreas F. Lowenfeld, *International Litigation and the Quest for Reasonableness: General Course on Private International Law*, 245 RECEUIL DES COURS (1994) [The Hague Academy of International Law].

Andreas F. Lowenfeld, *Thoughts About a Multinational Judgments Convention: A Reaction to the Von Mehren Report*, 57 LAW AND CONTEMP. PROBS. 289 (1994).

Robert E. Lutz, *Enforcement of Foreign Judgments, Part I: A Selected Bibliography of United States Enforcement of Judgments Rendered Abroad*, 27 INT'L LAW. 471 (1993).

Richard H. M. Maloy & Desamparados M. Nisi, *A Message to the Supreme Court: The Next Time You Get a Chance, Please Look at Hilton v. Guyot; We Think It Needs Repairing*, 5 J. INT'L LEGAL STUD. 1, 2 (1999).

Jeremy Maltby, *Juggling Comity and Self-Government: The Enforcement of Foreign Libel Judgments in U.S. Courts*, 94 COLUM. L. REV. 1978 (1994).

Katherine R. Miller, *Playground Politics: Assessing the Wisdom of Writing a Reciprocity Requirement into U.S. International Recognition and Enforcement Law*, 35 GEO. J. INT'L L. 239 (2004).

Karen E. Minehan, *The Public Policy Exception to the Enforcement of Foreign Judgments: Necessary or Nemesis?*, 18 LOY. L.A. INT'L & COMP. L.J. 795 (1996).

Jonathan S. Moore, *Enforcing Foreign Ownership Claims in the Antiquities Market*, 97 YALE L.J. 466 (1988).

Lawrence W. Newman, *Enforcement of Judgments*, 17 VAND J. TRANSNAT'L L. 77 (1984).

Lawrence W. Newman, *Jurisdiction to Enforce Foreign Judgments*, 225 N.Y.L.J. 3 (2001).

Robert Nicholas, *Reciprocal Enforcement of U.S. and Foreign Judgments*, 2 TEX. INT'L L.J. 75 (1971).

Arthur Nussbaum, *Jurisdiction and Foreign Judgments*, 41 COLUM. L. REV. 221 (1941).

Joel R. Paul, *Comity in International Law*, 32 HARV. INT'L L.J. 1 (1991).

Courtland H. Peterson, *Foreign Country Judgments and the Second Restatement of Conflict of Laws*, 72 COLUM. L. REV. 220 (1972).

Courtland H. Peterson, *Res Judicata and Foreign Country Judgments*, 24 OHIO ST. L.J. 291 (1963).

Johnathan H. Pittman, *The Public Policy Exception to the Recognition of Foreign Judgments*, 22 VAND. J. TRANSNAT'L. L. 969 (1989).

Willibald Posch, *Resolving Business Disputes Through Litigation or Other Alternatives: The Effects of Jurisdictional Rules and Recognition Practice*, 26 HOUS. J. INT'L L. 363 (2004).

Michael Quilling, Note, *The Recognition and Enforcement of Foreign Country Judgments and Arbitral Awards: A North-South Perspective*, 11 GA. J. INT'L & COMP. L. 635 (1981).

Alan Reed, *A New Model of Jurisdictional Propriety for Anglo-American Foreign Judgment Recognition and Enforcement: Something Old, Something Borrowed, Something New?*, 25 LOY. L.A. INT'L & COMP. L.J. 243 (2003).

Mark D. Rosen, *Should Un-American Judgments Be Enforced?*, 88 MINN. L. REV. 783 (2004).

Beth van Schaack, *In Defense of Civil Redress: The Domestic Enforcement of Human Rights Norms in the Context of the Proposed Hague Judgments Convention*, 42 HARV. INT'L L.J. 141 (2001).

Carolyn S. Schwartz, *Enforcement of Money Judgments: Debt Collection, Foreign Judgments and Effect of Bankruptcy, Commercial Law and Practice Course Handbook Series in Enforcing State and Federal Money Judgments and Commercial Claims, PLI Order No. A4–4454 April 12, 19, 26, and May 3, 1994*, 686 PLI/COMM. 7 (1994), *available on Westlaw.*

Eugene F. Scoles, *Interstate and International Distinctions in Conflict of Laws in the United States*, 54 CAL. L. REV. 1599 (1966).

Eugene F. Scoles & Laila E. Aarnas, *The Recognition and Enforcement of Foreign Nation Judgments: California, Oregon, and Washington*, 57 OR. L. REV. 377 (1978).

Elisabeth M. Senger-Weiss, *Enforcing Foreign Arbitration Awards*, 53 DISP. RESOL. J. 70 (1998).

Linda J. Silberman, *Enforcement and Recognition of Foreign Country Judgments in the United States, Litigation and Administrative Practice Course Handbook Series in International Commercial Litigation, PLI Order No. HO-001X February, 1998*, 579 PLI/LIT. (1998) 103, *available on Westlaw.*

Linda J. Silberman, *A Different Challenge for the ALI: Herein of Foreign Country Judgments, an International Treaty, and an American Statute*, 75 IND. L.J. 635 (2000).

Linda J. Silberman, *Enforcement and Recognition of Foreign Country Judgments in the United States*, 16 INT'L Q. 534 (2004).

Linda J. Silberman, *The Impact of Jurisdictional Rules and Recognition Practice on International Business Transactions: the U.S. Regime*, 26 HOUS. J. INT'L L. 327 (2004).

David H. Small, *Managing Extraterritorial Jurisdiction Problems: The United States Government Approach*, 50 LAW. & CONTEMP. PROBS. 283 (1987).

Hans Smit, *International Res Judicata and Collateral Estoppel in the United States*, 9 U.C.L.A. L. REV. 44 (1962).

Hans Smit, *Enforcement of Judgments in the United States of America*, 34 AM. J. COMP. L. Supp. 255 (1986).

Alan J. Sorkowitz, *Enforcing Judgments Under the Uniform Foreign Money-Judgments Recognition Act*, 37 PRAC. LAW. 57 (1991).

P. A. Stone, *The Civil Jurisdiction and Judgments Act 1982: Some Comments*, 32 INT'L & COMP. L.Q. 477 (1983).

Susan L. Stevens, *Commanding International Judicial Respect: Reciprocity and the Recognition and Enforcement of Foreign Judgments*, 26 HASTINGS INT'L & COMP. L. REV. 115 (2002).

William C. Sturm, *Enforcement of Foreign Judgments*, 95 COM. L.J. 200 (1990).

Louise Ellen Teitz, *Taking Multiple Bites of the Apple: A Proposal to Resolve Conflicts of Jurisdiction and Multiple Proceedings*, 26 INT'L LAW. 21 (1992).

Louise Ellen Teitz et al., *International Litigation*, 31 INT'L LAW. 317 (1997).

Louise Ellen Teitz, *International Litigation – Parallel Proceedings: Parallel Proceeding and the Guiding Hand of Comity*, 34 INT'L LAW. 545 (2000).

Louise Ellen Teitz, *International Litigation – Parallel Proceedings: Moving into Cyberspace*, 35 *Int'l Law.* 490 (2001).

Louise Ellen Teitz, *Both Sides of the Coin: A Decade of Parallel Proceedings and Enforcement of Foreign Judgments in Transnational Litigation*, 10 ROGER WILLIAMS U.L. REV. 1 (2004).

Loise Ellen Teitz, *Development in Parallel Proceedings: The Globalization of Procedural Responses*, 38 INT'L LAW. 303 (2004).

Lisa C. Thompson, *International Dispute Resolution in the United States and Mexico: A Practical Guide to Terms, Arbitration Clauses, and the Enforcement of Judgments and Arbitral Awards*, 24 SYRACUSE J. INT'L L. & COM. 1 (Fall 1997).

Robert B. von Mehren, *Transnational Litigation in American Courts: An Overview of Problems and Issues*, 3 DICK. J. INT'L L. 43 (1984).

Robert B. von Mehren, *Enforcement of Foreign Arbitral Awards in the United States, Litigation and Administrative Practice Course Handbook Series in International Commercial Litigation, PLI order no. ho-001x February, 1998*, 579 PLI/LIT. 147 (1998) *available on Westlaw*.

Robert B. von Mehren & Michael E. Patterson, *Recognition and Enforcement of Foreign-Country Judgments in the United States*, 6 LAW & POL'Y INT'L BUS. 37 (1974).

Arthur T. von Mehren, *Recognition and Enforcement of Sister-State Judgments: Reflections on General Theory and Current Practice in the European Economic Community and the United States*, 81 COLUM. L. REV. 1044 (1981).

Arthur T. von Mehren, *Recognition and Enforcement of Foreign Judgments: A New Approach for the Hague Conference?* 57 LAW & CONTEMP. PROBS. 271 (1994).

Arthur T. von Mehren & Donald T. Trautman, *Jurisdiction to Adjudicate: A Suggested Analysis*, 79 Harv. L. Rev. 1121 (1966).

Arthur T. von Mehren & Donald T. Trautman, *Recognition of Foreign Adjudications: A Survey and Suggested Approach*, 81 Harv. L. Rev. 1601 (1968).

Lawrence W. Newman & Michael Burrows, *Jurisdiction to Enforce Foreign-Country Money Judgments*, N.Y.L.J., AUG. 16, 1990, AT 3.

Michael Traynor, *Conflict of Laws, Comparative Law, and The American Law Institute*, 49 Am. J. Comp. L. 391, 396 (2001).

Russell J. Weintraub, *The Need for Awareness of International Standards When Construing Multilateral Conventions: The Arbitration, Evidence, and Service Conventions*, 28 Tex. Int'l L.J. 441 (1993).

Suzanne Raggio Westerheim, *The Uniform Foreign-Money Claims Act: No Solution to an Old Problem*, 69 Tex. L. Rev. 1203 (1991).

David Westin, *Enforcing Foreign Commercial Judgments and Arbitral Awards in the United States, West Germany, and England*, 19 Law & Pol'y Int'l Bus. 325 (1987).

John S. Willems, *Shutting the U.S. Courthouse Door? Forum non Conveniens in International Arbitration*, 58 Dispute Res. J. 54 (2003).

Katherine Birmingham Wilmore, Glen W. Rhodes, Lisa S. Buccino, *International Developments in Review: 2001 Business Transactions & Disputes, International Litigation*, 36 Int'l Law. 449 (2002).

David L. Woodward, *Reciprocal Recognition and Enforcement of Civil Judgments in the United States, the United Kingdom, and the European Economic Community*, 8 N.C. J. Int'l L. & Com. Reg. 299 (1983).

Hessel E. Yntema, *The Enforcement of Foreign Judgments in Anglo-American Law*, 33 Mich. L. Rev. 1129 (1935).

Hessel E. Yntema, *The Comity Doctrine*, 65 Mich. L. Rev. 9 (1966).

George A. Zaphiriou, *Transnational Recognition and Enforcement of Civil Judgments*, 53 Notre Dame L. Rev. 734 (1978).

***b. Unsigned***

*Appendix G: Federal Foreign Judgments Recognition and Enforcement Act*, 8 Transnat'l L. & Contemp. Probs. 105 (1998).

Comment, *Survey of International Law & Trade: Foreign Judgments Contrary to Public Policy of the Forum State Will Not Be Recognized or Enforced under Principles of Comity, Telnikoff* v. *Matusevich*, 347 Md. 561 (1997), 22 Md. J. Int'l L. & Trade 180 (1998).

*Foreign Currency Judgments: 1985 Report of the Committee on Foreign and Comparative Law*, 18 N.Y.U. J. Int'l L. & Pol. 791 (1986).

*Foreign Judgments-Enforcement*, dTahan v. Hodgson, 622 F.2d 862 (D.C. Cir. 1981), 3 J. Int'l. & Comp. L. 116 (1981).

*No Personal Jurisdiction over French Defendants in Yahoo! Case Regarding Nazi Material*, 21 COMPUTER & INTERNET LAW. 33 (2004).

Note, *Conversion Date of Foreign Money Obligations*, 65 COLUM. L. REV. 490 (1965).

### c. Annotations

Andrew M. Campbell, Annotation, *Refusal to Enforce Foreign Arbitration Awards on Public Policy Grounds*, 14 A.L.R. Federal. 481 (1998 & Supp. 2004).

Sara L. Johnson, *Validity, Construction, and Application of Uniform Enforcement of Foreign Judgments Act*, 31 A.L.R. 4th 706 (1984 & Supp. 2004).

E. H. Schopler, *Fraud as Defense to Action on Judgment of Sister State*, 55 A.L.R. 2d 673 (1957 & Supp. 2004).

Sheldon R. Shapiro, *Res Judicata or Collateral Estoppel Effect, in State Where Real Property Is Located, of Foreign Decree Dealing with Such Property*, 32 A.L.R. 3d 1330 (1970 & Supp. 2004).

Daniel J. Smith, *Invalidity of Judgment of a Court of Foreign Country*, 9 AM. JUR. PROOF OF FACTS 3d 687 (1990).

Gary D. Spivey, *Requirement of Full Faith and Credit to Foreign Judgment for Punitive Damages*, 44 A.L.R. 3d 960 (1972 & Supp. 2004).

Wanda Ellen Wakefield, *Judgment of Court of Foreign Country as Entitled to Enforcement or Extraterritorial Effect in State Court*, 13 A.L.R. 4th 1109 (1982 & Supp. 2004).

Charles A. Wright,Arthur R. Miller & Edward H. Cooper, Annotation, 18B FEDERAL. PRAC. & PROC. JURIS. 2d § 4473 (Supp. 2004).

Jay M. Zitter, *Construction and Application of Uniform Foreign Money-Judgments Recognition Act*, 88 A.L.R. 5th 545 (2001).

## 2. Federal

### a. Signed

Winston Anderson, *Enforcement of Foreign Judgments Founded upon a Cause of Action Unknown in the Forum*, 42 INT'L & COMP. L.Q. 697 (1993).

Stephen B. Burbank, *Federal Judgments Law: Sources of Authority and Sources of Rules*, 70 TEX. L. REV. 1551 (1992).

John D. Brummett, Jr., *The Preclusive Effect of Foreign-Country Judgments in the United States and Federal Choice of Law: The Role of the Erie Doctrine Reassessed*, 33 N.Y. L. SCH. L. REV. 83 (1988).

Jay Conison, *What Does Due Process Have to Do with Jurisdiction?* 46 RUTGERS L. REV. 1073 (1994).

Stephen J. Darmody, *An Economic Approach to Forum Non Conveniens Dismissals Requested by U.S. Multinational Corporations, The Bhopal Case*, 22 GEO. WASH. J. INT'L L. & ECON. 215 (1988).

David W. Hartmann, *Enforcing Foreign Judgments: Due Process Considerations*, 46 J. MO. B. 529 (1990).

Jerome A. Hoffman, *Recognition by Courts in the Eleventh Circuit of Judgments Rendered by Courts of Other Countries*, 29 CUMB. L. REV. 65 (1999).

Ernest C. Jett, Jr., *Recent Developments, Conflict of Laws – Recognition of Foreign Judgments – Federal Courts Are to Apply State Laws on Recognition of Foreign Judgments*, 8 TEX. INT'L L.J. 247 (1973).

Ramon P. Marks, Note, *Alternative Theories for Establishing a Federal Common Law of Foreign Judgments in Commercial Cases: The Foreign Affairs Power and the Dormant Foreign Commerce Clause*, 16 VA. J. INT'L L. 635 (1976).

Behrooz Moghaddam, *Recognition of Foreign Country Judgments – A Case for Federalization*, 22 TEX. INT'L L.J. 331 (1987).

Willis L. M. Reese, *The Status in This Country of Judgments Rendered Abroad*, 50 COLUM. L. REV. 783 (1950).

Hershel Shanks & Steven A. Standiford, *Schizophrenia in Federal Judgment Enforcement: Registration of Foreign Judgments Under 28 U.S.C. § 1963*, 59 NOTRE DAME L. REV. 851 (1984).

Allan Jay Stevenson, *Forum Non Conveniens and Equal Access Under Friendship, Commerce, and Navigation Treaties: A Foreign Plaintiff's Rights*, 13 HASTINGS INT'L & COMP. L. REV. 267 (1990).

Penny Zagalis, *Hartford Fire Insurance Company v. California: Reassessing the Application of the McCarran-Ferguson Act to Foreign Reinsurers*, 27 CORNELL INT'L L.J. 241 (1994).

### *b. Annotations*

Kristine Cordier Karnezis, *Registration in Federal District Court of Judgment of Another Federal Court Under 28 U.S.C.A. § 1963*, 194 A.L.R. FED. 531 (2004).

Russell G. Donaldson, *Proof of Foreign Official Record Under Rule 44(a)(2) of Federal Rules of Civil Procedure*, 41 A.L.R. FED. 784 (1973 & Supp. 2004).

Robin C. Miller, *Propriety of Federal Court Injunction Against Suit in Foreign Country*, 78 A.L.R. FED. 831 (1986 & Supp. 2004).

Sheldon R. Shapiro, *Federal or State Law as Governing Federal Court's Authority, in Diversity Action after Erie R. Co. v. Tompkins, to Take Judicial Notice of Law of Sister State or Foreign Country*, 7 A.L.R. FED. 921 (1971 & Supp. 2004).

Sheldon R. Shapiro, *Valid Judgment of Court of Foreign Country as Entitled to Extraterritorial Effect in Federal District Court*, 13 A.L.R. FED. 208 (1972 & Supp. 2004).

## 3. States and Possession (by State)

### *Arizona*

James O. Ehinger, *Enforcement of Foreign Country Judgments in Arizona*, 33 ARIZ. ATT'Y 20 (MAR. 1997).

Winton D. Woods, Jr. & Daniel J. Hochuli, *Attacking Foreign Judgments in Arizona: Full Faith and Credit Problems to Avoid*, 21 ARIZ. B.J., Jun.–July 1985, at 35.

### *California*

Comment, *Extraterritorial Jurisdiction: The Application of U.S. Antitrust Laws to Acts Outside the United States – Hartford Fire Insurance Co. v. California 113 S. Ct. 2891 (1993)*, 20 Wm. Mitchell L. Rev. 1109 (1994).

Stacy Adler Gordon, *California Ruling Limits Many Foreign Lawsuits*, 25 Bus. Ins., Dec. 23, 1991, at 1.

William P. Hogoboom & Donald B. King (Contributing editors: Michael Asimow, Kenneth A. Black and Bruce E. Cooperman), *Recognition and Enforcement of Foreign Judgments Generally (Other Than for Support or Custody)*, in California Practice Guide (family law chapter) 18:900 – 18:979–84 (1997).

Donald E. McKnight, Jr., *Enforcement of a Foreign Money Judgment in California*, 1 cal. Int'l Prac. no. 2 1 (1989–90).

Eugene F. Scoles & Laila E. Aarnas, *The Recognition and Enforcement of Foreign Nation Judgments: California, Oregon and Washington*, 57 Or. L. Rev. 377 (1978).

Penny Zagalis, *Hartford Fire Insurance Company v. California: Reassessing the Application of the McCarran-Ferguson Act to Foreign Reinsurers*, 27 Cornell Int'l L.J. 241 (1994).

### *Colorado*

Mark S. Caldwell, *Enforcing Foreign Country Judgments in Colorado*, 13 Colo. Law. 381 (1984).

### *Florida*

Ricardo J. Cata, *Uniform Foreign Money Judgments Recognition Act: An Idea Whose Time Has Come in Florida?*, 66 Fla. B.J. 94 (1992).

Thomas W. Franchino, *The Florida Enforcement* of *Foreign Judgments Act: What Time Limit Applies?*, 74 Fla. B.J. 22 (2000).

Hilarion Arnaldo Martinez Llanes, *Foreign Nation Judgments: Recognition and Enforcement of Foreign Judgments in Florida and the Status of Florida Judgments Abroad*, 31 U. Fla. L. Rev. 588 (1979).

### *Kansas*

John R. Schmertz & Mike Meier, *Applying Kansas Law on Enforcement of Foreign Country Judgments, Tenth Circuit Holds That Claim Preclusion Based on Prior Australian Judgment Barred Federal Court Action Arising out of Same Transactions*, 2 Int'l L. Update 90 (Aug., 1996).

### *Indianna*

Jack G. Hittle, *Foreign Judgments: To Docket or Not to Docket*, 31 Res Gestae 177 (1987).

### *Massachusetts*

J. W. Fitch, et al., *The Enforcement of Foreign Money Judgments in Massachusetts*, 81 Mass. L. Rev. 65 (1996).

*Missouri*

Stephen M. Boyd & John N. Ehlers, *Missouri's Uniform Foreign Country Money-Judgments Recognition Act*, 41 MO. B. 240 (1985).

*New Jersey*

Peter G. Ernster, *Recognition and Enforcement of Foreign Money-Judgments: A Clear Position for New Jersey*, 22 RUTGERS L. REV. 327 (1968).

*New York*

Cerisse Anderson, *New York Injunction Enforced in Dispute from English Court*, 227 N.Y. L.J. (2002).

Jennifer Freeman, *Judgments in Foreign Currency: A Little Known Change in New York Law*, 23 INT'L LAW. 737 (1989).

Adolf Homburger, *Recognition and Enforcement of Foreign Judgments: A New Yorker Reflects on Uniform Acts*, 18 AM. J. COMP. L. 367 (1970).

Barbara Kulzer, *Recognition of Foreign Country Judgments in New York: The Uniform Foreign Money-Judgments Recognition Act*, 18 BUFF. L. REV. 1 (1969).

Ellen J. Pollock & George Anders, *Libel Judgment from Britain Is Rejected*, WALL ST. J., April 16, 1992, at B11.

Fritz Weinschenk, *Cheap Imports: Foreign Judgments in New York*, N.Y. L.J., Mar. 16, 1989, at 5.

*Ohio*

Gregory A. Harrison, *Ohio Enacts an Enforcement of Foreign Judgments Law*, 9 U. DAYTON L. REV. 391 (1984).

Daniel J. Hoffheimer, *Recognition and Enforcement of Foreign Country Money Judgments*, OHIO STATE BAR ASSOC. REPORT, Aug. 12, 1985, V. 58 N.32 P.1288(5).

*Oklahoma*

Sylvia Marks-Barnett, *Enforcement of Foreign Support Orders, Judgments or Decrees*, 52 OKLA. B.J. 1801 (1981).

*Pennsylvania*

Zicherman & R. Brand, *Improving the Litigation Climate for Pennsylvania Business: The Uniform Foreign Money Judgments Recognition Act*, 7 PITT. LEGAL J. 36 (1989).

*Puerto Rico*

Jaime Toro-Monserrate, *Recognition of Foreign Judgments in Puerto Rico: Effectos Litograficos, C.A. v. Nat'l Paper Co. of Puerto Rico*, 21 TEX. INT'L L.J. 151 (1985).

*Texas*

R. Doak Bishop, *Obtaining Recognition and Enforcement of Foreign-Country Judgments in Texas*, 45 TEX. B.J. 287 (1982).

R. Doak Bishop, *Recent Amendments to the Texas Foreign Country Judgments Act*, 6 NEWSL. INT'L L. SEC. ST. B. TEX. 17 (1990).

Beverly May Carl, *Recognition of Texas Judgments in Courts of Foreign Nations and Vice Versa*, 13 HOUS. L. REV. 680 (1976).

Beverly May Carl, *Uniform Foreign Country Money Judgments Recognition Act*, 44 TEX. B.J. 60 (1981).

RICHARD J. GRAVING & JON H. SYLVESTER, *Is the Uniform Foreign Money Judgments Recognition Act Potentially Unconstitutional? If So, Should the Texas Cure Be Adopted Elsewhere?* 25 GEO. WASH. J. INT'L L. & ECON. 737 (1992).

Francis Rauer, *Uniform Foreign Money Judgments Recognition Act Amendments*, 52 TEX. B.J., January 1989, at 39.

Michael D. Schimek, *Anti-Suit and Anti-Anti-Suit Injunctions: A Proposed Texas Approach*, 45 BAYLOR L. REV. 499 (1993).

### 4. Specialized Areas

#### *a. Administration Orders and Public Rights*

William S. Dodge, *Breaking the Public Law Taboo*, 43 HARV. INT'L L.J. 161 (2002).

F. A. Mann, *The International Enforcement of Public Rights*, 19 N.Y.U. J. INT'L L. & POL. 603 (1987).

Antonio F. Perez, *The International Recognition of Judgments: The Debate Between Private and Public Law Solutions*, 19 BERK. J. INT'L J. 44 (2001).

#### *b. Admiralty*

J. Kodwo Bentil, *The Enforcement of Judgments of Foreign Admiralty Courts*, 128 SOLIC. J. 375 (1984).

Michael L. Bono, *Remedies for Wrongful Seizure in Admiralty Marastro Compania Naviera S.A. v. Canadian Maritime Carriers*, 17 MAR. LAW. 317 (1992).

William H. Theis, *Admiralty Proceedings and the Proposed Hague Convention on Jurisdiction and Judgments*, 32 J. MAR. L. & COM. 59 (2001).

James R. Ward, *Thorsteinsson v. The Drangur: The Eleventh Circuit's Unnecessary Scuttling of a Foreign Admiralty in Rem Judgment*, 27 TEX. INT'L L.J. 507 (1992).

#### *c. Antitrust*

M. A. Blythe, *The Extraterritorial Impact of Anti-Trust Laws: Protecting British Trading Interests*, 31 AM. J. COMP. L. 99 (1983).

Jeffrey L. Cotter, *Extraterritorial Jurisdiction: The Application of U.S. Antitrust Laws to Acts Outside the United States – Hartford Fire Insurance Co. v. California 113 S. Ct. 2891 (1993)*, 20 WM. MITCHELL L. REV. 1109 (1994).

Michael J. Danaher, *Anti-Antitrust Law: The Clawback and Other Features of the United Kingdom Protection of Trading Interests Act*, 12 LAW & POL'Y INT'L BUS. 947 (1980).

Thomas W. Dunfee & Aryeh S. Friedman, *The Extra-territorial Application of United States Antitrust Laws: A Proposal for an Interim Solution*, 45 OHIO ST. L.J. 883 (1984).

David A. Harris, *United States v. Pilkington plc and Pilkington Holdings, Inc.: The Expansion of International Antitrust Enforcement by the United States Justice Department*, 20 N.C. J. INT'L LAW & COM. REG. 415 (1995).

Tina J. Kahn, *The Protection of Trading Interests Act of 1980: Britain's Response to U.S. Extraterritorial Antitrust Enforcement*, 2 NW. J. INT'L L. & BUS. 476 (1980).

Lionel Kennedy, *Enforcing International Commercial Arbitration Agreements and Awards Not Subject to the New York Convention*, 23 VA. J. INT'L L. 75 (1982).

A. V. Lowe, *Blocking Extraterritorial Jurisdiction: The British Protection of Trading Interests Act, 1980*, 75 AM. J. INT'L L. 257 (1981).

Laurence W. Maher, *Antitrust Fall-out: Tensions in the Australian-American Relationship*, 13 FED. L. REV. 105 (1982).

P. C. F. Pettit & C.J.D. Styles, *The International Response to the Extraterritorial Application of United States Antitrust Laws*, 37 BUS. LAW. 697 (1982).

Spencer Weber Waller, *Special Defenses in International Antitrust Litigation*, ABA SECTION OF ANTITRUST LAW (1995).

Penny Zagalis, *Hartford Fire Insurance Company v. California: Reassessing the Application of the McCarran-Ferguson Act to Foreign Reinsurers*, 27 CORNELL INT'L L.J. 241 (1994).

### *d. Arbitration Awards/New York Convention*

Gerald Aksen, *American Arbitration Accession Arrives in the Age of Aquarius: United States Implements United Nations Convention on the Recognition and Enforcement of Foreign Arbitral Awards*, 3 S.W.U. L. REV. 1 (1971).

Werner F. Ebke & Mary E. Parker, *Foreign Country Money-Judgments and Arbitral Awards and the Restatement (Third) of Foreign Relations Law of the United States: A Conventional Approach*, 24 INT'L LAW. 21 (1990).

Ann Joyce, *Arbitration: United States Court Recognition of ICSID Arbitral Award Liberian Eastern Timber Corp. v. Republic of Liberia, 650 F. Supp. 73 (S.D.N.Y. 1986), aff'd mem., No. 86–9047 (2d Cir. May 19, 1987); Liberian Eastern Timber Corp. v. Republic of Liberia 659 F. Supp. 606 (D.D.C. 1987)*, 29 HARV. INT'L L.J. 135 (1988).

Lionel Kennedy, *Enforcing International Commercial Arbitration Agreements and Awards Not Subject to the New York Convention*, 23 VA. J. INT'L L. 75 (1982).

Stanley L. Levine, *United Nations Foreign Arbitral Awards Convention: United States Accession*, 2 CAL. W. INT'L L.J. 67 (1971).

Christine Lecuyer-Thieffry & Patrick Thieffrey, *Negotiating Settlement of Disputes Provisions in International Business Contracts: Recent Developments in Arbitration and Other Processes*, 45 BUS. LAW. 577 (1990).

John P. McCahon, *Implementation of the United Nations Convention on Foreign Arbitral Awards in the United States*, 2 J. MAR. L. & COM. 735 (1971).

J. Stewart McClendon, *Enforcement of Foreign Arbitral Awards in the United States*, 4. Nw. J. Int'l L. & Bus. 58 (1982).

Willibald Posch, *Resolving Business Disputes Through Litigation or Other Alternatives: The Effects of Jurisdictional Rules and Recognition Practice*, 26 Hous. J. Int'l L. 363 (2004).

Leonard V. Quigley, *Convention on Foreign Arbitral Awards*, 58 A.B.A. J. 821 (1972).

Javier H. Rubinstein, *International Commercial Arbitration: Reflections at the Crossroads of the Common Law and Civil Law Traditions*, 5 Chi. J. Int'l L. 303 (2004).

Patrick Thieffrey, *Europe 1992, New Incentives, Arbitration Expected to Increase*, Nat'l L.J., Mar. 19, 1990, at 21.

Kenneth T. Ungar, Note, *The Enforcement of Arbitral Awards Under UNCITRAL's Model Law on International Commercial Arbitration*, 25 Colum. J. Transnat'l L. 717 (1987).

### *e. Bankruptcy and Creditors' Rights*

Charles D. Booth, *Recognition of Foreign Bankruptcies: An Analysis and Critique of the Inconsistent Approaches of United States Courts*, 66 Am. Bankr. L.J. 135 (1992).

Douglass G. Boshkoff, *United States Judicial Assistance in Cross-Border Insolvencies*, 36 Int'l. & Comp. L.Q. 729 (1987).

Jenny Clift, *United Nations Commission on International Trade Law (UNCITRAL): The UNCITRAL Model Law on Cross-Border Insolvency: A Legislative Framework to Facilitate Coordination and Cooperation in Cross-Border Insolvency*, 12 Tul. J. Int'l & comp. L. 307 (2004).

Richard E. Coulson, *Choice of Law in United States Cross-Border Insolvencies*, 32 Denv. J. Int'l L. & Pol'y 275 (2004).

Brian J. Gallagher & John Hartje, *The Effectiveness of Section 304 in Achieving Efficient and Economic Equity in Transnational Insolvency*, 1983 Norton Ann. Surv. Bankr. L. 1 (1983).

Thomas C. Given & Victor A. Vilaplana, *Comity Revisited: Multinational Bankruptcy Cases Under Section 304 of the Bankruptcy Code*, 1983 Ariz. St. L.J. 325 (1983).

Mark Gross, *Foreign Creditor Rights: Recognition of Foreign Bankruptcy Adjudications in the United States and the Republic of Singapore*, 12 U. Pa. J. Int'l Bus. L. 125 (1991).

Ulrich Huber, *Creditor Equality in Transnational Bankruptcies: The United States Position*, 19 Vand. J. Transnat'l L. 741 (1986).

Stephen B. James, *International Bankruptcy: Limited Recognition in the New U.S. Bankruptcy Code*, 3 Hous. J. Int'l L. 241 (1986).

Ingo A. J. Klocker, *Foreign Debtors and Creditors under United States and West German Bankruptcy Laws: An Analysis and Comparison*, 20 Tex. Int'l L.J. 55 (1985).

Lynn M. LoPucki, *Cooperation in International Bankruptcy: A Post-Universalist Approach*, 84 Cornell L. Rev. 696 (1999).

Kurt H. Nadelmann, *Rehabilitating International Bankruptcy Law: Lessons Taught by Herstatt and Company*, 52 N.Y.U. L. L. Rev. 1 (1977).

Anne Norby Nielsen, *Section 304 of the Bankruptcy Code: Has It Fostered the Development of an International Bankruptcy System*, 22 COLUM. J. TRANSNAT'L L. 541 (1984).

Timothy E. Powers & Rona R. Mears, *Protecting a U.S. Debtor's Assets in International Bankruptcy: A Survey and Proposal for Reciprocity*, 10 N.C. J. INT'L L. & COM. REG. 303 (1985).

Pauline M. Stevens, *The Interpenetration of Foreign Bankruptcy Laws in Domestic Proceedings Under H.R. 8200*, 52 AM. BANKR. L.J. 61 (1978).

Donald T. Trautman, *Foreign Creditors in American Bankruptcy Proceedings*, 29 HARV. INT'L L.J. 49 (1988).

Barbara K. Unger, *United States Recognition of Foreign Bankruptcies*, 19 INT'L L. 1153 (1985).

### *f. Defamation and First Amendment Issues*

Derek Devgun, *United States Enforcement of English Defamation Judgments: Exploring the First Amendment*, 23 ANGLO-AM. L. REV. 1995 (1994).

Ken Kraus & Dan Polatsek, *Enforcement of Foreign Media Judgments in the Aftermath of Gutnick v. Dow Jones & Co.*, 21 SPG COMM. LAW. 1 (2003).

Jeremy Maltby, *Juggling Comity and Self-Government: The Enforcement of Foreign Libel Judgments in U.S. Courts*, 94 COLUM. L. REV. 1978 (1994).

Pollock & Anders, *Libel Judgment from Britain is Rejected*, WALL ST. J., Apr. 16, 1992, at B6.

Jeff Sanders, *Extraterritorial Application of the First Amendment to Defamation Claims Against American Media*, 19 N.C. J. INT'L L. & COM. REG. 515 (1994).

Craig A. Stern, *Foreign Judgments and the Freedom of Speech: Look Who's Talking*, 60 BROOK. L. REV. 999 (1994).

Molly S. Van Houweling, *Enforcement of Foreign Judgments, the First Amendment, and Internet Speech: Notes for the Next Yahoo! v. Licra*, 24 MICH. J. INT'L L. 697 (2003).

Kyu Ho Youm, *Suing American Media in Foreign Courts: Doing an End-Run Around U.S. Libel Law*, 16 HASTINGS COMM. & ENT. L.J. 235.

### *g. Domestic Relations*

Robert D. Arenstein, *Interjurisdictional Enforcement of Matrimonial Orders*, 2 AM. J. FAM. L. 7 (Spring 1988).

Christopher L. Blakesly, *Comparativist Ruminations from the Bayou on Child Custody Jurisdiction: The UCCJA, the PKPA, and the Hague Convention on Child Abduction*, 58 LA. L. REV. 449 (1998).

David F. Cavers, *International Enforcement of Family Support*, 81 COLUM. L. REV. 994 (1981).

R. F. Chase, *Domestic Recognition of Divorce Decree Obtained in Foreign Country and Attacked for Lack of Domicil or Jurisdiction of Parties*, 13 A.L.R. 3d 1419 (1967 & Supp. 1992).

Albert A. Ehrenzweig, *Recognition of Custody Decrees Rendered Abroad: Law and Reason Versus the Restatement*, 2 AM. J. COMP. L. 167 (1953).

Robin Jo Frank, *American and International Responses to International Child Abductions*, 16 N.Y.U. J. INT'L L. & POL. 415 (1984).

Rebecca O. Gillen,*Recent Developments, Domestic Relations-Jurisdiction: Extension of Comity to Foreign-Nations Divorce*, 46 TENN. L. REV. 238 (1978).

Erwin N. Griswold, *Divorce Jurisdiction and Recognition of Divorce Decrees: A Comparative Study*, 65 HARV. L. REV. 193 (1951).

INTERNATIONAL CHILD ABDUCTIONS: A GUIDE TO APPLYING THE HAGUE CONVENTION, WITH FORMS, 2nd ed. (Gloria F. Dehart ed., A.B.A. SECTION OF FAMILY LAW, 1993).

Jerome I. Karet, *The International Enforcement of Matrimonial Financial Orders*, 6 INT'L LEGAL PRAC. 8 (1981).

Joan M. Krauskopf, *International Recognition and Enforcement of Family Law Judgments*, 27 ST. LOUIS B.J. 6 (1980).

Sylvia Marks-Barnett, *Enforcement of Foreign Support Orders, Judgments, or Decrees*, 52 OKLA. B.J. 1801 (1981).

Note, *United States Recognition of Foreign, Nonjudicial Divorces*, 53 MINN. L. REV. 612 (1969).

Michael M. O'Hear, *Some of the Most Embarrassing Questions: Extra-territorial Divorces and the Problem of Jurisdiction Before Pennoyer*, 104 YALE L.J. 1507 (1995).

Michael Jay Simkin, *Choices in Enforcement of Foreign Marital Judgments*, 22 BEVERLY HILLS B. ASSN. J. 223 (1988).

*Special Issue: Divorce Law Around the World*, FAM ADVOC. (Spring 1987).

P. H. Vartanian, *Foreign Filiation or Support Order in Bastardy Proceedings, Requiring Periodic Payments, as Extraterritorially Enforceable*, 16 A.L.R. 2d 1098 (1951 & Supp. 1992).

***h. International Court of Justice***

Colton Brown, *Enforcement of ICJ Decisions in the United States Courts*, 11 MD. J. INT'L L. & TRADE 73 (1987).

Mary Ellen O'Connell, *The Prospects for Enforcing Monetary Judgments of the International Court of Justice: A Study of Nicaragua's Judgment Against the United States*, 30 VA. J. INT'L L. 891 (1990).

***i. Internet (E-Commerce)***

Mary Shannon Martin, *Keep It Online: the Hague Convention and the Need for Online Alternative Dispute Resolution in International Business-to-Consumer E-Commerce*, 20 BOSTON U. INT'L.J. 125 (2002).

***j. Non-Money Judgments (Equitable Remedies)***

David Buzard, *U.S. Recognition and Enforcement of Foreign Country Injunctive and Specific Performance Decrees*, 20 CAL. W. INT'L L.J. 91 (1990).

James Crawford, *Execution of Judgments and Foreign Sovereign Immunity*, 75 AM. J. INT'L L. 820 (1981).

Georges R. Delaume, *Long Arm Jurisdiction Under the Federal Sovereign Immunities Act*, 74 AM. J. INT'L L. 640 (1980).

Georges R. Delaume, *The Foreign Sovereign Immunities Act and Public Debt Litigation: Some Fifteen Years Later*, 88 AM. J. INT'L L. 257 (1994).

William N. Eskridge, Jr., *The Iranian Nationalization Cases: Toward a General Theory of Jurisdiction over Foreign States*, 22 HARV. INT'L L.J. 525 (1981).

Hazel Fox,*Enforcement Jurisdiction, Foreign State Property and Diplomatic Immunity*, 34 INT'L & COMP. L.Q. 115 (1985).

Thomas H. Hill, *A Policy Analysis of the American Law of Foreign State Immunity*, 50 FORDHAM L. REV. 155 (1981).

Gregory Jay, *Foreign Sovereign Immunity Act: Commercial Activity Exception United States May Exercise Jurisdiction over a Foreign Sovereign Who Has Issued Promissory Notes to a U.S. Corporation*, 21 GA. J. INT'L & COMP. L. 539 (1991).

M. P. A. Kindall, *Immunity of States for Noncommercial Torts: A Comparative Analysis of the International Law Commission's Draft*, 75 CAL. L. REV. 1849 (1987).

Wendlene K. Montgomery, *Jurisdiction and Sovereign Immunity: Jurisdiction over Foreign States Under the Alien Tort Claims Act: Amerada Hess Shipping Corp. v. Argentine Republic*, 830 F.2D 431 (2D CIR. 1987), 29 HARV. INT'L L.J. 215 (1988).

Matthew H. Murray, *The Torture Victim Protection Act: Legislation to Promote Enforcement of the Human Rights of Aliens in U.S. Courts*, 25 COLUM. J. TRANSNAT'L L. 673 (1987).

Jamison M. Selby & David P. Stewart, *Practical and Legal Aspects of Arbitrating Claims Before the Iran-United States Claims Tribunal*, 18 INT'L LAW. 211 (1984).

Marisa Silverman, *Karaha Bodas Co., L.L.C. v. Perusahan Pertambangan Minyak Dan Gas Vedara 313 F.3d 70 (2d Cir. 2002)*, 16 N.Y. INT'L L. REV. 223 (2003).

David L. Underhill, *Denying Enforcement of a Foreign Country Injunction: Solution or Symptom: Pilkington Bros. v. AFG Industries, Inc.*, 17 CONN. L. REV. 703 (1985).

Rhonda Wasserman, *Equity Renewed: Preliminary Injunctions to Secure Potential Money Judgments*, 67 WASH. L. REV. 257 (1992).

### *k. Sovereign Immunity*

Lawrence W. Newman & Michael Burrows, *Enforceability of Iran Tribunal Awards*, N.Y. L.J., Sept. 21, 1990, at 3.

Lawrence W. Newman & Michael Burrows, *Enforcement of Judgments Against Foreign States*, N.Y. L.J., Apr. 3, 1991 at 3.

Jeremy Ostrander, *The Last Bastion of Sovereign Immunity: A Comparative Look at Immunity from Execution of Judgments* 22 BERKELEY JOURNAL OF INTERNATIONAL LAW 541 (2004).

E. H. Schopler, *Modern Status of the Rules as to Immunity of Foreign Sovereign from Suit in Federal or State Courts*, 25 A.L.R.3D 322 (1969 & Supp. 1992).

*l. Brussels and Lugano Conventions*

John Fitzpatrick, *The Lugano Convention and Western European Integration: A Comparative Analysis of Jurisdiction and Judgments in Europe and the United States*, 8 CONN. J. INT'L L. 695 (1993).

Kathryn A. Russel, *Exorbitant Jurisdiction and Enforcement of Judgments: The Brussels System as an Impetus for United States Action*, 19 SYRACUSE J. INT'L L. & COM. 57 (1993).

*m. Antidilution*

David S. Welkowitz, *Preemption, Extraterritoriality, and the Problem of State Antidilution Laws*, 67 TUL. L. REV. 1 (1992).

*n. Comparative Studies*

Brandon B. Danford, *The Enforcement of Foreign Money Judgments in the United States and Europe: How Can We Achieve a Comprehensive Treaty?*, 23 REV. LITIG. 381 (2004).

Jenny S. Martinez, *Towards an International Judicial System*, 56 STAN. L. REV. 429 (2003).

Juan Carlos Martinez, *Recognizing and Enforcing Foreign Nation Judgments: The United States and Europe Compared and Contrasted: A Call for Revised Legislation in Florida*, 4 J. TRANSNAT'L L. & POL'Y 49 (1995).

Brian Richard Paige, *Foreign Judgments in American and English Courts: A Comparative Analysis*, 26 SEATTLE UNIV. L. R. 591 (2003).

*o. Transient or Tag Jurisdiction*

Eric B. Fastiff, *The Proposed Hague Convention on the Recognition and Enforcement of Civil Commercial Judgments: A Solution to Butch Reynolds's Jurisdiction and Enforcement Problems*, 28 CORNELL INT'L L.J. 469 (1995).

*p. Parallel Proceedings*

Lauretta Drake, *Stop the Madness! Procedural and Practical Defenses to Avoid Inconsistent Cross-Border Judgments Between Texas and Mexico*, 9 J. TRANSNAT'L L. & POL'Y 209 (1999).

James George, *Parallel Litigation*, 51 BAYLOR L. REV. 769 (1999).

James P. George, *International Parallel Litigation: A Survey of Current Conventions and Model Laws*, 37 TEX. INT'L L.J. 499 (2002).

Margarita Trevino de Coal, *Stay, Dismiss, Enjoin or Abstain: A Survey of Foreign Parallel Litigation in the Federal Courts of the United States*, 17 B.U. INT'L L.J. 79 (1999).

*q. Tax*

Jeffery C. Atik, *The Problem of Reciprocity in Transnational Enforcement of Tax Judgments*, 8 YALE J. WORLD PUB. ORD. 156 (1981).

Philip Burgess, *Globalization Comes to Tax Collection*, 34 TAX NOTES INT'L 645 (2004).

Richard A. Dachs, *Enforcement of Foreign Tax Judgments in the United States: The Queen Ex Rel. British Columbia v. Gilbertson*, 14 J. INT'L L. & ECON. 281 (1980).

Elizabeth J. Farnam, *Racketeering, RICO and the Revenue Rule in Attorney General of Canada v. R.J. Reynolds: Civil RICO Claims for Foreign Tax Law Violations*, 77 WASH. L. REV. 843 (2002).

Richard E. Smith, Note, *The Nonrecognition of Foreign Tax Judgments: International Tax Evasion*, 1981 U. ILL. L. REV. 241.

Thomas B. Stoel, Jr., *The Enforcement of Foreign Non-Criminal Penal and Revenue Judgments in England and the United States*, 16 INT'L & COMP. L.Q. 663 (1967).

### *r. U.S.-U.K. Convention*

Peter Hay & Robert J. Walker, *The Proposed Recognition-of-Judgments Convention Between the United States and the United Kingdom*, 11 TEX. INT'L L.J. 421 (1976).

Peter Hay & Robert J. Walker, *The Proposed U.S.-U.K. Recognition-of-Judgments Convention: Another Perspective*, 18 VA. J. INT'L L. 753 (1978).

## D. RECENT DOMESTIC CASES

### 1. Organized by Main Issue

***Personal Jurisdiction of Court of Origin***

| | |
|---|---|
| General | *Pure Fishing v. Silver Star Co.*, 202 F. Supp. 2d 905 (2002).<br>*Dresdner Bank AG v. Haque*, 161 F. Supp. 2d 259 (2001).<br>*Guardian Ins. Co. v. Bain Hogg Int'l Ltd.*, 52 F. Supp. 2d 536 (1999).<br>*CIBC Mellon Trust Co. v. Mora Hotel Corp. N.V.*, 792 N.E.2d 155 (2003).<br>*Electrolines Inc. v. Prudential Assur. Co.*, 260 Mich. App. 144 (2003).<br>*Wimmer Can. v. Abele Tractor & Equip. Co.*, 750 N.Y.S.2d 331 (2002).<br>*Kam-Tech Sys. v. Yardeni*, 340 N.J. Super. 414 (2001).<br>*Soc'y of Lloyd's v. Hudson*, 276 F. Supp. 2d 1110, (2003).<br>*Kohn v. American Metal Climax, Inc.*, 458 F.2d 255 (3d Cir. 1972), *cert. denied*, 409 U.S. 874 (1972).<br>*Bullen v. Her Majesty's Government*, 553 So.2d 1344 (Fla. App. 1989).<br>*Somportex Ltd. v. Philadelphia Chewing Gum Corporation*, 453 F.2d 435 at 443 (3d Cir. 1971), *cert. denied*, 405 U.S. 1017 (1972). |
| Default Judgments | *Constandinou v. Constandinou*, 695 N.Y.S.2d 844 (1999).<br>Appearance of Defendant/Consent to Foreign Notice/Service<br>*Constandinou v. Constandinou*, 695 N.Y.S.2d 844 (1999).<br>*AG of Can. ex rel. Her Majesty the Queen v. Gorman*, 769 N.Y.S.2d 369 (2003). |
| Personal Jurisdiction of the Recognizing Court | *Lenchyshyn v. Pelko Elec., Inc.*, 723 N.Y.S.2d 285 (2001).<br>Forum Selection Clauses/Choice of Law/Interpretation of Foreign Law |

| | |
|---|---|
| | *Soc'y of Lloyd's v. Mullin*, 255 F. Supp. 2d 468 (2003). |
| | *Films by Jove, Inc. v. Berov*, 250 F. Supp. 2d 156 (2003). |
| | *Int'l Nutrition Co. v. Horphag Research Ltd.*, 257 F.3d 1324 (2001). |
| | *Harris S.A. De C.V. v. Grupo Sistemas Integrales de Telecomunicacion S.A. De C.V. et al.*, 719 N.Y.S.2d 25 (2001). |
| | *Exter Shipping Ltd. v. Kilakos*, 310 F. Supp. 2d 1301 (2004). |
| | *Philips Electronics, N.V. v. New Hampshire Insurance Co.*, 692 N.E.2d 1268 (Ill. App. 1998). |
| Due Process | *Dresdner Bank AG v. Haque*, 161 F. Supp. 2d 259 (2001). |
| | *Soc'y of Lloyds v. Webb*, 156 F. Supp. 2d 632 (2001). |
| | *Society of Lloyd's v. Ashenden*, 233 F.3d 473 (2000). |
| | *Bridgeway Corp. v. Citibank*, 201 F.3d 134 (2000). |
| | *Guardian Ins. Co. v. Bain Hogg Int'l Ltd.*, 52 F. Supp. 2d 536 (1999). |
| | *Bank Melli Iran v. Pahlavi*, 58 F.3d 1406 (1995). |
| | *CIBC Mellon Trust Co. v. Mora Hotel Corp. N.V.*, 792 N.E.2d 155 (2003). |
| | *Kam-Tech Sys. v. Yardeni*, 340 N.J. Super. 414 (2001). |
| | *Society of Lloyd's v. Grace*, 718 N.Y.S.2d 327 (2000). |
| | *Soc'y of Lloyd's v. Hudson*, 276 F. Supp. 2d 1110, (2003). |
| | *Soc'y of Lloyd's v. Turner*, 303 F.3d. 325 (2002). |
| | *Watts v. Swiss Bank Corporation*, 27 N.Y.2d 270 (1970). |
| Inconvenience of Forum | *Aguinda v. Texaco, Inc.*, 303 F.3d 470 (2d Cir. 2002). |
| | *CIBC Mellon Trust Co. v. Mora Hotel Corp. N.V.*, 792 N.E.2d 155 (2003). |
| | *Alfadda v. Fenn (Alfadda II)*, 966 F. Supp. 1317, 1329 (S.D.N.Y. 1997), *aff'd on other grounds*, 159 F.3d 41 (1998). |
| | *Monegasque de Reassurances S.A.M. v. NAK Naftogaz of Ukraine*, 311 F.3d 488 (2d Cir. 2002). |
| | *Baldwin v. Iowa State Traveling Men's Association*, 283 U.S. 522 (1931). |
| | *Torres v. Southern Peru Copper Corp.*, 965 F. Supp. 899 (S. D. Tex. 1999), *aff'd*, 113 F.3d 540 (5th Cir. 1997). |
| Conclusiveness of Judgment | *Nicor Int'l. Corp. v. El Paso Corp.*, 292 F. Supp. 2d 1357 (2003). |
| | *Black Clawson Co. v. Kroenert Corp.*, 245 F.3d 759 (2001). |
| | *Huse v. Huse-Sporsem, A.S. (In re: Birting Fisheries, Inc.)*, 300 B.R. 489 (2003). |
| | *Korea Water Resources Corp. v. Lee*, 8 Cal. Rptr. 3d 853 (2004). |
| | *Gonzalez v. Lebensversicherung A.G.*, 761 N.Y.S.2d2 (2003). |
| | *Press Publ. v. Matol Botanical Int'l*, 37 P.3d 1121 (2001). |
| | *Alta. Secs. Comm'n v. Ryckman*, 30 P.3d 121 (2001). |
| | *S.C. Chimexim S.A. v. Velco Enters. Ltd.*, 36 F. Supp. 2d 206 (1999). |
| | *Mayekawa Mfg. Co. v. Sasaki*, 76 Wn. App. 791 (1995). |
| | *Bata v. Bata*, 163 A.2d 493 (Del., 1960). |
| | *Schoenbrod v. Siegler*, 20 N.Y.2d 403 (1967). |
| | *Stalinski v. Bakoczy*, 41 F. Supp. 2d 755 (S. D. Ohio 1998). |

| | |
|---|---|
| Burden of Proof | *Hernandez v. Seventh Day Adventist Corp.*, 54 S.W.3d 335 (2001). |
| Bankruptcy | *Huse v. Huse-Sporsem, A.S. (In re: Birting Fisheries, Inc.)*, 300 B.R. 489 (2003).<br>*Herbstein v. Bruetman (In re: Bruetman)*, 259 B.R. 649 (2001). |
| Foreign Dismissal | *Black Clawson Co. v. Kroenert Corp.*, 245 F.3d 759 (2001). |
| Arbitration Clause/ | *In Re: Int'l. Bechtel Co*, 2004 W.L. 225064 (2004). |
| Conflict with Arbitration Clause | *Courage Co. v. Chemshare Corp.*, 93 S.W.3d 323 (2002). |
| Public Policy | *Soc'y of Lloyd's v. Mullin*, 255 F. Supp. 2d 468 (2003).<br>*Soc'y of Lloyds v. Webb*, 156 F. Supp. 2d 632 (2001).<br>*Ackermann v. Levine*, 788 F.2d 830 (1986).<br>*Cantrade Privatbank AG Zurich v. Bangkok Bank Pub. Co.*, 681 N.Y.S.2d 21 (1998).<br>*In Re: Int'l. Bechtel Co.*, 2004 W.L. 225064 (2004).<br>*Soc'y of Lloyd's v. Turner*, 303 F.3d. 325 (2002).<br>*Larwex Enters. v. Bacharach*, 755 N.Y.S.2d 631 (2001).<br>*Glaverbel Societe Anonyme v. Northlake Mktg. & Supply*, 1998 U.S. Dist. Lexis 18820 (1998). |
| First Amendment/ Defamation Issues | *Yahoo! Inc. v. La Ligue Contre Le Racisme et L'antisemitisme*, 379 F.3d 1120 (2004).<br>*Matusevitch v. Telkinof*, 159 F.3d 636 (1998). |
| Full Faith and Credit Clause | *Hilton v. Guyot* 159 U.S. 113 (1895).<br>*Jaffe v. Accredited Sur. & Cas. Co.*, 294 F.3d 584 (2002).<br>*Herbstein v. Bruetman (In re: Bruetman)*, 259 B.R. 649 (2001). |
| Certainty of Amount Sought | *Nicor Int'l Corp. v. El Paso Corp.*, 292 F. Supp. 2d 1357 (2003).<br>*Cecuk v. MacAdoo*, 726 N.Y.S.2d 421 (2001). |
| Authenticity | *Hernandez v. Seventh Day Adventist Corp.*, 54 S.W.3d 335 (2001). |
| Impartial Tribunal | *Bridgeway Corp. v. Citibank*, 201 F.3d 134 (2000).<br>*S.C. Chimexim S.A. v. Velco Enters. Ltd.*, 36 F. Supp. 2d 206 (1999).<br>*Bank Melli Iran v. Pahlavi*, 58 F.3d 1406 (1995).<br>*Kwongyuen Hangkee Co. v. Starr Fireworks, Inc.*, 634 N.W.2d 95 (2001). |
| Statute of Limitations | *Logemann Holding, Inc. v. Lieber*, 793 N.E.2d 135 (2003).<br>*Pinilla v. Harza Eng'g Co.*, 755 N.E.2d 23 (2001).<br>*Nadd v. Le Credit Lyonnais*, 804 So.2d 1226 (2001).<br>*Soc'y of Lloyd's v. Estate of McMurray*, 274 F.3d 1133 (2001). |
| Foreign Judgment's Preclusive Effect Limited | *Weiss v. La Suisse Societe d'Assurances Sur La Vie*, 161 F. Supp. 2d 305 (2001). |
| Fraud | *Soc'y of Lloyd's v. Mullin*, 255 F. Supp. 2d 468 (2003).<br>*Fairchild, Arabatzis & Smith, Inc. v. Prometco*, 470 F. Supp. 610 (1979). |

| | |
|---|---|
| Damages Calculation/ Conversion | *Competex, S.A. v. LaBow*, 783 F.2d 333 (2d Cir. 1986).<br>*Manches & Co. v. Gilbey*, 646 N.E.2d 86 (1995). |
| Intellectual Property | *Int'l Nutrition Co. v. Horphag Research Ltd.*, 257 F.3d 1324 (2001).<br>*Black Clawson Co. v. Kroenert Corp.*, 245 F.3d 759 (2001).<br>*Pony Express Records, Inc. v. Springsteen*, 163 F. Supp. 2d 465 (2001). |
| Participation/Appearance in Prior Litigation as Preclusive | *Van Den Biggelaar v. Wagner*, 978 F. Supp. 848 (1997).<br>*Ackerman v. Levine*, 788 F.2d 830 (1986). |
| Burden of Proof | *Shen v. Leo A. Daly Co.*, 222 F.3d 472 (2000). |
| Reciprocity | *Banque Libanaise Pour Le Commerce v. Khreich*, 915 F.2D 1000 (1990). |
| Parallel Proceedings | *AAR Int'l, Inc. v. Nimelias Enters. S.A.*, 250 F.3d 510 (2001).<br>*Posner v. Essex Ins. Co.*, 178 F.3d 1209 (1999). |
| Taxation | *United States v. Pasquantino*, 305 F.3d 291 (4th Cir. 2002).<br>*Canada v. R. J. Reynolds Tobacco Holdings, Inc.*, 268 F.3d 103 (2d Cir. 2001), *cert. denied*, 123 S. Ct. 513 (2002). |

**2. Organized by U.S. State Where Enforcement Sought**

| | |
|---|---|
| Arizona | *Alta. Secs. Comm'n v. Ryckman*, 30 P.3d 121 (2001). |
| California | *Yahoo! Inc. v. La Ligue Contre Le Racisme et L'antisemitisme*, 379 F.3d 1120 (2004).<br>*Bank Melli Iran v. Pahlavi*, 58 F.3d 1406 (1995).<br>*Korea Water Resources Corp. v. Lee*, 8 Cal. Rptr. 3d 853 (2004). |
| Connecticut | *Int'l Nutrition Co. v. Horphag Research Ltd.*, 257 F.3d 1324 (2001). |
| Florida | *Nicor Int'l Corp. v. El Paso Corp.*, 292 F. Supp. 2d 1357 (2003).<br>*Posner v. Essex Ins. Co.*, 178 F.3d 1209 (1999).<br>*Nadd v. Le Credit Lyonnais*, 804 So.2d 1226 (2001).<br>*Diamond R. Fertilizer Co. v. Lake Packing Pshp.*, 743 So.2d 547 (1999). |
| Georgia | *Exter Shipping Ltd. v. Kilakos*, 310 F. Supp. 2d 1301 (2004). |
| Illinois | *Hyatt Int'l Corp. v. Coco*, 302 F.3d 707 (2002).<br>*Society of Lloyd's v. Ashenden*, 233 F.3d 473 (2000).<br>*Herbstein v. Bruetman (In re: Bruetman)*, 259 B.R. 649 (2001).<br>*Logemann Holding, Inc. v. Lieber*, 793 N.E.2d 135 (2003).<br>*Pinilla v. Harza Eng'g Co.*, 755 N.E.2d 23 (2001).<br>*Soc'y of Lloyd's v. Estate of McMurray*, 274 F.3d 1133 (2001). |
| Indiana | *Van Den Biggelaar v. Wagner*, 978 F. Supp. 848 (1997). |
| Iowa | *Pure Fishing v. Silver Star Co.*, 202 F. Supp. 2d 905 (2002).<br>*Black Clawson Co. v. Kroenert Corp.*, 245 F.3d 759 (2001). |

Maryland
*Matusevitch v. Telkinof*, 159 F.3d 636 (1998).
*Andes v. Versant Corp.*, 778 F.2d 1033 (1986).
*Koehler v. Bank of Berm. N.Y. Ltd.*, 209 F.3d 130 (2000).

Massachusetts
*Chase Manhattan Bank, N.A. v. Hoffman* 665 F. Supp. 73 (D.C. Mass. 1987).
*Manches & Co. v. Gilbey*, 646 N.E.2d 86 (1995).

Michigan
*Electrolines, Inc. v. Prudential Assur. Co.*, 260 Mich. App. 144 (2003).

Nebraska
*Shen v. Leo A. Daly Co.*, 222 F.3d 472 (2000).

Nevada
*Soc'y of Lloyd's v. Hudson*, 276 F. Supp. 2d 1110, (2003).

New Jersey
*Kam-Tech Sys. v. Yardeni*, 340 N.J. Super. 414 (2001)
*Pony Express Records, Inc. v. Springsteen*, 163 F. Supp. 2d 465 (2001).

New York
*Films by Jove, Inc. v. Berov*, 250 F. Supp. 2d 156 (2003).
*Weiss v. La Suisse Societe d'Assurances Sur La Vie*, 161 F. Supp. 2d 305 (2001).
*Dresdner Bank AG v. Haque*, 161 F. Supp. 2d 259 (2001).
*Bridgeway Corp. v. Citibank*, 201 F.3d 134 (2000).
*S.C. Chimexim S.A. v. Velco Enters. Ltd.*, 36 F. Supp. 2d 206 (1999).
*Ackerman v. Levine*, 788 F.2d 830 (1986).
*Fairchild, Arbatzis & Smith v. Prometco*, 470 F. Supp. 610 (1979).
*AG of Can. ex rel. Her Majesty the Queen v. Gorman*, 769 N.Y.S.2d 369 (2003).
*Gonzalez v. Lebensversicherung A.G.*, 761 N.Y.S.2d 2 (2003).
*CIBC Mellon Trust Co. v. Mora Hotel Corp. N.V.*, 792 N.E.2d 155 (2003).
*Wimmer Can. v. Abele Tractor & Equip. Co.*, 750 N.Y.S.2d 331 (2002).
*Cecuk v. MacAdoo*, 726 N.Y.S.2d 421 (2001).
*Lenchyshyn v. Pelko Elec., Inc.*, 723 N.Y.S.2d 285 (2001).
*Harris S.A. De C.V. v. Grupo Sistemas Integrales de Telecomunicacion S.A. De C.V. et al.*, 719 N.Y.S.2d 25 (2001).
*Society of Lloyd's v. Grace*, 718 N.Y.S.2d 327 (2000).
*Constandinou v. Constandinou*, 695 N.Y.S.2d 844 (1999).
*Cantrade Privatbank AG. Zurich v. Bangkok Bank Pub. Co.*, 681 N.Y.S.2d 21 (1998).
*Larwex Enters. v. Bacharach*, 755 N.Y.S.2d 631 (2001).
*Voreep v. Tarom Romanian Air Transport*, 1999 U.S. Dist. Lexis 7294 (1999).

North Carolina
*Wener v. Perrone & Cramer Realty, Inc.* 528 S.E.2d 65 (N.C. Ct. App. 2000).

Pennsylvania
*Soc'y of Lloyd's v. Mullin*, 255 F. Supp. 2d 468 (2003).

| | |
|---|---|
| South Dakota | *Kwongyuen Hangkee Co. v. Starr Fireworks, Inc.*, 634 N.W.2d 95 (2001). |
| Texas | *Soc'y of Lloyds v. Webb*, 156 F. Supp. 2d 632 (2001).<br>*Banque Libanaise Pour Le Commerce v. Khreich*, 915 F.2d 1000 (1990).<br>*Courage Co. v. Chemshare Corp.*, 93 S.W.3d 323 (2002).<br>*Soc'y of Lloyd's v. Turner*, 303 F.3d 325 (2002).<br>*Hernandez v. Seventh Day Adventist Corp.*, 54 S.W.3d 335 (2001). |
| Virgin Islands | *Guardian Ins. Co. v. Bain Hogg Int'l Ltd.*, 52 F. Supp. 2d 536 (1999). |
| Virginia | *Jaffe v. Accredited Sur. & Cas. Co.*, 294 F.3d 584 (2002). |
| Washington | *Huse v. Huse-Sporsem, A.S. (In re: Birting Fisheries, Inc.)*, 300 B.R. 489 (2003).<br>*Mayekawa Mfg. Co. v. Sasaki*, 76 Wn. App. 791 (1995). |
| Washington, D.C. | *In Re: Int'l. Bechtel Co*, 2004 W.L. 225064 (2004). |

### 3. Organized by Country of Rendering Court

| | |
|---|---|
| Abu Dhabi | *Banque Libanaise Pour Le Commerce v. Khreich*, 915 F.2d 1000 (1990). |
| Argentina | *Herbstein v. Bruetman (In re: Bruetman)*, 259 B.R. 649 (2001).<br>*Pinilla v. Harza Eng'g Co.*, 755 N.E.2d 23 (2001). |
| Australia | *Pure Fishing v. Silver Star Co.*, 202 F. Supp. 2d 905 (2002). |
| Bahamas | *Diamond R. Fertilizer Co. v. Lake Packing Pshp.*, 743 So.2d 547 (1999). |
| Bermuda | *Posner v. Essex Ins. Co.*, 178 F.3d 1209 (1999).<br>*Koehler v. Bank of Berm. N.Y. Ltd.*, 209 F.3d 130 (2000). |
| Canada | *AG of Can. ex rel. Her Majesty the Queen v. Gorman*, 769 N.Y.S.2d 369 (2003).<br>*Jaffe v. Accredited Sur. & Cas. Co.*, 294 F.3d 584 (2002).<br>*Wimmer Can. v. Abele Tractor & Equip. Co.*, 750 N.Y.S.2d 331 (2002).<br>*Lenchyshyn v. Pelko Elec. Inc.*, 723 N.Y.S.2d 285 (2001).<br>*Alta. Secs. Comm'n v. Ryckman*, 30 P.3d 121 (2001).<br>*Constandinou v. Constandinou*, 695 N.Y.S.2d 844 (1999).<br>*Larwex Enters. v. Bacharach*, 755 N.Y.S.2d 631 (2001). |
| Chile | *Cecuk v. MacAdoo*, 726 N.Y.S.2d 421 (2001). |
| China | *Kwongyuen Hangkee Co. v. Starr Fireworks, Inc.*, 634 N.W.2d 95 (2001).<br>*Hernandez v. Seventh Day Adventist Corp.*, 54 S.W.3d 335 (2001). |
| Dominican Republic | *Nicor Int'l Corp. v. El Paso Corp.*, 292 F. Supp. 2d 1357 (2003). |
| Dubai | *In Re: Int'l. Bechtel Co.*, 2004 W.L. 225064 (2004). |

| | |
|---|---|
| England/U.K. | *Soc'y of Lloyd's v. Mullin*, 255 F. Supp. 2d 468 (2003). |
| | *Soc'y of Lloyds v. Webb*, 156 F. Supp. 2d 632 (2001). |
| | *Society of Lloyd's v. Ashenden*, 233 F.3d 473 (2000). |
| | *Guardian Ins. Co. v. Bain Hogg Int'l Ltd.*, 52 F. Supp. 2d 536 (1999). |
| | *Matusevitch v. Telkinof*, 159 F.3d 636 (1998). |
| | *Andes v. Versant Corp.*, 778 F.2d 1033 (1986). |
| | *Fairchild, Arbatzis & Smith v. Prometco*, 470 F. Supp. 610 (1979). |
| | *Huse v. Huse-Sporsem, A.S. (In re: Birting Fisheries, Inc.)*, 300 B.R. 489 (2003). |
| | *CIBC Mellon Trust Co. v. Mora Hotel Corp. N.V.*, 792 N.E.2d 155 (2003). |
| | *Society of Lloyd's v. Grace*, 718 N.Y.S.2d 327 (2000). |
| | *Manches & Co. v. Gilbey*, 646 N.E.2d 86 (1995). |
| | *Soc'y of Lloyd's v. Hudson*, 276 F. Supp. 2d 1110, (2003). |
| | *Soc'y of Lloyd's v. Turner*, 303 F.3d. 325 (2002). |
| | *Pony Express Records, Inc. v. Springsteen*, 163 F. Supp. 2d 465 (2001). |
| | *Soc'y of Lloyd's v. Estate of McMurray*, 274 F.3d 1133 (2001). |
| France | *Yahoo! Inc. v. La Ligue Contre Le Racisme et L'Antisemitisme*, 379 F.3d 1120 (2004).<br>*Int'l Nutrition Co. v. Horphag Research Ltd.*, 257 F.3d 1324 (2001).<br>*Nadd v. Le Credit Lyonnais*, 804 So.2d 1226 (2001). |
| Germany | *Black Clawson Co. v. Kroenert Corp.*, 245 F.3d 759 (2001).<br>*Dresdner Bank AG v. Haque*, 161 F. Supp. 2d 259 (2001).<br>*Ackerman v. Levine*, 788 F.2d 830 (1986).<br>*Logemann Holding, Inc. v. Lieber*, 793 N.E.2d 135 (2003). |
| Greece | *Vagenas v. Continental Gin Co.*, 988 F.2d 104 (11th Cir.), *cert. denied*, 114 S. Ct. 389 (1993). |
| Iran | *Bank Melli Iran v. Pahlavi*, 58 F.3d 1406 (1995). |
| Israel | *Kam-Tech Sys. v. Yardeni*, 340 N.J. Super. 414 (2001). |
| Italy | *Hyatt Int'l Corp. v. Coco*, 302 F.3d 707 (2002). |
| Japan | *Mayekawa Mfg. Co. v. Sasaki*, 76 Wn. App. 791 (1995). |
| Korea | *Choi v. Kim*, 50 F.3d 244, 249–50 (3d Cir. 1995). |
| | *Korea Water Resources Corp. v. Lee*, 8 Cal. Rptr. 3d 853 (2004). |
| Liberia | *Bridgeway Corp. v. Citibank*, 201 F.3d 134 (2000).<br>*Electrolines Inc. v. Prudential Assur. Co.*, 260 Mich. App. 144 (2003). |
| Mexico | *Southwest Livestock & Trucking Co. v. Ramon*, 169 F.3d 317 (1999).<br>*Harris S.A. de C.V. v. Grupo Sistemas Integrales de Telecomunicacion S.A. de C.V. et al.*, 719 N.Y.S.2d 25 (2001). |

| | |
|---|---|
| Netherlands | *Van Den Biggelaar v. Wagner*, 978 F. Supp. 848 (1997). |
| Romania | *S.C. Chimexim S.A. v. Velco Enters. Ltd.*, 36 F. Supp. 2d 206 (1999).<br>*Voreep v. Tarom Romanian Air Transport*, 1999 U.S. Dist. Lexis 7294 (1999). |
| Russia | *Films by Jove, Inc. v. Berov*, 250 F. Supp. 2d 156 (2003). |
| Spain | *Gonzalez v. Lebensversicherung* A.G., 761 N.Y.S.2d 2 (2003). |
| Switzerland | *Weiss v. La Suisse Societe d'Assurances Sur La Vie*, 161 F. Supp. 2d 305 (2001). |
| Taiwan | *Shen v. Leo A. Daly Co.*, 222 F.3d 472 (2000). |
| Thailand | *Cantrade Privatbank AG Zurich v. Bangkok Bank Pub. Co.*, 681 N.Y.S.2d 21 (1998). |

# Instruments, Laws, and Other Materials – Part One

# REVISED UNIFORM ENFORCEMENT OF FOREIGN JUDGMENTS ACT

Drafted by the

NATIONAL CONFERENCE OF COMMISSIONERS
ON UNIFORM STATE LAWS

and by it

APPROVED AND RECOMMENDED FOR ENACTMENT
IN ALL THE STATES

at its

ANNUAL CONFERENCE
MEETING IN ITS SEVENTY-THIRD YEAR
AT NEW YORK, NEW YORK
AUGUST 3 – 8, 1964

*WITH PREFATORY NOTE*

Approved by the American Bar Association at its Meeting
at New York, New York, August 13, 1964

# REVISED UNIFORM ENFORCEMENT OF FOREIGN JUDGMENTS ACT

## PREFATORY NOTE

Court congestion is a problem common to all states. Overcrowded dockets, overworked judges and court officials, with attendant delays, inevitably tend to lower standards for the administration of justice. One of the things that contributes to calendar congestion is the Federal necessity of giving full faith and credit to the judgments of courts of other states. U.S. Const. art IV § 1. While there is no constitutional requirement that a debtor who has had a full due process trial in one state need be given a second full scale trial on the judgment in another state, this is the only course generally available to creditors. The usual practice requires that an action be commenced on the foreign judgment. The full procedural requirements apply to the second action.

In 1948 the National Conference of Commissioners on Uniform State Laws approved the original Uniform Enforcement of Foreign Judgments Act. This act was a distinct advance over the usual method. It provided a summary judgment procedure for actions on foreign judgments. Even this advance, however, fell far short of the method provided by Congress in 1948 for the inter-district enforcement of the judgments of the Federal District Courts. 28 U.S.C., § 1963. Further, widespread adoption by the states of some form of the Federal Rules of Civil Procedure which include regular summary judgment practice made special summary judgment acts superfluous.

This 1964 revision of the Uniform Enforcement of Foreign Judgments Act adopts the practice which, in substance, is used in Federal courts. It provides the enacting state with a speedy and economical method of doing that which it is required to do by the Constitution of the United States. It also relieves creditors and debtors of the additional cost and harassment of further litigation which would otherwise be incident to the enforcement of the foreign judgment. This act offers the states a chance to achieve uniformity in a field where uniformity is highly desirable. Its enactment by the states should forestall Federal legislation in this field.

# REVISED UNIFORM ENFORCEMENT OF FOREIGN JUDGMENTS ACT

**SECTION 1. [*Definitions.*]** In this Act "foreign judgment" means any judgment, decree, or order of a court of the United States or of any other court which is entitled to full faith and credit in this state.

**SECTION 2. [*Filing and Status of Foreign Judgments.*]** A copy of any foreign judgment authenticated in accordance with the act of Congress or the statutes of this state may be filed in the office of the Clerk of any [District Court of any city or county] of this state. The Clerk shall treat the foreign judgment in the same manner as a judgment of the [District Court of any city or county] of this state. A judgment so filed has the same effect and is subject to the same procedures, defenses and proceedings for reopening, vacating, or staying as a judgment of a [District Court of any city or county] of this state and may be enforced or satisfied in like manner.

**SECTION 3. [*Notice of Filing.*]**

(a) At the time of the filing of the foreign judgment, the judgment creditor or his lawyer shall make and file with the Clerk of Court an affidavit setting forth the name and last known post office address of the judgment debtor, and the judgment creditor.

(b) Promptly upon the filing of the foreign judgment and the affidavit, the Clerk shall mail notice of the filing of the foreign judgment to the judgment debtor at the address given and shall make a note of the mailing in the docket. The notice shall include the name and post office address of the judgment creditor and the judgment creditor's lawyer, if any, in this state. In addition, the judgment creditor may mail a notice of the filing of the judgment to the judgment debtor and may file proof of mailing with the Clerk. Lack of mailing notice of filing by the Clerk shall not affect the enforcement proceedings if proof of mailing by the judgment creditor has been filed.

[(c) No execution or other process for enforcement of a foreign judgment filed hereunder shall issue until [__________] days after the date the judgment is filed.]

**SECTION 4. [*Stay.*]**

(a) If the judgment debtor shows the [District Court of any city or county] that an appeal from the foreign judgment is pending or will be taken, or that a stay of execution has been granted, the court shall stay enforcement of the foreign judgment until the appeal is concluded, the time for appeal expires, or the stay of execution expires or is vacated, upon proof that the judgment debtor has furnished the security for the satisfaction of the judgment required by the state in which it was rendered.

(b) If the judgment debtor shows the [District Court of any city or county] any ground upon which enforcement of a judgment of any [District Court of any city or county] of this state would be stayed, the court shall stay enforcement of the foreign judgment for an appropriate period, upon requiring the same security for satisfaction of the judgment which is required in this state.

**[SECTION 5. [*Fees.*]** Any person filing a foreign judgment shall pay to the clerk of Court __________ dollars. Fees for docketing, transcription or other enforcement proceedings shall be as provided for judgments of the [District Court of any city or county of this state].]

**SECTION 6. [*Optional Procedure.*]** The right of a judgment creditor to bring an action to enforce his judgment instead of proceeding under this Act remains unimpaired.

**SECTION 7. [*Uniformity of Interpretation.*]** This Act shall be so interpreted and construed as to effectuate its general purpose to make uniform the law of those states which enact it.

**SECTION 8. [*Short Title.*]** This Act may be cited as the Uniform Enforcement of Foreign Judgments Act.

**SECTION 9. [*Repeal.*]** The following Acts and parts of Acts are repealed:

(1)

(2)

(3)

**SECTION 10. [*Taking Effect.*]** This Act takes effect on
____________________ .

1964 Uniform Enforcement of Foreign Judgments Act – Jurisdictions Wherein the 1964 Act Has Been Adopted

**STATE ADOPTIONS:**

Alabama
Alaska
Arizona
Arkansas
Colorado
Connecticut
Delaware
District of Columbia
Florida
Georgia
Hawaii
Idaho
Illinois
Iowa
Kansas
Kentucky
Louisiana
Maine
Maryland
Michigan
Minnesota
Mississippi
Missouri
Montana
Nebraska
Nevada
New Hampshire
New Jersey
New Mexico
New York
North Carolina
North Dakota
Ohio
Oklahoma
Oregon
Pennsylvania
Puerto Rico
Rhode Island
S. Carolina
South Dakota
Tennessee
Texas
U.S. Virgin Islands
Utah
Virginia
Washington
West Virginia
Wisconsin
Wyoming

# UNIFORM FOREIGN MONEY-JUDGMENTS RECOGNITION ACT

Drafted by the

NATIONAL CONFERENCE OF COMMISSIONERS
ON UNIFORM STATE LAWS

and by it

APPROVED AND RECOMMENDED FOR ENACTMENT
IN ALL THE STATES

at its

ANNUAL CONFERENCE
MEETING IN ITS SEVENTY-FIRST YEAR
MONTEREY, CALIFORNIA
JULY 30 – AUGUST 4, 1962

*WITH PREFATORY NOTE AND COMMENTS*

Approved by the American Bar Association
February 4, 1963

# UNIFORM FOREIGN MONEY-JUDGMENTS RECOGNITION ACT

## PREFATORY NOTE

In most states of the Union, the law on recognition of judgments from foreign countries is not codified. In a large number of civil law countries, grant of conclusive effect to money-judgments from foreign courts is made dependent upon reciprocity. Judgments rendered in the United States have in many instances been refused recognition abroad either because the foreign court was not satisfied that local judgments would be recognized in the American jurisdiction involved or because no certification of existence of reciprocity could be obtained from the foreign government in countries where existence of reciprocity must be certified to the courts by the government. Codification by a state of its rules on the recognition of money-judgments rendered in a foreign court will make it more likely that judgments rendered in the state will be recognized abroad.

The Act states rules that have long been applied by the majority of courts in this country. In some respects the Act may not go as far as the decisions. The Act makes clear that a court is privileged to give the judgment of the court of a foreign country greater effect than it is required to do by the provisions of the Act. In codifying what bases for assumption of personal jurisdiction will be recognized, which is an area of the law still in evolution, the Act adopts the policy of listing bases accepted generally today and preserving for the courts the right to recognize still other bases. Because the Act is not selective and applies to judgments from any foreign court, the Act states that judgments rendered under a system which does not provide impartial tribunals or procedures compatible with the requirements of due process of law shall neither be recognized nor enforced.

The Act does not prescribe a uniform enforcement procedure. Instead, the Act provides that a judgment entitled to recognition will be enforceable in the same manner as the judgment of a court of a sister state which is entitled to full faith and credit.

In the preparation of the Act codification efforts made elsewhere have been taken into consideration, in particular, the [British] Foreign Judgments (Reciprocal Enforcement) Act of 1933 and a Model Act produced in 1960 by the International Law Association. The Canadian Commissioners on Uniformity of Legislation, engaged in a similar endeavor, have been kept informed of the progress of the work. Enactment by the states of the Union of modern uniform rules on recognition of foreign money-judgments will support efforts toward improvement of the law on recognition everywhere.

# UNIFORM FOREIGN MONEY-JUDGMENTS RECOGNITION ACT

[Be it enacted . . . . ]

**SECTION 1. [*Definitions.*]** As used in this Act:

(1) "foreign state" means any governmental unit other than the United States, or any state, district, commonwealth, territory, insular possession thereof, or the Panama Canal Zone, the Trust Territory of the Pacific Islands, or the Ryukyu Islands;

(2) "foreign judgment" means any judgment of a foreign state granting or denying recovery of a sum of money, other than a judgment for taxes, a fine or other penalty, or a judgment for support in matrimonial or family matters.

**SECTION 2. [*Applicability.*]** This Act applies to any foreign judgment that is final and conclusive and enforceable where rendered even though an appeal therefrom is pending or it is subject to appeal.

**Comment**

Where an appeal is pending or the defendant intends to appeal, the court of the enacting state has power to stay proceedings in accordance with section 6 of the Act.

**SECTION 3. [*Recognition and Enforcement.*]** Except as provided in section 4, a foreign judgment meeting the requirements of section 2 is conclusive between the parties to the extent that it grants or denies recovery of a sum of money. The foreign judgment is enforceable in the same manner as the judgment of a sister state which is entitled to full faith and credit.

**Comment**

The method of enforcement will be that of the Uniform Enforcement of Foreign Judgments Act of 1948 in a state having enacted that Act.

**SECTION 4. [*Grounds for Non-Recognition.*]**

(a) A foreign judgment is not conclusive if

(1) the judgment was rendered under a system which does not provide impartial tribunals or procedures compatible with the requirements of due process of law;

(2) the foreign court did not have personal jurisdiction over the defendant; or

(3) the foreign court did not have jurisdiction over the subject matter.

(b) A foreign judgment need not be recognized if

(1) the defendant in the proceedings in the foreign court did not receive notice of the proceedings in sufficient time to enable him to defend;

(2) the judgment was obtained by fraud;

(3) the [cause of action] [claim for relief] on which the judgment is based is repugnant to the public policy of this state;

(4) the judgment conflicts with another final and conclusive judgment;

(5) the proceeding in the foreign court was contrary to an agreement between the parties under which the dispute in question was to be settled otherwise than by proceedings in that court; or

(6) in the case of jurisdiction based only on personal service, the foreign court was a seriously inconvenient forum for the trial of the action.

**Comment**

The first ground for non-recognition under subsection (a) has been stated authoritatively by the Supreme Court of the United States in *Hilton v. Guyot*, 159 U.S. 113, 205 (1895). As indicated in that decision, a mere difference in the procedural system is not a sufficient basis for non-recognition. A case of serious injustice must be involved.

The last ground for non-recognition under subsection (b) authorizes a court to refuse recognition and enforcement of a judgment rendered in a foreign country on the basis only of personal service when it believes the original action should have been dismissed by the court in the foreign country on grounds of *forum non conveniens*.

**SECTION 5. [*Personal Jurisdiction.*]**

(a) The foreign judgment shall not be refused recognition for lack of personal jurisdiction if

(1) the defendant was served personally in the foreign state;

(2) the defendant voluntarily appeared in the proceedings, other than for the purpose of protecting property seized or threatened with seizure in the proceedings or of contesting the jurisdiction of the court over him;

(3) the defendant prior to the commencement of the proceedings had agreed to submit to the jurisdiction of the foreign court with respect to the subject matter involved;

(4) the defendant was domiciled in the foreign state when the proceedings were instituted, or, being a body corporate had its principal place of business, was incorporated, or had otherwise acquired corporate status, in the foreign state;

(5) the defendant had a business office in the foreign state and the proceedings in the foreign court involved a [cause of action] [claim for relief] arising out of business done by the defendant through that office in the foreign state; or

(6) the defendant operated a motor vehicle or airplane in the foreign state and the proceedings involved a [cause of action] [claim for relief] arising out of such operation.

(b) The courts of this state may recognize other bases of jurisdiction.

**Comment**

New bases of jurisdiction have been recognized by courts in recent years. The Act does not codify all these new bases. Subsection (b) makes clear that the Act does not prevent the courts in the enacting state from recognizing foreign judgments rendered on the bases of jurisdiction not mentioned in the Act.

**SECTION 6. [*Stay in Case of Appeal.*]** If the defendant satisfies the court either that an appeal is pending or that he is entitled and intends to appeal from the foreign judgment, the court may stay the proceedings until the appeal has been determined or until the expiration of a period of time sufficient to enable the defendant to prosecute the appeal.

**SECTION 7. [*Saving Clause.*]** This Act does not prevent the recognition of a foreign judgment in situations not covered by this Act.

**SECTION 8. [*Uniformity of Interpretation.*]** This Act shall be so construed as to effectuate its general purpose to make uniform the law of those states which enact it.

**SECTION 9. [*Short Title.*]** This Act may be cited as the Uniform Foreign Money-Judgments Recognition Act.

**SECTION 10. [*Repeal.*]** [The following Acts are repealed:

(1)

(2)

(3) .]

**SECTION 11. [*Time of Taking Effect.*]** This Act shall take effect . . . .

# UNIFORM FOREIGN-COUNTRY MONEY JUDGMENTS RECOGNITION ACT

drafted by the

NATIONAL CONFERENCE OF COMMISSIONERS
ON UNIFORM STATE LAWS

and by it

APPROVED AND RECOMMENDED FOR ENACTMENT
IN ALL THE STATES

at its

ANNUAL CONFERENCE
MEETING IN ITS ONE-HUNDRED-AND-FOURTEENTH YEAR
PITTSBURGH, PENNSYLVANIA

July 21-28, 2005

*WITH PREFATORY NOTE AND COMMENTS*



February 10, 2006

## UNIFORM FOREIGN-COUNTRY MONEY JUDGMENTS RECOGNITION ACT

**SECTION 1. SHORT TITLE.** This [act] may be cited as the [Uniform Foreign-Country Money Judgments Recognition Act].

**SECTION 2. DEFINITIONS.** In this [act]:

(1) "Foreign country" means a government other than:

(A) the United States;

(B) a state, district, commonwealth, territory, or insular possession of the United States; or

(C) any other government with regard to which the decision in this state as to whether to recognize a judgment of that government's courts is initially subject to determination under the Full Faith and Credit Clause of the United States Constitution.

(2) "Foreign-country judgment" means a judgment of a court of a foreign country.

**SECTION 3. APPLICABILITY.**

(a) Except as otherwise provided in subsection (b), this [act] applies to a foreign-country judgment to the extent that the judgment:

(1) grants or denies recovery of a sum of money; and

(2) under the law of the foreign country where rendered, is final, conclusive, and enforceable.

(b) This [act] does not apply to a foreign-country judgment, even if the judgment grants or denies recovery of a sum of money, to the extent that the judgment is:

(1) a judgment for taxes;

(2) a fine or other penalty; or

(3) a judgment for divorce, support, or maintenance, or other judgment rendered in connection with domestic relations.

(c) A party seeking recognition of a foreign-country judgment has the burden of establishing that this [act] applies to the foreign-country judgment.

**SECTION 4. STANDARDS FOR RECOGNITION OF FOREIGN-COUNTRY JUDGMENT.**

(a) Except as otherwise provided in subsections (b) and (c), a court of this state shall recognize a foreign-country judgment to which this [act] applies.

(b) A court of this state may not recognize a foreign-country judgment if:

(1) the judgment was rendered under a judicial system that does not provide impartial tribunals or procedures compatible with the requirements of due process of law;

(2) the foreign court did not have personal jurisdiction over the defendant; or

(3) the foreign court did not have jurisdiction over the subject matter.

(c) A court of this state need not recognize a foreign-country judgment if:

(1) the defendant in the proceeding in the foreign court did not receive notice of the proceeding in sufficient time to enable the defendant to defend;

(2) the judgment was obtained by fraud that deprived the losing

party of an adequate opportunity to present its case;

(3) the judgment or the [cause of action] [claim for relief] on which the judgment is based is repugnant to the public policy of this state or of the United States;

(4) the judgment conflicts with another final and conclusive judgment;

(5) the proceeding in the foreign court was contrary to an agreement between the parties under which the dispute in question was to be determined otherwise than by proceedings in that foreign court;

(6) in the case of jurisdiction based only on personal service, the foreign court was a seriously inconvenient forum for the trial of the action;

(7) the judgment was rendered in circumstances that raise substantial doubt about the integrity of the rendering court with respect to the judgment; or

(8) the specific proceeding in the foreign court leading to the judgment was not compatible with the requirements of due process of law.

(d) A party resisting recognition of a foreign-country judgment has the burden of establishing that a ground for nonrecognition stated in subsection (b) or (c) exists.

**SECTION 5. PERSONAL JURISDICTION.**

(a) A foreign-country judgment may not be refused recognition for lack of personal jurisdiction if:

(1) the defendant was served with process personally in the

foreign country;

(2) the defendant voluntarily appeared in the proceeding, other than for the purpose of protecting property seized or threatened with seizure in the proceeding or of contesting the jurisdiction of the court over the defendant;

(3) the defendant, before the commencement of the proceeding, had agreed to submit to the jurisdiction of the foreign court with respect to the subject matter involved;

(4) the defendant was domiciled in the foreign country when the proceeding was instituted or was a corporation or other form of business organization that had its principal place of business in, or was organized under the laws of, the foreign country;

(5) the defendant had a business office in the foreign country and the proceeding in the foreign court involved a [cause of action] [claim for relief] arising out of business done by the defendant through that office in the foreign country; or

(6) the defendant operated a motor vehicle or airplane in the foreign country and the proceeding involved a [cause of action] [claim for relief] arising out of that operation.

(b) The list of bases for personal jurisdiction in subsection (a) is not exclusive. The courts of this state may recognize bases of personal jurisdiction other than those listed in subsection(a) as sufficient to support a foreign-country judgment.

**SECTION 6. PROCEDURE FOR RECOGNITION OF FOREIGN-COUNTRY JUDGMENT.**

(a) If recognition of a foreign-country judgment is sought as an original matter, the issue of recognition shall be raised by filing an action seeking recognition of the foreign-country judgment.

(b) If recognition of a foreign-country judgment is sought in a pending action, the issue of recognition may be raised by counterclaim, cross-claim, or affirmative defense.

**SECTION 7. EFFECT OF RECOGNITION OF FOREIGN-COUNTRY JUDGMENT.** If the court in a proceeding under Section 6 finds that the foreign-country judgment is entitled to recognition under this [act] then, to the extent that the foreign-country judgment grants or denies recovery of a sum of money, the foreign-country judgment is:

(1) conclusive between the parties to the same extent as the judgment of a sister state entitled to full faith and credit in this state would be conclusive; and

(2) enforceable in the same manner and to the same extent as a judgment rendered in this state.

**SECTION 8. STAY OF PROCEEDINGS PENDING APPEAL OF FOREIGN-COUNTRY JUDGMENT.** If a party establishes that an appeal from a foreign-country judgment is pending or will be taken, the court may stay any proceedings with regard to the foreign-country judgment until the appeal is concluded, the time for appeal expires, or the appellant has had sufficient time to prosecute the appeal and has failed to do so.

**SECTION 9. STATUTE OF LIMITATIONS.** An action to recognize a foreign-country judgment must be commenced within the earlier of the time during which the foreign-country judgment is effective in the foreign country or 15 years from the date that the foreign-country judgment became effective in the foreign country.

**SECTION 10. UNIFORMITY OF INTERPRETATION.** In applying and construing this uniform act, consideration must be given to the need to promote uniformity of the law with respect to its subject matter among states that enact it.

**SECTION 11. SAVING CLAUSE.** This [act] does not prevent the recognition under principles of comity or otherwise of a foreign-country judgment not within the scope of this [act].

**SECTION 12. EFFECTIVE DATE.**

[(a) This [act] takes effect … .

[(b) This [act] applies to all actions commenced on or after the effective date of this [act] in which the issue of recognition of a foreign-country judgment is raised.]

**SECTION 13. REPEAL.** The following [acts] are repealed:

(a) Uniform Foreign Money-Judgments Recognition Act,

(b)

.]

Uniform Foreign Money-Judgments Recognition Act – Jurisdictions Wherein the Act Has Been Adopted

**STATE ADOPTIONS:**
Alaska
California
Colorado
Connecticut
Delaware
District of Columbia
Florida
Georgia
Hawaii
Idaho
Illinois
Iowa
Maine
Maryland
Massachusetts
Michigan
Minnesota
Missouri
Montana
New Jersey
New Mexico
New York
North Carolina
North Dakota
Ohio
Oklahoma
Oregon
Pennsylvania
Texas
U.S. Virgin Islands
Virginia
Washington

# UNIFORM FOREIGN-MONEY CLAIMS ACT

Drafted by the

NATIONAL CONFERENCE OF COMMISSIONERS
ON UNIFORM STATE LAWS

and by it

APPROVED AND RECOMMENDED FOR ENACTMENT
IN ALL THE STATES

at its

ANNUAL CONFERENCE
MEETING IN ITS NINETY-EIGHTH YEAR
IN KAUAI, HAWAII
JULY 28 – AUGUST 4, 1989

*WITH PREFATORY NOTE AND COMMENTS*

Approved by the American Bar Association
Los Angeles, California, February 13, 1990

# UNIFORM FOREIGN-MONEY CLAIMS ACT

## PREFATORY NOTE

This Act facilitates uniform judicial determination of claims expressed in the money of foreign countries. It requires judgments and arbitration awards in these cases to be entered in the foreign money rather than in United States dollars. The debtor may pay the judgment in dollars on the basis of the rate of exchange prevailing at the time of payment.

A Uniform Act governing foreign-money claims has become desirable because:

> These claims have increased greatly as a result of the growth in international trade.
>
> Values of foreign moneys as compared to the United States dollar fluctuate more over shorter periods of time than was formerly the case.
>
> United States jurisdictions treat recoveries on foreign-money claims differently than most of our major trading partners.
>
> A lack of uniformity among the states in resolving foreign-money claims stimulates forum shopping and creates a lack of certainty in the law.

American courts historically follow one of two different rules in selecting a time during litigation for converting foreign money into United States dollars. These are called the "breachdayrule"– the date the money should have been paid – and the "judgment date rule"– when judgment is entered. Many other countries use the "payment day rule" – when the judgment is paid. See *Miliangos v. George Frank (Textiles) Ltd.*, (1976) A.C. 1007. The merits of this approach have begun to be recognized in this country. The payment day rule is endorsed by this Act.

The three rules produce wildly disparate results in terms of making an injured person whole. This is illustrated by the following example:

> An American citizen (A) owes 18,790 pounds sterling to a British corporation (BCo) suing in New York, and the pound is falling against the dollar. Due to the declining value of the pound, the three rules worked out as follows:

| Date | Rate of Exchange | BCo Gets |
|---|---|---|
| Breach day | Pound = $2.20 | $41,338 |
| Judgment day | Pound = $1.50 | $28,185 |
| Payment day | Pound = $1.20 | $22,548 |

A judgment of $41,338 may be entered based on the breach day rule. However, the payment in dollars was worth 34,449 pounds ($41,338 divided by $1.20) when eventually received, an excess of L15,659 over the actual loss.

This example is adapted from an actual case. See *Comptex v. LaBow*, 783 F.2d 333 (2d Cir. 1986). The facts are simplified.

If conversion is delayed until the date of actual payment, the creditor is recompensed with its own money or the financial equivalent in United States dollars; the debtor bears the risk of a fall in the debtor's money or reaps the benefit of a rise therein. If conversion is made at breach or judgment date, the risk of fluctuation in value of a money not of its selection falls on the creditor.

The real issue is where the risk of exchange rate fluctuation should be placed. This Act recognizes the right of the parties to agree upon the money that governs their relationship. In the absence of an agreement, the Act adopts the rule of giving the aggrieved party the amount to which it is entitled in its own money or the money in which the loss was suffered.

The principle of the Act is to restore the aggrieved party to the economic position it would have been in had the wrong not occurred. Thus, for example, if oil is spilled on the coast of France by an American ship, the loss is felt by the French in francs and a judgment of an American court for damages should reflect this fact. Courts should enter judgments in the money customarily used by the injured person.

The payment day rule, on which the Act is based, meets the reasonable expectations of the parties involved. It places the aggrieved party in the position it would have been in financially but for the wrong that gave rise to the claim. States which adopt it will align themselves with most of the major civilized countries of the world.

The Act also covers other issues that may arise in connection with foreign-money claims. These include revalorization and interest. In order to determine aliquot shares for distributions from funds created in insolvency and estate proceedings, the Act specifies use of the date the distribution proceeding was initiated for conversion of foreign money into United States dollars.

# UNIFORM FOREIGN-MONEY CLAIMS ACT

SECTION 1. DEFINITIONS. In this [Act]:

(1) "Action" means a judicial proceeding or arbitration in which a payment in money may be awarded or enforced with respect to a foreign-money claim.

(2) "Bank-offered spot rate" means the spot rate of exchange at which a bank will sell foreign money at a spot rate.

(3) "Conversion date" means the banking day next preceding the date on which money, in accordance with this [Act], is:

(i) paid to a claimant in an action or distribution proceeding;

(ii) paid to the official designated by law to enforce a judgment or award on behalf of a claimant; or

(iii) used to recoup, set-off, or counterclaim in different moneys in an action or distribution proceeding.

(4) "Distribution proceeding" means a judicial or nonjudicial proceeding for the distribution of a fund in which one or more foreign-money claims is asserted and includes an accounting, an assignment for the benefit of creditors, a foreclosure, the liquidation or rehabilitation of a corporation or other entity, and the distribution of an estate, trust, or other fund.

(5) "Foreign money" means money other than money of the United States of America.

(6) "Foreign-money claim" means a claim upon an obligation to pay, or a claim for recovery of a loss, expressed in or measured by a foreign money.

(7) "Money" means a medium of exchange for the payment of obligations or a store of value authorized or adopted by a government or by inter-governmental agreement.

(8) "Money of the claim" means the money determined as proper pursuant to Section 4.

(9) "Person" means an individual, a corporation, government or governmental subdivision or agency, business trust, estate, trust, joint venture, partnership, association, two or more persons having a joint or common interest, or any other legal or commercial entity.

(10) "Rate of exchange" means the rate at which money of one country may be converted into money of another country in a free financial market convenient to or reasonably usable by a person obligated to pay or to state a rate of conversion. If separate rates of exchange apply to different kinds of transactions, the term means the rate applicable to the particular transaction giving rise to the foreign-money claim.

(11) "Spot rate" means the rate of exchange at which foreign money is sold by a bank or other dealer in foreign exchange for immediate or next day availability or for settlement by immediate payment in cash or equivalent, by charge to an account, or by an agreed delayed settlement not exceeding two days.

(12) "State" means a State of the United States, the District of Columbia, the Commonwealth of Puerto Rico, or a territory or insular possession subject to the jurisdiction of the United States.

**Comment**

1. "Action." A suit or arbitration may be legal or equitable in nature, but it must be based on a pecuniary claim.

2. "Bank-offered spot rate" is the rate at which a bank will sell the requisite amount of foreign money for immediate or nearly immediate use by the buyer.

3. "Conversion date." Exchange rates may fluctuate from day to day. A date must be picked for calculating the value of foreign money in terms of United States dollars. As used in the Act, 'conversion date' means the day before a foreign-money claim is paid or set-off. The day refers to the time period of the place of the payor, not necessarily that of the recipient. The exchange rate prevailing at or near the close of business on the banking day before the day payment is made will be well known at the time of payment. See Comment 2 to Section 7.

4. "Distribution proceeding." In keeping with the concept underlying Section 2, the coverage of this statute is limited to judicial actions and nonjudicial proceedings which involve the creation of a fund from which pro-rata distributions are made to claimants. As provided in Section 8, a different conversion date is required where either input to or outgo from a fund involves two or more different

moneys. Thus, the term includes a mortgage foreclosure proceeding, judicial or under a trust deed, distribution of property in divorce and child support proceedings, distributions in the administration of a trust or a decedent's estate, an assignment for the benefit of creditors, an equity receivership, a liquidation by a statutory successor, a voluntary dissolution of a business or a nonprofit enterprise or the like when in each case a fund must be shared among claimants and where, usually, the fund will not satisfy all claimants of the same class. An asset or a liability of the fund must also involve one or more foreign-money claims, but not all of the claims can be in the same money.

5. "Foreign money." Since only the federal government has the power to coin money and regulate the value thereof, the term "foreign" means a government other than that of the United States of America. Special Drawing Rights of the International Monetary Fund are foreign money even though the United States is a member of the Fund. Foreign governments included are all those whose moneys are, in the currency markets of the world, exchangeable for the money of other currencies even though the government is not recognized by the United States.

6. "Foreign-money claim." The term "claim" is not limited to any one party to an action or a distribution proceeding and may be asserted by a plaintiff or a defendant or by a party to an arbitration or distribution proceeding. It may be based on a foreign judgment, or sound in contract, quasi-contract, or tort.

7. "Money." The definition includes composite currencies such as European Currency Units created by agreement of the governments that are members of the European Monetary System or the Special Drawing Rights created under the auspices of the International Money Fund. These are "stores of value" used to determine the quantity of payment in some international transactions.

8. "Money of the claim." See Section 4 and the Comment thereto.

9. "Party." This combines the Uniform Commercial Code's definitions of "person" and "organization," but is limited to those who are parties to transactions or involved in events which could give rise to a foreign-money claim.

10. "Rate of Exchange." A free market rate is to be used rather than an official rate if both exist. Some countries have transactional differences in exchange rates with slightly different rates; for example, in Belgium one rate prevails for commercial and another for financial transactions. Both rates are recognized in money market transactions. The last sentence of the definition indicates that the rate appropriate to the transaction is the rate to be used.

11. "Spot rate" is the term used in the financial markets of the United States for the rate of exchange for immediate or nearly immediate transfers from one money to another, as distinguished from the rates for future options or future deliveries.

In the foreign exchange markets, as in the stock markets, quotations are either "bid" or "ask," and the spread between is where the dealer makes a profit. An "offered spot rate" is the rate at which the offeror will sell the particular money. It is, of course, higher than the rate at which that person will buy the same money. "Spot" refers to the time the trade is made, not the time for settlement, which in spot transactions is often two days after the date of the trade.

12. "State." The definition, as in other Uniform Laws, is extended to include areas given the same, or nearly the same, treatment in law as the states.

**SECTION 2. SCOPE.**

(a) This [Act] applies only to a foreign-money claim in an action or distribution proceeding.

(b) This [Act] applies to foreign-money issues even if other law under the conflict of laws rules of this State applies to other issues in the action or distribution proceeding.

**Comment**

Under the rules of the conflict of laws, the determination of when a foreign money is converted to United States dollars is generally considered a procedural matter for the law of the forum. Subsection (b) removes any doubt.

**SECTION 3. VARIATION BY AGREEMENT.**

(a) The effect of this [Act] may be varied by agreement of the parties made before or after commencement of an action or distribution proceeding or the entry of judgment.

(b) Parties to a transaction may agree upon the money to be used in a transaction giving rise to a foreign-money claim and may agree to use different moneys for different aspects of the transaction. Stating the price in a foreign money for one aspect of a transaction does not alone require the use of that money for other aspects of the transaction.

**Comment**

1. A basic policy of the Act is to preserve freedom of contract and to permit parties to resolve disputed matters by contract at any time, even as to choice of law problems. The parties may agree upon the date and time for conversion. After entry of judgment the parties may agree upon how the judgment is to be satisfied.

2. Subsection (b) covers cases where, for example, claims for petroleum may be settled in United States dollars but settlement for joint costs of exploration may be in pounds sterling. The parties also may agree on the money to be used for damages. The second sentence recognizes that a price stated in a particular money does not indicate, without more evidence, an intent that all damages from breach are to be in the same money. The principle of freedom of contract allows the parties to allocate the risks of currency fluctuations between foreign moneys as they desire. Sections 4 and 5 provide rules in the absence of special agreements by the parties for determining the money to be used. Parties may by agreement select a particular market or foreign exchange dealer to be used for exchange purposes.

**SECTION 4. DETERMINING MONEY OF THE CLAIM.**

(a) The money in which the parties to a transaction have agreed that payment is to be made is the proper money of the claim for payment.

(b) If the parties to a transaction have not otherwise agreed, the proper money of the claim, as in each case may be appropriate, is the money:

(1) regularly used between the parties as a matter of usage or course of dealing;

(2) used at the time of a transaction in international trade, by trade usage or common practice, for valuing or settling transactions in the particular commodity or service involved; or

(3) in which the loss was ultimately felt or will be incurred by the party claimant.

**Comment**

1. Subsection (a) uses "payment" in a broad sense not related to just the price, but to any obligation arising out of a contract to transfer money. See also Section 3(b).

2. Subsection (b) states rules to fill gaps in the agreement of the parties with rules as to the allocation of risks of fluctuations in exchange rates. The three rules will normally apply in the order stated. Prior dealings may indicate the desired money. If there are none, it is appropriate to use the money indicated by trade usage or custom for transactions of like kind. The final rule of subsection (a) is one established in English cases. See *The Despina R and the Folias*, (1979) A.C. 685. An example is the use of an operating account in United States dollars by a French company to buy Japanese yen for ship repairs; the loss is felt in the depletion of the dollar bank account. Appropriateness of a rule is to be determined by the judge from the facts of the case. See Section 6(d).

**SECTION 5. DETERMINING AMOUNT OF THE MONEY OF CERTAIN CONTRACT CLAIMS.**

(a) If an amount contracted to be paid in a foreign money is measured by a specified amount of a different money, the amount to be paid is determined on the conversion date.

(b) If an amount contracted to be paid in a foreign money is to be measured by a different money at the rate of exchange prevailing on a date before default, that rate of exchange applies only to payments made within a reasonable time after default, not exceeding 30 days. Thereafter, conversion is made at the bank-offered spot rate on the conversion date.

(c) A monetary claim is neither usurious nor unconscionable because the agreement on which it is based provides that the amount of the debtor's obligation to be paid in the debtor's money, when received by the creditor, must equal a specified amount of the foreign money of the country of the creditor. If, because of unexcused delay in payment of a judgment or award, the amount received by the creditor does not equal the amount of the foreign money specified in the agreement, the court or arbitrator shall amend the judgment or award accordingly.

**Comment**

1. Subsections (a) and (b) cover different interpretation problems. One arises where the amount of the money to be paid is measured by another money, one of which is foreign. An example is "pay 5,000 Swiss francs in pounds sterling." The issue is the time at which the rate of exchange into pounds sterling is to be applied. Subsection (a) says in a "measured by" situation with no rate specified, the rate of exchange that controls is the one prevailing at or near the close of business on the day before the day of payment. See Section 1(2), the definition of "conversion date."

2. Another problem arises when an exchange rate in effect before a default is used, as in "pay on November 30, 1989, 5,000 Swiss francs in pounds sterling at the exchange rate prevailing on June 30, 1989." In this case, the issue is how long does the specified exchange rate control in the absence of a clear expression of intent?

Inclusion of a fixed rate as of a date before default, under subsection (b), remains effective only if payment is made within a reasonable time after default, not to exceed 30 days. The 30-day limitation accords usually with the expectation of the parties. Parties may agree to a longer time.

3. The most common application of subsection (c) will be found in international loan transactions. For example, a loan by a Japanese bank to an American company could be made with dollars purchased by yen for the purpose. The loan agreement could provide for repayment in dollars of an amount which, when received by the lender, would repurchase the amount of yen used to acquire the dollars advanced.

An exemption is needed from the application of usury laws that may be interpreted to hold that the indexing of the principal amount creates additional interest. See *Aztec Properties, Inc. v. Union Planters National Bank*, 530 S.W.2d 756 (Tenn. Sup. Ct. 1975). The subsection removes all doubts as to the legal enforceability of such agreements under theories such as usury, merger in a judgment, unconscionability, or the like.

**SECTION 6. ASSERTING AND DEFENDING FOREIGN-MONEY CLAIM.**

(a) A person may assert a claim in a specified foreign money. If a foreign-money claim is not asserted, the claimant makes the claim in United States dollars.

(b) An opposing party may allege and prove that a claim, in whole or in part, is in a different money than that asserted by the claimant.

(c) A person may assert a defense, set-off, recoupment, or counterclaim in any money without regard to the money of other claims.

(d) The determination of the proper money of the claim is a question of law.

## Comment

1. Subsection (a) covers not only the claim of a plaintiff but also the assertion by a defendant of a defense, set-off, or counterclaim. Subsection (b) provides that the money asserted as the money of its defenses by the defendant need not be the same as that of the plaintiff.

2. The money to be used as the money of the claim is a threshold issue to be determined, if contested, by the court after any factual issues as to expenditures, custom, usage, or course of dealing are decided. See subsection (b). If a payment is made or a debt incurred in a money other than that in which the loss was felt, the party asserting the foreign-money claim should establish the amount of the money of the claim used to procure the money of expenditure and the applicable exchange rate used.

3. Judgments may be entered in more than one money when dealings impact on more than one area. An inn-keeper in Mexico, for example, in taking in customers from many countries, should be held to foresee that treatment for injuries at the inn would occur not only in Mexico, but also in the native land of the injured party or in a third country.

## SECTION 7. JUDGMENTS AND AWARDS ON FOREIGN-MONEY CLAIMS; TIMES OF MONEY CONVERSION; FORM OF JUDGMENT.

(a) Except as provided in subsection (c), a judgment or award on a foreign-money claim must be stated in an amount of the money of the claim.

(b) A judgment or award on a foreign-money claim is payable in that foreign money or, at the option of the debtor, in the amount of United States dollars which will purchase that foreign money on the conversion date at a bank-offered spot rate.

(c) Assessed costs must be entered in United States dollars.

(d) Each payment in United States dollars must be accepted and credited on a judgment or award on a foreign-money claim in the amount of the foreign money that could be purchased by the dollars at a bank-offered spot rate of exchange at or near the close of business on the conversion date for that payment.

(e) A judgment or award made in an action or distribution proceeding on both (i) a defense, set-off, recoupment, or counterclaim and (ii) the adverse party's claim, must be netted by converting the money of the smaller into the money of the larger, and by subtracting the smaller from the larger, and specify the rates of exchange used.

(f) A judgment substantially in the following form complies with subsection (a):

[IT IS ADJUDGED AND ORDERED, that Defendant (insert name) pay to Plaintiff (insert name) the sum of (insert amount in the foreign money) plus interest on that sum at the rate of (insert rate – seeSection 9) percent a year or, at the option of the judgment debtor, the number of United States dollars which will purchase the (insert name of foreign money) with interest due, at a bank-offered spot rate at or near the close of business on the banking day next before the day of payment, together with assessed costs of (insert amount) United States dollars.] [Note: States should insert their customary forms of judgment with appropriate modifications.]

(g) If a contract claim is of the type covered by Section 5(a) or (b), the judgment or award must be entered for the amount of money stated to measure the obligation to be paid in the money specified for payment or, at the option of the debtor, the number of United States dollars which will purchase the computed amount of the money of payment on the conversion date at a bank-offered spot rate.

(h) A judgment must be [filed] [docketed] [recorded] and indexed in foreign money in the same manner, and has the same effect as a lien, as other judgments. It may be discharged by payment.

**Comment**

1. Subsection (a) changes a number of statutes in the states which can be construed to require all values in legal proceedings to be expressed in United States dollars. Professor Brand, in his article in the Yale Journal of International Law, Vol. 11:139 at page 169, identified 18 states having statutes which could require all judgments to be entered in dollars. They are Arkansas, California, Idaho, Iowa, Louisiana, Maryland, Michigan, Montana, Nevada, New Jersey, New Mexico, New York, South Carolina, Tennessee, Vermont, Virginia, West Virginia, and Wisconsin. Brand, *ibid.* fn. 166. Hence, direct statutory authority must be given the courts in those states, and will be helpful in other states. In some states other statutes may need amendments. See, *e.g.*, Wisc. Stats. §§ 138.01, 138.02, 138.03, and 779.05.

2. Subsection (d) gives defendants the option of paying in dollars which are, at the payment date, practically the economic equivalent of the foreign money awarded. The judgment creditor should be indifferent to whether the debtor

exercises the right to pay in dollars as the only difference is a small bank charge for exchanging the dollars for the foreign money. The concept of the rate of the banking day next before the payment day is taken from Section 131 of the Province of Ontario, Canada, Courts of Justice Act (Ch. 11 Ont. Stats. (1984) as recently amended). It gives the defendant and the sheriff conducting the sale the necessary conversion rate comfortably ahead of its use. Newspaper quotations are usually said to be "at or near the close of business" on the stated date, so that phrase is used in this Act.

3. Subsection (e) provides for netting the affirmative recoveries of a defendant and plaintiff, whether in the same money or in different moneys, but preserving the quantum of each for appellate purposes. The theory is that when claims are reduced to money, they become mutual debts and should be set-off, so that a person's exchange rate fluctuation risk continues only for the surplus in its money of the claim. The set-off is made by the judge or arbitrator.

4. The form of judgment in subsection (f) should be varied appropriately where the money to be paid is measured by a foreign money. See Section 5.

**SECTION 8. CONVERSIONS OF FOREIGN MONEY IN DISTRIBUTION PROCEEDING.** The rate of exchange prevailing at or near the close of business on the day the distribution proceeding is initiated governs all exchanges of foreign money in a distribution proceeding. A foreign-money claimant in a distribution proceeding shall assert its claim in the named foreign money and show the amount of United States dollars resulting from a conversion as of the date the proceeding was initiated.

**Comment**

All claims must be in the same money when determining aliquot shares in a distribution proceeding. The Act requires use of the date the proceeding was initiated for applying the exchange rate to convert foreign-money claims into United States dollars. See *Re Lines Bros. Ltd.*, (1982) 2 All E.R. 99. A claim may be amended to show the proper conversion rate and the proper amount of United States dollars.

**SECTION 9. PRE-JUDGMENT AND JUDGMENT INTEREST.**

(a) With respect to a foreign-money claim, recovery of pre-judgment or pre-award interest and the rate of interest to be applied in the action or distribution proceeding, except as provided in subsection (b), are matters of the substantive law governing the right to recovery under the conflict-of-laws rules of this State.

(b) The court or arbitrator shall increase or decrease the amount of pre-judgment or pre-award interest otherwise payable in a judgment or award in foreign-money to the extent required by the law of this State governing a failure to make or accept an offer of settlement or offer of judgment, or conduct by a party or its attorney causing undue delay or expense.

(c) A judgment or award on a foreign-money claim bears interest at the rate applicable to judgments of this State.

**Comment**

1. As to pre-judgment interest, the Act adopts the majority rule in the United States that pre-judgment interest follows the substantive law of the case under conflict of laws rules, both as to the right to recover and the rate. English courts use a different rule, *i.e.*, the borrowing rate used by plaintiff or prevailing in the country issuing the money of the judgment. See *Helmsing Schiffarts G.M.B.H. v. Malta Drydock Corp.* (1977) 2 Lloyd's Rep. 44 (Maltese money but borrowed in West Germany; German rate); *Miliangos v. George Frank (Textiles) Ltd. (No. 2)* (1976) 1 QB 487 at 489 (Swiss money, Swiss interest rate). Although pre-judgment interest is one form of damages, provision for pre-judgment interest is not to be taken as indicating that no other damages for delay in payment can be awarded under the substantive law applicable to the determination of damages. *Cf. Isaac Naylor & Sons, Ltd. v. New Zealand Co-operative Wool Marketing Association, Ltd.* (1981) 1 N.Z.L.R. 361 (exchange loss due to delay as additional damages).

2. Allowances of pre-judgment interest in some states depend upon a party's conduct with respect to settlement or delay of the proceeding. Subsection (b) treats these state laws as either procedural in nature or expressions of a significant policy, in either case to be governed by the law of the forum state.

3. Interest on a judgment is considered to be procedural and also goes by the law of the forum. There is a problem here in that there is great discrepancy among the states in the rates for judgment interest. When a judgment is in a foreign money, United States interest rates may result in some overcompensation or undercompensation as compared to what would be awarded in the jurisdiction issuing the foreign money. But in both the United States and in foreign countries, most jurisdictions have fixed statutory rates that do not readily respond to the inflation or deflation of the value of their money in the world market. Hence it was decided to apply the usual rules of the conflict of laws.

## SECTION 10. ENFORCEMENT OF FOREIGN JUDGMENTS.

(a) If an action is brought to enforce a judgment of another jurisdiction expressed in a foreign money and the judgment is recognized in this State as enforceable, the enforcing judgment must be entered as provided in Section 7, whether or not the foreign judgment confers an option to pay in an equivalent amount of United States dollars.

(b) A foreign judgment may be [filed] [docketed] [recorded] in accordance with any rule or statute of this State providing a procedure for its recognition and enforcement.

(c) A satisfaction or partial payment made upon the foreign judgment, on proof thereof, must be credited against the amount of foreign money specified in the judgment, notwithstanding the entry of judgment in this State.

(d) A judgment entered on a foreign-money claim only in United States dollars in another state must be enforced in this State in United States dollars only.

### Comment

1. Some states have special acts that simply cover the recognition, entry, and enforcement of foreign judgments. Common law enforcement is by action. Subsection (a) refers to the common law method; it is subject to subsection (b) which refers to statutory procedures. Subsection (c) applies to both procedures.

2. Subsection (d) avoids constitutional issues under the full faith and credit clause by requiring that judgments of sister states be enforced as entered in the sister state.

## SECTION 11. DETERMINING UNITED STATES DOLLAR VALUE OF FOREIGN-MONEY CLAIMS FOR LIMITED PURPOSES.

(a) Computations under this section are for the limited purposes of the section and do not affect computation of the United States dollar equivalent of the money of the judgment for the purpose of payment.

(b) For the limited purpose of facilitating the enforcement of provisional remedies in an action, the value in United States dollars of assets to be seized or restrained pursuant to a writ of attachment, garnishment, execution, or other legal process, the amount of United States dollars at issue for assessing costs, or the amount of United States dollars involved for a surety bond or other court-required undertaking, must be ascertained as provided in subsections (c) and (d).

(c) A party seeking process, costs, bond, or other undertaking under subsection (b) shall compute in United States dollars the amount of the foreign money claimed from a bank-offered spot rate prevailing at or near the close of business on the banking day next preceding the filing of a request or application for the issuance of process or for the determination of costs, or an application for a bond or other court-required undertaking.

(d) A party seeking the process, costs, bond, or other undertaking under subsection (b) shall file with each request or application an affidavit or certificate executed in good faith by its counsel or a bank officer, stating the market quotation used and how it was obtained, and setting forth the calculation. Affected court officials incur no liability, after a filing of the affidavit or certificate, for acting as if the judgment were in the amount of United States dollars stated in the affidavit or certificate.

**Comment**

This section protects those who must determine how much should be held subject to a levy or other collection process or what the dollar amount of a supersedeas or other surety bond should be. If the judgment debtor is damaged by a gross overstatement of the dollar amount in the affidavit or certificate of counsel for the judgment creditor or the bank officer, recovery should be against that person.

## SECTION 12. EFFECT OF CURRENCY REVALORIZATION.

(a) If, after an obligation is expressed or a loss is incurred in a foreign money, the country issuing or adopting that money substitutes a new money in place of that money, the obligation or the loss is treated as if expressed or incurred in the new money at the rate of conversion the issuing country establishes for the payment of like obligations or losses denominated in the former money.

(b) If substitution under subsection (a) occurs after a judgment or award is entered on a foreign-money claim, the court or arbitrator shall amend the judgment or award by a like conversion of the former money.

**Comment**

1. Subsection (a) refers to situations in which a country authorizes the issue of a new money to take the place of the old money at a stated ratio. An example is

Brazil's recent abolition of cruzieros for cruzados. The subsection mandates that foreign money claims should be subjected to the same ratio.

2. The Act takes no position on the effect of money repudiations or revalorizations so drastic as to be, in effect, confiscations. Remedy, if any, for these is usually found through diplomatic channels. Equally, the Act takes no position on the effect of exchange control laws. The effect, if any, on obligations to pay is left to other law.

**SECTION 13. SUPPLEMENTARY GENERAL PRINCIPLES OF LAW.** Unless displaced by particular provisions of this [Act], the principles of law and equity, including the law merchant, and the law relative to capacity to contract, principal and agent, estoppel, fraud, misrepresentation, duress, coercion, mistake, bankruptcy, or other validating or invalidating causes supplement its provisions.

**Comment**

The section is taken from Section 1-103 of the Uniform Commercial Code.

**SECTION 14. UNIFORMITY OF APPLICATION AND CONSTRUCTION.** This [Act] shall be applied and construed to effectuate its general purpose to make uniform the law with respect to the subject of this [Act] among states enacting it.

**SECTION 15. SHORT TITLE.** This [Act] may be cited as the Uniform Foreign-Money Claims Act.

**SECTION 16. SEVERABILITY CLAUSE.** If any provision of this [Act] or its application to any person or circumstance is held invalid, the invalidity does not affect other provisions or applications of this [Act] which can be given effect without the invalid provision or application, and to this end the provisions of this [Act] are severable.

**SECTION 17. EFFECTIVE DATE.** This [Act] becomes effective on January 1st following its enactment.

**SECTION 18. TRANSITIONAL PROVISION.** This [Act] applies to actions and distribution proceedings commenced after its effective date.

[**SECTION 19. REPEALS.** The following acts and parts of acts are repealed:

(1) [Any statute requiring judgments to be entered in United States dollars.]

(2) ________________________________.

(3) ________________________________.]

## Uniform Foreign-Money Claims Act – Jurisdictions Wherein the Act Has Been Adopted

**STATE ADOPTIONS:**

California
Colorado
Connecticut
Delaware
District of Columbia
Hawaii
Idaho
Illinois
Minnesota
Montana
Nevada
New Jersey
New Mexico
North Carolina
North Dakota
Ohio
Oklahoma
Oregon
U.S. Virgin Islands
Utah
Virginia
Washington
Wisconsin

http://uscode.house.gov/download/pls/28C115.txt

TITLE 28 – JUDICIARY AND JUDICIAL PROCEDURE
PART V – PROCEDURE
CHAPTER 115 – EVIDENCE; DOCUMENTARY

Sec. 1738. State and Territorial statutes and judicial proceedings; full faith and credit

The Acts of the legislature of any State, Territory, or Possession of the United States, or copies thereof, shall be authenticated by affixing the seal of such State, Territory or Possession thereto.

The records and judicial proceedings of any court of any such State, Territory or Possession, or copies thereof, shall be proved or admitted in other courts within the United States and its Territories and Possessions by the attestation of the clerk and seal of the court annexed, if a seal exists, together with a certificate of a judge of the court that the said attestation is in proper form.

Such Acts, records and judicial proceedings or copies thereof, so authenticated, shall have the same full faith and credit in every court within the United States and its Territories and Possessions as they have by law or usage in the courts of such State, Territory or Possession from which they are taken.

## CONSTITUTION OF THE UNITED STATES,

## ARTICLE IV.--SECTION 1.

1. Full faith and credit shall be given in each State to the public acts, records, and judicial proceedings of every other State. And the Congress may, by general laws, prescribe the manner in which such acts, records, and proceedings shall be proved, and the effect thereof.

## FRCP Rule 4. Summons

### (a) Form.

The summons shall be signed by the clerk, bear the seal of the court, identify the court and the parties, be directed to the defendant, and state the name and address of the plaintiff's attorney or, if unrepresented, of the plaintiff. It shall also state the time within which the defendant must appear and defend, and notify the defendant that failure to do so will result in a judgment by default against the defendant for the relief demanded in the complaint. The court may allow a summons to be amended.

### (b) Issuance.

Upon or after filing the complaint, the plaintiff may present a summons to the clerk for signature and seal. If the summons is in proper form, the clerk shall sign, seal, and issue it to the plaintiff for service on the defendant. A summons, or a copy of the summons if addressed to multiple defendants, shall be issued for each defendant to be served.

### (c) Service with Complaint; by Whom Made.

(1) A summons shall be served together with a copy of the complaint. The plaintiff is responsible for service of a summons and complaint within the time allowed under subdivision (m) and shall furnish the person effecting service with the necessary copies of the summons and complaint.

(2) Service may be effected by any person who is not a party and who is at least 18 years of age. At the request of the plaintiff, however, the court may direct that service be effected by a United States marshal, deputy United States marshal, or other person or officer specially appointed by the court for that purpose. Such an appointment must be made when the plaintiff is authorized to proceed in forma pauperis pursuant to 28 U.S.C. § 1915 or is authorized to proceed as a seaman under 28 U.S.C. § 1916.

### (d) Waiver of Service; Duty to Save Costs of Service; Request to Waive.

(1) A defendant who waives service of a summons does not thereby waive any objection to the venue or to the jurisdiction of the court over the person of the defendant.

(2) An individual, corporation, or association that is subject to service under subdivision (e), (f), or (h) and that receives notice of an action in the manner provided in this paragraph has a duty to avoid unnecessary costs of serving the summons. To avoid costs, the plaintiff may notify such a defendant of the commencement of the action and request that the defendant waive service of a summons. The notice and request

(A) shall be in writing and shall be addressed directly to the defendant, if an individual, or else to an officer or managing or general agent (or other agent authorized by appointment or law to receive service of process) of a defendant subject to service under subdivision (h);

(B) shall be dispatched through first-class mail or other reliable means;

(C) shall be accompanied by a copy of the complaint and shall identify the court in which it has been filed;

(D) shall inform the defendant, by means of a text prescribed in an official form promulgated pursuant to Rule 84, of the consequences of compliance and of a failure to comply with the request;

(E) shall set forth the date on which request is sent;

(F) shall allow the defendant a reasonable time to return the waiver, which shall be at least 30 days from the date on which the request is sent, or 60 days from that date if the defendant is addressed outside any judicial district of the United States; and

(G) shall provide the defendant with an extra copy of the notice and request, as well as a prepaid means of compliance in writing.

If a defendant located within the United States fails to comply with a request for waiver made by a plaintiff located within the United States, the court shall impose the costs subsequently incurred in effecting service on the defendant unless good cause for the failure be shown.

(3) A defendant that, before being served with process, timely returns a waiver so requested is not required to serve an answer to the complaint until 60 days after the date on which the request for waiver of service was sent, or 90 days after that date if the defendant was addressed outside any judicial district of the United States.

(4) When the plaintiff files a waiver of service with the court, the action shall proceed, except as provided in paragraph (3), as if a summons and complaint had been served at the time of filing the waiver, and no proof of service shall be required.

(5) The costs to be imposed on a defendant under paragraph (2) for failure to comply with a request to waive service of a summons shall include the costs subsequently incurred in effecting service under subdivision (e), (f), or (h), together with the costs, including a reasonable attorney's fee, of any motion required to collect the costs of service.

## (e) Service Upon Individuals Within a Judicial District of the United States.

Unless otherwise provided by federal law, service upon an individual from whom a waiver has not been obtained and filed, other than an infant or an incompetent person, may be effected in any judicial district of the United States:

(1) pursuant to the law of the state in which the district court is located, or in which service is effected, for the service of a summons upon the defendant in an action brought in the courts of general jurisdiction of the State; or

(2) by delivering a copy of the summons and of the complaint to the individual personally or by leaving copies thereof at the individual's dwelling house or usual place of abode with some person of suitable age and discretion then residing therein or by delivering a copy of the summons and of the complaint to an agent authorized by appointment or by law to receive service of process.

## (f) Service Upon Individuals in a Foreign Country.

Unless otherwise provided by federal law, service upon an individual from whom a waiver has not been obtained and filed, other than an infant or an incompetent person, may be effected in a place not within any judicial district of the United States:

(1) by any internationally agreed means reasonably calculated to give notice, such as those means authorized by the Hague Convention on the Service Abroad of Judicial and Extrajudicial Documents; or

(2) if there is no internationally agreed means of service or the applicable international agreement allows other means of service, provided that service is reasonably calculated to give notice:

(A) in the manner prescribed by the law of the foreign country for service in that country in an action in any of its courts of general jurisdiction; or

(B) as directed by the foreign authority in response to a letter rogatory or letter of request; or

(C) unless prohibited by the law of the foreign country, by

(i) delivery to the individual personally of a copy of the summons and the complaint; or

(ii) any form of mail requiring a signed receipt, to be addressed and dispatched by the clerk of the court to the party to be served; or

(3) by other means not prohibited by international agreement as may be directed by the court.

**(g) Service Upon Infants and Incompetent Person.**

Service upon an infant or an incompetent person in a judicial district of the United States shall be effected in the manner prescribed by the law of the state in which the service is made for the service of summons or like process upon any such defendant in an action brought in the courts of general jurisdiction of that state. Service upon an infant or an incompetent person in a place not within any judicial district of the United States shall be effected in the manner prescribed by paragraph (2)(A) or (2)(B) of subdivision (f) or by such means as the court may direct.

**(h) Service Upon Corporations and Associations.**

Unless otherwise provided by federal law, service upon a domestic or foreign corporation or upon a partnership or other unincorporated association that is subject to suit under a common name, and from which a waiver of service has not been obtained and filed, shall be effected:

(1) in a judicial district of the United States in the manner prescribed for individuals by subdivision (e)(1), or by delivering a copy of the summons and of the complaint to an officer, a managing or general agent, or to any other agent authorized by appointment or by law to receive service of process and, if the agent is one authorized by statute to receive service and the statute so requires, by also mailing a copy to the defendant, or

(2) in a place not within any judicial district of the United States in any manner prescribed for individuals by subdivision (f) except personal delivery as provided in paragraph (2)(C)(i) thereof.

**(i) Serving the United States, Its Agencies, Corporations, Officers, or Employees.**

(1) Service upon the United States shall be effected

(A) by delivering a copy of the summons and of the complaint to the United States attorney for the district in which the action is brought or to an assistant United States attorney or clerical employee designated by the United States attorney in a writing filed with the clerk of the court or by sending a copy of the summons and of the complaint by registered or certified mail addressed to the civil process clerk at the office of the United States attorney and

(B) by also sending a copy of the summons and of the complaint by registered or certified mail to the Attorney General of the United States at Washington, District of Columbia, and

(C) in any action attacking the validity of an order of an officer or agency of the United States not made a party, by also sending a copy of the summons and of the complaint by registered or certified mail to the officer or agency.

(A) Service on an agency or corporation of the United States, or an officer or employee of the United States sued only in an official capacity, is effected by serving the United States in the manner prescribed by Rule 4(i)(1) and by also sending a copy of the summons and complaint by registered or certified mail to the officer, employee, agency, or corporation.

(B)Service on an officer or employee of the United States sued in an individual capacity for acts or omissions occurring in connection with the performance of duties on behalf of the United States - whether or not the officer or employee is sued also in an official capacity - is effected by serving the United States in the manner prescribed by Rule 4(i)(1) and by serving the officer or employee in the manner prescribed by Rule 4 (e), (f), or (g).

(3) The court shall allow a reasonable time to serve process under Rule 4(i) for the purpose of curing the failure to serve:

(A) all persons required to be served in an action governed by Rule 4(i)(2)(A), if the plaintiff has served either the United States attorney or the Attorney General of the United States, or

(B) the United States in an action governed by Rule 4(i)(2)(B), if the plaintiff has served an officer or employee of the United States sued in an individual capacity.

**(j) Service Upon Foreign, State, or Local Governments.**

(1) Service upon a foreign state or a political subdivision, agency, or instrumentality thereof shall be effected pursuant to 28 U.S.C. § 1608.

(2) Service upon a state, municipal corporation, or other governmental organization subject to suit, shall be effected by delivering a copy of the summons and of the complaint to its chief executive officer or by serving the summons and complaint in the manner prescribed by the law of that state for the service of summons or other like process upon any such defendant.

**(k) Territorial Limits of Effective Service.**

(1) Service of a summons or filing a waiver of service is effective to establish jurisdiction over the person of a defendant

(A) who could be subjected to the jurisdiction of a court of general jurisdiction in the state in which the district court is located, or

(B) who is a party joined under Rule 14 or Rule 19 and is served at a place within a judicial district of the United States and not more than 100 miles from the place from which the summons issues, or

(C) who is subject to the federal interpleader jurisdiction under 28 U.S.C. § 1335, or

(D) when authorized by a statute of the United States.

(2) If the exercise of jurisdiction is consistent with the Constitution and laws of the United States, serving a summons or filing a waiver of service is also effective, with respect to claims arising under federal law, to establish personal jurisdiction over the person of any defendant who is not subject to the jurisdiction of the courts of general jurisdiction of any state.

**(l) Proof of Service.**

If service is not waived, the person effecting service shall make proof thereof to the court. If service is made by a person other than a United States marshal or deputy United States marshal, the person shall make affidavit thereof. Proof of service in a place not within any judicial district of the United States shall, if effected under paragraph (1) of subdivision (f), be made pursuant to the applicable treaty or convention, and shall, if effected under paragraph (2) or (3) thereof, include a receipt signed by the addressee or other evidence of delivery to the addressee satisfactory to the court. Failure to make proof of service does not affect the validity of the service. The court may allow proof of service to be amended.

### (m) Time Limit for Service.

If service of the summons and complaint is not made upon a defendant within 120 days after the filing of the complaint, the court, upon motion or on its own initiative after notice to the plaintiff, shall dismiss the action without prejudice as to that defendant or direct that service be effected within a specified time; provided that if the plaintiff shows good cause for the failure, the court shall extend the time for service for an appropriate period. This subdivision does not apply to service in a foreign country pursuant to subdivision (f) or (j)(1).

### (n) Seizure of Property; Service of Summons not Feasible.

(1) If a statute of the United States so provides, the court may assert jurisdiction over property. Notice to claimants of the property shall than be sent in the manner provided by the statute or by service of a summons under this rule.

(2) Upon a showing that personal jurisdiction over a defendant cannot, in the district where the action is brought, be obtained with reasonable efforts by service of summons in any manner authorized by this rule, the court may assert jurisdiction over any of the defendant's assets found within the district by seizing the assets under the circumstances and in the manner provided by the law of the state in which the district court is located.

**FRCP 69**

VIII. PROVISIONAL AND FINAL REMEDIES > **Rule 69.**

## Rule 69. Execution

### (a) In General.

Process to enforce a judgment for the payment of money shall be a writ of execution, unless the court directs otherwise. The procedure on execution, in proceedings supplementary to and in aid of a judgment, and in proceedings on and in aid of execution shall be in accordance with the practice and procedure of the state in which the district court is held, existing at the time the remedy is sought, except that any statute of the United States governs to the extent that it is applicable. In aid of the judgment or execution, the judgment creditor or a successor in interest when that interest appears of record, may obtain discovery from any person, including the judgment debtor, in the manner provided in these rules or in the manner provided by the practice of the state in which the district court is held.

### (b) Against Certain Public Officers.

When a judgment has been entered against a collector or other officer of revenue under the circumstances stated in Title 28, U.S.C., § 2006, or against an officer of Congress in an action mentioned in the Act of March 3, 1875, ch. 130, § 8 (18 Stat. 401), U.S.C., Title 2, § 118, and when the court has given the certificate of probable cause for the officer's act as provided in those statutes, execution shall not issue against the officer or the officer's property but the final judgment shall be satisfied as provided in such statutes.

# CODE OF CIVIL PROCEDURE SECTION 1713-1713.8

1713. This chapter may be cited as the Uniform Foreign Money-Judgments Recognition Act.

1713.1. As used in this chapter:
(1) "Foreign state" means any governmental unit other than the United States, or any state, district, commonwealth, territory, insular possession thereof, or the Panama Canal Zone, or the Trust Territory of the Pacific Islands;
(2) "Foreign judgment" means any judgment of a foreign state granting or denying recovery of a sum of money, other than a judgment for taxes, a fine or other penalty, or a judgment for support in matrimonial or family matters.

1713.2. This chapter applies to any foreign judgment that is final and conclusive and enforceable where rendered even though an appeal therefrom is pending or it is subject to appeal.

1713.3. Except as provided in Section 1713.4, a foreign judgment meeting the requirements of Section 1713.2 is conclusive between the parties to the extent that it grants or denies recovery of a sum of money. The foreign judgment is enforceable in the same manner as the judgment of a sister state which is entitled to full faith and credit, except that it may not be enforced pursuant to the provisions of Chapter 1 (commencing with Section 1710.10) of this title.

1713.4. (a) A foreign judgment is not conclusive if
(1) The judgment was rendered under a system which does not provide impartial tribunals or procedures compatible with the requirements of due process of law;
(2) The foreign court did not have personal jurisdiction over the defendant; or
(3) The foreign court did not have jurisdiction over the subject matter.
(b) A foreign judgment need not be recognized if
(1) The defendant in the proceedings in the foreign court did not receive notice of the proceedings in sufficient time to enable him to defend;
(2) The judgment was obtained by extrinsic fraud;
(3) The cause of action or defense on which the judgment is based is repugnant to the public policy of this state;
(4) The judgment conflicts with another final and conclusive judgment;
(5) The proceeding in the foreign court was contrary to an agreement between the parties under which the dispute in question was

to be settled otherwise than by proceedings in that court; or
(6) In the case of jurisdiction based only on personal service, the foreign court was a seriously inconvenient forum for the trial of the action.

1713.5. (a) The foreign judgment shall not be refused recognition for lack of personal jurisdiction if
(1) The defendant was served personally in the foreign state;
(2) The defendant voluntarily appeared in the proceedings, other than for the purpose of protecting property seized or threatened with seizure in the proceedings or of contesting the jurisdiction of the court over him;
(3) The defendant prior to the commencement of the proceedings had agreed to submit to the jurisdiction of the foreign court with respect to the subject matter involved;
(4) The defendant was domiciled in the foreign state when the proceedings were instituted, or, being a body corporate had its principal place of business, was incorporated, or had otherwise acquired corporate status, in the foreign state;
(5) The defendant had a business office in the foreign state and the proceedings in the foreign court involved a cause of action arising out of business done by the defendant through that office in the foreign state; or
(6) The defendant operated a motor vehicle or airplane in the foreign state and the proceedings involved a cause of action arising out of such operation.
(b) The courts of this state may recognize other bases of jurisdiction.

1713.6. If the defendant satisfies the court either that an appeal is pending or that he is entitled and intends to appeal from the foreign judgment, the court may stay the proceedings until the appeal has been determined or until the expiration of a period of time sufficient to enable the defendant to prosecute the appeal.

1713.7. This chapter does not prevent the recognition or nonrecognition of a foreign judgment in situations not covered by this chapter.

1713.8. This chapter shall be so construed as to effectuate its general purpose to make uniform the law of those states which enact it.

# CODE OF CIVIL PROCEDURE SECTION 676-676.16

676. This title shall be known and may be cited as the Uniform Foreign-Money Claims Act.

676.1. As used in this title:

(1) "Action" means a judicial proceeding or arbitration in which a payment in money may be awarded or enforced with respect to a foreign-money claim.

(2) "Bank-offered spot rate" means the spot rate of exchange at which a bank will sell foreign money at a spot rate.

(3) "Conversion date" means the banking day next preceding the date on which money, in accordance with this title, is (i) paid to a claimant in an action or distribution proceeding, (ii) paid to the official designated by law to enforce a judgment or award on behalf of a claimant, or (iii) used to recoup, setoff, or counterclaim in different moneys in an action or distribution proceeding.

(4) "Distribution proceeding" means a judicial or nonjudicial proceeding for the distribution of a fund in which one or more foreign-money claims is asserted and includes an accounting, an assignment for the benefit of creditors, a foreclosure, the liquidation or rehabilitation of a corporation or other entity, and the distribution of an estate, trust, or other fund.

(5) "Foreign money" means money other than money of the United States of America.

(6) "Foreign-money claim" means a claim upon an obligation to pay, or a claim for recovery of a loss, expressed in or measured by a foreign money.

(7) "Money" means a medium of exchange for the payment of obligations or a store of value authorized or adopted by a government or by intergovernmental agreement.

(8) "Money of the claim" means the money determined as proper pursuant to Section 676.4.

(9) "Person" means an individual, a corporation, government or governmental subdivision or agency, business trust, estate, trust, joint venture, partnership, association, two or more persons having a joint or common interest, or any other legal or commercial entity.

(10) "Rate of exchange" means the rate at which money of one country may be converted into money of another country in a free financial market convenient to or reasonably usable by a person obligated to pay or to state a rate of conversion. If separate rates of exchange apply to different kinds of transactions, the term means the rate applicable to the particular transaction giving rise to the foreign-money claim.

(11) "Spot rate" means the rate of exchange at which foreign money is sold by a bank or other dealer in foreign exchange for immediate or next day availability or for settlement by immediate payment in cash or equivalent, by charge to an account, or by an agreed delayed settlement not exceeding two days.

(12) "State" means a State of the United States, the District of Columbia, the Commonwealth of Puerto Rico, or a territory or insular possession subject to the jurisdiction of the United States.

676.2. (a) This title applies only to a foreign-money claim in an action or distribution proceeding.
(b) This title applies to foreign-money issues even if other law under the conflict-of-laws rules of this state applies to other issues in the action or distribution proceeding.

676.3. (a) The effect of this title may be varied by agreement of the parties made before or after commencement of an action or distribution proceeding or the entry of judgment.
(b) Parties to a transaction may agree upon the money to be used in a transaction giving rise to a foreign-money claim and may agree to use different moneys for different aspects of the transaction. Stating the price in a foreign money for one aspect of a transaction does not alone require the use of that money for other aspects of the transaction.

676.4. (a) The money in which the parties to a transaction have agreed that payment is to be made is the proper money of the claim for payment.
(b) If the parties to a transaction have not otherwise agreed, the proper money of the claim, as in each case may be appropriate, is one of the following:
(1) The money regularly used between the parties as a matter of usage or course of dealing.
(2) The money used at the time of a transaction in international trade, by trade usage or common practice, for valuing or settling transactions in the particular commodity or service involved.
(3) The money in which the loss was ultimately felt or will be incurred by the party claimant.

676.5. (a) If an amount contracted to be paid in a foreign money is measured by a specified amount of a different money, the amount to be paid is determined on the conversion date.
(b) If an amount contracted to be paid in a foreign money is to be measured by a different money at the rate of exchange prevailing on a date before default, that rate of exchange applies only to payments made within a reasonable time after default, not exceeding 30 days. Thereafter, conversion is made at the bank-offered spot rate on the conversion date.
(c) A monetary claim is neither usurious nor unconscionable because the agreement on which it is based provides that the amount of the debtor's obligation to be paid in the debtor's money, when received by the creditor, shall equal a specified amount of the foreign money of the country of the creditor. If, because of unexcused delay in payment of a judgment or award, the amount received by the creditor does not equal the amount of the foreign money specified in the agreement, the court or arbitrator shall amend the judgment or award accordingly.

676.6. (a) A person may assert a claim in a specified foreign money. If a foreign-money claim is not asserted, the claimant makes the claim in United States dollars.

(b) An opposing party may allege and prove that a claim, in whole or in part, is in a different money than that asserted by the claimant.

(c) A person may assert a defense, setoff, recoupment, or counterclaim in any money without regard to the money of other claims.

(d) The determination of the proper money of the claim is a question of law.

676.7. (a) Except as provided in subdivision (c), a judgment or award on a foreign-money claim shall be stated in an amount of the money of the claim.

(b) A judgment or award on a foreign-money claim is payable in that foreign money or, at the option of the debtor, in the amount of United States dollars which will purchase that foreign money on the conversion date at a bank-offered spot rate.

(c) Assessed costs shall be entered in United States dollars.

(d) Each payment in United States dollars shall be accepted and credited on a judgment or award on a foreign-money claim in the amount of the foreign money that could be purchased by the dollars at a bank-offered spot rate of exchange at or near the close of business on the conversion date for that payment.

(e) A judgment or award made in an action or distribution proceeding on both (1) a defense, setoff, recoupment, or counterclaim and (2) the adverse party's claim, shall be netted by converting the money of the smaller into the money of the larger, and by subtracting the smaller from the larger, and specify the rates of exchange used.

(f) A judgment substantially in the following form complies with subdivision (a):

"IT IS ADJUDGED AND ORDERED, that Defendant ________(insert name) pay to Plaintiff _______(insert name) the sum of ____________________ (insert amount in the foreign money) plus interest on that sum at the rate of ____________________(insert rate--see Section 676.9) percent a year or, at the option of the judgment debtor, the number of United States dollars which will purchase the ____________________ (insert name of foreign money) with interest due, at a bank-offered spot rate at or near the close of business on the banking day next before the day of payment, together with assessed costs of ___________(insert amount) United States dollars."

(g) If a contract claim is of the type covered by subdivision (a) or (b) of Section 676.5, the judgment or award shall be entered for the amount of money stated to measure the obligation to be paid in the money specified for payment or, at the option of the debtor, the number of United States dollars which will purchase the computed amount of the money of payment on the conversion date at a bank-offered spot rate.

(h) A judgment shall be entered in foreign money in the same manner, and has the same effect as a lien, as other judgments. It may be discharged by payment.

676.8. The rate of exchange prevailing at or near the close of business on the day the distribution proceeding is initiated governs all exchanges of foreign money in a distribution proceeding. A foreign-money claimant in a distribution proceeding shall assert its claim in the named foreign money and show the amount of United States dollars resulting from a conversion as of the date the proceeding was initiated.

676.9. (a) With respect to a foreign-money claim, recovery of prejudgment or pre-award interest and the rate of interest to be applied in the action or distribution proceeding, except as provided in subdivision (b), are matters of the substantive law governing the right to recovery under the conflict-of-laws rules of this state.

(b) The court or arbitrator shall increase or decrease the amount of prejudgment or pre-award interest otherwise payable in a judgment or award in foreign money to the extent required by the law of this state governing a failure to make or accept an offer of settlement or offer of judgment, or conduct by a party or its attorney causing undue delay or expense.

(c) A judgment or award on a foreign-money claim bears interest at the rate applicable to judgments of this state.

676.10. (a) If an action is brought to enforce a judgment of another jurisdiction expressed in a foreign money and the judgment is recognized in this state as enforceable, the enforcing judgment shall be entered as provided in Section 676.7, whether or not the foreign judgment confers an option to pay in an equivalent amount of United States dollars.

(b) A foreign judgment may be enforced in accordance with Title 11 (commencing with Section 1710.10) of Part 3.

(c) A satisfaction or partial payment made upon the foreign judgment, on proof thereof, shall be credited against the amount of foreign money specified in the judgment, notwithstanding the entry of judgment in this state.

(d) A judgment entered on a foreign-money claim only in United States dollars in another state shall be enforced in this state in United States dollars only.

676.11. (a) Computations under this section are for the limited purposes of the section and do not affect computation of the United States dollar equivalent of the money of the judgment for the purpose of payment.

(b) For the limited purpose of facilitating the enforcement of provisional remedies in an action, the value in United States dollars of assets to be seized or restrained pursuant to a writ of attachment, garnishment, execution, or other legal process, the amount of United States dollars at issue for assessing costs, or the amount of United States dollars involved for a surety bond or other court-required undertaking, shall be ascertained as provided in subdivisions (c) and (d).

(c) A party seeking process, costs, bond, or other undertaking under subdivision (b) shall compute in United States dollars the amount of the foreign money claimed from a bank-offered spot rate prevailing at or near the close of business on the banking day next preceding the filing of a request or application for the issuance of process or for the determination of costs, or an application for a bond or other court-required undertaking.

(d) A party seeking the process, costs, bond, or other undertaking under subdivision (b) shall file with each request or application an affidavit or certificate executed in good faith by its counsel or a bank officer, stating the market quotation used and how it was obtained, and setting forth the calculation. Affected court officials incur no liability, after a filing of the affidavit or certificate, for acting as if the judgment were in the amount of United States dollars stated in the affidavit or certificate.

676.12. (a) If, after an obligation is expressed or a loss is incurred in a foreign money, the country issuing or adopting that money substitutes a new money in place of that money, the obligation or the loss is treated as if expressed or incurred in the new money at the rate of conversion the issuing country establishes for the payment of like obligations or losses denominated in the former money.

(b) If substitution under subdivision (a) occurs after a judgment or award is entered on a foreign-money claim, the court or arbitrator shall amend the judgment or award by a like conversion of the former money.

676.13. Unless displaced by particular provisions of this title, the principles of law and equity, including the law merchant, and the law relative to capacity to contract, principal and agent, estoppel, fraud, misrepresentation, duress, coercion, mistake, bankruptcy, or other validating or invalidating causes supplement its provisions.

676.14. This title shall be applied and construed to effectuate its general purpose to make uniform the law with respect to the subject of this title among states enacting it.

676.15. If any provision of this title or its application to any person or circumstance is held invalid, that invalidity does not affect other provisions or applications of this title which can be given effect without the invalid provision or application, and to this end the provisions of this title are severable.

676.16. This title applies to actions and distribution proceedings commenced on or after January 1, 1992.

# EVIDENCE CODE SECTION 1450-1454

1450. The presumptions established by this article are presumptions affecting the burden of producing evidence.

1451. A certificate of the acknowledgment of a writing other than a will, or a certificate of the proof of such a writing, is prima facie evidence of the facts recited in the certificate and the genuineness of the signature of each person by whom the writing purports to have been signed if the certificate meets the requirements of Article 3 (commencing with Section 1180) of Chapter 4, Title 4, Part 4, Division 2 of the Civil Code.

1452. A seal is presumed to be genuine and its use authorized if it purports to be the seal of:
(a) The United States or a department, agency, or public employee of the United States.
(b) A public entity in the United States or a department, agency, or public employee of such public entity.
(c) A nation recognized by the executive power of the United States or a department, agency, or officer of such nation.
(d) A public entity in a nation recognized by the executive power of the United States or a department, agency, or officer of such public entity.
(e) A court of admiralty or maritime jurisdiction.
(f) A notary public within any state of the United States.

1453. A signature is presumed to be genuine and authorized if it purports to be the signature, affixed in his official capacity, of:
(a) A public employee of the United States.
(b) A public employee of any public entity in the United States.
(c) A notary public within any state of the United States.

1454. A signature is presumed to be genuine and authorized if it purports to be the signature, affixed in his official capacity, of an officer, or deputy of an officer, of a nation or public entity in a nation recognized by the executive power of the United States and the writing to which the signature is affixed is accompanied by a final statement certifying the genuineness of the signature and the official position of (a) the person who executed the writing or (b) any foreign official who has certified either the genuineness of the signature and official position of the person executing the writing or the genuineness of the signature and official position of another foreign official who has executed a similar cetificate in a chain of such certificates beginning with a certificate of the genuineness of the signature and official position of the person executing the writing. The final statement may be made only by a secretary of an embassy or legation, consul general, consul, vice consul, consular agent, or other officer in the foreign service of the United States stationed in the nation, authenticated by the seal of his office.

1530. (a) A purported copy of a writing in the custody of a public entity, or of an entry in such a writing, is prima facie evidence of the existence and content of such writing or entry if:

(1) The copy purports to be published by the authority of the nation or state, or public entity therein in which the writing is kept;

(2) The office in which the writing is kept is within the United States or within the Panama Canal Zone, the Trust Territory of the Pacific Islands, or the Ryukyu Islands, and the copy is attested or certified as a correct copy of the writing or entry by a public employee, or a deputy of a public employee, having the legal custody of the writing; or

(3) The office in which the writing is kept is not within the United States or any other place described in paragraph (2) and the copy is attested as a correct copy of the writing or entry by a person having authority to make attestation. The attestation must be accompanied by a final statement certifying the genuineness of the signature and the official position of (i) the person who attested the copy as a correct copy or (ii) any foreign official who has certified either the genuineness of the signature and official position of the person attesting the copy or the genuineness of the signature and official position of another foreign official who has executed a similar certificate in a chain of such certificates beginning with a certificate of the genuineness of the signature and official position of the person attesting the copy. Except as provided in the next sentence, the final statement may be made only by a secretary of an embassy or legation, consul general, consul, vice consul, or consular agent of the United States, or a diplomatic or consular official of the foreign country assigned or accredited to the United States. Prior to January 1, 1971, the final statement may also be made by a secretary of an embassy or legation, consul general, consul, vice consul, consular agent, or other officer in the foreign service of the United States stationed in the nation in which the writing is kept, authenticated by the seal of his office. If reasonable opportunity has been given to all parties to investigate the authenticity and accuracy of the documents, the court may, for good cause shown, (i) admit an attested copy without the final statement or (ii) permit the writing or entry in foreign custody to be evidenced by an attested summary with or without a final statement.

(b) The presumptions established by this section are presumptions affecting the burden of producing evidence.

NY CLS CPLR § 3213 (2004)

§ 3213. Motion for summary judgment in lieu of complaint

When an action is based upon an instrument for the payment of money only or upon any judgment, the plaintiff may serve with the summons a notice of motion for summary judgment and the supporting papers in lieu of a complaint. The summons served with such motion papers shall require the defendant to submit answering papers on the motion within the time provided in the notice of motion. The minimum time such motion shall be noticed to be heard shall be as provided by subdivision (a) of rule 320 for making an appearance, depending upon the method of service. If the plaintiff sets the hearing date of the motion later than the minimum time therefor, he may require the defendant to serve a copy of his answering papers upon him within such extended period of time, not exceeding ten days, prior to such hearing date. No default judgment may be entered pursuant to subdivision (a) of section 3215 prior to the hearing date of the motion. If the motion is denied, the moving and answering papers shall be deemed the complaint and answer, respectively, unless the court orders otherwise.

NY CLS CPLR § 5222 (2004)

§ 5222. Restraining notice

(a) Issuance; on whom served; form; service. A restraining notice may be issued by the clerk of the court or the attorney for the judgment creditor as officer of the court, or by the support collection unit designated by the appropriate social services district. It may be served upon any person, except the employer of a judgment debtor or obligor where the property sought to be restrained consists of wages or salary due or to become due to the judgment debtor or obligor. It shall be served personally in the same manner as a summons or by registered or certified mail, return receipt requested or if issued by the support collection unit, by regular mail, or by electronic means as set forth in subdivision (g) of this section. It shall specify all of the parties to the action, the date that the judgment or order was entered, the court in which it was entered, the amount of the judgment or order and the amount then due thereon, the names of all parties in whose favor and against whom the judgment or order was entered, it shall set forth subdivision (b) and shall state that disobedience is punishable as a contempt of court, and it shall contain an original signature or copy of the original signature of the clerk of the court or attorney or the name of the support collection unit which issued it. Service of a restraining notice upon a department or agency of the state or upon an institution under its direction shall be made by serving a copy upon the head of the department, or the person designated by him or her and upon the state department of audit and control at its office in Albany; a restraining notice served upon a state board, commission, body or agency which is not within any department of the state shall be made by serving the restraining notice upon the state department of audit and control at its office in Albany. Service at the office of a department of the state in Albany may be made by the sheriff of any county by registered or certified mail, return receipt requested, or if issued by the support collection unit, by regular mail.

(b) Effect of restraint; prohibition of transfer; duration. A judgment debtor or obligor served with a restraining notice is forbidden to make or suffer any sale, assignment, transfer or interference with any property in which he or she has an interest, except upon direction of the sheriff or pursuant to an order of the court, until the judgment or order is satisfied or vacated. A restraining notice served upon a person other than the judgment debtor or obligor is effective only if, at the time of service, he or she owes a debt to the judgment debtor or obligor or he or she is in the possession or custody of property in which he or she knows or has reason to believe the judgment debtor or obligor has an interest, or if the judgment creditor or support collection unit has stated in the notice that a specified debt is owed by the person served to the judgment debtor or obligor or that the judgment debtor or obligor has an interest in specified property in the possession or custody of the person served. All property in which the judgment debtor or obligor is known or believed to have an interest then in and thereafter coming into the possession or custody of such a person, including any specified in the notice, and all debts of such a person, including any specified in the notice, then due and thereafter coming due to the judgment debtor or obligor, shall be subject to the notice. Such a person is forbidden to make or suffer any sale, assignment or transfer of, or any interference with, any such property, or pay over or otherwise dispose of any such debt, to any person other than the sheriff or the support collection unit, except upon direction of the sheriff or pursuant to an order of the court, until the expiration of one year after the notice is served upon him or her, or until the judgment or order is satisfied or vacated, whichever event first occurs. A judgment creditor [fig 1] or support collection unit which has specified personal property or debt in a restraining notice shall be liable to the owner of the property or the person to whom the debt is owed, if other than the judgment debtor or obligor, for any damages sustained by reason of the restraint. If a garnishee served with a restraining notice withholds the payment of money belonging or owed to the judgment debtor or obligor in an amount equal to twice the amount due on the judgment or order, the restraining notice is not effective as to other property or money.

(c) Subsequent notice. Leave of court is required to serve more than one restraining notice upon the same person with respect to the same judgment or order.

(d) Notice to judgment debtor or obligor. If a notice in the form prescribed in subdivision (e) has not been given to the judgment debtor or obligor within a year before service of a restraining notice, a copy of the restraining notice together with the notice to judgment debtor or obligor shall be mailed by first class mail or personally delivered to each judgment debtor or obligor who is a natural person within four days of the service of the restraining notice. Such notice shall be mailed to the defendant at his or her residence address; or in the event such mailing is returned as undeliverable by the post office, or if the residence address of the defendant is unknown, then to the defendant in care of the place of employment of the defendant if known, in an envelope bearing the legend "personal and confidential" and not indicating on the outside thereof, by the return address or otherwise, that the communication is from an attorney or concerns a judgment or order; or if neither the residence address nor the place of employment of the defendant is known then to the defendant at any other known address.

(e) Content of notice. The notice required by subdivision (d) shall be in substantially the following form and may be included in the restraining notice:

NOTICE TO JUDGMENT DEBTOR OR OBLIGOR

Money or property belonging to you may have been taken or held in order to satisfy a judgment or order which has been entered against you. Read this carefully.

YOU MAY BE ABLE TO GET YOUR MONEY BACK

State and federal laws prevent certain money or property from being taken to satisfy judgments or orders. Such money or property is said to be "exempt". The following is a partial list of money which may be exempt:

1. Supplemental security income, (SSI);

2. Social security;

3. Public assistance (welfare);

4. Alimony or child support;

5. Unemployment benefits;

6. Disability benefits;

7. Workers' compensation benefits;

8. Public or private pensions; and

9. Veterans benefits.

If you think that any of your money that has been taken or held is exempt, you must act promptly because the money may be applied to the judgment or order. If you claim that any of your money that has been taken or held is exempt, you may contact the person sending this notice.

Also, YOU MAY CONSULT AN ATTORNEY, INCLUDING LEGAL AID IF YOU QUALIFY. The law (New York civil practice law and rules, article four and sections fifty-two hundred thirty-nine and fifty-two hundred forty) provides a procedure for determination of a claim to an exemption.

(f) For the purposes of this section "order" shall mean an order issued by a court of competent jurisdiction directing the payment of support, alimony or maintenance upon which a "default" as defined in paragraph seven of subdivision (a) of section fifty-two hundred forty-one of this article has been established subject to the procedures established for the determination of a "mistake of fact" for income executions pursuant to subdivision (e) of section fifty-two hundred forty-one of this article except that for the purposes of this section only a default shall not be founded upon retroactive child support obligations as defined in paragraph (a) of subdivision one of section four hundred forty of the family court act and subdivision one of section two hundred forty and paragraph b of subdivision nine of section two hundred thirty-six of the domestic relations law.

(g) Restraining notice in the form of magnetic tape or other electronic means. Where such person consents thereto in writing, a restraining notice in the form of magnetic tape or other electronic means, as defined in subdivision (f) of rule twenty-one hundred three of this chapter, may be served upon a person other than the judgment debtor or obligor. A restraining notice in such form shall contain all of the information required to be specified in a restraining notice under subdivision (a), except for the original signature or copy of the original signature of the clerk or attorney who issued the restraining notice. The provisions of this subdivision notwithstanding, the notice required by subdivisions (d) and (e) shall be given to the judgment debtor or obligor in the written form set forth therein.

NY CLS CPLR § 5223 (2004)

§ 5223. Disclosure

At any time before a judgment is satisfied or vacated, the judgment creditor may compel disclosure of all matter relevant to the satisfaction of the judgment, by serving upon any person a subpoena, which shall specify all of the parties to the action, the date of the judgment, the court in which it was entered, the amount of the judgment and the amount then due thereon, and shall state that false swearing or failure to comply with the subpoena is punishable as a contempt of court.

NY CLS CPLR R 5224 (2004)

R 5224. Subpoena; procedure

(a) Kinds and service of subpoena. Any or all of the following kinds of subpoenas may be served:

1. a subpoena requiring attendance for the taking of a deposition upon oral or written questions at a time and place named therein; or

2. a subpoena duces tecum requiring the production of books and papers for examination at a time and place named therein; or

3. an information subpoena, accompanied by a copy and original of written questions and a prepaid, addressed return envelope. Service of an information subpoena may be made by registered or certified mail, return receipt requested. Answers shall be made in writing under oath by the person upon whom served, if an individual, or by an officer, director, agent or employee having the information, if a corporation, partnership or sole proprietorship. Each question shall be answered separately and fully and each answer shall refer to the question to which it responds. Answers shall be returned together with the original of the questions within seven days after receipt.

4. an information subpoena in the form of magnetic tape or other electronic means. Where the person to be served consents thereto in writing, an information subpoena in the form of magnetic tape or electronic means, as defined in subdivision (f) of rule twenty-one hundred three of this chapter, may be served upon the individual, or if a corporation, partnership, limited liability company, or sole proprietorship, upon the officer, director, agent or employee having the information. Answers shall be provided within seven days.

(b) Fees. A judgment debtor served with a subpoena under this section and any other person served with an information subpoena shall not be entitled to any fee. Any other person served with a subpoena requiring attendance or the production of books and papers shall be paid or tendered in advance authorized traveling expenses and one day's witness fee.

(c) Time and place of examination. A deposition on oral or written questions or an examination of books and papers may proceed upon not less than ten days' notice to the person subpoenaed, unless the court orders shorter notice, before any person authorized by subdivision (a) of rule 3113. An examination shall be held during business hours and, if taken within the state, at a place specified in rule 3110. Upon consent of the witness, an examination may be held at any other place within the state and before any officer authorized to administer an oath.

(d) Conduct of examination. The officer before whom the deposition is to be taken shall put the witness on oath. If requested by the person conducting the examination, the officer shall personally, or by some one acting under his direction, record and transcribe the testimony and shall list all appearances by the parties and attorneys. Examination and cross-examination of the witness shall proceed as permitted in the trial of actions in open court. Cross-examination need not be limited to the subject matter of the examination in chief. All objections made at the time of the examination to the qualifications of the officer taking the deposition, or of a person recording it, or to the manner of taking it, or to the testimony presented, or to the conduct of any person, and any other objection to the proceedings, shall be noted by the officer upon the deposition and the deposition shall proceed subject to the right of a person to apply for a protective order. The deposition shall be taken continuously and without unreasonable adjournment, unless the court orders or the witness agrees otherwise. If the witness does not understand the English language, the judgment creditor shall, at his own expense, provide a translation of all questions and answers. Unless the court orders otherwise, a person other than the judgment debtor served with a subpoena duces tecum requiring the production of books of account may produce in place of the original books of account a sworn transcript of such accounts as are relevant.

(e) Signing deposition; physical preparation. At the request of the person conducting the examination, a deposition on written questions or a deposition on oral questions which has been transcribed shall be submitted to the witness and shall be read to or by him, and any changes in form or substance which the witness desires to make shall be entered upon the deposition with a statement of the reasons given by the witness for making them; and the deposition shall then be signed by the witness before any officer authorized to administer an oath. If the witness fails to sign the deposition, the officer before whom the deposition was taken shall sign it and state on the record the fact of the witness's failure or refusal to sign together with any reason given. The deposition may then be used as fully as though signed. Where testimony is transcribed, the officer before whom the deposition was taken shall certify on the deposition that the witness was duly sworn by him and that the deposition is a true record of the testimony given by the witness.

(f) Subsequent examination. Leave of court is required to compel a judgment debtor to appear for the taking of his deposition or to compel the production by him of books and papers within one year after the conclusion of a previous examination of him with respect to the same judgment.

NY CLS CPLR § 5225 (2004)

§ 5225. Payment or delivery of property of judgment debtor

(a) Property in the possession of judgment debtor. Upon motion of the judgment creditor, upon notice to the judgment debtor, where it is shown that the judgment debtor is in possession or custody of money or other personal property in which he has an interest, the court shall order that the judgment debtor pay the money, or so much of it as is sufficient to satisfy the judgment, to the judgment creditor and, if the amount to be so paid is insufficient to satisfy the judgment, to deliver any other personal property, or so much of it as is of sufficient value to satisfy the judgment, to a designated sheriff. Notice of the motion shall be served on the judgment debtor in the same manner as a summons or by registered or certified mail, return receipt requested.

(b) Property not in the possession of judgment debtor. Upon a special proceeding commenced by the judgment creditor, against a person in possession or custody of money or other personal property in which the judgment debtor has an interest, or against a person who is a transferee of money or other personal property from the judgment debtor, where it is shown that the judgment debtor is entitled to the possession of such property or that the judgment creditor's rights to the property are superior to those of the transferee, the court shall require such person to pay the money, or so much of it as is sufficient to satisfy the judgment, to the judgment creditor and, if the amount to be so paid is insufficient to satisfy the judgment, to deliver any other personal property, or so much of it as is of sufficient value to satisfy the judgment, to a designated sheriff. Costs of the proceeding shall not be awarded against a person who did not dispute the judgment debtor's interest or right to possession. Notice of the proceeding shall also be served upon the judgment debtor in the same manner as a summons or by registered or certified mail, return receipt requested. The court may permit the judgment debtor to intervene in the proceeding. The court may permit any adverse claimant to intervene in the proceeding and may determine his rights in accordance with section 5239.

(c) Documents to effect payment or delivery. The court may order any person to execute and deliver any document necessary to effect payment or delivery.

NY CLS CPLR § 5302 (2004)

§ 5302. Applicability

This article applies to any foreign country judgment which is final, conclusive and enforceable where rendered even though an appeal therefrom is pending or it is subject to appeal.

NY CLS CPLR § 5303 (2004)

§ 5303. Recognition and enforcement

Except as provided in section 5304, a foreign country judgment meeting the requirements of section 5302 is conclusive between the parties to the extent that it grants or denies recovery of a sum of money. Such a foreign judgment is enforceable by an action on the judgment, a motion for summary judgment in lieu of complaint, or in a pending action by counterclaim, cross-claim or affirmative defense.

NY CLS CPLR § 5304 (2004)

§ 5304. Grounds for non-recognition

(a) No recognition. A foreign country judgment is not conclusive if:

1. the judgment was rendered under a system which does not provide impartial tribunals or procedures compatible with the requirements of due process of law;

2. the foreign court did not have personal jurisdiction over the defendant.

(b) Other grounds for non-recognition. A foreign country judgment need not be recognized if:

1. the foreign court did not have jurisdiction over the subject matter;

2. the defendant in the proceedings in the foreign court did not receive notice of the proceedings in sufficient time to enable him to defend;

3. the judgment was obtained by fraud;

4. the cause of action on which the judgment is based is repugnant to the public policy of this state;

5. the judgment conflicts with another final and conclusive judgment;

6. the proceeding in the foreign court was contrary to an agreement between the parties under which the dispute in question was to be settled otherwise than by proceedings in that court; or

7. in the case of jurisdiction based only on personal service, the foreign court was a seriously inconvenient forum for the trial of the action.

NY CLS CPLR § 5401 (2004)

§ 5401. Definition

In this article "foreign judgment" means any judgment, decree, or order of a court of the United States or of any other court which is entitled to full faith and credit in this state, except one obtained by default in appearance, or by confession of judgment.

9 USC § 201

§ 201. Enforcement of Convention

The Convention on the Recognition and Enforcement of Foreign Arbitral Awards of June 10, 1958, shall be enforced in United States courts in accordance with this chapter [9 USCS §§ 201 et seq.].

9 USC § 202

§ 202. Agreement or award falling under the Convention

An arbitration agreement or arbitral award arising out of a legal relationship, whether contractual or not, which is considered as commercial, including a transaction, contract, or agreement described in section 2 of this title [9 USCS § 2], falls under the Convention. An agreement or award arising out of such a relationship which is entirely between citizens of the United States shall be deemed not to fall under the Convention unless that relationship involves property located abroad, envisages performance or enforcement abroad, or has some other reasonable relation with one or more foreign states. For the purpose of this section a corporation is a citizen of the United States if it is incorporated or has its principal place of business in the United States.

9 USC § 203

§ 203. Jurisdiction; amount in controversy

An action or proceeding falling under the Convention shall be deemed to arise under the laws and treaties of the United States. The district courts of the United States (including the courts enumerated in section 460 of title 28 [28 USCS § 460]) shall have original jurisdiction over such an action or proceeding, regardless of the amount in controversy.

9 USC § 204

§ 204. Venue

An action or proceeding over which the district courts have jurisdiction pursuant to section 203 of this title [9 USCS § 203] may be brought in any such court in which save for the arbitration agreement an action or proceeding with respect to the controversy between the parties could be brought, or in such court for the district and division which embraces the place designated in the agreement as the place of arbitration if such place is within the United States.

9 USC § 205

§ 205. Removal of cases from State courts

Where the subject matter of an action or proceeding pending in a State court relates to an arbitration agreement or award falling under the Convention, the defendant or the defendants may, at any time before the trial thereof, remove such action or proceeding to the district court of the United States for the district and division embracing the place where the action or proceeding is pending. The procedure for removal of causes otherwise provided by law shall apply, except that the ground for removal provided in this section need not appear on the face of the complaint but may be shown in the petition for removal. For the purposes of Chapter 1 of this title [9 USCS §§ 1 et seq.] any action or proceeding removed under this section shall be deemed to have been brought in the district court to which it is removed.

9 USC § 206

§ 206. Order to compel arbitration; appointment of arbitrators

A court having jurisdiction under this chapter [9 USCS §§ 201 et seq.] may direct that arbitration be held in accordance with the agreement at any place therein provided for, whether that place is within or without the United States. Such court may also appoint arbitrators in accordance with the provisions of the agreement.

9 USC § 207

§ 207. Award of arbitrators; confirmation; jurisdiction; proceeding

Within three years after an arbitral award falling under the Convention is made, any party to the arbitration may apply to any court having jurisdiction under this chapter [9 USCS §§ 201 et seq.] for an order confirming the award as against any other party to the arbitration. The court shall confirm the award unless it finds one of the grounds for refusal or deferral of recognition or enforcement of the award specified in the said Convention.

9 USC § 208

§ 208. Chapter 1 [9 USCS §§ 1 et seq.]; residual application

Chapter 1 [9 USCS §§ 1 et seq.] applies to actions and proceedings brought under this chapter [9 USCS §§ 201 et seq.] to the extent that chapter is not in conflict with this chapter [9 USCS §§ 201 et seq.] or the Convention as ratified by the United States.

## United Nations Convention on the Recognition and Enforcement of Foreign Arbitral Awards (New York, 10 June 1958)

### Article I

**1.** This Convention shall apply to the recognition and enforcement of arbitral awards made in the territory of a State other than the State where the recognition and enforcement of such awards are sought, and arising out of differences between persons, whether physical or legal. It shall also apply to arbitral awards not considered as domestic awards in the State where their recognition and enforcement are sought.

**2.** The term "arbitral awards" shall include not only awards made by arbitrators appointed for each case but also those made by permanent arbitral bodies to which the parties have submitted.

**3.** When signing, ratifying or acceding to this Convention, or notifying extension under article X hereof, any State may on the basis of reciprocity declare that it will apply the Convention to the recognition and enforcement of awards made only in the territory of another Contracting State. It may also declare that it will apply the Convention only to differences arising out of legal relationships, whether contractual or not, which are considered as commercial under the national law of the State making such declaration.

### Article II

**1.** Each Contracting State shall recognize an agreement in writing under which the parties undertake to submit to arbitration all or any differences which have arisen or which may arise between them in respect of a defined legal relationship, whether contractual or not, concerning a subject matter capable of settlement by arbitration.

**2.** The term "agreement in writing" shall include an arbitral clause in a contract or an arbitration agreement, signed by the parties or contained in an exchange of letters or telegrams.

**3.** The court of a Contracting State, when seized of an action in a matter in respect of which the parties have made an agreement within the meaning of this article, at the request of one of the parties, refer the parties to arbitration, unless it finds that the said agreement is null and void, inoperative or incapable of being performed.

**Article III**

Each Contracting State shall recognize arbitral awards as binding and enforce them in accordance with the rules of procedure of the territory where the award is relied upon, under the conditions laid down in the following articles. There shall not be imposed substantially more onerous conditions or higher fees or charges on the recognition or enforcement of arbitral awards to which this Convention applies than are imposed on the recognition or enforcement of domestic arbitral awards.

**Article IV**

**1.** To obtain the recognition and enforcement mentioned in the preceding article, the party applying for recognition and enforcement shall, at the time of the application, supply:

**(a)** The duly authenticated original award or a duly certified copy thereof;

**(b)** The original agreement referred to in article II or a duly certified copy thereof.

**2.** If the said award or agreement is not made in an official language of the country in which the award is relied upon, the party applying for recognition and enforcement of the award shall produce a translation of these documents into such language. The translation shall be certified by an official or sworn translator or by a diplomatic or consular agent.

**Article V**

**1.** Recognition and enforcement of the award may be refused, at the request of the party against whom it is invoked, only if that party furnishes to the competent authority where the recognition and enforcement is sought, proof that:

**(a)** The parties to the agreement referred to in article II were, under the law applicable to them, under some incapacity, or the said agreement is not valid under the law to which the parties have subjected it or, failing any indication thereon, under the law of the country where the award was made; or

**(b)** The party against whom the award is invoked was not given proper notice of the appointment of the arbitrator or of the arbitration proceedings or was otherwise unable to present his case; or

**(c)** The award deals with a difference not contemplated by or not falling within the terms of the submission to arbitration, or it contains decisions on matters beyond the scope of the submission to arbitration, provided that, if the decisions on matters submitted to arbitration can be separated from those not so submitted, that part of the award which contains decisions on matters submitted to arbitration may be recognized and enforced; or

**(d)** The composition of the arbitral authority or the arbitral procedure was not in accordance with the agreement of the parties, or, failing such agreement, was not in accordance with the law of the country where the arbitration took place; or

**(e)** The award has not yet become binding on the parties, or has been set aside or suspended by a competent authority of the country in which, or under the law of which, that award was made.

**2.** Recognition and enforcement of an arbitral award may also be refused if the competent authority in the country where recognition and enforcement is sought finds that:

**(a)** The subject matter of the difference is not capable of settlement by arbitration under the law of that country; or

**(b)** The recognition or enforcement of the award would be contrary to the public policy of that country.

**Article VI**

If an application for the setting aside or suspension of the award has been made to a competent authority referred to in article V (1) (e), the authority before which the award is sought to be relied upon may, if it considers it proper, adjourn the decision on the enforcement of the award and may also, on the application of the party claiming enforcement of the award, order the other party to give suitable security.

**Article VII**

**1.** The provisions of the present Convention shall not affect the validity of multilateral or bilateral agreements concerning the recognition and enforcement of arbitral awards entered into by the Contracting States nor deprive any interested party of any right he may have to avail himself of an arbitral award in the manner and to the extent allowed by the law or the treaties of the country where such award is sought to be relied upon.

**2.** The Geneva Protocol on Arbitration Clauses of 1923 and the Geneva Convention on the Execution of Foreign Arbitral Awards of 1927 shall cease to have effect between Contracting States on their becoming bound and to the extent that they become bound, by this Convention.

**Article VIII**

**1.** This Convention shall be open until 31 December 1958 for signature on behalf of any Member of the United Nations and also on behalf of any other State which is or hereafter becomes a member of any specialized agency of the United Nations, or which is or hereafter becomes a party to the Statute of the International Court of Justice, or any other State to which an invitation has been addressed by the General Assembly of the United Nations.

**2.** This Convention shall be ratified and the instrument of ratification shall be deposited with the Secretary-General of the United Nations.

**Article IX**

**1.** This Convention shall be open for accession to all States referred to in article VIII.

**2.** Accession shall be effected by the deposit of an instrument of accession with the Secretary-General of the United Nations.

**Article X**

**2.** At any time thereafter any such extension shall be made by notification addressed to the Secretary-General of the United Nations and shall take effect as from the ninetieth day after the day of receipt by the Secretary-General of the United Nations of this notification, or as from the date of entry into force of the Convention for the State concerned, whichever is the later.

**3.** With respect to those territories to which this Convention is not extended at the time of signature, ratification or accession, each State concerned shall consider the possibility of taking the necessary steps in order to extend the application of this Convention to such territories, subject, where necessary for constitutional reasons, to the consent of the Governments of such territories.

**Article XI**

In the case of a federal or non-unitary State, the following provisions shall apply:

**(a)** With respect to those articles of this Convention that come within the legislative jurisdiction of the federal authority, the obligations of the federal Government shall to this extent be the same as those of Contracting States which are not federal States;

**(b)** With respect to those articles of this Convention that come within the legislative jurisdiction of constituent states or provinces which are not, under the constitutional system of the federation, bound to take legislative action, the federal Government shall bring such articles with a favourable recommendation to the notice of the appropriate authorities of constituent states or provinces at the earliest possible moment;

**(c)** A federal State Party to this Convention shall, at the request of any other Contracting State transmitted through the Secretary-General of the United Nations, supply a statement of the law and practice of the federation and its constituent units in regard to any particular provision of this Convention, showing the extent to which effect has been given to that provision by legislative or other action.

**Article XII**

**1.** This Convention shall come into force on the ninetieth day following the date of deposit of the third instrument of ratification or accession.

**2.** For each State ratifying or acceding to this Convention after the deposit of the third instrument of ratification or accession, this Convention shall enter into force on the ninetieth day after deposit by such State of its instrument of ratification or accession.

**Article XIII**

**1.** Any Contracting State may denounce this Convention by a written notification to the Secretary-General of the United Nations. Denunciation shall take effect one year after the date of receipt of the notification by the Secretary-General.

**2.** Any State which has made a declaration or notification under article X may, at any time thereafter, by notification to the Secretary-General of the United Nations, declare that this Convention shall cease to extend to the territory concerned one year after the date of the receipt of the notification by the Secretary-General.

**3.** This Convention shall continue to be applicable to arbitral awards in respect of which recognition and enforcement proceedings have been instituted before the denunciation takes effect.

**Article XIV**

A Contracting State shall not be entitled to avail itself of the present Convention against other Contracting States except to the extent that it is itself bound to apply the Convention.

**Article XV**

The Secretary-General of the United Nations shall notify the States contemplated in article VIII of the following:

**(a)** Signatures and ratifications in accordance with article VIII;

**(b)** Accessions in accordance with article IX;

**(c)** Declarations and notifications under articles I, X and XI;

**(d)** The date upon which this Convention enters into force in accordance with article XII;

**(e)** Denunciations and notifications in accordance with article XIII.

**Article XVI**

**1.** This Convention, of which the Chinese, English, French, Russian and Spanish texts shall be equally authentic, shall be deposited in the archives of the United Nations.

**2.** The Secretary-General of the United Nations shall transmit a certified copy of this Convention to the States contemplated in article VIII.

**Ratification/Accession/Succession Convention on the Recognition and Enforcement of Foreign Arbitral Awards Done at New York on 10 June 1958**

ENTRY INTO FORCE: 7 June 1959, in accordance with article XII.
REGISTRATION: 7 June 1959, No. 4739.
TEXT: United Nations, Treaty Series, vol. 330, p. 3 .
STATUS: Signatories: 24. Parties: 121.

Note: The Convention was prepared and opened for signature on 10 June 1958 by the United Nations Conference on International Commercial Arbitration, convened in accordance with resolution 604 (XXI)1 of the Economic and Social Council of the United Nations adopted on 3 May 1956. The Conference met at the Headquarters of the United Nations in New York from 20 May to 10 June 1958. For the text of the Final Act of this Conference, see United Nations, Treaty Series, vol. 330, p. 3.

Participant/Signature [Ratification, accession (a), succession (d)]

Algeria 7 Feb 1989 a
Antigua and Barbuda 2 Feb 1989a
Argentina 26 Aug 1958 14 Mar 1989 Armenia 29 Dec 1997 a
Australia 26 Mar 1975 a
Austria 2 May 1961 a
Bahrain 6 Apr 1988 a
Bangladesh 6 May 1992 a
Barbados 16 Mar 1993 a
Belarus 29 Dec 1958 15 Nov 1960 Belgium 10 Jun 1958 18 Aug 1975 Benin 16 May 1974 a
Bolivia 28 Apr 1995 a
Bosnia and Herzegovina 1 Sep 1993 d Botswana 20 Dec 1971 a
Brunei Darussalam 25 Jul 1996 a
Bulgaria 17 Dec 1958 10 Oct 1961 Burkina Faso 23 Mar 1987 a
Cambodia 5 Jan 1960 a
Cameroon 19 Feb 1988 a
Canada 12 May 1986 a
Central African Republic 15 Oct 1962 a
Chile 4 Sep 1975 a
China2 22 Jan 1987 a
Colombia 25 Sep 1979 a
Costa Rica 10 Jun 1958 26 Oct 1987 Ctte d'Ivoire 1 Feb 1991 a
Croatia 26 Jul 1993 d Cuba 30 Dec 1974 a
Cyprus 29 Dec 1980 a
Czech Republic3 30 Sep 1993 d Denmark 22 Dec 1972 a
Djibouti 14 Jun 1983 d Dominica 28 Oct 1988 a
Ecuador 17 Dec 1958 3 Jan 1962 Egypt 9 Mar 1959 a
El Salvador 10 Jun 1958 26 Feb 1998 Estonia 30 Aug 1993 a
Finland 29 Dec 1958 19 Jan 1962 France 25 Nov 1958 26 Jun 1959 Georgia 2 Jun 1994 a
Germany4,5 10 Jun 1958 30 Jun 1961 Ghana 9 Apr 1968 a
Greece 16 Jul 1962 a
Guatemala 21 Mar 1984 a
Guinea 23 Jan 1991 a
Haiti 5 Dec 1983 a

Participant/Signature [Ratification, accession (a), succession (d)]

Holy See 14 May 1975 a
Hungary 5 Mar 1962 a
India 10 Jun 1958 13 Jul 1960 Indonesia 7 Oct 1981 a
Ireland 12 May 1981 a
Israel 10 Jun 1958 5 Jan 1959 Italy 31 Jan 1969 a
Japan 20 Jun 1961 a
Jordan 10 Jun 1958 15 Nov 1979 Kazakhstan 20 Nov 1995 a
Kenya 10 Feb 1989 a
Kuwait 28 Apr 1978 a
Kyrgyzstan 18 Dec 1996 a
Lao People's Democratic Republic 17 Jun 1998 a
Latvia 14 Apr 1992 a
Lebanon 11 Aug 1998 a
Lesotho 13 Jun 1989 a
Lithuania 14 Mar 1995 a
Luxembourg 11 Nov 1958 9 Sep 1983 Madagascar 16 Jul 1962 a

Malaysia 5 Nov 1985 a
Mali 8 Sep 1994 a
Mauritania 30 Jan 1997 a
Mauritius 19 Jun 1996 a
Mexico 14 Apr 1971 a
Monaco 31 Dec 1958 2 Jun 1982 Mongolia 24 Oct 1994 a
Morocco 12 Feb 1959 a
Mozambique 11 Jun 1998 a
Nepal 4 Mar 1998 a
Netherlands 10 Jun 1958 24 Apr 1964 New Zealand 6 Jan 1983 a
Niger 14 Oct 1964 a
Nigeria 17 Mar 1970 a
Norway 14 Mar 1961 a
Oman 25 Feb 1999 a
Pakistan 30 Dec 1958 Panama 10 Oct 1984 a
Paraguay 8 Oct 1997 a
Peru 7 Jul 1988 a
Philippines 10 Jun 1958 6 Jul 1967 Poland 10 Jun 1958 3 Oct 1961 Portugal 18 Oct 1994 a
Republic of Korea 8 Feb 1973 a
Republic of Moldova 18 Sep 1998 a
Romania 13 Sep 1961 a
Russian Federation 29 Dec 1958 24 Aug 1960 San Marino 17 May 1979 a

Participant/Signature [Ratification, accession (a), succession (d)]

Saudi Arabia 19 Apr 1994 a
Senegal 17 Oct 1994 a
Singapore 21 Aug 1986 a
Slovakia 28 May 1993 d Slovenia 6 Jul 1992 d South Africa 3 May 1976 a
Spain 12 May 1977 a
Sri Lanka 30 Dec 1958 9 Apr 1962 Sweden 23 Dec 1958 28 Jan 1972 Switzerland 29 Dec 1958 1 Jun 1965 Syrian Arab Republic6 9 Mar 1959 a
Thailand 21 Dec 1959 a
the former Yugoslav Republic of Macedonia 10 Mar 1994 d Trinidad and Tobago 14 Feb 1966 a
Tunisia 17 Jul 1967 a
Turkey 2 Jul 1992 a
Uganda 12 Feb 1992 a
Ukraine 29 Dec 1958 10 Oct 1960 United Kingdom 24 Sep 1975 a
United Republic of Tanzania 13 Oct 1964 a
United States of America 30 Sep 1970 a
Uruguay 30 Mar 1983 a
Uzbekistan 7 Feb 1996 a
Venezuela 8 Feb 1995 a
Viet Nam 12 Sep 1995 a
Yugoslavia 26 Feb 1982 a
Zimbabwe 29 Sep 1994 a

**Declarations and Reservations**

(Unless otherwise indicated, the declarations and reservations were made upon ratification, accession or succession. For objections thereto and territorial applications, see hereinafter.)

Algeria

Declaration: Referring to the possibility offered by article I, paragraph 3, of the Convention, the People's Democratic Republic of Algeria declares that it will apply the Convention, on the basis of reciprocity, to the recognition and enforcement of arbitral awards made only in the territory of another Contracting State and only where such awards have been made with respect to differences arising out of legal relationships whether contractual or not, which are considered as commercial under Algerian law.

Antigua and Barbuda

Declarations: "In accordance with article I, the Government of Antigua and Barbuda declares that it will apply the Convention on the basis of reciprocity only to the recognition and enforcement of awards made in the territory of another contracting state.

The Government of Antigua and Barbuda also declares that it will apply the Convention only to differences arising out of legal relationships, whether contractual or not, which are considered as commercial under the laws of Antigua and Barbuda."

Argentina

Upon signature:
Subject to the declaration contained in the Final Act.

Upon ratification:
On the basis of reciprocity, the Republic of Argentina will apply the Convention only to the recognition and enforcement of foreign arbitral awards made in the territory of another Contracting State. It will also apply the Convention only to differences arising out of legal relationships, whether contractual or not, which are considered as commercial under its national law.

The Convention will be interpreted in accordance with the principles and clauses of the National Constitution in force or those resulting from modification made by virtue of the Constitution.

Armenia

Declarations:
"1. The Republic of Armenia will apply the Convention only to recognition and enforcement of awards made in the territory of another Contracting State.

2. The Republic of Armenia will apply the Convention only t differences arising out of legal relationships, whether contractual or not, which are considered as commercial under the laws of the Republic of Armenia."
Austria

Bahrain

"1. The accession by the State of Bahrain to the Convention on the Recognition and Enforcement of Foreign Arbitral Awards, 1958 shall in no way constitute recognition of Israel or be a cause for the establishment of any relations of any kind therewith.

In accordance with article 1 (3) of the Convention, the State of Bahrain will apply the Convention, on the basis of reciprocity, to the recognition and enforcement of only those awards made in the territory of another Contracting State party to the Convention.

In accordance with article 1 (3) of the Convention, the State of Bahrain will apply the Convention only to differences arising out of legal relationships, whether contractual or not, which are considered as commercial under the national law of the State of Bahrain."

Barbados

Declaration:
"(i) In accordance with article 1 (3) of the Convention, the Government of Barbados declares that it will apply the Convention on the basis of reciprocity to the recognition and enforcement of awards made only in the territory of another Contracting State.

(ii) The Government of Barbados will also apply the Convention only to differences arising out of legal relationships, whether contractual or not which are considered as commercial under the laws of Barbados."

Belarus

The Byelorussian Soviet Socialist Republic will apply the provisions of this Convention in respect to arbitral awards made in the territories of non-contracting States only to the extent to which they grant reciprocal treatment.

Belgium

In accordance with article I, paragraph 3, the Government of the Kingdom of Belgium declares that it will apply the Convention to the recognition and enforcement of arbitral awards made only in the territory of a Contracting State.

Bosnia and Herzegovina

Declaration:
"The Convention will be applied to the Republic of Bosnia and Herzegovina only relating those arbitral awards that have been brought after entering into force of the Convention.

The Republic of Bosnia and Herzegovina will apply the Convention, on the basis of reciprocity, to the recognition and enforcement of only those awards made in the territory of another Contracting State.

The Republic of Bosnia and Herzegovina will apply the Convention only to differences arising out of legal relationships, whether contractual or not, which are considered as commercial under the national law of the Republic of Bosnia and Herzegovina."

Botswana

"The Republic of Botswana will apply the Convention only to differences arising out of legal relationship, whether contractual or not, which are considered commercial under Botswana law."

"The Republic of Botswana will apply the Convention to the Recognition and Enforcement of Awards made in the territory of another Contracting State."

Brunei Darussalam

Declaration:
"... Brunei Darussalam will on the basis of reciprocity apply the said Convention to the recognition and enforcement of only those awards which are made in the territory of another Contracting State."

Bulgaria

"Bulgaria will apply the Convention to recognition and enforcement of awards made in the territory of another contracting State. With regard to awards made in the territory of non-contracting States it will apply the Convention only to the extent to which these States grant reciprocal treatment."

Canada

27 May 1987
"The Government of Canada declares that it will apply the Convention only to differences arising out of legal relationships, whether contractual or not, which are considered as commercial under the laws of Canada, except in the case of the Province of Quebec where the law does not provide for such limitation."

Central African Republic

Referring to the possibility offered by paragraph 3 of article I of the Convention, the Central African Republic declares that it will apply the Convention on the basis of reciprocity, to the recognition and enforcement of awards made only in the territory of another contracting State; it further declares that it will apply the Convention only to differences arising out of legal relationships, whether contractual or not, which are considered as commercial under its national law.

China

1. The People's Republic of China will apply the Convention, only on the basis of reciprocity, to the recognition and enforcement of arbitral awards made in the territory of another Contracting State;

2. The People's Republic of China will apply the Convention only to differences arising out of legal relationships, whether contractual or not, which are considered as commercial under the national law of the People's Republic of China.

Cuba

Cuba will apply the Convention to the recognition and enforcement of arbitral awards made in the territory of another Contracting State. With respect to arbitral awards made by other noncontracting States it will apply the Convention only in so far as those States grant reciprocal treatment as established by mutual agreement between the parties. Moreover, it will apply the Convention only to differences arising out of legal relationships, whether contractual or not, which are considered as commercial under Cuban legislation.

Cyprus

"The Republic of Cyprus will apply the Convention, on the basis of reciprocity, to the recognition and enforcement of awards made only in the territory of another Contracting State; furthermore it will apply the Convention only to differences arising out of legal relationships, whether contractual or not, which are considered as commercial under its national law."

Czech Republic 3

Denmark

In accordance with the terms of article I, paragraph 3, [the Convention] shall have effect only as regards the recognition and enforcement of arbitral awards made by another Contracting State and [it] shall be valid only with respect to commercial relationships.

Ecuador

Ecuador, on a basis of reciprocity, will apply the Convention to the recognition and enforcement of arbitral awards made in the territory of another contracting State only if such awards have been made with respect to differences arising out of legal relationships which are regarded as commercial under Ecuadorian law.

France

Referring to the possibility offered by paragraph 3 of article I of the Convention, France declares that it will apply the Convention on the basis of reciprocity, to the recognition and enforcement of awards made only in the territory of another contracting State.

Referring to paragraphs 1 and 2 of article X of the Convention, France declares that this Convention will extend to all the territories of the French Republic.

Germany

Greece

8 April 1980
The present Convention is approved on condition of the two limitations set forth in article I (3) of the Convention.

Guatemala

On the basis of reciprocity, the Republic of Guatemala will apply the above Convention to the recognition and enforcement of arbitral awards made only in the territory of another contracting State; and will apply it only to differences arising out of legal relationships, whether contractual or not, which are considered as commercial under its national law.

Holy See

The State of Vatican City will apply the said Convention on the basis of reciprocity, on the one hand, to the recognition and enforcement of awards made only in the territory of another Contracting State, and on the other hand, only to differences arising out of legal relationships, whether contractual or not, which are considered as commercial under Vatican law.

Hungary

"The Hungarian People's Republic shall apply the Convention to the recognition and enforcement of such awards only as have been made in the territory of one of the other Contracting States and are dealing with differences arising in respect of a legal relationship considered by the Hungarian law as a commercial relationship."

India

"In accordance with Article I of the Convention, the Government of India declare that they will apply the Convention to the recognition and enforcement of awards made only in the territory of a State, party to this Convention. They further declare that they will apply the Convention only to differences arising out of legal relationships, whether contractual or not, which are considered as commercial under the law of India."

Indonesia

"Pursuant to the provision of article I (3) of the Convention, the Government of the Republic of Indonesia declares that it will apply the Convention on the basis of reciprocity, to the recognition and enforcement of awards made only in the territory of another Contracting State, and that it will apply the Convention only to differences arising out of legal relationships, whether contractual or not, which are considered as commercial under the Indonesian Law."

Ireland

"In accordance with article I (3) of the said Convention the Government of Ireland declares that it will apply the Convention to the recognition and enforcement of arbitral awards made only in the territory of another Contracting State."

Japan

"It will apply the Convention to the recognition and enforcement of awards made only in the territory of another Contracting State."

Jordan

The Government of Jordan shall not be bound by any awards which are made by Israel or to which an Israeli is a party.

Kenya

Declaration:
"In accordance with article I (3) of the said Convention the Government of Kenya declares that it will apply the Convention to the recognition and enforcement of arbitral awards made only in the territory of another contracting state."

Kuwait

The State of Kuwait will apply the Convention to the recognition and enforcement of awards made only in the territory of another Contracting State.

It is understood that the accession of the State of Kuwait to the Convention on the Recognition and Enforcement of Foreign Arbitral Awards, done at New York, on the 10th of June 1958, does not mean in any way recognition of Israel or entering with it into relations governed by the Convention thereto acceded by the State of Kuwait.

Lebanon

Declaration:
The Government of Lebanon declares that it will apply the Convention, on the basis of reciprocity, to the recognition and enforcement of awards made only in the territory of another Contracting State.

Lithuania

Declaration:
[The Republic of Lithuania] will apply the provisions of the said Convention to the recognition of arbitral awards made in the territories of the Non-Contracting States, only on the basis of reciprocity."

Luxembourg

Declaration:
The Convention is applied on the basis of reciprocity to the recognition and enforcement of only those arbitral awards made in the territory of another Contracting State.

Madagascar

The Malagasy Republic declares that it will apply the Convention on the basis of reciprocity, to the recognition and enforcement of awards made only in the territory of another contracting State; it further declares that it will apply the Convention only to differences arising out of legal relationships, whether contractual or not, which are considered as commercial under its national law.

Malaysia

Declaration:
The Government of Malaysia will apply the Convention on the basis of reciprocity, to the recognition and enforcement of awards made only in the territory of another Contracting State. Malaysia further declares that it will apply the Convention only to differences arising out of legal relationships, whether contractual or not, which are considered as commercial under Malaysian law.

Mauritius

Declarations:
"In accordance with paragraph 3 of article 1 of the Convention, the Republic of Mauritius declares that it will, on the basis of reciprocity, apply the Convention only to the recognition and enforcement of awards made in the territory of another Contracting State.

Referring to paragraphs 1 and 2 of article X of the Convention, the Republic of Mauritius declares that this Convention will extend to all the territories forming part of the Republic of Mauritius."

Monaco

Referring to the possibility offered by article I (3) of the Convention, the Principality of Monaco will apply the Convention, on the basis of reciprocity, to the recognition and enforcement of awards made only in the territory of another contracting State; furthermore, it will apply the Convention only to differences arising out of legal relationship, whether contractual or not, which are considered as commercial under its national law.

Mongolia

Declaration:
"1. Mongolia will apply the Convention, on the basis of reciprocity, to the recognition and enforcement of arbitral awards made only in the territory of another Contracting State.

2. Mongolia will apply the Convention only to differences arising out of legal relationships, whether contractual or not, which are considered as commercial under the national law of Mongolia."

Morocco

The Government of His Majesty the King of Morocco will apply the Convention to the recognition and enforcement of awards made only in the territory of another Contracting State.

Mozambique

Reservation:
"The Republic of Mozambique reserves itself the right to enforce the provisions of the said Convention on the base of reciprocity, where the arbitral awards have been pronounced in the territory of another Contracting State."

Nepal

Declaration:
"The Kingdom of Nepal will apply the Convention, on the basis of reciprocity, to the recognition and enforcement of awards made only in the territory of another contracting state. [The Government of Nepal] further declares that the Kingdom of Nepal will apply the Convention only to the differences arising out of legal relationship, whether contractual or not, which are considered as commercial under the law of the Kingdom of Nepal."

Netherlands

Referring to paragraph 3 of article I of the Convention on the Recognition and Enforcement of Foreign Arbitral Awards, the Government of the Kingdom declares that it will apply the Convention to the recognition and enforcement of awards made only in the territory of another Contracting State.

New Zealand

Declarations:
"In accordance with paragraph 3 of article 1 of the Convention, the Government of New Zealand declares that it will apply the Convention, on the basis of reciprocity, to the recognition and enforcement of awards made only in the territory of another Contracting State.

"Accession to the Convention by the Government of New Zealand shall not extend for the time being, pursuant to article X of the Convention, to the Cook Islands and Niue."

Nigeria

"In accordance with paragraph 3 of article I of the Convention, the Federal Military Government of the Federal Republic of Nigeria declares that it will apply the Convention on the basis of reciprocity to the recognition and enforcement of awards made only in the territory of a State party to this Convention and to differences arising out of legal relationships, whether contractual or not, which are considered as commercial under the laws of the Federal Republic of Nigeria."

Norway

"1. [The Government of Norway] will apply the Convention only to the recognition and enforcement of awards made in the territory of one of the Contracting States."

"2. [The Government of Norway] will not apply the Convention to differences where the subject matter of the proceedings is immovable property situated in Norway, or a right in or to such property."

Philippines

Upon signature:
Reservation:
"The Philippine delegation signs ad referendum this Convention with the reservation that it does so on the basis of reciprocity."

Declaration:
"The Philippines will apply the Convention to the recognition and enforcement of awards made only in the territory of another contracting State pursuant to Article I, paragraph 3 of the Convention."

Declaration made upon ratification: "The Philippines, on the basis of reciprocity, will apply the Convention to the recognition and enforcement of awards made only in the territory of another Contracting State and only to differences arising out of legal relationships, whether contractual or not, which are considered as commercial under the national law of the State making such declaration."

Poland

"With reservations as mentioned in article I, para. 3."

Portugal

Declaration:
Within the scope of the principle of reciprocity, Portugal will restrict the application of the Convention to arbitral awards pronounced in the territory of a State bound by the said Convention.

Republic of Korea

"By virtue of paragraph 3 of article I of the present Convention, the Government of the Republic of Korea declares that it will apply the Convention to the recognition and enforcement of arbitral awards made only in the territory of another Contracting State. It further declares that it will apply the Convention only to differences arising out of legal relationships, whether contractual or not, which are considered as commercial under its national law.

Republic of Moldova

"The Convention will be applied to the Republic of Moldova only relating those arbitral awards that have been brought after entering into force of the Convention.

The Convention will be applied to the Republic of Moldova, on the basis of reciprocity, only relating those awards made in the territory of another Contracting State."

Romania

The Romanian People's Republic will apply the Convention only to differences arising out of legal relationships, whether contractual or not, which are considered as commercial under its legislation.

The Romanian People's Republic will apply the Convention to the recognition and enforcement of awards made in the territory of another Contracting State. As regards awards made in the territory of certain non-contracting States, the Romanian People's Republic will apply the Convention only on the basis of reciprocity established by joint agreement between the parties.

Russian Federation

The Union of Soviet Socialist Republics will apply the provisions of this Convention in respect to arbitral awards made in the territories of non-contracting States only to the extent to which they grant reciprocal treatment.

Saudi Arabia

Declaration:
On the Basis of reciprocity, the Kingdom declares that it shall restrict the application of the Convention to the recognition and enforcement of arbitral awards made in the territory of a Contracting State.

Singapore

"The Republic of Singapore will on the basis of reciprocity apply the said Convention to the recognition and enforcement of only those awards which are made in the territory of another Contracting State."

Slovakia

Switzerland

Trinidad and Tobago

"In accordance with article I of the Convention, the Government of Trinidad and Tobago declares that it will apply the Convention to the recognition and enforcement of awards made only in the territory of another Contracting State. The Government of Trinidad and Tobago further declares that it will apply the Convention only to differences arising out of legal relationships, whether contractual or not, which are considered as commercial under the Law of Trinidad and Tobago."

Tunisia

With the reservations provided for in article I, paragraph 3, of the Convention, that is to say, the Tunisian State will apply the Convention to the recognition and enforcement of awards made only in the territory of another Contracting State and only to differences arising out of legal relationships, whether contractual or not, which are considered as commercial under the Tunisian law.

Turkey

Declaration:
In accordance with the Article I, paragraph 3 of the Convention, the Republic of Turkey declares that it will apply the Convention on the basis of reciprocity, to the recognition and enforcement of awards made only in the territory of another contracting State. It further declares that it will apply the Convention only to differences arising out of legal relationships, whether contractual or not, which are considered as commercial under its national law.

Uganda

Declaration:
"The Republic of Uganda will only apply the Convention to recognition and enforcement of awards made in the territory of another Contracting State."

Ukraine

The Ukrainian Soviet Socialist Republic will apply the provisions of this Convention in respect to arbitral awards made in the territories of non-contracting States only to the extent to which they grant reciprocal treatment.

United Kingdom of Great Britain and Northern Ireland

5 May 1980
"The United Kingdom will apply the Convention only to the recognition and enforcement of awards made in the territory of another Contracting State. This declaration is also made on behalf of Gibraltar, Hong Kong and the Isle of Man to which the Convention has been extended."

United Republic of Tanzania

"The Government of the United Republic of Tanganyika and Zanzibar will apply the Convention, in accordance with the first sentence of article I (3) thereof, only to the recognition and enforcement of awards made in the territory of another Contracting State."

United States of America

"The United States of America will apply the Convention, on the basis of reciprocity, to the recognition and enforcement of only those awards made in the territory of another Contracting State.

"The United States of America will apply the Convention only to differences arising out of legal relationships, whether contractual or not, which are considered as commercial under the national law of the United States."

Venezuela

Declarations:
(a) The Republic of Venezuela will apply the Convention only to the recognition and enforcement of foreign arbitral awards made in the territory of another Contracting State.

(b) The Republic of Venezuela will apply the present Convention only to differences arising out of legal relationships, whether contractual or not, which are considered as commercial under its national law.

Vietnam

Declarations:
1. [The Socialist Republic of Viet Nam] considers the Convention to be applicable to the recognition and enforcement of arbitral awards made only in the territory of another Contracting State. With respect to arbitral awards made in the territories of non-contracting States, it will apply the Convention on the basis of reciprocity.

2. The Convention will be applied only to differences arising out of legal relationships which are considered as commercial under the laws of Viet Nam.

3. Interpretation of the Convention before the Vietnamese Courts or competent authorities should be made in accordance with the Constitution and the law of Viet Nam.

Yugoslavia

Reservation:
"1. The Convention is applied in regard to the Socialist Federal Republic of Yugoslavia only to those arbitral awards which were adopted after the coming of the Convention into effect.

"2. The Socialist Federal Republic of Yugoslavia will apply the Convention on a reciprocal basis only to those arbitral awards which were adopted on the territory of the other State Party to the Convention.

"3. The Socialist Federal Republic of Yugoslavia will apply the Convention [only] with respect to the disputes arising from the legal relations, contractual and non-contractual, which, according to its national legislation are considered as economic."

**Objections**

(Unless otherwise indicated, the objections were received upon ratification, accession or succession).

Germany

29 December 1989
The Federal Republic of Germany is of the opinion that the second paragraph of the declaration of the Argentine Republic represents a reservation and as such is not only contradictory to article I (3) of the Convention but is also vague and hence inadmissible; it therefore raises an objection to that reservation.

In all other respects this objection is not intended to prevent the entry into force of the Convention between the Argentine Republic and the Federal Republic of Germany.

**Territorial Application**

Participant Date of receipt of Territories the notification

Australia 26 Mar 1975 All the external territories for the international relations of which Australia is responsible other than Papua New Guinea
Denmark16 10 Feb 1976 Faeroe Islands, Greenland
France 26 Jun 1959 All the territories of the French Republic
Netherlands17 24 Apr 1964 Netherlands Antilles, Surinam
United Kingdom2, 18 24 Sep 1975 Gibraltar
21 Jan 1977 Hong Kong
22 Feb 1979 Isle of Man
14 Nov 1979 Bermuda
26 Nov 1980 Belize, Cayman Islands
19 Apr 1985 Guernsey
United States of America Nov 1970 All the territories for the international relations of which the United States of America is responsible

Declarations and reservations made upon notification of territorial application

United Kingdom of Great Britain and Northern Ireland

Belize, Bermuda, Cayman Islands, Guernsey

[The Convention will apply] . . . "in accordance with article I, paragraph 3 thereof, only to the recognition and enforcement of awards made in the territory of another Contracting State."

# CONVENTION ON THE SERVICE ABROAD OF JUDICIAL AND EXTRAJUDICIAL DOCUMENTS IN CIVIL OR COMMERCIAL MATTERS

*(Concluded 15 November 1965)*
*(Entered into force 10 February 1969)*

The States signatory to the present Convention,
Desiring to create appropriate means to ensure that judicial and extrajudicial documents to be served abroad shall be brought to the notice of the addressee in sufficient time,
Desiring to improve the organisation of mutual judicial assistance for that purpose by simplifying and expediting the procedure,
Have resolved to conclude a Convention to this effect and have agreed upon the following provisions:

*Article 1*
The present Convention shall apply in all cases, in civil or commercial matters, where there is occasion to transmit a judicial or extrajudicial document for service abroad.
This Convention shall not apply where the address of the person to be served with the document is not known.

## CHAPTER I — JUDICIAL DOCUMENTS

*Article 2*
Each Contracting State shall designate a Central Authority which will undertake to receive requests for service coming from other Contracting States and to proceed in conformity with the provisions of Articles 3 to 6.
Each State shall organise the Central Authority in conformity with its own law.

*Article 3*
The authority or judicial officer competent under the law of the State in which the documents originate shall forward to the Central Authority of the State addressed a request conforming to the model annexed to the present Convention, without any requirement of legalisation or other equivalent formality.
The document to be served or a copy thereof shall be annexed to the request. The request and the document shall both be furnished in duplicate.

*Article 4*
If the Central Authority considers that the request does not comply with the provisions of the present Convention it shall promptly inform the applicant and specify its objections to the request.

*Article 5*
The Central Authority of the State addressed shall itself serve the document or shall arrange to have it served by an appropriate agency, either —
*a)* by a method prescribed by its internal law for the service of documents in domestic actions upon persons who are within its territory, or
*b)* by a particular method requested by the applicant, unless such a method is incompatible with the law of the

State addressed.
Subject to sub-paragraph *(b)* of the first paragraph of this Article, the document may always be served by delivery to an addressee who accepts it voluntarily.
If the document is to be served under the first paragraph above, the Central Authority may require the document to be written in, or translated into, the official language or one of the official languages of the State addressed.
That part of the request, in the form attached to the present Convention, which contains a summary of the document to be served, shall be served with the document.

*Article 6*
The Central Authority of the State addressed or any authority which it may have designated for that purpose, shall complete a certificate in the form of the model annexed to the present Convention.
The certificate shall state that the document has been served and shall include the method, the place and the date of service and the person to whom the document was delivered. If the document has not been served, the certificate shall set out the reasons which have prevented service.
The applicant may require that a certificate not completed by a Central Authority or by a judicial authority shall be countersigned by one of these authorities.
The certificate shall be forwarded directly to the applicant.

*Article 7*
The standard terms in the model annexed to the present Convention shall in all cases be written either in French or in English. They may also be written in the official language, or in one of the official languages, of the State in which the documents originate.
The corresponding blanks shall be completed either in the language of the State addressed or in French or in English.

*Article 8*
Each Contracting State shall be free to effect service of judicial documents upon persons abroad, without application of any compulsion, directly through its diplomatic or consular agents.
Any State may declare that it is opposed to such service within its territory, unless the document is to be served upon a national of the State in which the documents originate.

*Article 9*
Each Contracting State shall be free, in addition, to use consular channels to forward documents, for the purpose of service, to those authorities of another Contracting State which are designated by the latter for this purpose.
Each Contracting State may, if exceptional circumstances so require, use diplomatic channels for the same purpose.

*Article 10*
Provided the State of destination does not object, the present Convention shall not interfere with —
*a)* the freedom to send judicial documents, by postal channels, directly to persons abroad,
*b)* the freedom of judicial officers, officials or other competent persons of the State of origin to effect service of judicial documents directly through the judicial officers, officials or other competent persons of the State of destination,
*c)* the freedom of any person interested in a judicial proceeding to effect service of judicial documents directly through the judicial officers, officials or other competent persons of the State of destination.

*Article 11*
The present Convention shall not prevent two or more Contracting States from agreeing to permit, for the purpose of service of judicial documents, channels of transmission other than those provided for in the preceding Articles and, in particular, direct communication between their respective authorities.

*Article 12*
The service of judicial documents coming from a Contracting State shall not give rise to any payment or reimbursement of taxes or costs for the services rendered by the State addressed.
The applicant shall pay or reimburse the costs occasioned by-
*a)* the employment of a judicial officer or of a person competent under the law of the State of destination,
*b)* the use of a particular method of service.

*Article 13*
Where a request for service complies with the terms of the present Convention, the State addressed may refuse to comply therewith only if it deems that compliance would infringe its sovereignty or security.
It may not refuse to comply solely on the ground that, under its internal law, it claims exclusive jurisdiction over the subject-matter of the action or that its internal law would not permit the action upon which the application is based.
The Central Authority shall, in case of refusal, promptly inform the applicant and state the reasons for the refusal.

*Article 14*
Difficulties which may arise in connection with the transmission of judicial documents for service shall be settled through diplomatic channels.

*Article 15*
Where a writ of summons or an equivalent document had to be transmitted abroad for the purpose of service, under the provisions of the present Convention, and the defendant has not appeared, judgment shall not be given until it is established that —
*a)* the document was served by a method prescribed by the internal law of the State addressed for the service of documents in domestic actions upon persons who are within its territory, or
*b)* the document was actually delivered to the defendant or to his residence by another method provided for by this Convention,
and that in either of these cases the service or the delivery was effected in sufficient time to enable the defendant to defend.
Each Contracting State shall be free to declare that the judge, notwithstanding the provisions of the first paragraph of this Article, may give judgment even if no certificate of service or delivery has been received, if all the following conditions are fulfilled-
*a)* the document was transmitted by one of the methods provided for in this Convention,
*b)* a period of time of not less than six months, considered adequate by the judge in the particular case, has elapsed since the date of the transmission of the document,
*c)* no certificate of any kind has been received, even though every reasonable effort has been made to obtain it through the competent authorities of the State addressed.
Notwithstanding the provisions of the preceding paragraphs the judge may order, in case of urgency, any provisional or protective measures.

*Article 16*
When a writ of summons or an equivalent document had to be transmitted abroad for the purpose of service, under the provisions of the present Convention, and a judgment has been entered against a defendant who has not appeared, the judge shall have the power to relieve the defendant from the effects of the expiration of the time for appeal from the judgment if the following conditions are fulfilled —
*a)* the defendant, without any fault on his part, did not have knowledge of the document in sufficient time to defend, or knowledge of the judgment in sufficient time to appeal, and

*b)* the defendant has disclosed a *prima facie* defence to the action on the merits.
An application for relief may be filed only within a reasonable time after the defendant has knowledge of the judgment.
Each Contracting State may declare that the application will not be entertained if it is filed after the expiration of a time to be stated in the declaration, but which shall in no case be less than one year following the date of the judgment.
This Article shall not apply to judgments concerning status or capacity of persons.

CHAPTER II – EXTRAJUDICIAL DOCUMENTS
*Article 17*
Extrajudicial documents emanating from authorities and judicial officers of a Contracting State may be transmitted for the purpose of service in another Contracting State by the methods and under the provisions of the present Convention.

CHAPTER III – GENERAL CLAUSES
*Article 18*
Each Contracting State may designate other authorities in addition to the Central Authority and shall determine the extent of their competence.
The applicant shall, however, in all cases, have the right to address a request directly to the Central Authority.
Federal States shall be free to designate more than one Central Authority.

*Article 19*
To the extent that the internal law of a Contracting State permits methods of transmission, other than those provided for in the preceding Articles, of documents coming from abroad, for service within its territory, the present Convention shall not affect such provisions.

*Article 20*
The present Convention shall not prevent an agreement between any two or more Contracting States to dispense with –
*a)* the necessity for duplicate copies of transmitted documents as required by the second paragraph of Article 3,
*b)* the language requirements of the third paragraph of Article 5 and Article 7,
*c)* the provisions of the fourth paragraph of Article 5,
*d)* the provisions of the second paragraph of Article 12.

*Article 21*
Each Contracting State shall, at the time of the deposit of its instrument of ratification or accession, or at a later date, inform the Ministry of Foreign Affairs of the Netherlands of the following –
*a)* the designation of authorities, pursuant to Articles 2 and 18,
*b)* the designation of the authority competent to complete the certificate pursuant to Article 6,
*c)* the designation of the authority competent to receive documents transmitted by consular channels, pursuant to Article 9.
Each Contracting State shall similarly inform the Ministry, where appropriate, of –
*a)* opposition to the use of methods of transmission pursuant to Articles 8 and 10,
*b)* declarations pursuant to the second paragraph of Article 15 and the third paragraph of Article 16,
*c)* all modifications of the above designations, oppositions and declarations.

*Article 22*
Where Parties to the present Convention are also Parties to one or both of the Conventions on civil procedure signed at The Hague on 17th July 1905, and on 1st March 1954, this Convention shall replace as between them

Articles 1 to 7 of the earlier Conventions.

*Article 23*
The present Convention shall not affect the application of Article 23 of the Convention on civil procedure signed at The Hague on 17th July 1905, or of Article 24 of the Convention on civil procedure signed at The Hague on 1st March 1954.
These Articles shall, however, apply only if methods of communication, identical to those provided for in these Conventions, are used.

*Article 24*
Supplementary agreements between Parties to the Conventions of 1905 and 1954 shall be considered as equally applicable to the present Convention, unless the Parties have otherwise agreed.

*Article 25*
Without prejudice to the provisions of Articles 22 and 24, the present Convention shall not derogate from Conventions containing provisions on the matters governed by this Convention to which the Contracting States are, or shall become, Parties.

*Article 26*
The present Convention shall be open for signature by the States represented at the Tenth Session of the Hague Conference on Private International Law.
It shall be ratified, and the instruments of ratification shall be deposited with the Ministry of Foreign Affairs of the Netherlands.

*Article 27*
The present Convention shall enter into force on the sixtieth day after the deposit of the third instrument of ratification referred to in the second paragraph of Article 26.
The Convention shall enter into force for each signatory State which ratifies subsequently on the sixtieth day after the deposit of its instrument of ratification.

*Article 28*
Any State not represented at the Tenth Session of the Hague Conference on Private International Law may accede to the present Convention after it has entered into force in accordance with the first paragraph of Article 27. The instrument of accession shall be deposited with the Ministry of Foreign Affairs of the Netherlands.
The Convention shall enter into force for such a State in the absence of any objection from a State, which has ratified the Convention before such deposit, notified to the Ministry of Foreign Affairs of the Netherlands within a period of six months after the date on which the said Ministry has notified it of such accession.
In the absence of any such objection, the Convention shall enter into force for the acceding State on the first day of the month following the expiration of the last of the periods referred to in the preceding paragraph.

*Article 29*
Any State may, at the time of signature, ratification or accession, declare that the present Convention shall extend to all the territories for the international relations of which it is responsible, or to one or more of them. Such a declaration shall take effect on the date of entry into force of the Convention for the State concerned.
At any time thereafter, such extensions shall be notified to the Ministry of Foreign Affairs of the Netherlands.
The Convention shall enter into force for the territories mentioned in such an extension on the sixtieth day after the notification referred to in the preceding paragraph.

*Article 30*

The present Convention shall remain in force for five years from the date of its entry into force in accordance with the first paragraph of Article 27, even for States which have ratified it or acceded to it subsequently.

If there has been no denunciation, it shall be renewed tacitly every five years.

Any denunciation shall be notified to the Ministry of Foreign Affairs of the Netherlands at least six months before the end of the five year period.

It may be limited to certain of the territories to which the Convention applies.

The denunciation shall have effect only as regards the State which has notified it. The Convention shall remain in force for the other Contracting States.

*Article 31*

The Ministry of Foreign Affairs of the Netherlands shall give notice to the States referred to in Article 26, and to the States which have acceded in accordance with Article 28, of the following —

*a)* the signatures and ratifications referred to in Article 26;

*b)* the date on which the present Convention enters into force in accordance with the first paragraph of Article 27;

*c)* the accessions referred to in Article 28 and the dates on which they take effect;

*d)* the extensions referred to in Article 29 and the dates on which they take effect;

*e)* the designations, oppositions and declarations referred to in Article 21;

*f)* the denunciations referred to in the third paragraph of Article 30.

In witness whereof the undersigned, being duly authorised thereto, have signed the present Convention.

Done at The Hague, on the 15th day of November, 1965, in the English and French languages, both texts being equally authentic, in a single copy which shall be deposited in the archives of the Government of the Netherlands, and of which a certified copy shall be sent, through the diplomatic channel, to each of the States represented at the Tenth Session of the Hague Conference on Private International Law.

## Conclusions and Recommendations of the Special Commission on the practical operation of The Hague Apostille, Evidence and Service Conventions

***(28 October to 4 November 2003)***

1. A Special Commission met in The Hague from 28 October to 4 November 2003 to review the practical operation of the Hague Conventions of *5 October 1961 Abolishing the Requirement of Legalisation for Foreign Public Documents*, of *15 November 1965 on the Service Abroad of Judicial and Extrajudicial Documents in Civil or Commercial Matters*, and of *18 March 1970 on the Taking of Evidence Abroad in Civil or Commercial Matters*. The Special Commission, which was attended by 116 delegates representing 57 Member States, States party to one or more Convention under review, and observers, unanimously approved the following conclusions and recommendations:

### I. GENERAL COMMENTS

2. The Special Commission (SC) noted and emphasised the *continued importance* of the Hague Apostille, Evidence and Service Conventions.

3. In light of the value of the continued monitoring of the Conventions' practical operation, the need to promote uniform interpretation, foster mutual confidence and enhance the mutual benefits for States party to the Convention to exchange their respective experiences in operating the Conventions, as well as to promote the benefits of the Conventions to non-party States, the SC recommended to have *more frequent meetings* to review the practical operation of the Apostille, Evidence and Service Conventions. The Special Commission recommended that review meetings on the practical operation of these three Conventions be held *every five years*, subject to the availability of the additional resources needed. Also, consideration should be given to the possibility of reviewing the practical operation of the *Hague Convention of 25 October 1980 on International Access to Justice*.

4. The SC emphasised that the Apostille, Evidence and Service Conventions operate in an environment which is subject to important *technical developments*. Although this evolution could not be foreseen at the time of the adoption of the three Conventions, the SC underlined that modern technologies are an integral part of today's society and their usage a matter of fact. In this respect, the SC noted that the spirit and letter of the Conventions do not constitute an obstacle to the usage of modern technology and that their application and operation can be further improved by relying on such technologies. The Workshop held prior to the SC (*i.e.*, on 27 October 2003) clearly revealed the means, possibilities and advantages of using modern technologies in subject matters falling within the scope of the Conventions[1].

---

[1] The Workshop was structured around the following presentations: MR THOMAS GOTTWALD & MR PETER FRANK (Federal Ministry of Justice, Austria): *eJustice – Datahighway to Austrian Courts – Electronic Legal Communication (ELC) – Transmission of Legal Documents*; MS JULIE NIND (Ministry of Justice, New Zealand): *Taking evidence by video link across Tasman*; MS DORY MCKENZIE & MR JAMES MASON (Foreign and Commonwealth Office, United Kingdom): *The issuance of Apostilles by the Foreign and Commonwealth Office*; MR OZIE STALLWORTH & MR KEVIN MENDELSON (National Notary Association, United States of America): *enjoa – The Electronic Notary Journal of Official Acts.*

## II. APOSTILLE CONVENTION

*General considerations*

5. Examination of practice under the Apostille Convention confirmed its *very wide use and effectiveness*, as well as the absence of any major practical obstacle. Against this background, the SC recommended strongly that States party to the Convention should continue to *promote* it to other States. In particular, Member States of the Conference which are not already party to the Convention are encouraged to consider actively becoming party to the Convention.

6. The SC also stressed the *usefulness of linking the application of the Hague Adoption Convention of 1993 to the Apostille Convention*. In light of the high number of public documents included in a typical adoption procedure, the SC recommended that States that are party to the Adoption Convention but not to the Apostille Convention consider actively becoming party to the latter.

7. The SC emphasised that the *use of information technology (IT) could have a positive impact on the operation of the Convention*, in particular through lowering costs and increasing the efficiency of the creation and registration of Apostilles.

8. The SC noted the difficulties some States face with the recognition of Apostilles issued in States with numerous competent authorities (difficulties in identifying and verifying the competence of individual issuing authorities; differences in Apostilles issued within the same State). With a view to further promoting knowledge about the practical operation of the Convention, the SC recommended that States party send all *relevant information to the Permanent Bureau to be publicised on the Hague Conference's website, and that particular consideration to a FAQ-section be given.*

9. Furthermore, the SC recommended that a *Handbook* on the practical operation of the Convention be prepared by the Permanent Bureau, subject to adequate resources being available for the purpose.

*Scope of the Convention*

10. With regard to *commercial and customs documents*, which are excluded from the scope of the Convention, the SC noted that despite some isolated concerns there were no developments that would justify the need to reconsider this exclusion. The SC suggested that the matter be further explored in the Handbook (see recommendation 9 above).

11. Regarding the application of an Apostille on a *certified copy* of a public document, the SC concluded that Article 1 of the Convention applies. Individual States, however, may decline to issue an Apostille to the certified copy of a document on the grounds of public policy.

*Competent Authorities*

12. In addition to the obligation mentioned in Article 6 (of the Convention), the SC recommended that States party make available to the Permanent Bureau a list of *all* competent authorities to issue Apostilles, including their full contact details (postal address, telephone and fax numbers, e-mail). The SC noted the importance of keeping this information updated.

*Formal requirements*

13. The SC underlined the importance of the *principle that an Apostille that has been established according to the requirements of the Convention in the State of issuance must be accepted and produce its effects in any State of production*. With a view to further facilitating free circulation of Apostilles, the SC recalled the importance of the *Model certificate* annexed to the Convention. The SC recommended that Apostilles issued by competent authorities should conform as closely as possible to this model. However, variations in the form of an Apostille among issuing authorities should not be a basis for rejection as long as the Apostille is clearly identifiable as an Apostille issued under the Convention. *The SC firmly rejects, as contrary to the Convention, isolated practices among States party that require Apostilles to be legalised.*

14. The SC took note of some reports of *successful use of electronically or non-manually reproduced signatures of issuing authorities* and that the use of such signatures has not led to an increased incidence of fraud. At the same time, it was noted that most States party remained reticent towards the use of such signatures. The SC recommended the advantages of increased automation, but stressed the importance of applying appropriate anti-fraud measures to the production of automated signatures.

15. The SC agreed that it was important to maintain *mutual confidence* where electronically or non-manually reproduced signatures are used. In this respect, the SC underlined the important role that the *register* – which up to now has not often been called upon to verify the relevant information contained in a specific Apostille – could play in resolving any doubt in relation to an Apostille. The SC noted that maintenance of electronic registers could facilitate the process of verification.

16. The SC noted the *variety of means for affixing Apostilles* to the public document. These means may include rubber stamp, glue, (multi-coloured) ribbons, wax seals, impressed seals, self-adhesive stickers, etc.; as to an allonge, these means may include glue, grommets, staples, etc. The SC noted that all these means are acceptable under the Convention, and that, therefore, these variations cannot be a basis for the rejection of Apostilles.

17. As regards Apostilles to be issued for a *multi-page document*, the SC recommended that the Apostille be affixed to the signature page(s) of the document. When using an allonge, the Apostille may be affixed to the front or the back of the document.

18. The SC stressed that Apostilles may *not be refused in a State of production on the grounds that they do not comply with that State's national formalities and modes of issuance*. The only relevant consideration in this respect is that referred to in paragraph 13 above.

*Language*

19. The SC concluded that Article 4 of the Convention permitted the *use of more than one language* in the Apostille and that this might well assist in the circulation of documents. In the light of examples given by delegations it was clear that it was possible to create a form of Apostille with a number of languages and yet retain conformity with the model of the Apostille provided in the Convention. The SC recommended that States party give information on this to the PB for inclusion on the Hague Conference's website.

*Costs*

20. The SC recalled that the fees charged in connection with the issuing of the Apostille should be *reasonable*, particularly for situations like cross-border adoptions and maintenance procedures. One way of dealing with this could be to charge a single fee for a cluster of related documents rather than an individual fee for each document in a particular case.

*Retention of records in a Register*

21. As regards the issue of the retention and disposal of records in a register or card index established under Article 7, the SC did not suggest a minimum period during which records in a register should be kept. It concluded that it was a matter for each State party to develop *objective criteria* in this respect. The SC agreed that holding of information in electronic form would assist this process by making it easier to store and retrieve records.

*Effects of an Apostille*

22. The SC recalled that under the Convention, the effect of an Apostille is to "certify the authenticity of the signature, the capacity in which the person signing the document has acted and, where appropriate, the identity of the seal or stamp which it bears" (Art. 3). In particular, the *effect of an Apostille does not extend to the content of the public document* to which it is attached.

*Use of IT in issuing Apostilles*

23. The SC identified the following four stages in the issuing of an Apostille in respect of which the application of IT might be considered and thought that there was no reason in principle – as far as the use of IT proves to be cost-efficient – why IT should not be applied:

    1. maintenance of a secure electronic database of signatures for the purpose of verifying the signatures appearing on public documents for which an Apostille is requested;
    2. use of word-processing technology to complete the information to appear on the Apostille;
    3. use of electronically reproduced signatures of the issuing authority to be inserted through secure electronic means and printed on the Apostille;
    4. maintenance of an electronic register.

*E-Apostille?*

24. The SC recommended that States party and the PB should work towards the development of techniques for the generation of electronic Apostilles taking into account *inter alia* the UNCITRAL model laws on electronic commerce and on electronic signatures, both being based on the principles of non-discrimination and functional equivalence.

*Multi-unit States and Regional Economic Integration Organisations (REIOs)*

25. The SC took note of the position of one Member State that the existence of a Multi-unit State clause might assist that State to accede to the Convention, but there was insufficient priority for this to be the subject of a protocol on its own; if there were to be a Protocol on other issues, then such a clause might be considered.

26. The SC accepted that, at this point, there was no need to consider the application of the Convention to documents issued by REIOs.

## III. EVIDENCE CONVENTION

*General considerations*

27. The SC recalled the importance of the Evidence Convention as a *bridge between common law and civil law* procedures relating to the taking of evidence in civil and commercial litigation.

28. With a view to overcoming some of the differences that have arisen among States party in interpreting the Convention, in particular the scope of a possible reservation under Article 23, the SC carefully reviewed some of the principles and practices relating to the Convention.

*Reservations under Article 23*

29. The SC recognised that the terms of Article 23, which permits a Contracting State to "declare that it will not execute Letters of Request issued for the purpose of obtaining pre-trial discovery of documents", are a continued source of misunderstandings. Having regard to the history of the provision, the SC agreed that Article 23 was intended to permit States to ensure that a request for the production of documents must be *sufficiently substantiated* so as to avoid requests whereby one party merely seeks to find out what documents may generally be in the possession of the other party to the proceeding. The SC noted that the wording of the particularised declaration submitted by the UK (*i.e.,* the proponent of the provision) reflected this purpose more adequately than the wording of Article 23. The UK declaration reads as follows:

> "In accordance with Article 23 Her Majesty's Government declare that the United Kingdom will not execute Letters of Request issued for the purpose of obtaining pre-trial discovery of documents. Her Majesty's Government further declare that Her Majesty's Government understand "Letters of Request issued for the purpose of obtaining pre-trial discovery of documents" for the purposes of the foregoing Declaration as including any Letter of Request which requires a person:
>
> a. to state what documents relevant to the proceedings to which the Letter of Request relates are, or have been, in his possession, custody or power; or
> b. to produce any documents other than particular documents specified in the Letter of Request as being documents appearing to the requested court to be, or to be likely to be, in his possession, custody or power."

30. Equally, the SC noted that Article 16 of the *Additional Protocol of 1984 to the Inter-American Convention on the Taking of Evidence Abroad* also more adequately reflects the concern of the proponents of Article 23 of the Evidence Convention. Article 16 of the Additional Protocol reads as follows:

> "The States Parties to this Protocol shall process a letter rogatory that requests the exhibition and copying of documents if it meets the following requirements:
>
> a. The proceeding has been initiated;
> b. The documents are reasonably identified by date, contents, or other appropriate information, and
> c. The letter rogatory specifies those facts and circumstances causing the requesting party reasonably to believe that the requested documents are or were in the possession, control, or custody of, or are known to the person from whom the documents are requested.

The person from whom documents are requested may, where appropriate, deny that he has possession, control, or custody of the requested documents, or may object to the exhibition and copying of the documents, in accordance with the rules of the Convention.

At the time of signing, ratifying or acceding to this Protocol a State may declare that it will process the letters rogatory to which this article applies only if they identify the relationship between the evidence or information requested and the pending proceeding."

31. The SC noted that in some instances where States have made a general, non-particularised declaration under Article 23, they may have mistakenly believed that they are only objecting to evidence requests submitted prior to the *opening of a proceeding in the State of origin*. In fact, "pre-trial discovery" means evidence requests submitted after the filing of a claim but before the final hearing on the merits.

32. Compounding the misunderstandings that may have prompted Contracting States to make a general declaration under Article 23 denying the "pre-trial discovery of documents", the SC noted that in some cases the judicial authorities of a State of origin have concluded that no requests for the production of documents were permitted under the Convention in a State having made such a general declaration. This may result in the State of origin applying its own domestic law for the taking of evidence against foreign parties.

33. The SC took note of the fact that following the discussion of the same issue during the SC meeting in 1989, some States revised their declaration under Article 23 to reflect the more particularised terms on the UK declaration. At the same time, another State party informed the SC about changes in its internal law to further limit the scope of pre-trial discovery, including by increasing the control of judges over discovery proceedings.

34. Against this background, the SC recommended that States which have made a general, non-particularised declaration under Article 23 *revisit their declaration* by considering an amendment adopting terms such as those contained in the UK declaration or in Article 16 of the Inter-American Protocol. In this connection, the SC further recommended the production of a new edition of the *practical Handbook* on the operation of the Convention.

*Scope of Article 23*

35. The SC noted that Article 23 expressly refers to "documents" and that the scope of the provision should not be extended to oral testimony.

*Article 1(2)*

36. The SC recommended that States party submit information to the Permanent Bureau as to how Article 1(2) was interpreted and, in particular, what national judicial proceedings would be regarded as "contemplated" for purposes of this provision.

*Mandatory and / or Exclusive character of the Convention*

37. The SC noted that there were still differing views among States party as to the obligatory and/or exclusive character of the Convention.

---

[2] Reference was also made to the treatment of pretrial discovery of documents under Art. 9 of the *Inter-American Convention of 1975 on the Taking of Evidence Abroad.*

*Arbitration*

38. The SC noted that in some instances, and in accordance with the internal law of some States, the Convention has been made available for use in arbitration proceedings. The SC stressed that a request for the taking of evidence under the Convention would have to be presented by the relevant judicial authority of the State where the arbitration proceedings take place.

*Time issues*

39. The SC recommended that requests for evidence be presented as soon as practically possible so as to provide sufficient time for their execution in the State addressed.

40. The SC also urged States party to communicate to their Central Authorities and to the authorities receiving letters of request, the importance of expeditious execution of the requests.

41. With a view to avoiding unnecessary delays where a letter of request is deficient, the SC recommended that Central Authorities or executing authorities encourage the requesting authority to reformulate and resubmit its letter of request. In cases where the request appears to be partially deficient, the executing authorities should, wherever appropriate, execute the portion of a letter that is not deficient rather than to reject the entire request.

*Modern technologies*

42. The SC expressed general support for the use of modern technologies to further facilitate the efficient operation of the Convention. The SC noted that there seems to be no legal obstacle to the usage of modern technologies under the Convention. However, the use of some techniques may be subject to different legal requirements in different States (*e.g.*, obtaining the consent of all parties involved in the execution). In this respect, the SC recommended that States party make relevant information on legal requirements relating to specific techniques available to the Permanent Bureau

43. The SC stressed where a special method or procedure is requested for the taking of evidence (Art. 9(2)), the *exception* for methods that are "incompatible with the internal law of the State of execution or [...] impossible of performance by reason of its internal practice and procedure or by reason of practical difficulties" should be interpreted narrowly to permit, to the greatest possible extent, the use of modern information technology.

44. The SC stressed that early informal contact among appropriate authorities to coordinate the presentation and execution of Letters of request might be facilitated by the use of modern information technology such as e-mail.

*Multi-unit States and Regional Economic Integration Organisations (REIOs)*

45. The SC took note of the position of one Member State that the existence of a Multi-unit State clause might assist that State to accede to the Convention, but there was insufficient priority for this to be the subject of a protocol on its own; if there were to be a Protocol on other issues, then such a clause might be considered.

46. The SC accepted that, at this point, there was no need to consider the application of the Convention in relation to REIOs.

## IV. SERVICE CONVENTION

*Forwarding Authorities*

47. The SC recalled that it is for the law of the requesting State to determine the competence of the forwarding authorities (Art. 3). Furthermore, the SC took note of information provided by number of experts about the position of forwarding authorities and concluded that most practical problems have been solved.

48. The SC invited all States party to provide information on the forwarding authorities and their competences to the Permanent Bureau for posting on the Conference's website. The SC also accepted a suggestion that such information be included on the Standard Form for a Request for Service[3].

49. The SC recommended that in any question of doubt as to the competence of the forwarding authority, rather than rejecting the request, the authorities in the State requested should seek to confirm that competence by either consulting the Conference's website or by making expeditious informal inquiries of the forwarding authorities, including by way of e-mail.

*Designation of Central Authorities*

50. The SC reaffirmed the requirement on States party to the Service Convention to designate a Central Authority under Article 2 and noted the serious difficulties which can arise in operating the Convention if such a designation is not made known to the depositary at the time of the deposit of the instrument of ratification or accession. The SC urged all States party which have not yet done so to designate, as soon as possible, a Central Authority. If delays may not be avoided in the designation of the Central Authority(ies), the SC urged that such States give full information to the Permanent Bureau about the arrangements provided to facilitate the functioning of the Convention pending such designation.

51. The SC requested all States party to provide to the Permanent Bureau complete contact information (postal address, telephone and fax numbers, e-mail and website addresses) for their Central Authorities, particularly for States that have designated more than one Central Authority or other authorities under Article 18. The SC noted the importance of regularly updating of this information on the Conference's website.

*Functioning of the Central Authorities*

52. The SC reaffirmed that it is for a State party to determine its own model for the organisation of the Central Authority functions. In particular, the SC noted that the terms of the Convention do not preclude a Central Authority from contracting activities under the Convention to a private entity, while retaining its status as Central Authority and ultimate responsibility for its obligations under the Convention[4].

53. The SC reaffirmed that according to Article 12(1), a State party shall not charge for its services rendered under the Convention. Nevertheless, under Article 12(2), an applicant shall pay or reimburse the costs occasioned by the employment of a judicial officer or other competent person. The SC urged States to ensure that any such costs reflect actual expenses and be kept at a reasonable level[5].

---

3 The Russian Federation did not support this recommendation and reserved its position.
4 The Russian Federation did not support this recommendation and reserved its position.
5 The Russian Federation did not support this recommendation and reserved its position.

54. The SC invited States party to make available to the Permanent Bureau all relevant information relating to costs, the availability and modalities of service by delivery under Article 5(2), as well as information relating to the alternative modes of transmission under the Convention, for posting on the Conference's website.

*Alternative channels of transmission*

55. The SC reaffirmed its clear understanding that the term "send" in Article 10(a) is to be understood as meaning "service" through postal channels.

56. The SC considered the increasing use of private courier services for the expeditious transmission of documents in a variety of business settings and heard reports that such couriers have been used to serve process under Article 10(a) of the Convention. In light of that, the SC concluded that for the purposes of Article 10(a) the use of a private courier was the equivalent of the postal channel.

57. The SC noted the further clarification submitted by the Japanese delegation on its position regarding Article 10(a):

> "Japan has not declared that it objects to the sending of judicial documents, by postal channels, directly to addressees in Japan. As the representative of Japan made clear at the Special Commission of April 1989 on the practical operation of the Service and Evidence Conventions, Japan does not consider that the use of postal channels for sending judicial documents to persons in Japan constitutes an infringement of its sovereign power.
> Nevertheless, as the representative also indicated, the absence of a formal objection does not imply that the sending of judicial documents by postal channels to addressees in Japan is always considered valid service in Japan. In fact, sending documents by such a method would not be deemed valid service in Japan in circumstances where the rights of the addressee were not respected."

58. The SC noted that the UK confirmed its position expressed at the Special Commission meeting of 1989, indicating its preference for the use of direct service through English solicitors on residents of England and Wales.

*Use of IT technology*

59. The SC stressed that the operation of the Convention was to be considered in light of a business environment in which use of modern technology was now all pervasive, and that the electronic transmission of judicial communications is a growing part of that environment. In this light, conclusions could be reached as follows:

60. The Convention does not on its terms prevent or prescribe the use of modern technologies to assist in further improving its operation.

61. The Convention does not on its terms deal with internal procedures but there is a link between domestic law systems and the functioning of the Convention.

62. It can be concluded, however, that the transmission of documents internationally for the purposes of the Convention can and should be undertaken by IT-Business methods including e-mail; this is already happening and the SC recommends that States party to the Convention explore all ways in which they can use modern technology for this purpose.

63. In this light, the SC identified a variety of steps for which the use of electronic means may be immediately explored: communication between a requesting party and a forwarding authority, communication between a forwarding authority and a Central Authority of a requested State, and retransmission of the certificate of execution by the designated authority.
64. The SC also recognised that in many domestic legal systems the relevant legal procedures and technological conditions did not allow for service by electronic means, although in certain systems the use of e-mail and fax was permitted in certain circumstances, particularly where approved by judicial authority in advance or agreed by the parties. Nevertheless, the SC recognised that given the pace of technological developments, existing problems might well be overcome so as to enable service by these methods to become more widely used. States party to the Convention are therefore encouraged to explore ways in which such innovations can be achieved.

*Translation requirements*

65. The SC recognised that no translation is required, under the Convention, for transmission under alternative channels provided by the Convention; the SC noted, however, that in isolated cases such translation requirements are imposed by a State's internal law.

66. The SC noted that the vast majority of States party do not require a translation for service by way of informal delivery (Art. 5(2)).

67. As to the translation requirement for service under Article 5(1), the SC also noted the importance of respecting the various requirements provided in the national laws of States party.

68. The SC invited the States party to make available to the Permanent Bureau all relevant information (incl. any declaration) regarding the extent of any translation requirement for execution of requests under Article 5. The SC also invited States party to provide information as to the consequences under their domestic law when acting as requesting State of a refusal of an addressee to accept service under the Convention.

*Scope of application*

69. As to the meaning of the terms "civil or commercial matters", the SC urged for a broad interpretation of these terms and reaffirmed the following conclusions adopted in 1989:

   a. The Commission considered it desirable that the words "civil or commercial matters" should be interpreted in an *autonomous* manner, without reference exclusively either to the law of the requesting State or to the law of the requested State, or to both laws cumulatively.
   b. In the "grey area" between private and public law, the historical evolution would suggest the possibility of a more *liberal interpretation* of these words. In particular, it was accepted that matters such as bankruptcy, insurance and employment might fall within the scope of this concept.

70. In addition, the SC took note of the fact that while in some States tax issues were considered as falling within the scope of the Convention, in others this was not the case.

71. The SC also noted that in some States party, the Convention had been applied in proceedings relating to the recovery of proceeds of crime.

72. Finally, the SC cautioned that the meaning of "civil and commercial" appearing in other instruments should not be relied on for interpretation without considering the object and purpose of such other instruments.

*Mandatory and/or exclusive character of the Convention*

73. Recalling the conclusions and recommendations of 1989, the SC confirmed the prevailing view that the Convention was of a non-mandatory, but exclusive character as described in more detail in the provisional version of the new edition of the Practical Handbook, without prejudice to international law on the interpretation of treaties.

74. The SC recalled the purpose and fundamental importance of Article 15(2), which is designed to ensure actual notice to a defender in sufficient time to organise his or her defence.

*Double-date*

75. The SC considered and rejected a proposal that States party adopt a recommendation to implement a system of double-date, according to which the interests of the plaintiff (*e.g.*, limitation periods) and those of the defendant (*e.g.*, time to file his or her defence) have to be protected by assigning different dates. The SC took note that many legal systems have effective means to protect the interests of the plaintiff without having to rely on the actual date of service.

*Exclusion of the application of the Convention between the parties*

76. The SC took note of the practice reported in one State party to the Convention whereby contractual arrangements were entered into and upheld in the courts of that State which excluded the application of the Convention for service of documents as regards parties to such contracts, including parties outside that State.

77. Several experts commented to the effect that this would not be allowed in their States and be considered as contrary to their internal law. Some experts indicated, however, that a judgment rendered pursuant to service in accordance with any such contractual arrangements would not necessarily be refused execution.

*Exequatur*

78. The SC recalled that the Convention does not address the issue of recognition and enforcement of judgments. In addition, experts reaffirmed the need for the Convention to operate so as to sustain the procedural rights of the defender. In particular, the SC recalled again the principle that the defender should be given actual notice in sufficient time to allow him or her to organise a defence. This was significant notably where in the State addressed consideration was given to the validity of service.

*Reservations and reciprocity*

79. The SC noted that States party do not assert reciprocity against other States party that have made declarations under Articles 8 and 10.

*Regional Economic Integration Organisations (REIOs)*

80. The SC accepted that, at this point, there was no need to consider the application of the Convention in relation to REIOs.

*Future Work: Form and Handbook*

81. The SC accepted that future work on the forms be undertaken by the PB in conjunction with a representative group of experts to be designated by the Secretary General, in particular with a view to assessing the necessity of amending the forms and to develop guidelines for completing those forms.

82. The SC welcomed the draft version of the new edition of the Practical Handbook prepared by the Permanent Bureau. The SC invited the Permanent Bureau to finalise the new edition, taking into account the conclusions and recommendations adopted by the SC and emphasised the desirability of maintaining and enhancing the practical utility of the Handbook in conjunction with the information provided on the ConferenceÕs website.

The Hague / 20 November 2003

**Status table**

**Convention of 15 November 1965 on the Service Abroad of Judicial and Extrajudicial Documents in Civil or Commercial Matters**

Entry into force: 10-II-1969

1) S = Signature
2) R/A = Ratification or Accession
3) Type = R: Ratification;
A: Accession;
A*: Accession giving rise to an acceptance procedure; click on A* for details of acceptances of the accession;
C: Continuation;
Su: Succession;
D: Denunciation;
4) EIF = Entry into force
5) Ext = Extensions of application
6) Auth = Designation of Authorities
7) Res/D/N = Reservations, declarations or notifications

**Member States of the Organisation (click here for the non-Member States)**

| States | S [1] | R/A [2] | Type [3] | EIF [4] | Ext [5] | Auth [6] | Res/D/N [7] |
|---|---|---|---|---|---|---|---|
| Argentina | | 2-II-2001 | A | 1-XII-2001 | | 1 | Res, D |
| Belarus | | 6-VI-1997 | A | 1-II-1998 | | 1 | |
| Belgium | 21-I-1966 | 19-XI-1970 | R | 18-I-1971 | | 2 | D |
| Bulgaria | | 23-XI-1999 | A | 1-VIII-2000 | | 3 | D |
| Canada | | 26-IX-1988 | A | 1-V-1989 | | 4 | D |
| China (People's Republic of) | | 6-V-1991 | A | 1-I-1992 | | 8 | D, N |
| Cyprus | | 26-X-1982 | A | 1-VI-1983 | | 4 | D |
| Czech Republic | | 23-IX-1981 | Su | 1-VI-1982 | | 2 | Res, D |
| Denmark | 7-I-1969 | 2-VIII-1969 | R | 1-X-1969 | | 3 | D |
| Egypt | 1-III-1966 | 12-XII-1968 | R | 10-II-1969 | | 1 | Res |
| Estonia | | 2-II-1996 | A | 1-X-1996 | | 1 | D |
| Finland | 15-XI-1965 | 11-IX-1969 | R | 10-XI-1969 | | 2 | |
| France | 12-I-1967 | 3-VII-1972 | R | 1-IX-1972 | | 3 | D |
| Germany | 15-XI-1965 | 27-IV-1979 | R | 26-VI-1979 | | 3 | D |
| Greece | 20-VII-1983 | 20-VII-1983 | R | 18-IX-1983 | | 1 | D |
| Hungary | | 13-VII-2004 | A | 1-IV-2005 | | | D |
| Ireland | 20-X-1989 | 5-IV-1994 | R | 4-VI-1994 | | 2 | Res, D |
| Israel | 25-XI-1965 | 14-VIII-1972 | R | 13-X-1972 | | 2 | Res, D |
| Italy | 25-I-1979 | 25-XI-1981 | R | 24-I-1982 | | 3 | D |
| Japan | 12-III-1970 | 28-V-1970 | R | 27-VII-1970 | | 3 | D |
| Latvia | | 28-III-1995 | A | 1-XI-1995 | | 1 | |
| Lithuania | | 2-VIII-2000 | A | 1-VI-2001 | | 1 | Res, D |
| Luxembourg | 27-X-1971 | 9-VII-1975 | R | 7-IX-1975 | | 1 | Res, D |
| Mexico | | 2-XI-1999 | A | 1-VI-2000 | | 1 | D |
| Netherlands | 15-XI-1965 | 3-XI-1975 | R | 2-I-1976 | 1 | 4 | D |
| Norway | 15-X-1968 | 2-VIII-1969 | R | 1-X-1969 | | 3 | Res, D |
| Poland | | 13-II-1996 | A | 1-IX-1996 | | 4 | Res |
| Portugal | 5-VII-1971 | 27-XII-1973 | R | 25-II-1974 | | 2 | D |
| Republic of Korea | | 13-I-2000 | A | 1-VIII-2000 | | 2 | Res, D |
| Romania | | 21-VIII-2003 | A | 1-IV-2004 | | 2 | D |
| Russian Federation | | 1-V-2001 | A | 1-XII-2001 | | 2 | Res, D |
| Slovak Republic | | 23-IX-1981 | Su | 1-VI-1982 | | 3 | D |

| | | | | | | | |
|---|---|---|---|---|---|---|---|
| Slovenia | | 18-IX-2000 | A | 1-VI-2001 | | 1 | |
| Spain | 21-X-1976 | 4-VI-1987 | R | 3-VIII-1987 | | 1 | D |
| Sri Lanka | | 31-VIII-2000 | A | 1-VI-2001 | | 3 | D |
| Sweden | 4-II-1969 | 2-VIII-1969 | R | 1-X-1969 | | 2 | D |
| Switzerland | 21-V-1985 | 2-XI-1994 | R | 1-I-1995 | | 3 | Res, D |
| Turkey | 11-VI-1968 | 28-II-1972 | R | 28-IV-1972 | | 3 | Res, D |
| Ukraine | | 1-II-2001 | A | 1-XII-2001 | | 3 | Res, D |
| United Kingdom of Great Britain and Northern Ireland | 10-XII-1965 | 17-XI-1967 | R | 10-II-1969 | 14 | 4 | D |
| United States of America | 15-XI-1965 | 24-VIII-1967 | R | 10-II-1969 | 1 | 1 | D |
| Venezuela | | 29-X-1993 | A | 1-VII-1994 | | 1 | Res, D |

**Non-Member States of the Organisation (click here for the Member States)**

| States | S [1] | R/A [2] | Type [3] | EIF [4] | Ext [5] | Auth [6] | Res/D/N [7] |
|---|---|---|---|---|---|---|---|
| Antigua and Barbuda | | | Su | 1-XI-1981 | | 1 | |
| Bahamas | | 17-VI-1997 | A | 1-II-1998 | | 1 | |
| Barbados | | 10-II-1969 | A | 1-X-1969 | | 1 | |
| Botswana | | 10-II-1969 | A | 1-IX-1969 | | 3 | D |
| Kuwait | | 8-V-2002 | A | 1-XII-2002 | | 1 | |
| Malawi | | 24-IV-1972 | A | 1-XII-1972 | | 1 | |
| Pakistan | | 7-XII-1988 | A | 1-VIII-1989 | | 3 | D |
| Saint Vincent and the Grenadines | | | Su | 27-X-1979 | | 1 | |
| San Marino | | 15-IV-2002 | A | 1-XI-2002 | | 3 | D |
| Seychelles | | 18-XI-1980 | A | 1-VII-1981 | | 1 | D |

FORMS (REQUEST AND CERTIFICATE)
SUMMARY OF THE DOCUMENT TO BE SERVED
(annexes provided for Articles 3, 5, 6 and 7)
ANNEX TO THE CONVENTION
*Forms*
REQUEST FOR SERVICE ABROAD OF JUDICIAL OR EXTRAJUDICIAL DOCUMENTS
Convention on the Service Abroad of Judicial and Extrajudicial Documents in Civil or Commercial Matters,
signed at The Hague, the 15th of November 1965.
Identity and address
of the applicant
Address of receiving
authority
The undersigned applicant has the honour to transmit - in duplicate - the documents listed below and, in
conformity with Article 5 of the above-mentioned Convention, requests prompt service of one copy thereof on the
addressee, *i.e*,
(identity and address) ..........................................................................................
*a)* in accordance with the provisions of sub-paragraph *(a)* of the first paragraph of Article 5 of the Convention*.
*b)* in accordance with the following particular method (sub-paragraph *(b)* of the first paragraph of Article 5)*:
...........................................................................
*c)* by delivery to the addressee, if he accepts it voluntarily (second paragraph of Article 5)*.
The authority is requested to return or to have returned to the applicant a copy of the documents - and of the
annexes* - with a certificate as provided on the reverse side.
*List of documents*
........................................................................
........................................................................
........................................................................
........................................................................
........................................................................

.......................................................................
Done at . . . . . . . . . . . , the . . . . . . . .
Signature and/or stamp.
* Delete if inappropriate.
*Reverse of the request*
CERTIFICATE
The undersigned authority has the honour to certify, in conformity with Article 6 of the Convention,
1) that the document has been served*
• the (date)
.............................................
• at (place, street, number)
.............................................
.............................................
- in one of the following methods authorised by Article 5:
*a)* in accordance with the provisions of sub-paragraph *(a)* of the first paragraph of Article 5 of the Convention*.
*b)* in accordance with the following particular method*:
.........................................................................................
....................................................................................
*c)* by delivery to the addressee, who accepted it voluntarily* .
The documents referred to in the request have been delivered to:
• (identity and description of person)
• ..........................................................
.............................................................
• relationship to the addressee (family, business or other):
• ..............................................................................
.................................................................................
.................................................................................
2) that the document has not been served, by reason of the following facts*:
..............................................................................
..............................................................................
..............................................................................
In conformity with the second paragraph of Article 12 of the Convention, the applicant is requested to pay or
reimburse the expenses detailed in the attached statement*.
*Annexes*
Documents returned: ..............................................................................
..............................................................................
..............................................................................
In appropriate cases, documents establishing the service:
..............................................................................
..............................................................................
Done at . . . . . . . . . . . , the . . . . . . . .
Signature and/or stamp.
* Delete if inappropriate.

SUMMARY OF THE DOCUMENT TO BE SERVED
Convention on the Service Abroad of Judicial and Extrajudicial Documents in Civil or Commercial Matters,
signed at The Hague, the 15th of November 1965.
(Article 5, fourth paragraph)
Name and address of the requesting authority:
.........................................................................
.........................................................................
Particulars of the parties*:
.........................................................................
.........................................................................
JUDICIAL DOCUMENT**
Nature and purpose of the document:
.........................................................................
.........................................................................
Nature and purpose of the proceedings and, where appropriate, the amount in dispute:
.........................................................................
.........................................................................
Date and place for entering appearance**:
.........................................................................
.........................................................................
Court which has given judgment**:
.........................................................................
.........................................................................
Date of judgment**:
.........................................................................
Time-limits stated in the document**:
.........................................................................
.........................................................................
EXTRAJUDICIAL DOCUMENT**
Nature and purpose of the document:
.........................................................................
.........................................................................
Time-limits stated in the document**:
.........................................................................
.........................................................................
* If appropriate, identity and address of the person interested in the transmission of the document.
** Delete if inappropriate.

CONVENTION ON THE CHOICE OF COURT

*(Concluded November 25, 1965)*

The States signatory to the present Convention,
Desiring to establish common provisions on the validity and effects of agreements on the choice of court,
Have resolved to conclude a Convention to this effect and have agreed upon the following provisions:

*Article 1*
In the matters to which this Convention applies and subject to the conditions which it prescribes, parties may by an agreement on the choice of court designate, for the purpose of deciding disputes which have arisen or may arise between them in connection with a specific legal relationship, either –
(1) the courts of one of the Contracting States, the particular competent court being then determined (if at all) by the internal legal system or systems of that State, or
(2) a court expressly named of one of the Contracting States, provided always that this court is competent according to the internal legal system or systems of that State.

*Article 2*
This Convention shall apply to agreements on the choice of court concluded in civil or commercial matters in situations having an international character.
It shall not apply to agreements on the choice of court concluded in the following matters –
(1) the status or capacity of persons or questions of family law including the personal or financial rights or obligations between parents and children or between spouses;
(2) maintenance obligations not included in sub-paragraph (1);
(3) questions of succession;
(4) questions of bankruptcy, compositions or analogous proceedings, including decisions which may result therefrom and which relate to the validity of the acts of the debtor;
(5) rights in immovable property.

*Article 3*
This Convention shall apply whatever the nationality of the parties.

*Article 4*
For the purpose of this Convention the agreement on the choice of court shall have been validly made if it is the result of the acceptance by one party of a written proposal by the other party expressly designating the chosen court or courts.
The existence of such an agreement shall not be presumed from the mere failure of a party to appear in an action brought against him in the chosen court.
The agreement on the choice of court shall be void or voidable if it has been obtained by an abuse of economic power or other unfair means.

*Article 5*
Unless the parties have otherwise agreed only the chosen court or courts shall have jurisdiction.
The chosen court shall be free to decline jurisdiction if it has proof that a court of another Contracting State could avail itself of the provisions of Article 6(2).

*Article 6*
Every court other than the chosen court or courts shall decline jurisdiction except –
(1) where the choice of court made by the parties is not exclusive,
(2) where under the internal law of the State of the excluded court, the parties were unable, because of the subject-matter, to agree to exclude the jurisdiction of the courts of that State,
(3) where the agreement on the choice of court is void or voidable in the sense of Article 4,
(4) for the purpose of provisional or protective measures.

*Article 7*
Where, in their agreement, the parties have designated a court or the courts of a Contracting State without excluding the jurisdiction of other courts, proceedings already pending in any court thus having jurisdiction and which may result in a decision capable of being recognised in the State where the defence is pleaded, shall constitute the basis for the defence of *lis pendens*.

*Article 8*
Decisions given by a chosen court in the sense of this Convention in one of the Contracting States shall be recognised and enforced in the other Contracting States in accordance with the rules for the recognition and enforcement of foreign judgments in force in those States.

*Article 9*
Where the conditions for recognition and enforcement of a decision rendered on the basis of an agreement on the choice of court are not fulfilled in another Contracting State, the agreement shall not preclude any party from bringing a new action in the courts of that State.

*Article 10*
Settlements made in the chosen court in the course of proceedings there pending which are enforceable in the State of that court shall be treated in the same manner as decisions made by that court.

*Article 11*
This Convention shall not derogate from Conventions containing provisions on the matters governed by this Convention to which the Contracting States are, or shall become, Parties.

*Article 12*
Any Contracting State may reserve the right not to recognise agreements on the choice of court concluded between persons who, at the time of the conclusion of such agreements, were its nationals and had their habitual residence in its territory.

*Article 13*
Any Contracting State may make a reservation according to the terms of which it will treat as an internal matter the juridical relations established in its territory between, on the one hand, physical or juridical persons who are there and, on the other hand, establishments registered on local registers, even if such establishments are branches, agencies or other representatives of foreign firms in the territory in question.

*Article 14*
Any Contracting State may make a reservation according to the terms of which it may extend its exclusive jurisdiction to the juridical relations established in its territory between, on the one hand, physical or juridical persons who are there and on the other hand establishments registered on local registers, even if such establishments are branches, agencies or other representatives of foreign firms in the territory in question.

*Article 15*

Any Contracting State may reserve the right not to recognise agreements on the choice of court if the dispute has no connection with the chosen court, or if, in the circumstances, it would be seriously inconvenient for the matter to be dealt with by the chosen court.

*Article 16*

The present Convention shall be open for signature by the States represented at the Tenth Session of the Hague Conference on Private International Law.

It shall be ratified, and the instruments of ratification shall be deposited with the Ministry of Foreign Affairs of the Netherlands.

*Article 17*

The present Convention shall enter into force on the sixtieth day after the deposit of the third instrument of ratification referred to in the second paragraph of Article 16.

The Convention shall enter into force for each signatory State which ratifies subsequently on the sixtieth day after the deposit of its instrument of ratification.

*Article 18*

Any State not represented at the Tenth Session of the Hague Conference on Private International Law may accede to the present Convention after it has entered into force in accordance with the first paragraph of Article 17. The instruments of accession shall be deposited with the Ministry of Foreign Affairs of the Netherlands.

The Convention shall enter into force for such a State in the absence of any objection from a State, which has ratified the Convention before such deposit, notified to the Ministry of Foreign Affairs of the Netherlands within a period of six months after the date on which the said Ministry has notified it of such accession.

In the absence of any such objection, the Convention shall enter into force for the acceding State on the first day of the month following the expiration of the last of the periods referred to in the preceding paragraph.

*Article 19*

Any State may, at the time of signature, ratification or accession, declare that the present Convention shall extend to all the territories for the international relations of which it is responsible, or to one or more of them. Such a declaration shall take effect on the date of entry into force of the Convention for the State concerned.

At any time thereafter, such extensions shall be notified to the Ministry of Foreign Affairs of the Netherlands.

The Convention shall enter into force for the territories mentioned in such an extension on the sixtieth day after the notification referred to in the preceding paragraph.

*Article 20*

Any State may, not later than the moment of its ratification or accession, make one or more of the reservations mentioned in Articles 12, 13, 14 and 15 of the present Convention. No other reservation shall be permitted.

Each Contracting State may also, when notifying an extension of the Convention in accordance with Article 19, make one or more of the said reservations, with its effect limited to all or some of the territories mentioned in the extension.

Each Contracting State may at any time withdraw a reservation it has made. Such a withdrawal shall be notified to the Ministry of Foreign Affairs of the Netherlands.

Such a reservation shall cease to have effect on the sixtieth day after the notification referred to in the preceding paragraph.

*Article 21*

The present Convention shall remain in force for five years from the date of its entry into force in accordance with the first paragraph of Article 17, even for States which have ratified it or acceded to it subsequently.

If there has been no denunciation, it shall be renewed tacitly every five years.

Any denunciation shall be notified to the Ministry of Foreign Affairs of the Netherlands at least six months before the end of the five year period.
It may be limited to certain of the territories to which the Convention applies.
The denunciation shall have effect only as regards the State which has notified it. The Convention shall remain in force for the other Contracting States.

*Article 22*
The Ministry of Foreign Affairs of the Netherlands shall give notice to the States referred to in Article 16, and to the States which have acceded in accordance with Article 18, of the following –
*a)* the signatures and ratifications referred to in Article 16;
*b)* the date on which the present Convention enters into force in accordance with the first paragraph of Article 17;
*c)* the accessions referred to in Article 18 and the dates on which they take effect;
*d)* the extensions referred to in Article 19 and the dates on which they take effect;
*e)* the reservations and withdrawals referred to in Article 20;
*f)* the denunciations referred to in the third paragraph of Article 21.

In witness whereof the undersigned, being duly authorised thereto, have signed the present Convention.
Done at The Hague, on the 25th day of November, 1965, in the English and French languages, both texts being equally authentic, in a single copy which shall be deposited in the archives of the Government of the Netherlands, and of which a certified copy shall be sent, through the diplomatic channel, to each of the States represented at the Tenth Session of the Hague Conference on Private International Law.

# CONVENTION ON THE RECOGNITION AND ENFORCEMENT OF FOREIGN JUDGMENTS IN CIVIL AND COMMERCIAL MATTERS

*(Concluded 1 February 1971)*
*(Entered into force 20 August 1979)*

The States signatory to the present Convention,
Desiring to establish common provisions on mutual recognition and enforcement of judicial decisions rendered in their respective countries,
Have resolved to conclude a Convention to this effect and have agreed on the following provisions:

## CHAPTER I – SCOPE OF THE CONVENTION

*Article 1*

This Convention shall apply to decisions rendered in civil or commercial matters by the courts of Contracting States.
It shall not apply to decisions the main object of which is to determine –
(1) the status or capacity of persons or questions of family law, including personal or financial rights and obligations between parents and children or between spouses;
(2) the existence or constitution of legal persons or the powers of their officers;
(3) maintenance obligations, so far as not included in sub-paragraph (1) of this Article;
(4) questions of succession;
(5) questions of bankruptcy, compositions or analogous proceedings, including decisions which may result therefrom and which relate to the validity of the acts of the debtor;
(6) questions of social security;
(7) questions relating to damage or injury in nuclear matters.
This Convention does not apply to decisions for the payment of any customs duty, tax or penalty.

*Article 2*

This Convention shall apply to all decisions given by the courts of a Contracting State, irrespective of the name given by that State to the proceedings which gave rise to the decision or of the name given to the decision itself such as judgment, order or writ of execution.
However, it shall apply neither to decisions which order provisional or protective measures nor to decisions rendered by administrative tribunals.

*Article 3*

This Convention shall apply irrespective of the nationality of the parties.

## CHAPTER II – CONDITIONS OF RECOGNITION AND ENFORCEMENT

*Article 4*

A decision rendered in one of the Contracting States shall be entitled to recognition and enforcement in another Contracting State under the terms of this Convention –
(1) if the decision was given by a court considered to have jurisdiction within the meaning of this Convention, and
(2) if it is no longer subject to ordinary forms of review in the State of origin.
In addition, to be enforceable in the State addressed, a decision must be enforceable in the State of origin.

*Article 5*

Recognition or enforcement of a decision may nevertheless be refused in any of the following cases –

(1) if recognition or enforcement of the decision is manifestly incompatible with the public policy of the State addressed or if the decision resulted from proceedings incompatible with the requirements of due process of law or if, in the circumstances, either party had no adequate opportunity fairly to present his case;
(2) if the decision was obtained by fraud in the procedural sense;
(3) if proceedings between the same parties, based on the same facts and having the same purpose —
*a)* are pending before a court of the State addressed and those proceedings were the first to be instituted, or
*b)* have resulted in a decision by a court of the State addressed, or
*c)* have resulted in a decision by a court of another State which would be entitled to recognition and enforcement under the law of the State addressed.

*Article 6*
Without prejudice to the provisions of Article 5, a decision rendered by default shall neither be recognized nor enforced unless the defaulting party received notice of the institution of the proceedings in accordance with the law of the State of origin in sufficient time to enable him to defend the proceedings.

*Article 7*
Recognition or enforcement may not be refused for the sole reason that the court of the State of origin has applied a law other than that which would have been applicable according to the rules of private international law of the State addressed.
Nevertheless, recognition or enforcement may be refused if, to reach its decision, the court of the State of origin had to decide a question relating either to the status or the capacity of a party or to his rights in other matters excluded from this Convention by sub-paragraphs (1)-(4) of the second paragraph of Article 1, and has reached a result different from that which would have followed from the application to that question of the rules of private international law of the State addressed.

*Article 8*
Without prejudice to such review as is required by the terms of the preceding Articles, there shall be no review of the merits of the decision rendered by the court of origin.

*Article 9*
In questions relating to the jurisdiction of the court of the State of origin, the authority addressed shall be bound by the findings of fact on which that court based its jurisdiction, unless the decision was rendered by default.

*Article 10*
The court of the State of origin shall be considered to have jurisdiction for the purposes of this Convention —
(1) if the defendant had, at the time when the proceedings were instituted, his habitual residence in the State of origin, or, if the defendant is not a natural person, its seat, its place of incorporation or its principal place of business in that State;
(2) if the defendant had, in the State of origin, at the time when the proceedings were instituted, a commercial, industrial or other business establishment, or a branch office, and was cited there in proceedings arising from business transacted by such establishment or branch office;
(3) if the action had as its object the determination of an issue relating to immovable property situated in the State of origin;
(4) in the case of injuries to the person or damage to tangible property, if the facts which occasioned the damage occurred in the territory of the State of origin, and if the author of the injury or damage was present in that territory at the time when those facts occurred;
(5) if, by a written agreement or by an oral agreement confirmed in writing within a reasonable time, the parties agreed to submit to the jurisdiction of the court of origin disputes which have arisen or which may arise in respect of a specific legal relationship, unless the law of the State addressed would not permit such an agreement because of the subject-matter of the dispute;

of the subject-matter of the dispute;
(6) if the defendant has argued the merits without challenging the jurisdiction of the court or making reservations thereon; nevertheless such jurisdiction shall not be recognized if the defendant has argued the merits in order to resist the seizure of property or to obtain its release, or if the recognition of this jurisdiction would be contrary to the law of the State addressed because of the subject-matter of the dispute;
(7) if the person against whom recognition or enforcement is sought was the plaintiff in the proceedings in the court of origin and was unsuccessful in those proceedings, unless the recognition of this jurisdiction would be contrary to the law of the State addressed because of the subject-matter of the dispute.

*Article 11*
The court of the State of origin shall be considered to have jurisdiction for the purposes of this Convention to try a counterclaim–
(1) if that court would have had jurisdiction to try the action as a principal claim under sub-paragraphs (1)-(6) of Article 10, or
(2) if that court had jurisdiction under Article 10 to try the principal claim and if the counterclaim arose out of the contract or out of the facts on which the principal claim was based.

*Article 12*
The jurisdiction of the court of the State of origin need not be recognized by the authority addressed in the following cases –
(1) if the law of the State addressed confers upon its courts exclusive jurisdiction, either by reason of the subject-matter of the action or by virtue of an agreement between the parties as to the determination of the claim which gave rise to the foreign decision;
(2) if the law of the State addressed recognizes a different exclusive jurisdiction by reason of the subject-matter of the action, or if the authority addressed considers itself bound to recognize such an exclusive jurisdiction by reason of an agreement between the parties;
(3) if the authority addressed considers itself bound to recognize an agreement by which exclusive jurisdiction is conferred upon arbitrators.

CHAPTER III – RECOGNITION AND ENFORCEMENT PROCEDURES
*Article 13*
The party seeking recognition or applying for enforcement shall furnish –
(1) a complete and authenticated copy of the decision;
(2) if the decision was rendered by default, the originals or certified true copies of the documents required to establish that the summons was duly served on the defaulting party;
(3) all documents required to establish that the decision fulfills the conditions of sub-paragraph (2) of the first paragraph of Article 4, and, where appropriate, of the second paragraph of Article 4;
(4) unless the authority addressed otherwise requires, translations of the documents referred to above, certified as correct either by a diplomatic or consular agent or by a sworn translator or by any other person so authorized in either State.
If the terms of the decision do not permit the authority addressed to verify whether the conditions of this Convention have been complied with, that authority may require the production of any other necessary documents.
No legalisation or other like formality may be required.

*Article 14*
The procedure for the recognition or enforcement of foreign judgments is governed by the law of the State addressed so far as this Convention does not provide otherwise.
If the decision contains provisions which can be dissociated, any one or more of these may be separately

recognized or enforced.

*Article 15*
Recognition or enforcement of an award of judicial costs or expenses may be accorded by virtue of this Convention only if this Convention is applicable to the decision on the merits.
This Convention shall apply to decisions relating to judicial costs or expenses even if such decisions do not proceed from a court, provided that they derive from a decision which may be recognized or enforced under this Convention and that the decision relating to costs or expenses could have been subject to judicial review.

*Article 16*
A judgment for costs or expenses given in connection with the granting or refusal of recognition or enforcement of a decision may be enforced under this Convention only if the applicant in the proceedings for recognition or enforcement relied on this Convention.

*Article 17*
No security, bond or deposit, however termed under the law of the State addressed, shall be required by reason of the nationality or domicile of the applicant to guarantee the payment of judicial costs or expenses if the applicant, being a natural person, has his habitual residence in or, not being a natural person, has a place of business in a State which has concluded with the State addressed a Supplementary Agreement in accordance with Article 21.

*Article 18*
A party granted legal aid in the State of origin shall be extended such aid in accordance with the law of the State addressed in any proceedings for the recognition or for the enforcement of a foreign decision.

*Article 19*
Settlements made in court in the course of a pending proceeding which may be enforced in the State of origin shall be enforceable in the State addressed under the same conditions as decisions falling within this Convention, so far as those conditions apply to settlements.

CHAPTER IV – CONCURRENT ACTIONS
*Article 20*
If two States have concluded a Supplementary Agreement pursuant to Article 21, the judicial authorities of either State may dismiss an action brought before them or may stay such an action when other proceedings between the same parties, based on the same facts and having the same purpose, are pending in a court of another State and these proceedings may result in a decision which the authorities of the State in which the first mentioned action was brought would be bound to recognize under the terms of this Convention.
The authorities of these States may nevertheless order provisional or protective measures regardless of proceedings elsewhere.

CHAPTER V – SUPPLEMENTARY AGREEMENTS
*Article 21*
Decisions rendered in a Contracting State shall not be recognized or enforced in another Contracting State in accordance with the provisions of the preceding Articles unless the two States, being Parties to this Convention, have concluded a Supplementary Agreement to this effect.

*Article 22*
This Convention shall not apply to decisions rendered before the entry into force of the Supplementary Agreement provided for in Article 21 unless that Agreement otherwise provides.
The Supplementary Agreement shall continue to be applicable to decisions in respect of which recognition or

enforcement proceedings have been instituted before any denunciation of that Agreement takes effect.

*Article 23*

In the Supplementary Agreements referred to in Article 21 the Contracting States may agree –

(1) to clarify the meaning of the expression "civil and commercial matters", to determine the courts whose decisions shall be recognized and enforced under this Convention, to define the expression "social security" and to define the expression "habitual residence";

(2) to clarify the meaning of the term "law" in States with more than one legal system;

(3) to include within the scope of this Convention questions relating to damage or injury in nuclear matters;

(4) to apply this Convention to decisions ordering provisional or protective measures;

(5) not to apply this Convention to decisions rendered in the course of criminal proceedings;

(6) to specify the cases under which a decision is no longer subject to ordinary forms of review;

(7) to recognize and enforce decisions upon which enforcement could be obtained in the State of origin even if such decisions are still subject to ordinary forms of review and in such a case to define the conditions under which a stay of proceedings for recognition or enforcement is possible;

(8) not to apply Article 6 if the decision rendered by default was notified to the defaulting party and the latter had the opportunity to lodge a timely appeal against such a decision;

(8 *bis*) that the Authority addressed shall not be bound by the findings of fact on which the court of the State of origin based its jurisdiction;

(9) to consider the courts of the State in which the defendant has his "domicile" as having jurisdiction under Article 10:

(10) that the court of origin shall be considered as having jurisdiction under the terms of this Convention in cases where its jurisdiction is admitted by another Convention in force between the State of origin and the State addressed if that other Convention contains no special rules relating to the recognition or enforcement of foreign judgments;

(11) that the court of origin shall be considered as having jurisdiction under the terms of this Convention either when its jurisdiction is admitted by the law of the State addressed relating to the recognition or enforcement of foreign judgments, or on grounds additional to those in Article 10;

(12) to define, for the purposes of the application of Article 12, the bases of jurisdiction which are exclusive by reason of the subject-matter of the action;

(13) to exclude, in cases where jurisdiction is based on an agreement between the parties, the application of sub-paragraph (1) of Article 12 as well as to exclude that of sub-paragraph (3) of Article 12;

(14) to regulate the procedure for obtaining recognition or enforcement;

(15) to regulate the enforcement of judgments other than those which order the payment of a sum of money;

(16) that the enforcement of a foreign judgment may be refused when a specified period has elapsed from its date;

(17) to fix the rate of interest payable from the date of the judgment in the State of origin;

(18) to adapt to the requirements of their legal systems the list of documents required by Article 13, but with the sole object of enabling the authority addressed to verify whether the conditions of this Convention have been fulfilled;

(19) to subject the documents referred to in Article 13 to legalisation or to a similar formality;

(20) to depart from the provisions of Article 17 and to depart from the provisions of Article 18;

(21) to make the provisions of the first paragraph of Article 20 obligatory;

(22) to include within the scope of this Convention "actes authentiques", including documents upon which immediate enforcement can be obtained, and to specify those documents.

CHAPTER VI – FINAL CLAUSES

*Article 24*

This Convention shall not affect other Conventions relating to the recognition and enforcement of judgments to which the Contracting States are already Parties so long as those States have not concluded a Supplementary

Agreement under the terms of Article 21.
Unless it is otherwise agreed, the provisions of a Supplementary Agreement concluded under Article 21 shall prevail over the terms of any prior Conventions in force between the Parties relating to the recognition and enforcement of judgments to the extent that their terms are mutually inconsistent.

*Article 25*
Whether or not they have concluded a Supplementary Agreement under Article 21, the Contracting States shall not conclude between themselves other Conventions relating to the recognition and enforcement of judgments within the scope of this Convention unless they consider it necessary, in particular, because of economic ties or of particular aspects of their legal systems.

*Article 26*
Notwithstanding the provisions of Articles 24 and 25, this Convention and the Supplementary Agreements made under Article 21 shall not prevail over Conventions to which the Contracting States are or may become Parties in special fields and which contain provisions for the recognition and enforcement of judgments.

*Article 27*
This Convention shall be open for signature by the States represented at the Tenth Session of the Hague Conference on Private International Law and Cyprus, Iceland and Malta.
It shall be ratified and the instruments of ratification shall be deposited with the Ministry of Foreign Affairs of the Netherlands.

*Article 28*
This Convention shall enter into force on the sixtieth day after the deposit of the second instrument of ratification.
This Convention shall enter into force for each State which ratifies it subsequently on the sixtieth day after the deposit of its instrument of ratification.

*Article 29*
Any State not falling within the provisions of the first paragraph of Article 27 may accede to this Convention after it has entered into force in accordance with the first paragraph of Article 28. The instrument of accession shall be deposited with the Ministry of Foreign Affairs of the Netherlands.
This Convention shall enter into force for such a State in the absence of any objection from a State which has ratified this Convention before such deposit, notified to the Ministry of Foreign Affairs of the Netherlands within a period of six months after the date on which the said Ministry has notified it of such accession.
In the absence of any such objection, this Convention shall enter into force for the acceding State on the first day of the month following the expiration of the last of the periods referred to in the preceding paragraph.

*Article 30*
Any State may, at the time of signature, ratification or accession, declare that this Convention shall extend to all the territories for the international relations of which it is responsible, or to one or more of them. Such a declaration shall take effect on the date of entry into force of this Convention for the State concerned.
At any time thereafter, such extensions shall be notified to the Ministry of Foreign Affairs of the Netherlands.
This Convention shall enter into force for the territories mentioned in such an extension on the sixtieth day after the notification referred to in the preceding paragraph.
The Parties to a Supplementary Agreement concluded under Article 21 shall determine its territorial application.

*Article 31*
This Convention shall have a duration of five years from the date on which it enters into force under the first paragraph of Article 28, even in its application to States which have subsequently ratified or acceded to it.

In the absence of any denunciation, this Convention shall be renewed tacitly every five years.
Any denunciation shall be notified to the Ministry of Foreign Affairs of the Netherlands at least six months before the end of the five year period.
Such denunciation may be limited to any one of the territories to which this Convention applies.
Such denunciation shall affect only the notifying State. This Convention shall remain in force for the other Contracting States.

*Article 32*
Each Supplementary Agreement concluded under Article 21 shall take effect from the date specified in such Agreement; a certified copy and, if necessary, a translation into French or English shall be communicated to the Ministry of Foreign Affairs of the Netherlands.
Any Contracting State may, without denouncing this Convention, denounce a Supplementary Agreement either under any provision for denunciation in such Agreement or, if such Agreement contains no such provision, by giving six months' notice to the other State. Any State denouncing a Supplementary Agreement shall so inform the Ministry of Foreign Affairs of the Netherlands.
Notwithstanding the denunciation of this Convention, it shall nevertheless continue to have effect between the denouncing State and any other State with which the former has concluded a Supplementary Agreement under Article 21, unless such Agreement provides otherwise.

*Article 33*
The Ministry of Foreign Affairs of the Netherlands shall give notice to the States referred to in Article 27, and to the States which have acceded in accordance with Article 29, of the following –
*a)* the signatures and ratifications referred to in Article 27;
*b)* the date on which the present Convention enters into force in accordance with the first paragraph of Article 28;
*c)* the accessions referred to in Article 29 and the dates on which they take effect;
*d)* the extensions referred to in Article 30 and the dates on which they take effect;
*e)* a translation or a copy of the text in English or French of Supplementary Agreements concluded under Article 21;
*f)* the denunciations referred to in the third paragraph of Article 31 and the second paragraph of Article 32.

In witness whereof the undersigned, being duly authorised thereto, have signed this Convention.
Done at The Hague, on the first day of February, 1971, in the English and French languages, both texts being equally authentic, in a single copy which shall be deposited in the archives of the Government of the Netherlands, and of which a certified copy shall be sent, through the diplomatic channel, to each of the States represented at the Tenth Session of the Hague Conference on Private International Law, and to Cyprus, Iceland and Malta.

# CONVENTION ON THE TAKING OF EVIDENCE ABROAD IN CIVIL OR COMMERCIAL MATTERS

*(Concluded 18 March 1970)*
*(Entered into force 7 October 1972)*

The States signatory to the present Convention,
Desiring to facilitate the transmission and execution of Letters of Request and to further the accommodation of the different methods which they use for this purpose,
Desiring to improve mutual judicial co-operation in civil or commercial matters,
Have resolved to conclude a Convention to this effect and have agreed upon the following provisions:

## CHAPTER I — LETTERS OF REQUEST

*Article 1*

In civil or commercial matters a judicial authority of a Contracting State may, in accordance with the provisions of the law of that State, request the competent authority of another Contracting State, by means of a Letter of Request, to obtain evidence, or to perform some other judicial act.
A Letter shall not be used to obtain evidence which is not intended for use in judicial proceedings, commenced or contemplated.
The expression "other judicial act" does not cover the service of judicial documents or the issuance of any process by which judgments or orders are executed or enforced, or orders for provisional or protective measures.

*Article 2*

A Contracting State shall designate a Central Authority which will undertake to receive Letters of Request coming from a judicial authority of another Contracting State and to transmit them to the authority competent to execute them. Each State shall organize the Central Authority in accordance with its own law.
Letters shall be sent to the Central Authority of the State of execution without being transmitted through any other authority of that State.

*Article 3*

A Letter of Request shall specify-
*a)* the authority requesting its execution and the authority requested to execute it, if known to the requesting authority;
*b)* the names and addresses of the parties to the proceedings and their representatives, if any;
*c)* the nature of the proceedings for which the evidence is required, giving all necessary information in regard thereto;
*d)* the evidence to be obtained or other judicial act to be performed.
Where appropriate, the Letter shall specify, *inter alia* —
*e)* the names and addresses of the persons to be examined;
*f)* the questions to be put to the persons to be examined or a statement of the subject-matter about which they are

to be examined;
*g)* the documents or other property, real or personal, to be inspected;
*h)* any requirement that the evidence is to be given on oath or affirmation, and any special form to be used;
*i)* any special method or procedure to be followed under Article 9.
A Letter may also mention any information necessary for the application of Article 11.
No legalization or other like formality may be required.

*Article 4*
A Letter of Request shall be in the language of the authority requested to execute it or be accompanied by a translation into that language.
Nevertheless, a Contracting State shall accept a Letter in either English or French, or a translation into one of these languages, unless it has made the reservation authorized by Article 33.
A Contracting State which has more than one official language and cannot, for reasons of internal law, accept Letters in one of these languages for the whole of its territory, shall, by declaration, specify the language in which the Letter or translation thereof shall be expressed for execution in the specified parts of its territory. In case of failure to comply with this declaration, without justifiable excuse, the costs of translation into the required language shall be borne by the State of origin.
A Contracting State may, by declaration, specify the language or languages other than those referred to in the preceding paragraphs, in which a Letter may be sent to its Central Authority.
Any translation accompanying a Letter shall be certified as correct, either by a diplomatic officer or consular agent or by a sworn translator or by any other person so authorized in either State.

*Article 5*
If the Central Authority considers that the request does not comply with the provisions of the present Convention, it shall promptly inform the authority of the State of origin which transmitted the Letter of Request, specifying the objections to the Letter.

*Article 6*
If the authority to whom a Letter of Request has been transmitted is not competent to execute it, the Letter shall be sent forthwith to the authority in the same State which is competent to execute it in accordance with the provisions of its own law.

*Article 7*
The requesting authority shall, if it so desires, be informed of the time when, and the place where, the proceedings will take place, in order that the parties concerned, and their representatives, if any, may be present. This information shall be sent directly to the parties or their representatives when the authority of the State of origin so requests.

*Article 8*
A Contracting State may declare that members of the judicial personnel of the requesting authority of another Contracting State may be present at the execution of a Letter of Request. Prior authorization by the competent authority designated by the declaring State may be required.

*Article 9*
The judicial authority which executes a Letter of Request shall apply its own law as to the methods and procedures to be followed.
However, it will follow a request of the requesting authority that a special method or procedure be followed, unless this is incompatible with the internal law of the State of execution or is impossible of performance by reason of its internal practice and procedure or by reason of practical difficulties.

A Letter of Request shall be executed expeditiously.

*Article 10*
In executing a Letter of Request the requested authority shall apply the appropriate measures of compulsion in the instances and to the same extent as are provided by its internal law for the execution of orders issued by the authorities of its own country or of requests made by parties in internal proceedings.

*Article 11*
In the execution of a Letter of Request the person concerned may refuse to give evidence in so far as he has a privilege or duty to refuse to give the evidence –
*a)* under the law of the State of execution; or
*b)* under the law of the State of origin, and the privilege or duty has been specified in the Letter, or, at the instance of the requested authority, has been otherwise confirmed to that authority by the requesting authority.
A Contracting State may declare that, in addition, it will respect privileges and duties existing under the law of States other than the State of origin and the State of execution, to the extent specified in that declaration.

*Article 12*
The execution of a Letter of Request may be refused only to the extent that –
*a)* in the State of execution the execution of the Letter does not fall within the functions of the judiciary; or
*b)* the State addressed considers that its sovereignty or security would be prejudiced thereby.
Execution may not be refused solely on the ground that under its internal law the State of execution claims exclusive jurisdiction over the subject-matter of the action or that its internal law would not admit a right of action on it.

*Article 13*
The documents establishing the execution of the Letter of Request shall be sent by the requested authority to the requesting authority by the same channel which was used by the latter.
In every instance where the Letter is not executed in whole or in part, the requesting authority shall be informed immediately through the same channel and advised of the reasons.

*Article 14*
The execution of the Letter of Request shall not give rise to any reimbursement of taxes or costs of any nature.
Nevertheless, the State of execution has the right to require the State of origin to reimburse the fees paid to experts and interpreters and the costs occasioned by the use of a special procedure requested by the State of origin under Article 9, paragraph 2.
The requested authority whose law obliges the parties themselves to secure evidence, and which is not able itself to execute the Letter, may, after having obtained the consent of the requesting authority, appoint a suitable person to do so. When seeking this consent the requested authority shall indicate the approximate costs which would result from this procedure. If the requesting authority gives its consent it shall reimburse any costs incurred; without such consent the requesting authority shall not be liable for the costs.

CHAPTER II – TAKING OF EVIDENCE BY DIPLOMATIC OFFICERS, CONSULAR AGENTS AND COMMISSIONERS

*Article 15*
In civil or commercial matters, a diplomatic officer or consular agent of a Contracting State may, in the territory of another Contracting State and within the area where he exercises his functions, take the evidence without compulsion of nationals of a State which he represents in aid of proceedings commenced in the courts of a State which he represents.
A Contracting State may declare that evidence may be taken by a diplomatic officer or consular agent only if

permission to that effect is given upon application made by him or on his behalf to the appropriate authority designated by the declaring State.

*Article 16*
A diplomatic officer or consular agent of a Contracting State may, in the territory of another Contracting State and within the area where he exercises his functions, also take the evidence, without compulsion, of nationals of the State in which he exercises his functions or of a third State, in aid of proceedings commenced in the courts of a State which he represents, if –
*a)* a competent authority designated by the State in which he exercises his functions has given its permission either generally or in the particular case, and
*b)* he complies with the conditions which the competent authority has specified in the permission.
A Contracting State may declare that evidence may be taken under this Article without its prior permission.

*Article 17*
In civil or commercial matters, a person duly appointed as a commissioner for the purpose may, without compulsion, take evidence in the territory of a Contracting State in aid of proceedings commenced in the courts of another Contracting State, if –
*a)* a competent authority designated by the State where the evidence is to be taken has given its permission either generally or in the particular case; and
*b)* he complies with the conditions which the competent authority has specified in the permission.
A Contracting State may declare that evidence may be taken under this Article without its prior permission.

*Article 18*
A Contracting State may declare that a diplomatic officer, consular agent or commissioner authorized to take evidence under Articles 15, 16 or 17, may apply to the competent authority designated by the declaring State for appropriate assistance to obtain the evidence by compulsion. The declaration may contain such conditions as the declaring State may see fit to impose.
If the authority grants the application it shall apply any measures of compulsion which are appropriate and are prescribed by its law for use in internal proceedings.

*Article 19*
The competent authority, in giving the permission referred to in Articles 15, 16 or 17, or in granting the application referred to in Article 18, may lay down such conditions as it deems fit, *inter alia*, as to the time and place of the taking of the evidence. Similarly it may require that it be given reasonable advance notice of the time, date and place of the taking of the evidence; in such a case a representative of the authority shall be entitled to be present at the taking of the evidence.

*Article 20*
In the taking of evidence under any Article of this Chapter persons concerned may be legally represented.

*Article 21*
Where a diplomatic officer, consular agent or commissioner is authorized under Articles 15, 16 or 17 to take evidence –
*a)* he may take all kinds of evidence which are not incompatible with the law of the State where the evidence is taken or contrary to any permission granted pursuant to the above Articles, and shall have power within such limits to administer an oath or take an affirmation;
*b)* a request to a person to appear or to give evidence shall, unless the recipient is a national of the State where the action is pending, be drawn up in the language of the place where the evidence is taken or be accompanied by a translation into such language;

*c)* the request shall inform the person that he may be legally represented and, in any State that has not filed a declaration under Article 18, shall also inform him that he is not compelled to appear or to give evidence;
*d)* the evidence may be taken in the manner provided by the law applicable to the court in which the action is pending provided that such manner is not forbidden by the law of the State where the evidence is taken;
*e)* a person requested to give evidence may invoke the privileges and duties to refuse to give the evidence contained in Article 11.

*Article 22*
The fact that an attempt to take evidence under the procedure laid down in this Chapter has failed, owing to the refusal of a person to give evidence, shall not prevent an application being subsequently made to take the evidence in accordance with Chapter I.

CHAPTER III – GENERAL CLAUSES
*Article 23*
A Contracting State may at the time of signature, ratification or accession, declare that it will not execute Letters of Request issued for the purpose of obtaining pre-trial discovery of documents as known in Common Law countries.

*Article 24*
A Contracting State may designate other authorities in addition to the Central Authority and shall determine the extent of their competence. However, Letters of Request may in all cases be sent to the Central Authority.
Federal States shall be free to designate more than one Central Authority.

*Article 25*
A Contracting State which has more than one legal system may designate the authorities of one of such systems, which shall have exclusive competence to execute Letters of Request pursuant to this Convention.

*Article 26*
A Contracting State, if required to do so because of constitutional limitations, may request the reimbursement by the State of origin of fees and costs, in connection with the execution of Letters of Request, for the service of process necessary to compel the appearance of a person to give evidence, the costs of attendance of such persons, and the cost of any transcript of the evidence.
Where a State has made a request pursuant to the above paragraph, any other Contracting State may request from that State the reimbursement of similar fees and costs.

*Article 27*
The provisions of the present Convention shall not prevent a Contracting State from –
*a)* declaring that Letters of Request may be transmitted to its judicial authorities through channels other than those provided for in Article 2;
*b)* permitting, by internal law or practice, any act provided for in this Convention to be performed upon less restrictive conditions;
*c)* permitting, by internal law or practice, methods of taking evidence other than those provided for in this Convention.

*Article 28*
The present Convention shall not prevent an agreement between any two or more Contracting States to derogate from –
*a)* the provisions of Article 2 with respect to methods of transmitting Letters of Request;
*b)* the provisions of Article 4 with respect to the languages which may be used;

*c)* the provisions of Article 8 with respect to the presence of judicial personnel at the execution of Letters;
*d)* the provisions of Article 11 with respect to the privileges and duties of witnesses to refuse to give evidence;
*e)* the provisions of Article 13 with respect to the methods of returning executed Letters to the requesting authority;
*f)* the provisions of Article 14 with respect to fees and costs;
*g)* the provisions of Chapter II.

*Article 29*
Between Parties to the present Convention who are also Parties to one or both of the Conventions on Civil Procedure signed at The Hague on the 17th of July 1905 and the 1st of March 1954, this Convention shall replace Articles 8-16 of the earlier Conventions.

*Article 30*
The present Convention shall not affect the application of Article 23 of the Convention of 1905, or of Article 24 of the Convention of 1954.

*Article 31*
Supplementary Agreements between Parties to the Conventions of 1905 and 1954 shall be considered as equally applicable to the present Convention unless the Parties have otherwise agreed.

*Article 32*
Without prejudice to the provisions of Articles 29 and 31, the present Convention shall not derogate from conventions containing provisions on the matters covered by this Convention to which the Contracting States are, or shall become Parties.

*Article 33*
A State may, at the time of signature, ratification or accession exclude, in whole or in part, the application of the provisions of paragraph 2 of Article 4 and of Chapter II. No other reservation shall be permitted.
Each Contracting State may at any time withdraw a reservation it has made; the reservation shall cease to have effect on the sixtieth day after notification of the withdrawal.
When a State has made a reservation, any other State affected thereby may apply the same rule against the reserving State.

*Article 34*
A State may at any time withdraw or modify a declaration.

*Article 35*
A Contracting State shall, at the time of the deposit of its instrument of ratification or accession, or at a later date, inform the Ministry of Foreign Affairs of the Netherlands of the designation of authorities, pursuant to Articles 2, 8, 24 and 25.
A Contracting State shall likewise inform the Ministry, where appropriate, of the following –
*a)* the designation of the authorities to whom notice must be given, whose permission may be required, and whose assistance may be invoked in the taking of evidence by diplomatic officers and consular agents, pursuant to Articles 15, 16 and 18 respectively;
*b)* the designation of the authorities whose permission may be required in the taking of evidence by commissioners pursuant to Article 17 and of those who may grant the assistance provided for in Article 18;
*c)* declarations pursuant to Articles 4, 8, 11, 15, 16, 17, 18, 23 and 27;
*d)* any withdrawal or modification of the above designations and declarations;
*e)* the withdrawal of any reservation.

*Article 36*
Any difficulties which may arise between Contracting States in connection with the operation of this Convention shall be settled through diplomatic channels.

*Article 37*
The present Convention shall be open for signature by the States represented at the Eleventh Session of the Hague Conference on Private International Law.
It shall be ratified, and the instruments of ratification shall be deposited with the Ministry of Foreign Affairs of the Netherlands.

*Article 38*
The present Convention shall enter into force on the sixtieth day after the deposit of the third instrument of ratification referred to in the second paragraph of Article 37.
The Convention shall enter into force for each signatory State which ratifies subsequently on the sixtieth day after the deposit of its instrument of ratification.

*Article 39*
Any State not represented at the Eleventh Session of the Hague Conference on Private International Law which is a Member of this Conference or of the United Nations or of a specialized agency of that Organization, or a Party to the Statute of the International Court of Justice may accede to the present Convention after it has entered into force in accordance with the first paragraph of Article 38.
The instrument of accession shall be deposited with the Ministry of Foreign Affairs of the Netherlands.
The Convention shall enter into force for a State acceding to it on the sixtieth day after the deposit of its instrument of accession.
The accession will have effect only as regards the relations between the acceding State and such Contracting States as will have declared their acceptance of the accession. Such declaration shall be deposited at the Ministry of Foreign Affairs of the Netherlands; this Ministry shall forward, through diplomatic channels, a certified copy to each of the Contracting States.
The Convention will enter into force as between the acceding State and the State that has declared its acceptance of the accession on the sixtieth day after the deposit of the declaration of acceptance.

*Article 40*
Any State may, at the time of signature, ratification or accession, declare that the present Convention shall extend to all the territories for the international relations of which it is responsible, or to one or more of them. Such a declaration shall take effect on the date of entry into force of the Convention for the State concerned.
At any time thereafter, such extensions shall be notified to the Ministry of Foreign Affairs of the Netherlands.
The Convention shall enter into force for the territories mentioned in such an extension on the sixtieth day after the notification indicated in the preceding paragraph.

*Article 41*
The present Convention shall remain in force for five years from the date of its entry into force in accordance with the first paragraph of Article 38, even for States which have ratified it or acceded to it subsequently.
If there has been no denunciation, it shall be renewed tacitly every five years.
Any denunciation shall be notified to the Ministry of Foreign Affairs of the Netherlands at least six months before the end of the five year period.
It may be limited to certain of the territories to which the Convention applies.
The denunciation shall have effect only as regards the State which has notified it. The Convention shall remain in force for the other Contracting States.

*Article 42*
The Ministry of Foreign Affairs of the Netherlands shall give notice to the States referred to in Article 37, and to the States which have acceded in accordance with Article 39, of the following –
*a)* the signatures and ratifications referred to in Article 37;
*b)* the date on which the present Convention enters into force in accordance with the first paragraph of Article 38;
*c)* the accessions referred to in Article 39 and the dates on which they take effect;
*d)* the extensions referred to in Article 40 and the dates on which they take effect;
*e)* the designations, reservations and declarations referred to in Articles 33 and 35;
*f)* the denunciations referred to in the third paragraph of Article 41.

In witness whereof the undersigned, being duly authorized thereto, have signed the present Convention.
Done at The Hague, on the 18th day of March, 1970, in the English and French languages, both texts being equally authentic, in a single copy which shall be deposited in the archives of the Government of the Netherlands, and of which a certified copy shall be sent, through the diplomatic channel, to each of the States represented at the Eleventh Session of the Hague Conference on Private International Law.

**Member States**

The following 64 States are Members of the Hague Conference on Private International Law:

- A
- Albania
- Argentina
- Australia
- Austria
- B
- Belarus
- Belgium
- Bosnia and Herzegovina
- Brazil
- Bulgaria
- C
- Canada
- Chile
- China (People's Republic of)
- Croatia
- Cyprus
- Czech Republic
- D
- Denmark
- E
- Egypt
- Estonia
- F
- Finland
- France
- G
- Georgia
- Germany
- Greece
- H
- Hungary
- I
- Iceland
- Ireland
- Israel
- Italy
- J
- Japan
- Jordan
- L
- Latvia
- Lithuania
- Luxembourg
- M
- Malaysia
- Malta
- Mexico
- Monaco
- Morocco
- N
- Netherlands
- New Zealand
- Norway
- P
- Panama
- Peru
- Poland
- Portugal
- R
- Republic of Korea
- Romania
- Russian Federation
- S
- Serbia and Montenegro
- Slovak Republic
- Slovenia
- South Africa
- Spain
- Sri Lanka
- Suriname
- Sweden
- Switzerland
- T
- The former Yugoslav Republic of Macedonia
- Turkey
- U
- Ukraine
- United Kingdom of Great Britain and Northern Ireland
- United States of America
- Uruguay
- V
- Venezuela

## CONVENTION ABOLISHING THE REQUIREMENT OF LEGALISATION FOR FOREIGN PUBLIC DOCUMENTS

*(Concluded 5 October 1961)*
*(Entered into force 24 January 1965)*

The States signatory to the present Convention,
Desiring to abolish the requirement of diplomatic or consular legalisation for foreign public documents,
Have resolved to conclude a Convention to this effect and have agreed upon the following provisions:

*Article 1*
The present Convention shall apply to public documents which have been executed in the territory of one Contracting State and which have to be produced in the territory of another Contracting State.
For the purposes of the present Convention, the following are deemed to be public documents:
*a)* documents emanating from an authority or an official connected with the courts or tribunals of the State, including those emanating from a public prosecutor, a clerk of a court or a process-server ("huissier de justice");
*b)* administrative documents;
*c)* notarial acts;
*d)* official certificates which are placed on documents signed by persons in their private capacity, such as official certificates recording the registration of a document or the fact that it was in existence on a certain date and official and notarial authentications of signatures.
However, the present Convention shall not apply:
*a)* to documents executed by diplomatic or consular agents;
*b)* to administrative documents dealing directly with commercial or customs operations.

*Article 2*
Each Contracting State shall exempt from legalisation documents to which the present Convention applies and which have to be produced in its territory. For the purposes of the present Convention, legalisation means only the formality by which the diplomatic or consular agents of the country in which the document has to be produced certify the authenticity of the signature, the capacity in which the person signing the document has acted and, where appropriate, the identity of the seal or stamp which it bears.

*Article 3*
The only formality that may be required in order to certify the authenticity of the signature, the capacity in which the person signing the document has acted and, where appropriate, the identity of the seal or stamp which it bears, is the addition of the certificate described in Article 4, issued by the competent authority of the State from which the document emanates.
However, the formality mentioned in the preceding paragraph cannot be required when either the laws, regulations, or practice in force in the State where the document is produced or an agreement between two or more Contracting States have abolished or simplified it, or exempt the document itself from legalisation.

more Contracting States have abolished or simplified it, or exempt the document itself from legalisation.

*Article 4*
The certificate referred to in the first paragraph of Article 3 shall be placed on the document itself or on an "allonge", it shall be in the form of the model annexed to the present Convention.
It may, however, be drawn up in the official language of the authority which issues it. The standard terms appearing therein may be in a second language also. The title "Apostille (Convention de La Haye du 5 octobre 1961)" shall be in the French language.

*Article 5*
The certificate shall be issued at the request of the person who has signed the document or of any bearer.
When properly filled in, it will certify the authenticity of the signature, the capacity in which the person signing the document has acted and, where appropriate, the identity of the seal or stamp which the document bears.
The signature, seal and stamp on the certificate are exempt from all certification.

*Article 6*
Each Contracting State shall designate by reference to their official function, the authorities who are competent to issue the certificate referred to in the first paragraph of Article 3.
It shall give notice of such designation to the Ministry of Foreign Affairs of the Netherlands at the time it deposits its instrument of ratification or of accession or its declaration of extension. It shall also give notice of any change in the designated authorities.

*Article 7*
Each of the authorities designated in accordance with Article 6 shall keep a register or card index in which it shall record the certificates issued, specifying:
*a)* the number and date of the certificate,
*b)* the name of the person signing the public document and the capacity in which he has acted, or in the case of unsigned documents, the name of the authority which has affixed the seal or stamp.
At the request of any interested person, the authority which has issued the certificate shall verify whether the particulars in the certificate correspond with those in the register or card index.

*Article 8*
When a treaty, convention or agreement between two or more Contracting States contains provisions which subject the certification of a signature, seal or stamp to certain formalities, the present Convention will only override such provisions if those formalities are more rigorous than the formality referred to in Articles 3 and 4.

*Article 9*
Each Contracting State shall take the necessary steps to prevent the performance of legalisations by its diplomatic or consular agents in cases where the present Convention provides for exemption.

*Article 10*
The present Convention shall be open for signature by the States represented at the Ninth Session of the Hague Conference on Private International Law and Iceland, Ireland, Liechtenstein and Turkey.
It shall be ratified, and the instruments of ratification shall be deposited with the Ministry of Foreign Affairs of the Netherlands.

*Article 11*
The present Convention shall enter into force on the sixtieth day after the deposit of the third instrument of ratification referred to in the second paragraph of Article 10.

The Convention shall enter into force for each signatory State which ratifies subsequently on the sixtieth day after the deposit of its instrument of ratification.

*Article 12*
Any State not referred to in Article 10 may accede to the present Convention after it has entered into force in accordance with the first paragraph of Article 11. The instrument of accession shall be deposited with the Ministry of Foreign Affairs of the Netherlands.
Such accession shall have effect only as regards the relations between the acceding State and those Contracting States which have not raised an objection to its accession in the six months after the receipt of the notification referred to in sub-paragraph *d)* of Article 15. Any such objection shall be notified to the Ministry of Foreign Affairs of the Netherlands.
The Convention shall enter into force as between the acceding State and the States which have raised no objection to its accession on the sixtieth day after the expiry of the period of six months mentioned in the preceding paragraph.

*Article 13*
Any State may, at the time of signature, ratification or accession, declare that the present Convention shall extend to all the territories for the international relations of which it is responsible, or to one or more of them. Such a declaration shall take effect on the date of entry into force of the Convention for the State concerned.
At any time thereafter, such extensions shall be notified to the Ministry of Foreign Affairs of the Netherlands.
When the declaration of extension is made by a State which has signed and ratified, the Convention shall enter into force for the territories concerned in accordance with Article 11. When the declaration of extension is made by a State which has acceded, the Convention shall enter into force for the territories concerned in accordance with Article 12.

*Article 14*
The present Convention shall remain in force for five years from the date of its entry into force in accordance with the first paragraph of Article 11, even for States which have ratified it or acceded to it subsequently.
If there has been no denunciation, the Convention shall be renewed tacitly every five years.
Any denunciation shall be notified to the Ministry of Foreign Affairs of the Netherlands at least six months before the end of the five year period.
It may be limited to certain of the territories to which the Convention applies.
The denunciation will only have effect as regards the State which has notified it. The Convention shall remain in force for the other Contracting States.

*Article 15*
The Ministry of Foreign Affairs of the Netherlands shall give notice to the States referred to in Article 10, and to the States which have acceded in accordance with Article 12, of the following:
*a)* the notifications referred to in the second paragraph of Article 6;
*b)* the signatures and ratifications referred to in Article 10;
*c)* the date on which the present Convention enters into force in accordance with the first paragraph of Article 11;
*d)* the accessions and objections referred to in Article 12 and the date on which such accessions take effect;
*e)* the extensions referred to in Article 13 and the date on which they take effect;
*f)* the denunciations referred to in the third paragraph of Article 14.

In witness whereof the undersigned, being duly authorised thereto, have signed the present Convention.
Done at The Hague the 5th October 1961, in French and in English, the French text prevailing in case of divergence between the two texts, in a single copy which shall be deposited in the archives of the Government of the Netherlands, and of which a certified copy shall be sent, through the diplomatic channel, to each of the States represented at the Ninth Session of the Hague Conference on Private International Law and also to Iceland, Ireland, Liechtenstein and Turkey.

## Annex to the Convention

*Model of certificate*

The certificate will be in the form of a square with sides at least 9 centimetres long

APOSTILLE

(Convention de La Haye du 5 octobre 1961)

1. Country: ..............
   This public document
2. has been signed by ...........................
3. acting in the capacity of .......................
4. bears the seal/stamp of ........................
   ..........................................

Certified

5. at .............. 6. the ................
7. by ..........................................
8. N°................
9. Seal/stamp: 10. Signature:
   .............. ....................

# U.S. Department of State

## HAGUE CONVENTION ON THE SERVICE ABROAD OF JUDICIAL AND EXTRA-JUDICIAL DOCUMENTS IN CIVIL AND COMMERCIAL MATTERS

**DISCLAIMER:** THE INFORMATION IN THIS CIRCULAR RELATING TO THE LEGAL REQUIREMENTS OF SPECIFIC FOREIGN COUNTRIES IS PROVIDED FOR GENERAL INFORMATION ONLY AND MAY NOT BE TOTALLY ACCURATE IN A PARTICULAR CASE. QUESTIONS INVOLVING INTERPRETATION OF SPECIFIC FOREIGN LAWS SHOULD BE ADDRESSED TO FOREIGN COUNSEL OR THE FOREIGN CENTRAL AUTHORITY FOR THE CONVENTION.

**IN FORCE** :..ANGUILLA [3] , ANTIGUA AND BARBUDA, ARGENTINA [7] , ARUBA [5] , BAHAMAS, BARBADOS, BELARUS, BELGIUM, *BELIZE* [1] , BERMUDA [3] , BOTSWANA, BRITISH VIRGIN ISLANDS [3] , BULGARIA [7,13] , CANADA, CAYMAN ISLANDS [3] , CHINA [2, 7] , CYPRUS, CZECH REPUBLIC [2, 7] , DENMARK, *DJIBOUTI (formerly Afars and Issas)* [1] , EGYPT [7] , ESTONIA, FALKLAND ISLANDS AND DEPENDENCIES [3] , *FIJI* [1,3] , FINLAND, FRANCE (including French Overseas Departments), FRENCH POLYNESIA [4] , GERMANY [7, 8, 9] , GIBRALTAR [3] , GREECE [10] , GUERNSEY [3] , HONG KONG SAR [3] , IRELAND, ISLE OF MAN [3] , ISRAEL, ITALY, JAPAN, JERSEY [3] , *KIRIBATI (formerly Gilbert Islands and Central and Southern Line Islands)* [1, 3] , KOREA, Republic of (SOUTH KOREA) [7,14] , LATVIA, LITHUANIA [7] , LUXEMBOURG [11] , MACAU SAR [6] , MALAWI, MEXICO, MONTSERRRAT [3] , NETHERLANDS, *NEVIS* [1] , NORWAY [7] , PAKISTAN, PITCAIRN [3] , POLAND, PORTUGAL, RUSSIAN FEDERATION, *ST. CHRISTOPHER (KITTS)* [1] , ST. HELENA AND DEPENDENCIES [3] , *ST. LUCIA* [1] , *ST. VINCENT AND THE GRENADINES* [1] , SEYCHELLES, SLOVAK REPUBLIC [2, 7, SLOVENIA] , *SOLOMON ISLANDS* [1] , SPAIN, SRI LANKA [7] , SWEDEN, SWITZERLAND [7] , TURKEY [7] , TURKS AND CAICOS ISLANDS [3] , *TUVALU (formerly Ellice Islands)* [1] , UKRAINE, UNITED KINGDOM, UNITED STATES [12] , VENEZUELA [7] .

[1] *This country achieved independence. No declaration has been made on the continuation in force of the Convention. We have requested the assistance of the Hague Conference on Private International Law in ascertaining from these countries whether they are applying the Convention.*

[2] *In accordance with Article 34(1) of the Vienna Convention on Succession of States in Respect of Treaties, the U.S. view is that when a country which is a party to a multilateral treaty or convention has dissolved, the successor state(s) inherit the treaty obligations of the former government, consistent with Article 34 of the Vienna Convention on Succession of States in Respect of Treaties. However, as a practical matter, the custom is for depositaries to expect a notice of succession to confirm that the new entity is*

*performing its treaty obligations. Many newly independent states may not really be implementing such conventions at this time in that they may be performing the functions set forth in the Convention. We continue to work with these governments and the depositories to obtain confirmation that the respective successor state is complying with treaty obligations.*

[3] *The Convention was extended to this territory, possession or other jurisdiction by the United Kingdom.*

[4] *The Convention was extended to this territory, possession or other jurisdiction by France.*

[5] *The Convention was extended to this territory, possession or other jurisdiction by the Netherlands.*

[6] *The Convention was extended to this territory, possession or other jurisdiction by Portugal.*

[7] *Argentina, China, the Czech Republic, Egypt, Germany, Greece, Latvia, Lithuania, Luxembourg, Norway, Poland, the Republic of South Korea, the Slovak Republic, Sri Lanka, Switzerland, Turkey, Ukraine, and Venezuela have notified the Hague Conference on Private International Law on accession, ratification or subsequently that they object to service in accordance with Article 10, sub-paragraph a of the Convention, via postal channels.*

[8] *The Hague Service Convention provision for service by a Central Authority is the exclusive method for service of process in the Federal Republic of Germany.*

[9] *On November 19, 1992, the Federal Republic of Germany advised the depositary for the Convention that notwithstanding the provisions of the first paragraph of Article 15, a German judge may give judgment even if no certificate of service or delivery has been received, if all the following conditions are fulfilled: the document was transmitted by one of the methods provided for in the Convention; a period of time of not less than six months, considered adequate by the judge in the particular case, has elapsed since the date of the transmission of the document; no certificate of any kind has been received, even though every reasonable effort has been made to obtain it through the competent authorities of the State addressed. In addition, Germany advised that an application for relief in accordance with Article 16 will not be entertained if it is filed after the expiration of one year following the termination of the time-limit which has not been observed.*

[10] *On November 23, 1989, Greece informed the depositary government for the Convention that the judges of Greece may give judgment if all the conditions in Article 15, paragraph 2(a),(b) and (c) of the Convention are fulfilled even if no certificate of service or delivery has been received.*

[11] *Luxembourg communicated the withdrawal of its declaration opposing service through postal channels in accordance with Article 10(a) of the Convention in a Note to the Government of the Netherlands dated June 2, 1978.*

[12] *As of June 28, 1978, the United States will not charge a fee for service of judicial documents which it receives from any State Party to the Convention which does not impose a charge for service of documents sent from the United States for service under the Convention. On March 31, 1994, the Government of the United States declared that the Convention shall also be extended to the Commonwealth of the Northern Mariana Islands.*

[13] *In accordance with Article 28, second paragraph, the Convention will enter into force for the Republic of Bulgaria in the absence of any objection from a State which has ratified the Convention before the deposit of the accession, notified to the Ministry of Foreign Affairs of the Netherlands within a period of six months after the date on which the Ministry has notified it of the accession. For practical reasons, this six months" period will run from January 31, 2000 to July 31, 2000. The Republic of Bulgaria objects to the use of channels of transmission for service mentioned in Article 10 of the Convention. The Republic of Bulgaria requires the document, which is to be served, to be written in or accompanied by a translation into the Bulgarian language. The Republic of Bulgaria designates the district courts as authorities which are competent to complete the certificate (Article 6, paragraphs 1 and 2).*

[14] *Ratified Convention January 13, 2000; in accordance with Article 28, second paragraph, the Convention will enter into force for the Republic of Korea in the absence of any objections from a State which has ratified the Convention before the deposit of the accession, notified to the Ministry of Foreign Affairs of the Netherlands within a period of six months after the date on which the Ministry has notified it of the accession. For practical reasons, this six month"s period will run from January 31, 2000 to July 31, 2000. Pursuant to Article 10, the Republic of Korea objects to the following:* ***a)*** *the freedom to send judicial documents, by postal channels, directly to persons abroad,* ***b)*** *the freedom of judicial officers, officials or other competent persons of the State of origin to effect service of judicial documents directly through the judicial officials or other competent persons of the State of destination,* ***c)*** *the freedom of any person interested in a judicial proceeding to effect service of judicial documents directly through judicial officers, officials or other competent persons of the State of destination.*

**CITATIONS**

20 U.S.T. 1361

658 U.N.T.S. 163

T.I.A.S. No. 6638

28 U.S.C.A. (Appendix following Rule 4 FRCvP)

16 I.L.M. 1339 (1977)

Martindale-Hubbell Law Directory, Law Digest Volume, Selected International Conventions

**U.S. CENTRAL AUTHORITY**

Office of International Judicial Assistance
Civil Division
Department of Justice
1100 L Street, NW
Room 11006
Washington, D.C. 20530
(202) 307-0983

**PURPOSE**

The Hague Service Convention codifies service of process by international registered mail and by agent. The treaty also provides for service of process by a Central Authority (usually the Ministry of Justice) in the Convention countries pursuant to a request submitted on a form USM-94, available at the office of any United States Marshal. The text of the treaty is self-explanatory, but see the reservations and declarations each country made on accession to the treaty. Some countries made specific reservations against particular methods of service. The Convention method should be employed in all countries party to it.

**SCOPE OF THE CONVENTION**

This question was raised at the first Special Commission meeting on the operation of the Convention. The applicability of the Convention to administrative cases is generally decided on a case-by-case basis. See Commission Reported, cited under References.

**REQUEST FOR SERVICE FORM (USM-94)**

You may obtain a copy of the Request for Service form (USM-94) from the local office of the U.S. Marshal's Service. Further information on the treaty may be obtained from the Supervisory Deputy for process at the nearest U.S. Marshal's office. You may also contact Headquarters, U.S. Marshal's Service, 202-307-9110. (See also Memo No. 386, Revision No. 3, at the U.S. Marshal's office or at Vol. 16, Intl Legal Materials, 1331, (1977) Am. Soc. Intl. Law).

**COMPLETE THE FORM**

The completed request form and documents to be served, with accompanying translations (2 copies of each), should be mailed directly to the foreign central authority as provided by Article 3 of the Convention.

**FEDERAL AUTHORITY FOR ATTYS TO COMPLETE AND SEND FORM**

Effective February 26, 1983 Public Law 97-462 amended Rule 4 of the Federal Rules of CivilProcedure regarding service of process. Pursuant to this change in Rule 4(c)2(A) the U.S. Marshal will no longer transmit Form USM-94 directly to the foreign central authority of a country party to the Hague Service Convention. Rather, the attorney representing the party seeking service should execute the portion of Form USM-94 marked "Identity and Address of the Applicant" and the "Name and Address of the Requesting Authority" portion of the Summary of the Document to be Served.

**CITE AUTHORITY**

A reference to the statutory authority to serve the document should appear prominently on the request, stating that "service is requested pursuant to Rule 4(c)2(A), U.S. Federal Rules of Civil Procedure" which authorizes any person who is not a party and is not less than 18 years of age to serve a summons and complaint.

**STATE COURT ACTIONS**

In actions pending in state courts, state law designates the person authorized to effect service. Requests pend ing in state courts should specify that the request is made pursuant to Rule 4(c)2(A) of the U.S. Federal Rules of Civil Procedure and any pertinent state law. See U.S. Marshal's Memo 386, [p. 14, footnote 11,] 16 I.L.M. 1331 et seq. (1977) for guidance on service requests in actions pending in state courts.

**DESIGNATING METHOD OF SERVICE TO BE USED BY CENTRAL AUTHORITY**

Fill in the USM-94 in duplicate, designating the method of service to be used by the foreign Central Authority.

**FORMAL SERVICE**

(Article 5, paragraph 1, sub-paragraph a)The Central Authority itself serves or arranges to have served "by a method prescribed by its internal law for the service of documents in domestic actions upon persons who are within its territory". Generally, documents to be served in accordance with this method must be translated into the official language of the country. See the Practical Handbook on the Convention for specific information, or consult the U.S. Central Authority.

**INFORMAL DELIVERY**

(Article 5, paragraph 2)Unless a particular method is requested, the document may always be served by delivery to an addressee who accepts it voluntarily. This method of informal delivery is by far the most broadly used approach in a substantial number of Contracting States. The person who delivers the document is often a police official. In most cases, the addressees accept the document voluntarily or come down to pick it up at the police station, which dispenses with the need for translation of the documents to be served.

**PERSONAL SERVICE**

(Article 5, paragraph 1, sub-paragraph b)If personal service is required, delete methods (a) and (c) on the Request for Service form (USM-94) and indicate method (b) on the form, noting that the documents should be served personally upon the person or company to be served.

**TRANSLATIONS**

Unless the party to be served will accept service voluntarily, the documents to be served must be accompanied by a translation into the official language of the foreign country. See Ristau, International Judicial Assistance (Civil and Commercial), International Law Institute, 1995, Vol. 1, Section 4-2-3(5), pp. 133-138. See Teknekron Management Inc. v. Quante Fernmeldtechnik Gmbh, 115 F.R.D. 175 (D. Nev. 1987); Vornees v. Fischer & Krecke, 697 F. 2d 574, 575 (4th Cir. 1983)

**COSTS**

There are generally no costs incurred in connection with service through the central authority under the Convention. However, if personal service is made and the person to be served resides in some remote location, some fees may be charged. The fees will be billed to the requester by the foreign central authority.

**TIME FRAME**

There is no specific time frame for serviceprovided for in the Convention. However, the Hague Conference on Private International Law advises that most Convention central authorities generally accomplish service within two months.

**PROOF OF SERVICE**

On the reverse side of the Request for Service form is a Certificate of Service form. The certificate, which serves as proof of service, is completed and mailed directly to the requesting party by the foreign central authority after service has been effected.

**SERVICE OTHER THAN BY CONVENTION CENTRAL AUTHORITY SERVICE THRU CONSULAR & DIPLOMATIC CHANNELS**

(Articles 8 and 9)U.S. consular officers are prohibited by Federal regulations from effecting service of process in private matters. See 22 CFR 92.85.

**SERVICE BY POSTAL CHANNELS**

(Article 10, sub-paragraph a)American courts have consistently held that international mail service of civil summonses is not proper in the case of States party to the Hague Service Convention which have entered an appropriate reservation under Article 10 thereof. See Ristau, Vol. 1, Section. 4-1-6, pp. 121.3-121.9. See also, Epstein, International Litigation, A Guide to Jurisdiction, Practice and Strategy, 2nd., 1994, Section 4.04(3), pp. 4-14-4-19.

*Argentina, China, the Czech Republic, Egypt, Germany, Greece, the Republic of South Korea, Latvia, Lithuania, Luxembourg, Norway, Poland, the Slovak Republic, Sri Lanka, Switzerland, Turkey, Ukraine, and Venezuela have notified the Hague Conference on Private International Law on accession, ratification or subsequently that they object to service in accordance with Article 10, sub-paragraph a of the Convention, via postal channels.*

**SELECTED CASES:** Re Hunt's Pier Associates Debtor, 156 Bankr, 464 (E.D. Pa. 1993); Grand Entertainment v. Star Media Sales, 988 F. 2d 476 (3rd Cir. 1993); Peabody Holding Co. v. Lotain Group PLC, 808 F. Supp. 1425 (E.D. Mo. 1992); Perfumer's Workshop, Ltd. v. Roure Bertrand du Pont, S.A., 737 F. Supp. 785 (S.D.N.Y. 1990); Wilson v. Honda Motor Co. Ltd, 766 F. Supp. 339 (E.D. Tenn 1991); Honda Motor Co., Ltd., v. Superior Court (10 Cal. App. 4th 1043, 12 Cal. Rptr 2d 861 (1992); Sheets v. Yamaha Motor Co. Ltd., (891 F. 2d 533 (5th Cir. 1990)); Bankston v. Toyota Motor Corp. (889 Fed. Rptr, 2d Series, 172, (8th Cir. 1989; W.D. Ark., 4 Jan 1989); Suzuki Motor CO., Ltd. v. Superior Court (200 Cal. App. 3d 1476, 249 Cal. Rptr. 376 (1988); Hantover Inc. v. Omet S.N.A., 688 F. Supp. 1377 (W.D. Mo. 1988); Turick v. Yamaha, (121 F.R.D. 32 (S.D.N.Y. 1988)); Cooper v. Makita Electric Works Ltd., 117 F.R.D. 16 (1987); Ackermann v. Levine (788 F. wd 830 (2d Cir. 1986); , Pochop v. Toyota Motor Co. Ltd., 111 F.R.D. 464 (1986), Mommsen v. Toro Co., 108 F.R.D. 444 (1985); DeJames v. Magnificence Carriers, Inc., 654 F.2d 280 (3d Cir. 1981); Porsche v. Superior Court, 177 Cal. Rptr. 155 (1981); Cintron v. W&D Machinery Co. Inc., 182 N.J. Super. 126, 440 (A. 2d 76 (1981)); Kadota v. Hosogai, 608 P. 2d 68 (Ct. of Appeals, Ariz, 1980); Shoei Kako Co. v. Superior Court, 33 Cal. App. 3d 808, 109 Cal. Rptr. 402 (1973).

**But see,** Umbenhauer v. Woog, 959 F. 2d 25, (3rd Cir, 1992) which held that objections from foreign governments cannot justify non-compliance with the Federal Rules of Civil Procedure for service of process by international mail. It should be noted that the country in question, Switzerland, was not a party to the Hague Service Convention at that time, and thus did not file formal objection to service by postal channels under Article 10(a). Formal objections to this method of service made at the time of accession or subsequently in accordance with the Convention are honored as a Treaty obligation.

**Note:** With respect to the debate in the courts regarding the validity of service by mail in Japan, see our country specific flyer, Service of Process in Japan, via our autofax service or at our Internet Home Page.

**BUT SEE** , FTC v. Compagnie de Saint-Gobain-Pont-a-Mousson, 636 F. 2d 1327, n. 150 (D.C. Cir. 1980) on the issue of service via international registered mail when the document to be served is not compulsory or punitive when there is no treaty obligation to refrain from such methods of service. See also, Digest of United States Practice in International Law, Department of State, Office of the Legal Adviser, 1980 p. 457.

**TRANSLATIONS AND SERVICE BY MAIL**

Translation of documents to be served by registered mail is not strictly required by the Convention. Courts have ruled that the translation requirement of Article 5 applies only to service of documents by the foreign Central Authority, and not direct postal service. See Lemme v. Wine of Japan Import, Inc., 631 F. Supp. 456, 463-64 (E.D.N.Y. 1986). See also Greenfield v. Suzuki Motor Co., Ltd., 776 F. Supp. 698, 701-703 (E.D.N.Y. 1991). See Epstein, International Litigation: A Guide to Jurisdiction, Practice and Strategy, , 2nd, 1994, Section 4.04(1), p. 4-13. But see, Ristau, Vol 1, Section 4-3-1(2), p. 142 for a discussion of challenges which can occur if documents are not served in the language the recipient understands.

**SERVICE THRU JUDICIAL OFFICERS**

(Article 10, sub-paragraphs b and c)Permits the judicial officers, officials and other competent persons of the state of origin to effect service of judicial documents through the efforts of the judicial officials of the state of destination, unless the latter state objects to this method.

**SEE ALSO** Volkswagenwerk Aktiengesellschaft v. Schlunk, 108 S. Ct. 2104, 100 L. Ed. 2d 722, 27 I.L.M. 1093 (15 June 1988) on the issue of service on an agent for a foreign corporation in the United States.

**FOREIGN CENTRAL AUTHORITIES**

The Hague Conference on Private International Law Handbook on the Operation of the Hague Service Convention provides the following addresses of foreign central authorities:

**ANDORRA:**

1. El Ministre d"Afers Exteriors

2. El Ministre de Justícia i Interior

All legalization requests are centralized through the following address:

Ministeri d"Afers Exteriors
Prat de la Creu
Edifici del Govern

Andorra la Vella
Principat d''Andorra

Tel.: 376-875-700
Fax: 376-869-559
E-mail: exteriors.gov@andorra.ad

**ANGUILLA:**
The Registrar of the Supreme Court
Anguilla

**ANTIGUA & BARBUDA:**
(1) The Governor General
Antigua and Barbuda;

(2) Registrar of the High Court
High Street
St. John''s, Antigua, West Indies
tel: 809-462-3147

**ARGENTINA:**
Acceded to the Convention: February 2, 2001
Enters into Force: December 1, 2001

Central Authority: Ministry of Foreign Affairs, International Trade and Worship
Treaty Bureau
Esmeralda 1212 - 15th. Fl.
1007 Buenos Aires
Tel: (5411) 4819-7000
4819-8015

Argentina made the following declarations:

1 - To Article 5, third paragraph: "The ARGENTINE REPUBLIC shall not accept documents to be served or transmitted unless they are accompanied by a translation into the Spanish language."

2 - To Article 21, first paragraph, a): "The Argentine Government designates the Ministry of Foreign Affairs, International Trade and Worship as the Central Authority."

3 - To Article 21, second paragraph, a): "The ARGENTINE REPUBLIC opposes to the use of methods of transmission pursuant to Article 10."

4 - To Article 21, second paragraph, b): "The Argentine Government accepts declarations pursuant to second paragraph of Article 15 and third paragraph of Article 16."

5 - The ARGENTINE REPUBLIC rejects the claimed extension of application of the Convention on the Service Abroad of Judicial and Extrajudicial Documents in Civil or Commercial Matters, adopted at The Hague on November 14, 1965, to the Malvinas, South Georgias and South Sandwich Islands as notified on May 20, 1970 by the UNITED KINGDOM OF GREAT BRITAIN AND NORTHERN IRELAND to the KINGDOM OF THE NETHERLANDS as Depositary of the Convention under the "Falkland Islands and dependencies" inaccurate denomination. Therefore, the ARGENTINE REPUBLIC similarly rejects the designation of the "Registrar of the Supreme Court" in the Malvinas Islands as application authority of this Convention which was made on that same opportunity, as well as any other act derived or that may be derived from this claimed territorial extension.

The General Assembly of the United Nations has recognized the existence of a dispute on the Malvinas, South Georgias and South Sandwich Islands sovereignty and has urged the ARGENTINE REPUBLIC and the UNITED KINGDOM OF GREAT BRITAIN AND NORTHERN IRELAND to hold negotiations in order to find, as soon as possible, a peaceful and definite solution to such dispute, with United Nations Secretary General's good offices mediation, who shall inform the General Assembly about the progress made (Resolutions 2065 (XX), 3160 (XXVIII), 31/49, 37/9, 38/12, 39/6, 40/21, 41/40, 42/19 and 43/25). The Special Committee on Decolonization having equally declared, has annually adopted a resolution which proclaims that to put an end to this colonial situation the negotiations must be resumed in order to peacefully and definitely solve this sovereignty dispute. The last of these resolutions was adopted on July 1, 1999.

The ARGENTINE REPUBLIC reaffirms its sovereignty on the Malvinas, South Georgias and South Sandwich Islands and its maritime surrounding areas which are an integral part of its national territory."

**ARUBA:**
The Kingdom of the Netherlands declared that the application of the Convention shall extend to *Aruba* on 28 May 1986. Entry into Force for *Aruba: 27 July 1986* . Effective November 1, 2000, the Central Authority is:

Procurator General
L.G. Smith Boulevard 42-44
Oranjestad, Aruba
Tel: (279) 834-387 / 829-132
Fax: (279) 838-891

**BAHAMAS:**

Entered into Force: February 1, 1998. Designated Central Authority: "The Honorable Attorney General."

Bahamian Central Authority for the Hague Service
Rhonda Bain

The Attorney General's Office
PO Box N3007
East Hill Street
Nassau, Bahamas
Tel: (242)-502-0400

**BARBADOS:**
The Registrar of the Supreme Court of Barbados
Law Courts, Bridgetown, Barbados
tel: 809-42-75537

**BELARUS:**
Ministry of Justice
Division of Execution of International Treaties
Department of Legal Provis ion of Foreign Relations
Kollektornaya St. 10
220048 Minsk
Belarus
Contact: Ms. Marina Zhandarova
Telephone: 375-17-211-0185

**BELGIUM:**
Le Ministere de la Justice
Administration de la Legislation
Place Poelaert 4
1000 Bruxelles
tel: 511-42-00
telex: 62.440 Min Jus

**BELIZE:**
Now Independent. No formal confirmation to depositary government that Convention applies. Government of Belize authorities have advised the U.S. Embassy that the Convention does apply and that requests for service should be sent to the following central authority:

The General Registry
Supreme Court Building
P.O. Box 87
Belize City, Belize

**BERMUDA:**
The Registrar of the Supreme Court
Sessions House
21 Parliament St.
Hamilton HM 12, Bermuda
tel: 809-292-1350

**BOTSWANA:**
The Minister of State in the Office of the President of the Republic of Botswana
Lobatse, Botswana

**BRITISH VIRGIN ISLANDS:**
The Registrar of the Supreme Court
British Virgin Islands

**BULGARIA:**
The Republic of Bulgaria designates the Minstry of Justice and European Legal Integration as Central Authority. The same authority is competent to receive the documents forwarded under Article 9, paragraph 1.

**CANADA:**
To save time, requests should be forwarded directly to the Central Authority of the province or territory concerned. They may, however, also be forwarded to the Federal Central Authority which will transmit them to the relevant Central Authority in the province or territory.

**Federal Central Authority:**
Director, Legal Advisory Division
Department of External Affairs
125 Sussex Drive
Ottawa, Ontario
Canada K1A 0G2
(613) 995-0119

**For Alberta:**
Attorney-General for Alberta
Attn: Executive Director - Court Services
9833-109th Street
Edmonton, Alberta
Canada T5K 2E8
tel: (403) 427-4992

**For British Columbia:**
Ministry of the Attorney-General
for British Columbia
Office of the Deputy Minister
Fifth Floor, 910 Government Street
Victoria, British Columbia
Canada V8V 1X4
tel: (604) 387-5211

**For Manitoba:**
Attorney-General for Manitoba

c/o Director - Civil Legal Services
Woodsworth Building
6th Floor
405 Broadway
Winnipeg, Manitoba
Canada, R3C 0V8
tel: (204) 945-2847

**For New Brunswick:**
Attorney-General for New Brunswick
P.O.Box 6000
Fredericton, New Brunswick
Canada, E3B 5H1
tel: (506) 453-2208

**For Newfoundland:**
Department of Justice
Confederation Building
St. John's, Newfoundland
Canada A1C 5T7
tel: (709) 576-2869

**For Nova Scotia:**
Attorney General of Nova Scotia
Legal Services Division
P.O. Box 7
Halifax, Nova Scotia
tel: (902) 424-4024

**For Ontario:**
Ministry of the Attorney General for Ontario Reciprocity Office: Civil Law Division
18 King St. East
Toronto, Ontario
Canada M5C 1C5
tel: (416) 965-2570

**For Prince Edward Island:**
Attorney General of Prince Edward Island
Office of the Deputy Minister
P.O. Box 2000
Charlottetown, Prince Edward Island
Canada C1A 7N8
tel: (902) 368-4570

**For Quebec:**
Ministre de la Justice du Quebec

a/s Le service juridique
1200 route de l"Eglise
5eme etage
Ste-Foy, Quebec
Canada G1V 4M1
(418) 643-1436

**For Saskatchewan:**
Minister of Justice for Saskatchewan Att. of Director of Sheriff Services
1874 Scarth St., 10th Floor
Regina, Saskatchewan
Canada S4P 3V7
(306) 787-5488

**For Yukon:**
Director of Court Services
Department of Justice
Box 2703
Whitehorse, Yukon Y1A 2C6
(403) 667-5942

**For Northwest Territories:**
Deputy Minister of Justice
Government of the Northwest Territories
Box 1320
Yellowknife, Northwest Territories
Canada X1A 2L9
tel: (613) 995-0119

**CAYMAN ISLANDS:**
Clerk of the Courts
Grand Cayman, Cayman Islands

**CHINA:**
Bureau of International Judicial Assistance
Ministry of Justice of the People"s Republic of China
10 Chaoyangmen Nandajie
Chaoyang District
BEIJING, 100020
China

**CYPRUS:**
Ministry of Justice & Public Order
Office of Permanent Secretary
125 Athalassa Avenue
2024 Nicosia,Cyprus

Tel: 357-22-805955
Fax: 357-22-518356

**CZECH REPUBLIC:**
Ministerstvo Spravedlnosti Ceske Republiky/ Ministry of Justice of the Czech Republic
128 10 Praha 2, Vysehradska 16
Prague, Czech Republic

**DENMARK:**
Ministry of Justice
Justitsministeriet
Slotsholmsgade 10
1216 Kobenhavn K.
Copenhagen, Denmark
tel: 120906
telex: 15530

***DJIBOUTI:***
*Unknown. Now Independent. Formerly French territory of Afars and Issas. No formal confirmation to depositary government that Convention applies.*

**EGYPT:**
Ministry of Justice
Office of International Judicial Cooperation
New Annex Building 7th Floor
Nobar Street
Abdin, Cairo, Egypt
tel. 011-20-2-795-6059

**ESTONIA:**
The Ministry of Justice of the Republic of Estonia

**FALKLAND ISLANDS:**
The Registrar of the Supreme Court
Stanley, Falkland Islands

***FIJI:***
*Chief Registrar of the High Court of Fiji*
*Government Buildings*
*Suva, Fiji*

*Fiji became an independent State October 10, 1970. Prior to that time, Fiji was a dependency of the United Kingdom which extended its accession to the Convention to Fiji. Fiji has never confirmed to the Hague Conference on Private International Law or the Government of the Netherlands whether it considers the Hague Service Convention to apply to Fiji. However, Fijian authorities have provided the U.S. Embassy with the name and address of the Central Authority noted above to whom requests for service under the Hague Convention may be transmitted.*

**FINLAND:**
Ministry of Justice
10 Etelaesplanadi
Helsinki 13, Finland
tel: 358-0-1601

**FRANCE:**
Ministere de la Justice
Bureau de l'Entraide Judi ciaire Internationale D4
13 Place Vendome
75042 Paris (1er), Cedex 01, France
tel: 261-80-22
telex: 211-802F

**GERMANY:**

**For Baden-Wurttemberg:**
Justizministerium Baden-Wurttemberg
Schillerplatz 4
70173 Stuttgart, Federal Republic of Germany

**For Bavaria**
Bayerisches Staatsministerium der Justiz
Justizpalast
Prielmeyerstrasse 7
80335 Muenchen
Munich, Germany
(this is the street address)

(For correspondence the following address should be used):

Bayerisches Staatsministerium der Justiz
80097 Muenchen
Munich, Germany

**For Berlin:**
Senator fur Justiz
Salzburger Strasse 21-25
10825 Berlin, Germany

**For Brandenburg:**
Das Ministerium der Justiz
des Landes Brandenburg

Heinrich-Mann-Alee 107
14460 Potsdam, Germany

**For Bremen:**
Prasident des Landgerichts Bremen
Domsheide 16
28195 Bremen, Germany

**For Hamburg:**
Prasident des Amtsgerichtes Hamburg
Sievekingplatz 1
20335 Hamburg

**For Hesse:**
Hessischer Minister der Justiz
Luisenstrasse 13
65185 Wiesbaden, Germany

**For Lower Saxony:**
Niedersachsisher Minister der Justiz
Am Waterlooplatz 1
30169 Hannover, Germany

**For Mecklenburg-Western Pomerania:**
Der Minister fur Justiz
Bundes- und Europaangelegenheiten
des Landes Mecklenburg-Vorpommern
Demmlerplatz 14
19053 Schwerin, Germany

**For Northrhine-Westphalia:**
Justizminister des Landes Nordrhein-Westfalen
Cecilienallee 3
40474 Dusseldorf, Germany

**For Rhineland-Palatinate:**
Ministerium der Justiz
Ernst-Ludwig-Strasse 3
55116 Mainz, Germany

**For Saarland:**
Minister der Justiz des Saarlandes
Zahringerstrasse 12
66119 Saarbrucken, Germany

**For Saxony:**
Sachsisches Staatsministerium der Justiz
Archivstrasse 1
01097 Dresden, Germany

**For Saxony-Anhalt:**
Ministerium der Justiz
des Landes Sachsen-Anhalt
Wilhelm-Hopfner-Ring 6
39116 Magdeburg, Germany

**For Schleswig-Holstein:**
Der Justizminister
des Landes Schleswig-Holstein
Lorentzendamm 35
24103 Kiel, Germany

**For Thuringia:**
Thuringer Justizministerium
Alfred-Hess Strasse 8
99094 Erfurt, Germany

**GIBRALTAR:**
The Registrar of the Supreme Court
Gibraltar

**GREECE:**
Ministry of Foreign Affairs
Department of Administrative and Judicial Affairs
D-3 Section, Department 2
Zalakosta 1, Athens, Greece

**GUERNSEY:**
The Bailiff
Bailiff's Office
Royal Court House
Guernsey
Channel Islands

**HONG KONG SAR (CHINA) / CHINA (HONG KONG SAR):**
The Chief Secretary of Hong Kong
Central Government Offices
Lower Albert Road
Hong Kong, tel: 011-852-8102954

**ISLE OF MAN:**
The First Deemster and Clerk of the Rolls
Roll's Office
Douglas, Isle of Man

**IRELAND:**
Master of the High Court
Dublin, Ireland

or

- a practising Solicitor; or
- a Country Registrar; or
- a District County Clerk

**ISRAEL:**
Director of Courts
Directorate of Courts
Russian Compound
Jerusalem
tel: 246919

**ITALY:**
The Registry of the Court of Appeal
Rome, Italy

L''Ufficio unico degli ufficiali
giudiziari presso la corte d''appello la corte
d''appello di Roma
Rome, Italy

**JAPAN:**
The Minister of Foreign Affairs
2-2-1 Kasumigaseki, Chiyoda-ku
Tokyo 100, Japan
tel: 81-3-3581-4015

**JERSEY:**
The Attorney General
Jersey, Channel Islands

***KIRIBATI:***
*Unknown. Now Independent. No formal confirmation to depositary government that Convention applies. Former Central Authority: Registrar of the High Court*

**KOREA, REPUBLIC OF (SOUTH KOREA):**
Ministry of Court Administration, Attn.: Director of International Affairs, 967, Seocho-dong, Seocho-gu, SEOUL 137-750, Republic of Korea

**LATVIA:**
Ministry of Justice
Brivibas Boulevard 34
LV - 1536 Riga

**LITHUANIA:**
Signatory: August 2, 2000
Accession: May 15, 2001
Entry into Force: June 1, 2001

Central Authority: Ministry of Justice
Dept. of International Law
Gedimino 30
Vilnius, Lithuania.

An alternative central authority is the District Attorney, Procuracy General, Smetonos 4, Vilnius, Lithuania.

The instrument of accession of Lithuania contains the following declarations:

And whereas it is provided in Article 2 of the said Convention, the Republic of Lithuania designates the Ministry of Justice of the Republic of Lithuania as a Central Authority to receive requests for service coming from other Contracting States;

And whereas it is provided in Article 8 of the said Convention, the Republic of Lithuania declares that it opposes to the ways of service of documents provided in this Article, unless the documents are to be served upon a national of the State in which the documents originate;

And whereas it is provided in Article 10 of the said Convention, the Republic of Lithuania declares that it is opposed to the ways of service of documents provided in this Article;

And whereas it is provided in paragraph 2 of Article 15 of the said Convention, the Republic of Lithuania declares that the judge of the Republic of Lithuania may give judgment even if no certificate of service or delivery has been received, if all conditions of paragraph 2 of Article 15 are fulfilled;

And whereas it is provided in paragraph 2 of Article 16 of the said Convention, the Republic of Lithuania declares that an application for relief will not be entertained if it is filed after the expiration of one year following the date of the final judgment;...".

**LUXEMBOURG:**
Parquet general pres la Cour superieure de Justice
12 Cote d"Eich
Luxembourg-Ville
tel: 475981 or 26765 or 41464

**MACAU SAR (CHINA) / CHINA (MACAU SAR):**
Portugal extended its accession to Macau. Requests for service of process in Macau may be transmitted to the Portuguese Central Authority for forwarding to the Competent Authority in Macau to effect service. See Portugal.

**MALAWI:**
The Registrar of the High Court of Malawi
P.O. Box 30244
Chichiri
Blantyre 3
Malawi

**MEXICO:**
Secretaria de Relaciones Exteriores
Direccion General de Asuntos Juridicos
Av. Ricardo Flores Magon No. 1 - Anexo 2
Planta Alta
Colonia Tlatelolco
06995 Mexico, D.F.
tel: 011-52-55-5782-4144

By a Note dated 7 May 2001, the Embassy of Mexico at The Hague informed the depositary of the following: besides English and French, request forms addressed to the Mexican Central Authority should be filled in Spanish, according to Article 7 of the Convention.

**MONTSERRAT:**
The Registrar of the High Court
Montserrat

**NETHERLANDS:**
The Public Prosecutor
District Court of the Hague
Juliana van Stoleberglaan 2-4
The Hague, the Netherlands
tel: 82-40-41

***NEVIS:***
*Ministry of Legal Affairs*
*P.O. Box 186*

*Government Headquarters*
*St. Kitts-Nevis, West Indies*
*tel: 809-465-2521*

**NORWAY:**
Ministry of Justice
Boks 8005
Oslo/Dep
Oslo 1, Norway

**PAKISTAN:**
Solicitor
Ministry of Law and Justice
Islamabad, Pakistan

Other Authorities in addition to Central Authority
Within Their Respective Territorial Jurisdictions:

Registrars of:
Lahore High Court, Lahore
Peshawar High Court, Peshawar
Baluchistan High Court, Quetta
High Court of Sind, Karachi

**PITCAIRN:**
The Governor and Commander-in-Chief, Pitcairn
British High Commission
Reserve Bank of New Zealand Building (9th Floor)
2 The Terrace (P.O. Box 1812)
Wellington 1
New Zealand

**POLAND:**
Ministry of Justice
Department of International Cooperation and European Law
Al. Ujazdowskia 11
00-950 Warsaw, Poland
tel: 48-22-628-4431 (ext. 247)
fax: 48-22-628-0949

**PORTUGAL:**
Director General of the Judicial Service of the Ministry of the
Ministry of Justice (Direccao-Geral dos Servicas Judiciarios,
Ministerio de Justica)
Av. Casal Ribeiro 48
1098 Lisboa Codex

Lisbon, Portugal
tel: 351-21-315-52 82
fax: 351-21-353-87 02

**RUSSIAN FEDERATION:**
Accession: May 1, 2001
Entry into Force: December 1, 2001
Central Authority: Unknown. Seeking clarification from the Russian Federation and the Hague Conference on Private International Law.

**SLOVENIA:**
Signatory: September 18, 2000
Accession: May 15, 2001
Entry into Force: June 1, 2001
Central Authority unknown

**SRI LANKA:**
Signatory: August 31, 200
Accession: May 15, 2001
Entry into Force: June 1, 2001

Central Authority: Secretary/Ministry of Justice and Constitutional Affairs. Seeking clarification regarding address and phone number from Sri Lanka and Hague Conference on Private International law.

The instrument of accession of Sri Lanka contains the following declarations:

In terms of Article 2, the Secretary/Ministry of Justice and Constitutional Affairs is designated the Central Authority.

The authority competent to act upon a Letter of Request pursuant to Article 6 would be the Secretary, Ministry of Justice and Constitutional Affairs/Registrar of the Court of Appeal.

For purposes of Article 7, the documents should be in the English language.

For purposes of Article 10, Sri Lanka has no objection to the procedure set out in paragraph (b) thereof. However it does not agree to the procedure set out in paragraphs (a) and (c).

In terms of Article 15, Sri Lanka wishes to declare that the Judge may proceed to give judgement even if no certificate of service or delivery has been received, provided the conditions set out in Article 15 are fulfilled.

**ST. CHRISTOPHER (St. Kitts):**
Ministry of Legal Affairs

P.O. Box 186
Government Headquarters
St. Kitts-Nevis, West Indies
tel: 809-465-2521

Now Independent. No formal confirmation to depositary government that Convention applies, however local government has provided information to the U.S. Embassy regarding central authority competent to receive Hague Service Convention requests noted above.

**ST. HELENA:**
The Supreme Court
Saint Helena

***ST. LUCIA:***
*Now Independent. No formal confirmation to depositary government that Convention applies, however local government has provided the following information to the U.S. Embassy regarding central authority competent to receive Hague Service Convention requests.*

*Registrar of the High Court*
*Attn: Miss Isabella Shillingford*
*Registry Department*
*Peynier Street*
*Castries, St. Lucia, W.I.*
*tel: 809-452-1257*
*There is no standard fee for service.*

***ST. VINCENT:***
*Now Independent. No formal confirmation to depositary government that Convention applies, however local government has provided the following information to the U.S. Embassy regarding central authority competent to receive Hague Service Convention requests.*

*Ministry of Foreign Affairs*
*St. Vincent and the Grenadines*
*W.I.*
*tel: 809-456-1111*

*There is no fee. The Ministry of Foreign Affairs forwards the request for service to the Registrar's Office which effects service.*

**SEYCHELLES:**
The Registrar
Supreme Court

Victoria
Mahe, Republic des Seychelles

**SLOVAK REPUBLIC:**
Ministerstvo Spravodlivosti Slovenskej Republicky
Zupne namestie 13, 813 11 Bratislava
Slovak Republic
Fax: (00427) 5316035

**SLOVENIA:**
Signatory: September 18, 2000
Accession: May 15, 2001
Entry into Force: June 1, 2001
the Ministry of Justice of the Republic of Slovenia
Zupanciceva 3
1000 LJUBLJANA
tel.: +386 1 478 5244
fax: +386 1 426 1050

***SOLOMON ISLANDS:***
*Unknown. Now Independent. No formal confirmation to depositary government that Convention applies. Former Central Authority: Registrar of the High Court, Honiara*

**SPAIN:**
Secretaria General Tecnica
Subdireccion de Cooperacion Juridica Internacional
Ministerio de Justicia
San Bernardo, 45
28015 Madrid, Spain
tel: (34)(1) 390-2328

**SWEDEN:**
Ministry of Justice
Division for Criminal and International Judicial Cooperation
Central Authority
SE-103 33 Stockholm, Sweden
tel: (46)(8) 405-5057
fax: (46)(8) 405-4676

**SWITZERLAND:**
Switzerland designates the cantonal authorities listed below as Central Authorities as referred to in the respective conventions. Requests for the service of documents may also be addressed to:

The Federal Justice and Police Department
Federal Office for Police Matters

International Judicial and Extrajudicial Assistance
Bundesrain 20
3003 Bern
Switzerland
Tel. 011-41-31-322-4310
Fax 011-41-31-322-5380

That office will forward the requests for service to the Central Authority in the appropriate canton.

Requests for service under the Hague Convention may also be sent directly to the Central Authority for the appropriate Canton. The following list provides the canton, official language of the canton, address and telephone number.

**Authorized Swiss Central Authorities for each Canton**

*Cantonal Central Authorities (list up to date as per 14 September 2001)*
The competent cantonal Central Authority to whom a request may be addressed can be ascertained on-line at the following address: <http://www.elorge.admin.ch/>

Official Language(s) (G=German F=French I=Italian)

| Canton | Language | Address | Phone/Fax |
|---|---|---|---|
| Aargau (AG) | G | Obergericht des Kantons Aargau Obere Vorstadt 40 5000 Aarau | tel.: +41.62-835.3850 fax: +41.62-835.3949 |
| Appenzell Ausserrhoden (AR) | G | Kantonsgericht Appenzell A.Rh. 9043 Trogen | tel.: +41.71-343.6399 fax: +41.71-343.6359 |
| Appenzell Innerrhoden (AI) | G | Kantonsgericht Appenzell I.Rh. 9050 Appenzell | tel.: +41.71-788.9551 fax: +41.71-788.9554 |
| Basel-Landschaft (BL) | G | Obergericht des Kantons Basel-Landschaft 4410 Liestal | tel.: +41.61-925.5111 fax: +41.61-925.6964 |

| | | | |
|---|---|---|---|
| Basel-Stadt (BS) | G | Appellationsgericht Basel-Stadt 4051 Basel | tel.: +41.61-267.8181 fax: +41.61-267.6315 |
| Bern (BE) | G/F | Justiz-, Gemeinde- und Kirchendirektion des Kantons Bern M,nstergasse 2 3011 Bern | tel.: +41.31-633.7676 fax: +41.31-633.7626 |
| Fribourg (FR) | F/G | Tribunal cantonal 1700 Fribourg | tel.: +41.26-305.3910 fax: +41.26-305.3919 |
| Genève (GE) | F | Parquet du Procureur gènèral 1211 Genève 3 | tel.: +41.22-319.2797 fax: +41.22-781.4365 |
| Glarus (GL) | G | Obergericht des Kantons Glarus 8750 Glarus | tel.: +41.55-645.2525 fax: +41.55-645.2500 |
| Graubünden (GR) | G | Justiz-, Polizei- und Sanitätsdepartement Graubünden 7001 Chur | tel.: +41.81-257.2121 fax: +41.81-257.2166 |
| Jura (JU) | F | Dèpartement de la Justice Service juridique 2800 Delèmont | tel.: +41.32-421.5111 fax: +41.32-421.5555 |
| Luzern (LU) | G | Obergericht des Kantons Luzern Hirschengraben 16 6003 Luzern | tel.: +41.41-228.6262 fax: +41.41-228.6264 |
| Neuchâtel (NE) | F | Dèpartement de la justice, de la santè et de la sècuritè Service | tel.: +41.32-889.4110 fax: +41.32 |

| | | | |
|---|---|---|---|
| | | de la justice Château 2001 Neuchâtel | 889.6064 |
| Nidwalden (NW) | G | Kantonsgericht Nidwalden 6370 Stans | tel.: +41.41-618.7950 fax: +41.41-618.7963 |
| Obwalden (OW) | G | Kantonsgericht Obwalden Postfach 1260 6061 Sarnen | tel.: +41.41-666.6222 fax: +41.41-660.8286 |
| St. Gallen (SG) | G | Kantonsgericht St. Gallen Klosterhof 1 9001 St. Gallen | tel.: +41.71-229.3898 fax: +41.71-229.3787 |
| Schaffhausen (SH) | G | Obergericht des Kantons Schaffhausen Postfach 568 8201 Schaffhausen | tel.: +41.52-632.7422 fax: +41.52-636.7836 |
| Schwyz (SZ) | G | Kantonsgericht Schwyz 6430 Schwyz | tel.: +41.41-819.1124 |
| Solothurn (SO) | G | Obergericht des Kantons Solothurn 4500 Solothurn | tel.: +41.32-627.7311 fax: +41.32-627.2298 |
| Tessin (TI) | I | Tribunale di appello 6901 Lugano | tel.: +41.91-815.5111 fax: +41.91-815.5478 |
| Thurgau (TG) | G | Obergericht des Kantons Thurgau 8500 Frauenfeld | tel.: +41.52-722.3121 fax: +41.52-722.3125 |
| Uri (UR) | G | Landgericht Uri Am Rathausplatz 2 6460 Altdorf | tel.: +41.41-875.2244 fax: +41.41 |

| | | | |
|---|---|---|---|
| | | | 875.2277 |
| Valais (VS) | F/G | Tribunal cantonal 1950 Sion | tel.: +41.27-322.9393 fax: +41.27-322.6351 |
| Vaud (VD) | F | Tribunal cantonal 1014 Lausanne | tel.: +41.21-316.1511 fax: +41.21-316.1328 |
| Zug (ZG) | G | Obergericht des Kantons Zug Rechtshilfe 6300 Zug | tel.: +41.41-728.3154 fax: +41.41-728.3144 |
| Zürich (ZH) | G | Obergericht des Kantons Zürich, Rechtshilfe 8023 Zürich | tel.: +41.1-257.9191 fax: +41.1-261.1292 |

**TURKEY:**
General Service of Civil Affairs
Ministry of Justice
Ankara, Turkey

(Adalet Bakanligi Hukuk Isleri Genel Mudurlugu, Ankara, Turkey)

**TURKS & CAICOS:**
The Registrar of the Supreme Court
Turks and Caicos Islands

***TUVALU:***
*Now Independent. No formal confirmation to depositary government that Convention applies. Former Central Authority: Registrar of the High Court.*

**UKRAINE:**
Accession: February 1, 2001; Entry into Force: December 1, 2001.

Central Authority: Ministry of Justice of Ukraine. Seeking clarification regarding address and phone number from Ukraine and the Hague Conference on Private International Law.

The instrument of accession of Ukraine contains the following declarations and reservations:

"1) on Article 2 of the Convention: the Ministry of Justice of Ukraine is the Central Authority of Ukraine;

2) on Article 6 of the Convention: the Ministry of Justice of Ukraine and its territorial departments of justice are competent to complete the certificate of service;

3) on Article 8 of the Convention: service of judicial documents through diplomatic or consular agents of another State within the territory of Ukraine may be effected only upon nationals of the State in which the documents originate;

4) on Article 9 of the Convention: the Ministry of Justice of Ukraine is the authority competent to receive documents transmitted by consular channels or, if exceptional circumstances so require, by diplomatic channels;

5) on Article 10 of the Convention: Ukraine will not use methods of transmission of judicial documents provided for in Article 10 of the Convention;

6) on Article 15 of the Convention: if all the conditions provided for in the second paragraph of Article 15 of the Convention are fulfilled, the judge, notwithstanding the provisions of the first paragraph of Article 15 of the Convention, may give judgment even if no certificate of service or delivery has been received;

7) on Article 16 of the Convention: application for relief will not be entertained in Ukraine if it is filed after the expiration of one year following the date of the judgment."

**UNITED KINGDOM:**
Her Majesty's Principal Secretary of State for
Foreign and Commonwealth Affairs
London SW1A 2AL

**For England and Wales:**
The Senior Master of the Supreme Court of Judicature
Royal Courts of Justice
Strand
London WC2A 2LL, United Kingdom

**For Scotland:**
By a Note of 21 March 2000, the British Government notified that, with effect from 1 April 2000, the designated authority for Scotland will be:

The Scottish Executive Justice Department
Civil Justice and International Division
Hayweight House

23 Lauriston Street
Edinburgh, EH3 9DQ
Telephone: +44.131.221.6815
Fax: +44.131.221.6894

**For Northern Ireland:**
By a Note of 10 June 1980, the British Government notified that instead of the Registrar of the Supreme Court of Northern Ireland, designated in 1967 as the additional authority for Northern Ireland in conformity with Article 18 of the Convention, the Master (Queen's Bench and Appeals) is designated as the said additional authority. The address of the Master (Queen's Bench and Appeals) is Royal Courts of Justice, Belfast 1.

**VENEZUELA:**
Ministry of Foreign Affairs
Caracas, Venezuela

**REFERENCE**

"Checklist for the Discussions of the Special Commission of April 1989 on the Operation of the Hague Convention on the Service of Process Abroad", Preliminary Document No. 1 of March 1989, Hague Conference on Private International Law, 28 I.L.M. 1556 (1989).

"Report on the Work of the Special Commission on the Operation of the Service Convention", 17 I.L.M. 312, 312 (1978).

Practical Handbook on the Operation of the Hague Convention of 15 November 1965 on the Service Abroad of Judicial and Extrajudicial Documents in Civil or Commercial Matters, Hague Conference on Private International Law, Maarten Kluwer"s Internationale Uitgeversonderneming, Antwerp 1983. U.S. Distributor: Butterworth Publishers Inc., 10 Tower Office Park, Woburn, Boston, Massachusetts 01801. Contact U.S. Central Authority for addresses of other distributors.

Cumulative Digest of United States Practice in International Law, 1981-1988, Vol. II, Department of State, Office of the Legal Adviser, pp. 1530-1547 (1994).

Digest of United States Practice in International Law, 1976, Department of State, Office of the Legal Adviser, p. 307.

Digest of United States Practice in International Law, 1977, Department of State, Office of the Legal Adviser, pp. 477-490; pp. 501-504.

Digest of United States Practice in International Law, 1980, Department of State, Office of the Legal Adviser, p. 457.

Amram, "The Proposed International Convention on the Service of Documents Abroad", 51 A.B.A. J. 650 (1965).

Baeck & Ginsberg, "Service of Process Abroad", 4 Int"l. Law. 145 (1969).

Basarrate, Note: "International Service of Process: Reconciling the Federal Rules of Civil Procedure with the Hague Convention on the Service Abroad of Judicial and Extrajudicial Documents in Civil or Commercial Matters", Vanderbilt Journal of Transnational Law", Vol. 22, No. 5, pp. 1071-1096 (1988).

Beucher & Sandage, "United States Punitive Damage Awards in German Courts: The Evolving German position on Service and Enforcement", Vanderbilt Journal of Transnational Law, Vol. 23, No. 5, pp. 967-991 (1991).

Boyd, "Contemporary Practice of the United States Relating to International Law - The Hague Service Convention", 72 American Journal of International Law, 130 (1978).

Downs, "Note: The Effect of the Hague Convention on Service Abroad of Judicial and Extrajudicial Documents in Civil or Commercial Matters", 1 Cornell Intl L. J., 125 (1969).

Epstein, International Litigation: A Guide to Jurisdiction, Practice and Strategy, 2nd, Prentice Hall Law & Business, 1994.

Gordon, Comment: "Service of Process by Registered Mail on a Japanese Defendant is Ineffective Under Article 10(a) of the Hague Convention of November 15, 1965 on the Service Abroad of Judicial and Extrajudicial Documents in Civil and Commercial Matters, Bankston v. Toyota Motor Corp. 889 F. 2nd 172 (8th Cir. 1989)" Vanderbilt Journal of Transnational Law, Vol. 23, No. 4, pp. 851-869.

Horlick, "Service of Process and other Documents Abroad, American Bar Association, Problems in Transnational Litigation, 23 (1980).

Horlick, "A Practical Guide to Service of Process Abroad", 14 Int"l. Law. 637 (1980).

Hoyal, "The Hague Service Convention and Agency Concepts: Lamb v. Volkswagenwerk Aktiengesellschaft", Cornell International Law Journal, Vol. 20, pp. 391-412.

Leo, Note: "The Interplay Between Domestic Rules Permitting Service Abroad by Mail and the Hague Convention on Service: Proposing an Amendment to the Federal Rules of Civil Procedure", Cornell International Law Journal, Vol. 22, No. 2, pp. 335-370 (1989).

Miller and Pionk, "The practical aspects of litigating against foreign corporations", 54 Journal of Air Law and Commerce 123 (Fall 1988), esp. pp. 128-137.

Mitsui, "Ratification of Convention Relating to Civil Procedure on the Service Abroad of Judicial and Extra-Judicial Documents in Civil and Commercial Matters", 16 Japanese Annual Int"l. L. 7 (1972).

Nanda and Pansius, Litigation of International Disputes in U.S. Courts, Vol. 4, International Business and Law Series, (1996), Sec. 2.02(2), pp. 2-4 - 2-15.

Note, "Closing the Chasm of International Judicial Assistance: Extraterritorial Service of Documents, 12 How. L. J. 238 (1966).

Ristau, International Judicial Assistance (Civil and Commercial), International Law Institute (1984, supp. 1990, 1995).

Schwartz, "Obtaining Evidence Overseas: Discovery on Foreign Shores", 9 Family Advocate 28 (1987) [includes discussion of service abroad].

Vazquez, "Hague Service Convention - scope and application - role of internal law: Volkswagen Aktiengesellschaft v. Schlunk, 82 American Journal of International Law 816 (1988).

**ADDITIONAL INFORMATION** :

The Office of American Citizens Services has available general information flyers on international judicial assistance . These topics include country-specific information about service of process and obtaining evidence abroad.

**Using the Internet:** Many of our judicial assistance flyers are available on the Internet via the Department of State, Bureau of Consular Affairs home page . See also, the Department of State, Office of the Legal Adviser for Private International Law home page for information regarding the work of the Hague Conference on Private International Law. See also the home pages for many of our embassies . As noted above, the text of the Convention and updatedinformation concerning countries which have acceded to the Convention can be found in the Martindale-Hubbell Law Directory, Law Digest Volume .

**QUESTIONS** :

1. U.S. Central Authority: Additional questions regarding the operation of the Hague Service Convention should be addressed to the U.S. Central Authority, the Office of International Judicial Assistance, Civil Division, Department of Justice, tel: (202) 307-0983.

2. General questions may also be addressed to the appropriate geographic division of the Office of American Citizens Services, at telephone (202) 647-5225 or 202-647-5226.

This site is managed by the Bureau of Consular Affairs, U.S. Department of State. External links to other Internet sites should not be construed as an endorsement of the views contained therein.

# U.S. Department of State

## Hague Convention on Legalization of Foreign Public Documents

**DISCLAIMER: THE INFORMATION IN THIS CIRCULAR RELATING TO THE LEGAL REQUIREMENTS OF SPECIFIC FOREIGN COUNTRIES IS PROVIDED FOR GENERAL INFORMATION ONLY. QUESTIONS INVOLVING INTERPRETATION OF SPECIFIC FOREIGN LAWS SHOULD BE ADDRESSED TO FOREIGN COUNSEL.**

**Frequently Asked Questions**

- Q. What countries follow the Hague Legalization Convention?
- Q. Who is the foreign central authority for a particular country?
- Q. In the United States, who can put the Hague Legalization Convention "apostille" certificate on a document?

**Learn About the Hague Legalization Convention**

**Q. I have a document which has the seal of a notary, state or federal official in the United States. What do I need to do to be able to use this document overseas?**

A. The document must be authenticated for use abroad. This is also called legalization of the document. Authentication means that a seal is placed on the document which will be recognized in the foreign country where the document will be used.

**Q. How do I get the document authenticated or legalized?**

A. That depends on whether the country where the document will be used in a party to a treaty on this subject called the "Hague Convention Abolishing the Requirement of Legalization for Foreign Public Documents".

**Q. What procedures should be followed if the Hague Legalization Convention does not apply?**

A. If the country is not a party to the Hague Convention, see our general information on Authentication of Documents for Use Abroad available via our home page.

**Q. What is a Public Document under the Hague Legalization Convention?**

A. For the purposes of the Convention, public documents include:

a. documents issued by a state court;
b. administrative documents;
c. documents executed before a notary public;

d. official certificates which are placed on documents signed by persons in their private capacity, such as official certificates recording the registration of a document or the fact that it was in existence on a certain date and official and notarial authentications of signatures.

**Q. Where does the Hague Legalization Convention apply?**

A. The Hague Legalization Convention is in force in the following countries. But see the next question regarding how the change of status of a country affects treaty obligations. Click on the name of the country for specific information about the competent authority to issue apostille certificates and other details on how the Hague Legalization Convention works in that country.

- ANDORRA
- ANGOLA
- ANGUILLA
- ANTIGUA AND BARBUDA
- ARGENTINA
- ARMENIA
- ARUBA
- AUSTRALIA
- AUSTRIA
- BAHAMAS
- BARBADOS
- BELARUS
- BELGIUM
- BELIZE
- BERMUDA
- BOSNIA-HERZEGOVINA
- BOTSWANA
- BRITISH VIRGIN ISLANDS
- BRUNEI
- BULGARIA
- CAYMAN ISLANDS
- CHINA *(Hong Kong SAR (Special Administrative Region) ONLY)*
  CHINA *(Macau SAR (Special Administrative Region) ONLY)*
- COLOMBIA
- COMOROS ISLANDS
- CROATIA
- CYPRUS
- CZECH REPUBLIC
- DJIBOUTI
- DOMINICA
- EL SALVADOR
- ESTONIA
- FALKLAND ISLANDS

- FIJI
- FINLAND
- FRANCE

***Extended to:***

- NEW CALEDONIA
- WALLIS AND FUTUNA
- FRENCH POLYNESIA

- GERMANY
- GIBRALTAR
- GREECE
- GRENADA
- GUERNSEY
- HONG KONG SAR (China, Hong Kong SAR)
- HUNGARY
- IRELAND
- ISLE OF MAN
- ISRAEL
- ITALY
- JAPAN
- JERSEY
- KAZAKHSTAN
- LATVIA
- LESOTHO
- LIBERIA
- LIECHTENSTEIN
- LITHUANIA
- LUXEMBOURG
- MACAU SAR (China, Macau SAR)
- MACEDONIA
- MALAWI
- MALTA
- MARSHALL ISLANDS
- MAURITIUS
- MEXICO
- MONTSERRAT
- MOZAMBIQUE
- NAMIBIA
- NETHERLANDS

***Extended to:***

- ARUBA

- NETHERLANDS ANTILLES (Curacao, Bonaire, St. Martin, St. Eustatius and Saba)
- SURINAME

- NEW ZEALAND
- NIUE
- NORWAY
- PANAMA
- PORTUGAL

***Extended to:***

- ANGOLA
- MOZAMBIQUE

- ROMANIA
- RUSSIAN FEDERATION
- ST. CHRISTOPHER (Kitts) AND NEVIS
- ST. GEORGIA AND SOUTH SANDWICH ISLANDS
- ST. HELENA
- ST. LUCIA
- ST. PIERRE AND MIQUELON
- ST. VINCENT AND THE GRENADINES
- SAMOA
- SAN MARINO
- SEYCHELLES
- SLOVAKIA
- SLOVENIA
- SOLOMON ISLANDS
- SOUTH AFRICA
- SPAIN
- SURINAME
- SWAZILAND
- SWEDEN
- SWITZERLAND
- TONGA
- TRINIDAD AND TOBAGO
- TURKEY
- TUVALU
- UNITED KINGDOM

***Extended to:***

- JERSEY
- GUERNSEY
- ISLE OF MAN

- ANTIGUA
- BAHAMAS
- BARBADOS
- BERMUDA
- BRUNEI
- CAYMAN ISLANDS
- DOMINICA
- FALKLAND ISLANDS
- FIJI
- GIBRALTAR
- GRENADA
- HONG KONG
- MAURITIUS
- MONTSERRAT
- ST. HELENA
- ST. KITTS
- NEVIS
- ANGUILLA
- ST. LUCIA
- ST. VINCENT
- SEYCHELLES
- TURKS AND CAICOS
- VIRGIN ISLANDS, BRITISH

- UNITED STATES

***Extended to:***

- 50 STATES
- THE DISTRICT OF COLUMBIA
- AMERICAN SAMOA
- GUAM (TERRITORY OF)
- NORTHERN MARIANA ISLANDS (COMMONWEALTH OF)
- PUERTO RICO
- U.S. VIRGIN ISLANDS

- VANUATU
- VENEZUELA
- YUGOSLAVIA

**Q. Where can I find the text of the Convention?**

**A.** See 527 U.N.T.S. 189, T.I.A.S. 10072, 20 I.L.M. 1405, 1407, Martindale-Hubbell Law Director, Law Digest Volume, Selected International Conventions or see the web site for the Hague Convention on Private International Law.

**Q. How can I keep track when new countries join the Hague Legalization Convention?**

**A.** The easiest way to find out whether a new country has become a party to the Hague Legalization Convention is to check out the web site on the Internet for the Hague Conference on Private International Law at http://www.hcch.net/ for up to date information about recent accessions to the Convention. The U.S. Department of State Consular Affairs home page and U.S. State Department Authentications Office home page are updated periodically after the Government of the Netherlands notifies the United States that a new country has deposited its instruments of accession to the Convention.

**Q. Does a change of status of a country affect whether the Hague Legalization Convention is still in force?**

**A.** This is a complex question. The following notes may assist you in understanding how the change of status of a country can affect treaty obligations.

1. When the Hague Legalization Convention first entered into force, many countries declared that the treaty also applied in foreign dependencies which have since declared independence We have requested the assistance of the Hague Conference on Private International Law to confirm whether these countries continue to consider themselves bound by the treaty.
2. In accordance with Article 34(1) of the Vienna Convention on Succession of States in Respect of Treaties, the U.S. view is that when a country which is a party to a multilateral treaty or convention has dissolved, the successor state(s) inherit the treaty obligations of the former government, consistent with Article 34 of the Vienna Convention on Succession of States in Respect of Treaties. However, as a practical matter, the custom is for depositaries to expect a notice of succession to confirm that the new entity is performing its treaty obligations. Many newly independent states may not really be implementing such conventions at this time in that they may not be performing the functions set forth in the Convention. We continue to work with these governments and the depositories to obtain confirmation that the respective successor state is complying with treaty obligations.
3. On September 4, 1991, the Union of Soviet Socialist Republics (USSR) deposited an instrument of accession to the Convention. The Convention was to have entered into force for the USSR on April 1, 1992. Prior to that date, the USSR dissolved. Three members of the Newly Independent States (NIS), the Russian Federation, the Belarus Republic and Armenia have informed the depositary for the Convention that the Convention applies in those jurisdictions. We have requested the assistance of the Hague Conference on Private International Law in ascertaining from the other NIS countries whether they are applying the Convention. Even if other NIS countries were to consider the Convention to apply, it may not be operational. Each jurisdiction must designate an authority competent to issue the Convention certificate (apostille) before the Convention can be operational. It may be wise to have documents prepared for use in

jurisdictions which have not yet designated an authority competent to affix the Convention apostille in two sets, one using the apostille and one using the chain authentication method, including the seal of the foreign embassy or consulate if possible. Local authorities in such jurisdictions may question the validity of the apostille due to lack of familiarity with the certificate. In addition, the some states, for example, the Russian Federation, have declined to affix the Convention apostille to administrative or commercial documents. Such documents would have to be authenticated using the chain authentication method.

4. Former Yugoslavia was a party to the Convention. Slovenia, Macedonia, Bosnia-Herzegovina and Croatia have informed the depositary that they consider the Convention to apply and have designated a competent authority to issue the Convention certificate (apostille). The names of the competent authorities designated by the remaining segments of former Yugoslavia (Serbia-Montenegro) continue to be listed in this flyer as a point of reference.

**Q. How does the Hague Legalization Convention make dealing with documents between countries easier?**

**A.** The Convention simplifies the old "chain" authentication procedure which requires multiple seals to be place on documents, by eliminating many links in the chain. Documents which have the special Hague Legalization Certificate are acceptable in other countries where the treaty is in force without any other authentication.

**Q. What certificate is used under the Hague Legalization Convention?**

**A.** If you have a document you want legalized for use in another country which is also a party to the treaty, a special certification called an "apostille" must be affixed to the document by a competent authority. The apostille is a pre-printed form prescribed by the Convention. See a copy of the apostille certificate in Volume 7, Department of State, Foreign Affairs Manual, Section 847.2 (Exhibit) on the State Department Freedom of Information Act (FOIA) site. On that site, select Foreign Affairs Regulations, and then, 7 FAM - Consular Affairs. You may also go to the web site for the Hague Convention on Private International Law . See also, Digest, United States Practice in International Law, 1981-1988, Office of the Legal Adviser, U.S. Department of State, Vol 2, 1548 (1994); Ristau, International Judicial Assistance, Civil and Commercial, International Law Institute, Vol 1, Section 6-2-6 (1995).

**Q. Is there a fee for the Apostille Certificate?**

**A.** Fees vary depending on where the certificate is issued. Fees are subject to change without notice. For federal documents authenticated by the U.S. Department of State, the fee is $5.00 (effective January 1, 1997). See references to fees under specific countries and U.S. states noted below.

**Q. Who are the U.S. "Competent Authorities" to issue the apostille certificate?**

**A.** There are three levels of U.S. competent authorities, one for Federal agencies, one for U.S. (federal) courts, and one for state documents, including documents executed before notaries.

**1. Federal Executive and Administrative Agencies:** Authentications Office, Department of State, 518 23rd St., N.W., Washington, D.C. 20520, (202) 647-5002 Fee: $5.00. For additional information, call the Federal Information Center: 1-800-688-9889, and choose option 6 after you press 1 for touch tone phones. Walk-in service is available from the Authentications Office from 8 a.m. to 12 noon Monday-Friday, except holidays. Walk-in service is limited to 15 documents per person per day (documents can be multiple pages). Processing time for authentication requests sent by mail is 5 working days or less. See also, the State Department home page : http://www.state. See also in general, 22 C.F.R. 131.

**2. U.S. Courts:** Clerks and Deputy Clerks of the Federal Court System. Fee: $5.00.

For the purposes of the Convention, clerks and deputy clerks of the U.S. Courts shall include the clerks and deputy clerks of the following: The Supreme Court of the United States, the Courts of Appeals for the First through the Eleventh Circuits and the District of Columbia Circuit, the United States District Courts, the United States Court of Claims, the United States Court of Customs and Patent Appeals, the United States Court of International Trade, the United States District Court for the District of the Canal Zone, the District Court of Guam, the District Court of the Virgin Islands, and the District Court for the Northern Mariana Islands.

**3. States, Territories and Other Jurisdictions:** Each state and other jurisdiction in the United States (District of Columbia, Puerto Rico, American Samoa, U.S. Virgin Islands, Commonwealth of the Northern Mariana Islands, Guam)

**Q. How can I contact that Competent Authorities to issue the Apostille Certificate in Each State or other Jurisdiction in the United States?**

**A.** Click here for the name, address and telephone number of the Competent authority and fee information.

**Q. Where Can I Read More About the Hague Legalization Convention?**

**A.** This is a selected list of references which may be helpful.

Administrative Office of the United States Courts, Addendum (Section 4, paragraphs 304.1-304.7) to Guide to Judiciary Policies and Procedures (Vol. IV, Ch. 3).
American Bar Association, The Hague Convention Abolishing the Requirement of Legalisation for Foreign Public Documents (Report of the Committee on the International Unification of Private Law, with Action by the Section of International Law and the House of Delegates); 9 International Lawyer, No. 4, 755 (1975).
Amram, Toward Easier Legalisation of Foreign Public Documents; 60 American Bar

Association Journal, 310, (1974).
Apostilles: Jet-Age Authentication, Nat'l Notary Mag., 10, 14 (July 1996).
Apostilles: Authenticating Documents for Use in Foreign Countries, Am. Notary, 7 (Apr. - June 1997).
Authentication: Proving Your Powers: The Time-Saving "Apostille", The National Notary, 24-25, January (1990)
Clerk's Manual, United States Disrict Courts,Vol 1, Section 17.06 - Apostilles.
Deukmejian, United States: State of California Attorney General's Opinion on the Hague Convention Abolishing the Requirement of Legalization for Foreign Public Documents, 21 I.L.M. 357, 362 (1982)
Deukmejian, California Attorney General's Opinion No. 88-802, January 5, 1989, 89 Daily Journal D.A.R. 148 (recordability of an apostille in the French language).
Griew, Hague Draft Convention on the Legalisation of Foreign Documents and the Form of Wills, 8 Int'l and Comp. L.Q. 559 (1959).
Hague Convention Abolishing the Requirement for Legalization of Foreign Public Documents, Patent and Trademark Review 39, January (1982).
Harvey, The United States and The Hague Convention Abolishing the Requirement of Legalization for Foreign Public Documents, 11 Harv. Int'l. L.J. 476 (1970).
Lowry, Doc. 6, Critical Documents Sourcebook Annotated, International Commercial Law and Arbitration 157 (1991).
Meszaros, Notarial Services Provided by U.S. Consuls, 33 American Notary, No. 2, 1, 9 (1998).
Nash-Leich, The Hague Convention Abolishing the Requirement of Legalization for Foreign Public Documents, 76 Am. J. Int'l L. 182 (1982).
Pfund, P.H., Chapter, "Legalization of Documents for Use Abroad" in The International Lawyer's Deskbook, edited by Lowe, Norton and Drory, ABA (Section of International Law and Practice) 1996, ISBN 1-57073-166-7.
Ristau, International Judicial Assistance (Civil and Commercial), Vol. 1, International Law Institute, Washington, D.C., Sec. 6.1-1 - 6-2-7, 241-256 (1995).
Sherry, Old Treaties Never Die, They Just Lose Their Teeth: Authentication Needs of a Global Community Demand Retirement of the Hague Public Documents Convention, 31 John Marshall Law Review 1045 (1998).
Sinnott, A Practical Guide to Document Authentication: Legalization of Notarized and Certified Documents 464 (1997).
Untangling the Red Tape of Authentication, The National Notary, 34-35, January/February (1981).
Zamora and Brand, II Basic Documents of International Economic Law, 845-854, (1990).

**Q. Who Can I Talk to If I Have Questions About the Hague Legalization Convention?**

**A.** Responsibility for the Hague Legalization Convention is shared by various offices in the U.S. Department of State. Contact the office responsible for the issue in which you are interested.

1. **How to Authenticate a Federal Document in the United States** - U.S. Department of State, Authentications Office: 1-800-688-9889 (Option #6).
2. **How to Get a Foreign Document Authenticated for Use in the United States** - U.S. Department of State, Overseas Citizens Services, American Citizens Services and Crisis Management - (202) 647-5225.
3. **How to interpret the Hague Legalization Convention** - U.S. Department of State, Overseas Citizens Services, Office of Policy Review and Inter-Agency Liaison, (202) 647-3666.
4. **Negotiation History** - U.S. Department of State, Office of the Legal Adviser, Private International Law.

**Q. Where Can I Find The State Department's Publications About the Hague Legalization Convention?**

**A.** We have information available via our home page on the Internet, our automated fax service and by mail.

**Internet Resources**

U.S. State Department Consular Affairs home page at http://travel.state.gov

Authentications Office home page at http://www.state.gov/

Office of the Legal Adviser, Treaty Affairs home page at http://www.state.gov/

**Q. Where can I find the Hague Conference on Private International Law information about the Hague Legalization Convention?**

**A.** Hague Conference on Private International Law home page on the Internet is http://www.hcch.net/

State Authentication Authorities

***Alabama***
Office of the Secretary of State
Authentication Section
State Capitol, Room E-204
600 Dexter Ave.
Montgomery, AL 36104
334-242-7210
http://www.sos.state.al.us/authenticate/index.htm
**Fee: $5.00**
Designated Authority: Secretary of State

***Alaska***
Notary Administrator

Office of the Lieutenant Governor
P.O. Box 110015
Juneau, AK 99811- 0015
907-465-3509
http://www.gov.state.ak.us/ltgov/notary/authentications.htm
**Fee: $2.00**
Designated Authority: Lieut enant Governor; Attorney General; Clerk of the Supreme Court

***Arizona***
Office of the Secretary of State
Business Services Division, Notary Section
1700 W. Washington, 7th Floor
Phoenix, AZ 85007-2888
602 542-4086/ 602 542-4758
http://www.sosaz.com/notary
**Fee: $3.00**
Designated Authority: Secretary of State; Assistant Secretary of State.

***Arkansas***
Office of Secretary of State
Corporations Division
State Capitol
Little Rock, AR 72201-1094
501-682-3409
http://www.sosweb.state.ar.us/business.html
**Fee: $10.00**
Designated Authority: Secretary of State; Chief Deputy Secretary of State.

***California***
Office of the Secretary of State
Business Programs Division
Notary Public Section
P.O. Box 942877
Sacramento, CA 94277-0001
916-653-3595
http://www.ss.ca.gov/business/notary/notary.htm
**Fee: $20.00**
Designated Authority: Secretary of State; any Assistant Secretary of State; any Deputy Secretary of State.

***Colorado***
Office of Secretary of State
1560 Broadway, Suite 200
Denver, CO 80202
303-894-2680

http://www.sos.state.co.us/pubs/info_center/2001fees.htm
**Fee: By Mail: $2.00 While You Wait: $17.00**
Designated Authority: Secretary of State; Deputy Secretary of State.

***Connecticut***
Office of the Secretary of State
Authentication Unit
30 Trinity St.
Hartford, CT 06106
860-509-6135
http://www.sots.state.ct.us/recordslegislativeservices/authen.html#orders
**Fee: $20.00**
Designated Authority: Secretary of State; Deputy Secretary of State.

***Delaware***
Office of Secretary of State
Notary Division
401 Federal St., Suite 3
Dover, DE 19901
302- 302/739-4111
http://www.state.de.us/sos/sos.htm
**Fee: $10.00**
Designated Authority: Secretary of State; Acting Secretary of State.

***District of Columbia***
Office of the Secretary, D.C.
Notary Commissions & Authentications Section
441 4th St. N.W. (One Judiciary Square)
Washington, D.C.
202-727-3117
http://os.dc.gov/info/notary/notary.shtm#document
**Fee: $10.00**
Designated Authority: Executive Secretary; Assistant Executive Secretary; Mayor's Special Assistant and Assistant to the Executive Secretary; Secretary of the District of Columbia.

***Florida***
Department of State
Office of International Affairs
Notary Certification/Apostille Section
The Capitol Building
Suite 1902
Tallahassee, FL 32399-0250
804-488-7521
http://notaries.dos.state.fl.us/notproc7.htm

**Fee: $10.00**
Designated Authority: Secretary of State

***Georgia***
Georgia Superior Court Clerks' Cooperative Authority
Notary Division
1875 Century Boulevard, Suite 100
Atlanta, GA 30345
404-327-6023
http://www2.gsccca.org/projects/apost.html

or

Office of Secretary of State
Administrative Procedures Unit
2 Martin Luther King Jr. Drive
Suite 820 - West Tower
Atlanta, Georgia 30334
404-656-2885
http://www.sos.state.ga.us/administration/notary.htm
**Fee: $3.00**
Designated Authority: Secretary of State; Georgia Superior Court Clerks' Cooperative Authority.

***Hawaii***
Office of the Lieutenant Governor
State Capitol, 5 th Floor,
Honolulu, Hawaii 96813
808-586-0255
http://www.state.hi.us/ltgov/page8.html
**Fee: $1.00**
Designated Authority: Lieutenant Governor of the State of Hawaii.

***Idaho***
Office of Secretary of State
Notary Department
Box 83720
Boise, ID 83720
208- 332-2810
http://www.idsos.state.id.us/notary/apostill.htm
**Fee: $10.00**
Designated Authority: Secretary of State; Chief Deputy Secretary of State; Deputy Secretary of State; Notary Public Clerk.

***Illinois***
Office of the Secretary of State

Index Department, Notaries Public Division
111 E. Monroe St.
Springfield, IL 62756
217- 217-782-7017
http://www.sos.state.il.us/departments/index/division.html
**Fee: $2.00**
Designated Authority: Secretary of State; Assistant Secretary of State; Deputy Secretary of State.

***Indiana***
Office of Secretary of State
Statehouse
Suite 201
Indianapolis, IN 46204
317-232-6532
http://www.in.gov/sos/notary/seal.html
**Fee: no charge**
Designated Authority: Secretary of State; Deputy Secretary of State

***Iowa***
Office of Secretary of State
Lucas Building
First Floor, Public Service
Des Moines, IA 50319
515-281-5204
http://www.sos.state.ia.us
**Fee: $5.00**
Designated Authority: Secretary of State; Deputy Secretary of State

***Kansas***
Office of Secretary of State
State Capitol
Second Floor
Topeka, KS 66612
913-296-2744
http://www.kssos.org
**Fee: $5.00**
Designated Authority: Secretary of State; Assistant Secretary of State; any Deputy Assistant Secretary of State.

***Kentucky***
Office of Secretary of State
Capitol Building
P.O. Box 718
Frankfort, KY 40602-0178
502-564-7330

**Fee: $5.00**
http://www.kysos.com
Designated Authority: Secretary of State; Assistant Secretary of State.

***Louisiana***
Office of Secretary of State
P.O. Box 94125
Baton Rouge, LA 70804-9125
504-342-4981
**Fee: $5.00**
http://www.sec.state.la.us/comm/comm- index.htm
Designated Authority: Secretary of State.

***Maine***
Office of Secretary of State
Bureau of Corporations
Elections and Commissions
101 State House Station
Augusta, ME 04333-0101
207-624-7650
http://www.state.me.us/sos/cec/rcn/notary/authapos.htm
**Fee: $10.00**
Designated Authority: Secretary of State; Deputy Secretary of State.

***Maryland***
Office of Secretary of State
Statehouse
Annapolis, MD 21401
410-974-5520
http://www.sos.state.md.us/sos/certif/html/certif2c.html#apos
**Fee: $5.00**
Designated Authority: Secretary of State.

***Massachusetts***
Secretary of the Commonwealth
Public Records Division
Commissions Section
McCormack Building, Room 1719
One Ashburton Place
Boston, MA 02108
617-727-2832
http://www.state.ma.us/sec/pre/precom/comidx.htm
**Fee: $3.00**

***Michigan***
Department of State

Office of the Great Seal
7064 Crowner Boulevard
Lansing, MI 48918
517-373-2531
http://www.michigan.gov/sos/1,1607,7-127-1638_8734---,00.html
**Fee: $1.00**
Designated Authority: Secretary of State; Deputy Secretary of State.

***Minnesota***
Secretary of State's Office
180 State Office Bldg.
St. Paul, MN 55155
651-296-2803
http://www.sos.state.mn.us/uccd/authinfo.html
**Fee: $5.00**
Designated Authority: Secretary of State; Deputy Secretary of State.

***Mississippi***
Office of Secretary of State
P.O. Box 136
Jackson, MS 39205-0136
601-359-1615
http://www.sos.state.ms.us/busserv/notaries/notaries.html
**Fee: $5.00**
Designated Authority: Secretary of State; any Assistant Secretary of State.

***Missouri***
Office of Secretary of State
Commission Division
600 West Main, Room 367
Jefferson City, MO 65102
573-751-2783
http://www.sos.state.mo.us/business/commissions/certify.asp
Fee: $10.00
Designated Authority: Secretary of State; Deputy Secretary of State.

***Montana***
Office of Secretary of State
Room 225
Box 202801
State Capitol
Helena, MT 59602
406-444-5379
http://sos.state.mt.us/css/index.asp
**Fee: $2.00**

Designated Authority: Secretary of State; Chief Deputy Secretary of State; Government Affairs Bureau Chief.

***Nebraska***
Office of Secretary of State
Notary Division
Box 95104
State Capitol
Lincoln, NE 68509
402-471-2558
http://www.sos.state.ne.us/Notary/notauth.htm
**Fee: $10.00**
Designated Authority: Secretary of State; Deputy Secretary of State.

***Nevada***
Secretary of State
101 N. Carson Street, #3
Carson City, NV 89701-4786
775-684-5708
http://sos.state.nv.us/notary/apostille.htm
**Fee: $20.00**
Designated Authority: Secretary of State; Chief Deputy Secretary of State; Deputy Secretary of State.

***New Hampshire***
Office of Secretary of State
Statehouse
Room 204
Concord, NH 03301
603-271-3242
http://www.state.nh.us/sos/certific.htm
**Fee: $5.00**
Designated Authority: Secretary of State; Deputy Secretary of State

***New Jersey***
Department of State
Notary Public Unit
Division of Commercial Recording
PO Box 452
Trenton, NJ 08625
609-530-6421
http://www.state.nj.us/treasury/revenue/dcr/programs/notary.html
**Fee: Regular Service: $25.00 Expedited Service: $35.00**
Designated Authority: NJ Department of the Treasury, Division of Revenue

*New Mexico*
Office of the Secretary of State
State Capitol North Annex, Suite 300
Santa Fe, NM 87503
505-827-3600
http://www.sos.state.nm.us/notary-cert.htm
**Fee: $3.00**
Designated Authority: Secretary of State

*New York*

- **Upstate Counties**
  Miscellaneous Records
  162 Washington Ave.
  Albany, NY 12231
  518-474-4770
  http://www.dos.state.ny.us
  **Fee: $10.00**
  Designated Authority: Secretary of State; Executive Deputy Secretary of State; any Deputy Secretary of State; any Special Deputy Secretary of State.
- **Down State Counties**
  New York authorities in Albany advise that documents issued in the nine down state counties are authenticated under the Convention by the New York City office. The nine down state counties are New York, Kings, Queens, Bronx, Westchester, Nassau, Suffolk, Rockland and Richmond. The address of the New York Department of State, Certification Unit is 6th Floor, 270 Broadway, New York, New York 10007, tel: 212-417-5684. **Fee: $10.00**

*North Carolina*
Office of Secretary of State
Authentication Division
PO Box 29622
Raleigh, NC 27626-0622
919-807-2140
http://www.secretary.state.nc.us/authen
**Fee: $10.00**
Designated Authority: Secretary of State; Deputy Secretary of State

*North Dakota*
Office of Secretary of State
Capitol Building
600 E Boulevard Ave., Dept 108
Bismarck, ND 58505
701-328-2900
http://www.state.nd.us/sec

**Fee: $10.00**
Designated Authority: Secretary of State; Deputy Secretary of State.

***Ohio***
Office of the Secretary of State
30 East Broad St.
15th Fl.
Columbus, OH 43266-0418
877-767-6446
http://www.state.oh.us/sos/authentication_of_documents_stat.htm
**Fee: $5.00**
Designated Authority: Secretary of State; Assistant Secretary of State.

***Oklahoma***
Office of Secretary of State
2300 N. Lincoln
Room 101
Oklahoma City, OK 73105
405-521-4211
http://www.sos.state.ok.us
**Fee: $25.00 (cashiers check or money order)**
Designated Authority: Secretary of State; Assistant Secretary of State; Budget Officer of the Secretary of State.

***Oregon***
Office of Secretary of State
255 Capitol St.
Suite 151
Salem OR 97310
503-986-2200.
http://www.filinginoregon.com/notary/index.htm
**Fee: $10.00**
Designated Authority: Secretary of State; Deputy Secretary of State; Acting Secretary of State; Assistant to the Secretary of State.

***Pennsylvania***
Department of State
Bureau of Commissions
Elections and Legislation
North Office Building
Room 304
Harrisburg, PA 17120
717-787-5280
http://www.dos.state.pa.us/bcel/certifications/certifications.html
**Fee: $15.00**

Designated Authority: Secretary of the Commonwealth; Executive Deputy Secretary of the Commonwealth.

***Rhode Island***
Office of Secretary of State
Notary Division
100 N. Main St.
Providence, RI 02903
401-277-1487
http://www.corps.state.ri.us/notaries/notaries.htm
**Fee: $5.00**
Designated Authority: Secretary of State; First Deputy Secretary of State; Deputy Secretary of State

***South Carolina***
Office of Secretary of State
P.O. Box 11350
Columbia, SC 29211
803-734-2119
http://www.scsos.com/notariesbc.htm
**Fee: $2.00**
Designated Authority: Secretary of State

***South Dakota***
Office of Secretary of State
500 East Capitol
Pierre, SD 57501-5077
605-773-5004
http://www.state.sd.us/sos/Notaries/apostilles_and_authentications.htm
**Fee: $2.00**
Designated Authority: Secretary of State; Deputy Secretary of State

***Tennessee***
Office of Secretary of State
James K. Polk Building
Division of Business Services
312 Eighth Avenue North
6th Floor, William R. Snodgrass Tower
Nashville, TN 37243
615-741-3699
http://www.state.tn.us/sos/service.htm#apostilles
**Fee: $2.00**
Designated Authority: Secretary of State.

***Texas***
Office of Secretary of State

P.O. Box 12079
Austin, TX 78711
512-463-5705
http://txsos-7.sos.state.tx.us/authfaqs.shtml
**Fee: $10.00**
Designated Authority: Secretary of State; Assistant Secretary of State

***Utah***
Office of the Lieutenant Governor
210 State Capitol
Salt Lake City, UT 84145-8414
801-538-1040
http://governor.state.ut.us/lt_gover/internationaltemplate.html
**Fee: Certifying Notary's Seal: $10.00 Apostille: $5.00**
Designated Authority: Lieutenant Governor; Deputy Lieutenant Governor; Administrative Assistant.

***Vermont***
Office of Secretary of State
109 State St.
Montpelier, VT 05609-1103
802-828-2308
http://www.sec.state.vt.us
**Fee: $2.00**
Designated Authority: Secretary of State; Deputy Secretary of State.

***Virginia***
Office of Secretary of Commonwealth
Authentications Division
830 East Main Street, 14th Floor
Richmond, VA 23219
804-786-2441
http://www.soc.state.va.us
**Fee: $10.00**
Designated Authority: Secretary of the Commonwealth; Chief Clerk, Office of the Secretary of Commonwealth.

***Washington***
Office of the Secretary of State
Corporations Division
Apostille and Certificate Program
PO Box 40228
Olympia, WA 98504-0228
360-586-2268
http://www.secstate.wa.gov/apostilles
**Fee: $15.00**

Designated Authority: Secretary of State; Assistant Secretary of State; Director, Department of Licensing.

***West Virginia***
Office of Secretary of State
Capitol Building
1900 Kanawha Blvd. East
No. 157-K
Charleston, WV 25305-0770
304-558-6000
http://www.wvsos.com/execrecords/other/authentication.htm
**Fee: $10.00**
Designated Authority: Secretary of State; Under Secretary of State; any Deputy Secretary of State.

***Wisconsin***
Office of Secretary of State
P.O. Box 7848
Madison, WI 53707-7848
608-266-3159
http://badger.state.wi.us/agencies/sos/authen.htm
**Fee: $10.00**
Designated Authority: Secretary of State; Assistant Secretary of State.

***Wyoming***
Office of Secretary of State
The Capitol
Cheyenne, WY 82002-0020
307-777-5342
http://soswy.state.wy.us/authenti/authenti.htm
**Fee: $3.00**
Designated Authority: Secretary of State; Deputy Secretary of State.

***American Samoa***
Office of the Governor
Pago Pago, AS 96799
011-684-633-4116
http://www.amsamoa.com
Designated Authority: Secretary of American Samoa; Attorney General of American Samoa.

***Guam (Territory of)***
Office of the Governor
P.O. Box 2950
Agana, GU 96910
011-671-472-1537

http://www.admin.gov.gu/doa
Designated Authority: Department of Administration

***Northern Mariana Islands (Commonwealth of the)***
Designated Authority: Attorney General; Acting Attorney General; Clerk of the Court, Commonwealth Trial Court; Deputy Clerk, Commonwealth Trial Court
http://www.saipan.com/gov

***Puerto Rico (Commonwealth of)***
Supreme Court of Puerto Rico
Office of Notarial Inspection
P.O. Box 190860
San Juan, PR 00919-0860
787-763-8816
http://www.lexjuris.com/lexnotaria.htm
Designated Authority: Supreme Court of Puerto Rico

***U.S. Virgin Islands***
Office of the Lieutenant Governor
7 & 8 King St.
Christiansted, St. Croix, USVI 00802
340-774-2991
http://www.ltg.gov.vi/Departments/Administration/index.html
No authority designated: refer requests to the U.S. Department of State, Authentications Office, 2400 M Street, NW, Washington, DC 20520. 202-647-5002

**FOREIGN CENTRAL AUTHORITIES**

**Andorra:** Entered into force for Andorra 12/31/96. **Competent Authority:** On December 13, 2001, Andorra advised that the competent authorities to issue the certificate in accordance with Article 3, paragraph 1 are:

1. El Ministre d'Afers Exteriors
2. El Ministre de JustÌcia i Interior

All legalization requests are centralized through the following address:

Ministeri d'Afers Exteriors
Prat de la Creu
Edifici del Govern
Andorra la Vella
Principat d'Andorra

Tel.: 376-875-700
Fax: 376-869-559
E-mail: exteriors.gov@andorra.ad

**Angola:** Now Independent. **No confirmation issued by Angola that Convention is deemed to apply.** On October 22, 1969, Portugal extended Convention to Angola. Portugal declared the competent authority to be the Governor General ("Les Gouverneurs generaux ("Governadores Gerais"). Current Competent Authority Unknown.

**Anguilla:** On February 24, 1965, the United Kingdom extended the Convention to the Saint Christopher, Nevis and Anguilla which entered into force April 25, 1965. Antigua achieved independence on November 1, 1981 as Antigua and Barbuda. Antigua and Barbuda declared on May 1, 1985 that it considered itself bound by the Convention effective the date of independence. Extended by the United Kingdom to Anguilla February 24, 1965. **Competent Authority:** the Governor of Anguilla.

**Antigua and Barbuda:** On February 24, 1965, the United Kingdom extended the Convention to Antigua which entered into force April 25, 1965. Achieved independence in 1981 and Antigua and Barbuda. Antigua and Barbuda declared that it considers itself bound by the Convention. **Competent Authority:** a. Governor-General, Antigua-Barbuda; b. Registrar of the The High Court; High Street; St. John's, Antigua, West Indies; tel: 809-462-3147

**Argentina:** Entered into force 2/18/88. **Competent Authority:** Ministerio de Relaciones Exteriores y Culto, Reconquista 1088, 1003 Buenos Aires, Argentina

**Armenia:** Entered into force 8/14/94. **Competent Authority:** Ministry of Foreign Affairs and Ministry of Justice

**Australia:** Entered into force 3/16/95. **Competent Authority:** Secretary to the Department of Foreign Affairs and Trade of the Commonwealth

**Austria:** Entered into force 1/13/68. **Competent Authority:** 1. Federal Ministry of Foreign Affairs (Bundesministerium fur auswartige Angelegenheiten; 2. The Presidents of any Civil Court of First Instances, with the exception of the Commercial Court (Handelsgericht) of Vienna and the Juvenile Court (Jugendgerichtshof) of Vienna, or their representatives authorized to issue the apostille; 3. The Governors of the Provinces (Landeshauptmanner); 4. Governments of the Provinces (Landesregierungen)

**Bahamas:** On February 24, 1965, the United Kingdom extended the Convention to the Bahamas which entered into force April 25, 1965. Bahamas achieved independence on July 10, 1973. On April 30, 1976 the Bahamas declared that it considered itself bound by the Convention effective the date of independence. **Competent Authority:** Ministry of Foreign Affairs, East Hill Street, P. O. Box N-3746, Nassau, Bahamas, tel: (242) 328-4145. The minister with responsibility for the Central Authority is the Honorable Frederick A. Mitchell, MP. The Permanent Secretary at the Central Authority is Mrs. A. Missouri Sherman-Peter.

**Barbados:** On February 24, 1965, the United Kingdom extended the Convention to Barbados which entered into force April 25, 1965. Barbados achieved independence

November 30, 1966. By a note of August 1995 to the depositary, the Government of Barbados declared that it considers itself bound by the Convention effective the date of independence. **Competent Authority:** 1. Solicitor-General; 2. Deputy Solicitor General; 3. Registrar of the Supreme Court of Barbados Law Courts, Bridgetown, Barbados, tel: 809-42-75537; 4. The Permanent Secretary - Foreign Affairs, Ministry of Foreign Affairs, Tourism and International Transport; 5. The Chief of Protocol, Ministry of Foreign Affairs, Tourism and International Transport

**Belarus:** Entered into Force May 31, 1992. **Competent Authority:** Ministry of Justice (judicial/court documents); Ministry of National Education(educational documents); Committee for Archives and Administration (state archives documents); Ministry of Foreign Affairs (all other documents)

**Belgium:** Entered into force 2/9/76. **Competent Authority:** Ministry of Foreign Affairs, External Trade and Cooperation in Development (Ministere des Affaires Etrangeres, du Commerce exterieur et de la Cooperation au Developpement)

**Belize:** Entered into force 4/11/93. **Competent Authority:** The Registrar General

**Bermuda:** On February 24, 1965, the United Kingdom extended the Convention to the Bermuda which entered into force April 25, 1965. **Competent Authority:** On October 17, 1968 the competent authority was declared to be the Governor and Commander-in-Chief of the Bermudas or Somers Islands or any member of his staff signing on his behalf and using his official seal.

**Bosnia-Herzegovina:** Entered into Force: December 20, 1991. **Competent Authority:** By Note dated 17 August 2000, the Ministry of Foreign Affairs of Bosnia and Herzegovina informed the depositary of the following:

"(...) the authorities designated by Bosnia and Herzegovina who are competent to issue the certificate referred to in the first paragraph of Article 3 of the Convention Abolishing the Requirement of Legalisation for Foreign Public Documents concluded at The Hague on 5th October 1961, are Municipal Courts in the Federation of Bosnia and Herzegovina and in the Republic of Srpska. These certificates shall be subject to certification by the Ministry of Civil Affairs and Communications of Bosnia and Herzegovina and the Minstry of Foreign Affairs of Bosnia and Herzegovina."

**Botswana:** On February 24, 1965, the United Kingdom extended the Convention to the Bechuanaland Protectorate which entered into force April 25, 1965. The Bechuanaland Protectorate achieved independence September 30, 1966 as Botswana. On September 16, 1968, Botswana declared that it considered itself bound by the Convention effective the date of independence. **Competent Authority:** 1. Permanent Secretary; 2. Registrar of the High Court; 3. District Commissioner; 4. Any person appointed or empowered to hold a subordinate court of the first class; 5. Such other person as the President may appoint by notice in the Gazette.

**British Virgin Islands:** On February 24, 1965, the United Kingdom extended the Convention to the British Virgin Islands which entered into force April 25, 1965. **Competent Authority:**

Registrar of Courts
Tortola, BVI
Phone: 284-494-3492
Fax: 284-494-6664

**Brunei:** On February 24, 1965, the United Kingdom extended the Convention to Brunei which entered into force April 25, 1965. Brunei achieved independence January 1, 1984. Brunei declared that it considers itself bound by the Convention December 3, 1987. **Competent Authority:** Chief Registrar, Deputy Chief Registrar and Registrars of the Supreme Court of Brunei Darussalam; Chief Magistrate, Magistrates and Registrars of subordinate Courts of Brunei Darussalam.

**Bulgaria:** Entry into force April 29, 2001. **Competent Authority:** Ministry of Justice regarding documents of the courts and notaries; Ministry of Foreign Affairs regarding other documents.

**Cayman Islands:** On February 24, 1965, the United Kingdom extended the Convention to the Cayman Islands which entered into force April 25, 1965. **Competent Authority:** declared October 17, 1968 to be the Governor of the Cayman Islands

**China, Hong Kong S.A.R. ONLY:** Entered into force 6/3/97 in accordance with an exchange of diplomatic notes. Applies only to the Hong Kong Special Administrative Region. The Convention is **not/not** in force for other jurisdictions in the People's Republic of China. **Competent Authority:** Registrar, Supreme Court; Deputy Registrar or Assistant Registrar, Supreme Court; and Deputy Chief Secretary, Supreme Court, Registrar, Hong Kong Supreme Court, 38 Queensway, Hong Kong, tel: (852) 2825-4254. See Hong Kong SAR.

**Colombia:** Entered into force January 30, 2001. **Colombian Competent Authority to Issue Apostille:**

Ministerio de Relaciones Exteriores
Oficina de Legalizaciones
Doctor Carlos Guillermo DIAZ BUITRAGO
Transversal 17A, NO. 9-45
Santafe de Bogota, Colombia
tel: (1) 525-1862, 525-1860, 522-3697

**Comoros Islands:>** Now Independent. **No formal confirmation that Convention is deemed to apply.** When France extended its accession to the Convention to the Comoros Islands (Moroni), the competent authority to affix the Convention "apostille" certificate was the General Procecutor of the Republic at the High Court of Appeal at Moroni (le Procureur de la Republique pres le Tribunal Superieur d'appel de Moroni.)

**Croatia:** Entered into force October 8, 1991. **Competent Authority:** Municipal courts or the Ministry of Justice and Administration of the Republic of Croatia

**Cyprus: Competent Authority:** Ministry of Justice of the Republic of Cyprus

**Czech Republic:** Signed the Convention June 23, 1998; ratified the Convention January 8, 1999. Entered into force: May 1, 1999. **Competent Authority:** Designation of the competent authorites to issue the certificate in accordance with Article 6, paragraph 1: 1. the Ministry of Justice, International Department (certificates issued by authorities of justice, including certificates issued or certified by notaries); 2. the Ministry of Foreign Affairs, Consular Department (documents issued by authorities of State Administration or by the other ones).

**Djibouti:** Now Independent. **No confirmation issued by newly independent country that Convention is deemed to apply.** When France extended its accession to the Convention to the Affars and the Issas (now Djibouti), the competent authority to affix the Convention "apostille" certificate was the General Procecutor of the Republic at the High Court of Appeal at Djibouti (le Procureur de la Republique pres le Tribunal Superieur d'appel de Djibouti.) Current Competent Authority: Unknown.

**Dominica: No confirmation issued by newly independent country that Convention is deemed to apply.** On February 24, 1965, the United Kingdom extended the Convention to Dominica which entered into force April 25, 1965. Dominica achieved independence November 3, 1978 and became the Commonwealth of Dominica. **Competent Authority:** Unknown.

**El Salvador: Competent Authority:**

Minisisterio de Relaciones Exteriores de El Salvador
Departamento de Tramites Registrales
Seccion Autenticas y Apostillado
Plan Maestro Centro de Gobierno
17 Ave Norte
Edificio 4, 1er Piso
San Salvador, El Salvador
Cost: No fee
Tel: 271-3266 x 2138 or 231-1336/1337

**Estonia:** Accession - December 11, 2000; Entry into Force - October 1, 2001. Designation of the competent authorities to issue the certificate in accordance with Article 6, paragraph 1:

1. The Ministry of Foreign Affairs, Legal Division, Consular Department, Islandi väljak

1, 15049 Tallinn, phone +372 6317 440, fax +372 631 7454;
2. Estonian Ministry of Education, Administrative Department, Room 104, Tönismägi 11, 15192 Tallin, phone +372 6 281 243, fax +372 6 281 390;
3. Administrative Department, Munga 18, 51007 Tartu, phone +372 7 350 252, fax +372 7 350 250;
4. Monitoring Department, Munga 18, Tartu, phone +372 7 350 231, fax +372 7 350 250;
5. Ministry of Justice, Courts' Department, Tartu mnt 85, Room 103, 10115 Tallinn, phone +372 612 7810, fax +372 612 7811;
6. Ministry of Internal Affairs, General Administrative Department, Legal Services office, Lai 40 , 10133 Tallinn, phone +372 612 5199, fax +372 5198;
7. Ministry of Social Affairs, Public Relations and Training Department, Gonsiori 29, 15027 Tallinn, phone +372 626 9875, fax +372 699 2209.

**Falkland Islands:** On February 24, 1965, the United Kingdom extended the Convention to the Falkland Islands which entered into force April 25, 1965. **Competent Authority:** On October 17, 1968 competent authority declared to be the Governor of the Falkland Islands

**Fiji:** Now independent. On February 24, 1965, the United Kingdom extended the Convention to Fiji which entered into force April 25, 1965. Fiji achieved independence October 10, 1970. Fiji declared on March 29, 1971 that it considered itself bound by the Convention. Fiji's accession to the Convention was effective the date of Fijian independence. **Competent Authority:** The Chief Registrar of the Supreme Court of Fiji.

**Finland:** As of September 21, 2000, Finland announced multiple new authorities competent to issue the apostille certificate. See the Hague Conference on Private International Law website at http://www.hcch.net/e/status/stat12e.html

**France:** Departments in Europe and Overseas Departments (Guadeloupe, French Guiana, Martinique and Reunion): The General Prosecutors at the Courts of Appeal (Les Procureurs generaux pres les cours d' appel

**French Overseas Territories:**

**New Caledonia:** Extended by France 11/25/64. **Competent Authority:** The General Prosecutor at the Court of Appeal of Noumea (le Procureur general pres la Cour d'appel de Noumea

**Wallis and Futuna:** The Judge of the Section of the Court of First Instance of Noumea at Mata Utu (le Juge de la Section du Tribunal de premiere instance de Noumea siegeant a Mata Utu)

**French Polynesia:** The Prosecutor of the Republic at the High Court of Appeal at Papeete (le Procureur de la Republique pres le Tribunal superieur d'appel de Papeete)

**St. Pierre and Miquelon:** The President of the High Court of Appeal of Saint-Pierre (le President du Tribunal Superieur d'appel de Saint-Pierre)

**Germany, Federal Republic of: Competent Authorities:** (a) Federal Authorities: 1. Federal Administrative Office (Bundesverwaltungsamt in Koln); 2. President of the German Patent Office (Prasident des Deutschen Patentamtes); (b) Authorities of the "Lander"; 3. Minister of Justice (Ministerium (Senator) fur Justiz Land-, (Amts-) gerichtsprasident); 4. President of the Provincial Court (Landgerichtsprasident); 5. President of the District Court/Court of First Instance (Amtsgerichsprasident); 6. Minister of Home Affairs, Ministerium (Senator) fur Innere Regierungsprasident (Prasident des Verwaltungsbezirks); 7. Ministerium (Senator) fur Inneres Regierungsprasident (Prasident des Verwaltungsbezirks); 8. Head of the Provincial Government (Regierungsprasident); 9. Head of the Administrative District (Prasident des Verwaltungsbezirks)

**With the reunification of Germany on October 3, 1990** , Convention apostille certificates from the new federal Lander of Brandenburg, Mecklenburg-West Pomerania, Saxony, Saxony-Anhalt and Thuringia is the responsibility of the following Land authorities: 1. Minister of Justice, Die Ministerien fur Justiz sowie die Prasidenten der Langerichte (Bezirksgerichte); 2. Head of the Provincial Government, Die Ministerien fur Inneres sowie die Regierungsprasidenten (Bezirksregierungen) und das Landesverwaltungsamt (Thuringen); 3. Minister of Home Affairs, Die Ministerien fur Inneres; 4. Die Regierungsprasidenten (Bezirksregierungen), die Ministerien fur Justiz sowie die Prasidenten der Landgerichte (Bezirksgerichte)

**Gibraltar:** On February 24, 1965, the United Kingdom extended the Convention to Gibraltar which entered into force April 25, 1965. **Competent Authority:** declared on October 17, 1968 to be the Governor and Commander-in-Chief of the City and Garrison of Gibraltar

**Greece: Competent Authority:** local nomarchy (department). Specifically, for Athens, administrative documents come from the Athens Nomarchy, Stadiou 29, Athens, Greece. All judicial documents, both penal and civil, as well as notarial deeds, are legalized by the local court of first instance, in the area where the decision or the notarial deed was issued.

**Grenada:** Now Independent. **No confirmation issued by newly independent country that Convention is deemed to apply.** On February 24, 1965, the United Kingdom extended the Convention to Grenada which entered into force April 25, 1965. Grenada achieved independence February 7, 1974. **Competent Authority:** Unknown.

**Guyana:** On February 24, 1965, the United Kingdom extended the Convention to British Guyana which entered into force April 25, 1965. British Guyana achieved independence in May 26, 1966 and became Guyana. Confirmation to U.S. Embassy in Georgetown,Guyana December, 1996 that Guyana considers itself bound by the Convention. **Competent Authority:** Legal Adviser, Ministry of Foreign Affairs, Takuba

Lodge 254 South Road Bourda, Georgetown, Guyana, Tel: 011-592-2-54166 or 011-592-2-54151, Fax: 011-592-2-59192

**Guernsey:** Extended to Guernsey by the United Kingdom January 24, 1965. Competent authority declared January 17, 1968. **Competent Authority:** The Lieutenant Governor of the Bailiwick of Guernsey

**Hong Kong SAR:** On February 24, 1965, the United Kingdom extended the Convention to Hong Kong which entered into force for Hong Kong April 25, 1965. Sovereignty of Hong Kong reverted to the People's Republic of China on July 1, 1998. China declared the Hague Legalization Convention shall continue to apply to Hong Kong SAR effective July 1, 1998. **Competent Authority** : first declared October 17, 1968. On October 18, 1986, the then Governor of Hong Kong delegated authority to the Registrar, High Court; Deputy Registrar or Assistant Registrar, High Court; and Deputy Chief Secretary, High Court, Registrar, Hong Kong High Court, 38 Queensway, Hong Kong, tel: (852) 2825-4226. The Competent Authority did not change following reversion to Chinese sovereignty.

**Hungary: Competent Authority:** 1. Minister of Justice regarding public documents and judicial documents; 2. Minister of Foreign Affairs regarding public documents and legalizations executed by other authorities

**Ireland:** Signed the Convention October 29, 1996; ratified the Convention January 8, 1999. Entered into force: March 9, 1999. **Competent Authority:** Designation of the competent authorities to issue the certificate in accordance with Article 6, paragraph 1: the Department of Foreign Affairs in Dublin.

**Israel: Competent Authority:** 1. Ministry of Foreign Affairs; 2. Registrars of Magistrates Courts and Civil Servants appointed by the Minister of Justice under Notaries Law, 1976.

**Italy: Competent Authority:** 1. The Public Prosecutor (I Procurators della Reppublica); 2. The Competent Prefetti (Heads) of the Territories for the Valley of Aosta; Il Presidente della Regione (The Head of the District for the Provinces of Trente and Bolzano; Il Commissario di Governo (The Commissioner of the Government)

**Japan: Competent Authority:** Ministry of Foreign Affairs, Authentications Division (Shomei-han) 2-1 Kasumigaseki 2-chome, Chiyoda Ku, Tokyo 100, Japan. Request an application for obtaining an apostille from the Ministry. The letter must include an explanation as to why you need this document. After you receive the application, you must complete it and send it back to the Japanese authority with the "original" document to be authenticated bearing the appropriate seal of the issuing authority. The "original" document must have been certified by the issuing office within the past six months. You should also send a photocopy of the document and a self addressed stamped envelope. You will receive the authenticated documents directly from the Ministry. There is no fee for this service. You may also contact the Japanese Embassy or Consulate in the U.S. nearest you for additional information.

**Jersey:** Extended by the United Kingdom January 24, 1965. **Competent Authority:** declared October 17, 1968, the Lieutenant Governor of the Bailiwick of Jersey.

**Kazakhstan:** Entry into force January 30, 2001. **Competent Authority:** By Note dated 19 September 2001, the Republic of Kazakhstan informed the depositary of the following:

"... and has the honour to inform that the new authorities have been designated to issue the apostille in accordance with the Decree of the Government of the Republic of Kazakhstan N 545 dated 24.04.01:
The Ministry of Justice of the Republic of Kazakhstan - for official documents issued by the bodies for justice and other state bodies, including the notary offices;
The Ministry of Education and Science of the Republic of Kazakhstan - for official documents issued by the bodies for education, science and the educational institutions of the Republic;
The Ministry of Internal Affairs of the Republic of Kazakhstan - for official documents issued by the structural subdivisions of the Migration Police;
The Committee on administration of the archives and documentation to the Ministry of Culture, Information and Public Consent of the Republic of Kazakhstan - for archive certificates and copies of archive documents issued by the state archives of the Republic of Kazakhstan;
The Committee for forensic (legal) administration to the Supreme Court (to be co-ordinated) for official documents issued by the law-enforcement bodies and the bodies for execution of law;
The Ministry on State Income of the Republic of Kazakhstan - for official documents issued by the structural and territorial subdivisions of the Ministry on State Income of the Republic of Kazakhstan;
The General Office of Public Prosecutors of the Republic of Kazakhstan (to be co-ordinated) - for official documents issued by the bodies of Public Prosecutors, investigation agencies and inquest;
The Ministry of Defence of the Republic of Kazakhstan - for archive certificates and copies of archive documents issued by the special state archives of the Ministry of Defence of the Republic of Kazakhstan;
The Committee for National Security of the Republic of Kazakhstan (to be co-ordinated) - for archive certificates and copies of archive documents issued by the special archives of the Committee for National Security of the Republic of Kazakhstan;
The designated bodies are entitled to delegate the authority to their territorial bodies to issue the apostille.
Attachment: The Hague Convention dtd 05.10.1961 abolishing the legalisation for foreign public documents stipulates the apostille of 9 x 9 cm in size.
It is expedient to have a stamp of the apostille, which size is 13 x 13 cm.
A script of the text can be enlarged for the comfort of its representation and reading. It is not allowed to change (translate) a language document, text and its order of placing on

the stamp.
The stamp can be fulfilled in the language of the Republic of Kazakhstan only."

**Kiribati:** Now Independent. **No confirmation issued by newly independent country that Convention is deemed to apply.** On February 24, 1965, the United Kingdom extended the Convention to the Gilbert Islands which entered into force April 25, 1965. The Gilbert Islands achieved independence as Kiribati July 12, 1979. **Competent Authority:** Unknown.

**Korea, Republic of (South Korea):** Ratified Convention January 13, 2000; in accordance with Article 28, second paragraph, the Convention will enter into force for the Republic of Korea in the absence of any objections from a State which has ratified the Convention before the deposit of the accession, notified to the Ministry of Foreign Affairs of the Netherlands within a period of six months after the date on which the Ministry has notified it of the accession. For practical reasons, this six month's period will run from January 31, 2000 to July 31, 2000. Pursuant to Article 10, the Republic of Korea objects to the following: **a)** the freedom to send judicial documents, by postal channels, directly to persons abroad, **b)** the freedom of judicial officers, officials or other competent persons of the State of origin to effect service of judicial documents directly through the judicial officials or other competent persons of the State of destination, **c)** the freedom of any person interested in a judicial proceeding to effect service of judicial documents directly through judicial officers, officials or other competent persons of the State of destination. **Competent Authority:** Ministry of Court Administration, Attn.: Director of International Affairs, 967, Seocho-dong, Seocho-gu, SEOUL 137-750, Republic of Korea

**Latvia:** Entered into force: May 11, 1995. **Competent Authority:** The Ministry of Foreign Affairs, Consular Department, 57 Elizbietes Street, Riga, LV 1510, Latvia, tel: 728-9505, Cost: $10.00 (for individuals, 10 day processing), $20.00 (for individuals, one day service), $20.00 (for organizations, 10 day processing), $40.00 (for organizations, one day service)

**Lesotho:** On February 24, 1965, the United Kingdom extended the Convention to Basutoland which entered into force April 25, 1965. Basutoland achieved independence on October 4, 1966 as Lesotho. On April 24, 1972, Lesotho declared that it considers itself bound by the Convention. The effective date of Lesotho's accession is the date of independence. **Competent Authority:** 1. The Attorney General; 2. The Permanent Secretary of a Ministry or Department; 3. The Registrar of the High Court; 4. A Resident Magistrate; 5. A Magistrate of the First Class; 6. By appointment of the Minister, noticed in Gazette

**Liberia: CONVENTION NOT IN FORCE BETWEEN U.S. AND LIBERIA** as U.S. concluded Liberia cannot fulfill responsibilities of competent authority to issue Convention "apostille" at present.

**Liechtenstein: Competent Authority:** Office of the Government of the Prince at Vaduz (Regierungskanzlei der furstlichen Regierung)

**Lithuania:** Entered into force November 5, 1996. **Competent Authority:** Dalia Salkauskiene, Head of Consular Assistance, Ministry of Foreign Affairs, Consular Division, J. Tumo-Vaizganto g.2, 2600 Vilnius, Republic of Lithuania.

**Luxembourg: Competent Authority:** Ministry of Foreign Affairs (Ministere des Affaires Etrangeres)

**Macau SAR:** Extended to Macau by Portugal at the time of Portugal's accession to the Convention on October 22, 1969. **Competent Authority:** 1. The Governor of Macau, Palacio do Governo, Av. da Praia Grande, Macau; 2. The Assistant Secretary for Justice of Macau, R. de S. Lourenco, Edificio dos Secretarios Adjuntos, 1 andar, Macau 3. The Head of the Justice Department of Macau Av. da Praia Grande, 594, Edificio BCM, 8 andar, Macau. **NOTE:** Macau will revert to Chinese sovereignty December 20, 1999. By letter of 10 December 1999, the Ambassador of them People's Republic to the Netherlands informed the Minister of Foreign Affairs of the Netherlands of the following:

The Convention abolishing the requirement of legalisation for foreign public documents, done at the Hague on 5 October 1961 (hereinafter referred to as the Convention), which applies to Macau at present, shall continue to apply to the Macau Special Administrative Region with effect from 20 December 1999. The Government of the People's Republic of China also wishes to make the following declaration: In accordance with Article 6 of the Convention, it designates the Chief Executive, the Secretary for Administration and Justice, and the Director of Justice Affairs Department of the Macau Special Administrative Region as the authorities competent to issue the certificate referred to in the first paragraph of Article 3 of the Convention in the Macau Special Administrative Region.

**Macedonia:** Entered into force September 30, 1993. **Competent Authority:** Ministry of Justice

**Malawi:** Malawi acceded to the Convention February 24, 1967. The Convention entered into force for Malawi on December 2, 1967. **Competent Authority:** 1. The Attorney General or the Solicitor General; 2. The Permanent Secretary of a Government Ministry; 3. The Registrar of the High Court; 4. The Registrar General; 5. A Government Agent; 6. A notary public; 7. A Resident Magistrate

**Malta: Competent Authority:** Ministry of Commonwealth and Foreign Affairs

**Man, Isle of:** Extended by the United Kingdom on January 24, 1965. Competent Authority declared October 17, 1968. **Competent Authority:** The Lieutenant Governor of the Isle of Man

**Marshall Islands, Republic of:** Acceded to the Convention November 18, 1991. The Convention entered into force for the RMI on August 14, 1992. **Competent Authority:** 1. Minister of Foreign Affairs of the Marshall Islands; 2. Attorney General and Acting Attorney General; 3. Clerk and Deputy Clerk of the High Court; 4. Registrars and Deputy Registrars of Corporations; 5. Maritime Administrator and Special Agents thereof; 6. Commissioner and Deputy Commissioner of Maritime Affairs or Special Agents thereof.

**Mauritius:** On December 20, 1968, Mauritius declared it considers itself bound by the Convention. On February 24, 1965, the United Kingdom extended the Convention to Mauritius which entered into force April 25, 1965. The effective date of accession is March 12, 1968, the date of independence. **Competent Authority:** In a note to the depositary dated September 17, 1973, Mauritius declared the competent authority is now: 1. The Permanent Secretary, or in his absence, 2. A Principal Assistant Secretary of the Prime Minister's Office

**Mexico:**

**Competent Authorities:**

A. Federal Documents: 1. Direccion General de Gobierno, Bucareli No. 99, Planta Baja, 06600 Mexico, D.F., tel: 535-31-12; 535-43-92, fax: 535-26-88; 2. Direccion de Coordinacion Politica Con Los Poderes de la Union, Abraham Gonzalez No. 48, Planta Baja, 06600 Mexico, D.F., tel: 535-51-31, fax: 566-12-25; 3. Subdireccion de Formalizacion Y Control Abraham Gonzalez No. 48, Planta Baja, 06600 Mexico, D.F., tel: 535-53-84; 546-57-32, fax: 566-12-25

B. Secretaria De Gobernacion Directorio Representaciones de la Subsecretaria de Gobierno

BAJA CALIFORNIA: Servicios Migratorios, Linea, Internacional, Agustin Melgar No. 1, Col. Centro, 21100 Mexicali, B.C., tel: 65-556665, fax: 65-529050
BAJA CALIFORNIA SUR: Bravo No. 406, entre Aquiles Serdan y Guillermo Preito, 23000 La Paz, B.C.S., tel: 112-32083, fax: 112-32280
CAMPECHE: Av. de las Palmas S/N junto al centro, Bizantino Bartimeo, 24020 Campeche, Camp., tel: 91-981-53150; 53186, fax: 91-981-53149
CHIAPAS: Libramiento Norte S/N a un costado de Esq. Pablo Guardado Chavez, Tuxtla Gutierrez, Chis., tel: 91-961-43288, fax: 91-961-899091
CHIHUAHUA: Doblado y 3a No. 117, Despacho 2 y 3, Col. Centro, 3100 Chihuahua, Chih., tel: 14-167499, fax: 14-370149
COAHUILA: Victoria No. 406-1, Zona, Centro, 2500 Saltillo, Coah., tel: 18-175506, fax: 18-175334; 178951
COLIMA: Gabino Barrera No. 159-a, Zona Centro, 28000 Colima, Col., tel: 91-331-45912, fax: 91-331-45912
DURANGO: Constitucion No. 210-1, Norte Altos, Zona Centro, 34000, Durango, Dgo., tel: 18-17506, fax: 18-178951
GUANAJUATO: Agora del Baratillo Despacho 8, Zona Centro, 36000 Guanajuato, Gto.,

tel: 91-473-29446, fax: 91-473-29110; 29111
GUERRERO: Av. Ignacio Ramirez No. 22-a, Col. Centro, 39000, Chilpancingo, Gro., tel: 91-74-711772, fax: 91-74-721144; Calle Mina No. 120 Esq., Morelos, Col. Centro, 39300, Acapulco, Gro., tel: 91-74-828751, fax: 91-74-800341
HIDALGO: Torre Coby, Art. 3 No. 97-7, piso, Fracc, Constitution, 42080 Pachuco, Hgo., tel: 91-771-34026, fax: 91-771-34026
JALISCO: Chesterton 184, Jardines Vallarta, 45030 Guadalajara, Jal., tel: 91-3-6732394, fax: 91-3-6732138
MEXICO: Chaoco No. 703-8, Col. Sanchez, 50140 Toluca, Mexico, tel: 91-72-134679, fax: 91-72-134768; 158325
MICHOACAN: Av. Siervo de la Nacion S/N, Col. del Valle, 58260 Morelia, Mich., tel: 91-43-267
MORELOS: Galeana No. 2-8 piso Edificio, Ocampo, Col. Centro, 62000, Cuernavaca, Mor., tel: 91-73- 188594, fax: 91-73-188708
NAYARIT: Zacatecas No. 16 sur 1 y 2, piso entre Allende y Abasolo, 63000 Tepic, Nayarit, tel: 91-321-46269, fax: 91-321-46271
NUEVO LEON: Zaragoza No. 1000 Sur, Condominio Acero PH, 64000, Monterrey, N.L., tel: 8-3403000, fax: 8-3403000
OAXACA: Calzada de la Republica No. 402-B, Jalatlaco, 33606, Oaxaca, Oax., tel: 91-951-42145, fax: 91-951-42145
PUEBLA: Calla Italia No. 2224, Fracc., Las Hadas entre 15 de mayo y, 26 Pte., 72070 Puebla, Pue., tel: 91-22-494082, fax: 91-22-494072
QUERETARO: Boulevard Hernando Quintana, No. 168 Desp. 203 y 204, 76050 Queretaro, Qro., tel: 91-42-234960 or 91-42-234660, fax: 91-42-234960
QUINTANA ROO: Av. Primo de Verdad No. 181, int. 1 Esp. Av. Heroes, 67000 Chetumal, Q. Roo, tel: 91-983-27347, fax: 91-983-22744
SAN LUIS POTOSI: Av. Venustiano Carranza 707-402, Col. Centro 78250, San Luis Potosi, S.L.P., tel: 91-48-144092, fax: 91-48-173988
SINALOA: Lazaro Cardenas No. 913 Sur, Primer piso, Zona Centro, 80129 Culiacan, Sin., tel: 67-173988, fax: 67-173988
SONORA: Blvd. Navarrete No. 125, Despacho 2, Edif. Sonmol. Col. Valle Verde, 83200, Hermosillo, Son., tel: 62-165044, fax: 62-165044
TABASCO: Centro Admvo. Del Estado, Tabasco 2000, 86035, Villahermosa, Tab., tel: 91-93-165152, fax: 91-93-165152
TAMAULIPAS: Matamoros 11 y 12 No. 613, Cd. Victoria, Tamps., tel: 131-20462, fax: 131-20462
TLAXCALA: Kilometro 1 1/2 Carretera, federal Tlaxcala-Puebla S/N, 90000 Tlaxcala, Tlax., tel: 91-246-27147, fax: 91-246-27264
VERACRUZ: Zaragoza No. 2 Esq. Miguel, Barragan, 91000 Xalapa, Ver., tel: 91-28-189303, fax: 91-28-189395
YUCATAN: Calle 51 No. 459 x 50, Zona, Centro, 97000 Merida, Yuc., tel: 91-99-239142, 91-99-239636, 91-99-239671, 91-99-240815, fax: 91-99-235535
ZACATECAS: Calle Sabino No. 114 Fracc., La Penuela, 98060 Zacatecas, Zac., tel: 492-42318, fax: 492-42318

**Montserrat:** On February 24, 1965, the United Kingdom extended the Convention to Montserrat which entered into force April 25, 1965. **Competent Authority:** declared October 17, 1968 to be the Governor of Montserrat

**Mozambique:** Now Independent. **No confirmation issued by newly independent country that Convention is deemed to apply.** On October 22, 1969, Portugal extended the Convention to Mozambique. **Competent Authority:** designated to be the Governor General ("Les Gouverneurs generaux ("Governadores Gerais"). Competent Authority Unknown.

**Namibia:** Entry into force January 30, 2001. **Competent Authority: Unknown**

**Netherlands: Competent Authority:** Kingdom in Europe: Registrars of the Courts of First Instance (Griffiers van de arrondissementsrechtbanken)

**Netherlands Antilles:** Extended by the Netherlands March 1, 1967. Entered into force for the Netherlands Antilles April 30, 1967. **Competent Authority:** declared to be Lieutenant Governor of an Island or Group of Islands (Gezaghebber van het eilandgebied)

**Curacao: Competent Authority:** the Lieutenant Governor of the Island of Curacao -- has delegated his authority to: (1) the Head of the Births, Deaths and Marriages, Population and Electoral Registers of the island of Curacao, and (2) the acting Head of the Births, Deaths, Marriages, Population and Electoral Registers of the island of Curacao.

**Aruba: Competent Authority:** Centraal Bureau Juridische Zaken en Algemene Zaken (Central Bureau Legal and General Affairs), Att. Ms. Cecilia Solagnier, Vondellaan 19-C, Oranjestad, Aruba; tel: 011-297-835002; fax: 011-297-831772

**Nevis:** On February 24, 1965, the United Kingdom extended the Convention to Saint Christopher (Kitts), Nevis, and Anguilla which entered into force April 25, 1965. Now independent, Saint Kitts and Nevis (formerly Saint Christopher and Nevis) acceded to the Convention on February 26, 1994. The Convention entered into force on December 14, 1994. **Competent Authority:** 1. The Chief Secretary in the Office of the Premier. 2. The Legal Adviser in the Legal Department or 3. The Deputy Registrary of the Supreme Court. Ministry of Legal Affairs, P.O. Box 186, Government Headquarters, St. Kitts-Nevis, West Indies, tel: 809-465-2521

**New Zealand:** Signature - February 7, 2001; Accession - September 23, 2001; Entry into Force - November 22, 2001. With the following declaration: This accession shall not extend to Tokelau unless and until a declaration to that effect is lodged by the Government of New Zealand with the depository, in accordance with Article 13 of the Convention; and designates the New Zealand Department of Internal Affairs as its competent authority for the purposes of Article 6 of the Convention.

**Niue:** Signed the Convention June 10, 1998; ratified the Convention January 1, 1999. Entered into force: March 2, 1999. By Note dated 22 June 1999, the Government of Niue informed the depositary that in accordance with Article 6, paragraph 1, of the Convention, the designated authorities are: (a) the Attorney General; (b) the Financial Secretary; (c) Crown Counsel; (d) the Registrar International Business Companies; (e) Deputy Registrar International Business Companies; (f) the Registrar, High Court of Niue; (g) Secretary to Government.

**Norway: Competent Authority:** Royal Norwegian Ministry of Foreign Affairs; the County Governors, namely:

Fylkesmannen i Oslo og Akershus, Postboks 8111 Dep., N-0032 Oslo 1, tel: 02-42-90-85
Fylkesmannen i Ostfold, Postboks 325, N-1501 Moss, tel: 032-54-100
Fylkesmannen i Hedmark, Postboks 308, N-2301 Hamar, tel: 065-26-080
Fylkesmannen i Oppland, N-2600 Lillehammer, tel: 062-66-000
Fylkesmannen i Budkerud, N-3000 Drammen, tel: 03-83-81-50
Fylkesmannen i Vestfold, N-3100 Tonsberg, tel: 033-17-515
Fylkesmannen i Telemark, N-3700 Skien, tel: 03-52-70 20/52 82 74
Fylkesmannen i Aust-Agder, Postboks 55, N-4801 Arendal, tel: 041-25-860
Fylkesmannen i Vest-Agder, Tinghuset, N-4600 Kristiansand S, tel: 042-28-000
Fylkesmannen i Rogaland, Postboks 59, N-4001 Stavanger, tel: 04-52-70-60
Fylkesmannen i Hordaland, Postboks 106, N-5001 Bergen, tel: 05-23-70 00
Fylkesmannen i Sogn og Fjordane, N-5840 Hermansverk, tel: 056-55-000
Fylkesmannen i More og Romsdal, Fylkeshuset, N-6400 Molde, tel: 072-58 000
Fylkesmannen i Sor-Trondelag, N-7000 Trondheim, tel: 07-51-08 11
Fylkesmannen i Nord-Trondelag, N-7700 Steinkjer, tel: 077-66-722
Fylkesmannen i Nordland, N-8000 Bode, tel: 081-62-1000
Fylkesmannen i Troms, Postboks 595, N-9001 Tromso, tel: 083-87530
Fylkesmannen i Finnmark, N-9800 Vadso, tel: 085-51 761/53 001

**Panama: Competent Authority:** 1. Concerning documents authorized by competent court authorities or officials, the Secretary of the Supreme Court or his legal substitutes; 2. Concerning deeds drawn up by a notary or private documents authenticated by a notary, the officials of the Department of Administrative Service of the Ministry of Justice; 3. Regarding documents issued by any central government bodies, any autonomous or semi-autonomous bodies, municipal or police authorities or a Public Ministry, the officials of the Consular and Legalization Department of the Ministry of Foreign Affairs; 4. Regarding all other public documents, any of the three preceeding procedures are allowed.

**Portugal:** Entered into force October 22, 1969. **Competent Authority:** Applicable on entry into force to entire territory of the Republic of Portugal Portugal:General Prosecutor of the Republic (Procurador General de Republica) and Prosecutors of the Republic at the Courts of Appeal (Procuradores da Republica junto dos Tribunals da Relacao), Other Overseas Departments: Les gouverneurs ("Governadores")

Macau, territory of: see Macau

Angola and Mozambique: see Angola and Mozambique

**Romania:** Entry into force March 16, 2001. **Competent Authority:** Ministry of Justice for the certificates referred to in Article 1 a,c,d, and the Ministry of Foreign Affairs for the official certificates referred to in Article 1 b.

**Russian Federation:**

**Competent Authority:**

1. Ministry of Justice (documents of organizations and institutions directly subordinate to the Ministry)
2. Ministries of Justice of the Republics within the Russian Federation and judicial bodies of the administration of krais, regions and autonomous formations as well as of the towns of Moscow and St. Petersburg shall certify documents of judicial bodies subordinate to them and institutions and corresponding bodies of law of the republic, krai, region, district or town.
3. Republican registry offices of the republics within the Russian Federation, central registry offices of krais, regions and districts as well as of the towns of Moscow and St. Petersburg shall certify certificates of civil status of the above-mentioned bodies or registry offices subordinate to them;
4. The Department of documentary and reference work of the Archives Committee of the Russian Federation shall certify documents issued by the central state archives of Russia;
5. Archives bodies of autonomous formations and archive departments of krais and regions shall certify documents issued by archives subordinate to them;
6. The Department of Procurator General's Office of the Russian Federation shall certify documents made through the channels of the bodies of prosecution.

**St. Georgia and the South Sandwich Islands: Competent Authority:** declared by the United Kingdom October 17, 1968, the Commissioner for South Georgia and the South Sandwich Islands.

**Saint Helena:** On February 24, 1965, the United Kingdom extended the Convention to Saint Helena which entered into force for Saint Helena April 25, 1965. **Competent Authority:** declared October 17, 1968. The Governor and Commander-in-Chief of the Island of St. Helena and its Dependencies.

**St. Kitts (Christopher):** On February 24, 1965, the United Kingdom extended the Convention to Saint Kitts which entered into force for Saint Kitts April 25, 1965. Competent authority declared October 17, 1968. Now independent, Saint Kitts and Nevis (formerly Saint Christopher and Nevis) acceded to the Convention on February 26, 1994. The Convention entered into force on December 14, 1994. **Competent Authority:** 1. The Attorney General; 2. The Solicitor General; 3. The Chief Secretary of the Office of the

Prime Minister; 4. The Permanent Secretary in the Ministry of Foreign Affairs; or 5. The Registrar of the Supreme Court, Ministry of Legal Affairs, P.O. Box 186, Government Headquarters, St. Kitts-Nevis, West Indies, Tel: 809-465-2521.

**Saint Lucia:** On February 24, 1965, the United Kingdom extended the Convention to Saint Lucia which entered into force for Saint Lucia April 25, 1965. Achieved independence in 1979. On December 5, 2001, Saint Lucia acceded to the Convertion in its own right. The Convention enters into force in Saint Lucia June 1, 2002. **Competent Authority:**

On accession, December 5, 2001, Saint Lucia designated the following competent authorities to issue the certificate in accordance with Article 6, paragraph 1:

The Permanent Secretary, Ministry of Foreign Affairs and International Trade
The Deputy Permanent Secretary, Ministry of Foreign Affairs and International Trade
The Permanent Secretary, Ministry of Commerce, International Financial Services and Consumer Affairs
The Deputy Permanent Secretary, Ministry of Commerce, International Financial Services and Consumer Affairs
The Registrar of Companies and Intellectual Property
The Registrar of the Supreme Court
The Solicitor General

**St. Vincent and the Grenadines:** On February 24, 1965, the United Kingdom extended the Convention to Saint Vincent which entered into force for Saint Vincent April 25, 1965. St. Vincent achieved independence October 27, 1979 as St. Vincent and the Grenadines. Confirmation provided by local authorities to U.S. Embassy in Bridgetown, Barbados (whose consular district includes St. Vincent and the Grenadines) that country considers itself bound by Convention. **Competent Authority:** Ministry of Foreign Affairs, St. Vincent and the Grenadines, W.I., tel: 809-456-1111. Ministry of Foreign Affairs forwards to Registrar's Office

**Samoa:** On January 18, 1999, Samoa signed the Convention. Samoa ratified the Convention July 15, 1999 and the Convention entered into force September 13, 1999. In accordance with Article 6, paragraph 1, of the Convention, the Independent State of Samoa has designated as its competent authority: The Secretary for Foreign Affairs, Ministry of Foreign Affairs, P.o. Box L1861, Apia, Samoa; telephone: 685-63333; fax: 685-21504.

**San Marino:** Acceded to Convention May 26, 1994. Convention entered into force February 13, 1995. **Competent Authority:** 1. The Minister for Foreign Affairs (Il Segretario di Stato per gli Affari Esteri della Repubblica di San Marino) or 2. a person delegated and officially authorized by him/her to sign and authenticate legal instruments and documents issued by the Department of Foreign Affairs and other of the Republic's public bodies.

**Seychelles:** On February 24, 1965, the United Kingdom extended the Convention to the Seychelles which entered into force for the Seychelles April 25, 1965. Now independent. Acceded to Convention June 9, 1978. Convention entered into force March 31, 1979. **Competent Authority:** The Registrar, Supreme Court, Victoria, Mahe

**Slovakia:** Accession - June 6, 2001; Enters into Force - December 20, 2001. With the following declaration:

"The Slovak Republic, under Article 6 of the Convention, designates for purposes of Article 3 of the Convention as authorities competent to issue the certificate the following:

1. The Ministry of Justice of the Slovak Republic ( *Ministerstvo spravodlivosti Slovenskej republiky* ) for:
    a. public documents issued or certified by courts, notaries, hussiers de justice or other judicial officers;
    b. translations executed by official (court appointed) translators;
2. The Ministry of Interior of the Slovak Republic ( *Ministerstvo vnutra Slovenskej republiky* ) for public documents emanating from authorities within its jurisdiction with the exception of documents specified in point 6 lit. a) below;
3. The Ministry of Education of the Slovak Republic ( *Ministerstvo srkolstva Slovenskej republiky* ) for public documents emanating from authorities within its jurisdiction;
4. The Ministry of Health of the Slovak Republic ( *Ministerstvo zdravotnictva Slovenskej republiky* ) for public documents emanating from authorities within its jurisdiction with the exception of documents specified in point 6 lit. b) below;
5. The General Headquarters of the Army of the Slovak Republic ( *Generalny stab Armady Slovenskej republiky* ) for public documents emanating from authorities within the jurisdiction of the Ministry of Defence of the Slovak Republic;
6. Office of the Regional Administration ( *krajsky urad* ) for:
    a. documents from the Register of Births, Deaths and Marriages ( *matrika* ) with the exception of decisions on civil status;
    b. documents issued by health facilities established by the Office of Regional Administration;
7. The Ministry of Foreign Affairs of the Slovak Republic ( *Ministerstvo zahranicnych veci Slovenskej republiky* ) for any other public documents issued in the Slovak Republic not specified above."

**Slovenia, Republic of:** Entered into Force June 25, 1991. **Competent Authority:** Ministry of Justice and Administration, Republic of Slovenia

**Solomon Islands: No confirmation issued by country that Convention is deemed to apply.** On February 24, 1965, the United Kingdom extended the Convention to the British Solomon Islands Protectorate which entered into force April 25, 1965. The British Solomon Islands Protectorate achieved independence July 7, 1978 as the Solomon Islands. **Competent Authority:** Unknown.

**South Africa:** Entered into force August 3, 1994. Convention entered into force April 30, 1995. **Competent Authority:** 1. Any magistrate or additional magistrate. 2. Any registrar or assistant registrar of the Supreme Court of South Africa 3. Any person designated by the Director-General: Justice 4. Any person designated by the Director-General: Foreign Affairs

**Spain:** Entered into force September 25, 1978. **Competent Authority:** by a note to the depositary dated November 10, 1978, Spain notified a modification in the designated competent authorities: 1. For documents drawn up by competent judicial authorities or officials: the Secretaries of "Territorial Courts" (Secretarios de Gobierno de las Audiencias) or their deputies; 2. For documents authenticated by a notary public, or private documents where the signatures have been authenticated by a notary public: the President of the relevant Association of notaries public or the person legally responsible for its affairs; 3. For other public documents, excepting those issued by central administrative bodies: any of the officials referred to in paragraphs 1 and 2, above; 4. For documents issued by authorities of the central administration: Head of the Central Section of the Ministry of Justice (Jefe de la Seccion Central de la Subsecretaria) Ministerios de Justicia Registro General c/ San Bernardo 45 28015 Madrid, Spain, tel: 34-1-390-2000

**Suriname:** Extended by the Kingdom of the Netherlands May 16, 1967. Achieved independence November 25, 1975. Suriname declared on October 29, 1976 that it considers itself bound by the Convention. Effective date of accession is date of independence. **Competent Authority:** Registrar at the Court of Justice of Suriname (Griffier by het Hof van Justitie in Suriname)

**Swaziland:** On February 24, 1965, the United Kingdom extended the Convention to Swaziland which entered into force for Swaziland April 25, 1965. Achieved independence September 6, 1968. Swaziland declared on July 3, 1978 that it considers itself bound by the Convention. **Competent Authority:** 1. The Deputy Prime Minister; 2. The Attorney General; 3. The Registrar of the High Court; 4. The Head of Department not specified in paragraphs 2 and 3; 5. A District Commissioner; 6. A Magistrate; 7. Such other officer as the Deputy Prime Minister may, by notice published in the Gazette, specify.

**Sweden:** Signed the Convention March 2, 1999; ratified the Convention March 2, 1999. Entered into force: May 1, 1999. **Competent Authority:** The instrument of ratification contains the following declaration: "The Government of Sweden declares, in accordance with Article 6, that the competent authorities to issue certificates are all Notaries Public and the Ministry of Foreign Affairs."

**Switzerland: Competent Authority:** (a) Federal Authorities: The Federal Office (La Chandellerie federale); (b) Cantonal Authorities: Canton of.State Office (Die Staatskanzlei): State Office (Die Staatskanzlei): Aargau, Basel-Stadt, Lucerne, St. Gallen, Schaffhausen, Solothurn, Thurgau, Zug, Zurich.

State Office (Die Staatskanzlei): Nidwalden, Obwalden, Schwyz, Uri.
State Office (Die Staatskanzlei/La Chancellerie d'Etat): Bern, Freiburg, Wallis.
Government Office (Die Regierungskanzlei): Glarus.
Office of the Land (Die Landeskanslei): Basel-Landschaft.
State Office (La Chancellerie d'Etat): Geneva, Neuchatel, Vaud.
Canton Office (Die Kantonskanzlei): Appenzell Z.-Rh.
Council Office (Die Ratskanzlei): Appenzell I.-Rh.
State Office (Die Standeskanzlei/La Cancelleria dello Stato): Graubuden.
State Office (La Chancelleria dello Stato): Ticino.

**Tonga:** Tonga declared on October 28, 1971 that it considers itself bound by the Convention. On February 24, 1965, the United Kingdom extended the Convention to Tonga which entered into force for Tonga April 25, 1965. **Competent Authority:** The Secretary to Government, Prime Minister's Office, Nuku'alofa

**Trinidad and Tobago:** Signed the Convention October 28, 1999, ratifed or acceded to the Convention May 15, 2000 for which the Convention entered into force July 14, 2000. **Competent Authority:** By Note dated 27 July 2000, the Republic of Trinidad and Tobago informed the depositary of the following: "(...)the Registrar General (in Port-of-Spain) has been designated the competent authority to affix the Convention Apostille. By Note dated 9 March 2001, the Republic of Trinidad and Tobago informed the depositary of the following:

"... further to Note ... informing that the Registrar General has been designated the competent authority to affix the Convention Apostille, the Permanent Secretary, Ministry of Education and the Chief of Protocol, Ministry of Enterprise Development, Foreign Affairs and Tourism, have also been designated competent authorities to issue certificates of authenticity under Article 3 of the Convention. Each competent authority may delegate his function to a deputy or deputies as circumstances warrant.

**Turkey: Competent Authority:** 1. Administrative documents: a. In Provinces: Governor, Deputy-Governor, Director of Juridical Matters; b. In towns: Vice-Governor; 2. Judicial Documents: Presidencies of the Judicial Commissions where the high criminal courts exist.

**Turks and Caicos Islands:** On February 24, 1965, the United Kingdom extended the Convention to the Turks and Caicos Islands which entered into force for the Turks and Caicos Islands April 25, 1965. **Competent Authority:** The Governor of the Turks and Caicos Islands

**Tuvalu:** Now Independent. **No confirmation issued by newly independent country that Convention is deemed to apply.** On February 24, 1965, the United Kingdom extended the Convention to Ellice Islands which entered into force April 25, 1965. The Ellice Islands achieved independence as Tuvalu on October 1, 1978. **Competent Authority:** Unknown.

**United Kingdom: Competent Authority:** Her Majesty's Principal Secretary of State for Foreign and Commonwealth Affairs, Foreign and Commonwealth Office, London SW1, United Kingdom

**Vanuatu:** Now Independent. **No confirmation issued by newly independent country that Convention is deemed to apply.** In notes of April 1, 1970, the British and French Embassies notified the depositary that the respective governments have reached an agreement whereby he extension of the Convention to the Anglo-French Condominium of the New Hebrides with effect from February 15, 1966 has been confirmed, and the competent authorities to issue the certificate designated. On February 24, 1965, the United Kingdom extended the Convention to the New Hebrides which entered into force for the New Hebrides April 25, 1965. The New Hebrides achieved independence on July 30, 1980 and became the Republic of Vanuatu . **Competent Authority:** Unknown.

**Venezuela:** Signed the Convention July 1, 1998; ratified the Convention January 15, 1999. Entered into force: March 16, 1999. **Competent Authority:** Designation of the competent authorities to issue the certificate in accordance with Article 6, paragraph 1: the Ministry of Foreign Affairs, Directorate General of Consular Affairs. The address is:

Embajadora Edna Figueira
Directora General de Relaciones Consulares
Ministerio de Relaciones Exteriores
Torre MRE, Piso 6, Conde a Carmelitas, Caracas
Telephone: (582) 862-1145

**Yugoslavia, former: (Serbia-Montenegro):** The former Socialist Federal Republic of Yugoslavia became a Party to the Convention on 24 January 1965. Successor states which have confirmed the continued application of the Convention include: Bosnia and Herzegovina, Croatia, Macedonia (Former Yugoslav Republic of), and Slovenia. See the listings under each of these countries for information about their competent authorities. The Federal Republic of Yugoslavia (FRY) has NOT confirmed the continued applicability of the Convention in Serbia-Montenegro.

**Zimbabwe:** On February 24, 1965, the United Kingdom extended the Convention to South Rhodesia which entered into force for South Rhodesia April 25, 1965. Achieved independence as Republic of Zimbabwe April 18, 1980. No confirmation Convention continues to apply **Competent Authority:** Unknown.

*Department of State*
*Bureau of Consular Affairs*
*Overseas Citizens Services*

**Other Government Websites**

- First Gov Service Locator
- U.S. Department of Justice
- The White House
- more >

This site is managed by the Bureau of Consular Affairs, U.S. Department of State. External links to other Internet sites should not be construed as an endorsement of the views contained therein.

# U.S. Department of State

## Hague Convention on Taking of Evidence Abroad in Civil or Commercial Matters

**DISCLAIMER:** THE INFORMATION IN THIS CIRCULAR RELATING TO THE LEGAL REQUIREMENTS OF SPECIFIC FOREIGN COUNTRIES IS PROVIDED FOR GENERAL INFORMATION ONLY AND MAY NOT BE TOTALLY ACCURATE IN A PARTICULAR CASE. QUESTIONS INVOLVING INTERPRETATION OF SPECIFIC FOREIGN LAWS SHOULD BE ADDRESSED TO FOREIGN COUNSEL OR THE FOREIGN CENTRAL AUTHORITY FOR THE CONVENTION.

**IN FORCE** : ANGUILLA [1] , ARGENTINA (excludes recognition of the extension of the Convention by the United Kingdom to the MALVINAS, SOUTH GEORGIA and SOUTH SANDWICH ISLANDS), ARUBA [2] , AUSTRALIA, BARBADOS, BULGARIA, CAYMAN ISLANDS [1] , CHINA [8] , CYPRUS, CZECH REPUBLIC [3] , DENMARK, DJIBOUTI [4,5] , ESTONIA, FALKLAND ISLANDS [1] , FINLAND, FRANCE, FRENCH GUIANA [5] , FRENCH POLYNESIA [5] , GERMANY, GIBRALTAR [1] , GUADELOUPE [5] , GUERNSEY [1] , HONG KONG SAR [7,1] , ISLE OF MAN [1] , ISRAEL, ITALY, JERSEY [1] , LATVIA, LUXEMBOURG, MACAO SAR [6] , MARTINIQUE [5] , MEXICO, MONACO, NETHERLANDS, NORWAY, POLAND, PORTUGAL, SAINT PIERRE AND MIQUELON [5] , SINGAPORE, SLOVAK REPUBLIC [3] , SOVEREIGN BASE AREAS OF AKROTIRI AND DHEKELIA [1] , SPAIN, SWEDEN, SWITZERLAND, UNITED KINGDOM, UNITED STATES, VENEZUELA.

[1] The Convention was extended to this territory, possession or other jurisdiction by the United Kingdom.

[2] The Convention was extended to this territory, possession or other jurisdiction by the Netherlands.

[3] In accordance with Article 34(1) of the Vienna Convention on Succession of States in Respect of Treaties, the U.S. view is that when a country which is a party to a multilateral treaty or convention has dissolved, the successor state(s) inherit the treaty obligations of the former government, consistent with Article 34 of the Vienna Convention. However, as a practical matter, the custom is for depositories to expect a notice of succession to confirm that the new entity is performing its treaty obligations. Many newly independent states may not really be implementing such conventions at this time in that they may not be performing the functions set forth in the Convention. We continue to work with these governments and the depositories to obtain confirmation that the respective successor state is complying with treaty obligations.

[4] This country has achieved independence. No declaration has been made on the continuation in force of the Convention. We have requested the assistance of the Hague Conference on Private International Law in ascertaining from these countries whether they are applying the Convention.

[5] The Convention was extended to this territory, possession or other jurisdiction by France.

[6] The Convention was extended to this territory, possession or other jurisdiction by Portugal.

[7] Hong Kong became a Special Administrative Region (SAR) of the People's Republic of China on July 1, 1997 in accordance with the 1984 Sino-British Joint Declaration. The People's Republic of China has

advised the United States that the Hague Service and Evidence Conventions remain in effect for Hong Kong and that the Hong Kong Central Authorities continue to be located in Hong Kong. See list of Central Authorities.

[8] Upon its accession to the Hague Evidence Convention, China declared that the provisions of Chapter II of the Convention except for Article 15 will not be applicable. The United States is seeking clarification from the People's Republic of China regarding its interpretation and implementation of the Convention.

**CITATIONS** : 23 U.S.T. 2555; T.I.A.S. 7444; 847 UNTS 231; 28 U.S.C.A. 1782 (1975 Cum. Supp.); 28 U.S.C.A. following 1781 (Supp. 1979); 8 I.L.M. 37 (1969); Martindale-Hubbell Law Directory, Law Digest Volume, Selected International Conventions; Ristau, International Judicial Assistance (Civil and Commercial), International Law Institute, (1995 supp.), Appendix C, A-50 *ff.*

**PURPOSE** : The Hague Evidence Convention codifies the taking of depositions on notice and commission before consuls and court appointed commissioners, providing minimum standards with which contracting states agree to comply. The Convention's primary purpose is to reconcile different, often conflictive, discovery procedures in civil and common law countries. The Convention also streamlines procedures for compulsion of evidence, utilizing a form "letter of request" which can be sent directly by the court in the U.S. to a foreign central authority, eliminating the cumbersome "diplomatic channel". (See International Soc'y for Krishna Consciousness, Inc. v. Lee, 105 F.R.D. 435, 442-443 (S.D.N.Y. 1984) and Philadelphia Gear Corp. v. American Pfauter Corp., 100 F.R.D. 58, 59 (E.D. Pa. 1983). The foreign central authorities are listed below. (Note: Rule 28(b) F.R.Cv.P. provides for depositions to be taken abroad pursuant to "any applicable treaty or convention.") For a general discussion of the Convention, see, Restatement (Third) Foreign Relations Law of the United States Sec. 473 (2) (1987); Ristau, International Judicial Assistance (Civil and Commercial), International Law Institute, Sec. 5-1-1 - 5-3-4, pp. 159-237, (1995 Supp.); Epstein & Snyder, International Litigation: A Guide to Litigation, Practice & Strategy, 2nd, Prentice Hall Law & Business, Sec. 10.10 - pp. 10-17 - 10-33 (1994 Supp.); Moore's Federal Practice, 3rd, Sec. 28.11, p. 28-9 - 28-22 (March 1997); Digest of United States Practice in International Law, U.S. Department of State, Office of the Legal Adviser, 1973, p. 210-213; 1976, p. 309; 1977, p. 490-492; 1978, p. 870-878, 1709; 1979, 891; 1980, 504-505; 1981-1988 Cumulative Digest, 1409, 1419, 1425-1426, 1509, 1510-1516. 1550, 1557, 1564.

**DECLARATIONS AND RESERVATIONS:** Each country had the opportunity of making reservations and declarations regarding the applicability of each article of the Convention. This makes the Convention different for each country, so it is important to review our country-specific judicial assistance flyers.

**EXCLUSIVITY:** The nonexclusivity of the Hague Evidence Convention procedures was at issue in **Societe Nationale Industrielle Aerospatiale v. U.S. District Court, 482 U.S. 522, 96 L.Ed.2d 461, 107 S.Ct. 2542 (1987)** , where the U.S. Supreme Court held that the Convention did not bar a district court, pursuant to the Federal Rules of Civil Procedure, from ordering a foreign litigant over which that court exercised personal jurisdiction to produce evidence located within the foreign litigant"s own territory. **But see** , "Selected Cases" below. For a discussion of the *Aerospatiale* case and the nonexclusivity of the Convention, see Cumulative Digest of United States Practice in International Law, 1981-1988,

U.S. Department of State, Office of the Legal Adviser, Vol. 2, p. 1516-1524 (1994) and Vol. 3, p. 3704-3707 (1995), Ristau, Sec. 5-2-7, pp. 229-231.5 (1995 Supp.), Born & Westin, 319,334; Epstein & Snyder, Sec. 10.11 - 10.12, pp. 10-20, 10-27; Wright, Miller & Marcus, Federal Practice and Procedure, Civil, Sec. 2005.1, p. 68-76 (1994) and 1996 pocket part; Moore's Federal Practice, Sec. 28.11[3], p. 28-11- 28-12, and other treatises on the subject, some of which are noted under "Selected References" below.

**SCOPE OF THE CONVENTION:** Article 1 of the Convention provides that assistance is to be provided in "civil and commercial" matters. The term "civil and commercial" is not defined. See Ristau, Sec. 5-1-4, p. 162-168, (1995 Supp.), Born & Westin 310,312; and the Reports of the Special Commissions on the operation of the Convention noted below.

**U.S. CENTRAL AUTHORITY:** Office of International Judicial Assistance, Civil Division, Department of Justice, 1100 L St., N.W., Room 11006, Washington, D.C. 20530, tel: (202) 307-0983; fax: (202) 514-6584.

**TAKING DEPOSITIONS OF WILLING WITNESSES:** Each country party to the Convention made specific reservations and declarations when they deposited their instruments of accession to the Convention. Some countries allow the taking of depositions of willing witnesses only under certain specific conditions. For example, some countries require case-by-case permission from the foreign central authority before a voluntary deposition can be taken. See our country-specific flyers for details. The declarations and reservations made by countries party to the Convention can be found in the Martindale-Hubbell Law Directory, Selected International Conventions (via the Internet, Martindale-Hubbell website: **http://www.martindale.com/products/intl law dir.html)** and in the Practical Handbook on the Operation of the Hague Convention on the Taking of Evidence Abroad. See Ristau, Sec. 5-3-1- 5-2-4, pp. 232-238.4, (1995 Supp.) and Born & Westin, 315-317; Epstein & Snyder, Sec. 10.10[4], pp. 10.18 -10-20. Consult our country-specific flyers; see "Additional Information" below.

**DEPOSITIONS TAKEN BY COURT APPOINTED COMMISSIONERS OTHER THAN CONSULAR OFFICERS:** Article 17 provides for the possibility of court appointed commissioners to take depositions under restrictions similar to those confronting consular officers. To date, only Finland and the United States have given broad permission for court appointed commissioners to take depositions. The United Kingdom approves such depositions on a reciprocal basis. But see our country specific flyers for additional details. Some countries, such as Denmark and Portugal, made specific declarations prohibiting such activities by court appointed commissioners. In other countries, specific permission must be sought from the foreign central authority for a commissioner other than a consular officer to conduct depositions. See Ristau, Sec. 5-3-3, pp. 236-238, (1995 Supp.); Born & Westin 316.

**ARRANGING CONSULAR DEPOSITIONS:** When a U.S. consular officer is needed to preside at the taking of a voluntary deposition at an American embassy or consulate scheduling depositions is done directly by our embassies and consulates at a time and date mutually convenience to the participants and the consular officer. The U.S. consular officer generally administers the oaths to the witnesses, court reporter and interpreter and withdraws, subject to recall. The actual questions are posed by the attorneys. (See 22 C.F.R. 92.56, consular officers will comply with special instructions which accompany the request for deposition on notice or commission.) Requesting counsel must make arrangements with the witness to insure his or her appearance for the deposition (travel fees, witness fees, etc.) The U.S. Embassy/Consulate may be able to provide information concerning interpreters, translators and audio/video operators. Private counsel must make their own arrangements to retain the services of interpreters, translators and audio/video operators. Note: not all foreign countries have court reporters, interpreters and translators. American embassies and consulates do not have staff personnel available to perform such functions. It may be necessary to bring your own experts in these fields from the United States. Consult the U.S. embassy or consulate or the embassy or consulate of the foreign country regarding foreign Customs restrictions concerning bringing video and other equipment into a the foreign country. Consult our general information flyer "Obtaining Evidence Abroad" for detailed information about arranging consular depositions, telephone depositions, depositions on written questions, videotaping depositions, etc. See Ristau, Sec. 5-3-2, pp. 234-236 (1995 Supp.) for a discussion of consular depositions.

**U.S. FEDERAL, STATE OR LOCAL GOVERNMENT PARTICIPANTS:** . U.S. federal, state and local government officials interested in obtaining evidence abroad should contact the Office of American Citizens Services (ACS) at (202) 647-5226. ACS assists these officials in making the necessary arrangements for testimony of foreign officials, host country clearance and can assist them in retaining the services of stenographers, interpreters and video operators, where available. A copy of the host country clearance questionnaire will be faxed to you. It will also be available via our Internet Home Page and Autofax Service.

**PRE-TRIAL DISCOVERY OF DOCUMENTS** : Most countries party to the Convention, with the exception of the Czech Republic, Israel, the Slovak Republic and the United States, made specific declarations objecting to the Article 23 provision on pre-trial discovery of documents. See Ristau, Sec. 5-2-5, p. 205-223 (1995 Supp.); Born & Westin, 313, 315.

**COMPULSION OF EVIDENCE:** Testimony and documentary or physical evidence may be compelled using the "Model Letter of Request" provided in the Hague Evidence Convention. The court in the U.S. transmits the request with appropriate translations directly to the foreign central authority. See Moore"s Federal Practice, 3d, Section 28.12[8].

**MODEL REQUEST FORM:** Article 3 provides mandatory provisions concerning the content of the letter of request. See Ristau, Sec. 5-2-1(1), p. 173-175 (1995 Supp.). See Martindale-Hubbell Law Directory, Selected International Conventions; Ristau, Appendix C, DS-64 through DS-65 (1995 Supp.) for the model letter of request form to compel evidence. For a sample application to a U.S. court for issuance of a letter of request under the Convention, see Ristau, Sec. 5-2-1(3) p. 177-178 (1995 Supp.). For a sample completed letter of request using the recommended form see Ristau, Sec. 5-2-1(4), p. 179-184 (1995 Supp.) The request should include any specific procedures desired by the requesting court, such as verbatim transcripts or participation in the proceedings before the foreign court by American counsel or local counsel representing the American firm. See also Born & Westin, 317; Moore"s Federal Practice, 3d, Sec. 28.12[4] and 28.12[9].

**NUMBER OF COPIES:** The Evidence Convention, unlike the Service Convention, does not require that a letter of request be submitted in duplicate. In practice, however, countries prefer that the request be prepared in duplicate (one English text bearing the seal of the court, one photocopy of the English text; two copies of a translation of the request an any accompanying documents.) If testimony is desired of two or more witnesses, separate letters of request should be issued for each witness. See Ristau, Sec. 5-2-1, p. 185, (1995 Supp.).

**TRANSLATIONS** : Articles 4 and 33 of the Convention concern translations. The Convention requires a letter of request in the language of the receiving state, but English or French is acceptable unless the receiving state has expressly stated to the contrary. See Moore's Federal Practice, Sec. 28.12[3], p. 28-15. See also S&S Screw Mach. Co. v. Cosa Corp., 647 F. Supp. 600, 613 n.23 (M.D. Tenn. 1986). Consult the declarations and reservations made by each country. See the Martindale-Hubbell Law Directory, Selected International Conventions, Law Digest Volume or the Practical Handbook on the Operation of the Hague Convention on the Taking of Evidence Abroad. See also, Ristau, Sec. 5-2-1(8), p. 185-187 (1995 Supp.), or Epstein, International Litigation, a Guide to Jurisdiction, Practice and Strategy, Section 10.10; Moore's Federal Practice, 3d, Sec. 28.12[3] (1997). Translations should be a notarized certification by the translator. See Ristau, Sec. 5-2-1, p. 187 (1995 Supp.).

**TRANSMITTING REQUEST:** The requesting court in the United States transmits the model letter of request and accompanying documents and appropriate translations, in duplicate, directly to the central authority. See Ristau, Sec. 5-1-5(2), p. 168-171, (1995 Supp); Moore's Federal Practice, 3d, Sec. 28.12[2] (1997).

**EXECUTION OF THE REQUEST:** Article 9 provides that letters of request will be executed in accordance with local foreign law. See Ristau, Sec. 5-2-2, p. 188-200 (1995 Supp.); Born & Westin 317-318, and Moore's Federal Practice, 3d, Sec. 28.12[7] for a discussion on how requests are executed in civil and common law countries.

**TIME:** Article 9 provides that requests be executed "expeditiously." Requests under the Hague Evidence Convention are executed somewhat faster than letters rogatory. This is due in part to the direct channel from the U.S. court to the foreign central authority. However, the general estimate of 6 months to a year to execute the request is still used. See Ristau, Sec. 5-2-2(3), p. 192 (1995, Supp.); Born & Westin, 312 and Moore"s Federal Practice, 3d, Sec. 28.12[7].

**COSTS:** Articles 14, 26 and 28(f) govern costs and fees for execution of letters of request. Generally speaking, there is no fee. However, if the executing country incurs expense for fees paid to "experts and interpreters" reimbursement can be sought in accordance with paragraph 2 of Article 14. For a discussion of fees, see Ristau, Sec. 5-2-4, p. 201-204 (1995 Supp.).

**RETURN OF EXECUTED REQUEST:** Article 13(1) provides that the executed request shall be returned to the issuing authority (requesting court) by the foreign central authority. See Ristau, Sec. 5-1-5(4), p. 171, (1995 Supp.).

## FOREIGN CENTRAL AUTHORITIES

## COUNTRY AND CENTRAL AUTHORITY

***ANGUILLA***
Governor of Anguilla

***ARGENTINA***
Ministry of Foreign Relations and Culture (Ministerio de Relaciones Exteriores y Culto)
Recoquista 1088, Buenos Aires, Argentina

***ARUBA***
Convention Extended by the Netherlands. Central Authority Unknown. Consult Local Counsel.

***AUSTRALIA***
Secretary of the Attorney General's Department
Commonwealth of Australia
Canberra, ACT, Australia

***BARBADOS***
Registrar of the Supreme Court of Barbados
Law Courts
Bridgetown, Barbados
tel: 809-427-5537

***BULGARIA***
**Central Authority:** Ministry of Justice and European Legal Integration

***CAYMAN ISLANDS***
His Excellency the Governor
Cayman Islands

***CHINA***
Bureau of International Judicial Assistance
Ministry of Justice of the People's Republic of China
10 Chaoyangmen Nandajie, Chaoyang District
Beijing 100020
China

***CYPRUS***
Ministry of Justice

***CZECH REPUBLIC***
Ministerstvo Spravedlnosti Ceske republicky
The Ministry of Justice of the Czech Republic

128 Praha 2, Vysehradska 16
Prague, Czech Republic

***DENMARK***
Justitsministeriet
Ministry of Justice
Slotsholmsgade 10
1216 Kobenhavn K.
Copenhagen, Denmark
tel: 120906; telex: 15530

***ESTONIA***
Ministry of Justice
Suur Karja #19
Tallinn, Estonia EE0001
tel: (6) 28-2648

***FALKLAND ISLANDS***
The Governor
Stanley, Falkland Islands

***FINLAND***
Ministry of Justice
10 Etelaesplanadi
Helsinki 13, Finland
tel: 358-0-1601

***FRANCE***
Ministere de la Justice
Ministry of Justice
Service Civil de L"Entraide Judiciaire Internationale
13, Place Vendome
75042 Paris Cedex 01, France
tel: 261-80-22; telex: 211802

***GERMANY***

***For Baden-Wurttemberg***
Justizministerium Baden-Wurttemberg
Justice Ministry
Schillerplatz 4
70173 Stuttgart, Germany
tel: 21931

***For Bavaria***
Das Bayerisches Staasministerium der Justiz
Justizpalast
Prielmayerstrasse 7
80335 Munchen

Munich, Germany
tel: 55971

***For Berlin***
Senatsverwaltung fur Justiz von Berlin
Salzburger Strasse 21-25
10825 Berlin, Germany
tel: 7831

***For Brandenburg***
Das Ministerium der Justiz
des Landes Brandenburg
Heinrich-Mann-Allee 107
14460 Potsdam, Germany

***For Bremen***
Der Prasident des Landgerichts Bremen
Domsheide 16
28195 Bremen, Germany
tel: 3614204

***For Hamburg***
Der Prasident des Amtsgerichtes Hamburg
Sievekingplatz 1
20335 Hamburg, Germany
tel: 34971

***For Hesse***
Der Hessische Minister der Justiz
Luisenstrasse 13
65185 Wiesbaden, Germany
tel: 321<<P> ***For Lower Saxony***
Der Niedersachsisher Minister der Justiz
Am Waterlooplatz 1
30169 Hannover, Germany
tel: 1901

***For Mecklenburg-Western Pomerania***
Der Minister fur Justiz
Bundes- und Europaangelegenheiten
des Landes Mecklenburg-Vorpommern
Demmlerplatz 14
19053 Schwerin, Germany

***For Northrhine-Westphalia***
Prasident des Oberlandesgerichts
Dusseldorf
Cecilienallee 3

40474 Dusseldorf, Germany
tel: 87921

***For Rhineland-Palatinate***
Das Ministerium der Justiz
Ernst-Ludwig-Strasse 3
55116 Mainz, Germany
tel: 161

***For Saarland***
Ministerium der Justiz des Saarlandes
Zahringerstrasse 12
66119 Saarbrucken, Germany
tel: 5051

***For Saxony***
Das Sachsische Stattsministerium
der Justiz
Archivstrasse 1
66119 Dresden, Germany

***For Saxony-Anhalt***
Das Ministerium der Justiz
des Landes Sachsen-Anhalt
Wilhelm-Hopfner-Ring 6
39116 Magdeburg, Germany

***For Schleswig-Holstein***
Der Justizminister des Landes Schleswig-Holstein
Lorentzendamm 35
34103 Kiel, Germany
tel: 51371

***For Thuringia***
Das Justizministerium Thuringen
Alfred-Hess-Strasse 8
99094 Erfurt, Germany

***Gibraltar***
The Deputy Governor
Gibraltar

***Guernsey***
Bailiff, Deputy Bailiff, any Jurat of the Royal Court
of Guernsey, the Chairman or a Jurat of the Court
of Alderney and the Seneschal (or deputy) of the
Court of the Seneschal of Sark
Guernsey, United Kingdom

***Hong Kong SAR***
Chief Secretary of Hong Kong
Central Government Offices
Lower Albert Road
Hong Kong; tel: (011) (852) 8102954

***Isle of Man***
1. See United Kingdom.
2. Her Majesty"s First Deemster and Clerk of the
Rolls is designated as an additional authority to receive letters of request for execution in the Isle of Man

***Israel***
Director of the Courts
19 Jaffa Road
Jerusalem

***Italy***
Ministerio degliAffari Esteri
Rome, Italy

***Jersey***
Royal Court of Jersey

***Latvia***
Ministry of Justice
Brivibas Boulevard 34
LV - 1536 Riga, Latvia

***Luxembourg***
Parquet General Pres La Cour Superieure de Justice
12 Cote d'Eich
Luxembourg-Ville, Luxembourg
tel: 475981 or 26767 or 41464

***Macau SAR***
On December 16, 1999, the Government of the People's Republic of China declared: "In accordance with the Joint Declaration of the Governemnt of the People's Republic of China and the Government of the Republic of Portugal on the Question of Macau signed on 13 April 1987, the Government of the People's Republic of China will resume the exercise of sovereignty over Macau with effect from 20 December 1999. **Central Authority:** Procurator of the Procuratorate of Macau SAR, Alameda Dr. Carlos D'Assumpcao, NAPE, Edificio Comercial Tai Fung, 13, Regiao Administrativa Especial de Macau; tel: 853-797-8271, fax: 853-727-621. The official languages in Macau SAR are Chinese and Portugese. Foreign judical assistance requests pursuant to the Convention written in English will be accepted and processed, though the preference is for a copy to be submitted in one of the two official languages - Chinese or Portugese.

***Mexico***
Secretaria de Relaciones Exteriores
Dirreccion General de Asuntos Juridicos
Ricardo Flores Magon No. 1
Mexico City, Mexico
tel: 782-34-40
telex: 01762090

***Monaco***
Directorate of Judicial Services
MC 98025
Monaco Cedex, Monaco

***Netherlands***
De Officier van Justitie bij de Arrondissementsrechtbank te "s Gravenhage
The Public Prosecutor With the District Court of the Hague
Juliana van Stolberglaan 2-4
The Hague, the Netherlands tel: 82-40-41

***Norway***
The Royal Ministry of Justice and Police
Toks 8005
Oslo Dep
Oslo 1, Norway

***Poland***
Ministry of Justice
Department of International Cooperation and European Law
Al. Ujazdowskie 11
Warsaw, Poland 00-950
tel: (48)(22) 628-4431
fax: (48)(22) 628-0949

***Portugal***
Direccao-Geral dos Servicas Judiciarios
Ministerio da Justica
The Director-General of the Judiciary Deparment
Ministry of Justice
Prace do Comercio
1194 Lisboa Codex
Lisbon, Portugal
tel: 360786

***Singapore***
The Registrar of the Supreme Court
St. Andrews Road

Singapore 0617, Singapore
tel: 65-3324021; fax: 65-3379450

***Slovak Republic***
Ministerstvo spravodlivosti Slovenskej republicky
The Ministry of Justice of the Slovak Republic
Zupne namestie 13,
813 11 Brtislava, Slovak Republic
Fax: 00427-531035

***Sovereign Base Areas of Akrotiri & Dhekelia***
Senior Registrar of the Judge"s Court of the Sovereign Base Areas

***Spain***
The Ministry of Justice (El Ministerio Justicia)
La Direccion General de Codificacion y Cooperacion Juridica Internacional
Ministerio de Justicia e Interior
Technical Secretariat General (Secretaria General Tecnica)
Calle San Bernardo 62
28071 Madrid, Spain

***Sweden***
Ministry of Justice
Division for Criminal and International Judicial Cooperation
Central Authority
SE-103 33 Stockholm, Sweden
tel: (46)(8) 405-5048
fax: (46)(8) 405-4676

***Switzerland***
Federal Justice and Police Department
Federal Office for Police Matters
International Judicial and Extrajudicial Assistance
Bundesrain 20
3003 Bern, Switzerland
Fax: 011-41-31-322-5380

The Swiss Federal Justice and Police Department will forward the requests to the Central Authority in the appropriate canton. Requests for evidence may also be sent directly to the Central Authority for the appropriate Canton, as noted below.

**Authorized Swiss Central Authorities for each Canton**

*Language: (G=German); (F=French); (I-Italian)*

***Canton: Appenzell Ausserhoden (G)***
Kantonsgerich Appenzell A. Rh., 9043 Trogen, Switzerland
tel: 011-41-71-94-24-61

***Canton: Aargau (G)***
Obergericht des Kantons Aargau, 5000 Aargau, Switzerland
tel: 011-41-64-21-19-40

***Canton: Basel-Landschaft (G)***
Obergericht des Kantons Basel-Landschaft, 4410 Liestal, Switzerland
tel: 011-41-61-925-51-11

***Canton: Basel-Stadt (G)***
Apellationsgericht Basel-Stadt, 4054 Basel, Switerzland
tel: 011-41-61-267-81-81

***Canton: Bern (G/F)***
Justizdirektion des Kantons Bern, 3011 Bern, Switzerland
tel: 011-41-31-633-76-76

***Canton: Fribourg (F/G)***
Tribunal cantonal, 1700 Fribourg, Switzerland
tel: 011-41-37-25-39-10

***Canton: Geneve (F)***
Parquet du Procureur general, 1211 Geneve 3, Switzerland
tel: 011-41-22-319-21-11

***Canton: Glarus (G)***
Obergericht des Kantons Glarus, 8750 Glarus, Switzerland
tel: 011-41-58-61-15-32

***Canton: Graubuenden (G)***
Justiz-, Polizei- und Sanitaets- departement, Graubunden, 7001 Chur, Switzerland
tel: 011-41-81-21-21-21

***Canton: Jura (F)***
Department de la Justice, 2800 Delemont, Jura, Switzerland
tel: 011-41-66-21-51-11

***Canton: Luzern (G)***
Obergericht des Kantons Luzern, 6002 Luzern, Switzerland
tel: 011-41-41-24-51-11

***Canton: Neuchatel (F)***
Departement de Justice, 2001 Neuchatel, Switzerland
tel: 011-41-38-22-31-11

***Canton: Nidwalden (G)***
Kantonsgericht Nidwalden, 6370 Stans, Switzerland
tel: 011-41-41-63-79-50

***Canton: Obwalden (G)***
Kantonsgericht des Kantons, Obwalden, 6060 Sarnen, Switzerland
tel: 011-41-41-66-92-22

***Canton: St. Gallen (G)***
Kantonsgericht St. Gallen, 9001 St. Gallen, Switzerland
tel: 011-41-71-21-31-11

***Canton: Schaffhausen (G)***
Obergericht des Kantons, Schaffhausen, 8201 Schaffhausen, Switzerland
tel: 011-41-53-82-74-22

***Canton: Schwyz (G)***
Kantonsgericht Schwyz, 6430 Schwyz; Switzerland
tel: 011-41-43-24-11-24

***Canton: Solothurn (G)***
Obergericht des Kantons Solothurn, 4500 Solothurn, Switzerland
tel: 011-41-65-21-73-11

***Canton: Tessin (I)***
Tribunale di appello, 6901 Lugano, Switzerland
tel: 011-41-91-21-51-11

*Canton: Thurgau (G)*
Obergericht des Kantons Thurgau, 8500 Frauenfeld, Switzerland
tel: 011-41-54-22-31-21

***Canton: Uri (G)***
Gerichtskanzlei Uri, 6460 Altdorf, Switzerland
tel: 011-41-44-4-22-44

***Canton: Valais (F/G)***
Tribunal cantonal, 1950 Sion, Switzerland
tel: 011-41-27-22-93-93

***Canton: Vaud (F)***
Tribunal cantonal, 1014 Lausanne, Switzerland
tel: 011-41- 21-313-15-11

***Canton: Zug (G)***
Obergericht des Kantons Zug, Rechtshilfe, 6300 Zug, Switzerland
tel: 011-41-42-25-33-11

***Canton: Zurich (G)***
Obergericht des Kantons Zurich, Rechtshilfe, 8023 Zurich, Switzerland
tel: 011-41-1-257-91-91

***United Kingdom***
The Foreign and Commonwealth Office
London SW1A 2AL, United Kingdom

***For England and Wales***
The Senior Master of the Supreme Court of Judicature (Queen's Bench Division)
Royal Courts of Justice Strand
London WC2A 2LL, United Kingdom

***For Scotland***
The Crown Agent for Scotland
Lord Advocate's Department
Crown Office
5/7 Regent Road
Edinburgh EH7 5BL, Scotland

***For Northern Ireland***
Registrar of the Supreme Court of Northern Ireland

-or-

Master (Queens's Bench and Appeals)
Royal Courts of Justice
Belfast 1, Northern Ireland

***Venezuela***
el Miniterio Relaciones Exteriores the Ministry of External Relations

**SEE ALSO** :

- "Checklist for the Discussions of the Special Commission of April 1989 on the Operation of the Hague Convention on the Taking of Evidence Abroad", Hague Conference on Private International Law, Preliminary Document No. 1 of March 1989, 28 I.L.M. 1556 (1989).

- "Report of the Second Meeting of the Special Commission on the Operation of the Hague Convention on the Taking of Evidence Abroad in Civil or Commercial Matters, July 1985", 24 I.L.M. 1668 (1985).

- Practical Handbook on the Operation of the Hague Convention of 18 March 1970 on the Taking of Evidence Abroad in Civil Or Commercial Matters, Hague Conference on Private International Law, Maarten Kluwer's Internationale Uitgeversonderneming, Antwerp, 1984. U.S. Distributor: Butterworth Publishers Inc., 10 Tower Office Park, Woburn, Boston, Massachusetts 01801. Contact the U.S. Central Authority for addresses of other distributors.

- "Report on the Work of the Special Commission on the Operation of the Hague Convention on the Taking of Evidence Abroad in Civil or Commercial Matters Prepared by the United States Delegation", 17 I.L.M. 1417 (1978).

- "Report on the Work of the Special Commission on the Operation of the Convention of 18 March 1970 on the Taking of Evidence Abroad in Civil or Commercial Matters June 12-15, 1978 Prepared by the Permanent Bureau", 17 I.L.M. 1425 (1978).

- "Message from the President of the United States Transmitting the Convention on the Taking of Evidence Abroad in Civil or Commercial Matters", S. Exec. Doc. No. A 92d Cong., 2d Sess. (1972), 12 I.L.M. 323 (1973).

- "Letter of Submittal from Secretary of State William P. Rogers to the President Regarding the Evidence Convention", S. Exec. Doc. No. A, 1, 92d Cong., 2d Sess. (1972), 12 I.L.M. 324 (1973).

-"Report of the U.S. Delegation on the Taking of Evidence Abroad in Civil and Commercial Matters", 8 I.L.M. 785, 804 (1969).

**BUT SEE** :

Societe Nationale Industrielle Aerospatiale, et al., v. United States District Court for the Southern District of Iowa, 1987 U.S. LEXIS 2615; 96 Law. Ed. 2d 461; 107 Sup. Ct. 2542; 55 U.S. Law Week 4842; 7 Federal Rules of Service 3d 1105; 482 U.S. (page unassigned) (1987), 26 I.L.M. 1021 (1987).

Supreme Court Proceedings in Societe Nationale Industrielle Aerospatiale, et al., v. United States District Court for the Southern District of Iowa (Hague Evidence Convention; Extraterritorial Discovery in the U.S. Courts.) 25 I.L.M. 1475 (1986).

In re Anschuetz and Company, 838 F. 2d 1362, 7 March 1988.

Anschuetz & Co. v. Mississippi River Bridge Authority, et al.; Messerschmitt Bolkow Blohm v. Virginia Walker, et al., Brief for United States as Amicus Curiae and Petitioner's Response. 25 I.L.M. 803 (1986).

Club Mediterranee v. Dorin, 469 U.S. 1019 (1984), 23 I.L.M. 1332 (1984). Brief for United States as Amicus Curiae. (Appeal Dismissed.)

Volkswagenwerk v. Falzon, 464 U.S. 811 (1983), 23 I.L.M. 412 (1984). Brief for United States as Amicus Curiae. (Appeal Dismissed).

Hudson v. Hermann Pfauter GmbH & Co., 117 F.R.D. 33, 9 September 1987.

In re Benton Graphics v. Uddeholm Corp., 118 F.R.D. 386, D.N.J. 30 November 1987.

Sandsend Financial Consultants v. Wood, 743 SW2d 364, Tex. Civ. App., 1st Dist. Houston, 7 January 1988.

Scarminach v. Goldwell GmbH, 531 N.Y.S. 2d 188, Sup., Monroe County, 22 June 1988.

Cf. Rich v. KIS California, Inc., 121 F.R.D. 254, M.D.N.C., 22 June 1988.

John Jenco v. Martech International, Inc., 1988 U.S. Dist. LEXIS 4727, E.D. La., 20 May 1988, reversing 1988 U.S. Dist. LEXIS 3991.

"Hague Evidence Convention in the U.S. Courts", Laker Airways Ltd. v. Pan American World Airways, et al., U.S. District Court for the District of Columbia;

Graco v. Kremlin, Inc., U.S. District Court for the Northern District of Illinois (Eastern Division), 23 I.L.M. 748-781 (1984).

Laker Airways, Ltd. v. Sabena, Belgian World Airlines, 731 F. 2d 909, 937 (D.C. Cir. 1984).

In re Westinghouse Litigation, 563 F. 2d 992 (10th Cir. 1977).

In re Marc Rich & Co., A.G., 707 F. 2d 663, 667 (2d Cir.), cert. denied, 463 U.S. 1215 (1983). Marc Rich & Co., A.G. v. United States, 736 F. 2d 864 (2d Cir. 1984).

In re Grand Jury Proceedings: The Bank of Nova Scotia, 740 F. 2d 817 (11th Cir. 1984), cert. denied, U.S. , 105 S. Ct. 788 (1985).

**SEE ALSO** :

Alley, E.R., New Developments under the Hague Evidence and Service Conventions: 1989 Special Commission, International Business Lawyer, 380 (1989).

Amram, Explanatory Report on the Convention on the Taking of Evidence Abroad in Civil or Commercial Matters, Message from the President of the United States", Sen. Exec. A., 92nd Cong., 2d Sess. (Feb. 1, 1972).

Amram, The Proposed Convention on the Taking of Evidence Abroad, 55 A.B.A. J. 651 (1969).

Amram, Report on the Eleventh Session of the Hague Conference on Private International Law, 63 Am. J. Int'l Law 521 (1969).

Amram, United States Ratification of the Hague Convention on the Taking of Evidence Abroad, 67 Am. J. Int"l Law 104 (1973).

Augustine, Obtaining International Judicial Assistance Under the Federal Rules and the Hague Convention on the Taking of Evidence Abroad in Civil and Commercial Matters: An Exposition of the Procedures and a Practical Example: In re Westinghouse Uranium Contract Litigation, 10 Ga. J. Int'l & Comp. L. 101 (1980).

Bailey, Stephen R., "Depositions and Discovery - Hague Convention on the Taking of Evidence Abroad in Civil or Commercial Matters", 54 Journal of Air Law and Commerce, 381 (1988).

Bermann, The Hague Evidence Convention in the Supreme Court: A critique of the Aerospatiale Decision, 63 Tul. L. Rev. 525 (1989).

Bishop, Significant Issues in the Construction of The Hague Evidence Convention, 1 Int'l Litigation Q. 2, 38 (1985).

Black, United States Transnational Discovery: The Rise and Fall of the Hague Evidence Convention, 40 Int'l and Comparative L.Q. 901-906 (1991).

Born, The Hague Evidence Convention Revisited: Reflections on Its Role in U.S. Civil Procedure, 57 Law & Contemp. Probs. 77, 90-96 (1994).

Boyd, Contemporary Practice of the United States Relating to International Law - The Hague Evidence Convention, 72 Am. J. Int'l Law 133 (1978).

Comment, The Hague Convention on the Taking of Evidence Abroad in Civil or Commercial Matters: The Exclusive and Mandatory Procedures for Discovery Abroad, 132 U. Pa. L. Rev. 1461 (1984)

Edwards, Taking of Evidence Abroad in Civil or Commercial Matters, 18 Int'l. and Comp. L. Q. 646 (1969)

Gerber, International Discovery after Aerospatiale: the Quest for an Analytical Framework, 82 Am, J. Int'l L. 521, 555 (1988).

Griffin & Bravin, Beyond Aerospatiale: A Commentary on Foreign Discovery Provisions, 25 Int'l Law. No. 2, 315 (1991).

Guzman, Rick, Interplay between the Discovery Provisions of the Hague Evidence Convention and the Federal Rules of Civil Procedure: Societe Nationale Industrielle Aerospatiale, 9 Hous. J. Int'l. L., 333 (1987).

Hayne, Hague Convention and the Federal Rules of Civil Procedure, 9 Hous. J. Int'l L. 333 (1987).

Heck, U.S. Misinterpretation of the Hague Evidence Convention, 24 Colum. J. Transnat'l. L. 231 (1986).

McLean, The Hague Evidence Convention: Its Impact on American Civil Procedure, 9 Loy. L.A. Int'l & Comp. J.J. 17, 62 (1986).

McLean & McLachlan, The Hague Convention on the Taking of Evidence Abroad. Explanatory Documentation prepared for Commonwealth Jurisdictions, Commonwealth Secretariat, (September 1985).

Maier, Extraterritorial Discovery: Cooperation, Coercion, and the Hague Evidence Convention, 19 Vand. J. Transnat'l L. 239, 252-255 (1986).

Martens, D.H., German Civil Procedure and the Implementation of the Hague Evidence Convention,1 International Litigation Quarterly, No. 2, 115 (September 1985).

Matthews, The Role of the Hague Convention for Gathering Evidence Abroad: Societe Nationale Industrielle Aerospatiale v. United States District Court for the Southern District of Iowa, Stanford J. Int'l. L. 309 (1987).

Minch, U.S. Obligations Under the Hague Evidence Convention, 22 Int'l Law. 511, 528 (1988).

Nadelmann, The United States Joins the Hague Conference on Private International Law: A "History" with Comments, 30 Law & Contemp. Probs 291 (1965).

Noonan, Lori A., Societe Nationale Industrielle Aerospatiale v. United States District Court for the Southern District of Iowa: The Supreme Court of the United States Adopts a Case-by-Case Standard in Applying the Hague Convention on the Taking of Evidence Abroad, 1 The Transnational Lawyer, No. 1, 367, (1988).

Note, Gathering Evidence Abroad: The Hague Evidence Convention Revisited, 16 L. & Pol'y in Int'l. Bus. 963 (1984).

Note, Hague Evidence Convention: A Practical Guide to the Convention, United States Case Law, Convention-Sponsored Review Commission (1978 & 1985), and Responses of Other Signatory Nations: With Digest of Cases and Bibliography, 16 Ga. J. Int'l & Comp. L. 73, 99, App. A (1986).

Note, The Hague Convention on the Taking of Evidence Abroad in Civil or Commercial Matters: The Exclusive and Mandatory Procedures for Discovery Abroad, 132 U. Pa. L. Rev. 1461-1485 (1984).

Note, The Hague Convention on the Taking of Evidence Abroad in Civil or Commercial Matters: The Exclusive and Mandatory Procedures for Discovery Abroad, 132 U. Pa. L. Rev. 1461-1485 (1984).

Note, Obtaining International Judicial Assistance Under the Federal Rules and the Hague Convention on the Taking of Evidence Abroad: An Exposition of the Procedures and a Practical Example -- In Re Westinghouse Uranium Contract Litigation, 10 Ga. J. Int'l & Comp. L. (1980).

Note, The Securities Acts and International Discovery: The Hague Evidence Convention After Anschuetz and Messerschmitt Bolkow Blohm, 12 Syracuse J. Int'l L. and Com. 600 (1986).

Note, United States Ratification of the Hague Convention on the Taking of Evidence Abroad, 67 Am J. Int'l L. 104.

Notes & Comments, United States Ratification of the Hague Convention on the Taking of Evidence Abroad, 67 Am. J. Int'l Law 104, 105 (1973).

Oxman, The Choice Between Direct Discovery and Other Means of Obtaining Evidence Abroad: The Impact of the Hague Evidence Convention, 37 U. Miami L. Rev. 733 (1983).

Plaster, The Hague Evidence Convention: The Need for Guidance on Procedures and Resolution of Conflicts in International Discovery, Vand. J. Trans. L., Vol. 27, No. 1, pp. 185-217 (1994).

Prescott & Alley, Effective Evidence-Taking Under the Hague Convention, 22 The Int'l Law. 939 (Winter 1988).

Radvan, The Hague Convention on Taking of Evidence Abroad in Civil or Commercial Matters: Several Notes Concerning its Scope, Methods and Compulsion, 16 N.Y.U. J. Int'l L. & Pol. 1031 (1984).

Rogers, On the Exclusivity of the Hague Evidence Convention, 37 U. Miami L. Rev. 733 (1983).

Sadoff, The Hague Evidence Convention: Problems at Home of Obtaining Foreign Evidence, 20 Int'l Law. 659 (1986).

Shemanski, Obtaining Evidence in the Federal Republic of Germany: The Impact of the Hague Evidence Convention on German-American Judicial Co-operation, 17 Int'l Law. 465 (1983).

Weis, The Federal Rules and the Hague Conventions: Concerns of Conformity and Comity, 50 U. Pittsburgh L.R., 903 (1989).

Wotman, The Hague Convention on the Taking of Evidence Abroad in Civil or Commercial Matters - A Comparison with Federal Rules Procedures, 7 Brooklyn J. of Intl. L. 365 (1981).

**ADDITIONAL INFORMATION:** The Office of American Citizens Services has available general information flyers on international judicial assistance many of which are available via our Internet Consular Affairs home page. These topics include country-specific information about service of process and obtaining evidence abroad.

**Using the Internet:** Many of our judicial assistance flyers are also available on the Internet via the Department of State, Bureau of Consular Affairs home page under Judicial Assistance . See also, the Department of State, Office of the Legal Adviser for Private International Law home page for information regarding private international law unification. See also the home pages for many of our embassies . See also the Authentications Office home page .

**TREATY DATABASES ON THE INTERNET:**

United States Department of State, Office of the Legal Adviser, Treaty Affairs, List of Treaties and Other International Agreements of the United States In Force

**United Nations (UN):** Databases/Treaties

Council of Europe **(COE)** under Texts/Treaties

Organization of American States **(OAS):** under Documents/Treaties and Conventions.

**QUESTIONS:** Additional questions may be addressed to the appropriate geographic division of the U.S. Department of State, Bureau of Consular Affairs, Office of American Citizens Services at (202) 647-5225 or 202-647-5226. Questions regarding the operation of the Hague Evidence Convention may also be addressed to the U.S. Central Authority, the Office of International Judicial Assistance, Civil Division, Department of Justice, 1100 L St., N.W., Room 11006, Washington, D.C. 20530, tel: 202) 307-0983; fax: (202) 514-6584.

CONVENTION ON CHOICE OF COURT AGREEMENTS
(Concluded 30 June 2005)

The States Parties to the present Convention,
Desiring to promote international trade and investment through enhanced judicial co-operation,
Believing that such co-operation can be enhanced by uniform rules on jurisdiction and on recognition and enforcement of foreign judgments in civil or commercial matters,
Believing that such enhanced co-operation requires in particular an international legal regime that provides certainty and ensures the effectiveness of exclusive choice of court agreements between parties to commercial transactions and that governs the recognition and enforcement of judgments resulting from proceedings based on such agreements,
Have resolved to conclude this Convention and have agreed upon the following provisions -

CHAPTER I – SCOPE AND DEFINITIONS

*Article 1 Scope*
1. This Convention shall apply in international cases to exclusive choice of court agreements concluded in civil or commercial matters.
2. For the purposes of Chapter II, a case is international unless the parties are resident in the same Contracting State and the relationship of the parties and all other elements relevant to the dispute, regardless of the location of the chosen court, are connected only with that State.
3. For the purposes of Chapter III, a case is international where recognition or enforcement of a foreign judgment is sought.

Article 2 Exclusions from scope
1. This Convention shall not apply to exclusive choice of court agreements -

a) to which a natural person acting primarily for personal, family or household purposes (a consumer) is a party;
b) relating to contracts of employment, including collective agreements.
2. This Convention shall not apply to the following matters -

a) the status and legal capacity of natural persons;
b) maintenance obligations;
c) other family law matters, including matrimonial property regimes and other rights or obligations arising out of marriage or similar relationships;
d) wills and succession;
e) insolvency, composition and analogous matters;
f) the carriage of passengers and goods;
g) marine pollution, limitation of liability for maritime claims, general average, and emergency towage and salvage;
h) anti-trust (competition) matters;
i) liability for nuclear damage;
j) claims for personal injury brought by or on behalf of natural persons;
k) tort or delict claims for damage to tangible property that do not arise from a contractual relationship;
l) rights in rem in immovable property, and tenancies of immovable property;
m) the validity, nullity, or dissolution of legal persons, and the validity of decisions of their organs;

n) the validity of intellectual property rights other than copyright and related rights;
o) infringement of intellectual property rights other than copyright and related rights, except where infringement proceedings are brought for breach of a contract between the parties relating to such rights, or could have been brought for breach of that contract;
p) the validity of entries in public registers.
3. Notwithstanding paragraph 2, proceedings are not excluded from the scope of this Convention where a matter excluded under that paragraph arises merely as a preliminary question and not as an object of the proceedings. In particular, the mere fact that a matter excluded under paragraph 2 arises by way of defence does not exclude proceedings from the Convention, if that matter is not an object of the proceedings.
4. This Convention shall not apply to arbitration and related proceedings.
5. Proceedings are not excluded from the scope of this Convention by the mere fact that a State, including a government, a governmental agency or any person acting for a State, is a party thereto.
6. Nothing in this Convention shall affect privileges and immunities of States or of international organisations, in respect of themselves and of their property.

Article 3 Exclusive choice of court agreements
For the purposes of this Convention -

a) "exclusive choice of court agreement" means an agreement concluded by two or more parties that meets the requirements of paragraph c) and designates, for the purpose of deciding disputes which have arisen or may arise in connection with a particular legal relationship, the courts of one Contracting State or one or more specific courts of one Contracting State to the exclusion of the jurisdiction of any other courts;
b) a choice of court agreement which designates the courts of one Contracting State or one or more specific courts of one Contracting State shall be deemed to be exclusive unless the parties have expressly provided otherwise;
c) an exclusive choice of court agreement must be concluded or documented -

i) in writing; or
ii) by any other means of communication which renders information accessible so as to be usable for subsequent reference;
d) an exclusive choice of court agreement that forms part of a contract shall be treated as an agreement independent of the other terms of the contract. The validity of the exclusive choice of court agreement cannot be contested solely on the ground that the contract is not valid.

Article 4 Other definitions
1. In this Convention, "judgment" means any decision on the merits given by a court, whatever it may be called, including a decree or order, and a determination of costs or expenses by the court (including an officer of the court), provided that the determination relates to a decision on the merits which may be recognised or enforced under this Convention. An interim measure of protection is not a judgment.
2. For the purposes of this Convention, an entity or person other than a natural person shall be considered to be resident in the State -

a) where it has its statutory seat;
b) under whose law it was incorporated or formed;
c) where it has its central administration; or
d) where it has its principal place of business.

CHAPTER II – JURISDICTION

Article 5 Jurisdiction of the chosen court
1. The court or courts of a Contracting State designated in an exclusive choice of court agreement shall have jurisdiction to decide a dispute to which the agreement applies, unless the agreement is null and void under the law of that State.
2. A court that has jurisdiction under paragraph 1 shall not decline to exercise jurisdiction on the ground that the dispute should be decided in a court of another State.
3. The preceding paragraphs shall not affect rules -

a) on jurisdiction related to subject matter or to the value of the claim;
b) on the internal allocation of jurisdiction among the courts of a Contracting State. However, where the chosen court has discretion as to whether to transfer a case, due consideration should be given to the choice of the parties.

Article 6 Obligations of a court not chosen
A court of a Contracting State other than that of the chosen court shall suspend or dismiss proceedings to which an exclusive choice of court agreement applies unless -

a) the agreement is null and void under the law of the State of the chosen court;
b) a party lacked the capacity to conclude the agreement under the law of the State of the court seised;
c) giving effect to the agreement would lead to a manifest injustice or would be manifestly contrary to the public policy of the State of the court seised;
d) for exceptional reasons beyond the control of the parties, the agreement cannot reasonably be performed; or
e) the chosen court has decided not to hear the case.

*Article 7 Interim measures of protection*

Interim measures of protection are not governed by this Convention. This Convention neither requires nor precludes the grant, refusal or termination of interim measures of protection by a court of a Contracting State and does not affect whether or not a party may request or a court should grant, refuse or terminate such measures.

CHAPTER III – RECOGNITION AND ENFORCEMENT

*Article 8 Recognition and enforcement*
1. A judgment given by a court of a Contracting State designated in an exclusive choice of court agreement shall be recognised and enforced in other Contracting States in accordance with this Chapter. Recognition or enforcement may be refused only on the grounds specified in this Convention.
2. Without prejudice to such review as is necessary for the application of the provisions of this Chapter, there shall be no review of the merits of the judgment given by the court of origin. The court addressed shall be bound by the findings of fact on which the court of origin based its jurisdiction, unless the judgment was given by default.
3. A judgment shall be recognised only if it has effect in the State of origin, and shall be enforced only if it is enforceable in the State of origin.
4. Recognition or enforcement may be postponed or refused if the judgment is the subject of review in the State of origin or if the time limit for seeking ordinary review has not expired. A refusal does not prevent a subsequent application for recognition or enforcement of the judgment.
5. This Article shall also apply to a judgment given by a court of a Contracting State pursuant to a transfer of the case from the chosen court in that Contracting State as permitted by Article 5, paragraph 3. However, where the

chosen court had discretion as to whether to transfer the case to another court, recognition or enforcement of the judgment may be refused against a party who objected to the transfer in a timely manner in the State of origin.

Article 9 Refusal of recognition or enforcement

Recognition or enforcement may be refused if -

a) the agreement was null and void under the law of the State of the chosen court, unless the chosen court has determined that the agreement is valid;
b) a party lacked the capacity to conclude the agreement under the law of the requested State;
c) the document which instituted the proceedings or an equivalent document, including the essential elements of the claim,

i) was not notified to the defendant in sufficient time and in such a way as to enable him to arrange for his defence, unless the defendant entered an appearance and presented his case without contesting notification in the court of origin, provided that the law of the State of origin permitted notification to be contested; or
ii) was notified to the defendant in the requested State in a manner that is incompatible with fundamental principles of the requested State concerning service of documents;
d) the judgment was obtained by fraud in connection with a matter of procedure;
e) recognition or enforcement would be manifestly incompatible with the public policy of the requested State, including situations where the specific proceedings leading to the judgment were incompatible with fundamental principles of procedural fairness of that State;
f) the judgment is inconsistent with a judgment given in the requested State in a dispute between the same parties; or
g) the judgment is inconsistent with an earlier judgment given in another State between the same parties on the same cause of action, provided that the earlier judgment fulfils the conditions necessary for its recognition in the requested State.

*Article 10 Preliminary questions*

1. Where a matter excluded under Article 2, paragraph 2, or under Article 21, arose as a preliminary question, the ruling
on that question shall not be recognised or enforced under this Convention.
2. Recognition or enforcement of a judgment may be refused if, and to the extent that, the judgment was based on a ruling on a matter excluded under Article 2, paragraph 2.
3. However, in the case of a ruling on the validity of an intellectual property right other than copyright or a related right, recognition or enforcement of a judgment may be refused or postponed under the preceding paragraph only where -

a) that ruling is inconsistent with a judgment or a decision of a competent authority on that matter given in the State under the law of which the intellectual property right arose; or
b) proceedings concerning the validity of the intellectual property right are pending in that State.
4. Recognition or enforcement of a judgment may be refused if, and to the extent that, the judgment was based on a ruling on a matter excluded pursuant to a declaration made by the requested State under Article 21.

*Article 11 Damages*

1. Recognition or enforcement of a judgment may be refused if, and to the extent that, the judgment awards damages, including exemplary or punitive damages, that do not compensate a party for actual loss or harm suffered.

2. The court addressed shall take into account whether and to what extent the damages awarded by the court of origin serve to cover costs and expenses relating to the proceedings.

Article 12 Judicial settlements (transactions judiciaires)
Judicial settlements (transactions judiciaires) which a court of a Contracting State designated in an exclusive choice of court agreement has approved, or which have been concluded before that court in the course of proceedings, and which are enforceable in the same manner as a judgment in the State of origin, shall be enforced under this Convention in the same manner as a judgment.

Article 13 Documents to be produced
1. The party seeking recognition or applying for enforcement shall produce -

a) a complete and certified copy of the judgment;
b) the exclusive choice of court agreement, a certified copy thereof, or other evidence of its existence;
c) if the judgment was given by default, the original or a certified copy of a document establishing that the document which instituted the proceedings or an equivalent document was notified to the defaulting party;
d) any documents necessary to establish that the judgment has effect or, where applicable, is enforceable in the State of origin;
e) in the case referred to in Article 12, a certificate of a court of the State of origin that the judicial settlement or a part of it is enforceable in the same manner as a judgment in the State of origin.
2. If the terms of the judgment do not permit the court addressed to verify whether the conditions of this Chapter have been complied with, that court may require any necessary documents.
3. An application for recognition or enforcement may be accompanied by a document, issued by a court (including an officer of the court) of the State of origin, in the form recommended and published by the Hague Conference on Private International Law.
4. If the documents referred to in this Article are not in an official language of the requested State, they shall be accompanied by a certified translation into an official language, unless the law of the requested State provides otherwise.

*Article 14 Procedure*
The procedure for recognition, declaration of enforceability or registration for enforcement, and the enforcement of the judgment, are governed by the law of the requested State unless this Convention provides otherwise. The court addressed shall act expeditiously.

*Article 15 Severability*
Recognition or enforcement of a severable part of a judgment shall be granted where recognition or enforcement of that part is applied for, or only part of the judgment is capable of being recognised or enforced under this Convention.

CHAPTER IV – GENERAL CLAUSES

Article 16 Transitional provisions
1. This Convention shall apply to exclusive choice of court agreements concluded after its entry into force for the State of the chosen court.

2. This Convention shall not apply to proceedings instituted before its entry into force for the State of the court seised.

*Article17 Contracts of insurance and reinsurance*

1. Proceedings under a contract of insurance or reinsurance are not excluded from the scope of this Convention on the ground that the contract of insurance or reinsurance relates to a matter to which this Convention does not apply.

2. Recognition and enforcement of a judgment in respect of liability under the terms of a contract of insurance or reinsurance may not be limited or refused on the ground that the liability under that contract includes liability to indemnify the insured or reinsured in respect of -

a) a matter to which this Convention does not apply; or
b) an award of damages to which Article 11 might apply.

*Article 18 No legalisation*

All documents forwarded or delivered under this Convention shall be exempt from legalisation or any analogous formality, including an Apostille.

Article 19 Declarations limiting jurisdiction

A State may declare that its courts may refuse to determine disputes to which an exclusive choice of court agreement applies if, except for the location of the chosen court, there is no connection between that State and the parties or the dispute.

*Article 20 Declarations limiting recognition and enforcement*

A State may declare that its courts may refuse to recognise or enforce a judgment given by a court of another Contracting State if the parties were resident in the requested State, and the relationship of the parties and all other elements relevant to the dispute, other than the location of the chosen court, were connected only with the requested State.

Article 21 Declarations with respect to specific matters

1. Where a State has a strong interest in not applying this Convention to a specific matter, that State may declare that it will not apply the Convention to that matter. The State making such a declaration shall ensure that the declaration is no broader than necessary and that the specific matter excluded is clearly and precisely defined.

2. With regard to that matter, the Convention shall not apply -

a) in the Contracting State that made the declaration;
b) in other Contracting States, where an exclusive choice of court agreement designates the courts, or one or more specific courts, of the State that made the declaration.

Article 22 Reciprocal declarations on non-exclusive choice of court agreements

1. A Contracting State may declare that its courts will recognise and enforce judgments given by courts of other Contracting States designated in a choice of court agreement concluded by two or more parties that meets the requirements of Article 3, paragraph c), and designates, for the purpose of deciding disputes which have arisen or may arise in connection with a particular legal relationship, a court or courts of one or more Contracting States (a

non-exclusive choice of court agreement).
2. Where recognition or enforcement of a judgment given in a Contracting State that has made such a declaration is sought in another Contracting State that has made such a declaration, the judgment shall be recognised and enforced under this Convention, if -

a) the court of origin was designated in a non-exclusive choice of court agreement;
b) there exists neither a judgment given by any other court before which proceedings could be brought in accordance with the non-exclusive choice of court agreement, nor a proceeding pending between the same parties in any other such court on the same cause of action; and
c) the court of origin was the court first seised.

*Article 23 Uniform interpretation*
In the interpretation of this Convention, regard shall be had to its international character and to the need to promote uniformity in its application.

Article 24 Review of operation of the Convention
The Secretary General of the Hague Conference on Private International Law shall at regular intervals make arrangements for -

a) review of the operation of this Convention, including any declarations; and
b) consideration of whether any amendments to this Convention are desirable.

*Article 25 Non-unified legal systems*
1. In relation to a Contracting State in which two or more systems of law apply in different territorial units with regard to any matter dealt with in this Convention -

a) any reference to the law or procedure of a State shall be construed as referring, where appropriate, to the law or procedure in force in the relevant territorial unit;
b) any reference to residence in a State shall be construed as referring, where appropriate, to residence in the relevant territorial unit;
c) any reference to the court or courts of a State shall be construed as referring, where appropriate, to the court or courts in the relevant territorial unit;
d) any reference to a connection with a State shall be construed as referring, where appropriate, to a connection with the relevant territorial unit.
2. Notwithstanding the preceding paragraph, a Contracting State with two or more territorial units in which different systems of law apply shall not be bound to apply this Convention to situations which involve solely such different territorial units.
3. A court in a territorial unit of a Contracting State with two or more territorial units in which different systems of law apply shall not be bound to recognise or enforce a judgment from another Contracting State solely because the judgment has been recognised or enforced in another territorial unit of the same Contracting State under this Convention.
4. This Article shall not apply to a Regional Economic Integration Organisation.

*Article 26 Relationship with other international instruments*
1. This Convention shall be interpreted so far as possible to be compatible with other treaties in force for Contracting States, whether concluded before or after this Convention.

2. This Convention shall not affect the application by a Contracting State of a treaty, whether concluded before or after this Convention, in cases where none of the parties is resident in a Contracting State that is not a Party to the treaty.
3. This Convention shall not affect the application by a Contracting State of a treaty that was concluded before this Convention entered into force for that Contracting State, if applying this Convention would be inconsistent with the obligations of that Contracting State to any non-Contracting State. This paragraph shall also apply to treaties that revise or replace a treaty concluded before this Convention entered into force for that Contracting State, except to the extent that the revision or replacement creates new inconsistencies with this Convention.
4. This Convention shall not affect the application by a Contracting State of a treaty, whether concluded before or after this Convention, for the purposes of obtaining recognition or enforcement of a judgment given by a court of a Contracting State that is also a Party to that treaty. However, the judgment shall not be recognised or enforced to a lesser extent than under this Convention.
5. This Convention shall not affect the application by a Contracting State of a treaty which, in relation to a specific matter, governs jurisdiction or the recognition or enforcement of judgments, even if concluded after this Convention and even if all States concerned are Parties to this Convention. This paragraph shall apply only if the Contracting State has made a declaration in respect of the treaty under this paragraph. In the case of such a declaration, other Contracting States shall not be obliged to apply this Convention to that specific matter to the extent of any inconsistency, where an exclusive choice of court agreement designates the courts, or one or more specific courts, of the Contracting State that made the declaration.
6. This Convention shall not affect the application of the rules of a Regional Economic Integration Organisation that is a Party to this Convention, whether adopted before or after this Convention -

a) where none of the parties is resident in a Contracting State that is not a Member State of the Regional Economic Integration Organisation;
b) as concerns the recognition or enforcement of judgments as between Member States of the Regional Economic Integration Organisation.

## CHAPTER V – FINAL CLAUSES

### *Article 27 Signature, ratification, acceptance, approval or accession*

1. This Convention is open for signature by all States.
2. This Convention is subject to ratification, acceptance or approval by the signatory States.
3. This Convention is open for accession by all States.
4. Instruments of ratification, acceptance, approval or accession shall be deposited with the Ministry of Foreign Affairs of the Kingdom of the Netherlands, depositary of the Convention.

### Article 28 Declarations with respect to non-unified legal systems

1. If a State has two or more territorial units in which different systems of law apply in relation to matters dealt with in this Convention, it may at the time of signature, ratification, acceptance, approval or accession declare that the Convention shall extend to all its territorial units or only to one or more of them and may modify this declaration by submitting another declaration at any time.
2. A declaration shall be notified to the depositary and shall state expressly the territorial units to which the Convention applies.
3. If a State makes no declaration under this Article, the Convention shall extend to all territorial units of that

State.
4. This Article shall not apply to a Regional Economic Integration Organisation.

Article 29 Regional Economic Integration Organisations
1. A Regional Economic Integration Organisation which is constituted solely by sovereign States and has competence over some or all of the matters governed by this Convention may similarly sign, accept, approve or accede to this Convention. The Regional Economic Integration Organisation shall in that case have the rights and obligations of a Contracting State, to the extent that the Organisation has competence over matters governed by this Convention.
2. The Regional Economic Integration Organisation shall, at the time of signature, acceptance, approval or accession, notify the depositary in writing of the matters governed by this Convention in respect of which competence has been transferred to that Organisation by its Member States. The Organisation shall promptly notify the depositary in writing of any changes to its competence as specified in the most recent notice given under this paragraph.
3. For the purposes of the entry into force of this Convention, any instrument deposited by a Regional Economic Integration Organisation shall not be counted unless the Regional Economic Integration Organisation declares in accordance with Article 30 that its Member States will not be Parties to this Convention.
4. Any reference to a "Contracting State" or "State" in this Convention shall apply equally, where appropriate, to a Regional Economic Integration Organisation that is a Party to it.

*Article 30 Accession by a Regional Economic Integration Organisation without its Member States*
1. At the time of signature, acceptance, approval or accession, a Regional Economic Integration Organisation may declare that it exercises competence over all the matters governed by this Convention and that its Member States will not be Parties to this Convention but shall be bound by virtue of the signature, acceptance, approval or accession of the Organisation.
2. In the event that a declaration is made by a Regional Economic Integration Organisation in accordance with paragraph 1, any reference to a "Contracting State" or "State" in this Convention shall apply equally, where appropriate, to the Member States of the Organisation.

Article 31 Entry into force
1. This Convention shall enter into force on the first day of the month following the expiration of three months after the deposit of the second instrument of ratification, acceptance, approval or accession referred to in Article 27.
2. Thereafter this Convention shall enter into force -

a) for each State or Regional Economic Integration Organisation subsequently ratifying, accepting, approving or acceding to it, on the first day of the month following the expiration of three months after the deposit of its instrument of ratification, acceptance, approval or accession;
b) for a territorial unit to which this Convention has been extended in accordance with Article 28, paragraph 1, on the first day of the month following the expiration of three months after the notification of the declaration referred to in that Article.

*Article 32 Declarations*
1. Declarations referred to in Articles 19, 20, 21, 22 and 26 may be made upon signature, ratification, acceptance, approval or accession or at any time thereafter, and may be modified or withdrawn at any time.
2. Declarations, modifications and withdrawals shall be notified to the depositary.

3. A declaration made at the time of signature, ratification, acceptance, approval or accession shall take effect simultaneously with the entry into force of this Convention for the State concerned.
4. A declaration made at a subsequent time, and any modification or withdrawal of a declaration, shall take effect
on the first day of the month following the expiration of three months after the date on which the notification is received by the depositary.
5. A declaration under Articles 19, 20, 21 and 26 shall not apply to exclusive choice of court agreements concluded before it takes effect.

Article 33 Denunciation
1. This Convention may be denounced by notification in writing to the depositary. The denunciation may be limited to certain territorial units of a non-unified legal system to which this Convention applies.
2. The denunciation shall take effect on the first day of the month following the expiration of twelve months after the date on which the notification is received by the depositary. Where a longer period for the denunciation to take effect is specified in the notification, the denunciation shall take effect upon the expiration of such longer period after the date on which the notification is received by the depositary.

*Article 34 Notifications by the depositary*
The depositary shall notify the Members of the Hague Conference on Private International Law, and other States and Regional Economic Integration Organisations which have signed, ratified, accepted, approved or acceded in accordance with Articles 27, 29 and 30 of the following -

a) the signatures, ratifications, acceptances, approvals and accessions referred to in Articles 27, 29 and 30;
b) the date on which this Convention enters into force in accordance with Article 31;
c) the notifications, declarations, modifications and withdrawals of declarations referred to in Articles 19, 20, 21, 22, 26, 28, 29 and 30;
d) the denunciations referred to in Article 33.

In witness whereof the undersigned, being duly authorised thereto, have signed this Convention.
Done at The Hague, on 30 June 2005, in the English and French languages, both texts being equally authentic, in a single copy which shall be deposited in the archives of the Government of the Kingdom of the Netherlands, and of which a certified copy shall be sent, through diplomatic channels, to each of the Member States of the Hague Conference on Private International Law as of the date of its Twentieth Session and to each State which participated in that Session.
Annex to the Convention: recommended form

# PRELIMINARY DRAFT CONVENTION ON EXCLUSIVE CHOICE OF COURT AGREEMENTS

## DRAFT REPORT

*drawn up by Masato Dogauchi and Trevor C. Hartley*

December 2004

**Contents of the Report**

**PREFACE**

*References to other documents*

The following documents are referred to in the abbreviated form set out below:

**"Brussels Convention"** = *Convention on Jurisdiction and the Enforcement of Judgments in Civil and Commercial Matters*. It was opened for signature in Brussels on 27 September 1968. The original Parties were the six original Member States of what was then the EEC. As new States have joined the EU, as it is now called, they have become Parties to the Brussels Convention. The text has been amended on a number of occasions. An amended text may be found in the *Official Journal of the European Communities* ("*O.J.*"), 1998, Volume 27 of the "C" series, p. 1. Today, it has been largely superseded by the "Brussels Regulation" (below). It now applies only between Denmark and the other 14 old EU Member States.

**"Jenard Report"** = Report by Paul Jenard on the original Brussels Convention, published in *O.J.* 1979 C 59, p. 1.

**"Schlosser Report"** = Report by Professor Peter Schlosser on the Accession Convention of 9 October 1978, under which Denmark, Ireland and the United Kingdom acceded to the Brussels Convention, published in *O.J.* 1979 C 59, p. 71.[1]

**"Lugano Convention"** = *Convention on Jurisdiction and the Enforcement of Judgments in Civil and Commercial Matters*. It was originally opened for signature in Lugano, Switzerland on 16 September 1988. It contains similar provisions to the Brussels Convention, but the two Conventions are not identical. The Contracting States to the Lugano Convention are the 15 "old" EU Member States and certain other States in Europe. At the time of writing, these are Iceland, Norway, Poland and Switzerland. The demarcation between the Brussels and Lugano Conventions is laid down in Article 54B of the Lugano Convention. It is based on the principle that the Lugano Convention will not apply to relations among the EU Member States, but will apply where one of the other countries mentioned above is involved. The text may be found in *O.J.* 1988 L 319, p. 9.

**"Jenard / Möller Report"** = Report by Paul Jenard and Gustaf Möller on the Lugano Convention, published in *O.J.* 1990 C 189, p. 57.

**"Brussels Regulation"** = *Council Regulation (EC) No 44/2001 of 22 December 2000 on Jurisdiction and the Recognition and Enforcement of Judgments in Civil and Commercial Matters, O.J.* 2001 L 12, p. 1. It applies among all the EU Member States except Denmark and replaces the Brussels Convention in the mutual relations between those States to which it applies.

**"Preliminary draft Convention 1999"** = Preliminary draft Convention on Jurisdiction and Foreign Judgments in Civil and Commercial Matters of 1999. This was an earlier, much larger version of the present preliminary draft Convention drawn up within the Hague Conference on Private International Law in 1999. It covered much the same ground as the Brussels and Lugano Conventions. Work on it was put on hold when it became apparent that it would be difficult to obtain agreement at that time. Its text, together with a draft Report by the late Professor Peter Nygh and Professor Fausto Pocar, was published by the Permanent Bureau of the Hague Conference in August 2000.[2]

**"Nygh / Pocar Report"** = Report on the preliminary draft Convention 1999 (see footnote 2).

---

[1] There are also reports on the Accession Convention for Greece (D.I. Evrigenis & K.D. Kerameus), *O.J.* 1986 C 298, p. 1; and on the Accession Convention for Spain and Portugal (M. de Almeida Cruz, M. Desantes Real & P. Jenard), *O.J.* 1990 C 189, p. 35.

[2] "Preliminary draft Convention on jurisdiction and foreign judgments in civil and commercial matters, adopted by the Special Commission and Report" by P. Nygh & F. Pocar, Preliminary Document No 11 of August 2000, available at < www.hcch.net >.

**"Interim Text 2001"** = Summary of the Outcome of the Discussion in Commission II of the First Part of the Diplomatic Conference 6–20 June 2001.[3] The large number of square brackets in the text indicates that the delegates were unable to agree on many points.

**"Schulz Report"** = Report by Dr Andrea Schulz on the work of the informal working group on the Judgments Project, published by the Permanent Bureau of the Hague Conference in June 2003.[4]

**"2003 Draft"** = Draft text of the Convention, drawn up by the Special Commission on Jurisdiction, Recognition and Enforcement of Foreign Judgments in Civil and Commercial Matters in December 2003 (Work. Doc. No 49). This was the forerunner of the text discussed in this Report.[5]

**"The Convention"** = This refers to the current text of the preliminary draft Convention, officially known as the Draft on Exclusive Choice of Court Agreements. It was drawn up in April 2004 and published as Working Document No 110 (Revised).[6] This is the text discussed in this Report. The full text is set out below in the Annex II to this Report.

*Acknowledgements*

The authors of the present Report would like to acknowledge their debt to the authors of these earlier reports, especially to the authors of the Nygh / Pocar Report, the late Professor Nygh and Professor Pocar. They would also like to acknowledge the assistance given by Dr Andrea Schulz of the Permanent Bureau and Dr Gottfried Musger, Chairman of the Drafting Committee.

*Terminology*

The following terminology is used in the Convention:

**"Court of origin"** = the court which granted the judgment.

**"State of origin"** = the State in which the court of origin is situated.

**"Court addressed"** = the court which is asked to recognise or enforce the judgment.

**"Requested State"** = the State in which the court addressed is situated.[7]

In this Report:

**"State"** (upper-case "S") = a State in the international sense.

**"state"** (lower-case "s") = a territorial unit of a federal State (for example, a state in the United States)

Note: Passages in italics are intended to identify open issues and propose possible solutions in order to facilitate further work during the consultation period and at the Diplomatic Conference.

---

[3] Available at < www.hcch.net >.

[4] A. Schulz, "Report on the work of the Informal Working Group on the Judgments Project, in particular on the preliminary text achieved at its third meeting – 25-28 March 2003", Preliminary Document No 22 of June 2003, available at < www.hcch.net >.

[5] Available at < www.hcch.net >.

[6] Available at < www.hcch.net >.

[7] The preliminary draft Convention 1999 uses "State addressed" in the English version instead of "requested State" as used in this Report.

## INTRODUCTION

1 **Objective of the Convention**. The objective of the Convention is to make exclusive choice of court agreements as effective as possible in the context of international business. The hope is that the Convention will do for choice of court agreements what the New York Convention of 1958[8] has done for arbitration agreements.

2 **Three key obligations**. In order to achieve this objective, it is necessary to impose three obligations on the courts of Contracting States: the chosen court must be obliged to hear the dispute; all other courts must be obliged to decline jurisdiction; and the judgment given by the chosen court must be recognised and enforced by courts in other Contracting States.

3 **Three key provisions**. These obligations are laid down by three key provisions in the Convention, Articles 5, 7 and 9. Article 5, which is addressed to the chosen court, provides that the court designated in an exclusive choice of court agreement has jurisdiction and must exercise it; Article 7, which is addressed to all courts in other Contracting States, provides that those courts must suspend or dismiss the proceedings before them; and Article 9, which is addressed to the court in which recognition is sought, provides that a judgment given by the court of a Contracting State designated in an exclusive choice of court agreement must be recognised and enforced.

4 **The original project: a "mixed" convention**. The original project (the preliminary draft Convention 1999) was intended to be a "mixed" convention. This is a convention in which jurisdictional grounds are divided into three categories. There is a "white list", which contains a number of specified grounds of jurisdiction; there is a "black list", which contains other specified grounds of jurisdiction; and there is the so-called "grey area", which consists of all other grounds of jurisdiction under the national law of Contracting States. The idea is that where the court has jurisdiction on a "white" ground, it can hear the case, and the resulting judgment will be recognised and enforced in other Contracting States under the Convention (provided certain other requirements are satisfied). "Black list" grounds are prohibited: a court of a Contracting State cannot take jurisdiction on these grounds. Courts are permitted to take jurisdiction on the "grey area" grounds, but the resulting judgment will not be recognised under the Convention.[9]

5 As work proceeded on drafting, however, it became apparent that it would not be possible to draw up a satisfactory text for a "mixed" convention within a reasonable period of time. The reasons for this included the wide differences in the existing rules of jurisdiction in different States and the unforeseeable effects of technological developments, including the Internet, on the jurisdictional rules that might be laid down in the Convention. At the end of the First Part of the Nineteenth Session, held in June 2001, it was decided to postpone a decision on whether further work should be undertaken on the preliminary draft Convention. In order to find a way forward, the Commission on General Affairs and Policy of the Hague Conference, meeting in April 2002, decided that the Permanent Bureau, assisted by an informal working group, should prepare a text to be submitted to a Special Commission. It was decided that the starting point for this process would be such core areas as jurisdiction based on choice of court agreements in business-to-business cases, submission, defendant's forum, counterclaims, trusts, physical torts and certain other possible grounds.

---

[8] *Convention on the Recognition and Enforcement of Foreign Arbitral Awards of 10 June 1958.*

[9] The European instruments in this area (the Brussels Regulation, the Brussels Convention and the Lugano Convention) are based on a slightly different idea. Where the defendant is domiciled in another State to which the instrument applies, there is no grey area: jurisdiction may be exercised only on the grounds laid down in the instrument. Where the defendant is not domiciled in such a State, however, jurisdiction may, subject to certain exceptions, be exercised on any ground permitted by national law; the resulting judgment must nevertheless be recognised and enforced in the other States.

6 After three meetings, the informal working group proposed that the objective should be scaled down to a convention on choice of court agreements in business-to-business cases. After positive reactions from the Member States were received, a meeting of the Special Commission was held in December 2003 to discuss the draft that had been prepared by the informal working group. This meeting of the Special Commission produced a draft text that was published as Working Document No 49. The draft Explanatory Report on Working Document No 49 is contained in Preliminary Document No 25 of March 2004. A further meeting was held in April 2004, which reconsidered this document and dealt with the remaining issues. The April 2004 meeting produced the draft considered in this Report.[10]

7 **The relationship between the original project and the present draft**. If we apply the terminology explained in paragraph 4, we can say that the present draft provides for only one jurisdictional ground in the "white" list – an exclusive choice of court agreement. A court of a Contracting State selected in such an agreement must exercise jurisdiction, and other Contracting States must recognise and enforce the resulting judgment in accordance with the Convention. There is no "black" list in the sense previously explained, though courts of Contracting States other than that selected are not permitted to exercise jurisdiction in a case covered by the agreement. The "grey" area is accordingly very wide. It consists of all cases not covered by an exclusive choice of court agreement. Moreover, a "grey" area exists even where there *is* an exclusive choice of court agreement: since exclusive choice of court agreements concerning consumer contracts and employment contracts as well as some other subject matters are excluded from the scope of the Convention (Article 2), Contracting States are free to exercise, or not to exercise, jurisdiction in such cases. The courts of other Contracting States are free to recognise, or not to recognise, such judgments.

## ARTICLE-BY-ARTICLE COMMENTARY

### *Article 1 Scope*

8 Article 1 defines the scope of the Convention in a positive way by stating that it applies in international cases; Article 2 defines it in a negative way by laying down a number of specific exceptions. Moreover, "international" is defined in two different ways in Article 1(2) and 1(3): the former defines it for jurisdictional purposes; the latter defines it for the purpose of recognising and enforcing foreign judgments.

9 **Three limitations**. The first paragraph of Article 1 makes clear that the scope of the Convention is limited in three ways: it applies only in international cases; it applies only to exclusive choice of court agreements; and it applies only in civil or commercial matters.

10 **International cases**. The Convention is limited to international cases because the national law of the State in question should apply without restriction in domestic cases: other States have no legitimate interest in the outcome of such cases. However, in determining what constitutes an international case, one has to consider the meaning of "State" in the Convention. This is discussed further below.[11] At this point, it should simply be said that for some purposes "State" can refer to a territorial unit such as a US state or a Canadian province; for other purposes it can refer to a State in the international sense (the United States or Canada);[12] and for yet other purposes it can even refer to an international entity such as the European Community.[13] What constitutes an international case is, therefore, a matter of some complexity.

---

[10] The draft on Exclusive Choice of Court Agreements, Working Document No 110. It is set out in Annex II to this Report.

[11] See paragraphs 73–75 and 216–221 *infra*.

[12] See Article 22.

[13] See Article 26(5).

11 **Definition of "international" with regard to jurisdiction**. Article 1(2) defines "international" for the purposes of the rules on jurisdiction (found in Chapter II of the Convention). It states that a case is international unless both the following conditions are satisfied: first, the parties must be resident[14] in the Contracting State of the court seised (whether or not it is the chosen court); and, secondly, the relationship of the parties and all other elements relevant to the dispute (regardless of the location of the chosen court) must be connected only with that State.[15] This means that the rules of the Convention on jurisdiction will apply either if one or more of the parties is not resident in the State of the court seised, or if some other element relevant to the dispute (other than the location of the chosen court) has a connection with some other State.

12 This might be clearer if we give an example. Assume that two parties resident in Germany enter into a contract to be performed only in Germany, and agree that a Japanese court will have exclusive jurisdiction. If one of them brings proceedings before a German court, that court will not have to apply Article 7 (assuming that all other relevant elements are connected only with Germany). However, if proceedings were brought before the Japanese court, the position would be different. From its perspective, the case would be international because "the parties would not be resident in the Contracting State of the court seised" in terms of Article 1(2). As the Convention stands at present, therefore, the Japanese court would be bound under Article 5 to hear the case. This could result in the Japanese court acting inconsistently with the German court. At the Diplomatic Conference, delegates will have to consider whether this is the result they want.[16]

13 **Definition of "international" with regard to recognition and enforcement**. Article 1(3) defines "international" for the purposes of recognition and enforcement (Chapter III of the Convention). It states simply that a case is international for such purposes if the judgment to be recognised or enforced is foreign. This means that a case that was not international when the original judgment was granted becomes international if it is to be recognised or enforced in another Contracting State.

14 **Exclusive choice of court agreement**. The main reason for limiting the Convention to exclusive choice of court agreements was to simplify its structure. Article 5 (which requires the chosen court to hear the case) could not apply as it stands to non-exclusive choice of court agreements, since a court other than the chosen court might have been seised first, and it would be entitled to hear the case if the choice of court agreement was not exclusive. This would raise issues of *lis pendens* that would have been difficult to resolve in an acceptable way. Moreover, Article 7 (which prohibits courts other than that chosen from hearing the case) could not apply if the choice of court agreement was not exclusive.

15 **Civil or commercial matters**. The limitation to civil or commercial matters is standard in international conventions of this kind. It is clearly necessary to exclude public law and criminal law. The reason for using the word "commercial" as well as "civil" is that in some legal systems "civil" and "commercial" are regarded as separate and mutually exclusive categories. The use of both terms is necessary for those legal systems.[17] It

[14] The rules for determining the residence of an entity or person other than a natural person are set out in Article 4(2).

[15] The relevant date for the application of this test has not yet been settled: should it be applied to the facts as they stand when the agreement is concluded or when proceedings are commenced? Or should a case be regarded as international unless the conditions are satisfied at both times?

[16] *It might be one idea to replace the words "resident in the Contracting State of the court seised" in Article 1(2) by "resident in the same Contracting State". But this new wording would create another problem: When two Germans chose a German court in their agreement, the Japanese court which is seised in spite of the agreement would not be bound by Article 7 to dismiss the case since the case is not international. Accordingly, the meeting would have to reconsider the appropriate definition of an "international case" in light of the respective provisions.*

[17] It would not be possible to use "commercial" alone because in some systems it is too vague and in others it is too narrowly defined.

does no harm with regard to systems in which commercial proceedings are a sub-category of civil proceedings.[18] However, certain matters that clearly fall within the class of civil or commercial matters are nevertheless outside the scope of the Convention. These include: status and legal capacity of natural persons, family law matters, wills and succession, carriage of passengers or goods by sea, nuclear liability, rights *in rem* in immovable property, certain questions relating to legal persons (corporations) and some issues concerning certain intellectual property rights.

16 Article 1(1) of the preliminary draft Convention 1999 contained a further provision expressly stating that the Convention would not apply to revenue, customs or administrative matters. This provision was not included in the current draft because it was thought to be unnecessary: it was considered obvious that such matters could not be civil or commercial. The precise borderline between public-law and private-law matters is mainly a problem when a State or other public-law entity is a party to the contract. It is considered further below.[19]

*Article 2 Exclusions from scope*

17 **Consumer contracts**. Article 2(1)*(a)* provides that the Convention does not apply to choice of court agreements to which a natural person acting primarily for personal, family or household purposes (a consumer) is a party. Many legal systems have mandatory rules to protect consumers (including rules on exclusive jurisdiction), and these systems would not give effect to a choice of court agreement that required proceedings under a consumer contract to be brought in a foreign State. This exclusion would cover an agreement between a consumer and a non-consumer, as well as one between two consumers.

18 **Employment contracts**. Article 2(1)*(b)* excludes from the scope of the Convention choice of court agreements relating to individual or collective contracts of employment. The exclusion also applies to actions in tort arising out of the employment relationship – for example, if the employee suffers personal injury while at work.[20] Employment contracts are excluded for the same reason as consumer contracts. An individual contract of employment is one between an employer and an individual employee; a collective contract of employment is one between an employer or a group of employers and a group of employees or an organisation such as a trade union (labour union) representing them.

19 **Other excluded matters**. Article 2(2) states that the Convention does not apply to the matters listed in sub-paragraphs *a)* to *l)*.[21] However, as is made clear by Article 2(3), this exclusion applies only where one of the matters referred to in paragraph 2 is an "object" (the subject or one of the subjects)[22] of the proceedings This means that proceedings are not excluded from the scope of the Convention if one of these matters arises incidentally in proceedings that have some other matter as their object / subject.

---

[18] For further discussion of "civil or commercial matters", see pp. 29–31 of the Nygh / Pocar Report (*supra* footnote 2).

[19] See paragraphs 58 *et seq.*

[20] In some States, the law permits an employee to bring a direct action against the employer's in surer with regard to personal injury claims where the employer is insolvent. In this case, the Convention would also not apply to the employee's direct claim against the employer's insurer even if there was an exclusive choice of court agreement between the employer and the employee.

[21] This list is partly derived from Article 1(2), combined with Article 22, of the Brussels Regulation, and equivalent provisions in the Brussels and Lugano Conventions.

[22] The text uses the word "object", the word traditionally used in conventions of this kind (*cf.* Article 16 of the Brussels Convention), but it might just as well have said "subject". It is intended to mean a matter with which the proceedings are directly concerned. In French, there is a well understood distinction between proceedings that deal with a given matter *à titre principal* and those that deal with it *à titre incident*. This distinction cannot be expressed so clearly in English. In the English text of Article 2(3), the phrase "as an incidental question" is meant to convey the same idea as "*à titre incident*" in the French text, while the phrase "an object of the proceedings" in the English text is meant to convey the same idea as "*à titre principal*" in the French text.

20 There are various reasons why the matters referred to in Article 2(2) are excluded. In some cases, the public interest, or the interests of third parties, is involved, so that the parties have no right to dispose of the matter between themselves. In such cases, a particular court will often have exclusive jurisdiction that cannot be ousted by means of a choice of court agreement.

21 **Status and capacity**. Sub-paragraph *a)* concerns the status and capacity of natural persons.

22 **Family law and succession**. Sub-paragraphs *b)* to *d)* concern family law and succession.[23] In sub-paragraph *b)*, "maintenance" includes child support. In sub-paragraph *c)*, "matrimonial property" includes the special rights that a spouse has to the matrimonial home in some jurisdictions; while "similar relationships": covers a relationship between unmarried couples (including those of the same sex), to the extent that it is given legal recognition.[24]

23 **Insolvency**. Sub-paragraph *e)* excludes insolvency, composition and analogous matters. The term "insolvency" covers the bankruptcy of individuals as well as the winding-up or liquidation of corporations that are insolvent, but does not cover the winding-up or liquidation of corporations for reasons other than insolvency, which is dealt with by sub-paragraph *j)*. The term "composition" refers to procedures whereby the debtor may enter into agreements with creditors in respect of a moratorium on the payment of debts or on the discharge of those debts. The term "analogous matters" covers a broad range of other methods whereby insolvent persons or entities can be assisted to regain solvency while continuing to trade, such as Chapter 11 of the US Federal Bankruptcy Code.[25]

24 Only proceedings directly concerning insolvency are excluded from the scope of the Convention. Assume, for example, that A and B enter into a contract, under which B owes A a sum of money. The contract contains a choice of court agreement in favour of the courts of State X. B then becomes insolvent. The Convention would apply to any proceedings concerning the question whether B did in fact owe A the money, but it would not apply to proceedings concerned with the question where A ranks among B's creditors, even if the choice of court agreement was interpreted as covering them.

25 **Carriage of passengers or goods by sea**. Sub-paragraph *f)* excludes contracts for the carriage of passengers or goods[26] by sea. Contracts for the carriage of goods by sea were excluded because States that are parties to the Hague Rules on Bills of Lading[27] might be unwilling to accept a choice of court clause in a bill of lading if it granted jurisdiction to the courts of a State that was not a party to the Rules, since this could allow the ship owner to evade the mandatory provisions laid down in the Rules.[28] A second reason is that this matter forms the subject of a new project by UNCITRAL and the Conference did not want to interfere with that.[29] *The question of other maritime*

[23] Some of these matters are dealt with in other Hague Conventions.

[24] These provisions are largely taken from sub-paragraphs *a)* to *d)* of Article 1(2) of the preliminary draft Convention 1999, and their scope is further examined at pp. 32–34 of the Nygh / Pocar Report.

[25] There is an identical provision in Article 1(2)*(e)* of the preliminary draft Convention 1999, and its scope is further examined at pp. 34–35 of the Nygh / Pocar Report.

[26] Here "goods" includes passengers' luggage.

[27] They were adopted in 1924 and were amended by the Brussels Protocol of 1968. They are sometimes called the "Hague–Visby Rules".

[28] An alternative way of dealing with this problem would be to provide that, in proceedings concerning carriage of goods by sea, a Contracting State that was a Party to the Hague Rules (or any future agreement replacing them) would not be required to give effect to a choice of court agreement in favour of the courts of a State that was not a Party to those Rules.

[29] This could also be dealt with under Article 23.

*matters is still to be resolved. Proceedings, such as the limitation of ship owners' liability or general average, that affect the interests of third parties raise special issues.*

26 **Anti-trust / competition**. Anti-trust / competition matters are excluded by sub-paragraph *g)*. This refers to proceedings of the kind that may be brought under the Sherman and Clayton Acts in the United States, under Articles 81 and 82 (formerly Articles 85 and 86) of the EC Treaty, and under equivalent provisions in other countries. The standard term in the United States is "anti-trust law"; in Europe it is "competition law". It does not cover what Continental lawyers sometimes call "unfair competition" (*concurrence déloyale*).

27 Criminal anti-trust / competition proceedings are not civil or commercial matters; therefore, they are outside the scope of the Convention by virtue of Article 1(1).[30]

28 However, anti-trust / competition matters can form the subject of private-law proceedings. An action in tort for damages for breach of anti-trust / competition law, possible both in the United States and in the European Union, is a prime example. These actions are excluded by Article 2(2)*(g)* because, though they are between private parties, they nevertheless affect the public interest, since they discourage anti-competitive behaviour.

29 Another example is the rule laid down by the European Court of Justice in *Courage Ltd* v. *Crehan*,[31] under which an economically weak party, who is forced to accept terms in a contract that infringe EC competition law, can claim damages from the other party. The purpose of this rule is twofold: to do justice to the economically weak party and to benefit the public interest. It would be wrong to allow the economically strong party to avoid it by means of a choice of court agreement in favour of the court of a non-EU State, coupled with a choice-of-law clause in favour of the law of that State.

30 On the other hand, if a person sues someone under a contract, and the defendant claims that the contract is void because it infringes anti-trust / competition law, the proceedings are *not* outside the scope of the Convention, since anti-trust / competition matters are not the object / subject of the proceedings, but arise merely as an incidental question.[32] The object / subject of the proceedings is the claim under the contract: the principal issue before the court is whether judgment should be given against the defendant because he or she has committed a breach of contract.

31 **Nuclear liability**. This is the subject of various international conventions, which provide that the State where the nuclear accident takes place has exclusive jurisdiction over actions for damages for liability resulting from the accident.[33] Article 23 gives those conventions priority over this Convention. However, there are some States with nuclear power plants that are not parties to any of the nuclear-liability conventions.[34] Such States would be reluctant to allow legal proceedings to be brought in another State by virtue of a choice of court agreement, since, where the operators of the nuclear power plants benefit from limited liability under the law of the State in question, or where compensation for damage is paid out of public funds, a single collective procedure in that State under its internal law would be necessary in order to have a uniform solution in respect of liability and an equitable distribution of a limited fund among the victims.

---

[30] This applies both to criminal proceedings under US anti-trust law and to the quasi-criminal proceedings under Articles 81 and 82 of the EC Treaty.

[31] Case C-453/99, [2001] ECR I-6297; [2001] 3 WLR 1643.

[32] See Article 2(3).

[33] The *Paris Convention on Third-Party Liability in the Field of Nuclear Energy* 1960; the *Convention Supplementary to the Paris Convention* 1963; the Vienna Convention 1963; the *Joint Protocol relating to the Application of the Vienna Convention and the Paris Convention* 1988.

32 **Exclusive jurisdiction**. In the preliminary draft Convention 1999, there was a special provision on exclusive jurisdiction. It was contained in Article 12, and covered four matters: rights *in rem* in immovable property, legal persons, public registers, and the validity of certain intellectual property rights. Since the current preliminary draft Convention deals only with jurisdiction based on exclusive choice of court agreements, it was decided to exclude these matters from the scope of the Convention since choice of court agreements are not normally allowed with respect to them.

33 **Immovable property**. Sub-paragraph *i)* excludes rights *in rem* in immovable property. This concept should be interpreted as relating only to proceedings concerning ownership or possession of, or other rights *in rem* in, the immovable, not proceedings about immovables which do not have as their object / subject a right *in rem*.[35] It is said that one of the explanations for exclusive jurisdiction in this respect is the territorial sovereignty of the State where the immovable is situated. Thus, State A cannot allow the courts of State B to decide who is the owner of an immovable within State A's territory. Accordingly, it might be regarded as natural for the State in which the immovable is situated to have exclusive jurisdiction over proceedings which have as their object / subject rights *in rem* in immovable property; consequently, the Convention does not apply to choice of court agreements in such proceedings.

34 **Tenancies**. It has been proposed that tenancies in immovable property should also be covered by sub-paragraph *i)*.[36] This is because, in some countries, they are subject to special legislation designed to protect the tenant. To the extent that this legislation applies to private homes, the tenant would constitute a consumer under Article 2(1)*(a)* and the agreement would be excluded under that provision. However, the legislation may apply in other situations as well.

35 **Legal persons**. Sub-paragraph *j)* excludes the validity, nullity, or dissolution of legal persons, and the validity of decisions of their organs.[37] The reason for this exclusion is similar to that stated above with regard to immovable property. As legal persons are created by the sovereign power of the State, it might be regarded as natural for the courts of the State where they were established to have exclusive jurisdiction over proceedings which have as their object / subject the matters mentioned above. Accordingly, the Convention does not apply to choice of court agreements in such proceedings.

36 **Intellectual property**. The provisions on intellectual property in the 2003 Draft have been substantially reformulated, but no significant policy change was intended. They now constitute sub-paragraph *k)* to Article 2(2),[38] which draws a distinction between copyright and related rights, on the one hand, and all other intellectual property rights, on the other hand. These will be discussed separately.

37 **Copyright and related rights**. Copyright and related rights are fully covered by the Convention.

38 Examples of related rights include: rights of performers (such as actors and musicians) in their performances, rights of producers of sound recordings (for example, cassette recordings and CDs) in their recordings, and rights of broadcasting organisations in their radio and television programmes. Copyright as such is based on the creation of a new work (for example, the composition of a song or the writing of a book), while related

[35] For the meaning of a similar provision in Article 16(1)*(a)* of the Brussels Convention, see *Webb* v. *Webb*, C-294/92, [1994] ECR I-1717; *Reichert* v. *Dresdner Bank*, Case C-115/88, [1990] ECR I-27; *Lieber* v. *Göbel*, Case C-292/93, [1994] ECR I-2535; see further A. Dicey & J. Morris, *The Conflict of Laws* (13th ed., 2000 by L. Collins & specialist editors, Sweet and Maxwell, London), paragraphs 23-010 to 23-015 (pp. 941-943); H. Gaudemet-Tallon, *Compétence et exécution des jugements en Europe* (3rd ed., 2002, LGDJ, Paris) paragraph 102 (p. 74).

[36] This provision is in square brackets because it has not yet been agreed.

[37] This same phrase appears (with purely verbal differences) in Article 12(2) of the preliminary draft Convention 1999. The commentary on it in the Nygh / Pocar Report is at pp. 65-66.

[38] This sub-paragraph is in square brackets to indicate that it has not yet been agreed. One delegation raised the question whether there should be special consideration given to folklore and traditional knowledge as intellectual property rights. This has not yet been fully discussed.

rights protect a specific use of an existing work (for example, by performing, broadcasting or recording it) by someone other than the author of the work. They protect the additional contribution of the broadcaster, actor or record producer.

39 **Other intellectual property rights.**[39] Intellectual property rights other than copyright and related rights are excluded from the Convention, except in proceedings pursuant to a contract. This statement might, however, give a false impression. Since the Convention applies only to jurisdiction based on exclusive choice of court clauses, the normal run of piracy cases would not be covered in any event: pirates do not agree to choice of court clauses. Such clauses normally appear only in contracts that deal with intellectual property rights. Consequently, it is not very significant that the Convention covers intellectual property rights other than copyright and related rights only in proceedings pursuant to a contract: it is only in such proceedings that the possibility of applying the Convention is likely to arise.

40 "Proceedings pursuant to a contract" means proceedings to enforce substantive rights[40] under a contract (for example, by injunction)[41], to obtain damages for the breach of such rights, to obtain payment of royalties under a contract, to interpret a contract, to set it aside, to declare that it never existed, or to obtain a declaration of non-liability under it.

41 **Contracts covered**. The Convention is intended to cover a broad range of contracts dealing with intellectual property. Licence agreements and agreements to assign an intellectual property right are the most obvious examples, but distribution contracts, joint venture agreements and agency agreements are all intended to be covered in so far as they involve intellectual property. *Questions were raised in the plenary session whether the phrase "a contract which licenses or assigns such intellectual property rights" is wide enough to cover what was intended. A phrase considered earlier by the Intellectual Property Working Group, "a contract for the transfer or use of such intellectual property rights", might be better. Another possibility is "except in proceedings concerning a substantive right under a contract". This question will have to be reconsidered at the Diplomatic Conference.*

42 **Infringement proceedings**. It was intended that the Convention should apply to litigation concerning the scope of an intellectual property licence. Such proceedings may be brought either in contract or in tort. In some countries, the parties are required only to plead the facts: it is for the court to determine the appropriate legal characterization. Whether the court chooses contract or tort may depend on which is easier to prove. In other countries, the parties themselves decide whether to sue in contract or tort. They may have good reasons (such as the opportunity to obtain higher damages) for choosing one or the other. Most delegates felt that it should not depend on these accidental considerations whether or not a case was covered by the Convention. Some delegates thought that the wording of sub-paragraph *k)* was sufficient to cover proceedings in both contract and tort without the additional words in square brackets; others thought that the additional words were necessary to avoid misunderstanding.

43 **Validity as an incidental question**. Proceedings to revoke an intellectual property right are not "proceedings pursuant to a contract"; so they are not covered by

---

[39] The following paragraphs of this Report deal only with intellectual property rights other than copyright and related rights.

[40] A "substantive right" is a right other than a procedural right. The mere fact that the parties have concluded a choice of court agreement does not mean that any proceedings brought under that agreement are proceedings pursuant to a contract.

[41] By this is meant a final injunction. The Convention does not preclude the grant of interim injunctions, but this would not be covered by the Convention: see Article 8.

the Convention, even if brought as a counterclaim to contractual proceedings.[42] If the defendant raises invalidity as a defence to a claim covered by the Convention, the court can deal with that defence as a necessary step towards giving judgment on the claim. In the terminology of the Convention, it will be an "incidental question". This has two consequences: the first is that the proceedings are not taken outside the scope of the Convention by reason of the fact that the court deals with the invalidity defence;[43] the second is that the ruling on the validity of the intellectual property right is not enforceable as such under the Convention.[44]

44 An example will make this clearer. Assume that a licensor brings proceedings to enforce an intellectual property licensing agreement. The defendant claims that the intellectual property right is invalid. The court gives a ruling on this defence, holding the intellectual property right valid, and then gives judgment for the plaintiff, granting him an injunction plus damages. The judgment will be enforceable under the Convention, despite the fact that the court could give it only after deciding the incidental question of validity.[45] However, the ruling on validity will not itself be subject to recognition under the Convention,[46] nor will it create an estoppel or operate as issue preclusion under the Convention[47] in other Contracting States.

45 *The preceding paragraphs of this Report[48] set out the intention of the Conference. Doubts have, however, been raised as to whether the drafting of Article 2(2)*(k) *adequately expresses that intention, especially with regard to rulings on the validity of intellectual property rights other than copyright or related rights. These problems could be solved by deleting Article 2(2)*(k) *and inserting a new provision, Article 2(2* bis*), to read as follows:*

> *2 bis.*
>
> *a) The Convention shall not apply to intellectual property rights other than copyright or related rights, except —*
>
> > *i) in proceedings pursuant to a contract for the transfer or use of such intellectual property rights; or*
> >
> > *ii) in proceedings for infringement, provided that the infringement could have formed the basis of proceedings between the parties under sub-sub-paragraph* i) *above.*
>
> *b) The Convention shall not apply to judgments or rulings on the validity of intellectual property rights other than copyright or related rights, even if given in proceedings to which sub-paragraph* a)(i) *or* (ii) *applies.*

*Paragraph 2(3) would then have to be amended to read "Notwithstanding paragraphs 2* ***and 2 bis****, proceedings are not excluded from the scope of the Convention where a matter referred to in* ***those paragraphs*** *arises merely as an incidental question and not as the object of the proceedings."[49]*

46 **Public registers**. Sub-paragraph *l)* excludes the validity of entries in public registers.[50] Some people might not regard this as a civil or commercial matter. However,

---

[42] Article 2(2)*(k)*, footnote 1. This does not of course mean that the court cannot hear them.

[43] Article 2(3).

[44] See Article 10(1).

[45] This is subject to Article 10(2).

[46] Article 10(1). It might be recognised on some other basis.

[47] See also *infra* paragraph 56.

[48] Paragraphs 36-44.

[49] Article 10(1) would also have to be amended: see paragraph 167 *infra.*

[50] This same phrase appears (with purely verbal differences) in Article 12(3) of the preliminary draft Convention 1999. The commentary on it in the Nygh / Pocar Report is at p. 66.

as some international instruments[51] provide for exclusive jurisdiction over proceedings that have the validity of such entries as their object, it was thought better to exclude them explicitly in order to avoid any doubts.

47 **Insurance**. Contracts of insurance (or reinsurance) are not excluded from the scope of the Convention just because they relate to one of the matters referred to in paragraph 2. The fact that the risk covered is outside the scope of the Convention does not mean that the contract of insurance is outside the scope of the Convention. Thus, insurance of cargo carried by sea is not excluded by virtue of Article 2(2)*(f)* and insurance against liability for nuclear damage is not excluded by virtue of Article 2(2)*(h). In view of the importance of this question, it might be desirable, for the sake of clarity, to have an express provision to this effect. This could be added at the end of paragraph 3 and might read, "In particular, insurance (or reinsurance) is not excluded from the scope of this Convention merely because it relates to one of the matters referred to in paragraph 2 of this Article."*

48 **Procedural law**. It was not intended that the Convention would affect the procedural law of Contracting States, except in those areas expressly covered by it (jurisdiction, and recognition and enforcement of foreign judgments). Outside these areas, internal procedural law applies as before, even in proceedings under the Convention.[52] Examples are given in the following paragraphs, though these are far from exhaustive.

49 The Convention does not interfere with the rules of Contracting States on the service of documents (including writs) within their own territory or abroad. However, if the requirements of Article 9(1)*(c)* are not satisfied, other Contracting States may refuse to recognise the judgment.

50 The Convention does not require a Contracting State to grant a remedy that is not available under its law, even when called upon to enforce a foreign judgment in which such a remedy was granted. Contracting States do not have to create new kinds of remedies for the purpose of the Convention. However, they should apply the enforcement measures available under their internal law in order to give as much effect as possible to the foreign judgment.

51 Time limits within which proceedings must be brought or other steps taken under internal law remain unaffected by the Convention. Proceedings under a choice of court agreement, or proceedings to enforce a judgment under such an agreement, must be brought within the time limits laid down by internal law.

52 National rules regarding capacity to bring or defend legal proceedings are not affected by the Convention. Thus, if under the law of the requested State an entity with no legal personality lacks capacity to engage in litigation, it cannot bring proceedings under the Convention to enforce a judgment, even if the court that granted the judgment considered that it could bring such proceedings.

53 National law decides whether, and in what circumstances, appeals and similar remedies exist. Examples include: appeals to a higher court in the same State; references to the European Court of Justice to interpret provisions of Community law, including conventions to which the Community is a party; references to a special court to decide constitutional issues; and references to a patent office or other authority to decide the validity of a patent.

---

[51] For instance, Article 22(3) of the Brussels Regulation.

[52] In the case of recognition and enforcement, this is made clear by Article 14 of the preliminary draft Convention, which provides that the procedure for the recognition and enforcement of the judgment is governed by the law of the requested State.

54 National rules of evidence apply, even for proving the existence of a choice of court agreement.

55 **Incidental questions**. Article 2(3) provides that proceedings are not excluded from the scope of the Convention if a matter referred to in paragraph 2 arises merely as an incidental question. An incidental question is a question that is not the object (subject) of the proceedings but is a question that the court has to decide in order to give judgment.[53] For example, the plaintiff may claim a sum of money due under a patent-licensing agreement. The defendant may argue that the sum is not due because the patent is invalid. Then the validity of the patent would be an incidental question: the court would have to decide it in order to be able to decide the main question (whether the money is due). Another example is an action for breach of contract in which the defendant (who is a natural person, not a corporation) claims that he lacked capacity to enter into the contract: the main question would be whether he was liable for breach of contract; the incidental question would be whether he had capacity.

56 In some countries, parties are precluded in certain circumstances from re-litigating matters previously decided as incidental questions. In the United States, this is known as "issue preclusion" or "collateral estoppel"; in England it is called "issue estoppel". In other countries, such matters can be re-litigated. It is suggested below, however, that a ruling on an incidental question does not have to be recognised or enforced under the Convention: recognition is limited to the ruling on the principal question.[54] However, the Convention does not prevent a court from recognising or giving effect to such a ruling on the basis of internal law.[55]

57 **Arbitration**. Paragraph 4 excludes arbitration and proceedings relating thereto.[56] The purpose of this provision is to ensure that the present Convention does not interfere with existing instruments on arbitration.

58 **Governments**. Article 2(5) provides that proceedings are not excluded from the scope of the Convention by the mere fact that a government, a governmental agency or any person acting for a State is a party thereto.[57] The proceedings will, however, be excluded if they do not concern a civil or commercial matter. As a general rule of thumb, one can say that if a public authority is doing something that an ordinary citizen could do, the case probably involves a civil or commercial matter.[58]

59 Where a government or other public authority is involved, this can raise difficult questions, especially in the case of contracts. A contract does not cease to be civil or commercial just because a public authority is a party to it; nevertheless, it will not be civil or commercial if the public authority is exercising powers that a private person could not exercise. Thus, where a public authority uses its governmental powers to force a party to enter into a contract, the contract is probably not civil or commercial. For

---

[53] See paragraph 19 *supra*.

[54] See paragraphs 164 *et seq*.

[55] See paragraph 165 *infra*.

[56] An identical provision is found in Article 1(2)*(g)* of the preliminary draft Convention 1999: the relevant passage in the Nygh / Pocar Report is at p. 35.

[57] This provision is taken (with only verbal differences) from Article 1(3) of the preliminary draft Convention 1999. The commentary on it in the Nygh / Pocar Report is at pp. 35–36.

[58] For the interpretation by the Court of Justice of the European Communities of a similar provision in Article 1 of the Brussels Convention, see *LTU* v. *Eurocontrol*, Case 29/76, [1976] ECR 1541; [1977] 1 CMLR 88; *Netherlands* v. *Rüffer*, Case 814/79, [1980] ECR 3807; *Sonntag* v. *Waidmann*, Case C-172/91, [1993] ECR I-1963. See further A. Dicey & J. Morris, *The Conflict of Laws* (13th ed., 2000 by L. Collins & specialist editors, Sweet and Maxwell, London), paragraphs 11-013 to 11-016 (pp. 267–269); H. Gaudemet-Tallon, *Compétence et exécution des jugements en Europe* (3rd ed., 2002, LGDJ, Paris) paragraph 39 (pp. 26–28). The decisions of the Court of Justice of the European Communities on this issue would not necessarily apply to the Convention. Some courts might have a wider concept of what constitutes a civil or commercial matter: compare, for example, *United States of America* v. *Ivey* (1996) 130 DLR (4th) 674 (Ontario High Court, Canada), affirmed (1998) 139 DLR (4th) 570 (Ontario Court of Appeal) with *Netherlands* v. *Rüffer*, *supra*.

example, if a government authority offers to release an arrested person on condition that he enters into a contract under which he will pay a large sum of money if he does not appear for trial, the contract is probably too closely related to the criminal proceedings to come within the scope of the Convention.[59]

60 **Immunities of sovereign States**. Article 2(6) provides that nothing in the Convention affects the privileges and immunities of sovereign States or of entities of sovereign States, or of international organisations.[60]

*Article 3 Exclusive choice of court agreements*

61 **Definition: five requirements**. As mentioned above,[61] the Convention applies only to exclusive choice of court agreements. Article 3 *a)* gives a definition of such an agreement. The definition contains the following requirements: first, there must be an agreement between two or more parties; secondly, the formal requirements of paragraph *c)* must be satisfied; thirdly, the agreement must designate the courts of one State, or one or more specific courts in one State, to the exclusion of all other courts; fourthly, the designated court or courts must be in a Contracting State; and finally, the designation must be for the purpose of deciding disputes which have arisen or may arise in connection with a particular legal relationship.

62 **The first requirement**. A choice of court agreement cannot be established unilaterally: there must be agreement.[62] In interpreting a similar provision in the Brussels Convention,[63] the European Court of Justice has laid down autonomous, Community-law rules as to what constitutes consent for this purpose.[64] The application of autonomous rules may have been correct in the context of the Brussels Convention, but it is not correct with regard to the Hague Convention, under which the law of the State in question must decide whether there is consent: the explicit references in various Articles to State law clearly indicate this.[65]

63 Provided the original parties consent to the choice of court agreement, the agreement may bind third parties who did not expressly consent to it, if their standing to bring the proceedings depends on their taking over the rights and obligations of one of the original parties.[66] In some States, a "direct action" statute allows the victim of a tort to sue the tortfeasor's insurer without first proceeding against the tortfeasor. In such a case, the victim would be bound by any choice of court agreement contained in the insurance policy, if, under the relevant legislation, his or her right to bring the action is based on the fact that (s)he is regarded as having succeeded to the rights and obligations of the tortfeasor under the latter's contract with the insurer.[67]

---

[59] See *United States of America* v. *Inkley* [1989] QB 255; [1988] 3 WLR 304; [1988] 3 All ER 144 (Court of Appeal, England). See also *Attorney General for the United Kingdom* v. *Heinemann Publishers Australia Pty Ltd* (1988) 165 CLR 30 (High Court of Australia) (where a claim by the British Government, partly based on breach of contract, to compel the defendant not to reveal intelligence secrets was not enforced in Australia).

[60] This provision is taken from Article 1(4) of the preliminary draft Convention 1999. The commentary on it in the Nygh / Pocar Report is at p. 36.

[61] Paragraph 9.

[62] For this reason, the Convention does not apply to a choice of court made by a settlor in a trust instrument.

[63] Article 17.

[64] For example, in *Estasis Salotti and Colzani v. RÜWA*, Case 24/76, [1976] ECR 1831; [1977] 1 CMLR 345, it held that where a person signs a contract written on one side of a sheet of paper, he or she does not consent to a choice of court agreement on the other side, unless there is an explicit reference to it on the side that he signed. This decision was based on Community law, not on the law of any of the Contracting States.

[65] In Articles 5(1), 7 *a)* and 9(1)*(a)*, there is a reference to the law of the State of the chosen court; in Article 7 *b)* to the law of the State of the court seised, and in Article 9(1)*(b)* to the law of the requested State.

[66] For an example in an area outside the scope of the Convention (carriage of goods by sea), see *Russ* v. *Nova (The Tilly Russ)*, Case 71/83, [1984] ECR 2417 (Court of Justice of the European Communities).

[67] See *Youell* v. *Kara Mara Shipping* [2000] 2 Lloyd's Rep. 102 (High Court, Queen's Bench Division, England).

64 **The second requirement**. This concerns the form of the choice of court agreement. The relevant rules are laid down in paragraph *c)*, discussed below.

65 **The third requirement**. This requires the choice to be exclusive: the choice of court agreement must designate[68] the courts of one State or one or more specific courts in one State as having *exclusive* jurisdiction. This will be discussed below in connection with paragraph *b)*.

66 **The fourth requirement**. This requires reciprocity. The Convention applies only to choice of court agreements in favour of the courts of a Contracting State: agreements designating the courts (or one or more specific courts) of a non-Contracting State are not covered.

67 **The fifth requirement**. This is that the designation must be for the purpose of deciding disputes which have arisen or may arise in connection with a particular legal relationship. This makes clear that the choice of court agreement can be restricted to, or include, disputes that have already arisen. It can also cover future disputes, provided they relate to a particular legal relationship. It is not limited to claims in contract, but could, for example, cover claims in tort arising out of a particular relationship. Thus, a choice of court clause in a contract for the carriage of goods by road could cover a tort action for damage to the goods. Whether this would be so in any particular case would depend on the terms of the agreement.

68 **Agreements deemed exclusive**. Article 3 *b)* lays down the important rule (foreshadowed by the third requirement in paragraph *a)*) that a choice of court agreement which designates the courts of one Contracting State or one or more specific courts in one Contracting State will be deemed to be exclusive unless the parties have expressly provided otherwise.

69 The first element of this is that the choice of court agreement may refer either to the courts of a Contracting State in general, or to one or more specific courts in one Contracting State. Thus an agreement designating "the courts of France" is regarded as exclusive for the purposes of the Convention, even though it does not specify *which* court in France will hear the proceedings. In such a case, French law will be entitled to decide in which court or courts the action may be brought.[69] Subject to any such rule, the plaintiff can choose the court (in France) in which he brings the action.

70 An agreement referring to a particular court in France – for example, the Commercial Court of Paris – would also be exclusive.[70] The same is true of an agreement that designates two or more specific courts in the same Contracting State – for example, "either the Commercial Court of Paris or the Commercial Court of Lyons". This too would be an exclusive choice of court agreement.[71]

71 **One-sided (asymmetric) agreements**. Sometimes a choice of court agreement is drafted to be exclusive as regards proceedings brought by one party but not as regards proceedings brought by the other party. International loan agreements are often drafted in this way. A choice of court clause in such an agreement may provide, "Proceedings by the borrower against the lender may be brought exclusively in the courts of State X; proceedings by the lender against the borrower may be brought in the courts of State X or in the courts of any other State having jurisdiction under its law."

---

[68] Merely defending a case on the merits without objecting to jurisdiction would not itself give the court jurisdiction under the Convention, since this would not *designate* that court in terms of Article 3.

[69] See Article 5(3)*(b)*.

[70] The problems that arise where the court designated cannot hear the case under internal law are discussed *infra*: see paragraphs 101 *et seq.*

[71] An agreement stating that A may sue B only in the Commercial Court of Paris, and that B may sue A only in the Commercial Court of Lyons, would also be an exclusive choice of court agreement under the Convention. This would not be the case, however, if the two courts were in two different States.

72 Many lawyers would consider that, under Article 3 *a),* the question whether an agreement is exclusive must be determined at the time of its conclusion. In other words, it must be exclusive irrespective of the party bringing the proceedings. On the other hand, however, the question will arise for decision only when proceedings are brought. Consequently, it would be possible to wait until that occurs before answering it. If this latter approach were taken, the answer might depend on which party brought the proceedings. If they were brought by the borrower, the agreement would not be covered by the Convention, since the lender would remain free to bring proceedings elsewhere. If he did so, the Convention would not preclude the court from hearing them. The Convention would also not apply if the lender brought proceedings in a court other than that designated in the agreement. If, on the other hand, the lender brought proceedings in the designated court, the agreement would, from that moment onwards, become exclusive, since the borrower would not be entitled to bring them in any other court.

73 **Meaning of "State" in the case of a non-unified legal system**. It will be remembered that the word "State" can have different meanings in relation to a Contracting State in which two or more systems of law apply in different territorial units with regard to a matter dealt with by the Convention – for example, Canada, China, the United Kingdom or the United States. According to Article 22 (discussed below at paragraphs 215 *et seq.*) it can refer, as appropriate, either to the State as a whole – for example, Canada, China, the United Kingdom or the United States – or to a territorial unit within that State – for example, Ontario, Hong Kong, Scotland or New Jersey. Consequently, both a clause designating "the courts of the United States" and a clause designating "the courts of New Jersey" are exclusive choice of court agreements under the Convention.[72]

74 Although the Convention is restricted to exclusive choice of court agreements, Article 3 *b)* provides that an agreement which designates the courts of one Contracting State or one or more specific courts in one Contracting State is deemed to be exclusive unless the parties expressly provide otherwise. As a result, the following must be regarded as exclusive choice of court agreements:

- "The courts of State X shall have jurisdiction to hear proceedings under this contract."
- "Proceedings under this contract shall be brought before the courts of State X."

75 The following would not be exclusive:

- "The courts of State X shall have non-exclusive jurisdiction to hear proceedings under this contract."
- "Proceedings under this contract may be brought before the courts of State X, but this shall not preclude proceedings before the courts of any other State having jurisdiction under its law."

76 **Formal requirements**. Paragraph *c)* deals with formal requirements. These are both necessary and sufficient under the Convention: a choice of court agreement is not covered by the Convention[73] if it does not comply with them, but, if it does, no further requirements of a formal nature may be imposed under national law. Thus, for example, a court of a Contracting State cannot refuse to give effect to a choice of court agreement because:

- it is written in a foreign language;
- it is not in special bold type;

[72] A clause designating "the state courts of the state of New Jersey or the federal courts located in that state" would also be an exclusive choice of court agreement.

[73] If it is valid under the law of the State of the chosen court, that court may hear the case, but the courts of other States would not be obliged to apply the Convention with regard to the agreement (Article 7) or the resulting judgment (Article 9).

- it is in small type; or
- it is not signed by the parties separately from the main agreement.[74]

77 Paragraph *c)* provides that the choice of court agreement must be entered into or evidenced either (i) "in writing" or (ii) "by any other means of communication which renders information accessible so as to be usable for subsequent reference".

78 Where the agreement is in writing, its formal validity is not dependent on its being signed, though the lack of a signature might make it more difficult to prove the existence of the agreement. The other possible form is intended to cover electronic means of data transmission or storage. This includes all normal possibilities, provided that the data is retrievable so that it can be referred to on future occasions. It covers, for example, e-mail and fax.[75]

79 The agreement must either be concluded in one or other of these forms or it must be *evidenced* in them. The "evidenced in writing" requirement would be satisfied if the following facts were proved:

- there is an oral choice of court agreement;
- the agreement is confirmed in writing by one of the parties;
- the confirmation is received by the other party; and
- the latter raises no objection.[76]

80 It is not necessary for the party who received the confirmation expressly to accept it: if he or she did, that would constitute a new agreement in writing. It does not matter if the party who put the oral agreement into writing was the one who benefited from it – for example, because the chosen court was in his State.[77] In all cases, however, there must have been consent by both parties to the original oral agreement.

81 Article 3 *d)* provides that an exclusive choice of court agreement that forms part of a contract must be treated as an agreement independent of the other terms of the contract for the purpose of determining its validity: the validity of the exclusive choice of court agreement cannot be contested solely on the ground that the contract of which it forms part is not valid: the validity of the choice of court agreement must be determined independently, according to the criteria set out in the Convention.[78] Thus, it is possible for the designated court to hold the contract invalid without depriving the choice of court agreement of validity. On the other hand, of course, it is also possible for the ground on which the contract is invalid to apply equally to the choice of court agreement: it all depends on the circumstances. This approach is in accordance with that normally adopted with regard to the validity of arbitration agreements.

82 **Doctrine of consideration**. Under the common law, contracts are not valid unless there is consideration.[79] This means that each party must obtain something (however little) in return for what he promises the other party. If the choice of court agreement is treated as an independent contract, the question arises whether there is consideration. Normally, there would be. If A and B enter into a contract giving exclusive jurisdiction to the courts of State X, B's promise not to sue elsewhere would constitute consideration for A's promise not to do so either (and *vice versa*). However, there could be cases in which this would not be so. Assume that, if there had been no choice of court agreement, A could have sued B in the courts of State X or in those of State Y; B, on the other hand, could have sued A only in the courts of State X. If the parties were to agree that the courts of State X had exclusive jurisdiction, A would have given up the right to sue B in

[74] In some legal systems, these might be requirements of internal law: see, for example, *Trasporti Castelletti* v. *Hugo Trumpy*, Case C-159/97, [1999] ECR I-1597.

[75] The wording of this provision was inspired by Article 6(1) of the *UNCITRAL Model Law on Electronic Commerce* 1996.

[76] *Cf. Berghoefer* v. *ASA*, Case 221/84, [1985] ECR 2699; [1986] 1 CMLR 13.

[77] *Ibid.*

[78] See Articles 5(1), 7 and 9(1).

[79] This does not apply to contracts contained in a deed.

the courts of State Y, but he would have gained nothing in return, since, in any event, B could have sued him only in those courts. If such a choice of court agreement was part of the wider contract, consideration could be found in the other terms of the contract. However, if it was treated as a separate contract, it would be invalid for lack of consideration. *To solve this problem, the words "Where it would otherwise be invalid", could be inserted at the beginning of paragraph* d). *This would make clear that paragraph* d) *does not apply if its effect would be to make the contract invalid.*

*Article 4 Other definitions*

83 **"Judgment"**. Article 4 contains two further definitions. The first, in Article 4(1), is of "judgment". This is widely defined so as to cover any decision on the merits, regardless of what it is called.[80] It excludes a procedural ruling, but covers an order as to costs or expenses (even if given by an officer of the court, rather than by a judge) provided it relates to a judgment that may be recognised or enforced under the Convention. It does not cover a decision to grant interim relief (provisional and protective measures), as this is not a decision on the merits.[81]

84 **"Residence"**. Article 4(2) defines "residence" with regard to an entity or person other than a natural person. The definition is primarily intended to apply to corporations and will be explained on this basis.[82]

85 The concept of residence plays a role in Article 1 (definition of an "international" case for the purpose of jurisdiction), Article 19 (certain exceptions to recognition and enforcement) and Article 23 (relationship with other international instruments).

86 The problem faced by the Special Commission in defining the residence of entities other than natural persons was to reconcile the different conceptions of the common law and civil law countries, as well as those within the civil law countries.[83]

87 In the common law, the law of the place of incorporation is traditionally regarded as important for deciding issues relating to the internal affairs of the corporation.[84] It is the legal system that gives birth to it and endows it with legal personality. For jurisdictional purposes, however, the principal place of business and the place of its central management are also important.[85] The latter is the administrative centre of the corporation, the place where the most important decisions are taken. The principal place of business is the centre of its economic activities. Though normally in the same place, these two could be different. For example, a mining company with its headquarters in London (central administration) might carry on its mining activity in Namibia (principal place of business). Since all three concepts are important in the common law, the Convention provides that a corporation is resident in all three places.

88 Although some civil law systems also look to the law of the place of incorporation as the personal law of the company,[86] the dominant view favours the law of the "corporate seat" (*siège social*). The place of the corporate seat is also regarded as the domicile of

[80] It would cover a decision by a patent office exercising quasi-judicial functions.

[81] On interim relief, see Article 8.

[82] A State or a public authority of a State would be resident only in the territory of that State.

[83] For a comparative discussion of these matters, see S. Rammeloo, *Corporations in Private International Law* (Oxford University Press, Oxford, England, 2001), Chapters 4 and 5.

[84] For England, see A. Dicey & J. Morris, *The Conflict of Laws* (13th ed., 2000 by L. Collins & specialist editors, Sweet and Maxwell, London), Rules 152(1) and 153 (pp. 1101–1109); for the United States of America, see *First National City Bank* v. *Banco Para El Comercio Exterior de Cuba*, 462 US 611, 621; 103 S Ct 2591; 77 L Ed. 2d. 46 (1983).

[85] For English law, see A. Dicey & J. Morris, *The Conflict of Laws* (13th ed., 2000 by L. Collins & specialist editors, Sweet and Maxwell, London), Rule 152(2) (p. 1101). For the purpose of diversity jurisdiction in the United States (discussed *infra* at paragraphs 102 *et seq.*), a corporation is a citizen both of the state where it was incorporated and of that in which it has its principal place of business: 28 US Code § 1332*(c)*.

[86] For example, Japan and the Netherlands.

the corporation. However, there are two views as to how the corporate seat is to be determined. According to the first view, one looks to the legal document under which the corporation was constituted (the *statut* of the corporation). This will state where the corporate seat is, and should be regarded as decisive. The corporate seat thus determined is called the *siège statutaire*.

89 The *siège statutaire* may not, however, be the actual corporate headquarters. The second view is that one should look to the place where the company in fact has its central administration, sometimes called the *siège rèel*. This corresponds to the common-law concept of the place of central administration.

90 To cover all points of view, it was thus necessary to include the *siège statutaire*, which is translated into English as "statutory seat". However, this term does not refer to the corporation's seat as laid down by some statute (legislation)[87] but as laid down by the *statut*, the document containing the constitution of the company - for example, the articles of association. In United Kingdom law, the nearest equivalent is "registered office".[88] In practice, the State where the corporation has its statutory seat will almost always be the State under whose law it was incorporated or formed; while the State where it has its central administration will usually be that in which it has its principal place of business. On the other hand, it is not uncommon for a company to be incorporated in one State - for example, Panama - and to have its central administration and principal place of business in another.

*Article 5 Jurisdiction of the chosen court*

91 Article 5 is one of the "key provisions" of the Convention. A choice of court agreement would be of little value if the chosen court did not hear the case when proceedings were brought before it. For this reason, Article 5(1) provides that a court designated by an exclusive choice of court agreement has jurisdiction to decide a dispute to which the choice of court agreement applies, unless the agreement is null and void under the law of the State of the court designated. Article 5(2) provides that it must not decline to exercise jurisdiction on the ground that the dispute should be decided by a court in another State.

92 **Null and void**. The "null and void" provision is the only generally applicable exception to the rule that the chosen court must hear the case.[89] The question whether the agreement is null and void is decided according to the law of the State of the chosen court. The phrase "law of the State" includes the choice-of-law rules of that State as well as its rules of internal law.[90] Thus, if the chosen court considers that the law of another State should be applied under its choice-of-law rules, it will apply that law.

93 The "null and void" provision is intended to refer primarily to generally recognised grounds of invalidity like fraud, mistake, misrepresentation, duress and lack of capacity.[91]

94 **Declining jurisdiction**. Article 5(2) provides that the chosen court must not decline to exercise jurisdiction on the ground that the dispute should be decided in a court of another State. This provision reinforces the obligation laid down in Article 5(1). However, it applies only with regard to a court in another State, not to a court in the same State.[92]

95 **Meaning of "State"**. What is meant by "State" in this context? In the case of a State containing a single law-district, there is no problem. Where the State contains a

[87] The French for "statute" is "*loi*".

[88] See the Brussels Regulation, Article 60(2).

[89] For another exception that applies in special cases, see Article 18.

[90] If this had not been the intention, the text would have used the phrase "internal law of the State".

[91] In Articles 7 *b)* and 9(1)*(b)*, lack of capacity is dealt with separately because it is determined by a different system of law from other grounds of invalidity - that of the court seised, rather than that of the chosen court. In Article 5, on the other hand, the court seised *is* the chosen court; so there is no need to deal separately with it.

[92] On the transfer of cases between courts in the same State, see Article 5(3)*(b)*.

number of territories subject to different systems of law, such as the United States, Canada or the United Kingdom, the question is more difficult. Under Article 22(1)*(c)* of the Convention, a reference to "the court or courts of a State" means, where appropriate, the court or courts of the relevant territorial unit.[93] From this it follows, that the reference in Article 5(2) to "a court of another State" must be understood as referring to a court of another territorial unit where this is appropriate.

96 When is it appropriate to refer to a territorial unit within a State? This could depend on the terms of the choice of court agreement. If it referred to "the courts of England", England would be the relevant territorial unit, and Article 5(2) would preclude a transfer to a court in Scotland: Scotland would be another "State" for this purpose. If, on the other hand, the choice of court agreement referred to "the courts of the United Kingdom", "State" would mean the United Kingdom, and a court in England would not be precluded by Article 5(2) from transferring the case to a court in Scotland.[94]

97 In the case of the United States of America, the position could depend on whether the chosen court was a state[95] court or a federal court. If the choice of court agreement referred to "the courts of the state of New York", a transfer to a court in New Jersey would be precluded. Here, "State" would refer to the state of New York, not to the United States of America.[96] However, if the reference was to "the courts of the United States", Article 5(2) would not preclude a transfer to a federal court in a different state of the United States of America, since "State" would mean the United States of America.[97] The same would apply if the reference was to a specific federal court – for example, "the Federal District Court for the Southern District of New York". Here too, "State" would mean the United States of America; consequently, Article 5(2) would not preclude a transfer to a federal court in a different state of the United States of America.[98]

98 ***Forum non conveniens***. There are two legal doctrines on the basis of which a court might consider that the dispute should be decided in a court of another State. The first is *forum non conveniens.*[99] This is a doctrine mainly applied by common law countries.[100] Its precise formulation varies from country to country, but in general one can say that it permits a court having jurisdiction to stay (suspend) or dismiss the proceedings if it considers that another court would be a more appropriate forum.[101] The granting of a stay or dismissal is discretionary and involves weighing up all relevant factors in the particular case. It applies irrespective of whether or not proceedings have

---

[93] For the position with regard to Regional Economic Integration Organisations, such as the European Community, see Article 26(5).

[94] In this case, the Scottish judgment would be entitled to be recognised and enforced under the Convention, since the Scottish court would be "a court of a Contracting State designated in an exclusive choice of court agreement".

[95] It should be remembered that "state" with a lower-case "s" refers to a territorial unit of a federal State (for example, a state in the United States of America); "State" with an upper-case "S" refers to a State in the international sense.

[96] The same would be true if the agreement referred to "the state courts of New York or the federal courts located in that state".

[97] The resulting judgment would be entitled to recognition and enforcement under the Convention .

[98] Whether Article 5(3)*(b)* would have this effect is considered below.

[99] See J. Fawcett, (ed.), *Declining Jurisdiction in Private International Law* (Clarendon Press, Oxford, 1995).

[100] It actually originated in Scotland, a mixed common / civil-law country. It still applies in Scotland today and has also been adopted in civil-law jurisdictions such as Quebec. For the application of this doctrine and other statutory substitutes in the context of choice of court clauses, see A. Schulz, "Mechanisms for the Transfer of Cases within Federal Systems", Preliminary Document No 23 of October 2003.

[101] For the formulation in English law, see A. Dicey & J. Morris, *The Conflict of Laws* (13th ed., 2000 by L. Collins & specialist editors, Sweet and Maxwell, London), Rule 31(2) (p. 385); for the formulation in the United States of America, see The American Law Institute, *Second Restatement on Conflict of Laws* (The American Law Institute Publishers, St Paul, Minn., 1971), § 84. For further discussion of *forum non conveniens*, with special reference to its effect on choice of court agreements, see R. Brand, "Forum Selection and Forum Rejection in US Courts: One Rationale for a Global Choice of Court Convention", in J. Fawcett (ed.), *Reform and Development of Private International Law: Essays in Honour of Sir Peter North* (Oxford University Press, Oxford, 2002), p. 51.

been commenced in the other court (though this is a factor that may be taken into account).

99 ***Lis pendens***. The second doctrine is that of *lis pendens*. This is applied mainly by civil law countries. It requires a court to stay (suspend) or dismiss proceedings if another court has been seised first in proceedings involving the same cause of action between the same parties.[102] It is not discretionary, does not involve the weighing up of relevant factors to determine the more appropriate court and applies only when proceedings have already been commenced in the other court.

100 Article 5(2) precludes resort to either of these doctrines if the court in whose favour the proceedings would be stayed or dismissed is in another State, since under either doctrine the court would decline to exercise jurisdiction "on the ground that the dispute should be decided in a court of another State."

101 **Subject-matter jurisdiction**. Article 5(3)*(a)* provides that Article 5 does not affect internal rules on subject-matter jurisdiction or jurisdictional rules based on the value of the claim. The phrase "subject-matter jurisdiction" can have a variety of meanings. Here it refers to the division of jurisdiction among different courts in the same State on the basis of the subject matter of the dispute. It is not concerned with determining which State's courts will hear the case but with the question what kind of court *within* a State will hear it. For example, specialised courts may exist for matters such as divorce, tax or patents. Thus, a specialised tax court would lack subject-matter jurisdiction to hear an action for breach of contract. So even if the parties concluded an exclusive choice of court agreement designating such a court, it would not be obliged under the Convention to hear the case.

102 In the United States, subject-matter jurisdiction can also refer to the allocation of jurisdiction between state and federal courts.[103] As a general rule, one can say that state courts have subject-matter jurisdiction in all cases unless there is a specific rule depriving them of jurisdiction. Federal courts, on the other hand, have jurisdiction only if a specific rule grants them jurisdiction. The basic rules on federal jurisdiction are laid down in Article III, section 2 of the United States Constitution. The two most important cases in which federal courts have jurisdiction are cases arising under federal law[104] and cases in which there is diversity of citizenship. Diversity of citizenship arises if one party is a citizen of a different state from another party, or if one party is a citizen of a State of the United States of America and the other party is a foreign national.[105]

103 The parties cannot waive these rules. If subject-matter jurisdiction does not exist, a federal court cannot hear the case, even if the parties submit to its jurisdiction. Thus, if a Japanese citizen and a German citizen, both resident in their respective countries, enter into a contract for the sale of goods, and the contract contains a choice of court agreement designating "the Federal District Court for the Southern District of New York" as having exclusive jurisdiction to hear disputes arising out of the contract, the chosen court will not be able to hear the case. It will lack subject-matter jurisdiction because

[102] See, for example, Article 27 of the Brussels Regulation.

[103] For a detailed discussion of federal and state jurisdiction in Australia, Canada and the United States of America, see A. Schulz, "Mechanisms for the Transfer of Cases within Federal Systems", Preliminary Document No 23 of October 2003.

[104] Federal law covers the United States Constitution, federal statutes and international treaties concluded by the United States of America.

[105] There must be complete diversity: no party on one side can be a citizen of the same state as any party on the other side. To be a citizen of a state, a person must be a citizen of the United States of America (or an alien admitted for permanent residence) and must be resident in a state of the United States of America. In addition, the value of the claim must be above a specified minimum, at present $75,000. See 28 US Code § 1332. For the citizenship of a corporation, see footnote 85 *supra*.

federal law will not govern the case[106] and there will be no diversity of citizenship.[107] The Convention will not affect this outcome. The result is that the choice of court agreement will be void: there would be no justification for treating it as referring to the *state* courts of New York. If, on the other hand, the parties designated "the courts of New York" and the plaintiff brought proceedings in a federal court in New York, he could recommence them in the state courts of New York if the federal courts held that they had no subject-matter jurisdiction.

104 In some countries, certain courts have jurisdiction only if the value of the claim is greater, or less, than a specified amount. Since this concerns the internal allocation of jurisdiction within a single State, it is a question of subject-matter jurisdiction as defined above. However, some States do not use this terminology; so Article 5(3)*(a)* refers specifically to jurisdiction based on the value of the claim. The comments in the previous paragraph on subject-matter jurisdiction apply here as well.

105 **Internal procedural rules**. As was said above,[108] it was not intended that the Convention should affect rules of internal procedure that are not related to international jurisdiction or the recognition of foreign judgments. Some of these rules may preclude a court from hearing cases in certain circumstances. Rules on subject-matter jurisdiction are just one example. Other examples are: rules precluding certain parties (such a enemy aliens in time of war) from bringing proceedings; rules precluding proceedings being brought against certain parties (for example, rules on State / sovereign immunity); rules precluding courts from hearing certain disputes (for example, the act of state doctrine, as applied in the United States of America); rules precluding the application of foreign law in certain cases (for example, those based on public policy); rules requiring cases to be brought within a given period of time; and rules on capacity to sue or be sued (for example, rules that an entity lacking legal personality cannot bring legal proceedings). Some of these matters are expressly mentioned in the Convention;[109] others are not. However, even if they are not expressly mentioned – it is impossible to cover everything – it was not intended that they should be affected by Article 5.

106 **Internal allocation of jurisdiction**. Article 5(3)*(b)* provides that paragraphs 1 and 2 of Article 5 do not "affect the internal allocation of jurisdiction among the courts of a Contracting State [unless the parties designated a specific court]." The last seven words are in square brackets because they have not been agreed. If no specific court is designated by the parties – if, for example, the choice of court agreement refers merely to "the courts of the Netherlands" or "the courts of the state of New Jersey" – there is no reason why the normal rules on the internal allocation of jurisdiction question should not apply.

107 **A specific court**. What if the parties designate a specific court – for example, the Federal District Court for the Southern District of New York[110] or the Tokyo District Court? Should it still be possible to transfer the case to another court in the same Contracting State?[111] A number of States have rules permitting the transfer of cases between different courts in the same State, usually because a transfer would be in the interests of the parties or the good administration of justice. For example, if a hundred people were killed in the same air crash, and ninety-five of them had agreed to an exclusive choice of

---

[106] In general, state law governs most areas of commercial law, such as sale of goods and contracts.

[107] For diversity to exist, the parties must be citizens of different States of the United States of America; alternatively, one can be a citizen of a State of the United States of America and one a citizen of a foreign State. If both parties are citizens of foreign States, there is no diversity.

[108] Paragraphs 48-54.

[109] See, for example, Article 2(6).

[110] See *supra* paragraph 103.

[111] In the above example, "State" would refer to the United States of America as a whole: see paragraph 97 *supra*.

court clause specifying court X in State Z, while the remaining five had agreed that court Y, also in State Z, would have exclusive jurisdiction, it would make sense for the cases brought by the families of the five to be transferred to court X.[112]

108 If transfer or removal were permitted even where the parties designated a specific court, the question would arise whether the proceedings in the new court should still be covered by the Convention.[113] If it was decided that they should, further changes would have to be made to Article 7 (obligation of other courts not to hear the case) and Article 9 (recognition and enforcement of the resulting judgment).[114] These are indicated by words in square brackets in those provisions.[115]

109 *The Diplomatic Conference will have to decide whether local rules on transfer should remain unaffected by the Convention and, if so, whether Articles 7 and 9 should be altered so that the proceedings remain within the scope of the Convention.*

*Article 6 Stay of proceedings in the chosen court*

110 Article 6 states that nothing in the Convention prevents the chosen court from suspending the proceedings before it, in particular to allow the courts of the State under the law of which an intellectual property right arose to give judgment on its validity. It also permits the proceedings to be dismissed, provided that such dismissal does not prevent the proceedings from being recommenced. (This latter provision was included because it is said that, in some countries, it is difficult, if not impossible, to suspend proceedings.)

111 Article 6 does not *give* the courts of Contracting States the power to stay or dismiss proceedings. It merely *preserves* such powers as already exist under internal procedural law by making clear that they are not restricted by the Convention. It is not intended to restrict national powers in any way.

112 This Article is intended to apply in a number of situations,[116] the most important being where, in an intellectual-property licensing agreement, there is a choice of court clause giving jurisdiction to a court of a State other than that under the law of which the right arose. If proceedings were brought under the choice of court clause to enforce the licensing agreement and the defendant challenged the validity of the intellectual property right, the chosen court might want to stay the proceedings before it to allow the question of validity to be decided by the appropriate court of the State under the law of which the intellectual property right arose (in the case of a registered right, the State of registration). In some situations, this might be desirable in the interests of justice.

113 It is not easy to imagine circumstances in which a stay would be granted outside the intellectual property area,[117] but the following might constitute an example. A agrees to sell land in State X to B, and the contract contains a choice of court clause in favour of the courts of State Y. B fails to pay the price and A sues him in State Y. B defends the

---

[112] On the effect that such a transfer may have on the applicable substantive and procedural law, see A. Schulz, "Mechanisms for the Transfer of Cases within Federal Systems", Preliminary Document No 23 of October 2003, pp. 14 *et seq.*, 21, 26.

[113] Article 5(3)*(b)*, footnote 2.

[114] This is because the chosen court would have "decided not to hear the case" in terms of Article 7 *e)*, and a judgment given by the court to which the proceedings were transferred would not constitute a judgment given by a court "designated in an exclusive choice of court agreement" in terms of Article 9(1).

[115] See Article 7 *e)* and Article 9(1 *bis*).

[116] The words "in particular" indicate that the provision is not confined to intellectual property cases.

[117] References to another court or body (such as a patent office) in the *same* State could be made without the need for a special provision in the Convention: they would be matters of internal procedure (see paragraph 53 *supra*). The same would apply to references to a court of a Regional Economic Integration Organisation, such as the European Community (*ibid.*): it would be regarded as a State for this purpose (see Article 26(5)).

action by asserting that A does not have title to the land and cannot, therefore, transfer it to him. In this situation, the court might want to stay the proceedings to enable the courts of State X to decide the question of title.[118]

114 *Article 6 is in square brackets because it has not yet been agreed. Opponents of the provision argue that it might encourage dishonest parties to ask for proceedings to be suspended simply as a time-wasting tactic. It could also be regarded as negating, or at least weakening, the obligation in Article 5(2). It could even be argued that, in its present form, it might be understood as permitting a court to stay proceedings on the ground that another court would be more appropriate to decide the whole case (doctrine of* forum non conveniens*).*[119] *Furthermore, it might be misread as implying that the powers of national courts are restricted to the extent that they are not covered by Article 6.*

115 *The Diplomatic Conference will have to decide whether Article 6 should be retained and, if so, whether it should be amended.*

*Article 7 Obligations of a court not chosen*

116 Article 7 is the second "key provision" of the Convention. Like other provisions, it applies only if the choice of court agreement is exclusive and only if the chosen court is in a Contracting State.[120] It is addressed to courts other than that chosen, and requires them to refrain from hearing the case, even if they have jurisdiction under their national law. This is essential if the exclusive character of the choice of court agreement is to be respected.

117 Article 7 applies only if the parties to the proceedings are bound by the choice of court agreement. Normally they must be parties to the agreement, though, as we saw above,[121] there are circumstances in which someone who is not a party to the agreement will nevertheless be bound by it.

118 Problems can arise in multi-party cases. Assume that A, who is resident in State X, sells goods to B, who is resident in State Y. The contract contains a choice of court clause in favour of the courts of State X. The goods are delivered in State Y and B sells them to C, who is also resident in State Y. If C claims that the goods are defective, he can sue B in State Y. He could also sue A (in tort), since the choice of court agreement would not be binding between A and C. However, if he sues only B, and B wishes to join A as a third party, he will be unable to do so: the choice of court agreement is binding between A and B and the court will have to suspend or dismiss the proceedings against A.[122]

119 Article 7 requires the court to suspend or dismiss the "proceedings". It is not stated expressly what proceedings this refers to. However, it is clear from the context that it covers all proceedings inconsistent with the choice of court agreement. To determine what these are, the court must interpret the agreement. Under Article 3 *a)* of the Convention, the agreement applies to disputes "which have arisen or may arise in connection with a particular legal relationship". In interpreting the agreement, the court must decide what that relationship is, and which disputes the agreement applies to. It must decide, for example, whether a choice of court clause in a loan agreement covers a

---

[118] A contract for the sale of land (as distinct from a conveyance (transfer) of land) is not excluded from the scope of the Convention by Article 2(2)*(i)*: *cf.* Schlosser Report, paragraphs 169–172 (on the equivalent provision in the Brussels Convention).

[119] The words "in particular" indicate that proceedings may be suspended for purposes other than that referred to in the text.

[120] This follows from the definition of "exclusive choice of court agreement" in Article 3 *a)*.

[121] Paragraph 63.

[122] This could result in the proceedings being split in an undesirable way. Some courts, therefore, refuse to enforce choice of court agreements in such cases: see *Grecon Dimter Inc.* v. *Normand Inc.*, Quebec Court of Appeal, 12 January 2004 (available on < www.jugements.qc.ca >); *cf. Donohue* v. *Armco Inc.* [2001] UKHL 64; [2002] 1 All ER 749; [2001] 1 Lloyd's Rep. 425 (House of Lords, England).

tort action by the borrower against the lender for enforcing the agreement in an allegedly abusive manner.[123]

120 The most common situation in which Article 7 would apply is where a party brings an action covered by the choice of court agreement in a court other than that designated.[124]

121 Proceedings for an antisuit injunction to prevent one of the parties from suing in the chosen court would be inconsistent with the choice of court agreement. They too would be covered by Article 7.

122 If the proceedings are covered by Article 7, the court must either suspend or dismiss them, unless one of the exceptions applies. It would be appropriate to suspend the proceedings, if possible,[125] where further developments might occur that would change the situation - for example, if the chosen court has not yet heard the case and it is uncertain whether it will do so.

123 **Five exceptions**. Article 7 lays down five exceptions to the rule that the proceedings must be suspended or dismissed. The first two[126] are fairly standard, but the third and fourth[127] are intended to apply only in the most exceptional circumstances. If they were applied too widely, the whole purpose of the Convention would be undermined.

124 **The first exception: null and void**. The first exception is where the agreement is null and void under the law of the State of the chosen court.[128] This is the counterpart of the provision in Article 5(1).[129] However, while under Article 5(1) the court seised will be the chosen court, this will not be the case under Article 7 *a)*. In the latter case, therefore, the court seised will not be applying its own law.[130] Consequently, it becomes important to know whether incapacity is covered by Article 7 *a)* as well as by Article 7 *b)*. This is discussed below.

125 **The second exception: incapacity**. The second exception is where a party lacked capacity to enter into the agreement under the law of the State of the court seised. Here again "law" includes the choice-of-law rules of that State.[131] In deciding whether the choice of court agreement is null and void, the law of the chosen court must be applied by courts in all the Contracting States. In the case of capacity, however, it was considered too ambitious to lay down a uniform choice-of-law rule for all the Contracting States; accordingly, under Article 7 *b)* the court seised will apply the law designated by its own choice-of-law rules.[132] Since lack of capacity would also make the agreement null and void in terms of Article 7 *a)*, this could mean that capacity is determined *both* by the law of the chosen court *and* by the law of the court seised.[133] *There seems to be no objection to this view; however, it has been proposed that the situation should be clarified by adding the words "on any ground, including incapacity" to Article 7* a).[134]

---

[123] See *Continental Bank* v. *Aeakos Compania Naviera* [1994] 1 WLR 588; [1994] 2 All ER 540; [1994] 1 Lloyd's Rep. 505 (Court of Appeal, England).

[124] Article 11 provides that Article 7 also precludes recognition or enforcement of a judgment rendered in contravention of an exclusive choice of court agreement. This is discussed below.

[125] In some countries, the court has only limited powers to stay the proceedings. For example, under the Japanese Code of Civil Procedure, a court can stay the proceedings only where the court is unable to function because of a natural disaster or similar emergency (Article 130), or where a party is, for an indefinite period of time, not in a position to continue the proceedings (Article 131).

[126] In sub-paragraphs *a)* and *b)*.

[127] In sub-paragraphs *c)* and *d)*.

[128] It has been proposed that the words "under the law of the State of the chosen court" be deleted. The policy issues involved are discussed in Annex I to this Report.

[129] Discussed above at paragraphs 92 *et seq*.

[130] See footnote 91 *supra*.

[131] See paragraph 92 *supra*.

[132] In recognition or enforcement proceedings, the court addressed will also apply its own choice-of-law rules when deciding questions of capacity under Article 9(1)*(b)*.

[133] See footnote 91 *supra*.

[134] Article 7 *a)*, footnote 3.

126 **The third exception (first limb): injustice.**[135] The third exception is where giving effect to the agreement would lead to a "very serious injustice" or would be "manifestly contrary to fundamental principles of public policy of the State of the court seised". In some legal systems, the first phrase would be regarded as covered by the second. Lawyers from those systems would consider it axiomatic that an agreement leading to a very serious injustice would necessarily be contrary to public policy. In the case of such legal systems, the first phrase might be redundant.[136] In other legal systems, however, the concept of public policy refers to general interests – the interests of the public at large – rather than the interests of any particular individual, including a party. It is for this reason that both phrases are necessary.

127 The phrase "very serious injustice" would cover the case where one of the parties would not get a fair trial in the foreign State, perhaps because of bias or corruption, or where there were other reasons specific to that party that would preclude him or her from bringing or defending proceedings in the chosen court. It might also relate to the circumstances in which the agreement was concluded – for example, if it was the result of fraud.

128 **The third exception (second limb): public policy**. The phrase "manifestly contrary to fundamental principles of public policy of the State of the court seised" would cover situations where the chosen court would not apply some rule or principle that was regarded in the State of the court seised as being manifestly part of its fundamental public policy.[137]

129 **The fourth exception: incapable of performance.**[138] The fourth exception is where for exceptional reasons the agreement cannot reasonably be performed. This is intended to apply to cases where it would not be possible to bring proceedings before the chosen court. It need not be absolutely impossible, but the situation must be exceptional. One example would be where there is a war in the State concerned and its courts are not functioning. Another example would be where the chosen court no longer exists, or has changed to such a fundamental degree that it could no longer be regarded as the same court.[139] This exception could be regarded as an application of the doctrine of frustration (or similar doctrines), under which a contract is discharged if, due to a change of circumstances after its conclusion, it is no longer possible to carry it out.[140]

130 **The fifth exception: case not heard**. The fifth exception is where the chosen court has decided not to hear the case. This could be regarded as covered by the fourth exception, but it is sufficiently different to deserve separate treatment.[141]

*Article 8 Interim measures of protection*

131 Article 8 states that interim measures of protection are not governed by the Convention. It neither requires nor precludes the grant of such measures by a court of a Contracting State, nor does it affect the right of a party to request such measures. This refers primarily to interim (temporary) measures to protect the position of one of the parties, pending judgment by the chosen court,[142] though it could also cover measures

---

[135] The policy behind Article 7 *c)* needs further consideration: see footnote 4 to Article 7 *c)* of the preliminary draft Convention.

[136] For lawyers from these legal systems, it would seem natural to insert the word "otherwise" before "be manifestly contrary": see footnote 4 to the present text of the preliminary draft Convention.

[137] Here "public policy" includes the international public policy of the State concerned.

[138] It has been proposed that this provision should be deleted.

[139] See *Carvalho* v. *Hull Blyth* [1979] 1 WLR 1228; [1979] 3 All ER 280; [1980] 1 Lloyd's Rep. 172 (Court of Appeal, England).

[140] Under German law, for example, it could be covered by the doctrine of *Wegfall der Geschäftsgrundlage*.

[141] With regard to the exception in square brackets, see paragraphs 107-109.

[142] The measure might be granted either before, or after, proceedings are commenced in the chosen court.

granted after judgment that are intended to facilitate its enforcement. An order freezing the defendant's assets is an obvious example. Another example is an interim injunction preventing the defendant from doing something that is alleged to be an infringement of the plaintiff's rights. A third example is an antisuit injunction precluding a party from bringing proceedings in a court other than that chosen. A fourth example would be an order for the production of evidence for use in proceedings before the chosen court. All these measures are intended to support the choice of court agreement by making it more effective. They thus help to achieve the objective of the Convention.

132 Once the chosen court has given judgment, an interim measure that is inconsistent with the judgment must be rescinded. To allow it to continue in force would conflict with the requirement to recognise the judgment laid down in Article 9. For example, if a court other than that chosen grants an interim injunction to protect a right claimed by the plaintiff, it must lift the injunction if the chosen court rules that the plaintiff has no such right (unless that judgment is not subject to recognition under the Convention). Likewise, an asset-freezing order should be lifted if the chosen court gives judgment for the defendant (unless that judgment is not subject to recognition under the Convention).

133 A court that grants a measure of this kind does so under its own law. The Convention does not require the measure to be granted but it does not preclude the court from granting it. Courts in other Contracting States are not required to recognise or enforce it; however, they are not precluded from doing so. It all depends on national law.

134 It goes without saying that the court designated in the choice of court agreement can grant any interim measure it thinks appropriate. If an interim measure - for example, an injunction - granted by that court is subsequently made permanent, it will be enforceable under the Convention in other Contracting States.[143] If it is merely temporary, it will not constitute a "judgment" as defined by Article 4(1).[144] In such a case, courts in other Contracting States could enforce it under their national law, but would not be obliged to do so under the Convention.

*Article 9 Recognition and enforcement*

135 Article 9(1) is the third "key provision" in the Convention. It states that a judgment given by a court in a Contracting State designated in an exclusive choice of court agreement must be recognised and enforced in other Contracting States.[145] The first and most important condition for recognition and enforcement is, therefore, the existence of an exclusive choice of court agreement designating the court of origin.

136 **Six exceptions**. In addition to laying down the principle of recognition, Article 9(1) also sets out six exceptions to it in sub-paragraphs *a)* to *f)*.[146] Where these exceptions apply, the Convention does not require the court addressed to recognise or enforce the judgment, though it does not preclude it from doing so.[147]

---

[143] Article 9(1).

[144] See paragraph 83 *supra*.

[145] However, it was understood by the Conference that a Contracting State is not obliged to enforce a judgment for a non-monetary remedy if this is not possible under its legal system. Nevertheless, it should give the foreign judgment the maximum effect that is possible under its internal law. See paragraph 50 *supra*.

[146] Footnote 7 to the text of the preliminary draft Convention states that further consideration needs to be given to whether the matters covered in Articles 7 *c)* and *d)* are adequately reflected in Article 9(1).

[147] This is indicated by the use of "may", rather than "shall", in the second sentence of the "*chapeau*" to Article 9(1). The result is that each Contracting State may adopt legislation laying down rules as to whether and, if so, in what circumstances such judgments are to be recognised and enforced. In the absence of such rules (or if the rules themselves so provide) the court addressed may decide this matter for itself. In the discussion on Article 9, it should be remembered that this Report is concerned only with recognition and enforcement under the Convention, not with recognition or enforcement under internal law.

137 **The first exception: null and void**. The first two exceptions mirror those in Article 7. Sub-paragraph *a)* states that recognition or enforcement may be refused if the agreement was null and void under the law of the State of the chosen court.[148] However, it adds, "unless the chosen court has determined that the agreement is valid", thus indicating that the court addressed may not substitute its judgment for that of the chosen court.[149] The purpose of this is to avoid conflicting rulings on the validity of the agreement among different Contracting States: they are all required to apply the law of the State of the chosen court, and they must respect any ruling on the point by that court.

138 **The second exception: capacity**. The second exception, set out in sub-paragraph *b)*, follows the wording of Article 7 *b)*. In both Article 9(1)*(b)* and Article 7 *b)*, capacity is determined by the law of the forum (including its choice-of-law rules). However, the forum is different in the two cases: in Article 7 *b)* it is a court before which proceedings inconsistent with the agreement are brought; in Article 9(1)*(b)* it is the court asked to recognise or enforce the judgment of the chosen court. As mentioned previously, it was thought too ambitious to attempt to unify choice-of-law rules on capacity. The point made in paragraph 125, above, applies here too: since lack of capacity would also make the agreement null and void in terms of Article 9(1)*(a)*, there seems to be no objection to the view that capacity is determined both by the law of the chosen court and by the law of the court seised. It has been proposed that the matter should be clarified by adding the words "on any ground, including incapacity" to Article 9(1)*(a)*.

139 **The third exception: notification**. The third exception, set out in sub-paragraph *c)*, permits non-recognition if the defendant was not properly notified. Two rules are involved: the first, laid down in sub-paragraph *c)*(i), is concerned with the interests of the defendant; the second, laid down in sub-paragraph *c)*(ii), is concerned with the interests of the State of notification.[150]

140 **Protection of the defendant**. Sub-paragraph *c)*(i) lays down a purely factual test to ensure that the defendant was properly notified. It states that the court addressed may refuse to recognise or enforce the judgment if the document which instituted the proceedings or an equivalent document, including the essential elements of the claim, was not notified to the defendant in sufficient time and in such a way as to enable him to arrange for his defence. This rule does not apply, however, if the defendant entered an appearance and presented his or her case without contesting notification. This is to stop the defendant raising issues at the enforcement stage that he or she could have raised in the original proceedings. It would apply only where the defendant knew about the proceedings and entered an appearance, even though he or she might have had insufficient time to prepare his case properly. In such a situation, the obvious remedy would be for him or her to seek an adjournment. If he or she fails to do this, he or she should not be entitled to put forward the lack of proper notification as a ground for non-recognition of the judgment.[151]

141 **Protection of the State of notification**. Many States, including the major common-law countries, have no objection to the service of a foreign writ on their territory without any participation of their authorities. They see it simply as a matter of conveying information. Thus if a Japanese lawyer wants to serve a Japanese writ in England, he can fly to London, take a taxi to the defendant's home, knock on the door

---

[148] The law of the State of the chosen court includes the choice-of-law rules of that State: see paragraph 92 *supra*.

[149] The fact that the court of origin gave judgment does not necessarily mean that it considered the choice of court agreement to be valid: it may have taken jurisdiction on some other ground permitted by its internal law.

[150] Article 9 is addressed to the court called upon to recognise or enforce the judgment, not the court which gives it. The latter court has to apply its own procedural law. This law may provide for the application of the rules on service of the State in which notification takes place.

[151] This rule does not apply if it was not possible to contest notification in the court of origin.

and give it to him. He will have done nothing wrong. Other countries (in particular, those in which the civil law applies) take a different view. They consider the service of a writ to be a sovereign act (official act) and they consider that it infringes their sovereignty for a foreign writ to be served on their territory without their permission. Permission would normally be given through an international agreement laying down the procedure to be followed.[152] Such States would be unwilling to recognise a foreign judgment if the writ was served in a way that they regarded as an infringement of their sovereignty.[153] Sub-paragraph *c)*(ii) takes account of this point of view by providing that the court addressed may refuse to recognise or enforce the judgment if the writ was notified to the defendant in the requested State in a manner that violated the public policy of that State. Unlike the other grounds of non-recognition, sub-paragraph *c)*(ii) applies only to recognition or enforcement in the State in which service took place.

142 **The fourth exception: fraud**. The fourth exception, set out in sub-paragraph *d)*, is that the judgment was obtained by fraud in connection with a matter of procedure. Fraud is deliberate dishonesty or deliberate wrongdoing. Examples would be where the plaintiff deliberately serves the writ, or causes it to be served, on the wrong address; where the plaintiff deliberately gives the defendant wrong information as to the time and place of the hearing; or where either party seeks to corrupt a judge, juror or witness, or conceals evidence. The fraud might also relate to the choice of court agreement itself – for example, if the plaintiff forged the defendant's signature on a false document. For the purpose of sub-paragraph *d)*, fraud may be committed by either party or by the court.

143 **The fifth exception: public policy**. The fifth exception, set out in sub-paragraph *e)*, is that recognition or enforcement would be manifestly incompatible with the public policy of the requested State, including situations where the specific proceedings leading to the judgment were incompatible with fundamental principles of procedural fairness of that State. The first part of this provision simply repeats the public-policy exception normally found in conventions of this kind. The second part is intended to focus attention on serious procedural failings in the particular case at hand, thus discouraging an attack on the general procedural standards of the State that granted the judgment.[154]

144 It will be seen that there is considerable overlap among the last three exceptions, since they all relate, partly or wholly, to procedural fairness. Thus, for example, if, owing to the plaintiff's fraud, the writ was not served on the defendant and (s)he was unaware of the proceedings, the exceptions set out in sub-paragraphs *c)*, *d)* and *e)* could all be invoked. The reason for this emphasis on procedural fairness is that in some countries procedural fairness (also known as due process of law, natural justice or the right to a fair trial) is constitutionally mandated. In such countries, it might be unconstitutional to recognise a foreign judgment obtained in proceedings in which a fundamental breach of this principle occurred.

145 In Europe, some 46 States are parties to the European Convention on Human Rights,[155] Article 6 of which grants the right to a fair trial. The European Court of Human

---

[152] The *Hague Convention of 15 November 1965 on the Service Abroad of Judicial and Extrajudicial Documents in Civil or Commercial Matters* is the most important example. See also *Council Regulation (EC) No 1348/2000 of 29 May 2000 on the service in the Member States of judicial and extrajudicial documents in civil or commercial matters, O.J.* L 160, p. 37.

[153] In the judgment of the Japanese Supreme Court of 28 April 1998, *Minshu*, Vol. 52, No 3, p. 853 (English translation in the *Japanese Annual of International Law*, No 42, p. 155), it was held that the direct delivery of process by a Japanese lawyer, who was asked to do so by a Hong Kong lawyer, did not comply with the rules provided for in the Hague Service Convention, and did not satisfy the requirement of Article 118(ii) of the Japanese Code of Civil Procedure. Article 118(ii) provides as follows: "A final and conclusive judgment rendered by a foreign court shall have effect insofar as it satisfies the following conditions: ... (ii) The unsuccessful defendant was served with a summons or an order necessary for the commencement of the procedure other than by service by publication, or has voluntarily appeared without being so served. ..."

[154] The second part is not, however, intended to limit the first part: public policy can also be invoked where the foreign judgment conflicts with a provision of the substantive law of the requested State.

[155] An up-to-date list of States parties is available at < http.conventions.coe.int >.

Rights has held that this precludes a court in a Contracting State to the ECHR from recognising a judgment from a non-Contracting State if the proceedings that resulted in the judgment infringed the standard laid down in Article 6.[156] This means that none of these 46 States could recognise a judgment where the court that granted it infringed the right to a fair trial. Similar rights are laid down by the Fifth and Fourteenth Amendments to the United States Constitution and by the constitutions of many other countries. For these reasons, the Convention should be drafted in such a way that it does not oblige Contracting States to do something that they are not constitutionally able to do.

146 **The sixth exception: inconsistent judgments**. Sub-paragraph *f)* deals with the situation in which there is a conflict between the judgment for which recognition and enforcement are sought under the Convention and another judgment given between the same parties. It applies where the two judgments are "inconsistent". There are two views as to what this means. According to one view, sub-paragraph *f)* applies only if there is a conflict between the order (*dispositif*) in the two judgments: it is not concerned with a conflict between the reasoning on which they are based, nor is it concerned with rulings on incidental questions, a matter which is dealt with by Article 10. According to the other view, however, a conflict of this latter kind might also be covered. If the second view is correct, Article 10(2) would be unnecessary. The second view would considerably enlarge the scope of sub-paragraph *f)* and would widen the range of judgments that could be refused recognition or enforcement under it.

147 Sub-paragraph *f)* lays down two rules. The first is concerned with the case where the inconsistent judgment was granted by a court in the requested State. In such a situation, that judgment prevails, irrespective of whether it was given first: the court addressed is permitted to give preference to a judgment from its own State, even if that judgment was given after the judgment under the choice of court agreement. It is not necessary for the cause of action to be the same.

148 A conflict of judgments to which the first rule applies would normally arise only if the court that gave the judgment conflicting with the judgment under the choice of court agreement thought that one of the exceptions laid down in Article 7 applied. If this was not the case, it would have infringed the Convention by hearing the proceedings. However, if one of the exceptions did apply, the court addressed could refuse to recognise the judgment under the choice of court agreement on the basis of Article 9, paragraph 1, sub-paragraph *a)*, sub-paragraph *b)* or sub-paragraph *e)*, since all the exceptions under Article 7 are mirrored in these sub-paragraphs. Consequently, the most likely situation in which the application of sub-paragraph *f)* will be necessary is where the court which granted the conflicting judgment was mistaken in thinking that it was entitled to hear the case under Article 7.[157] In such a case, the court addressed is permitted to refuse recognition to the judgment under the choice of court agreement in order to avoid inconsistency between different judgments in the same State.

149 The second rule is concerned with the situation in which both judgments were given by foreign courts. Here, the judgment given under the choice of court agreement may be refused recognition and enforcement only if the following requirements are satisfied: first, the judgment under the choice of court agreement must have been given after the

---

[156] *Pellegrini* v. *Italy*, judgment of 20 July 2001, (2001) 35 EHRR 44 (available at < www.echr.coe.int >); but see the earlier cases of *Drozd and Janousek* v. *France and Spain*, judgment of 26 June 1992, Series A, No 240; (1992) 14 EHRR 745 (paragraph 110); and *Soering* v. *United Kingdom*, judgment of 7 July 1989, Series A, No 161; (1989) 11 EHRR 439 (paragraph 113), in which the (old) European Court of Human Rights, sitting in plenary session, held that recognition had to be refused only if there was a flagrant breach of the standards laid down in Article 6. See also *Lindberg* v. *Sweden*, admissibility decision of 15 January 2004 (available at < www.echr.coe.int >), which, however, concerned a slightly different question; and the judgment of the House of Lords (United Kingdom) in *United States Government* v. *Montgomery (No 2)*, [2004] UKHL 37; [2004] 1 WLR 2241, where the House of Lords held that the *Pellegrini* case applies only where proceedings are brought in Italy to recognise a judgment by a Vatican court.

[157] There might be cases in which the application of Article 7 by court A is different from the application of Article 9 by court B, or in which the situation at the time of the application of Article 7 is different from that at the time of the application of Article 9.

conflicting judgment; secondly, the parties must be the same;[158] thirdly, the cause of action must be the same; fourthly, the conflicting judgment must fulfil the conditions necessary for its recognition in the requested State [under an international agreement]; and fifthly, the conflicting judgment must not have been given in contravention of the Convention.

150 These requirements raise two issues. The first concerns the words "under an international agreement"[159] in the fourth requirement. The words are in square brackets because they have not been agreed. The problem is that the consequences of their inclusion would be different for different States. Some States[160] recognise and enforce foreign judgments only under an international agreement. For such States, it would make no difference at all whether the words were included or excluded. Other States[161] recognise and enforce foreign judgments under their own law, but they are also parties to international agreements. In the case of such States, the inclusion of the words in square brackets would limit the situations in which the rule would be applied, but it would still be applied in some cases. Yet other States[162] are parties to no international agreements on recognition and enforcement of foreign judgments. In such States, foreign judgments are recognised and enforced only on the basis of their own law. If the words in square brackets were included, the rule would never be applied by such States. In view of these differences, some delegates felt that it would be unfair to include in the Convention the words in square brackets; others felt that the words were justified because the main purpose of the provision is to avoid conflicting international obligations on the part of the requested State, not to protect its internal law.

151 The second point concerns the requirement that the judgment must not have been given in contravention of the Convention. This is an entirely reasonable requirement: it would be wrong if recognition and enforcement were refused to a judgment given under the Convention because it conflicted with a judgment that was given in contravention of the Convention.[163] However, the present wording gives an unjustifiable advantage to non-Contracting States, since their judgments can never be in contravention of the Convention: if they are not parties to the Convention, nothing they do will be a contravention of it. There is no reason why non-Contracting States should be given such an advantage. As it stands at present, sub-paragraph *f)* gives States an incentive not to become parties to the Convention.

152 *To avoid this, the second part of sub-paragraph* f) *could be modified to put non-Contracting States in the same position as Contracting States. The best way to do this would be to link sub-paragraph* f) *to Article 11. This latter Article precludes recognition or enforcement of judgments given in contravention of an exclusive choice of court agreement, unless a court in the requested State could itself have heard the case under one of the exceptions laid down in Article 7. If this link were made, sub-paragraph* f) *would read as follows:*

> Recognition or enforcement may be refused only on the following grounds -
>
> ...
>
> f) the judgment is inconsistent with a judgment given in a dispute between the same parties in the requested State, or it is inconsistent with an earlier judgment given in another State between the same parties and involving the same cause of action, provided that the earlier judgment fulfils the conditions necessary for its recognition in the requested State **and its recognition is not contrary to Article 11**.

---

158 This also applies under the first rule.

159 Unlike "international instrument" in Article 23(1), "international agreement" does not include rules made by an international organisation.

160 For example, Austria, China and Sweden (subject to certain exceptions).

161 For example, Germany and the United Kingdom.

162 For example, Japan and the United States (subject to certain exceptions).

163 Admittedly, the first rule laid down by sub-paragraph *f)* could be regarded as doing just that. However, a conflict between two courts in the same State as to the correct interpretation of a legal provision raises rather delicate issues.

153 **Transfer or removal**. If it is decided that a judgment given after the case has been transferred or removed from the chosen court to another court in the same Contracting State is to be recognised and enforced under the Convention even if the parties chose a specific court,[164] adjustments will have to be made to Article 9. Article 9(1 *bis*) indicates what those adjustments will have to be.[165]

154 ***Révision au fond.*** Article 9(2) prohibits review as to the merits of the judgment (though it permits such review as is necessary to apply the provisions of Chapter III of the Convention). This is a standard provision in conventions of this kind. Without it, foreign judgments might in some countries be reviewed by the court addressed as if it were an appellate court hearing an appeal from the court of origin.

155 **Findings of fact**. The second sentence of Article 9(2) provides that the court addressed is bound by the findings of fact on which the court of origin based its jurisdiction, unless the judgment was given by default. In this provision, "jurisdiction" means jurisdiction under the Convention. Since this will be based on the choice of court agreement, the provision applies to findings of fact that relate to the formal or substantive validity of the agreement, including the capacity of the parties to conclude it. It also applies to any findings of fact relevant to determining the scope of the agreement. Thus, when the court addressed is applying Article 9(1)*(a)* or 9(1)*(b)*, it will have to accept findings of fact made by the court of origin. However, the court addressed will not be bound by the legal evaluation made by the court of origin of the facts it has found. For example, if the court of origin found that the choice of court agreement was entered into by electronic means that satisfy the requirements of Article 3 *c)*(ii), the court addressed may, nevertheless, decide that Article 3 *c)*(ii) was not satisfied because the degree of accessibility was not sufficient to meet the requirements of Article 3 *c)*(ii).

156 The position is different with regard to the grounds of non-recognition laid down in sub-paragraphs *c)*, *d)* and *e)* of Article 9(1). These are not concerned with jurisdiction under the Convention, but with public policy and procedural fairness. Thus, the court addressed must be able to decide for itself whether the defendant was notified; whether there was fraud; or whether there was a fair trial: a finding by the judge of origin that he did not take a bribe, for example, cannot be binding on the court addressed.[166]

157 The same is true with regard to procedural fairness under sub-paragraph *e)*. Assume that the defendant resists recognition and enforcement on the ground that the proceedings were incompatible with the fundamental principles of procedural fairness of the requested State. He claims that he was not able to go to the State of origin to defend the case because he would have been in danger of imprisonment on political grounds. A finding by the court of origin that this was not true cannot be binding on the court addressed. Where matters of procedural fairness are concerned, the court addressed must be able to decide for itself.[167]

158 The result is as follows: rulings by the court of origin on the merits of the case cannot be reviewed by the court addressed, irrespective of whether they relate to questions of fact or law; rulings by the court of origin on the validity and scope of the choice of court agreement cannot be reviewed in so far as they relate to questions of fact; rulings by the court of origin on the grounds of non-recognition under sub-paragraphs *c)*, *d)* and *e)* are not binding on the court addressed, irrespective of whether they relate to fact or law.

---

[164] See paragraphs 107 *et seq. supra.*

[165] If the parties designated a specific court and the case was nevertheless transferred to another court in the same State, the resulting judgment would not have been given by the court "designated" in the choice of agreement, as required by the opening words of Article 9(1).

[166] The same applies to a finding by an appeal court that the first instance judge was not guilty of corruption.

[167] The international and constitutional provisions on the right to a fair trial mentioned above probably require this. In paragraph 40 of its judgment in the *Pellegrini* case (footnote 156 *supra*), the European Court of Human Rights held that the court addressed must "duly satisf[y] [itself] that the relevant proceedings fulfilled the guarantees of Article 6 [of the European Convention on Human Rights]." This would seem to preclude reliance on a finding by the court of origin, at least where the court of origin is in a State that is not a party to the European Convention on Human Rights.

159 **"Recognition" and "enforcement"**. Article 9(3) provides that a judgment will be recognised only if it has effect in the State of origin, and will be enforced only if it is enforceable in the State of origin. This raises the distinction between recognition and enforcement. Recognition means that the court addressed accepts the determination of the legal rights and obligations made by the court of origin. If the court of origin held that the plaintiff had, or did not have, a given right, the court addressed accepts that this is the case. Enforcement means the application of the legal procedures of the court addressed to ensure that the defendant obeys the judgment given by the court of origin. Thus, if the court of origin rules that the defendant must pay the plaintiff €1000, the court addressed will ensure that the money is handed over to the plaintiff. Since this would be legally indefensible if the defendant did not owe €1000 to the plaintiff, a decision to enforce the judgment must logically be preceded or accompanied by the recognition of the judgment. However, recognition need not be accompanied or followed by enforcement. For example, if the court of origin held that the defendant did not owe any money to the plaintiff, the court addressed may simply recognise this finding. Therefore, if the plaintiff sues the defendant again on the same claim before the court addressed, the recognition of the foreign judgment will be enough to dispose of the case.

160 In the light of this distinction, it is easy to see why Article 9(3) says that a judgment will be recognised only if it has effect in the State of origin. Having effect means that it is legally valid or operative. If it does not have effect, it will not constitute a valid determination of the parties' rights and obligations. Thus, if it does not have effect in the State of origin, it should not be recognised under the Convention in any other Contracting State. Moreover, if it ceases to have effect in the State of origin, the judgment should not thereafter be recognised under the Convention in other Contracting States.[168]

161 Likewise, if the judgment is not enforceable in the State of origin, it should not be enforced elsewhere under the Convention. It is of course possible that the judgment will be effective in the State of origin without being enforceable there. Enforceability may be suspended pending an appeal (either automatically or because the court so ordered). In such a case, enforcement will not be possible in other Contracting States until the matter is resolved in the State of origin. Moreover, if the judgment ceases to be enforceable in the State of origin, it should not thereafter be enforced in another Contracting State under the Convention.[169]

162 **Judgments subject to review**. Article 9(4) provides that recognition or enforcement may be postponed or refused if the judgment is the subject of review in the State of origin or if the time limit for seeking ordinary review has not expired.[170] This means that the court addressed may delay recognition or enforcement if the judgment might be set aside or amended by another court in the State of origin. It is not, however, obliged to do this.[171] Some courts might prefer to enforce the judgment. If it is subsequently set aside in the State of origin, the court addressed will rescind the enforcement. The judgment-creditor may be required to provide security to ensure that the judgment-debtor is not prejudiced.

163 If the court addressed does not want to enforce the judgment straight away, Article 9(4) gives it the option of either suspending the enforcement process or refusing

---

[168] At the Diplomatic Conference held in June 2001, the following text was inserted, in square brackets, into Article 25 of the preliminary draft Convention 1999: "A judgment referred to in paragraph 1 shall be recognised from the time, and for as long as, it produces its effects in the State of origin." The current text was intended by the Conference to have the same meaning.

[169] At the Diplomatic Conference held in June 2001, the following text was inserted, in square brackets, into Article 25 of the preliminary draft Convention 1999: "A judgment referred to in the preceding paragraphs shall be enforceable from the time, and for as long as, it is enforceable in the State of origin." The current text was intended by the Conference to have the same meaning.

[170] In enforcement cases, this rule will be applied only if enforcement of the judgment has not been suspended in the State of origin by reason of the appeal. If it has been suspended, the rule in Article 9(3) will be applicable: see paragraph 161 *supra*. On recognition see paragraph 160 *supra*.

[171] This assumes that the judgment is still enforceable in the State of origin.

to enforce the judgment.[172] It goes on to provide, however, that if the court addressed chooses the latter option, that will not prevent a new application for enforcement once the situation in the State of origin is clarified. Here, therefore, refusal means dismissal without prejudice.

*Article 10 Incidental questions*

164 **Estoppel and foreign judgments**. Often a court has to rule on various questions of fact or law as preliminary matters before it can rule on the plaintiff's claim. For example, in a patent infringement case, it might have to rule on whether the patent is valid. This is a preliminary ruling on an incidental question. It paves the way for the final judgment, which will be that the defendant is, or is not, liable to pay damages to the plaintiff. Clearly, the court addressed has to recognise this final judgment and, if damages are awarded, to enforce it (in so far as it was rendered under a choice of court agreement covered by the Convention); but is it required by the Convention to recognise the ruling on the incidental question?

165 In civil-law States, a judgment normally has effect only as regards the final ruling – for example, the *Tenor* or *Spruch* in Germany and Austria, and the *dispositif* in France. In the common-law world, however, the doctrine known variously as issue estoppel,[173] collateral estoppel or issue preclusion[174] requires a court in certain circumstances to recognise rulings on incidental questions given in an earlier judgment.[175] This can apply both where the original judgment was given by a court in the same State and where it was given by a court in another State.[176] It is suggested that the Convention never requires the recognition or enforcement of such rulings,[177] though it does not preclude Contracting States from recognising or enforcing them under their own law.[178]

---

[172] As stated in footnote 125 *supra*, in some civil law countries the judge has only limited powers to stay the proceedings.

[173] British terminology.

[174] These latter two expressions are both US terminology.

[175] These paragraphs are an attempt to explain the common law in terms that are easily understandable by a civil lawyer. In fact, however, this results in some distortion, since the common law uses different terminology and a different conceptual framework. For example, common lawyers do not talk in terms of "incidental questions", but rather of "issues".

[176] On the latter, see P. Barnett, *Res Judicata, Estoppel and Foreign Judgments* (Oxford University Press, Oxford, England, 2001).

[177] If a court was required to apply such doctrines as issue estoppel, etc., under the Convention, it would be faced with a difficult question: what law decides whether, in a given case, an incidental ruling by a foreign court is to be recognised? Should it be the law of the State of origin or that of the requested State? The only country where significant case law exists on this point is probably the United States, where there is authority for both views: see R. Casad, "Issue Preclusion and Foreign Country Judgments: Whose Law?" (1984) 70 *Iowa Law Rev.* 53; see also the Canadian decision of *Jacobs* v. *Beaver* (1908) 17 OLR 496 (Court of Appeal, Ontario), where there is a *dictum* by Garrow J.A. that supports the application of the law of the requested State. Since the Convention lays down no rule on this question, it is fair to assume that the Convention was not intended to apply to these various forms of estoppel or preclusion.

[178] It might be thought that these forms of estoppel or preclusion apply because the court of origin intended that its judgment should have this effect. This is not the way common lawyers look at it. These forms of estoppel are a small (and recent) addition to a large array of situations in which estoppel can apply. Estoppel is a doctrine originating in Equity and has no analogue in the civil law. Originally it was a rule of evidence. If a person made an assertion (either expressly or by implication), he was precluded (estopped) from denying it in subsequent legal proceedings (estoppel by representation). The idea is that a person should not be able to say different things at different times as it suits him, especially if another person acts in reliance on his representation. For example, if X tells Y that Z is his agent, and Y deals with Z, X cannot later deny liability on the ground that Z was not his agent. He is estopped from doing so. Estoppel resulting from a decision by a court is a development from this early form. Issue / collateral estoppel does not apply automatically, but depends on what the later court thinks just. For example, it may not apply if further evidence becomes available which the party could not have discovered with reasonable diligence at the time of the original case. The importance of these doctrines in private international law should not be exaggerated. They arise only if the same two parties engage in subsequent litigation in the requested State, and an issue arises that was decided in the previous case. This will not happen often. In the United States of America, collateral estoppel can also operate in favour of a third party, but even this will not arise very often.

166 **Rulings on incidental questions**. Article 10 is concerned with matters decided as incidental questions.[179] The first paragraph states that where a matter referred to in Article 2(2) arose as an incidental question, the ruling on that question will not be recognised or enforced under the Convention. If the suggestion in the previous paragraph is correct, this provision may be unnecessary. However, in the case of rulings on matters outside the scope of the Convention – in particular, the validity of certain intellectual property rights – the question is so important that it was thought desirable to have an express provision. This is why Article 10(1) is included in the Convention. It complements Article 2(3), which provides that proceedings are not excluded from the Convention just because the court gives a ruling on an excluded matter which arose as an incidental question.

167 *If, as was suggested in paragraph 45 above, Article 2(2)*(k) *is deleted and replaced by Article 2(2* bis*), Article 10(1) would have to be redrafted to read: "Where a matter referred to in Article 2, paragraphs 2* ***and 2 bis****, arose as an incidental question, the ruling on that question shall not be recognised and enforced under this Convention."*

168 **Judgments based on an incidental question**. Article 10(2) is not concerned with the non-recognition of rulings on incidental questions, but with the non-recognition of judgments based on such rulings. What it does is to lay down another ground of non-recognition, in addition to those set out in Article 9(1). Like Article 9(1)*(f)*, it deals with inconsistent judgments. However, it is concerned with a different kind of inconsistency – at least, if the first view as to the meaning of "inconsistency" is correct.[180] Article 9(1)*(f)* is concerned with inconsistency between two judgments, one under the Convention and one that was rendered in the requested State or is subject to recognition in that State. Article 10(2), on the other hand, is concerned with the case where the latter judgment is inconsistent, not with the judgment under the Convention, but with a ruling on an incidental question on which that judgment was based.

169 This is easier to understand if we take an example. Assume that A sues B in State X, claiming royalties under a patent-licensing agreement that contains an exclusive choice of court clause granting jurisdiction to the courts of State X. B responds by arguing that the patent is invalid. If we assume that A is entitled to claim the royalties only if the patent is valid, B's assertion would be a good defence if he could substantiate it; so the court must decide the validity of the patent as an incidental question. Let us assume it does so, and holds it valid. It gives judgment in favour of A for $1 million. A then brings proceedings under the Convention to enforce this judgment in State Y, another Contracting State. Now, if there was a judgment from the State of registration of the patent (which may be either State Y or a third State, State Z), holding it invalid, this judgment would conflict not with the actual judgment in the case under the Convention – this merely says that B must pay A $1 million – but with the incidental ruling that the patent was valid. However, since this incidental ruling provides the logical premise on which the judgment was based, there would be an inconsistency between the two judgments, though an inconsistency of a secondary nature. The purpose of Article 10(2) is to permit (but not oblige) the courts of State Y to refuse to recognise or enforce the judgment under the Convention in these circumstances.

170 Article 10(2) is concerned only with the case where the incidental ruling is on the validity of an intellectual property right other than copyright or related rights. The reason why it was proposed – it is in square brackets to show that it has not yet been accepted – is that some delegations attach special importance to the idea that the courts[181] of the State under the law of which the intellectual property right arose must have exclusive jurisdiction to give binding rulings on its validity.[182]

---

[179] On what is meant by an incidental question, see paragraphs 164–165 *supra*; see also footnote 22 *supra*.

[180] See paragraph 146 *supra*.

[181] It must be remembered that "court" includes a patent office. The definition of "judgment" in Article 4(1) includes a decision of a patent office or other authority exercising the functions of a court: see footnote 11 to Article 10(2) of the preliminary draft Convention.

[182] It has, however, been proposed to extend it to cover incidental rulings on all the matters excluded from the scope of the Convention under Article 2(2), provided that the judgment with which the incidental ruling conflicts

171 **Staying enforcement proceedings**. Article 10(3) takes the approach of Article 10(2) one step further by providing that if, when the enforcement proceedings are commenced, there are proceedings pending before the appropriate court (in the State under the law of which the intellectual property right arose) which could result in a ruling that the intellectual property right was invalid, the court hearing the enforcement proceedings is permitted (but not obliged) to suspend the proceedings before it until a judgment has been given on the question of validity.[183] This provision is in square brackets to indicate that it has not yet been agreed. Its opponents argue that it might encourage defendants to bring spurious revocation proceedings simply to delay enforcement.

*Article 11 Judgments in contravention of exclusive choice of court agreements*

172 Article 11 is intended to complement (or extend) Article 7. It was explained above that the objectives of the Convention would be prejudiced if a court other than the chosen court could hear proceedings to which the exclusive choice of court agreement applied.[184] For this reason, Article 7 requires any court in a Contracting State other than that of the chosen court to suspend or dismiss the proceedings in such a situation, unless the exceptions set out in Article 7 apply. However, the objectives of the Convention would also be prejudiced if that court recognised or enforced a judgment given in contravention of the exclusive choice of court agreement, irrespective of whether it was rendered in a Contracting or non-Contracting State. Apart from any other considerations, such recognition or enforcement might bar the recognition and enforcement of the judgment of the chosen court. For these reasons, Article 11 provides that the provisions of Article 7 also apply to proceedings for recognition or enforcement of a judgment rendered in contravention of an exclusive choice of court agreement. It is in square brackets because it has not yet been agreed.

173 Although the objective of Article 11 is eminently reasonable, the present drafting raises two problems. The first is that Article 7 applies only to a court in a Contracting State other than that of the chosen court. Consequently, Article 11, as at present drafted, also applies only when the court asked to recognise the judgment is not in the State of the chosen court. It does not, therefore, cover the case where proceedings are brought to recognise the judgment in such a court.

174 The second problem is that the requested State may be under a treaty obligation to recognise the judgment. If that treaty was concluded prior to the Convention and if the other party was not a Contracting State to the Convention, it would be unreasonable to prohibit the recognition or enforcement of the judgment. Article 23(5) covers this point; however, it goes further by giving priority to prior judgment-recognition treaties even between two Contracting States to the Convention.[185] This means that parties to the Convention are permitted to maintain in force between themselves a treaty provision that requires the recognition and enforcement of judgments that were given in contravention of the Convention.[186]

175 *One way of solving these problems, and making the provision clearer, would be to revise the text as follows:*

---

has effect not only as between the parties, but also as regards all other parties (*erga omnes*). On this, see the example given in paragraph 113 *supra*.

[183] This provision has something in common with Article 6. The comments made in connection with that provision in paragraph 114 *supra*, are also relevant here.

[184] Paragraph 116.

[185] See paragraphs 232-238 *infra*.

[186] On the position under international law, see A. Schulz, "The Relationship between the Judgments Project and other International Instruments", Preliminary Document No 24 of December 2003, available at < ww.hcch.net >.

*Article 11 Judgments in contravention of exclusive choice of court agreements*

**Variant 1**

1. If the parties have entered into an exclusive choice of court agreement, a court in a Contracting State other than that of the chosen court shall not recognize or enforce a judgment rendered in contravention of that agreement unless the judgment was granted consistently with Article 7 or, if the State of origin was a non-Contracting State, if it would have been so granted if that State had been a Contracting State.

2. Paragraph 1 shall not apply if the court addressed is obliged to recognize or enforce the judgment under an international agreement concluded prior to this Convention and the State of origin is not a party to this Convention.

**Variant 2**

1. If the parties have entered into an exclusive choice of court agreement, a court in a Contracting State other than that of the chosen court shall not recognize or enforce a judgment rendered in contravention of that agreement unless it could itself have heard the case consistently with Article 7.

2. If the parties have entered into an exclusive choice of court agreement, a court of the State of the chosen court shall not recognize or enforce a judgment rendered in contravention of that agreement unless [the chosen court refused, or could refuse, to hear the case consistently with Article 5] [the agreement is null and void under its law or the chosen court lacks subject-matter jurisdiction].

3. Paragraphs 1 and 2 shall not apply if the court addressed is obliged to recognize or enforce the judgment under an international agreement concluded prior to this Convention and the State of origin is not a party to this Convention.

176 *Variant 1 might seem more logical; however, it requires the court addressed to decide whether the choice of court agreement was contrary to the public policy of the State of origin, something that it would be ill equipped to do.*[187] *Variant 2 is based on the idea that recognizing a judgment contrary to an exclusive choice of court clause has the same effect as granting such a judgment.*

177 *Article 23(5) would have to be amended so that it did not affect this provision.*[188]

*Article 12 Settlements*

178 Article 12 provides that settlements which, in the course of proceedings, are approved by, or concluded before, a court of a Contracting State designated in an exclusive choice of court agreement, and which are enforceable in the same manner as a judgment in that State, must be enforced in other Contracting States in the same manner as a judgment.[189]

---

[187] The difference between the two Variants is that under Variant 1 the court has to apply the law of the State of origin under Article 7 *b)* and the public policy of that State under Article 7 *c)*; under Variant 2, it applies its own law and public policy.

[188] See paragraph 232-238 *infra.*

[189] The equivalent provision in the preliminary draft Convention 1999 is Article 36. The commentary in the Nygh / Pocar Report is at pp. 118–119.

179 Such a settlement is sometimes called a "judicial settlement", a translation of the French "*transaction judiciaire*".[190] In the sense in which the term is used here, judicial settlements are unknown in the common-law world. In France and other civil law countries, they are contracts concluded before a judge by which the parties put an end to litigation, usually by making mutual concessions. A judicial settlement is different from a consent order in the common law sense (an order made by the court with the consent of both parties), since a consent order is a judgment and may be recognised and enforced as such under Article 9 of the Convention. On the other hand, a judicial settlement is different from an out-of-court settlement, since it is made before a judge and puts an end to the proceedings. For these reasons, a special provision is devoted to it in the Convention.

180 Article 12 does not provide for the recognition of judicial settlements, but only for their enforcement.[191] The significance of this is best explained by an example.

> Assume that A and B conclude a contract with an exclusive choice of court clause in favour of the courts of State X. Subsequently, A sues B before a court in that State for €1000, a sum which he claims is due under the contract. The parties then enter into a judicial settlement under which B agrees to pay A €800, State X being a State where this may be done.

181 If B fails to pay, A may bring proceedings to enforce the settlement in State Y, another Contracting State. Such proceedings will be covered by Article 12 of the Convention. Assume, however, that B pays the money in compliance with the settlement without any need for enforcement proceedings. If A nevertheless brings a new action for the remaining €200 before the courts of State Y, B cannot ask the court to recognise the settlement under the Convention as a defence to the claim. The Convention does not provide for this, mainly because the effects of settlements are so different in different legal systems. However, the Convention does not preclude a court from treating the settlement as a contractual defence to the claim, and this is what most courts would do.

*Article 13 Documents to be produced*

182 Article 13(1) lists the documents to be produced by the party seeking recognition or enforcement of a judgment under the Convention.[192] The fact that recognition is mentioned in the "*chapeau*" to Article 13 does not mean that there has to be any special procedure.[193] However, if the other party disputes it, the party requesting recognition must produce the documents required by Article 13.

183 Article 13(1)*(a)* requires the production of a complete and certified copy of the judgment. This refers to the whole judgment (including, where applicable, the court's reasoning) and not just to the final order (*dispositif*). The words "or evidence of its existence" in Article 13(1)*(b)* were inserted to provide for agreements concluded electronically. In the case of such agreements, it is not possible to produce "the agreement" itself. Article 13(1)*(c)* requires documentary evidence that the defendant was notified, but this applies only in the case of a default judgment. In other cases, it is assumed that the defendant was notified unless he or she produces evidence to the contrary. The law of the requested State determines the consequences of failure to

---

[190] On an analogous provision in the Brussels Regulation, see H. Gaudemet-Tallon , *Compétence et exécution des jugements en Europe* (3rd ed., 2002, LGDJ, Paris), Chapter 4 (pp. 387 *et seq.*).

[191] On the distinction between recognition and enforcement, see paragraph 159 *supra*.

[192] This provision is similar to sub-paragraphs *a)* to *c)* of Article 29(1) in the preliminary draft Convention 1999. The commentary on the latter in the Nygh / Pocar Report is at pp. 109–110.

[193] See paragraph 188 *infra*.

produce the required documents. Excessive formalism should, however, be avoided: if the judgment-debtor was not prejudiced, the judgment-creditor should be allowed to rectify omissions.

184 Article 13(2) provides that the court addressed may require the production of further documents to the extent that it is necessary to verify that the requirements of Chapter III of the Convention have been satisfied. This makes clear that the list in paragraph 1 is not exhaustive. Unnecessary burdens on the parties should, however, be avoided.

185 Article 13(3) provides for the Hague Conference on Private International Law to recommend and publish a form which may be used by a person seeking recognition or enforcement of a judgment under the Convention. The use of such a form will not be obligatory. Information contained in it may be relied on by the court addressed in the absence of challenge. Even if there is no challenge, however, the information is not conclusive: the court addressed can decide the matter in the light of all the evidence before it. The Special Commission expressed the desire that the form should be published in the *Collection of Conventions*, though it also wanted to make it possible to amend it without undue difficulty, to meet new needs or to overcome problems that were not originally foreseen. For this reason, it was decided that the form should not constitute an Annex to the Convention.

186 *However, another option might be to follow the example of the 1980 Hague Convention on Access to Justice, which provides in Article 30, "The model forms annexed to this Convention may be amended by a decision of a Special Commission convoked by the Secretary General of the Hague Conference to which all Contracting States and all Member States shall be invited. Notice of the proposal to amend the forms shall be included in the agenda for the meeting."*

187 Article 13(4) provides that the court addressed may require a translation of any document referred to in Article 13. This depends on the rules of procedure of the requested State.

*Article 14 Procedure*[194]

188 Article 14 provides that the procedure for recognition, declaration of enforceability or registration for enforcement, and the enforcement of the judgment are governed by the law of the requested State unless the Convention provides otherwise.[195] Where the law of the requested State makes no provision for any special procedure for the recognition (as distinct from enforcement) of a foreign judgment, a judgment will be recognised automatically by operation of law, based solely on Article 9 of the Convention. Where, on the other hand, the law requires a mandatory procedure for the recognition of foreign judgments, such procedure will have to be followed in the case of foreign judgments covered by the Convention. *Delegates may want to consider whether the Convention should go further and expressly prohibit Contracting States from making any such procedure mandatory. This would not prevent them, for the purposes of legal certainty, from offering such a special procedure on a voluntary basis.*

*If it were decided that the Convention should go this way, the text could be amended as follows:*

> *No special procedure may be required for the recognition of a judgment under this Convention. The procedure for recognition, declaration of enforceability or registration for enforcement, and the enforcement of the judgment, are governed by the law of the requested State unless this Convention provides otherwise. The court addressed shall act expeditiously.*

---

[194] With regard to other procedural matters, see paragraphs 48 to 54 and 105.

[195] Except for purely verbal alterations, this is the same as Article 30 of the preliminary draft Convention 1999. The commentary on this Article is at p. 100 of the Nygh / Pocar Report.

189 In all proceedings covered by Article 14, the court addressed must act expeditiously, though there is no explicit sanction against delay. This means that the court must use the most expeditious procedure available to it. Contracting States should consider ways in which provision can be made to ensure that unnecessary delays are avoided.

*Article 15 Damages*

190 Article 15 deals with two issues: non-compensatory damages and excessive damages. The latter may be either compensatory or non-compensatory. The first paragraph applies only to non-compensatory damages. The second (which is concerned with excessive damages) appears to cover both, though the Nygh / Pocar Report states that it applies only to compensatory damages.[196] The third applies to both.

191 Compensatory damages are intended to compensate the plaintiff for loss suffered as a result of the wrongful act of the defendant. Non-compensatory damages are intended to serve a different purpose, usually to punish the defendant for his wrongdoing, or to deter others from doing something similar. They are sometimes called "exemplary" or "punitive" damages. However, Article 15(1) is not limited to damages so called: it applies to all damages that are not compensatory.

192 **Non-compensatory damages**. The first sentence of Article 15(1) requires a court in a Contracting State to recognise and enforce a judgment awarding non-compensatory damages if, and to the extent that, it could have awarded similar or comparable damages itself.[197] The test is whether it could have done so if the action had originally been brought before it. "Similar" damages are damages of the same kind; "comparable" damages are non-compensatory damages of a different kind that nevertheless fulfil a comparable function. Article 15 does not expressly say that a court is not obliged to recognise or enforce a judgment for non-compensatory damages if it could not itself have awarded similar or comparable damages, but this is what was intended.

193 If non-compensatory damages cannot be awarded in any circumstances in the State addressed,[198] the part of the foreign judgment awarding non-compensatory damages will never be recognised or enforced.[199] If non-compensatory damages could have been awarded only in special circumstances – for example, if the defendant deliberately commits the tort in the belief that the profit he or she will derive will outweigh any compensatory damages that could be awarded – the court would not be obliged to recognise or enforce the judgment if those circumstances did not pertain. Moreover, if it could have awarded non-compensatory damages in the circumstances of the case, but only for a small sum, it would not be obliged to recognise or enforce a judgment for a significantly greater sum. In all cases, however, it is permitted to recognise and enforce the judgment to the full amount.

194 **Excessive damages**. Article 15(2) deals with excessive damages. Even if it also applies to non-compensatory damages, its main importance derives from its application to compensatory damages. The purpose of Article 15(2)*(a)* is to allow the court

---

[196] See p. 111. In practice, at least, it will be applied only to compensatory damages, since non-compensatory damages are adequately dealt with by the first paragraph.

[197] It cannot, therefore, invoke the public policy exception in Article 9(1)*(e)* as a ground for refusing to recognise an award solely because the damages are non-compensatory.

[198] Generally speaking, this is the position in civil-law countries, where punishment is regarded as the business only of the criminal law.

[199] For judgments to this effect, see BGH 4 June 1992, BGHZ 118, 312 (*Bundesgerichtshof*, Germany); Supreme Court of Japan, judgment of 11 July 1997, *Minshu*, Vol. 51, No 6, p. 2578 (English translation in the *Japanese Annual of International Law*, No 41, p. 104). In both cases, the public policy exception was invoked to deny enforcement to the part of the award in an American judgment that represented punitive damages.

addressed to cut down an award of damages – even if they are purely compensatory – if it considers them to be grossly excessive. It may do this, however, only after proceedings have taken place in which the judgment-creditor has had the opportunity to be heard and only if the judgment-debtor satisfies the court – the onus is on him – that in all the circumstances, including those existing in the State of origin, the damages are grossly excessive. However, as is provided by Article 15(2)*(b)*, the court must in no event recognise or enforce the judgment in an amount less than that which could have been awarded in the requested State in the same circumstances, including those existing in the State of origin. This is to prevent the abuse of Article 15(2)*(a)*.

195 In applying Article 15(2), the court addressed cannot reduce the amount simply because things cost more in the State of origin. The cost of medical treatment is much greater in some States than in others. To the extent that the award reflects this, it cannot be deemed excessive. The same is true with regard to salaries. If the award is based on lost earnings, it will naturally reflect what the victim would have earned if the tort had not occurred. By the standards of the requested State, this might seem a great deal of money; nevertheless, the award cannot normally be reduced for this reason.

196 Article 15(2) will apply most often with regard to damages for matters that cannot be objectively assessed – for example, pain and suffering; loss of an arm, a leg or an eye; loss of reputation; hurt feelings; or similar matters. Here the court of origin will normally make an award guided solely by the level of past awards. If this level is grossly excessive, the court addressed will reduce the award.

197 The Nygh / Pocar Report states that, as a general principle, "grossly excessive" is likely to mean "grossly excessive according to the standards usually applied by the courts of the State of origin";[200] however, this view was strongly criticised by several delegations. If the court addressed had to apply the standards of the State of origin, Article 15(2) would be almost totally deprived of effect: if an award was "grossly excessive" by the standards of the State in which it was made, it would almost certainly be set aside on appeal, in which case the question of its enforcement would not arise.

198 It might be best not to use the word "standard", since it could suggest the application of rules, though if "standards" are to be applied, they must be those of the requested State. This does not, however, mean that the court addressed can refuse to enforce an award simply because it would itself have made a smaller one, or even none at all. The test is not one of rules but of judgment.

199 The test under Article 15(2) is similar to that of public policy. The question of damages could have been left to the public policy exception in Article 9(1)*(e)*, but it was decided to devote a special provision to it, partly to introduce greater certainty, and partly to reassure those States that might have been unwilling to sign the Convention if they had had to enforce awards they regarded as excessive.[201] Thus, though public policy is expressly mentioned only in Article 9(1)*(e)* as a ground for non-recognition of a judgment, the essential question that the court must ask when applying Article 15(2) is whether the award is so grossly excessive that its recognition or enforcement would be contrary to public policy.

---

[200] At p. 114.

[201] It was also intended to ensure that States would not use the public policy exception of the Convention to refuse to enforce an award of punitive damages if they could have awarded similar or comparable damages themselves.

200 This test must be applied to the total award: it should not be applied separately to each head of damages. It may well be that the court of origin awarded very large damages under one head, but this might have been to compensate for the fact that it could not, or did not, award damages under another head. For example, take the case of a wrongful-death action brought by the widow of the victim. One legal system might compensate her on the basis of the financial support she lost as a result of her husband's death. Another might compensate her for the emotional devastation she suffered. The final award might be much the same in both cases. It would be wrong, therefore, for the court addressed to apply the "grossly excessive" test individually to each item of compensation, since this might result in her receiving far less than she would have if the action had originally been brought before the court addressed.

201 The test is one of damages, not liability; therefore, the court addressed cannot refuse to enforce the judgment simply because it would not have regarded the defendant as liable, or because it could not have awarded damages for what he did. For example, in some legal systems defamation is a criminal offence but not a tort; in others, it is a tort but not a crime. If a court in a State where the latter system prevails grants an award of damages for libel, a court in a State that applies the former system cannot refuse to enforce it on the basis of Article 15(2)*(a)* simply because it could not have awarded damages in similar circumstances. However, if it feels that, in all the circumstances (including those in the State of origin), the sum awarded is grossly excessive in proportion to the wrong done, it will be entitled to reduce the award.[202]

202 The same would apply to actions in tort for inducing a breach of contract. Assume that A and B enter into a contract, and C induces B to break the contract. In these circumstances, most common law systems would consider that A can sue C in tort. In some other legal systems, this may not be possible. However, if a common law court were to award damages in such an action, another court ought not to refuse to enforce the judgment on the basis of Article 15(2)*(a)* simply because it would not have granted any damages if the action had originally been brought before it. However, it may cut the award down if it thinks that the amount of the award is so grossly excessive as to be out of all proportion to the harm inflicted on A.

203 **Legal costs and expenses**. The third paragraph of Article 15 applies to proceedings under both the first paragraph and the second paragraph. It provides that the court addressed must take into account whether, and to what extent, the award – whether stated to be compensatory or non-compensatory – is intended to cover costs and expenses relating to the proceedings. This provision was included because the rules regarding legal costs differ in different legal systems. In most countries, the successful plaintiff is entitled to "costs". This is a sum of money added to the damages to cover the costs and expenses of the legal proceedings. However, the rules for assessing costs can differ widely. In many countries, they cover lawyers' fees.[203] In the United States, they do not.[204] To compensate for this, juries in the United States often grant higher damages, sometimes designated as punitive damages. The court addressed is obliged by Article 15(3) to take this into account in deciding whether the award is grossly excessive:

---

[202] If the court addressed considers, on grounds other than the size of the award or the fact that it is non-compensatory, that it would be manifestly contrary to its public policy to recognise or enforce the judgment, it can invoke the public policy exception in Article 9(1)*(e)*. This might occur, for example, if it considered that a judgment for libel constituted an infringement of the right of free speech.

[203] There may, however, be considerable differences in the way in which these are assessed: they may cover more or less all that the successful party has had to pay his lawyer; or they may fall far short of this.

[204] There are a small number of exceptions.

it must take the amount of the judgment and compare it with the total amount it would have awarded, including costs. In doing this, it must also take into account the prevailing level of lawyers' fees in the State of origin.

204 **Insurance**. The effect of Article 15 on contracts of insurance (or reinsurance) needs explanation. Article 15 is concerned solely with the recognition or enforcement of a judgment for non-compensatory damages or excessive compensatory damages. The fact that an award of damages would not be recognised (in whole or in part) because the damages are non-compensatory or excessive does not mean that a judgment under a contract of insurance (or reinsurance) would not be recognised or enforced merely because the policy indemnified the insured against payment to a third party of such damages.

205 This distinction is made clearer by an example. Assume that a person enters into a contract of insurance under which the insurer agrees to indemnify him against an award of damages, including punitive or excessive damages.[205] Then a judgment awarding punitive damages is made against him. Article 15 would apply in proceedings to enforce that judgment in other Contracting States in so far as it was rendered under a choice of court agreement covered by the Convention (which rarely occurs). In some Contracting States, it might not be enforced. However, this would not affect the enforcement of a judgment against the insurer under the policy. Article 15 does not permit a Contracting State to refuse to enforce a judgment under an insurance contract just because the risk insured against is the payment of punitive damages. A judgment against an insurer requiring him to indemnify an insured against an award of punitive damages is not itself an award of punitive damages. Nor would it be an award of excessive damages, just because the loss against which the insurer agreed to indemnify the insured was an award of excessive damages. Therefore, Article 15 does not apply to the recognition and enforcement of the judgment against the insurer, if it was rendered under a choice of court agreement covered by the Convention.

206 *Although this may already be clear, it might be desirable, for the sake of certainty, to add a new paragraph to Article 15. This might read, "This Article does not permit a court of a Contracting State to limit recognition or enforcement of a judgment under a contract of insurance (or reinsurance) merely because the judgment requires the insurer to indemnify the insured against payment of non-compensatory damages or excessive compensatory damages."*

207 **Statutory and contractual (liquidated) damages**. Sometimes a statute lays down a formula for calculating damages, or specifies the sum to be paid. Sometimes a contract does so. This may be done to avoid lengthy disputes as to the correct amount. If this is a genuine attempt to estimate a fair level of compensation in advance, damages awarded on this basis would constitute compensatory damages, even if, in a given case, the resulting sum did not exactly reflect the amount of the plaintiff's loss. If, on the other hand, there was no genuine intention to estimate a fair level of compensation, but the intention was rather to punish the defendant, the damages would be non-compensatory.[206]

*Article 16 Severability*

208 Article 16 provides for the recognition and enforcement of a severable part of a judgment where this is applied for, or where only part of the judgment is capable of being recognised or enforced under the Convention.[207] For example, if an award of

---

[205] Whether the policy covers such damages would depend on its terms, as interpreted by the law governing it.

[206] See Interim Text 2001, p. 27, footnote 176.

[207] The equivalent provision in the preliminary draft Convention 1999 is Article 34. The commentary on this provision is at p. 115 of the Nygh / Pocar Report.

punitive damages is not enforced by reason of Article 15(1), the remainder of the award must be enforced if it satisfies the requirements of Article 9.[208] In order to be severable, the part in question must be capable of standing alone, and it must be reasonable and appropriate to recognise or enforce it independently of the rest of the judgment.[209] In so far as this depends on a rule of law, the law of the court addressed must be applied.

*Article 17 No legalisation*

209 Article 17 provides that all documents forwarded or delivered under the Convention must be exempt from legalisation or any analogous formality.[210] The latter would include, for example, an *apostille*.

*Article 18 Limitation of jurisdiction*

210 It was said above that it is the policy of the Convention to exclude wholly domestic situations from its scope.[211] Effect is given to this policy by Article 1. Article 18 pursues the opposite policy: it permits a State to make a declaration that its courts will not apply Article 5 of the Convention to cases that are wholly *foreign*. It states that upon ratification, acceptance, approval or accession, a State may declare that its courts may refuse to determine disputes covered by an exclusive choice of court agreement if, except for the location of the chosen court, there is no connection between that State and the parties or the dispute.[212]

211 In practice, parties sometimes choose the courts of a State with which neither they nor the facts of the case have any connection. The reason is that neither party wants to go before the courts of the other party's State; so they agree to choose the courts of a neutral State. Some countries welcome this.[213] Others feel that it imposes an undue burden on their judicial systems. The purpose of Article 18 is to accommodate States in the latter category.

*Article 19 Limitation of recognition and enforcement*

212 Article 19 provides that upon ratification, acceptance, approval or accession, a State may declare that its courts may refuse to recognise or enforce a judgment of a court in another Contracting State if the parties are resident in the requested State, and the relationship of the parties and all other elements relevant to the dispute, other than the location of the chosen court, are, at the time the agreement is concluded,[214] connected only with the requested State.[215] This provision pursues the policy, discussed above, of excluding wholly domestic situations from the scope of the Convention.

---

[208] See footnote 199 for cases in Germany and Japan where this occurred.

[209] This would normally depend on whether enforcing only one part of the judgment would significantly change the obligations of the parties: see the Nygh / Pocar Report, p. 115. If any questions of law arose, they would have to be decided by the law of the requested State: *ibid.*

[210] This is equivalent to Article 29(2) of the preliminary draft Convention 1999. The commentary on that provision in the Nygh / Pocar Report is at p. 110, where it is stated that this is a practice that is well established in the context of the Hague Conventions.

[211] Paragraph 10.

[212] Since the Convention uses the words "may refuse", the courts of a State that made such a declaration would have a discretion whether or not to exercise jurisdiction. Implementing legislation could introduce an obligation not to exercise jurisdiction in such cases.

[213] For example, English courts have for many years been willing to hear such cases, and in 1984 New York adopted special provisions to facilitate them: see New York Civil Practice Law and Rules, Rule 327(b) and New York General Obligations Law § 5-1402.

[214] The phrase "at the time the agreement is concluded" seems to apply to the residence of the parties, as well as to their relationship and to the other elements relevant to the dispute. However, further discussion may be necessary to clarify whether this is correct.

[215] Since the Convention uses the words "may refuse", the courts of a State that made such a declaration would have a discretion whether or not to recognise and enforce such judgments under the Convention. However, implementing legislation could introduce an obligation not to recognise or enforce foreign judgments in such circumstances.

213 To understand the purpose of Article 19, one must remember that the Convention applies only in international cases.[216] However, the definition of "international" for this purpose varies, depending on whether one is considering jurisdiction,[217] or the recognition and enforcement of a judgment.[218] For the purpose of jurisdiction, a case is not international if the parties are resident in the State of the court seised, and if all other elements relevant to the dispute (regardless of the location of the chosen court) are connected only with that State. However, for the purpose of recognition and enforcement, a case is always international if the judgment was given by a court in a State other than that in which recognition or enforcement is sought. That means that a case that is domestic when it is heard becomes international if proceedings are brought to enforce the judgment in another State. The purpose of Article 19 is to permit a Contracting State to declare that it will not recognise or enforce such a judgment if the case would have been wholly domestic to it, if the original proceedings had been brought in its courts. For example, assume that the parties are resident in State A and all other relevant elements are connected only with that State. They agree that a court in State B will have exclusive jurisdiction. If one of them brings proceedings before a court in State A, that court would not be obliged to decline jurisdiction under Article 7: the Convention would not be applicable because the case would not be international under Article 1(2). However, if proceedings were brought in State B, State A would be required by Article 9 to recognise the resulting judgment: the case would have become international in terms of Article 1(3). What Article 19 does is to make it possible for States to change this by entering an appropriate declaration. If it did that, State A would not be required to recognise the judgment.

*Article 20 Limitation with respect to asbestos related matters*

214 Article 20 provides that upon ratification, acceptance, approval or accession, a State may declare that it will not apply the provisions of the Convention to exclusive choice of court agreements in asbestos related matters.[219] This is because personal-injury and wrongful-death claims for asbestosis have caused serious problems in one particular State. This provision is intended to allow that State to opt out. It applies to actions concerning liability for injury, illness or death caused by exposure to asbestos.

*Article 21 Uniform interpretation*

215 Article 21 states that in the interpretation of the Convention regard must be had to its international character and to the need to promote uniformity in its application. This provision is addressed to courts applying the Convention. It requires them to interpret it in an international spirit so as to promote uniformity of application. Where reasonably possible, therefore, foreign decisions and writings should be taken into account. It should also be kept in mind that concepts and principles that are regarded as axiomatic in one legal system may be unknown or rejected in another. The objectives of the Convention can be attained only if all courts apply it in an open-minded way.[220]

[216] Article 1(1).

[217] Article 1(2).

[218] Article 1(3).

[219] Some delegations have proposed that further specific subject matters should be referred to in this provision, such as natural resources and joint ventures. These proposals are linked to issues that arise in relation to Articles 7 and 9.

[220] The equivalent provision in the preliminary draft Convention 1999 is Article 38(1). The commentary on this in the Nygh / Pocar Report is at pp. 118–119.

*Article 22 Non-unified legal system*

216 Article 22 is concerned with the problems that result from the fact that some States are composed of two or more territorial units, each with its own judicial system. It occurs most often in the case of federations – for example, Canada or the United States – but can also occur in other States as well – for example, China or the United Kingdom. This can create a problem because one has to decide in any particular case whether the appropriate unit is the State as a whole ("State" in the international sense) or whether it is a particular territorial unit within that State.

217 Article 22(1) solves this problem by providing that, where different systems of law apply in the territorial units with regard to any matter dealt with in the Convention,[221] the Convention is to be construed as applying either to the State in the international sense or to the relevant territorial unit, whichever is appropriate.[222] This might seem unsatisfactory, but in fact it is usually obvious what the answer is.

218 The most important situation in which the question arises is in connection with the definition of an exclusive choice of court agreement in Article 3. The way in which Article 22 applies in this situation has already been discussed.[223] Another situation is the determination of the residence of an individual or company.

219 Article 22(2) gives further effect to the policy of not applying the Convention to wholly domestic situations. It states that, notwithstanding the provisions of Article 22(1), a Contracting State with two or more territorial units in which different systems of law are applied is not bound to apply the Convention to situations involving solely such different territorial units. For this provision to apply, the chosen court must also be located in the State in question; if it is located in another Contracting State, Article 19 would apply.

220 Article 22(2) means that if, for example, the chosen court is in England and the situation is entirely internal to the United Kingdom, the United Kingdom is not required to apply the Convention by virtue of the fact that one of the parties is resident in Scotland. If, however, the chosen court were in Canada, United Kingdom courts would have to recognise and enforce any judgment given by that court, unless the United Kingdom had made a declaration under Article 19.

221 Article 22(3) provides that a court in a territorial unit of a Contracting State is not bound to recognise or enforce a judgment from another Contracting State solely because the judgment has been recognised or enforced under the Convention by a court in another territorial unit of the first Contracting State. This means, for example, that a court in New York is not bound to recognise a judgment from Japan solely because a court in New Jersey has done so. The New York court must decide for itself whether the conditions for recognition or enforcement under the Convention are fulfilled.

---

[221] The fact that some or all of the relevant territorial units in a Contracting State apply the common law does not necessarily mean that they do not apply different systems of law. They will do so if they have different legislation – for example, in the case of Australian states or the common law Canadian provinces.

[222] It was agreed that each Contracting State can provide in the legislation putting the Convention into effect how "appropriate" is to be understood.

[223] Paragraph 73.

*Article 23* *Relationship with other international instruments*

222 Article 23 is concerned with the relationship between the Convention and other international instruments that relate to jurisdiction, recognition and enforcement. The most important such instruments are the Brussels Convention, the Lugano Convention and the Brussels Regulation. The following discussion will be based mainly on those instruments, but Article 23 is not limited to them: it is general in application.[224]

223 The first paragraph of Article 23 defines an "international instrument". It means an international treaty, or rules made by an international organisation under an international treaty. It thus covers the Brussels Regulation (EU legislation) as well as the Brussels and Lugano Conventions.

224 The second and third paragraphs lay down two fairly non-controversial rules. Article 23(2) states that the Convention does not affect any *existing* international instruments to which Contracting States are parties, unless a declaration to the contrary is made by the States bound by such instrument. This rule is, however, subject to the provisions of paragraphs 4 and 5 (explained below).

225 Article 23(3) provides that the Convention does not affect the ability of one or more Contracting States to enter into future international instruments on jurisdiction and the recognition and enforcement of judgments, provided that those instruments do not affect the Convention in the relations between such States and other Contracting States. This permits a group of Contracting States ("special" Contracting States) to adopt among themselves a new international instrument that covers the same area as the Convention and even conflicts with it, provided that the new instrument does not affect relations between the special Contracting States and other Contracting States ("general" Contracting States).

226 This is a reasonable rule, and is in accordance with international law,[225] but it might not always be clear when relations with general Contracting States are involved. For example, if two special Contracting States enter into a treaty under which they agree to recognise each other's judgments, it might seem that this would not affect general Contracting States. However, if such a judgment was given in contravention of an exclusive choice of court agreement, it *would* affect them if the chosen court was located, or a party was resident, in a general Contracting State - at least, if Article 11 becomes part of the Convention.

227 Paragraph 4 is the most important provision in Article 23. As was said above, paragraph 2 provides that prior instruments are not affected by the Convention unless there is a contrary declaration. Paragraph 4, however, contains an exception to that rule, which applies in so far as jurisdiction is concerned. It is based on the principle, mentioned above, that the Convention should prevail when there is a significant contact with a "general" Contracting State.[226] For the purpose of this provision, a significant contact exists if either the chosen court is situated, or a party is resident, in the State in question. Consequently, the prior instrument prevails if both (a) the chosen court is situated in a "special" Contracting State or a non-Contracting State in which the

---

[224] Other conventions include the *Minsk Convention on Legal Aid and Legal Relations in Civil, Family and Criminal Cases* 1993 (English translation available at < http://www.coe.int/T/E/Legal_Affairs/Legal_co-operation/Transnational_criminal_justice/Information/OC_INF_44E.asp >) and various Latin American instruments.

[225] See Article 30(4) of the *Vienna Convention on the Law of Treaties* 1969. See also A. Schulz, "The Relationship between the Judgments Project and other International Instruments", Preliminary Document No 24 of December 2003.

[226] A "general" Contracting State, it will be remembered, is a State that is a Party to the Convention but not to the prior instrument.

instrument applies and (b) all the parties are resident [only][227] in a "special" Contracting State or in a non-Contracting State.[228] On the other hand, the Convention applies if *either* the chosen court is situated,[229] *or* a party is resident, in a "general" Contracting State.[230] Thus, for example, if a French party[231] and a Dutch party choose the courts of China, then as far as jurisdiction is concerned, the Convention will apply, not the Brussels Regulation. Likewise, if a French party and a Canadian party choose the courts of England, the Convention will prevail over the Brussels Regulation as far as jurisdiction is concerned.

228 Paragraph 4 works well with regard to the Brussels Convention and the Brussels Regulation.[232] This is because, as Member States of the European Community, all the States parties to those instruments will become parties to the Convention at one and the same time. However, this may not be the case with regard to other Conventions. Where some States that are parties to the prior instrument are also parties to the Convention, but others are not, a problem arises. We shall take the Lugano Convention as an example. If there is a State that is a party to the Lugano Convention but not to the[233] Convention, it would be entitled to expect that the other parties to the Lugano Convention would apply the Lugano Convention whenever there was a significant contact with it, even if there was also a significant contact with a "general" Contracting State. Article 23(4) does not, however, make provision for this. As a result, a State that was a party to both the Convention and the Lugano Convention could find itself in an impossible situation, since it would be required to apply the Lugano Convention with regard to States that were parties to the Lugano Convention but not the Convention, but it would be required to apply the Convention with regard to States that were parties to it. The following example shows some of the practical difficulties that could result.

229 The chosen court is in a State that is a party to both the Convention and to the Lugano Convention (say, Switzerland). One party is resident in a Contracting State to the Convention that is not a party to the Lugano Convention (say, New Zealand). The other party is resident in a State that is a party to the Lugano Convention but not to the Convention (we shall call it "Ruritania"). One party brings proceedings in a court in Ruritania, which hears the proceedings, despite the choice of court agreement;[234] subsequently, the other party brings proceedings in the designated court in Switzerland. In this situation, the Swiss court would be forbidden to hear the case by Article 21 of the Lugano Convention,[235] but would be required to hear it by Article 5 of the Convention.[236]

---

[227] It has not yet been settled what happens if a party is resident *both* in a general Contracting State *and* in a special Contracting State or non-Contracting State.

[228] The text actually says that the parties must be resident either in a State in which the instrument is applicable (which might be either a special Contracting State or a non-Contracting State) or in a non-Contracting State. However, this is the same as saying that the parties must be resident in either a special Contracting State or in a non-Contracting State.

[229] If the chosen court is in a non-Contracting State in which the instrument applies, the Convention will not in any event be applicable: under Article 1(1) combined with Article 3 *a)*, the Convention applies only if the chosen court is in a Contracting State.

[230] This is on the assumption that the word "only" is accepted in Article 23(4). If it is not, the Convention will not apply if every party is resident in a State other than a general Contracting State (even if also resident in a general Contracting State).

[231] By "French party", "Dutch party", etc. is meant a party resident [only] in France, the Netherlands, etc.

[232] It involves a limitation of these instruments, since, according to their terms, their provisions on choice of court agreements apply (in general) whenever one of the parties is domiciled in an EC State. However, if all the States to which these instruments apply become Parties to the Convention, it would be normal for prior treaty obligations among themselves to be affected: a State cannot conclude a law-making convention and expect its law on the same matter to remain unaffected.

[233] It should be remembered that references to "the" Convention are always references to the Hague Convention.

[234] In many cases, this would be contrary to Article 17 of the Lugano Convention; nevertheless, it could happen. The Ruritanian court might mistakenly think the choice of court agreement was invalid or did not cover the case; it might even decide to ignore Article 17. There might also be cases (if the agreement was drawn up or evidenced by electronic means) where a choice of court agreement meets the form requirements of the Hague Convention but not those of the Lugano Convention. In this case, the Ruritanian court would be entitled under the Lugano Convention to disregard the choice of court agreement.

[235] The Ruritanian court would have been seised first. It would make no difference if the Ruritanian court had taken jurisdiction contrary to Article 17(1) of the Lugano Convention. The rule in Article 21 of the Lugano

230 Admittedly, conflicts between the Convention and the Lugano Convention would be relatively rare. This is because the Convention is fairly similar to the Lugano Convention, having been partly modelled on it. However, the possibility of conflicts could be greater with other conventions.

231 *One possible solution would be to add a new paragraph (paragraph 4* bis*) to Article 23. Such a paragraph might read as follows:*

**Variant 1**

4. Where a Contracting State is also a party to an international instrument which contains provisions on matters governed by this Convention, this Convention shall prevail in matters relating to jurisdiction except where -

a) the chosen court is situated in a State in which the instrument is applicable; and

b) all the parties are resident[ only] either in a State in which the instrument is applicable or in a non-Contracting State.

4 *bis*. Notwithstanding paragraph 4 of this Article, a State that is a party to both the Convention and to the instrument shall not be required to apply the Convention if the chosen court is situated, or a party is resident, in a State that is a party to the instrument but not to the Convention.

*Another solution would be:*

**Variant 2**

4. Where a Contracting State is also a party to an international instrument which contains provisions on matters governed by this Convention, this Convention shall prevail in matters relating to jurisdiction **if there is a relevant connection with a Contracting State in which the instrument is not applicable; provided that a State that is a party to both the Convention and to the instrument shall not be required to apply the Convention if there is a relevant connection with a State that is a party to the instrument but not to the Convention**.

**4 *bis*. In this Article, a relevant connection exists with a State if either the chosen court is situated, or a party is resident, in that State.**

*A simpler solution is that proposed in the footnote to Article 23(4).*[237] *If this were adopted, the result would be as follows:*

**Variant 3**

4. Where a Contracting State is also a party to an international instrument which contains provisions on matters governed by this Convention, this Convention shall prevail in matters relating to jurisdiction except where –

a) the chosen court is situated in a State in which the instrument is applicable; and

---

Convention would apply even if the Swiss court thought that the Ruritanian court had violated the Lugano Convention by hearing the case: *Gasser* v. *MISRAT*, Case C-116/02, judgment of 9 December 2003 (available at < www.curia.eu.int >) (Court of Justice of the European Communities). This case was on the equivalent provision in the Brussels Convention, but would almost certainly be applicable to Article 17 of the Lugano Convention as well.

[236] Under Article 23(4) of the Convention, the Convention would prevail over the Lugano Convention because one party would be resident in a "general" Contracting State (New Zealand).

[237] Footnote 17 to the text of the preliminary draft Convention.

**b) a party is resident in a non-Contracting State in which the instrument is applicable, or there is some other relevant connection between the parties or the dispute and such a State.**

232 Article 23(5) is concerned with the recognition and enforcement of judgments. It states that if the international instrument is in force both in the State of origin and in the requested State, it will not be affected by the Convention. There is a proviso to this – which is in square brackets to indicate that it has not yet been agreed – that a judgment must not be recognised or enforced to a lesser extent than it would be under the Convention. If this proviso were not accepted, however, the Convention would be seriously undermined, since it would be possible for two Contracting States to apply an instrument that would block enforcement of a judgment under the Convention (for example, if it conflicted with a prior judgment given in contravention of an exclusive choice of court agreement), even if the judgment-creditor was resident in a Contracting State that was not a party to the instrument.

233 Article 23(5) applies only to international instruments "in force" between the State of origin and the requested State. It is not clear, though, at what time these instruments have to be in force in order not to be affected by the Convention. Article 30 of the *Vienna Convention on the Law of Treaties*, which contains a default rule on the relationship between successive treaties relating to the same subject matter, looks at the moment of adoption of the respective treaties in order to determine which is the earlier and which the later treaty.[238] States are free, however, to agree on different rules. In Hague Conventions, with the exception of four conventions (including the *Convention of 14 March 1978 on Celebration and Recognition of the Validity of Marriages*), the standard language does not normally refer to "earlier" and "later" treaties or to treaties "in force", but to "conventions to which Contracting States are parties". The point of reference is the moment when the convention containing the clause enters into force for the State concerned. Only conventions to which the State concerned is already a party when the new convention containing the clause enters into force would remain unaffected by it (unless the clause refers to "conventions to which Contracting States are or may become parties").

234 Article 21(1) of the *Convention on Celebration and Recognition of the Validity of Marriages* uses the "in force" language and makes it explicit which is the relevant point in time. The provision reads: "The Convention shall not affect the application of any convention on the celebration or recognition of the validity of marriages to which a Contracting State is a Party at the time this Convention enters into force for that State."

235 A. Malmström, in his Explanatory Report[239] on this provision, writes: "The first paragraph of Article 21 lays down a rule which is generally followed in previous Hague Conventions, namely that the Convention shall not affect the application of any convention containing provisions in the same field to which a Contracting State is a party at the time this new Convention enters into force for that State."

236 *If this is what delegates intended, the language could be made more explicit by adopting a wording similar to Article 21 of the* Convention on Celebration and Recognition of the Validity of Marriages.

237 *The reference to "international instruments to which Contracting States are parties" in Article 23(2) and (4) may also require a similar clarification.*

238 Article 23(5) is based on the assumption that the recognition and enforcement of foreign judgments are always to be encouraged. In general this is true. However, there is an exception in the case of a judgment given in contravention of an exclusive choice of

[238] According to I. Sinclair, *The Vienna Convention on the Law of Treaties*, 2nd ed. 1984, p. 98; M. Zuleeg, "*Vertragskonkurrenz im Völkerrecht, Teil I: Verträge zwischen souveränen Staaten*", *German Yearbook of International Law* (GYIL) 20 (1977), p. 246 (256), it is the date of the adoption of the text and not that of its entry into force which is decisive.
[239] *Acts and Documents of the Thirteenth Session*, Tome III, *Marriage*, p. 312.

court agreement. *If Article 11 were to be adopted, the Conference would have to ensure that it was not undermined by Article 23(5).*[240] *This could be done by limiting Article 23(5) to judgments under an exclusive choice of court agreement.*

239 Article 23(6) is concerned with both past and future international instruments (instruments concluded or adopted before or after the Convention). It provides that the Convention does not affect the ability of a Contracting State to continue to apply, or to enter into, international instruments which govern jurisdiction and the recognition and enforcement of foreign judgments in relation to specific subject matters. It applies even if all the parties to the instrument are also parties to the Convention. It was intended to apply to matters similar to those excluded from the scope of the Convention under Article 2(2). Carriage of goods by road might be an example. There is no agreement so far, however, as to whether or not paragraph 6 should be subject to the rules in paragraphs 4 and 5. This disagreement is expressed by the square brackets at the beginning of the paragraph: if paragraph 6 were "subject to" paragraphs 4 and 5, those rules (and therefore in many cases the Convention) would prevail. If paragraph 6 could be applied "notwithstanding" paragraphs 4 and 5, an international instrument on specific subject matters would take precedence in every case. Since European Community legislation counts as an "international instrument", Article 23(6) would allow the European Community to opt out of the Convention in any area, if it wanted to lay down different provisions. Other parties to the Convention could not do this, however, without entering into an international agreement.

*Article 24 Signature, ratification, acceptance, approval or accession*

240 Article 24 is concerned with the ways in which a State may become a party to the Convention. Any State may become a party to it either by signature followed by ratification, acceptance or approval, or by accession. The relevant instruments are deposited with the Dutch Ministry of Foreign Affairs, the depositary of the Convention.

*Article 25 Non-unified legal system*[241]

241 Article 25 is concerned with States that consist of two or more territorial units. It permits such a State to declare that the Convention will extend only to some of its territorial units. Such a declaration may be modified at any time. This provision is particularly important for States in which the legislation necessary to give effect to the Convention would have to be passed by the legislatures of the units (for example, by provincial legislatures in Canada), though it could also be of use to other States. Thus, the United Kingdom could ratify for England only, and China for Hong Kong only.

*Article 26 Regional Economic Integration Organisations*

242 Article 26 is concerned with Regional Economic Integration Organisations. The European Community is an example of such an organisation. The purpose of Article 26 is to allow Regional Economic Integration Organisations to become parties to the Convention if they possess external competence over some or all of the matters covered by it. To the extent that it has such external competence, the Regional Economic Integration Organisation has the same rights and obligations as a Contracting State. Where this is the case, it must notify the depositary of the matters for which it has external competence, and of any changes in this regard.[242]

243 **Paragraphs 1–3**. Article 26 envisages two possible situations. The first is where both the Regional Economic Integration Organisation and its Member States become parties to the Convention. This might occur if they enjoy concurrent external competence

[240] See the comments in paragraphs 174 *et seq. supra.*

[241] *Since this title has already been used for Article 22, it might be better to choose another title.*

[242] Article 26(2).

over the subject matter of the Convention (joint competence), or if some matters fall within the external competence of the Regional Economic Integration Organisation and others within that of the Member States (which would result in shared or mixed competence for the Convention as a whole). In this situation, any instrument deposited by the Regional Economic Integration Organisation does not count in addition to those deposited by its Member States for the purpose of determining when the Convention enters into force.[243]

244 **Paragraph 4**. The second situation is where the Regional Economic Integration Organisation alone becomes a party. This will occur where it has exclusive external competence over the subject matter of the Convention. In such a case, the Member States would be bound by the Convention by virtue of the agreement of the Regional Economic Integration Organisation. The Regional Economic Integration Organisation may then declare that its Member States are bound by the Convention.[244] In such a case, a reference in the Convention to a Contracting State will include, where appropriate, a reference to the Member States of the Regional Economic Integration Organisation.

245 **Paragraph 5**. In any case in which a Regional Economic Integration Organisation is a party to the Convention, a reference to a Contracting State includes, where appropriate, a reference to the Regional Economic Integration Organisation (with all necessary modifications).[245] In particular, references to a Contracting State in Articles 1(2), 18 and 19 must be read as references to the Regional Economic Integration Organisation.

246 **Paragraph 6**. Article 26(6) provides that Article 9 does not apply to the recognition and enforcement of judgments in cases where the State of origin and the requested State are Member States of a Regional Economic Integration Organisation that is a party to the Convention and has made a declaration under Article 26(4). There is, however, a proviso to this provision that the judgment must not be recognised or enforced to a lesser extent than under the Convention. The proviso is in square brackets to indicate that it has not yet been agreed. If the proviso were not accepted, however, it would mean that a judgment given under the Convention in one Member State could not be enforced under the Convention in another. Indeed, it might not be enforced at all. For example, if a Japanese party agrees with an English party that a German court would have exclusive jurisdiction, a judgment given by the German court might not be enforceable in England,[246] though it would be enforceable in States outside the European Union. *Since Article 23(5) would apply to a Regional Economic Integration Organisation that was a party to the Convention and this covers all the ground covered by Article 26(6), the best solution would be to delete Article 26(6).*

*Article 27 Entry into force*

247 Article 27 specifies when the Convention will enter into force. This will be on the first day of the month following the expiration of three months after the deposit of the [third][247] instrument of ratification, acceptance, approval or accession. Further rules are laid down for when it comes into force for a given State, Regional Economic Integration Organisation or territorial unit.

---

[243] Article 26(3).

[244] Article 26(4). This would be the case, for example, under Article 300(7) of the EC Treaty.

[245] Article 26(5).

[246] This would occur if a court in another EC State had given a prior judgment that was irreconcilable with the German judgment: Article 34(4) of the Brussels Regulation. The fact that such a judgment was contrary to both the Convention (Article 7) and to the Brussels Regulation (Article 23) would make no difference: the Brussels Regulation contains no provision prohibiting the recognition (or even permitting the non-recognition) of judgments given in contravention of an exclusive choice of court agreement.

[247] The required number of instruments deposited remains to be discussed, in particular with regard to Regional Economic Integration Organisations and their Member States.

*Article 28 Reservations*

248 This Article has not yet been adopted.

*Article 29 Declarations*

249 This Article has not yet been adopted.

*Article 30 Denunciation*

250 Article 30 provides that a Contracting State may denounce the Convention by a notification in writing to the depositary. The denunciation may be limited to certain territorial units of a non-unified legal system to which the Convention applies. The denunciation takes effect on the first day of the month following the expiration of twelve months after the date on which the notification is received by the depositary. Where a longer period for the denunciation to take effect is specified in the notification, the denunciation shall take effect upon the expiration of such longer period after the date on which the notification is received by the depositary.

*Article 31 Notifications by the depositary*

251 Article 31 requires the depositary to notify the Members of the Hague Conference on Private International Law, and other States and Regional Economic Integration Organisations which have signed, ratified, accepted, approved or acceded to the Convention, of various matters relevant to the Convention, such as signatures, ratifications, entry into force, declarations and denunciations.

# ANNEX I

*The problem of flexibility*

Some delegates have suggested that an element of flexibility should be introduced into the Convention to allow States to deal with special problems. The purpose of this Annex I is to examine possible ways of doing this and to explore their consequences.

(a) **Validity: choice of law**. One suggestion was to delete the words "under the law of the State of the chosen court" in Article 7 *a)*.[1] A similar deletion would have to be made in Article 9(1)*(a)*. Contracting States would then apply their own law (possibly including their choice-of-law rules) to determine whether a choice of court agreement was valid. Since all the provisions of the Convention are dependent on the existence of a valid choice of court agreement, this would mean that the application of the Convention in a given State would be entirely dependent on the law of that State. A Contracting State could opt out of the Convention with regard to any matter by passing a law providing that choice of court agreements with regard to that matter were invalid. Thus, if it felt that the Convention should not apply to choice of court agreements concerning carriage of goods by road, it could pass a law saying that choice of court agreements were invalid in so far as they applied to carriage of goods by road.

Such a provision would make it possible to delete Article 20 (asbestos), since States wishing to exclude the application of the Convention to asbestos-related matters could adopt a law on the lines suggested above. Moreover, there are other States that wish to exclude the application of the Convention to other matters, such as natural resources and joint ventures.[2] They too could adopt legislation.

The proposal would also avoid the problem of Article 23(6). This provision could be deleted from the Convention, and the Contracting States in question could instead adopt legislation declaring choice of court agreements invalid with regard to the subject matter in question.

These features might make the proposal seem attractive. However, the proposal would have other consequences. Contracting States could also introduce (or retain) provisions making choice of court agreements valid only if reasonable.[3] They could even declare all choice of court agreements invalid if the chosen court was in a foreign State. Not only would this not constitute any advance on the present situation, it would even make things worse, since businessmen might be given a false sense of security.

Another feature of the proposal is that it could lead to an imbalance between the rights and obligations of different Contracting States. Let us take the example of two imaginary States that both become parties to the Convention. One, "Negatonia", retains or adopts legislation making all choice of court agreements in favour of foreign courts invalid. It will never apply Article 7 or Article 9. The other State, "Positonia", accepts choice of court agreements as valid except in the case of generally recognised grounds of invalidity such as fraud and duress. If the parties choose the courts of Positonia, the courts of Negatonia will nevertheless be entitled, consistently with the Convention, to hear the case: they will not be bound by Article 7, since the choice of court agreement will be invalid under their law. If a court in Positonia gives a judgment, Negatonia will not be obliged to recognise it: the choice of court agreement will be invalid under its law. On the other hand, if the

[1] See footnote 3 to Article 7.

[2] See footnote 15 to Article 20.

[3] If the validity of a choice of court agreement was dependent on the general law of contract (as distinct from special rules applicable only to choice of court agreements), concepts such as fairness, justice or unequal bargaining power might also become relevant. Admittedly, this might also be the case under the law of the chosen court, but this would presumably be known to the parties when they chose that court.

parties choose the courts of Negatonia, and one of the parties brings proceedings before a court in Positonia, the latter would be required by Article 7 to decline jurisdiction: it would be bound by Article 7, since, under its law, the choice of court agreement would be valid. Moreover, if a court in Negatonia gave judgment, that judgment would have to be recognised in Positonia. In other words, if the proposal were accepted, Negatonia could gain all the advantages of the Convention without undertaking any obligations at all.

(b) **Declarations**. Another possibility would be to adopt a provision in the Convention permitting any Contracting State to make a declaration that it will not apply the Convention to a specific subject matter. In many ways, this would have the same effect.

It would also make it possible to delete Article 20, since a Contracting State could make a declaration that it will not apply the Convention to asbestos-related matters. Other Contracting States could make declarations regarding natural resources and joint ventures. This proposal would also make Article 23(6) unnecessary.

On the other hand, a system of declarations would make it possible to introduce an element of transparency. The Convention could provide that declarations would have to be made to the depositary who could be required to notify the Permanent Bureau and the States that are parties to the Convention. If suitable publicity were given to such declarations (for example, on the Permanent Bureau's website), it would be clear which States would not respect choice of court clauses with regard to any particular matter. The Convention could also provide that declarations would not take effect for 90 days after they were received by the depositary, and that they would not apply to choice of court agreements concluded before they took effect.[4]

The Convention could also provide that a Contracting State that made a declaration with regard to a given matter would be treated as a non-Contracting State with regard to that matter. This would eliminate the problem of non-reciprocity that could apply under the first proposal. Then, if one State made a declaration that it would not apply the Convention with regard to asbestos-related matters, other States would not be obliged to recognise that State's judgments in such cases, nor would their courts be obliged to decline jurisdiction if there was a choice of court agreement in favour of the courts of that State with regard to the matter covered by the declaration. This would discourage States from making declarations without good reason.

Such a system would not, however, be without drawbacks. For example, the declaration might be carefully worded to give the State making it almost all the benefits of the Convention without incurring many burdens. Other Contracting States might then be at a disadvantage. For example, the State of Ruritania might make a declaration covering "all contracts concerning widgets where the chosen court is outside Ruritania". If such a declaration were permitted, Ruritania would be entitled to refuse to recognise foreign judgments concerning widgets, but could still expect other States to recognise *its* judgments. In such a case, it might be reasonable to allow other States to treat Ruritania as a non-Contracting State with regard to *all* contracts concerning widgets, even those where the chosen court was in Ruritania.

[4] This rule might not apply to declarations made when the State in question signs or ratifies the Convention.

(c) **Other possibilities**. Further suggestions are put forward in footnote 4 to Article 7 of the text of the preliminary draft Convention. This lists three possibilities. These are:

> i) giving effect to the agreement would lead to a very [**delete: very**] serious injustice or would [**otherwise**] be manifestly contrary to fundamental principles of public policy of the State of the court seised;
>
> ii) under the mandatory rules on jurisdiction of the State of the court seised, the parties were unable to agree to exclude the jurisdiction of the courts of this State;
>
> iii) giving effect to the agreement would be manifestly contrary to public policy of the State of the court seised.

The proposals listed under sub-paragraphs (i) and (iii) do little more than tinker with the existing provisions. The proposal under sub-paragraph (ii), on the other hand, is much broader. It would have some of the same consequences as the first proposal discussed in this Annex (deleting the words "under the law of the State of the chosen court"), since a State could pass legislation precluding the parties from choosing a foreign court in a wide range of situations. However, it would be narrower in some respects since it would not necessarily bring in general grounds such as fairness.

## ANNEX II [Omitted]

RECOMMENDED FORM

(Sample form confirming the issuance and content of a judgment by the Court of Origin for the purposes of recognition and enforcement under the Convention on Exclusive Choice of Court Agreements (the "Convention"))

(THE COURT OF ORIGIN) ................................................................

(ADDRESS OF THE COURT OF ORIGIN) ............................................

(CONTACT PERSON AT THE COURT OF ORIGIN) ................................

(TEL./FAX/EMAIL OF THE COURT OF ORIGIN) ...................................

CASE / DOCKET NUMBER: ............................................................

___________________________________(PLAINTIFF)

v.

___________________________________(DEFENDANT)

(THE COURT OF ORIGIN) hereby confirms that it rendered a judgment in the above captioned matter on (DATE) in (CITY, STATE), which is a Contracting State to the Convention. Attached to this form is a complete and certified copy of the judgment rendered by (THE COURT OF ORIGIN).

1. This Court based its jurisdiction on an exclusive choice of court agreement:

YES________ NO________

If so, the agreement was found in or evidenced by the following document(s):

2. This Court awarded the following payment of money *(Please indicate any relevant categories of damages included):*

3. This Court awarded interest as follows (*Please specify the rate of interest, the portion(s) of the award to which interest applies, and the date from which interest is computed*):

4. This Court included within the judgment the following court costs and expenses (including lawyers' fees) related to the proceedings *(Please specify the amounts of any such awards, including where applicable, any amount(s) within a monetary award intended to cover costs and expenses relating to the proceedings)*:

5. This Court awarded, in whole or in part, the following non-monetary remedy *(Please describe the nature of the remedy)*:

6. This judgment was rendered by default:

YES________ NO________

*(If this judgment was rendered by default, please attach the original or a certified copy of the document verifying notice to the defendant of the proceedings.)*

7. This judgment (or a part thereof) is currently the subject of review in (STATE OF THE COURT OF ORIGIN):

YES________ NO________

**8. This judgment (or a part thereof) is enforceable in (STATE OF THE COURT OF ORIGIN):**

YES________ NO________

*List of documents annexed:*

Dated this __________ day of ___________, 20__.

Signature and/or stamp by an officer of the Court

THE CONFLICT OF JURISDICTION MODEL ACT

*Sec. 1. Declaration of Public Policy.* It is an important public policy of this State to encourage the early determination of the adjudicating forum for transnational civil disputes, to discourage vexatious litigation and to enforce only those foreign judgments which were not obtained in connection with vexatious litigation, parallel proceedings or litigation in inconvenient forums.

*Sec. 2. Discretion to Enforce Judgments.*

a. In cases where two or more proceedings arising out of the same transaction or occurrence were pending, the courts of this State shall enforce the judgments of any of such courts only if application for designation of an adjudicating forum was timely made to the first known court of competent jurisdiction where such a proceeding was commenced, or to the adjudicating forum after its selection, or to any court of competent jurisdiction if the foregoing courts were not courts of competent jurisdiction.

b. An application for designation of an adjudicating forum is timely if made within six months of reasonable notice of two such proceedings, or of reasonable notice of the selection of an adjudicating forum.

c. The determination of the adjudicating forum is binding for the purpose of enforcement of judgments in this State upon any person served with notice of an application to designate. The courts of this State shall enforce the judgments of the designated adjudicating forum pursuant to the ordinary rules for enforcement of judgments. The selection of the adjudicating forum shall be accorded presumptive validity in this State if the written decision determining the adjudicating forum evaluated the substance of the factors set forth in the following section.

d. Where no conclusive determination has been made by another court as provided above, the proper adjudicating forum shall be determined in accordance with the following sections by the courts of this State requested to enforce the judgment.

*Sec. 3. Factors in Selection of Adjudicating Forum.*

A determination of the adjudicating forum shall be made in consideration of the following factors:

a. the interests of justice among the parties and of worldwide justice;

b. the public policies of the countries having jurisdiction of the dispute, including the interest of the affected courts in having proceedings take place in their respective forums;

c. the place of occurrence, and of any effects, of the transaction or occurrence, and of any effects, of the transaction or occurrence out of which the dispute arose;

d. the nationality of the parties;

e. substantive law likely to be applicable and the relative familiarity of the affected courts with that law;

f. the availability of a remedy and the forum most likely to render the most complete relief;

g. the impact of the litigation on the judicial systems of the courts involved, and the likelihood of prompt adjudication in the court selected;

h. location of witnesses and availability of compulsory process;

i. location of documents and other evidence and ease or difficulty associated with obtaining, reviewing or transporting such evidence;

j. place of first filing and connection of such place to the dispute;

k. the ability of the designated forum to obtain jurisdiction over the persona and property that are the subject of the proceeding;

l. whether designation of an adjudicating forum is a superior method to parallel proceedings in adjudicating the dispute;

m. the nature and extent of litigation that has proceeded over the dispute and whether a designation of an adjudicating forum will unduly delay or prejudice the adjudication of the rights of the original parties; and

n. a realigned plaintiff's choice of forum should rarely be disturbed.

*Sec. 4. Evidence.* The court may consider any evidence admissible in the adjudicating forum or other court of competent jurisdiction, including but not limited to:

a. affidavits or declarations;

b. treaties to which the state of either forum is a party;

c. principles of customary international law;

d. testimony of fact or expert witnesses;

e. diplomatic notes or amicus submissions from the state of the adjudicating forum or other court of competent jurisdiction; and

f. statements of public policy by the state of the adjudicating forum or other court of competent jurisdiction set forth in legislation, executive or administrative action, learned treatises, or participation in intergovernmental organizations.

Reasonable written notice shall be given by any party seeking to raise an issue concerning the law of a forum of competent jurisdiction other than the adjudicating forum. In deciding questions of the law of another forum, the court may consider any relevant material or source, including testimony, whether or not admissible.

Restat 2d of Conflict of Laws, § 92

§ 92 Requisites of a Valid Judgment

A judgment is valid if
(a) the state in which it is rendered has jurisdiction to act judicially in the case; and

(b) a reasonable method of notification is employed and a reasonable opportunity to be heard is afforded to persons affected; and

(c) the judgment is rendered by a competent court; and

(d) there is compliance with such requirements of the state of rendition as are necessary for the valid exercise of power by the court.

Topic 2 - Recognition of Foreign Judgments

Introductory Note: This Topic is concerned with the "recognition" of foreign judgments while Topic 3 deals with the "enforcement" of such judgments. A foreign judgment is recognized, as the term is used in the Restatement of this Subject, when it is given the same effect that it has in the state where it was rendered with respect to the parties, the subject matter of the action and the issues involved. A foreign judgment is enforced when, in addition to being recognized, a party is given the affirmative relief to which the judgment entitles him. Recognition of a judgment is a condition precedent to its enforcement. Some foreign judgments cannot be enforced and can only be recognized. This is true of declaratory judgments and of judgments which give no affirmative relief, such as when the plaintiff's complaint is dismissed and judgment is rendered for the defendant. This is also true of judgments which determine the parties' interests in a thing or a status, such as a judgment clearing title to land or providing for an adoption or a divorce.

The effectiveness of various defense to the recognition or enforcement of a foreign judgment is discussed in Topic 4.

Restat 2d of Conflict of Laws, § 93

§ 93 Recognition of Sister State and Federal Court Judgments

A valid judgment rendered in one State of the United States must be recognized in a sister State, except as stated in §§ 103-121.

Topic 2 - Recognition of Foreign Judgments

Restat 2d of Conflict of Laws, § 94

§ 94 Persons Affected
What persons are bound by a valid State judgment is determined, subject to constitutional limitations, by the local law of the State where the judgment was rendered.

Restat 2d of Conflict of Laws, § 95

§ 95 Issues Affected

What issues are determined by a valid State judgment is determined, subject to constitutional limitations, by the local law of the State where the judgment was rendered.

Restat 2d of Conflict of Laws, § 96

§ 96 Res Judicata as to Jurisdiction Over the Person

When a defendant appears in an action to object that the court has no jurisdiction over him and the court overrules the objection and renders judgment against him, the local law of the State where the judgment was rendered determines, subject to constitutional limitations, whether the parties are precluded from attacking the judgment collaterally on the ground that the court had no jurisdiction over the defendant.

Restat 2d of Conflict of Laws, § 97

§ 97 Res Judicata as to Jurisdiction Over Thing or Status or as to Competence Over Subject Matter

When a court has jurisdiction over the parties, the local law of the State where the judgment was rendered determines, subject to constitutional limitations, whether the parties are precluded from collaterally attacking the judgment on the ground that the court had no jurisdiction over the thing or status involved or lacked competence over the subject matter of the controversy.

Restat 2d of Conflict of Laws, § 98

§ 98 Recognition of Foreign Nation Judgments

A valid judgment rendered in a foreign nation aftera fair trial in a contested proceeding will be recognized in the United States so far as the immediate parties and the underlying claim are concerned.

Restat 2d of Conflict of Laws, § 99

§ 99 Methods of Enforcement

The local law of the forum determines the methods by which a judgment of another state is enforced.

Restat 2d of Conflict of Laws, § 100

§ 100 Enforcement of Money Judgments

A valid judgment for the payment of money rendered in a State of the United States will be enforced in a sister State, except as stated in §§ 103-121.

Restat 2d of Conflict of Laws, § 101

§ 101 Amount for Which Judgment May Be Enforced

A valid judgment for the payment of money will be enforced in other states only in the amount for which it is enforceable in the state where it was rendered.

Restat 2d of Conflict of Laws, § 102

§ 102 Enforcement of Judgment Ordering or Enjoining Act

A valid judgment that orders the doing of an act other than the payment of money, or that enjoins the doing of an act, may be enforced, or be the subject of remedies, in other states.

Restat 2d of Conflict of Laws, § 103

§ 103 Limitations on Full Faith and Credit

A judgment rendered in one State of the United States need not be recognized or enforced in a sister State if such recognition or enforcement is not required by the national policy of full faith and credit because it would involve an improper interference with important interests of the sister State.

Restat 2d of Conflict of Laws, § 104

§ 104 Judgment Rendered Without Judicial Jurisdiction or Without Adequate Notice or Opportunity to Be Heard

A judgment rendered without judicial jurisdiction or without adequate notice or adequate opportunity to be heard will not be recognized or enforced in other states.

Restat 2d of Conflict of Laws, § 105

§ 105 Judgment Rendered by Court Lacking Competence

A judgment rendered by a court lacking competence to render it and for that reason subject to collateral attack in the state of rendition will not be recognized or enforced in other states.

Restat 2d of Conflict of Laws, § 106

§ 106 Erroneous Judgment

A judgment will be recognized and enforced in other states even though an error of fact or of law was made in the proceedings before judgment, except as stated in § 105.

§ 481 Recognition and Enforcement of Foreign Judgments

**(1) Except as provided in § 482, a final judgment of a court of a foreign state granting or denying recovery of a sum of money, establishing or confirming the status of a person, or determining interests in property, is conclusive between the parties, and is entitled to recognition in courts in the United States.**

**(2) A judgment entitled to recognition under Subsection (1) may be enforced by any party or its successors or assigns against any other party, its successors or assigns, in accordance with the procedure for enforcement of judgments applicable where enforcement is sought.**

§ 482 Grounds for Nonrecognition of Foreign Judgments

**(1) A court in the United States may not recognize a judgment of the court of a foreign state if:**
**(a) the judgment was rendered under a judicial system that does not provide impartial tribunals or procedures compatible with due process of law; or**

**(b) the court that rendered the judgment did not have jurisdiction over the defendant in accordance with the law of the rendering state and with the rules set forth in § 421.**

**(2) A court in the United States need not recognize a judgment of the court of a foreign state if:**
**(a) the court that rendered the judgment did not have jurisdiction of the subject matter of the action;**

**(b) the defendant did not receive notice of the proceedings in sufficient time to enable him to defend;**

**(c) the judgment was obtained by fraud;**

**(d) the cause of action on which the judgment was based, or the judgment itself, is repugnant to the public policy of the United States or of the State where recognition is sought;**

**(e) the judgment conflicts with another final judgment that is entitled to recognition; or**

**(f) the proceeding in the foreign court was contrary to an agreement between the parties to submit the controversy on which the judgment is based to another forum.**

§ 483 Recognition and Enforcement of Tax and Penal Judgments

**Courts in the United States are not required to recognize or to enforce judgments for the collection of taxes, fines, or penalties rendered by the courts of other states.**

§ 484 Recognition of Foreign Divorce Decrees

**(1) Courts in the United States will recognize a divorce granted in the state in which both parties to the marriage had their domicile or their habitual residence at the time of divorce, and valid and effective under the law of that state.**

**(2) Courts in the United States may, but need not, recognize a divorce, valid and effective under the law of the state where it was granted,**
**(a) if that state was, at the time of divorce, the state of domicile or habitual residence of one party to the marriage; or**

**(b) if the divorce was granted by a court having jurisdiction over both parties, and if at least one party appeared in person and the other party had notice of and opportunity to participate in the proceeding.**

**(3) A court that would not recognize a divorce that is within Subsection 2(a) or 2(b) may nevertheless recognize such a divorce if it would be recognized by the state where the parties were domiciled or had their habitual residence at the time of the divorce.**

§ 485 Recognition and Enforcement of Foreign Child Custody Orders

**(1) A court in the United States will recognize an order of a foreign court awarding or modifying an award of custody of a child, valid and effective in the state where it was issued, if, when the proceeding was commenced,**
**(a) the issuing state was the habitual residence of the child;**

**(b) the child and at least one party to the custody proceeding had a significant connection with that state; or**

**(c) the child was present in that state and emergency conditions required a custody order for protection of the child; provided that notice of the proceeding was given to each parent and to any other person having**

**physical custody of the child.**

**(2) Ordinarily, a court in the United States may modify a custody order entitled to recognition under this section only if the rendering court no longer has jurisdiction to modify the order, or has declined to exercise its jurisdiction to modify it.**

§ 486 Recognition and Enforcement of Foreign Support Orders

**(1) A court in the United States will recognize and enforce an order of a foreign court for support, valid and effective under the law of the state where it was issued, if the issuing state**
**(a) was the domicile or habitual residence of both parties to the marriage when the obligation for support accrued;**
**(b) was the domicile or habitual residence of the support debtor at the time the order was issued; or**
**(c) was the domicile or habitual residence of the support creditor, and the support debtor appeared in the proceedings.**

**(2) A court in the United States may modify a support order entitled to recognition under Subsection (1), at the initiative of either party, if the court has jurisdiction over the other party in accordance with § 421(2)(b), (c), or (g).**

§ 487 Recognition and Enforcement of Foreign Arbitral Agreements and Awards

**Under the Convention on the Recognition and Enforcement of Foreign Arbitral Awards, and subject only to the defenses set forth in § 488,**

**(1) a court in a state party to the Convention must recognize and enforce an arbitral award, rendered in a state party to the Convention pursuant to a valid written agreement to arbitrate, at least if the legal relationship that gave rise to the controversy was commercial in character;**

**(2) a court in a state party to the Convention must, at the request of any party to an action, stay or dismiss the action pending arbitration if an agreement to arbitrate falling under the Convention is in effect and covers the controversy on which the action is based.**

§ 488 Grounds for Nonrecognition of Foreign Arbitral Awards

**Under the Convention on the Recognition and Enforcement of Foreign Arbitral Awards,**

**(1) a court in a state party to the Convention may deny recognition or enforcement to a foreign arbitral award if**
**(a) the agreement to arbitrate was not valid under the applicable law;**

**(b) the party against which the award was rendered did not receive proper notice of the proceedings or was otherwise not afforded an opportunity to present its case;**

**(c) the award deals with matters outside the terms of the agreement to arbitrate;**

**(d) the constitution of the arbitral tribunal or the arbitral procedure was contrary to the agreement of the parties or to the law of the state where the arbitration took place; or**

**(e) the award has not yet become binding on the parties, or has been suspended or set aside by a competent court in the state where it was made.**

**(2) A court of a state party to the Convention may also deny recognition or enforcement to a foreign arbitral award that meets the requirements of § 487 if, under the law of that state,**
**(a) the subject matter of the controversy is not capable of settlement by arbitration; or**

**(b) recognition or enforcement of the award would be contrary to public policy.**

# The Foreign Judgments Recognition and Enforcement Act (without commentary)

## § 1. Scope and Definitions

(a) This Act applies to foreign judgments as herein defined other than:

(i) judgments for divorce, support, maintenance, custody, adoption, or other judgments rendered in connection with matters of domestic relations;

(ii) judgments of bankruptcy, liquidation, or similar proceedings; and

(iii) foreign arbitral awards or court orders in respect of agreements to arbitrate, except that if they are to be recognized or enforced, judgments of foreign courts confirming or setting aside foreign arbitral awards are subject to the criteria for recognition and enforcement set out in the Act.

(b) "Foreign judgment" means any final judgment or final order of the court of a foreign state granting or denying a sum of money, or determining a legal controversy. A judgment or order is final for purposes of the Act if it is enforceable in the state of origin, even though an appeal therefrom is pending or the judgment or order is subject to appeal.

(c) "Foreign state" or "foreign country" means any governmental unit outside the United States or outside any territory under control of the United States.

**§ 2. Recognition and Enforcement Generally**

(a) Except as provided in subsection (b), a foreign judgment shall be recognized and enforced by courts in the United States in accordance with this Act.

(b) (i) Judgments for taxes, fines, and penalties may, but need not, be recognized and enforced provided they meet the criteria of this Act.

(ii) Declaratory judgments and injunctions or comparable orders are not directly enforceable, but may be entitled to recognition provided they meet the criteria of this Act.

(c) An action or other proceeding to enforce a judgment shall be brought within [10] [15] years from the time the judgment becomes enforceable in the rendering state, or in the event of an appeal, from the time when the judgment is no longer subject to ordinary forms of review in the state of origin.

**§ 3. Effect of Foreign Judgment in the United States**

(a) A foreign judgment that meets the standards set out in this Act is entitled to recognition and enforcement by a court in the United States with respect to the liability or nonliability of the defendant, and with respect to the damages or other relief, whether monetary or non-monetary, as well as interest and costs, if any, awarded to the prevailing party. If the foreign judgment orders payment in a foreign currency, a court in the United States may order payment in that currency or in United States dollars at the exchange rate prevailing on the date of the judgment granting enforcement.

(b) A foreign judgment rendered in default of appearance of the defendant is entitled to recognition and enforcement, provided that the party seeking recognition satisfies the court in the United States that (i) the rendering court had jurisdiction over the defendant in accordance with the law of the state where the judgment was issued, and (ii) the rendering court had jurisdiction on a basis not unacceptable under § 6 of this Act, and (iii) that the defendant was duly served in the proceeding in the state of origin. The party resisting recognition or enforcement may raise the defenses set out in §§ 5 and 7, but may not raise defenses going to the merits of the controversy.

(c) A judgment of dismissal rendered by a foreign court, if otherwise entitled to recognition, shall be treated in the same way as a judgment for the defendant, except

(i) if the ground for dismissal was lack of jurisdiction of the rendering court;

(ii) if the ground for dismissal was that the action was time-barred, unless the party seeking to rely on the judgment of dismissal establishes that the claim is extinguished under the law applied to the claim by the rendering court;

(iii) if the dismissal was based on other grounds not regarded by courts in the United States as constituting dismissal with prejudice, including defective service, failure to pay the required filing fees, failure to post security, failure to join required parties, or similar defects.

### § 4. Claim and Issue Preclusion; Effect of Challenge to Jurisdiction in the Court of Origin

(a) Except as provided in § 3, a foreign judgment shall be given the same preclusive effect by a court in the United States that the judgment would be accorded in the state of origin, unless the rule of preclusion applicable in the state of origin would be manifestly incompatible with a superior interest in the United States in adjudicating or not adjudicating the claim or issue in question. The party seeking to rely on the preclusive effect of a foreign judgment shall have the burden to establish that the claim or issue is precluded.

(b) If an issue was raised and contested in the foreign court concerning the judicial jurisdiction of that court,

(i) findings of fact pertinent to the determination of jurisdiction are conclusive;

(ii) legal determinations are conclusive as to the jurisdiction of the rendering court under its own law, but the party resisting recognition or enforcement may show that such jurisdiction is unacceptable under § 6.

### § 5. Nonrecognition of a Foreign Judgment

(a) A foreign judgment shall not be recognized or enforced in a court in the United States if the person resisting recognition or enforcement establishes that:

(i) the judgment was rendered under a system that does not provide impartial tribunals or procedures compatible with fundamental principles of fairness;

(ii) the judgment was rendered in circumstances that raise substantial and justifiable doubt about the integrity of the rendering court with respect to the judgment in question;

(iii) the judgment was rendered on a basis of jurisdiction over the defendant unacceptable under § 6;

(iv) the judgment was rendered without notice reasonably calculated to inform the defendant of the pendency of the proceeding in a timely manner.

(v) the proceeding in the foreign court was undertaken contrary to an agreement between the parties under which the dispute giving rise to the judgment was to be determined in a forum (whether court or arbitration) other than the rendering court, unless the defendant submitted to the jurisdiction of the rendering court without raising the defense of the forum-selection agreement;

(vi) the judgment was obtained by fraud that had the effect of depriving the defendant of adequate opportunity to present its case to the court; or

(vii) the judgment or the claim on which the judgment is based is repugnant to the public policy of the United States, or to the public policy of a particular state of the United States where the relevant legal interest, right, or policy is regulated by state law.

(b) A foreign judgment need not be recognized or enforced in a court in the United States if the person resisting recognition or enforcement establishes that:

(i) the state of origin of the court that issued the foreign judgment did not have jurisdiction to prescribe or jurisdiction to adjudicate with respect to the subject matter of the controversy;

(ii) the judgment is irreconcilable with another judgment rendered between the same parties in the United States or with a judgment rendered in a foreign state that is entitled to recognition or enforcement under the Act;

(iii) the judgment results from a proceeding initiated after commencement in a court in the United States of a proceeding including the same parties and the same subject matter, and the proceeding in the United States was not stayed or dismissed; or

(iv) the judgment results from a proceeding undertaken with a view to frustrating a claimant's opportunity to have the claim adjudicated in a more appropriate court in the United States, whether by an anti-suit injunction or restraining order, by a declaration of nonliability, or by other means.

(c) The party resisting recognition or enforcement shall have the burden of proof with respect to the defenses set out in subsections (a) and (b), except that if a defense is raised pursuant to subsection (a)(v) that the judgment was rendered in contravention of a forum-selection clause, the party seeking recognition or enforcement shall have the burden of establishing the invalidity of the clause.

## § 6. Bases of Jurisdiction Not Recognized or Enforced

(a) A foreign judgment rendered on any of the following bases of jurisdiction shall not be recognized or enforced in the United States:

(i) except in admiralty and maritime actions, the presence or seizure of property belonging to the defendant in the forum state, when the claim does not involve a direct right to the property;

(ii) the nationality of the plaintiff;

(iii) the domicile, habitual residence, or place of incorporation of the plaintiff;

(iv) service of process based solely on the transitory presence of the defendant in the forum state, unless

(*a*) the defendant was a fugitive at the time of service; or

(*b*) the claim on which the judgment was given was based on gross violation of human rights under international law and the defendant could not have been sued on such a claim in a forum more closely linked to the events on which the claim is based.

(v) any other basis that is unreasonable or unfair given the nature of the claim and the identity of the parties. A basis of jurisdiction is not unreasonable or unfair solely because it is not an acceptable basis of jurisdiction for courts in the United States.

(b) A foreign judgment based on an assertion of an unacceptable basis of jurisdiction as defined in subsection (a) shall not be denied recognition or enforcement if the factual circumstances would clearly support jurisdiction not inconsistent with subsection (a).

(c) An appearance by the defendant in the state of origin, or an unsuccessful objection to the jurisdiction of the rendering court, does not deprive the defendant of the right to resist recognition or enforcement under this section, but factual determinations by the rendering court concerning jurisdiction are binding on the defendant.

### § 7. Reciprocal Recognition and Enforcement of Foreign Judgments

(a) A foreign judgment shall not be recognized or enforced in a court in the United States if the court finds that comparable judgments of courts in the United States would not be recognized or enforced in the courts of the state of origin.

(b) A judgment debtor or other person resisting recognition or enforcement of a foreign judgment in accordance with this section shall raise the defense of lack of reciprocity with specificity as an affirmative defense. Once the defense of lack of reciprocity is raised, [the judgment creditor or other person seeking to rely on the foreign judgment shall have the burden to show that the courts of the state of origin would grant recognition and enforcement to comparable judgments of courts in the United States.] [the party resisting recognition or enforcement shall have the burden to show that there is substantial doubt that the courts of the state of origin would grant recognition or enforcement to comparable judgments of courts in the United States.] Such showing may be made through expert testimony, or by judicial notice if the law of the state of origin or decisions of its courts are clear.

(c) In making the determination required under subsections (a) and (b), the court shall, as appropriate, inquire whether the courts of the state of origin deny enforcement to

(i) judgments against nationals of that state in favor of nationals of another state;

(ii) judgments originating in the courts of the United States or of a state of the United States;

(iii) judgments for compensatory damages rendered in actions for personal injury or death;

(iv) judgments for statutory claims;

(v) particular types of judgments rendered by courts in the United States similar to the foreign judgment for which recognition or enforcement is sought;

(vi) recognition practice of the state of origin with regard to judgments of other states.

(d) Denial by courts of the state of origin of enforcement of judgments for punitive, exemplary, or multiple damages shall not be regarded as denial of reciprocal enforcement of judgments for the purposes of this section if the courts of the state of origin would enforce the compensatory portion of such judgments.

(e) The Secretary of State is authorized to negotiate agreements with foreign states or groups of states setting forth reciprocal practices concerning recognition and enforcement of judgments rendered in the United States. The existence of such an agreement between a foreign state or group of foreign states and the United States establishes that the requirement of reciprocity has been met as to judgments within the agreement. The fact that no such agreement between the state of origin and the United States is in effect, or that the agreement is not applicable with respect to the judgment for which recognition or enforcement is sought, does not of itself establish that the state fails to meet the reciprocity requirement of this section.

(f) A party seeking to raise a defense under this section may, in appropriate cases, be required to give security.

**§ 8. Jurisdiction of Courts in the United States**

(a) The district courts of the United States shall have original jurisdiction, concurrently with the courts of the states, of an action brought to enforce a foreign judgment or to secure a declaration with respect to recognition under this Act, without regard to the citizenship or residence of the parties or the amount in controversy.

(b) Any such action brought in a state court may be removed by any defendant against whom the enforcement or declaration is sought to the United States District Court for the district and division embracing the place where the action is pending, without regard to the citizenship or residence of the parties or the amount in controversy. A notice of removal shall be filed in accordance with the time limits and procedures of 28 U.S.C. § 1446(b).

The district court may, in its discretion, remand any claim to which the foreign judgment does not apply. In exercising its discretion, the district court shall consider whether the claims involving the foreign judgment are so closely related to the other claims that it would be efficient to hear the entire action.

(c) Any action brought in a state court in which a foreign judgment asserted to be entitled to recognition under the Act is raised as a partial or complete defense, set-off, counterclaim, or otherwise, may be removed to the United States District Court for the district and division embracing the place where the action is pending, without regard to the citizenship or residence of the parties or the amount in controversy. Any party by or against whom such defense, set-off, counterclaim or other claim is asserted is entitled to remove the action. A notice of removal shall be filed by such party within 30 days after the close of pleadings.

(d) (i) When an action has been removed pursuant to subsection (c), the district court may, prior to determining whether the foreign judgment is entitled to recognition, decide to retain the entire action or, in its discretion, remand to the state court from which the action was removed, any claim with respect to which the defense of a foreign judgment is not invoked. In exercising the discretion to remand pursuant to this subsection, the district court shall consider whether claims involving the foreign-judgment defense are so closely related to other claims to which the foreign-judgment defense does not apply that it would be efficient to retain the entire action.

(ii) After making a determination as to whether the foreign judgment is entitled to recognition, the district court may decide to retain the action, or, in its discretion, remand all or part of the action to the state court from which the action was removed. In exercising the discretion to remand pursuant to this subsection, the district court shall consider the impact of the determination of the issue of recognition on the remaining claims and issues in the case, the interest of the parties, and judicial efficiency.

(iii) A remand pursuant to subsections (d)(i) and (d)(ii) shall not be subject to review by appeal or otherwise; however, in a case remanded under subsection (d)(ii), the determination by the district court on the issue of recognition of the foreign judgment under this Act shall be subject to immediate appellate review as a final order.

## § 9. Means of Enforcement of Foreign Judgments

(a) (i) Any foreign judgment entitled to recognition and enforcement under this Act may be enforced by means of a civil action, as provided in this section.

(ii) A foreign judgment for a sum of money only, entitled to enforcement under this Act, other than a judgment rendered by default or a judgment subject to appeal, may also be enforced by registration, as provided in § 10.

(b) An action to recognize or enforce a judgment under this Act may be brought in the appropriate state or federal court

(i) where the judgment debtor is subject to personal jurisdiction; or

(ii) where assets belonging to the judgment debtor are situated.

(c) Process in such actions may be served upon the judgment debtor in accordance with applicable state or federal law, including treaties to which the United States is a party.

(d) (i) When a judgment creditor brings more than one action to enforce a foreign judgment in the United States and the judgment debtor raises defenses under the Act, at least one such action shall be brought in the state or federal court for the place where the judgment debtor is domiciled or has its principal establishment in the United States, or where the judgment debtor's principal assets in the United States are situated.

(ii) If pursuant to paragraph (i) the judgment creditor brings an action where the judgment debtor is domiciled or has its principal establishment, that action shall be the "main enforcement action." If the judgment creditor has not brought an action in such place or there is no such place, the action brought at the place of the judgment debtor's principal assets in the United States shall be the "main enforcement action," and the court at such place shall be the "main enforcement court."

(iii) A judgment creditor bringing more than one action pursuant to this section shall inform each court in the United States where such action is brought of all other proceedings relating to the same judgment of which it has knowledge, and shall supplement such information as appropriate.

(iv) All issues concerning the recognition of a foreign judgment under the Act shall be decided by the main enforcement court, and proceedings relating to the issue of recognition shall be stayed in all other courts in the United States where an action to enforce the judgment may be pending. The decision on recognition shall be binding on all such courts or any other court in the United States where enforcement may thereafter be sought.

(e) The court may, in appropriate circumstances, require the person resisting enforcement to post security.

14

## § 10. Registration of Foreign Money Judgments in Federal Courts

(a) Except as provided hereafter, a foreign judgment [issued by the court of a state that has entered into an agreement with the United States for reciprocal recognition of judgments in accordance with § 7(e) of this Act] may be registered in accordance with this section in any United States court for a district in which the debtor has property. A judgment so registered shall have the same effect as a judgment of a United States court, and may be enforced in like manner, subject, however, to the defenses to enforcement of foreign judgments provided for in this Act. This section authorizes registration only of judgments for a sum of money, and does not authorize registration of judgments rendered by confession or default of appearance or upon failure to defend on the merits, or of judgment subject to appeal. [A judgment not eligible for registration under this section may not be registered in a state court.]

(b) A judgment creditor seeking to register a foreign judgment shall file with the clerk of the registering court (i) a certified copy of the judgment, together with a certified translation into English where necessary; [(ii) a statement setting forth the agreement between the state of origin of the judgment and the United States in accordance with § 7(e)]; and (iii) an affidavit pursuant to subsection (c).

An application for registration under this section does not expose the judgment creditor to jurisdiction of the registering court.

(c) The affidavit called for in subsection (b) shall set forth (i) grounds for the belief that the judgment debtor has property in the district where the federal court is located; (ii) that the judgment was not rendered in default of appearance or because of failure to defend on the merits; (iii) that all appeals from the judgment have been exhausted or the time for appeal has expired; (iv) that the judgment has not been satisfied; (v) that the judgment debtor has insufficient assets in the state of origin of the judgment to satisfy the judgment, or that the judgment debtor has taken steps to conceal assets in the state of origin. The affidavit shall also identify any other court in the United States in which registration or enforcement has been sought. The judgment creditor is under a duty to supplement or correct the affidavit in order to keep the required information current.

(d) Upon receipt of the application for registration and supporting documents, the clerk of the court shall register the foreign judgment on the judgment docket in the same manner as a judgment of the court in which it is registered. A judgment so registered shall have the same effect as a judgment of the registering court, including creation of a lien in accordance with state law.

(e) The clerk of the registering court shall promptly notify the judgment debtor of the registration of the judgment.

If the judgment debtor has a registered agent in the United States, notice of the registration shall be given to such agent; if the judgment debtor is a corporation with a branch office or other establishment in the United States, notice shall be given to a managing agent or other responsible person at any such branch or establishment; in other cases, notice shall be given at the last known address or addresses of the judgment debtor, as well as at other addresses of the debtor over the preceding five years known to the creditor, in the United States and elsewhere. The judgment creditor, upon certification under oath, shall furnish to the clerk a list of the addresses required by this section, and shall advance the costs of the notice.

The notice shall advise the judgment debtor that a writ of execution may be issued 60 days from the date of registration, unless within that time the judgment debtor files with the clerk a motion addressed to the court to vacate the judgment or the registration.

(f) A motion to vacate the registration shall be filed within 60 days from the date of registration, with a copy to the judgment creditor. Unless the court orders otherwise, any lien or other security entered pursuant to subsection (d) shall remain in effect, but may not be enforced before the motion to vacate is decided. Notice that a motion to vacate the registration has been filed shall be given by the clerk of the district court where the motion is pending to all other courts in the United States in which registration or enforcement has been sought, and no execution shall issue in any court while the motion to vacate is pending. The court may, in appropriate cases, require security to be furnished by the person seeking enforcement.

A motion to vacate does not have the effect of subjecting the judgment debtor to personal jurisdiction of the registering court.

(g) When a motion to vacate registration under this section raises a genuine issue with respect to recognition of the foreign judgment under the Act, the court shall vacate the registration and treat the matter as if it had been brought under § 9. In such case, the court may, if appropriate, continue any lien that may be in effect or may order the judgment debtor to give security under such conditions as may be necessary.

(h) In the case of multiple registrations under this Act, each federal court to which a motion to vacate is addressed shall decide issues focused on the property alleged to be situated within the district; for issues concerning recognition under the Act, the proceeding called for by subsection (g) shall be held in the court for the district where the judgment debtor is domiciled or has its principal establishment in the United States if the judgment debtor has property in that district and an application for registration has been filed there. If these conditions are not met, the proceeding called for by subsection (g) shall be held in the registering court where the greatest value of the judgment debtor's assets is situated. If the judgment creditor brings both an action under § 9 and applies for registration under this section, the proceeding called for by subsection (g) shall be held in the main enforcement court defined in § 9.

(i) Registrations entered pursuant to subsection (d) shall remain in effect pending decision on the motion to vacate, but no writ of execution may be issued while the motion is pending, and no other court shall hear or determine the issue of recognition. If the motion to vacate is granted, all courts before which registration or enforcement has been sought shall be notified, and all liens entered pursuant to subsection (d) shall be discharged, unless the ruling is appealed and a stay is issued, subject in appropriate cases to security furnished by the person seeking enforcement.

**§ 11. Declination of Jurisdiction When Prior Action Is Pending**

(a) Except as provided in subsection (b), when an action is brought in a court in the United States and it is shown that a proceeding including the same parties and the same subject matter has previously been brought and is pending in the courts of a foreign country, the court in the United States shall stay, or when appropriate, dismiss the action, if:

(i) the foreign court has jurisdiction on a basis not unacceptable under § 6; and

(ii) the foreign court is likely to render a timely judgment entitled to recognition under this Act.

(b) A court in the United States may decline to stay or dismiss the action under subsection (a) if the party bringing the action shows

(i) that the jurisdiction of the foreign court was invoked with a view to frustrating the exercise of jurisdiction of the court in the United

States, when that court would be the more appropriate forum;

(ii) that the proceedings in the first court are vexatious or frivolous; or

(iii) that there are other persuasive reasons for accepting the costs of parallel litigation.

**§ 12. Provisional Measures in Aid of Foreign Proceedings**

(a) A court in the United States may grant provisional relief in support of an order, whether or not it is final, issued by a foreign court

(i) to secure enforcement of a judgment entitled to recognition and enforcement under this Act; or

(ii) to provide security or disclosure of assets in connection with proceedings likely to result in a judgment entitled to recognition and enforcement under this Act.

(b) In granting provisional relief in accordance with this section,

(i) the court is authorized to make use of such remedies and procedures as are available to it in connection with ordinary proceedings in courts in the United States;

(ii) a federal court may grant an injunction freezing assets of the defendant situated anywhere in the United States.

(c) Notice of an order issued pursuant to this section shall be given to the defendant in the foreign action, whether or not the defendant is found in the United States or in the jurisdiction of the court issuing the order. Notice of an order issued pursuant to subsection (b)(i) shall be in accordance with the applicable state statute or rule; notice of an order issued pursuant to subsection (b)(ii) shall be in accordance with Rule 65 of the Federal Rules of Civil Procedure.

No order pursuant to this section shall be made unless it provides an opportunity for the defendant within a reasonable time to contest the issuance of the order or to apply for a modification.

(d) The applicant for provisional relief in accordance with this section may be required to give security.

(e) A court in the United States to which application has been made in accordance with this section for provisional relief in aid of an order of a foreign court may, in the interests of justice, communicate directly with the foreign court.

### § 13. Foreign Orders Concerning Litigation in the United States

Orders of a foreign court that may concern or affect litigation in the United States shall not be directly enforced by courts in the United States, but may be taken into account for purposes of determining motions to stay, dismiss, or otherwise regulate related proceedings in the United States.

## SUGGESTED FORMS

The following are suggested forms to be used in proceedings involving the recognition and enforcement of foreign country judgments. These forms are modified versions of American Jurisprudence Pleading and Practice Forms found in the 2004 annotated edition. The forms are:

a. For states requiring that an action be brought in order to enforce a foreign judgment:

  i. Suggested Form 1: Complaint, Petition or Declaration – Enforcement of a Foreign Judgment
  ii. Suggested Form 2a: Answer/Defense to Application for Filing Foreign Judgment – Generic
  iii. Suggested Form 2b: Answer/Defense to Application for Filing of Foreign Judgment – Extrinsic Fraud in Procuring the Foreign Judgment

b. For states requiring that a foreign judgment be registered in order to be enforceable:

  i. Suggested Form 3: Petition or Application for Registration ofa Foreign Judgment
  ii. Suggested Form 4a: Answer/Defense to Application for Filing of Foreign Judgment – Foreign Court Acted in Excess of Its Jurisdiction
  iii. Suggested Form 4b: Answer/Defense to Application for Filing of Foreign Judgment – Extrinsic Fraud in Procuring the Foreign Judgment

**Suggested Form 1:**
**Complaint, Petition or Declaration – Enforcement of a Foreign Judgment**

*[Caption, in troduction*]

1. Plaintiff is a resident of [city, *state and country]*
2. Defendant is a resident of *[city, state and country].*
3. Plaintiff was also plaintiff in a suit in *[court]* in *[country],* [case name, number or other identifying information].
4. Defendant in this action was also defendant in the above case.
5. The *[court]* is and was, at and prior to the time of the institution of that cause, and is at this time a court having general jurisdiction. Valid service of process was made on the defendant on *[date]* by *[mode of* service] , and the cause came for trial and judgment was rendered against the defendant and in favor if the plaintiff on *[date]* for the sum of *[amount and type ofcurrimcy].*
6. A legalized, certified copy of the judgment is attached, marked Exhibit - and incorporated by reference. The means of legalizing this copy were *[specijj; means, ie.., apostille, etc.j*
7. The judgment represents the sum of US. dollars as of *[date ofbreach or date of judgment].*
8. There is no defense to this action. *[Briefly list the possible defenses to the validity of original judgment or enforcement of it in the US., stating their inapplicability; a list ofpossible defenses with check boxes may be useful here]*
9. No part of the judgment described above has been paid.
10. Defendant is here and now on notice that plaintiff, on the trial of this cause, will introduce in evidence a certified, legalized copy of the proceedings, judgment, and orders in *[original case name and number].*

Wherefore, plaintiff requests that the defendant be cited to appear and answer this petition, and on filing this action plaintiff have judgment against defendant in the sum of US. dollars.

*[Signature, verification, etc.]*

**Suggested Form 2a:**
**Answer/Defense to Application for Filing of Foreign Judgment – Generic**

With respect to the action mentioned in *[reference to complaint in enforcement action],* *[Plaintiff or defendant]* has *[describe defense].*

Defendant thus had and has a good, substantial and sufficient defense to the action. Defendant is now willing, able and ready *to* show that *[describe actions creating defense* ].

*[Signature and verification]*

**Suggested Form 2b: Answer/Defense to Application for Filing of Foreign Judgment – Extrinsic Fraud in Procuring the Foreign Judgment**

After the commencement of the action mentioned in *[reference to complaint in enforcement action],* plaintiff came to the defendant with the intent to deceive defendant and prevent *[him or her]* from defending the action, and falsely and fraudulently represented *[state false representations, detailing fraud fully].*

Relying on those false and fraudulent representations, this defendant omitted to appear in the action and defend the same, as - *[he or she]* would otherwise have done but for the false representations.

Plaintiff thereafter and without knowledge of or any notice to defendant obtained judgment as of defendant's default.

Defendant had and has a g00d, substantial and sufficient defense to the action and would have shown at trial and is now willing, able and ready to show that *[describe actions creating defense].*

*[Signature and verification]*

**Suggested Form 3:**
**Petition or Application for Registration of a Foreign Judgment**

The *[petition or application]* for the registration of
of a foreign judgment respectfully shows:

1. In an action brought in the [court] in state and country] entitled *[name and identifYing information of case],* petitioner, as plaintiff, obtained a judgment against this defendant for *[amount and type offoreign currency].* This amount is equal to US. dollars on *[day of breach or day ofjudgment].*
2. The judgment was entered on *[date offoreign judgment].* An authenticated, legalized copy is attached marked Exhibit - and by reference made part of this petition. The means of legalizing this copy were *[specify means, i.e. apostille, etc.].*
3. The judgment was in no way deficient, *[list possible defenses to validity of judgment and sf£lte their inapplicability].* Nor is the judgment unenforceable by this court, . *[list possible reasons for non enforcement and state why they do not apply].*

Wherefore, petitioner requests that the judgment of *[specify foreign court]* be registered in the *[court].*

*[Signature and verification]*

**Suggested Form 4a: Answer/Defense to Application for Filing of Foreign Judgment – Foreign Court Acted in Excess of Its Jurisdiction**

The _______________ *[specifY foreign court]* of _______________ *[specft); foreign state and country]* in entering the judgment attempted to be registered in _______________ *[specft);, petition or application for registration]* acted in excess of its jurisdiction in the following particulars: *[specifY, for example, failure to obtain service on defendant in such action or, in the case of courts of limited jurisdiction, that the judgment is for a sum greater than it is authorized to give]*.

*[Signature and verification]*

**Suggested Form 4b: Answer/Defense to Application for Filing of Foreign Judgment – Extrinsic Fraud in Procuring the Foreign Judgment**

The *[specify foreign court]* of *[specify; foreign state and country]* in entering the judgment attempted to be registered in *[specft); petition or application for registration]* entered a judgment that was procured by extrinsic fraud in the following particulars: *[specify, for example, how the defendant was deceived and thereby prevented from presenting a defense]*.

*[Signature and verification]*

**PART TWO**

# Enforcement of Judgments Abroad

## I. OVERVIEW

Just as a practitioner in the United States may need to seek recognition and enforcement of foreign country money judgments in the United States, so may the U.S. practitioner require assistance in seeking a foreign jurisdiction's recognition and enforcement of a U.S.-rendered judgment. In this Part Two of the Handbook, the practitioner is taken through the companion process of obtaining an overseas jurisdiction's recognition and enforcement of a judgment rendered in the United States. This part describes the general approaches that the U.S. practitioner may confront abroad, and it analyzes the strategies and procedures that might be applicable in countries with which the United States has the most trade and investment activity. In addition, it summarizes the steps that the practitioner must take to prepare the case for the foreign court. While a complete survey of enforcement and recognition procedures of all countries is well beyond the scope of this and perhaps any text, Part Two seeks to alert the practitioner to the issues and areas that may require attention and further research in order to successfully enforce a U.S. judgment abroad.

A U.S. practitioner may have to seek enforcement of a U.S.-rendered judgment overseas if:

- The defendant resides overseas;
- The defendant has moved overseas before the judgment could be satisfied, restricting the U.S. court's jurisdictional basis over the defendant; or
- The defendant has assets in a foreign jurisdiction outside the United States and only those foreign assets can satisfy the U.S.-rendered judgment.

However, unless the U.S. practitioner who handled the original adjudication happens to be licensed to practice law in the jurisdiction where enforcement will be sought, the U.S. practitioner generally must identify and retain foreign counsel for enforcement proceedings overseas. Therefore, if your client has won a judgment, your task involves:

1. advising your client that it may be necessary to enforce the judgment overseas;
2. locating and retaining foreign counsel to represent your client in the foreign forum;
3. providing foreign counsel with the necessary documentation and information for foreign counsel to seek enforcement;
4. keeping your client advised of the case's progress;[1] and
5. obtaining the foreign court's recognition and/or enforcement of the U.S.-rendered judgment.

[1] This scenario assumes a typical enforcement case where a U.S. resident plaintiff has sued a defendant who is already overseas or who moves overseas during or after judgment is rendered. In some cases, however, the plaintiff might be a foreign resident or multinational corporation and able to seek out counsel overseas independently or, indeed, may have very close ties to the foreign jurisdiction where enforcement is sought. In this situation, U.S. counsel's representation would probably end once judgment has been rendered in the United States.

## II. HOW TO IDENTIFY AND SELECT FOREIGN COUNSEL

A U.S. lawyer qualified to practice in one or more states is subject to the competency requirement of each state's professional responsibility code. Similarly, lawyers qualified to practice in other countries are also subject to constraints.[1] Therefore, if an attorney seeks enforcement, recognition, and execution abroad of a judgment rendered in a U.S. court, precautions must be taken to avoid possible liability arising from the unlicensed practice of law ("unauthorized practice of law" or UPL). This concern applies both in the United States and abroad. In the United States, approximately half of the states permit an attorney to hire a "foreign legal consultant" (FLC) to advise on the applicable law in the country in which the FLC is licensed to practice law.[2] If an attorney does not engage a foreign legal consultant to render an opinion on the appropriate procedure, the attorney may be subject to discipline or malpractice liability under a state bar's ethical rule of competence. Similarly, if an American attorney does not engage a foreign attorney who is licensed to practice in the appropriate jurisdiction abroad, then the American attorney may be subject to liability under the foreign jurisdiction's prohibition against the unauthorized practice of law.[3] Moreover, the failure to be licensed in the jurisdiction where legal advice is rendered can result in the inability to collect fees or give rise to legal malpractice claims.[4]

> *Advice*: If your client requires representation in a foreign jurisdiction, be sure to *either* engage a foreign legal consultant (a foreign lawyer who is licensed as a FLC in your jurisdiction), if your state permits, *or* engage a foreign attorney located in the foreign jurisdiction who is licensed to practice in that jurisdiction.[5]

[1] Robert E. Lutz, *Ethics and International Practice: A Guide to the Professional Responsibilities of Practitioners*, Fordham Int'l L.J. 53, 68 (1992–3).

[2] As of this writing, 26 jurisdictions in the United States permit registration or certification of FLCs. These are Alaska, Arizona, California, Connecticut, Florida, Georgia, Hawaii, Idaho, Illinois, Indiana, Louisiana, Massachusetts, Michigan, Minnesota, Missouri, New Jersey, New Mexico, New York, North Carolina, Ohio, Oregon, Pennsylvania, Texas, Utah, Washington, and the District of Columbia. Many of these jurisdictions replicated some, but not all, of the provisions of the ABA Model Rule, proposed and endorsed by the ABA House of Delegates in 1993 and 2002. *See* http://www.abanet.org/cpr/mjp/201h.doc. A comparison chart of the ABA Model Rule with the individual state FLC rules can be found at http://www.abanet.org/cpr/jclr/silver_flc_chart.pdf. California's rule, which was promulgated in 1988, can be found at Cal. Rules of Court R. 988 (West 2004). In the early 1980s, New York was first to enact a FLC rule, and it remains probably the most liberal in terms of the FLC's allowable scope of practice. *See* http://www.abanet.org/cpr/jclr/silver_flc_chart.pdf.

[3] This concern – principally presented in the U.S. interstate context of temporary (as contrasted with permanent establisment) practice – gave rise to the formation of an ABA Commission on Multijurisdictional Practice (MJP Commission), which studied and made recommendations endorsed by the ABA House of Delegates regarding interstate and international MJP. *See* the General Agrementon Trade in Services (GATS) Web page at www.abanet.org/cpr. The recommendations endorsed state adoption of the ABA Model FLC Rule (*see supra* note 2 and accompanying text) and proposed state adoption of an ABA Model Foreign Lawyer Temporary Practice Rule. *See* www.abanet.org/cpr.

[4] *See Birbrower, Montalbano, Condon & Frank, P.C. v. Superior Court of Santa Clara County*, 949 P.2d 1 (Cal. 1998), holding that lawyers not licensed to practice law in California violated California's misdemeanor UPL provision when they assisted a California corporate client in connection with an impending California arbitration under California law and were therefore barred from recovering fees.

[5] Among the many directories offered as a resource for selecting of foreign counsel, *see* Guide to Foreign Law Firms (James R. Silkenat & William M. Hanney eds. 2004).

### A. SOURCES FOR IDENTIFYING FOREIGN COUNSEL

In order to enforce a U.S. judgment in a foreign country, the client must be represented by counsel qualified to practice in that jurisdiction and in the enforcement proceeding. If no hearing is involved, competent counsel must still handle the procedures for registration of the judgment.[6]

Thus, you must make several decisions before hiring foreign counsel. You must decide whether to refer the client to foreign local counsel, or to hire foreign counsel on the client's behalf. If you decide to hire counsel on the client's behalf, you have two options. You can hire local counsel in the foreign country, but evaluating the foreign attorney's competency and ability to control the litigation can be difficult at best.[7] Alternatively, you can hire counsel admitted to a foreign bar who is in the United States, but this can raise problems of aiding in UPL. However, as indicated, some states allow FLCs practitioners who are admitted to foreign bars who are allowed to render advice in the individual state after registering with the local state bar.[8] A list of these FLCs can usually be obtained from the state bar association.

Several resources are available to you to help you identify competent foreign counsel:

- Your firm may already have identified "foreign associates" or attorneys overseas who have represented your clients' interests on a regular basis. If your firm engages in such practice, you may refer the matter to the foreign associate or request further referral to other foreign counsel competent in the area of law underlying the judgment you are seeking to enforce.
- Your local or state bar association, whose International Law Section may have compiled a registry of FLCs and/or lawyers, is another possible source of foreign referrals. For example, many state bars and some metropolitan bar associations (*e.g.*, the Los Angeles County Bar Association and the Association of the Bar of the City of New York) have International Law Sections that may have foreign lawyers as associate members. You may also check the MARTINDALE-HUBBELL INTERNATIONAL LAW DIRECTORY for other state listings.
- The MARTINDALE-HUBBELL DIRECTORY lists attorneys and firms by country, along with their practice areas. An Internet search query containing the country and specialty you are seeking may also yield a list of attorneys. An additional source is James R. Silkenat and William M. Hanney's GUIDE TO FOREIGN LAW FIRMS.[9]
- You can contact the foreign country's embassy in Washington, D.C., or its consulate located in your state or nearby for a list of qualified and specialized attorneys.[10]
- You may wish to contact local law and business schools, as well as universities' international relations, political science, or public administration departments for referrals.[11]

[6] Regarding the duty of competence of U.S. practitioners handling foreign matters, *see* Lutz, *supra* note 1, at 62–8.

[7] *See* Lutz, *supra* note 1, at 68–85.

[8] *Id.* at 73–4.

[9] *See supra* note 5.

[10] *See* Lutz, *supra* note 1 at 78. The U.S. Department of State publishes a listing, "Foreign Consular Offices in the United States," which should be available in most law libraries. If all else fails, don't forget to check your local telephone listings for consulates if you live in a major city.

[11] For a general discussion of how to find foreign legal counsel, *see* Lutz, *supra* note 1, at 78–9.

- Foreign attorneys often attend annual meetings of specialty associations, such as the American Bar Association (ABA) Practice Sections, or the International Trademark Association or the International Bar Association meetings. Networking at these gatherings may be fruitful in establishing relationships with foreign attorneys who may be helpful in the future.[12]

## B. IS FOREIGN COUNSEL COMPETENT?

Unless you have dealt with the foreign lawyer before, you will not know if he or she is competent with respect to the enforcement of foreign judgments and, if relevant, with the area of law underlying your client's judgment. Not only must foreign counsel be expert in the procedural requirements of obtaining recognition, enforcement, and execution of a judgment rendered by a U.S. court, but he or she may have to argue the elements of the underlying cause of action to the foreign court, if necessary. If the particular cause of action is unknown in the foreign jurisdiction, you may have to explain the cause of action to foreign counsel and assist in research, if required. While an unfamiliar cause of action is not generally a bar to enforcement abroad, as long as the judgment meets the enforceability requirements in your jurisdiction,[13] foreign counsel must be prepared to argue the merits of the case underlying the judgment if required by the foreign jurisdiction's laws.[14]

## C. WHAT WILL FOREIGN REPRESENTATION COST?

After you have identified and selected the foreign representation, the first step is to establish an agreement on fees[15] and communicate the problem to the attorney. After initial conferences by telephone, you should institute regular telephone, email, and fax communication to minimize the possibilities of misunderstandings. You should provide all of the case documents to the foreign counsel, including pleadings and background information on U.S. court procedures, depending on the familiarity of foreign counsel with U.S. law. It may be useful to identify another attorney admitted to the bar of that country, perhaps locally, to consult with if a second opinion is needed.

[12] *See* ABA SECTION OF INTERNATIONAL LAW AND PRACTICE, INTERNATIONAL LITIGATION, 341–66 (Buffalo, NY, W. S. Hein 1993); *see also* Albert S. Pergam, *Symposium, Transnational Opinions: Selecting and Collaborating with Foreign Counsel*, 1989 COLUM. BUS. L. REV. 413 (1989); Ewell E. Murphy, *A Guide to Foreign Law Source Materials and Foreign Counsel*, 19 INT'L LAW. 39 (1985).

[13] These are, generally: final judgment rendered by a court of competent jurisdiction; judgment consistent with public policy in your jurisdiction; sufficient notice; no fraud; and no conflict with another final and conclusive judgment. *See infra* Part Two, IV, notes 2–4 and accompanying text.

Additionally, many countries require reciprocity, whereby the U.S. court must recognize the foreign jurisdiction's judgments under an equivalent or more lenient standard than that which the foreign court extends to U.S. judgments. On reciprocity on a country-by-country basis, *see generally* CENTER FOR INTERNATIONAL LEGAL STUDIES, INTERNATIONAL EXECUTION AGAINST JUDGMENT DEBTORS (Dennis Campbell & Suzanne Rodriguez eds. 2004) [hereinafter Campbell]; *see also* PAUL OMAR, PROCEDURES TO ENFORCE FOREIGN JUDGMENTS (Ashgate, Aldershot 2002).

[14] *See generally* Campbell, *supra* note 13.

[15] For more detail, see JOHN A. NILSSON, INTERNATIONAL BUSINESS PORTFOLIOS: DEALING EFFECTIVELY WITH LOCAL COUNSEL ABROAD (New York, Matthew Bender 1988).

Even if your firm has pre-established rates with foreign associates, the particular matter involving foreign recognition, enforcement, and execution of a U.S. court–rendered judgment may go beyond your regular agreement's scope. As part of the selection process, you can always discuss, and even compare, fees and forms of payment.[16]

[16] For further information on this issue, see Ivo Greiter, How to Get Your Money in Foreign Countries: A Survey of Court Costs and Lawyer's Fees in 151 Countries (1988). It is a helpful guide and is based on a questionnaire prepared and sent to law firms abroad regarding court costs and legal fees.

## III. DOCUMENTATION FOR ENFORCEMENT

Once foreign counsel has been retained, you will have to provide counsel with information and documentation necessary for enforcing the judgment. A copy of the judgment itself is universally required, and some courts may additionally require the principal pleadings of the case. This raises the issue of what requirements have to be met for authentication of those documents to be submitted to the foreign court, which will be a matter of local law in the enforcing jurisdiction. In addition to those documents that will be submitted to the foreign court, foreign counsel must have a clear understanding of the underlying adjudication in the United States. Defendant might raise issues regarding the law upon which the U.S. cause of action was based or question the U.S. court's jurisdiction to render the judgment. Therefore, all pleadings from the underlying adjudication not otherwise required for submission to the foreign court might still be required by foreign counsel in order to prepare pleadings for conversion of the judgment and to argue for enforcement, together with information on the court rules, practices, and law applied in the underlying U.S. adjudication.

Countries that require the legalization of documentation, otherwise known as "authentication," can be divided into two groups: those that are parties to the Hague Convention on Legalization for Foreign Public Documents[1] (which will accept the simplified *apostille* process of authentication of documents) and those that require more traditional and lengthy procedures.[2] The traditional procedure usually begins with notarization and winds through the state secretary of state's office and then through diplomatic channels where a "chain of certification" is constructed.

### A. THE HAGUE LEGALIZATION CONVENTION

In contrast to the traditional procedure, the *apostille* is a certification form that attaches to a document, such as a judgment. The *apostille* authenticates the document in lieu of an evidentiary chain of authentication and, thus, satisfies the authentication requirements in jurisdictions which are parties to the Hague Convention.[3,4] In the U.S., the Secretary of State of the state where the judgment is rendered usually issues the *apostille*. The Secretary of State requires some form of authentication of the judgment by the court clerk's office where the judgment was issued. However, if a federal court rendered the judgment, the federal court clerk has the power to issue the *apostille* directly.

[1] 527 U.N.T.S. 189 [hereinafter the Legalization Convention], *reprinted at* BRUNO RISTAU, INTERNATIONAL JUDICIAL ASSISTANCE, A-165 (2000) [hereinafter RISTAU]. *See* Part One, Instruments, Laws, and Other Materials for member nations and the *apostille* form.

[2] *See generally* JOHN P. SINNOTT, A PRACTICAL GUIDE TO DOCUMENT AUTHENTICATION: LEGALIZATION OF NOTARIZED AND CERTIFIED DOCUMENTS (1997).

[3] *See* RISTAU, *supra* note 1 at 344–5. *See* Documents Appendix for Convention on the Service Abroad of Judicial and Extrajudicial Documents in Civil or Commercial Matters 658 U.N.T.S. 163 (Nov. 15, 1965) [hereinafter Hague Service Convention], and an address list of foreign central authorities.

[4] *See* Christopher Cheng, *Translated Documents and Hague Service Convention Requirements*, 14 MICH. J. INT'L L. 383 (1993).

## B. TRADITIONAL CERTIFICATION

If the country where enforcement is sought is not a party to the Hague Convention, then you must follow local requirements for legalization of documents. This procedure may often approximate the following chain of authentications:

- Authentication by the clerk of the court (or some other designated officer of the court);
- Authentication by the state Secretary of State where judgment was issued (or by a government official at the state level who issues "official" documents);
- Authentication by the State Department;
- Authentication by the U.S. consulate or embassy located in the country where enforcement is sought and, possibly, by the consulate or embassy in the United States of the country where enforcement is sought.

Because the procedure varies from country to country, you should contact the consulate or embassy of the jurisdiction where enforcement is sought to determine the exact procedure, or you should obtain that information from foreign counsel. A listing of U.S. consular and diplomatic offices appears at the State Department's Web site, http://usembassy.state.gov.

## C. EVIDENCE OF THE JUDGMENT

The foreign court where enforcement is sought will require some properly authenticated documentary evidence of the judgment rendered in the U.S. court.[5] On behalf of your client, you have by now retained foreign counsel to handle the enforcement matter, so you will have to consult with foreign counsel regarding the necessary documents and required U.S. certifications of authenticity. Additionally, translations of the documents may be required; depending on local court rules, the translation may have to be done by designated official translators or may require separate guarantees of its authenticity. For example, in Italy, the court will examine the text of the judgment, or a translation of the text of the judgment if the judge does not understand the language of the judgment. If the defendant challenges the accuracy of the translation into Italian, the court may appoint an official translator. Therefore, Italy would not initially require a translation; if it were necessary later, local translators hired by foreign counsel could translate the text.[6]

## D. OTHER DOCUMENTATION AND INFORMATION

Depending on the foreign jurisdiction, the foreign court, where enforcement will be sought, may scrutinize the underlying adjudication. Therefore, foreign counsel must be thoroughly

[5] For a discussion of the documentary requirements of many major jurisdictions, *see* ENFORCEMENT OF FOREIGN JUDGMENTS (Lawrence W. Newman & Philip Weems eds. Release 19–2003) [hereinafter Weems] under Section II.B.2. of each country's survey.

[6] *Id.* at ITA-15.

familiar with the underlying adjudication, including the laws and procedures followed by the court. Hiring foreign counsel familiar with state or federal law is helpful; nevertheless, foreign counsel may require all of the pleadings, documents relating to notice (especially proof of service), legal research on the cause of action, evidentiary rules and relevant rules of civil procedure.

## IV. UNDERSTANDING FOREIGN ENFORCEMENT FRAMEWORKS

### A. GENERAL

Identifying and selecting a FLC or foreign counsel abroad is only the first step in obtaining foreign recognition of a U.S. judgment. Informed and effective representation of a U.S. plaintiff[1] seeking enforcement of an award overseas rests upon your understanding of other countries' enforcement systems. Other countries' frameworks for converting foreign awards to local awards for enforcement purposes share many common aspects. Most jurisdictions' applicable statutes or treaties bar judicial review of the merits of the underlying adjudication, but, as in the U.S., foreign jurisdictions have established some type of recognition proceeding granting the foreign court jurisdiction to determine whether a judgment rendered overseas can be converted to a domestic judgment. Foreign recognition, paralleling enforcement of foreign country money judgments[2] in the U.S., *commonly* requires:[3]

- A final U.S. judgment;
- That the rendering court had proper jurisdiction over the defendant;
- That standards of due process, including fraud, often defined by the law of the country where enforcement is sought, were not violated in the U.S. adjudication;
- That the underlying adjudication, including the law applied by the adjudicating court, is not offensive to the public policy[4] of the country where enforcement is sought; and
- Reciprocity, which means at a minimum the adjudicating jurisdiction has given *res judicata* or claim preclusion effect to judgments from the jurisdiction where enforcement is sought, or, at a minimum, a legal framework is in place that poses no impediments to enforcing such a judgment.[5]

This section gives an overview of four major enforcement frameworks in countries where enforcement of a U.S. judgment is frequently sought[6] and provides a guide for U.S.

[1] For reference to the professional responsibilities of counsel in international representations, *see* Lutz, *supra* Part Two, Section II, note 1.

[2] Some cases may require obtaining recognition and enforcement of non-money judgments, especially real property foreclosures. Non-money judgments may be available in both common law and civil law systems. For a general discussion, see Stefan A. Riesenfeld, *Availability of Relief in Form of Non-Money Judgments* in TRENDS IN THE ENFORCEMENT OF NON-MONEY JUDGMENTS AND ORDERS 71 (Ulla Jacobsson & Jack Jakob eds. 1988).

[3] For a broad discussion of the common characteristics of the law of enforcement overseas, see Philip R. Weems, *How to Enforce U.S. Money Judgments Abroad*, TRIAL, July 1988, at 72.

[4] "Public policy" grounds for invalidation in many countries, including the U.S., include a broad range of issues: irregularities in due process and notice; differences in substantive laws (the adjudicated cause of action does not exist in the country where enforcement is sought); and government policies of the country where enforcement is sought conflict with the policies of the adjudicating jurisdiction to the extent that courts of the jurisdiction where enforcement is sought cannot recognize the judgment.

[5] Evidence of "reciprocity" is facilitated by the fact that the rendering state has adopted the Uniform Foreign Money-Judgments Recognition Act, 13-II U.L.A. 39 (2002 & Supp. 2003) [hereinafter Recognition Act].

[6] No attempt is made here to explain the enforcement regimes of the nearly 200 countries in the world. What is attempted is an explanation of the basic problems or concerns experienced with the major kinds of recognition regimes. For additional information, *see generally* Weems, *supra* Part Two, Section III, note 5. Brief but also helpful works are: MARTINDALE-HUBBELL LAW DIGEST – INTERNATIONAL LAW DIGEST (1997);

practitioners to follow in obtaining overseas recognition, enforcement, and execution of a U.S.-rendered judgment.

## B. FOREIGN ENFORCEMENT FRAMEWORKS

### 1. Generally

The discussions of four major frameworks below outline the unique and salient features of several judgment enforcement systems.[7] Even among the countries grouped below there exist significant differences in procedures, so you should consult more detailed sources regarding the specific country where you are seeking enforcement.[8]

### 2. Common Law Countries: Action for Recognition (United Kingdom, British Commonwealth, and United States)

**a. Statutory approach:** Adopted in England in 1933, the Foreign Judgments (Reciprocal Enforcement) Act is in force in some form in England and in many Commonwealth countries.[9] This Act provides for registration and enforcement of judgments that meet the common law requirements mentioned earlier. The Act's purpose is to encourage reciprocity by enforcing foreign judgments in England, so as to obtain reciprocal enforcement of English judgments in other countries.

In contrast, the Uniform Foreign Money-Judgments Recognition Act[10] adopted in many U.S. jurisdictions has codified the recognition of foreign judgments law, but it has eliminated the reciprocity requirement.[11] In states that have also enacted the Uniform Enforcement of Foreign Judgments Act,[12] an efficient and simplified registration procedure is available.[13]

Common law jurisdictions may differ as to the applicable requirements, practices or rules – depending upon whether the country is a former British colony or Commonwealth member, a European nation, or an adherent to the Brussels Regulation.[14] Recognition of common law judgments in foreign jurisdictions is facilitated where the jurisdiction has adopted statutes codifying the common law. Generally, you must initiate proceedings at the trial court level by writ and motion for summary judgment to enforce a judgment under

ENFORCEMENT OF FOREIGN JUDGMENTS WORLDWIDE (Charles Platto ed. 1989) [hereinafter Platto]; ENFORCING FOREIGN JUDGMENTS IN THE UNITED STATES AND UNITED STATES JUDGMENTS ABROAD (Ronald A. Brand ed. 1992). All of these works are based upon contributions from practitioners in the jurisdictions discussed.

[7] *See generally* Platto, *supra* note 6, for a discussion of enforcement rules in different countries.

[8] *See* Part Two Bibliography.

[9] GEORGES R. DELAUME, LAW AND PRACTICE OF TRANSNATIONAL CONTRACTS §7.08, at 215 (1988).

[10] 13-II U.L.A. 39 (2002 & Supp. 2003) [hereinafter Recognition Act].

[11] As will be seen in Part Three, the American Law Institute (ALI) Project on "Recognition and Enforcement of Foreign Judgments," which proposes the adoption of a federal statute on enforcement of foreign judgments. That proposal includes a reciprocity provision in Section 7, which won support of the Institute by a very close vote at its annual meeting in 2004. *See* AMERICAN LAW INSTITUTE, RECOGNITION AND ENFORCEMENT OF FOREIGN JUDJMENTS: ANALYSIS AND PROPOSED FEDERAL STATUTE (Proposed Final Draft), April 11, 2005.

[12] 13-I U.L.A. 155 (2002 & Supp. 2003) [hereinafter Enforcement Act].

[13] *See supra* Part One, III.A.3.

[14] *See infra* Part Two, IV.B.4.b. (Brussels Regulation).

common law. However, Brussels Regulation countries require an application to register the judgment.[15]

Several issues arise in the United Kingdom and Commonwealth countries. First, the foreign court usually accepts that the U.S. court had *personal jurisdiction* over the defendant and the matter. In *Beals v. Saldanha*,[16] for example, the Supreme Court of Canada found that the "real and substantial connection" test for personal jurisdiction was satisfied by the defendant's purchase of property in Florida in a false representation suit regarding that transaction.

Because an action must be brought in the foreign court, the court must also be assured of its own personal jurisdiction over the defendant, which may prove difficult if the defendant is transient.[17] Once you file a complaint, a motion for summary judgment normally follows.[18] Furthermore, be aware that the court may reexamine some aspects of the merits of the underlying action if certain defenses apply,[19] such as improper notice or service, conflicting or non-final judgment, fraud, a pending appeal, and due process or public policy violations.

Next, the foreign country may require *reciprocity* by the United States in enforcing the foreign country's judgments in U.S. courts. Domestic statutes will define whether reciprocity is required.[20] Following is a brief list of countries' reciprocity requirements:[21]

**Requires Reciprocity by Foreign Courts**

| | |
|---|---|
| England | Only when either the AJA or FJREA applies |
| Australia | Based upon judgment reciprocity |
| Malaysia | Required by Government Proceedings Act 1956; not required under Common Law |
| Nigeria | Extended automatically to Commonwealth countries; discretionary with non-Commonwealth countries |

**Does not Require Reciprocity**

| | |
|---|---|
| Canada | (includes both Ontario and Quebec) |
| South Africa | Discretionary with the Court |

[15] *See* EU Regulation on Jurisdiction and the Recognition and Enforcement of Judgments in Civil and Commercial Matters, Council Regulation (EC) No. 44/2001 of 22 December 2000 [hereinafter *Brussels Regulation*]. For information about the predecessor of the Brussels Regulation – the Brussels and the Lugano Conventions – *see generally* ENFORCEMENT OF FOREIGN JUDGMENTS, at England and Wales-3 to England and Wales-16 (Lois Garb & Julian Lew eds. 1995 & Supp. 9 2003) [hereinafter ENFORCEMENT OF FOREIGN JUDGMENTS]; *see also* J.G. COLLIER, RECOGNITION AND ENFORCEMENT OF FOREIGN JUDGMENTS: ENGLAND, IN RECOGNITION AND ENFORCEMENT OF FOREIGN JUDGMENTS OUTSIDE THE SCOPE OF THE BRUSSELS AND LUGANO CONVENTIONS (The Hague, Kluwer Law Int'l., 2002).

[16] [2003] SCC 72 WL No. 28829 (Can. Dec. 18, 2003).

[17] ENFORCEMENT OF FOREIGN JUDGMENTS, *supra* note 15, at England and Wales-8 to England and Wales-9.

[18] DELAUME, *supra* note 9, § 7.08; this guide, Part One, I.

[19] *See* Part One, III.C.

[20] For example, in England and Wales, the Administration of Justice Act 1920 (AJA; applies to former British colonies and Commonwealth members) and Foreign Judgments (Reciprocal Enforcements) Act 1933 (FJREA) applies to some Commonwealth and European countries and requires reciprocity. *See* ENFORCEMENT OF FOREIGN JUDGMENTS, *supra* note 15, at England and Wales-4. For a listing of parties to the AJA or FJREA, see Annex and *id.* at England and Wales-11.

[21] *See id.* for the respective countries.

It is important to note that the foreign court *will not review the merits* of the underlying matter if all of the following formalities have been observed and the judgment is not subject to certain defenses, as noted earlier. If any of the defenses are asserted, the court is likely to review the U.S. judgment.[22] Furthermore, the defendant may raise a fraud defense for the first time, but he or she is under a heavy burden to show why the defense was not raised in the U.S. proceeding.[23]

**b. Documentary requirements:** Common law recognition requirements vary from jurisdiction to jurisdiction, but they generally include finality, proper jurisdiction over the matter and parties, notice, and the absence of fraud. Some jurisdictions may also require reciprocity, as discussed earlier. In order to comply with all formalities, you must also be aware of specific documentary requirements.

In **England**, you must provide[24]:

- A verified, certified or sealed copy of the judgment;
- An affidavit or application supporting statutory registration of the judgment or an affidavit supporting common law summary judgment;
- A judgment in English;
- Proof of service for a default judgment; and
- Evidence of any legal aid grant to your client.

**Canada** requires[25]:

- An original or authenticated copy of the judgment;
- An affidavit identifying the parties to the underlying action; and
- An affidavit stating that the defendant has exhausted all appeals, if the defendant is challenging the recognition action.

In **Australia**, you must file an application for enforcement, consisting of a motion and supporting affidavit with a copy of the judgment.[26] The affidavit must state:

- Plaintiff's and defendant's full names, titles, occupation, and last known place of residence or business;
- That plaintiff, as judgment creditor, is entitled to enforce the judgment;
- That the judgment is final and conclusive between the parties;
- That the foreign court is appropriate;
- That the judgment remains entirely or partially unsatisfied as of the application date;
- That the original court can enforce the judgment;

[22] FJREA § 4(1)(a) in HALISBURY'S STATUTES OF ENGLAND AND WALES, VOLUME 22 (London, Butterworths 1995, 2003 reissue).

[23] *See* ENFORCEMENT OF FOREIGN JUDGMENTS, *supra* note 15 at England and Wales-6.

[24] FJREA §10 in HALISBURY'S STATUTES OF ENGLAND AND WALES, VOLUME 22 (London, Butterworths 1995, 2003 reissue).

[25] Reciprocal Enforcement of Judgments Act, R.S.O. 1990 c. R.5; ENFORCEMENT OF FOREIGN JUDGMENTS, *supra* note 15 at Canada (Ontario)-8.

[26] Foreign Judgments (Reciprocal Enforcement) Act 1973 (NSW) §§5 & 6 [formal requirements]; ENFORCEMENT OF FOREIGN JUDGMENTS, *supra* note 15 at Australia-5 to Australia-6.

- That the judgment, if registered, cannot be set aside; and
- That interest, if any, is due as of the application date.[27]

### 3. Civil Law *Exequatur* (France, Germany, Spain, Italy, Latin America)

The *exequatur*[28] procedure, although resembling common law in substantive law recognition requirements, is unique in that recognition usually is sought through a special petition to a court that has exclusive jurisdiction over recognition proceedings, usually an appellate court and often the highest court of appeal.[29] For example, in Costa Rica the exequatur proceeding is brought before the Supreme Court of Justice; in Chile, before the Supreme Court; in Spain, the Supreme Court; and in Brazil, the Federal Supreme Court. The exequatur is also known as the *Vollstrekungsurteil* in Germany and the *delibazione* in Italy.[30]

**a. No reexamination on the merits:** Unlike common law courts, where the merits of the foreign adjudication may be reexamined under certain circumstances, the *exequatur* procedure limits the court to reviewing the judgment only on the basis of those elements for granting or denying recognition. In **France**, for example, these are similar to the elements required under common law, with slight variation:

- Proper jurisdiction in the original, rendering court;
- The court will apply French conflict of law rules to the decision or must find that the decision produced a result "equivalent" to what a French court would have rendered;
- There must be no violation of international public policy; and
- There must have been no fraud, but the defendant can raise fraud as a defense for the first time.[31]

Unlike some common law countries, reciprocity is not required.

**b. Documentary requirements:** You must submit an application to the designated court; its contents vary depending upon the country in which you are seeking enforcement.[32] Generally, courts require **originals**, although occasionally a court will accept a notarized copy. To date, facsimile copies are generally not accepted.

You must also show that the defendant received **proper notice** of the foreign proceedings. However, even if the defendant challenges proper notice, appearance in court will lead the court to conclude that the notice was sufficient.[33] An interesting example of refusal to

[27] For a country-by-country summary of recognition and enforcement requirements; *see generally* ENFORCEMENT OF FOREIGN JUDGMENTS, *supra* note 15.

[28] The word *exequatur* is from Latin, meaning "let it be enforced." *See* Francisco Ramos Romeu, *Litigation Under the Shadow of an* Exequatur: The *Spanish Recognition of U.S. Judgments*, 38 INT'L LAW. 945 (2004).

[29] DELAUME, *supra* note 9, § 7.07, at 212. Puerto Rico also applies the *exequatur* procedure. 31 P.R. LAWS ANN. § 7 (2002).

[30] *See* Part Two, Bibliography for general works as well as commentary on specific country procedures. Although these countries share the general approach under *exequatur*, you must check the application requirements for each country because procedures and documentary requirements differ.

[31] Decision of *Cour de Cassation*, *Munzer*, rendered on January 7, 1964 (Clunet 1964, 302; JCP64, II, 13590); ENFORCEMENT OF FOREIGN JUDGMENTS, *supra* note 15, at France-3, France-6.

[32] *See generally* ENFORCEMENT OF FOREIGN JUDGMENTS, *supra* note 15.

[33] Campbell, *supra* Part Two, Section II, note 13, at INT-10.

recognize a judgment on the basis of improper notice is a German case where Germany's highest constitutional court spoke. It refused to recognize service of process involving a New York class action judgment.[34]

The court reviews **certified translations**[35] of the **authenticated judgment**[36] and briefs in the case presented below, and renders a decision. *Exequatur* may be granted even if the defendant defaults, and once *exequatur* is granted, the judgment has *res judicata* or claim preclusion effect in the foreign jurisdiction.[37]

**c. Exclusive jurisdiction of the recognizing court:** In many civil law jurisdictions, such as Mexico[38] and France,[39] the court handling the *exequatur* procedure will deny recognition if the foreign adjudication was under the exclusive jurisdiction of the courts of the country where *exequatur* is sought. For example, French courts will not grant *exequatur* if:

- The defendant was a French citizen or permanent resident unless defendant waived his right to a French trial;
- A choice of forum clause gave France exclusive jurisdiction; or
- French property or a French patent, employment or insurance contract is at issue.[40]

**d. Enforcement in trial courts:** Once the court grants *exequatur*, which can take from four months for an unopposed action to several years if the action is opposed, the matter is usually sent to an execution judge for execution procedures. In civil law countries, the execution judges' range of enforcement measures allows them to: attach movable or immovable property; impose civil imprisonment; impose liquidation of an insolvent defendant company under bankruptcy laws to satisfy the judgment; or impose travel restrictions.

**e. The German example:** German law provides that a foreign judgment will be recognized and enforced in Germany if the following conditions are satisfied:

- it is a final judgment (that is, it is subject to the application of *res judicata*);
- the rendering court had jurisdiction;
- the defendant had proper notice;
- there was no conflicting domestic or foreign judgment exists;
- no prior proceeding was instituted;
- there is no incompatibility with German public policy; and
- reciprocity exists.[41]

A common problem with the enforcement of an American judgment is that most foreign jurisdictions, such as Germany, are reluctant to enforce one that involves the use of pretrial

[34] Einstweilige Anordnung vom 25 Juli 2003, BVerfG2.Senat [temporary court order of July 25, 2004].

[35] The court will usually have a list of certified translators.

[36] Either the clerk of the foreign court, or the country's consulate or *apostille* may authenticate the judgment.

[37] Delaume, *supra* note 9, § 7.07, at 213.

[38] Code of Civil Procedure for the Federal District, Art. 608; Weems, *supra* Part Two, III, note 5, at MEX-15.

[39] Decision of *Cour de Cassation*, *Simitch*, rendered February 6, 1985 (RCDIP, 369, et seq., 243, *et seq.*) (establishes additional requirement for recognition that French courts not have had exclusive jurisdiction over the claim).

[40] *Id.*; note, *The Enforcement of Foreign Judgments in France Under Noveau Code de Procedure Civile*, 4 B.C. Int'l & Comp. L. Rev. 149, 169–70, *cited in* Ved P. Nanda & David K. Pansius, Litigation of International Disputes in United States Courts §12.10 (2003).

[41] Zivilprocessordnung § 328.

discovery, contingency fees, and punitive damages. However, the German Federal Court of Justice made a remarkable ruling in 1992 recognizing the use of pretrial discovery and contingency fees, while carving out a rare exception for punitive damages.[42]

The German Court did not limit the American discovery to the more narrow fact-finding process under German procedure. Instead, the court looked to the importance of the evidence established through the American discovery process and determined that it did not violate German public policy.[43] American discovery was previously deemed too intrusive to be tolerated in Germany, but this decision allows the German Court "a high level of tolerance in cases involving discovery that goes beyond German procedural limits."[44] There have been only a handful of relevant cases before German courts since then, however.[45]

Generally, contingent fee arrangements and punitive damages are void as a matter of German public policy. Nevertheless, the German Court enforced a contingency fee arrangement in one case because, despite the procedural differences, the contingency fees are similar to the German policy of providing "government-funded legal aid for low income groups."[46] However, the Court refused to enforce punitive damages, but "[it] suggested in dicta that such damages may be enforceable if they serve legitimate compensatory purposes."[47]

### 4. Treaty Approach (European Union, Latin America, Nordic Countries, Austria)

**a. Uniform Substantive Law of Recognition (Bustamante Code):** Early European approaches and Inter-American approaches, such as the Bustamante Code,[48] stressed the adoption of common bases for recognition while at the same time leaving the national *procedures* of enforcement of each country intact.[49] The objective of these treaties was to ensure that judgments from party nations would automatically meet the reciprocity requirement, leaving recognition to be decided on bases such as the court's competency to render and execute the judgment, personal jurisdiction, notice, finality, or public policy.

In Bustamante Code countries,[50] an ***exequatur* proceeding** generally precedes counsel's presenting to the competent court the foreign judgment for which recognition is being

[42] Judgment of June 4, 1992, BGH Sen. Z., reprinted in 1992 ZIP 1256, (1269) (F.R.G.) as explained by Joachim Zekoll, *The Enforceability of American Money Judgments Abroad: A Landmark Decision by the German Federal Court of Justice*, 30 COL. J. TRANSNAT'L L. 641, 644–5 (1992).

[43] *Id.* at 648–9.

[44] *Id.* at 649.

[45] *See* Judgment of July 25, 2003, BVerfG 2. Senat (temporary order of the highest court denying recognition of service in an American class action); Judgment of February 13, 2001, O.L.G. Frankfurt 20.Zivilsenat (equivalent state supreme court denied recognition of an American judgment due to German public policy); and Judgment of November 24, 1999 L.G. Stuttgart 24. Zivilkammer (state court ruling regarding the effect in Germany of a pending class action suit in the United States).

[46] *Supra* note 42 at 650.

[47] *Id.* at 657.

[48] Convention on Private International Law (Bustamante Code), 86 L.N.T.S. 111; Inter-American Convention on Extraterritorial Validity of Foreign Judgments and Arbitral Awards, 18 I.L.M. 1224 (1979).

[49] ROBERT C. CASAD, CIVIL JUDGMENT RECOGNITION AND THE INTEGRATION OF MULTIPLE-STATE ASSOCIATIONS: CENTRAL AMERICA, THE UNITED STATES OF AMERICA, AND THE EUROPEAN COMMUNITY, ch. 3 (1981).

[50] Countries originally ratifying the Bustamante Code included those of Central and South America; however, Argentina, Colombia, Mexico, Paraguay, Uruguay, and the United States refused. *See* CASAD, *supra* note 49, at 50 & 236 n.5. For a review of foreign judgment recognition requirements, *see id.* at 53–66.

sought.[51] This high court decision will determine whether or not the foreign judgment is enforceable.[52] However, in Bustamante Code countries, the high court's order determining enforceability can be judicially reviewed, whereas in non-Code countries, the *exequatur* proceeding does not permit judicial review.

Next, counsel must **serve the judgment debtor** in either the enforcement action or *exequatur* proceeding, whichever is applicable. Service abroad, if the judgment debtor is a non-domiciliary of the enforcing jurisdiction, is accomplished either under the Hague Convention for Service Abroad[53] if the states are parties, or by letters rogatory. Additionally in Code countries, counsel must **notify the enforcing state's public representative** (generally an attorney who functions like a district attorney in the United States), providing a translation of the judgment.[54] The judgment debtor then has 20 days to appear; following this period, the court can issue an order granting or denying execution of the judgment, even if the judgment debtor defaults.[55] The foreign jurisdiction then executes the judgment as a domestic judgment, generally requiring reciprocity even with other Code signatories.[56]

**b. Modern streamlined procedures (The Brussels Regulation):** The Brussels Regulation[57] has generalized *exequatur* procedures to provide uniform streamlined procedures for automatic recognition of civil and commercial judgments among European Union (EU) countries.[58]

The Regulation assures automatic recognition without formalities when the judgment is proved in a collateral proceeding in an EU country.[59] To prove the judgment, the attorney must provide:

- An authenticated copy of the judgment;
- A certificate, provided in an Annex to the Regulation, filled out by a court of the rendering country.[60] This requirement may also temporarily be satisfied by an equivalent document.[61]

[51] "Competency" in Bustamante countries is generally synonymous with the concepts of personal and subject matter "jurisdiction" in common law countries, and includes venue. *Id.* at 45.

[52] *See id.* at 63–4. Compare with the Brussels Regulation, *supra* note 15, at Arts. 1(1) and 1(2), which except revenue, customs, administrative matters, domestic relations matters, bankruptcy, social security, and arbitration determinations.

[53] Convention on the Service Abroad of Judicial and Extrajudicial Documents in Civil or Commercial Matters 658 U.N.T.S. 163 (Nov. 15, 1965), *reprinted in* Ristau, *supra* Section III, note 1 at A-11 [hereinafter Service Abroad Convention]. See discussion in this handbook, Part One, III.C.2.b.

[54] Casad, *supra* note 49, at 64.

[55] *Id.* at 63–4.

[56] *Id.* An example of an unsuccessful enforcement attempt in a Bustamonte Code country is *Kappel Insut. Cal. & Equipt. v. Banco de Recife*, SE No. 4811, 85 Rev. de Direito 481 (1927) (Brazilian court's denial of New York judgment enforcement based on lack of jurisdiction by issuing court).

[57] *See* Brussels Convention, *Supra* note 15. *See also* Part Two, Bibliography.

[58] As indicated earlier, the Brussels Regulation excludes civil matters regarding marriage, wills, and bankruptcies, as well as revenue, customs, and administrative matters. EU Regulation, *supra* note 15, at Art. 1(1) and 1(2).

[59] Denmark's relations with other EU countries are still governed by the earlier promulgated instrument, the Brussels Convention. *See* generally P.L.C. Torremans, *The Uniform Interpretation of the Brussels and Lugano Conventions*, 28 Eur. L. Rev. 752 (2003).

[60] EU Regulation, *supra* note 15, at Art. 53 (1) and 53 (2).

[61] *Id.* at Art. 55(1).

Although the Brussels Regulation does not explicitly allow for *ex parte* proceedings, as did the Brussels Convention,[62] it does provide that "a judgment given in a member state and enforceable in that state shall be enforced in another member state when, *on the application of an interested party* it may be declared enforceable there."[63] There are no restrictions on whom the interested party can be, as long as the judgment satisfies the above criteria. Moreover, the Brussels Convention still applies as between Denmark and the other European states. Thus, *ex parte* petitions made per the Brussels Convention could be brought against Danish debtors.[64] The Brussels Convention also allows *ex parte* petitions for recognition, to ensure that the judgment debtor does not remove assets from the jurisdiction.[65]

The precursor agreement, the Brussels Convention, went into force in 1968 as the framework for enforcement of foreign judgments among the European Economic Community (EEC) countries. The Lugano Convention[66] was drafted in 1989 to allow the countries of the European Free Trade Association to accede to the terms of the Brussels Convention, thereby bringing those countries into the then-EEC framework. On December 22, 2000, the EU Council replaced the Brussels and Lugano Conventions with the Brussels Regulation discussed earlier.

The terms of the Brussels Regulation are not presently applicable to European enforcement of U.S. judgments. Under the auspices of the Hague Conference on Private International Law,[67] the United States considered negotiating a convention similar to the Brussels Convention with member countries, which would have enabled U.S.-rendered judgments to be enforced in EU and some other countries. However, the Hague Conference ultimately decided on a more modest undertaking, the Hague Convention on Choice of Courts Agreements, which was recently completed and is the subject of discussion in Part Three of this guide.[68]

If the following exceptions are present, courts will deny enforcement:[69]

- The rendering court disregarded the rules of exclusive jurisdiction under the convention[70];
- The judgment violates the public policy of the enforcing jurisdiction[71];
- Lack of due process[72];

[62] DELAUME, *supra* note 9, §7.09, at 221.

[63] Brussels Regulation, *supra* note 15, at Art. 38(1) (emphasis added).

[64] To the extent the Brussels Convention applies any more, it does allow for recognition to ensure that the judgment debtor does not remove assets from the jurisdiction. *See* DELAUME, *supra* note 9, §7.09, at 221.

[65] *See id.*

[66] European Communities-European Free Trade Association: Convention on Jurisdiction and Enforcement of Judgments in Civil and Commercial Matters (Lugano Convention), 28 I.L.M. 620 (1989) [hereinafter Lugano Convention].

[67] Hague Conference on Private International Law, http://www.hcch.net (last accessed Aug. 15, 2005).

[68] For suggested approaches to U.S. treaty participation, *see* Ronald A. Brand, *Enforcement of Foreign Money-Judgments in the United States: In Search of Uniformity and International Acceptance*, 67 NOTRE DAME L. REV. 253 (1991).

[69] Brussels Regulation, *supra* note 15, at Art. 34. These exceptions are to be considered after original recognition, however. The court thus automatically recognizes the judgment (when proper procedure is followed) and the parties may thereafter make submissions with respect to the exceptions; *id.* at Art. 41.

[70] *Id.* at Art. 35(1).

[71] *Id.* at Art. 34(1).

[72] *Id.* at Art. 34(2).

- Claim preclusion by a prior suit in the country where enforcement is sought[73]; or
- Claim preclusion or prior suit in another member state or third party state involving the same cause of action and between the same parties.[74]

Thus, the Brussels Regulation specifies in which courts enforcement actions are to be brought, and those courts have exclusive jurisdiction over the matter. The court in the enforcing country may not, under the terms of the Regulation, try the underlying matter *de novo*,[75] but will consider the defenses above which may deny enforcement.

Importantly, you should note that the Brussels Regulation extends only to EU members and, thus, excludes application to U.S. judgments. In order to obtain automatic recognition and enforcement of a U.S. court-rendered judgment in an EU country, a bilateral treaty providing for reciprocity of judgments would have to be in force between that country and the United States.

### c. Exclusive Treaties

1) **Generally:** Some nations require a treaty with the country where the judgment originated before granting recognition of the foreign judgment. For example, Sweden, Norway, Denmark, Iceland, and Finland will recognize and enforce a foreign-rendered judgment only if a ratified convention, such as the Brussels, Lugano, or the Nordic Convention Regarding the Recognition and Enforcement of Judgments, is in force.[76] The United States, on the other hand, is not a party to any international treaty regarding recognition and enforcement of foreign judgments.[77]

Nonetheless, the United States may have other types of agreements with foreign countries. Denmark and Austria illustrate two approaches.

2) **Denmark and the United States:** The relationship between the United States and Denmark illustrates one form of bilateral agreement for reciprocal recognition and enforcement of judgments. Specifically, Denmark and the United States entered into a Treaty of Friendship, Commerce, and Navigation in 1951[78]; additionally, Denmark and the United States are parties to the New York Convention on the Recognition and Enforcement of Arbitral Awards.[79] A Danish court will not review the merits where reciprocity exists, unless the relevant treaty so provides, but it has the discretion to do so where none exists.[80]

Thus, you must do the following under either bilateral agreement:

**Judgment Creditor**

- Submit an application for enforcement of the U.S. judgment, with a rendering court-certified copy showing enforceability, finality, and proper service on the defendant;

[73] *Id.* at Art. 34(3).
[74] *Id.* at Art. 34(4).
[75] *Id.* at Art. 36.
[76] Weems, *supra* note 5, at DEN-3. Denmark, Sweden, Norway, and Finland are parties to the Lugano Convention, which has supplanted the Nordic Convention except in certain uncovered areas. *See generally id.* for each country. The Nordic countries were brought into the EEC treaty framework through the Lugano Convention. The Brussels Regulation would now apply to all Nordic countries except Norway.
[77] *Id.* at US-13.
[78] *Id.* at DEN-16.
[79] *Id.* at DEN-5.
[80] *Id.* at DEN-11, DEN-13.

- Where the judgment issued by default, you must submit proof of service on the defendant of the application,[81] unless the defendant contractually waived service[82];
- The relevant treaty determines the court of proper jurisdiction[83];
- If the court grants interim relief, such as an injunction or attachment, upon filing of the application for enforcement, you must being proceedings before a Danish court immediately or the court will set aside the interim relief.[84]

### Judgment Debtor

- If an action is pending in another court, the Danish court will on its own motion decline jurisdiction;
- No limit to defenses.

3) **Austria and the United States:** In contrast, Austria recognizes foreign judgments on three bases: (1) a bilateral treaty with the originating country; (2) a multilateral treaty including Austria and the rendering country; or (3) an Austrian Government proclamation declaring the reciprocity exists.[85] Without either a treaty or a proclamation, an Austrian court will not enforce a foreign judgment.[86] Inasmuch as there is no bilateral U.S.-Austria treaty, the U.S. judgment creditor seeking recognition and enforcement of a U.S. court-rendered judgment would have to obtain an Austrian government proclamation.[87]

4) **Islamic countries:** The United States's relationship with most Islamic countries follows yet another pattern. Islamic law historically and modernly prescribes a code of legal conduct in civil and commercial matters that defines the parties' relationships, whether in private international law or public international law. Thus, it can be unfruitful for your client to seek to enforce a U.S. court-rendered civil money judgment in most Islamic countries because these countries' laws do not accept either consent or reciprocity as the basis for international litigation.[88] Even today, although accommodating to some Western or Anglo-American legal concepts, most Islamic countries will only enforce judgments of other Islamic nations based upon the Pact of the League of Arab States (the Arab League Treaty of 1952).[89] Otherwise, courts in Islamic countries may reexamine the merits of the case under principles of Islamic law.[90] Further, under Islamic law, interest on judgments may not be awarded.[91] This prohibition is based on the concept of unjust enrichment, which includes charging or awarding of interest in a monetary transaction.[92] The prohibition also relies on the concepts of fair bargaining in contractual relationships and freedom from usury, as well as disapproval of transfers of wealth from the poor to the

[81] Weems, *supra* note 5, at DEN-5, DEN-11.

[82] *Id.* at DEN-12.

[83] *Id.* at DEN-9.

[84] *Id.* at DEN-13.

[85] *Id.* at AUT-4.

[86] Weems, *supra* note 5, at AUT-5.

[87] *See generally id.* at AUT-4 to AUT-5.

[88] *See generally* Joseph Schacht, An Introduction to Islamic Law (1964); *see also* Al Mulla, *Conventions on Enforcement of Foreign Judgments in the Arab States*, 14 Arab L.Q. 33 (1999).

[89] 70 U.N.T.S. 237, 252. While Islamic law incorporates a fundamental rule of Western public international law, *pacta sunt servanda*, consent is not the basis of Islamic legal authority, C.G. Weeramantry, Islamic Jurisprudence 30–1, 65–6, 131–2 (1988); David A. Westbrook, *Islamic International Law and Public International Law: Separate Expressions of World Order*, 33 Va. J. Int'l L. 819, 877 (1993).

[90] For information on Islamic law and legal principles, *see generally* Jeanne Asherman, *Doing Business in Saudi Arabia: The Contemporary Application of Islamic Law*, 16 Int'l L. 321 (1982).

[91] Weems, *supra* note 22, at SAU-6.

[92] Schacht, *supra* note 88, at 145.

rich.[93] However, in certain cases Egypt permits interest to be awarded, as may other Islamic countries.

Egypt, moreover, is a future exception to the general Islamic rule of recognizing only judgments rendered in courts of other Islamic countries since concluding the 1979 peace treaty with Israel.[94] The Treaty provides that "the normal relationship established between [the Parties] will . . . guarantee the mutual enjoyment by citizens of the due process of law." Although the terms of the Treaty have not yet been fully implemented, it may provide a schema for future relations between Islamic and non-Islamic countries where recognition and enforcement of judgments is concerned. Israel, notwithstanding this treaty, already recognized foreign judgments based upon the common law, which permits a foreign judgment to serve as a basis for a cause of action or new litigation in an Israeli court.[95]

Egypt nonetheless applies the reciprocity principle in enforcing foreign judgments under the Arab League Treaty and separate bilateral treaties with France, Italy, Kuwait, and Jordan (the latter is also a party to the Arab League Treaty). However, there is no bilateral treaty between the United States and Egypt; therefore, your strategy might be to obtain recognition of the U.S. judgment in France or Italy, if there is any jurisdictional basis for doing so, and then obtain an order of enforcement from an Egyptian court based on reciprocity.[96] You may also be able to show that your state will enforce a judgment rendered by an Egyptian court under a uniform enforcement law. Generally, the procedural and jurisdictional requirements parallel those discussed in other enforcement regimes earlier in this Part: notice, authentication, and translation of the judgment; proper subject matter and personal jurisdiction of the rendering court; final judgment; and showing of reciprocity in the absence of a treaty.[97] The Egyptian court will allow an award of interest if it was part of the original judgment; even if it was not, the judgment creditor may submit a separate claim for interest when the judgment creditor submits its request for enforcement of the original judgment.[98]

Successful enforcement of foreign debts in Islamic countries may be more successfully pursued where there is an underlying arbitral award and enforcement of it can be employed.[99] For example, Saudi Arabia, one of the United States' principal trading partners in the Middle East, is a party to the New York Convention, as is the United States. Saudi Arabian courts will enforce contractual arbitration clauses inasmuch as arbitration is an acceptable dispute resolution method under Islamic law.[100] Thus, seeking to enforce an arbitral award will not meet with the obstacle of imposition of Saudi (Islamic) law on a court-awarded judgment,[101] although even this approach may not always succeed because it may violate Saudi public policy.[102]

[93] WEERAMANTRY, *supra* note 89, at 65–8.

[94] Treaty of Peace, March 18, 1979, Egypt-Israel, Art. III(3), 18 I.L. M. 362 (1979).

[95] Weems, *supra* note 5, at ISR-3 to ISR-4.

[96] *See generally id.* at EGY-4 to EGY-9, for detailed procedure.

[97] *Id.*

[98] *Id.* at EGY-6.

[99] Convention on the Recognition and Enforcement of Foreign Arbitral Awards, 21 U.S.T. 2517 (1970).

[100] David J. Karl, Note, *Islamic Law in Saudi Arabia: What Foreign Attorneys Should Know*, 25 GEO. WASH. J. INT'L L. & ECON. 131, 164 (1991); *see also* Asherman, *supra* note 90.

[101] Kristin T. Roy, *The New York Convention and Saudi Arabia: Can A Country Use the Public Policy Defense to Refuse Enforcement of Non-Domestic Arbitral Awards?*, 18 FORDHAM INT'L L.J. 920, 951–2 (1995).

[102] *Id.* at 953.

Consequently, when dealing with Islamic countries, you should explore the following strategies:

- Seek to obtain recognition and enforcement of the U.S. court-rendered judgment in a third country with which the Islamic country may have a bilateral treaty based on reciprocity; or
- Show that the U.S. jurisdiction will or has recognized judgments from the Islamic country as a basis for claiming reciprocity; or
- Ascertain if the Islamic country adheres to the New York Convention and, if so, determine, in a commercial matter, whether there is a contractual arbitration clause in the contract underlying the litigation;
- If a contractual arbitration clause applies, seek enforcement of an arbitral award.

**d. Supplemental treaties:** In EU and Inter-American Treaty countries, treaty approaches supplement statutory frameworks, allowing courts to consider recognition of judgments from any originating country. Therefore, a judgment creditor may seek enforcement under the national laws of a country and then take that judgment through the treaty procedures to another party to an enforcement treaty for recognition and enforcement. The Lugano Convention is an example of a supplemental treaty, insofar as it allowed European countries that are not members of the EEC to benefit from reciprocal recognition of judgments afforded to EEC members under the Brussels Convention.[103] Those countries, which belonged to the European Free Trade Association (EFTA), have now become members of the expanded EU, all of whose members benefit from the provisions of the Brussels Regulation, allowing automatic enforcement.

**e. Treaties vis-à-vis U.S. judgments:** The United States is not a party to any treaties for the enforcement of foreign judgments. Significant progress was made in the 1970s with the United Kingdom on a bilateral treaty for the enforcement of judgments[104]; however, no treaty was concluded.[105] Nevertheless, treaties may still provide protection to U.S. creditors in certain situations where they seek to enforce judgments. In some countries, exceptions occasionally appear allowing for enforcement of judgments from countries with which no treaty has been concluded. In these countries, enforcement treaties to which the country is a party may serve as helpful guides for the enforcement of U.S. treaties.[106]

### 5. East Asian Approach (Japan, Korea, and Taiwan)

**a. Uniform statutes:** Japan, South Korea, and the Republic of China have adopted identical statutes for the recognition of foreign judgments.[107] The statutes require that a judgment creditor bring a recognition and enforcement action for an "Execution

[103] *See supra* notes 57–75 and accompanying text.

[104] Draft Treaty Providing for U.S.-U.K. Reciprocal Recognition and Enforcement of Judgments in Civil Matters, 16 I.L.M. 71 (1976).

[105] *See* North, *The Draft U.S./U.K. Judgments Convention: A British Viewpoint*, 1 Nw. J. Int'l L. & Bus. 219 (1979).

[106] Regarding Sweden's *Vakis* rule, where enforcement of a Greek judgment was granted despite the requirement of a treaty on enforcement, *see* Platto, *supra* note 6 at 182–3.

[107] Japan: Minsōho, Art. 200 (Code of Civil Procedure); Korea: Civ. Enforcement Act, Arts. 26, 27; Code Civ. Proc., Arts. 476, 477; Taiwan: Civ. Proc. C., Art. 402.

Judgment"[108] by a trial court.[109] If the court recognizes the foreign judgment, the judgment creditor may immediately seek satisfaction of the judgment debt in the same court.[110] Jurisdiction can be obtained in a trial court where personal jurisdiction is available or where the subject matter property[111] is located. A judgment that is final and conclusive will be recognized if it meets the following conditions:

- Jurisdiction was proper under the laws of the country where recognition is now sought, and not contravened by treaty;
- The defendant, if a national of the country where enforcement is sought (Japan, Korea, Taiwan), received notice by personal summons and defaulted, or made an appearance at the proceedings (no recognition if default judgment was entered after notice by publication only);
- The foreign judgment is not contrary to the public order and morals of the country where enforcement is sought; and
- There is a guarantee of reciprocal enforcement in the courts of the nation where the judgment originated. (Inasmuch as these East Asian countries have no bilateral treaties, the "guarantee" is based upon the experiences of plaintiffs from these nations in the courts of the country of origin).

The unique features of this approach are the special protection given to defendants in the case of default judgments according to nationality and the very broad public policy exception. Although the statutes do not permit examination of the underlying merits of the foreign adjudication, the public policy exception in practice has allowed just that.[112]

## V. CONCLUSION

Part Two of this handbook is intended to outline for the U.S. practitioner how to obtain recognition and enforcement of a U.S. court-rendered judgment overseas. Once the practitioner has determined that the client requires foreign representation, the U.S. practitioner should become familiar with the recognition and enforcement regime to which the country in which recognition and enforcement are sought adheres: common law, *exequatur*, Bustamante Code, Brussels Regulation, or statutory scheme. If the country in which judgment is sought is Islamic, the U.S. practitioner should focus instead on obtaining an award under an international arbitration convention.

The practitioner has two goals in obtaining recognition and enforcement of a U.S. court-rendered judgment: the ethical goal to avoid the unlicensed practice of law (UPL) in an overseas jurisdiction (or in a domestic jurisdiction that does not permit the hiring of foreign legal consultants [FLCs]); and the professional goal of identifying, selecting, and informing foreign counsel of the underlying domestic action and validity of the U.S. judgment on the client's behalf.

[108] Weems, *supra* note 5, at JAP-8 to JAP-9, JAP-25, KOR-4, KOR-13.

[109] *Id.* at JAP-9 TO JAP-10, KOR-4 TO KOR-5, TAI-7.

[110] Minsōho, Art. 24 (Code of Civil Execution); Korean Code Civ. Proc. Art. 476.

[111] Subject matter jurisdiction is available where personal jurisdiction over the defendant is not available and attachable property is located in the jurisdiction. Weems, *supra* note 5, at JAP-6, KOR-4 to KOR-5, TAI-6.

[112] *Id.* at JAP-14 to JAP-15, JAP-18 to JAP-21.

As a practitioner, you have many resources available to you to help you meet these goals. This handbook provides a reference outline for beginning the process. However, before advising your client about foreign enforcement of a U.S. court-rendered judgment, you should review the resources particularly applicable to the country in which you will seek enforcement and recognition. By so doing, you will provide informed and efficient services to your client and minimize the risk of failing to obtain recognition and/or enforcement of your judgment.

# Bibliography

## INTRODUCTION

This is a selected bibliography of primary and secondary materials on the recognition and enforcement United States judgments in foreign countries. The time span represented by the cited publications is the nineteenth century through June 2004, with an emphasis on works published in the last three decades.[1] Works regarding enforcement of money judgments handed down from courts form the core of the bibliography. Therefore, although some general and introductory materials concerning non-money judgments (such as family law matters) and arbitral awards are included, an exhaustive listing of those materials is beyond the scope of this bibliography.

Only materials published in English are included, with the exception of a few materials in German. The anticipated user of this bibliography is a legal practitioner who seeks to enforce U.S. judgments overseas.

In each section the materials are divided by type, beginning with the primary materials and followed by secondary materials. Each type of material is subdivided into topics, with general topics presented first and specific topics following. The overall organization of materials in each section, as well as the order of citations in each topic area, follows rule 1.4 of *A Uniform System of Citation*. Citation forms are, wherever possible, in *Bluebook* format with additional information provided where available, such as publisher and publisher location.

Every effort was made to confirm sources cited. In order to provide the most complete listing, however, some citations have been taken from bibliographical listings of other materials and therefore may be subject to error from multiple transpositions. The author invites readers to bring mistakes and other useful sources to his attention.

[1] All primary treaty materials and secondary materials are cumulative (i.e., they are listed, although they may be subsequently superseded or outdated) with the exception of those treaties that have revised editions, in which case the most recent edition found is listed. U.S. statutes and foreign statutes are those in effect in 2004.

## A. APPLICABLE LAWS AND OTHER LEGAL INSTRUMENTS

### 1. Foreign State Statutes (country by country)[2]

| | |
|---|---|
| Argentina | CÓD. PROC. CIV. Y COM. arts. 517–19.<br>CÓD. PROC. CIV. Y COM. arts. 175–87 [expedited procedures].<br>CÓD. PROC. CIV. Y COM. arts. 617 [currency of judgment]. |
| Australia | |
| South Australia | Foreign Judgments Act 1971 (revised 1991) [unlike other Australian states, accepts judgments from any country, not only certain designated countries, which meets registration requirements]. |
| All Other States | Foreign Judgments (Reciprocal Enforcement) Act of 1991 [adopted under the same name by each state]. |
| Austria | Exekutionsordnung (Enforcement Code) §§ 79–86(a)(2002). |
| Belgium | JUD. CODE §§ 570, 635 (2002).<br>JUD. CODE §§ 1723 (arbitration) (2002). |
| Bermuda | Judgments (Reciprocal Enforcement) Act of 1958, Title 8/71 (1989 revision) (2002). |
| Bolivia | Code CIV. P. arts. 202–5, 552, 555 (2001). |
| Brazil | C.F. art. 102(h).<br>C.C. Law of Introduction arts. 12, 15–17 (1990).<br>Regimento Interno do Supremo Tribunal Federal, arts. 215–224 (1990).<br>C.P.C. arts. 88, 282, 483–4, 584, 737, 741 (1990). |
| Canada | |
| New Brunswick | R.S.N.B. chs. F-19, R-3, 1973 (2002). |
| Quebec | CODE CIV. PROC. §§ 178–179 (1995).<br>CIV. CODE § 1220 (1995).<br>All Other Provinces/Territories Reciprocal Enforcement of Judgments Act of 1980 (1995) [adopted by each government under the same name]. |
| Cayman Islands | Foreign Judgments Reciprocal Enforcement Law (Revised) 1976 (2002). |
| Chile | CODE CIV. P. arts. 242–51 (2004).<br>CODE CIV. P. arts. 15, 16, 995 [real property, marriage]. |
| China | CIV. P. CODE arts. 262–70 (2000). |
| China, People's | R.O.C. CIV. P. CODE arts. 145, 149, 401–2 (1999) arts. 12, 13 (2003). |

[2] In many instances these citations were compiled from secondary sources available to the author at the time of writing; these citations are only intended as a starting point for researching the law of recognition and enforcement for those countries listed. These laws are constantly changing; relevant statutes other than those statutes provided may exist in the countries listed, and relevant statutes may exist in countries not included in this listing.

| | |
|---|---|
| Republic of (Taiwan) | R.O.C. COMPUL. EXEC. L. art. 43 (2003). |
| Colombia | CODE CIV. P. §§ 302–39, 623, 693–7 (2003). |
| Costa Rica | CODE CIV. P. §§ 705–8 (2003). |
| Cyprus | Foreign Judgments (Reciprocal Enforcement) Law of 1935 (2003). |
| Czech Republic | Private International Law Code srts. 63–6 (2003). Code Civ. P. §§ 251–3 (2003). |
| Denmark* | Administration of Justice Act §§ 223A-B, 479 (2002). |
| Dominican Republic | CIV. CODE §§ 2123, 2134, Ley 1, 486 of 1938 (2002).<br>CODE CIV. P. §§ 116–65, 545–56 (2002). |
| Ecuador | CODE CIV. P. §§ 273–306, 423–8 (2003). |
| Egypt | CIV. & COM. PROC. arts. 296–8, 301 (2002).<br>Civil Procedures Law Chapter 4 No. 13 of (1968). |
| El Salvador | CODE CIV. P. §§ 441–53 (2003).<br>CODE CIV. P. § 170 [divorce]. |
| England | Judgments Extension Act, 1863, 31 & 32 Vict., ch. 54 (1998).<br>Administration of Justice Act, 1920, 10 & 11 Geo. 5, ch. 81 (1998).<br>Foreign Judgments (Reciprocal Enforcement) Act, 1933, 23 & 24 Geo. 5, ch. 81 (1998).<br>The Gaming Act, 1968, ch. 65.<br>Protection of Trading Interests Act, 1980, ch. 11 (1999).<br>Civil Jurisdiction and Judgments Act, 1982 (1999).<br>Order 71 Rules of the Supreme Court (1998). |
| Finland | Act on Cooperation Between Finnish and Foreign Authorities in Connection with Court Proceedings and Enforcement of Judgments Rendered by Foreign Courts (amended 1988) [attorney's fees] (2003). |
| France | NEW C. PR. CIV. art 509 (2001).<br>C. CIV. arts. 14–15, 2123, 2128 (2001). |
| Germany | Z.P.O. §§ 328(1), 722–723 (2000).<br>Z.P.O. §§ 1044 [arbitration] (2000). |
| Greece | CODE CIV. P. arts. 323, 905 (2003).<br>CODE CIV. P. arts. 903, 906 [arbitration] (2001). |
| Guatemala | CIV. & MERCANTILE PROC. CODE arts. 344–6 (2005).<br>Law of the Judicial Organism arts. 190–5 (2005).<br>International Private Law Code (Havana, 1928) (2004). |
| Honduras | CODE CIV. P. arts. 235–41 (2003). |
| Hungary | International Private Law Code of Hungary, ch. 4, arts. 70–74 (Act-Order 1979:13) (2000). |
| Iceland* | Act of Enforcement No. 90/1989 (2002). |

| | |
|---|---|
| India | INDIA CODE CIV. PROC. §§ 2, 13–14, 20–1, 34–5, 44, 47, 96, 100 (1991).<br>Foreign Rewards (recognition and enforcement) Act of 1961 (1999). |
| Indonesia | Reglement op de Rechtsvordering arts. 436, 440 (1999).<br>COMM. CODE art. 724 (1999). |
| Ireland | Jurisdiction of Courts and Enforcement of Judgments (European Communities) Act No. 2, 1988 (2001). |
| Israel | Foreign Judgments Enforcement Law 5718, 1958 (2002).<br>Israel Rules of Court §§ 352–9, 397 (1997).<br>Adjudication of Interest and Linkage Law 5721, 1961 (1998).<br>Evidence Ordinance (New Version) 5731, 1971 (1998). |
| Italy | C.P.C. §§ 39, 796–9 (2002).<br>Reform of Italian System of International Law No. 218/1995 (1999). |
| Japan | MINSOHŌ [Code of Civil Procedure] art. 188–200 [recognition] (2002).<br>MINPŌ [Civil Code] art. 24 [enforcement] (2002). |
| Kenya | Foreign Judgments (Reciprocal Enforcement) Act, ch. 43 (2003). |
| Korea, Republic of | CODE CIV. P. arts. 9, 203, 217, 476–7 (2002).<br>Civil Enforcement Act arts. 26, 27 (2002). |
| Lebanon | CODE CIV. P. arts. 1009–22 (2000).<br>CODE CIV. P. arts. 809–21 [arbitration] (2000). |
| Luxembourg | NEW CODE CIV. P. arts. 678–85 (2003).<br>CODE CIV. P. arts. 1224–51 [arbitration] (1981). |
| Malaysia | Reciprocal Enforcement of Judgments Act (Revised) 1972 (2003). |
| Malta | CODE ORG. & CIV. P. §§ 811–812, 826–828 (1990).<br>Maintenance Orders (Reciprocal Enforcement Act, ch. 242 (2002). |
| Mexico | C.P.C.D.F. arts. 24–5, 81, 85, 140, 156, 330, 604–8.<br>C.F.P.C. arts. 302, 355–6.<br>C.C.D.F. arts. 2814, 2817. |
| Netherlands | CODE CIV. P. arts. 431, 985–92 (2003).<br>CODE CIV. P. arts. 1074–76 [arbitration] (2003). |
| New Zealand | Reciprocal Enforcement of Judgments Act of 1934 (2003) |
| Nicaragua | CODE CIV. P. arts. 9–19, 542–52. |
| Nigeria | Foreign Judgments (Reciprocal Enforcement) Act of 1960 (2000). |
| Norway* | CODE CIV. P. §§ 167–8 (2003).<br>Enforcement Act §§ 3(10), 30, 78 (2003).<br>Act of Enforcement of Nordic Judgments Convention of 1971 (2003). |

| | |
|---|---|
| Pakistan | CODE CIV. P. §§ 2, 13, 20, 44A, 47 (2003). |
| Panama | CODE CIV. P. arts. 581–90, 1409–11 (2003).<br>Maritime Code arts. 419–28 (1982) (2002). |
| Paraguay | CODE CIV. P. §§ 532–7, 693(c) (2002) (693 only in EMJ 1992). |
| Peru | CIV CODE. arts. 1155–68 (2004).<br>CODE CIV. P. arts. 376, 410, 411, 749, 753–6 837–40, 1073, 24 I.L.M. 997 (1985) [English translation] (2002).<br>CIV. CODE JUR.COMPETENCE art. 1237, 2057–60, 2102–11 (1994). |
| Philippines | Rules of Court § 50, rule 40 (2004).<br>CIV. CODE. arts. 14, 16–17 (2004). |
| Poland | CODE CIV. P. arts. 1145–53 (2000). |
| Portugal | CODE CIV. P. arts. 65, 65A, 85, 558, 771, 1094–96, 1100–02 [generally] (2003).<br>CODE CIV. P. arts. 78–80 [admiralty] (1998).<br>CODE CIV. P. arts. 82 [bankruptcy] (1998).<br>CODE CIV. P. arts. 558 [currency] (1998). |
| Romania | Law No. 105/1992, art. 165–78.<br>Law No. 673/2002. |
| Russia | Arbitration Procedure Code of the Russian Federation (N 95-FZ 2002).<br>Civil Procedure Code of the Russian Federation (N 138-FZ 2002). |
| Saudi Arabia | Board of Grievances Regulation art. 8(1)(g) (1982) (2002).<br>Royal Order 235/2 of 9 May 1961 (2000) |
| Singapore | Reciprocal Enforcement of Foreign Judgments Act (1959), ch. 265, 1985 edition (2004).<br>Rules of Court (1996), Order 67 (2004). |
| South Africa | Protection of Businesses Act 99 of 1978 (2003).<br>Enforcement of Foreign Civil Judgments Act 32 of 1988 (2003). |
| Spain | CODE CIV. P. arts. 300, 523, 600–601, 921, 951–8, 1435–45 (L.E. Civ. 1881) (2004).<br>CODE CIV. P. art. (1.2 L.E. Civ. 2000).<br>Organic Act 20/2003, 62/2003.<br>Spanish Basic Law on Judiciary of 1985 §§ 7, 21–4 (2003). |
| Sri Lanka | Reciprocal Enforcement of Judgments Act, Ordinance No. 41 of 1921 (2004).<br>Enforcement of Foreign Judgments Act, ch. 93 (2004). |
| Sweden* | Act 1986:1042 on Enforcement of Certain Decisions Concerning Litigation Costs (1899:12, p. 9) (2002). |
| Switzerland | Swiss Act on Private International Law arts. 25–30, 149, 470–2 (1989) (2004).<br>GENEVA LAW CIV. P. arts. 472(a), 472(b) (2004). |

| | |
|---|---|
| Syria | SYRIAN. P. CODE §§ 195–218, 306–8, 311 (2002). |
| Tanzania | Foreign Judgment (Reciprocal Enforcement) Ordinance, ch. 8 (1936) (2003). |
| Thailand | CIV. & COM. CODE §§ 113, 164, 168, 150, 196, 224 655.<br>Act on Conflict of Laws, B.E. 2481 § 15, 1938 (1995).<br>CODE CIV. P. §§ 2, 4, 161, 170, 224, 229, 231, 247, 248, 253, 284–5, 287, 290 (1995). |
| Turkey | Enforcement and Recognition of Foreign Judgments and Arbitral Awards Act, No. 2675 of 1982 §§ 34–42 (1999). |
| United Arab Emirates | Abu Dhabi Code of Civil Procedure §§ 15–17, 21–26, 61–3.<br>U.A.E. Fed. Law No. 11 of 1992, art. 12 [between emirates] (1999). |
| Uruguay | CODE CIV. P. §§ 524–543 (2002). |
| Venezuela | CODE CIV. P. arts. 242–54, 850–8 (2000).<br>1998 Bill of Rules of Private International Law arts. 39–47, 53–7 (1999). |
| Zaire | Code of Judicial Organization and Competence, arts. 117, 144–5 (1992). |

**Note:* Foreign Judgments are generally unenforceable in the Nordic countries Denmark, Finland, Iceland, Norway, and Sweden except by treaty. The United States has no treaty for enforcement with these countries; therefore U.S. judgments generally are unenforceable, with the exception perhaps of judgments awarding attorney's fees in Finland and Sweden. The Nordic Judgments Convention of 1933 and 1977 provide for recognition and enforcement of judgments between these five countries.

### 2. Conventions[3]

#### *a. United Nations*

Convention on the Recognition of Foreign Arbitral Awards (New York Convention), June 10, 1958, 21 U.S.T. 2517, 330 U.N.T.S. 38 (1959).

Convention Concerning the Recognition and Enforcemnet of Decisions Involving Obligations to Support Minor Children, Apr. 15, 1958, 539 U.N.T.S. 27.

Convention on the Service Abroad of Judicial and Extrajudicial Documents in Civil and Commercial Matters, Nov. 15, 1965, 20 U.S.T. 361, T.I.A.S. No. 6638, 658 U.N.T.S. 163.

#### *b. Others*

Agreement on the Execution of Foreign Judgments (Acuerdo Boliviano), Caracas, Venezuela, July 18, 1911.

Arab League Convention on the Enforcement of Judgments, Sept. 14, 1952.

[3] Most of these conventions are inapplicable to the United States. For a list of those conventions to which the U.S. is a party, see Part One, Instruments, Laws, and Other Materials.

Convention on Accession of New Member States to the 1968 Convention on Jurisdiction of Courts, Oct. 9, 1978, O.J. (L 304) 1.

Convention on the Choice of Court, Nov. 25, 1965, Recueil de Conventions Hague [RCH] 96.

Convention on the Jurisdiction Applicable Law and Recognition of Adoptions, Nov. 15, 1965, [RCH] 64, U.K.T.S. 94 (1978) (Cmnd 7342).

Convention on Private International Law (Bustamante Code), Havana, Feb. 20, 1928, 86 L.N.T.S. 111.

Convention on the Recognition of Divorces and Legal Separations, June 1, 1970, RCH 138, U.K.T.S. 123 (Cmnd 6248), 8 I.L.M. 31.

Draft Treaty Providing for U.S.-U.K. Reciprocal Recognition and Enforcement of Judgments in Civil Matters, 16 I.L.M. 71 (1976); Third Consultive Paper, March 1979, *reprinted in* 8 N.C.J. INT'L. L. COM. REG. 322 (1983) [not in force].

European Communities – European Free Trade Association: Convention on Jurisdiction and Enforcement of Judgments in Civil and Commercial Matters (Lugano Convention), Sept. 16, 1988, 28 I.L.M. 620 (1989).

European Convention on the Accession of the Kingdom of Spain and the Portuguese Republic to the Brussels Convention (San Sebastion Convention), May 26, 1989, 29 I.L.M. 1413.

European Convention on International Commercial Arbitration, Geneva, Apr. 21, 1961, 484 U.N.T.S. 364 (1964).

European Convention on Jurisdiction and Enforcement of Judgments in Civil and Commercial Matters (Brussels Convention), Sept. 27, 1968, 1978 O.J. (L 304) 78, 8 I.L.M. 229 (1969).

European Convention on Recognition and Enforcement of Decisions Concerning Children and on Restoration of Custody of Children, Council of Europe, Luxembourg, May 20, 1980, EUROP. T.S. NO. 105.

Hague Convention Abolishing the Requirement of Legalization for Foreign Public Documents, Nov. 5, 1961 [supplemented by *Conclusions and Recommendations Adopted by the Special Commission on the Practical Operation of the Hague Apostille, Evidence and Service Conventions*, 28 October – 4 November, 2003].

Hague Convention on the Service Abroad of Judicial and Extrajudicial Documents in Civil and Commercial Matters, Nov. 15, 1965 [supplemented by *Conclusions and Recommendations Adopted by the Special Commission on the Practical Operation of the Hague Apostille, Evidence and Service Conventions*, 28 October – 4 November, 2003].

Hague Convention on the Taking of Evidence Abroad in Civil or Commercial Matters, Mar. 18, 1970 [supplemented by *Conclusions and Recommendations Adopted by the Special Commission on the Practical Operation of the Hague Apostille, Evidence and Service Conventions*, 28 October – 4 November, 2003].

Hague Convention on the Recognition and Enforcement of Decisions Relative to Maintenance Obligations, Oct. 2, 1973, RCH 203.

Hague Convention on the Recognition and Enforcement of Foreign Judgments in Civil and Commercial Matters, Apr. 26, 1966, 5 I.L.M. 636 (1966), 15 AM. J. COMP. L. 362 (1967).

Hague Convention on the Recognition and Enforcement of Foreign Judgments in Civil and Commercial Matters, Feb. 1, 1971, RCH 106.

Hague Conference on Private International Law, International Jurisdiction and Foreign Judgments in Civil and Commercial Matters (Hague Conference), Some Reflections on the Present State of Negotiations on the Judgments Project in the Context of the Future Work Programme of the Conference, Prel. Doc. No. 16 (Feb. 2002).

Hague Conference, The Impact of the Internet on the Judgments Project: Thoughts for the Future, Prel. Doc. No. 17 (Feb. 2002) (prepared by Avril D. Haines).

Hague Conference, Reflection Paper to Assist in the Preparation of a Convention on Jurisdiction and Recognition and Enforcement of Foreign Judgments in Civil and Commercial Matters, Prel. Doc. No. 19 (Aug. 2002) (prepared by Andrea Schulz).

Hague Conference, The Relationship Between the Judgments Project and Other International Instruments, Prel. Doc. No. 24 (Dec. 2003) (prepared by Andrea Schulz).

Inter-American Convention on the Extraterritorial Validity of Foreign Judgments and Arbitral Awards, May 18, 1979, OEA/Ser.A/28 (SEPF), PAN-AM T.S. 51, 18 I.L.M. 1224.

Inter-American Convention on International Commercial Arbitration, Panama, Jan. 30, 1975, 14 I.L.M. 336 (1976).

Inter-Americna Convention on Jurisdiction in the International Sphere for the Extraterritorial Validity of Foreign Judgments, Montevideo, May 24, 1984, OEA/Ser.A/39 (1980).

Inter-American Convention on Support Obligations, 29 I.L.M. 73 (1990).

The Proposed Hague Convention on Jurisdiction and Foreign Judgments: Trans-Atlantic Lawmaking for Transnational Litigation, Samuel P. Baumgartner (2003).

## B. TREATISES AND BOOKS

### 1. Conventions

#### *a. General*

COUNCIL OF EUROPE, THE PRACTICAL GUIDE TO RECOGNITION AND ENFORCEMENT OF FOREIGN DECISIONS IN CIVIL AND COMMERCIAL LAW PT. I (1975).

F. A. MANN, NOTES AND COMMENTS ON CASES IN INTERNATIONAL LAW, COMMERCIAL LAW, AND ARBITRATION (Oxford University Press, 1992).

ALAN REDFERN & MARTIN HUNTER, LAW AND PRACTICE OF INTERNATIONAL COMMERCIAL ARBITRATION (London, Sweet, & Maxwell, 2d ed., 1991).

ARTHUR T. VON MEHREN, RECOGNITION AND ENFORCEMENT OF FOREIGN JUDGMENTS: CONTEMPORARY PRACTICES AND THE ROLE OF CONVENTIONS, in PRIVATE INVESTORS ABROAD: PROBLEMS AND SOLUTIONS IN INTERNATIONAL BUSINESS IN 1980 (M. Landwehr ed., 1980).

RUSSELL J. WEINTRAUB, INTERNATIONAL LITIGATION AND ARBITRATION: PRACTICE AND PLANNING (Durham, NC, Carolina Academic Press, 4th ed., 2003).

*b. Brussels Convention and the EEC [EU]*

Peter Byrne, The E.E.C. Convention on Jurisdiction and the Enforcement of Judgments (Dublin, Round Hall Press, 1990).

Geoffrey Cheshire, Private Interntaional Law chs. 14, 16 (P.M. North ed., London, Butterworth's, 11th ed., 1987).

John G. Collier, Conflict of Laws 113–3 (Robert Y. Jennings ed., Cambridge, Cambridge University Press, 1987).

Alan Dashwood et al., A Guide to Civil Jurisdiction and Judgments Convention (Boston, Kluwer Law & Taxation Publishers, 1987).

Georges R. Delaume, Transnational Contracts Applicable Law and Settlement of Disputes ch. 10 (New York, Oceana Publications, 1992).

Ronald H. Graveson, Conflict of Laws: Private International Law 98–108 (London, Sweet & Maxwell, 7th ed., 1974) [Brussels Convention].

Joseph M. Lookofsky, Transnational Litigation and Commercial Arbitration, ch. 2 (Ardsley-on-Hudson, NY, Transnational Juris Publications, Inc., 1992).

Outside the Scope of the Brussels and Lugano Conventions (The Hague, Kluwer Law Int'l., 2002).

A. Tebbens, *Jurisdiction and Enforcement in International Contract Law (Selected Aspects of the Brussels Convention of 1968/1978)*, in International Contracts and Conflicts of Laws – A Collection of Essays (P. Šarĉević ed., 1990).

Gerhard Walter & Samuel P. Baugartner, *General Report: The Recognition and Enforcement of Judgments Outside the Scope of the Brussels and Lugano Conventions*, in Recognition and Enforcement of Foreign Judgments (Kluwer Law Int'l, 2000).

*c. Lugano and San Sebastian Conventions*

Michael Carpenter et al., the Lugano and San Sebastian Conventions (London, Butterworth's, 1990).

**2. General**

Bradford C. Cafrey, International Jurisdiction and the Recognition and Enforcement of Foreign Judgments in the Law Asia Region: A Comparative Study of the Laws of Eleven Asian Countries Inter-SE and with the E.E.C. Countries (North Ryde, N.S.W., C.C.H. Australia, 1985) [based on author's doctoral thesis, Universitaet Tuebingen].

Okezie Chukwumerije, Choice of Law in International Commercial Arbitration (Westport, CT, Quroum Books, 1994).

Jan H. Dalhuisen, Dalhuisen on International Insolvency and Bankruptcy §§ 1.03, 1.04, 1.06, 1.07 (New York, Matthew Bender, 1986).

Georges R. Delaume, Law and Practice of Transnational Contracts 199–222 (New York, Ocena Publications, 1988).

Albert V. Dicey & John H.C. Morris, the Conflict of Law (Collins, 13th ed., 2000).

EFFECTIVE DISPUTE RESOLUTION FOR THE INTERNATIONAL COMMERCIAL LAWYER 173–96 (P. Summerfield & D. Campbell eds., Boston, Kluwer Law & Taxation Publishers, 1989) [overview of Asian, civil and common law country approaches].

OLUSOJI ELIAS, JUDICIAL REMEDIES IN THE CONFLICT OF LAWS, CH. 7 (Oxford, Hart Publishing, 2001).

ENCYCLOPEDIA OF INTERNATIONAL COMMERCIAL LITIGATION (Anthony Colman ed., Graham & Trotman, Norwell, Kluwer Academic Publishers, 1991, updated 1997) [practice and procedure of each country with a section for each on enforcement].

ENFORCEMENT OF FOREIGN JUDGMENTS (Louis Garb & Julian Lew eds., Boston, Kluwer Law & Taxation Publishers, 1994, updated 2003) [country-by-country guide to laws and procedures].

ENFORCEMENT OF FOREIGN JUDGMENTS WORLDWIDE (Charles Platto ed., London, Graham & Trotman, 1993) [practice guide for 34 countries based on answers to questionnaires by practitioners in those countries].

INTERNATIONAL BAR ASSOCIATION, ENFORCEMENT OF FOREIGN JUDGMENTS WORLDWIDE (Charles Platto & William G. Horton eds., 2d ed., 1993).

INTERNATIONAL EXECUTION AGANINST JUDGMENT DEBTORS (Dennis Campbell ed., London, Sweet & Maxwell, 1993, updated 2004) [country-by-country guide to laws, procedures and recognition of foreign judgments].

INTERNATIONAL JUDICIAL ASSISTANCE (CIVIL AND COMMERCIAL) (Bruno Ristau ed., Washington, D.C., International Law Institute, 1984).

WILLIAM F. FOX, INTERNATIONAL COMMERCIAL AGREEMENTS: A FUNCTIONAL PRIMER ON DRAFTING, NEGOTIATING, AND RESOLVING DISPUTES 190–94 (Boston, Kluwer Law & Taxation Publishers, 1988).

VOLKMAR GESSNER, FOREIGN COURTS: CIVIL LITIGATION IN FOREIGN LEGAL CULTURES (The Oñati International Institute for the Sociology of Law, 1996).

JACK L. GOLDSMITH, INTERNATIONAL DISPUTE RESOLUTION: THE REGULATION OF FORUM SELECTION (Transnational Publishers, Inc., 1997).

RONALD H. GRAVESON, CONFLICT OF LAWS: PRIVATE INTERNATIONAL LAW 619–46 (London, Sweet & Maxwell, 1974).

ANDREAS F. LOWENFELD, INTERNATIONAL LITIGATION AND ARBITRATION CH. 5 (St. Paul, MN, West Publishing Co., 2d ed., 2002).

MARTINDALE-HUBBEL, MARTINDALE HUBBEL LAW DIGEST – INTERNATIONAL LAW DIGEST (New Providence, NJ, Martindale-Hubbel, 1992) [country-by-country general legal reference for 67 countries].

LESTER NELSON, DIGEST OF COMMERCIAL LAWS OF THE WORLD (Dobbs Ferry, NY, Oceana Publications, 1987).

LAWRENCE W. NEWMAN, ENFORCEMENT OF MONEY JUDGMENTS, Vol. 1–3 (2003).

FRANCIS T. PIGGOT, FOREIGN JUDGMENTS AND JURISDICTION (Hong Kong, Kelly & Walsch, 1908–1910).

Procedures to Enforce Foreign Judgments (Paul Omer ed., Ashgate, Aldershot, 2002) [English manual with bibliography of country-specific texts for several countries].

Thomas H. Reynolds & Arturo A. Flores, Foreign Law: Current Sources of Codes and Basic Legislation in Jurisdictions of the World (Littleton, CO, Fred B. Rothman & Co., 1989) [see entry for "foreign judgments" under each country].

Bruno Ristau, International Judicial Assistance, Vol. 1–2 (International Law Institute, Washington D.C., updated 1995) [an overview of which country has what multilateral and bilateral agreements, and blocking legislation].

George J. Roman, Recognition and Enforcement of Foreign Judgments in Various Foreign Countries (Washington, D.C., Library of Congress Law Library, 1984).

William Tetley, International Conflict of Laws: Common, Civil, or Maritime (International Shipping Publications, 1994) [ch. XXV, Recognition of Foreign Judgments].

David Westin, U.S. Judgments Abroad (New York, Matthew Bender, 1991) [country-by-country practice guide].

### 3. Regional

| | |
|---|---|
| Eastern Europe | Ivan Sipkov, The Codified Statutes on Private International Law of the East European Countries: A Comparative Study 27 (Washington, D.C., Library of Congress Law Library, 1986) [Czechoslovakia, Hungary, Yugoslavia].<br>Ivan Spikov, Legal Assistance Within the Socialist Commonwealth of Eastern European Countries 25 (Washington, D.C., Library of Congress Law Library, 1987). |
| Western Europe | Paul Cronheim, *Enforcing U.S. Judgments in Europe*, in International Litigation 487 (ABA Section of International Law and Practice, 1989). |
| Latin America | Robert C. Casad, Civil Judgment Recognition and the Integration of Multi-state Associations: Central America, The United States of America, and the European Economic Community (Lawrence, KS, The Regents Press of Kansas, 1981) [guide for Latin America only].<br>A. Golbert & Y. Nun, Latin American Laws and Institutions 565 (1982). |

### 4. Country-by-Country

| | |
|---|---|
| Argentina | Werner Goldschmidt & Jose Rodriguez-Novas, American-Argentine Private International Law 112 (Bilateral Studies in Private International Law No. 15, published for the Parker School of Foreign and Comparative Law, Columbia University, New York, Oceana Publications 1966).<br>Grigera Naon, The Recognition of Money Judgments in Civil and Commercial Matters, Asociacion Argenting de Derecho Comparado, Nat'l Rep. to Int'l Congress Comp. L. 54 (1986). |

MARTINDALE-HUBBELL, MARTINDALE-HUBBELL INTERNATIONAL LAW DIGEST, ARGENTINA LAW DIGEST (2004).

Australia

B. BAIRNES, AUSTRALIAN CIVIL PROCEDURE (1985).
D. BRYNE & J. HEYDON, CROSS ON EVIDENCE: THIRD AUSTRALIAN EDITION (1986).
Z. COWEN, AMERICAN-AUSTRALIAN PRIVATE INTERNATIONAL LAW 100 (Bilateral Studies in Private International Law No. 8, published for the Parker School of Foreign and Comparative Law, Columbia University, New York, Oceana Publications, 1957).
ALBERT V. DICEY, DICEY AND MORRIS ON THE CONFLICT OF LAWS (J. H. C. Morris ed., London, Lawrence, Stevens & Sons Ltd., 10th ed., 1980).
MARTINDALE-HUBBELL, MARTINDALE-HUBBELL INTERNATIONAL LAW DIGEST, AUSTRALIA LAW DIGEST (2004).
J. MCLEAN & K. PATCHETT, RECOGNITION AND ENFORCEMENT OF JUDGMENTS AND ORDERS AND THE SERVICE OF PROCESS WITHIN THE COMMONWEALTH (1977).
P.E. NYGH, CONFLICT OF LAWS IN AUSTRALIA (5th ed.).

Austria

MARTINDALE-HUBBELL, MARTINDALE-HUBBELL INTERNATIONAL LAW DIGEST, AUSTRIA LAW DIGEST (2004).
IGNAZ SEIDL-HOHENVELDERN, AMERICAN-AUSTRIAN PRIVATE INTERNATIONAL LAW 151 (Bilateral Studies in Private International Law No. 11, published for the Parker School of Foreign and Comparative Law, Columbia University, New York, Oceana Publications 1963).

Brazil

PAUL G. GARLAND, AMERICAN-BRAZILIAN PRIVATE INTERNATIONAL LAW 93 (Bilateral Studies in Private International Law No. 9, published for the Parker School of Foreign and Comparative Law, Columbia University, New York, Oceana Publications 1959).
MARTINDALE-HUBBELL, MARTINDALE-HUBBELL INTERNATIONAL LAW DIGEST, BRAZIL LAW DIGEST (2004).

Canada

IAN F. G. BAXTER, ESSAYS ON PRIVATE LAW: FOREIGN LAW AND JUDGMENTS (Toronto, University of Toronto Press, 1966).
J. G. CASTEL, PRIVATE INTERNATIONAL LAW: A COMPARATIVE STUDY OF THE RULES PREVAILING IN CANADA AND THE UNITED STATES 231 (Torronto, Canada, Law Book Co., 1960).
J. G. CASTEL, CANADIAN CONFLICT OF LAWS (5th ed., 2002).
WALTER S. JOHNSON, CONFLICT OF LAWS (Montreal, Wilson et Lafleur Limitée, 2d. ed., 1962).
MARTINDALE-HUBBELL, MARTINDALE-HUBBELL INTERNATIONAL LAW DIGEST, CANADA LAW DIGEST (2004).
MARTINDALE-HUBBELL, MARTINDALE-HUBBELL INTERNATIONAL LAW DIGEST, BRITISH COLUMBIA LAW DIGEST (2004).
MARTINDALE-HUBBELL, MARTINDALE-HUBBELL INTERNATIONAL LAW DIGEST, NEWFOUNDLAND AND LABRADOR LAW DIGEST (2004).
MARTINDALE-HUBBELL, MARTINDALE-HUBBELL INTERNATIONAL LAW DIGEST, ONTARIO LAW DIGEST (2004).

| | |
|---|---|
| | JAMES MACLEOD, THE CONFLICT OF LAWS (Calgary, Carswell Legal Publications, 1983).<br>RONALD E. MYRICK, WORLD LITIGATION AND PRACTICE UNIT A: NORTH AMERICA: CANADA § 8.02 (New York, Mathew Bender, 1986).<br>ROBERT J. SHARPE, *The Enforcement of Foreign Judgments*, in DEBTOR-CREDITOR LAW: PRACTICE AND DOCTRINE 641 (M. A. Springman & Eric Gertner eds., 1985). |
| | JEFFREY TALPIS, IF I'M FROM GRAND-MÈRE, WHY AM I BEING SUED IN TEXAS? (Les Éditions Thémis, 2001). |
| Cayman Islands | MARTINDALE-HUBBELL, MARTINDALE-HUBBELL INTERNATIONAL LAW DIGEST, CAYMAN ISLANDS LAW DIGEST (2004). |
| Chile | A. ETCHBERRY, AMERICAN-CHILEAN PRIVATE INTERNATIONAL LAW 94 (Bilateral Studies in Private International Law No. 10, published for the Parker School of Foreign and Comparative Law, Columbia University, New York, Oceana Publications, 1960). |
| China | MARTINDALE-HUBBELL, MARTINDALE-HUBBELL INTERNATIONAL LAW DIGEST, PEOPLE'S REPUBLIC OF CHINA LAW DIGEST (2004). |
| Cuba | MARTINDALE-HUBBELL, MARTINDALE-HUBBELL INTERNATIONAL LAW DIGEST, CUBA LAW DIGEST (2004). |
| Cyprus | MARTINDALE-HUBBELL, MARTINDALE-HUBBELL INTERNATIONAL LAW DIGEST, CYPRUS LAW DIGEST (2004). |
| Czechoslovakia | GEORGE E. GLOS, CZECHOSLOVAK PRIVATE INTERNATIONAL LAW (Washington, D.C., Library of Congress Law Library, 1983).<br>J. Vondracek, *The Recognition and Enforcement of Judgments Outside the Scope of the Application of the Brussels and Lugano Conventions: Czechoslovakia – Czech Republic* in RECOGNITION AND ENFORCEMENT OF FOREIGN JUDGMENTS OUTSIDE THE SCOPE OF THE BRUSSELS AND LUGANO CONVENTIONS (The Hague, Kluwer Law Int'l., 2002). |
| Colombia | P. EDLER, AMERICAN-COLOMBIAN PROVATE INTERNATIONAL LAW 94 (Bilateral Studies in Private International Law No. 5, published for the Parker School of Foreign and Comparative Law, Columbia University, New York, Oceana Publications, 1956). |
| Cyprus | LAW OF CYPRESS, CH. 10, 113 (1959). |
| Egypt | E. ABDALLAH, PRIVATE INTERNATIONAL LAW (1977).<br>A. ABDEL KERIM, LAW OF INTERNATIONAL PROCEDURE (1985).<br>FROUAD RIAD & SAMIA RASHED, CONFLICT OF LAWS AND CONFLICT OF JURISDICTION (1987).<br>H. SADEK, CONFLICT OF JURISDICTION (1978). |
| England and the Commonwealth of Nations | PETER BARNETT, RES JUDICATA, ESTOPPEL, AND FOREIGN JUDGMENTS (Oxford University Press, 2001).<br>A. BLACK, ENFORCEMENT OF A JUDGMENT (9th ed.)<br>GEOFFREY C. CHESHIRE, PRIVATE INTERNATIONAL LAW (P. M. North ed., London, Butterworth's, 11th ed., 1987). |

COLLEGE OF LAW, JURISDICTION AND ENFORCEMENT OF JUDGMENTS IN EUROPE (1985).
JOHN G. COLLIER, CONFLICT OF LAWS 63–112 (Robert Y. Jennings ed., Cambridge, Cambridge University Press, 1987).
J. G. Collier, *Recognition and Enforcement of Foreign Judgments: England*, in RECOGNITION AND ENFORCEMENT OF FOREIGN JUDGMENTS OUTSIDE THE SCOPE OF THE BRUSSELS AND LUGANO CONVENTIONS (The Hague, Kluwer Law Int'l., 2002).
GEORGES R. DELAUME, TRANSNATIONAL CONFLICTS APPLICABLE LAW AND SETTLEMENT OF DISPUTES CH. 9 (New York, Oceana Publishing, 1992).
ALBERT V. DICEY, DICEY AND MORRIS ON THE CONFLICT OF LAWS (J. H. C. Morris ed., London, Lawrence, Stevens & Sons Limited, 10th ed., 1980).
8 HALSBURY'S LAWS OF ENGLAND (London, Butterworth's, 4th ed., 1984).
22 HALSBURY'S STATUTES OF ENGLAND AND WALES (London, Butterworth's, 4th ed., 1985).
Michael James & Simpson Curtis, *Enforcing American and Other Foreign Judgments in England*, in THE COMPARATIVE LAW YEARBOOK OF INTERNATIONAL BUSINESS 1991 (Dennis Campbell ed., London, Graham & Trotman, 1991) [based upon and using for illustration *Adams v. Cape Industries PLC.*, 2 W.L.R. 657 (1990)].
J. F. JOSLING, EXECUTION OF A JUDGMENT 41 (Oyez Practice Notes No. 4, London, Oyez Publishing, 5th ed., 1974).
PETER KAYE, PRIVATE INTERNATIONAL LAW OF TORT AND PRODUCT LIABILITY – JURISDICTION APPLICABLE LAW & EXTRATERRITORIAL PROTECTIVE MEASURES (Brookfield, VT, Dartmouth Publishing Co., 1990).
MARTINDALE-HUBBELL, MARTINDALE-HUBBELL INTERNATIONAL LAW DIGEST, ENGLAND LAW DIGEST (2004).
JOHN O'HARE & ROBERT N. HILL, CIVIL LITIGATION (London, Oyez Publishing, 1981).
KEITH W. PATCHETT, RECOGNITION OF COMMERCIAL JUDGMENTS AND AWARDS IN THE COMMONWEALTH (Butterworth's, London, 1984).
HORACE E. READ, RECOGNITION AND ENFORCEMENT OF FOREIGN JUDGMENTS (Cambridge, MA, Harvard University Press, 1938).
THE SUPREME COURT PRACTICE 1985 (London, Sweet & Maxwell, 1984).
JOHN WESTLAKE, A TREATISE ON PRIVATE INTERNATIONAL LAW WITH PRINCIPLE REFERENCE TO ITS PRACTICE IN ENGLAND (Norman Bentwich ed., Littleton, CO, Fred B. Rothman & Co., 1986 [1859]).

Estonia

MARTINDALE-HUBBELL, MARTINDALE-HUBBELL INTERNATIONAL LAW DIGEST, ESTONIA LAW DIGEST (2004).

France

GEORGES R. DELAUME, AMERICAN-FRENCH PRIVATE INTERNATIONAL LAW (Bilateral Studies in Private International Law No. 2, published for the Parker School of Foreign and

| | |
|---|---|
| | Comparative Law, Columbia University, New York, Oceana Publications, 1961). |
| | Peter E. Herzog, Civil Procedure in France 586 (The Hague, Martinus Nijhoff, 1967). |
| | Martindale-Hubbell, Martindale-Hubbell International Law Digest, France Law Digest (2004). |
| | Siméon & Associés et al., Doing Business in France § 111119.02[8][b] (New York, Matthew Bender, 1986). |
| Finland | Juha Lappalainen, *The Recognition and Enforcement of Judgments Outside the Scope of the Application of the Brussels and Lugano Conventions: Finland*, in Recognition and Enforcement of Foreign Judgments Outside the Scope of the Brussels and Lugano Conventions (The Hague, Kluwer Law Int'l., 2002). |
| Germany | Ulrich Drobing, American German Private International Law 351 (Bilateral Studies in Private International Law No. 4, published for the Parker School of Foreign and Comparative Law, Columbia University, New York, Oceana Publications, 1974).<br>Reinhold Geimer, *The Recognition and Enforcement of Judgments Outside the Scope of the Application of the Brussels and Lugano Conventions: Germany*, in Recognition and Enforcement of Foreign Judgments Outside the Scope of the Brussels and Lugano Conventions (The Hague, Kluwer Law Int'l., 2002).<br>Martindale-Hubbell, Martindale-Hubbell International Law Digest, Germany: Law Digest of the Federal Republic of Germany (2004).<br>Rolf A. Schuetze, *Conceptual Differences and Areas of Potential Collision Between United States and "Civil Law" Procedure from the German Prospective*, in Litigation of Business Matters in the United States and International Legal Assistance (Roger Zaech ed., 1984).<br>Renfors van der Velden, Wagner Third Report on National Case Law on the Lugano Convention (2001).<br>Dr. Hartwig Graf, Von Westerholt & Peter Lautz, *Litigation in Civil Courts*, in Business Transactions in Germany (FRG) §§ 5.15–5.22 (B. Ruster gen. ed., 1983). |
| Greece | C. Beis, Lessons of Civil Procedure – Enforcement (1st ed.).<br>J. Brinias, The Enforcement (2d ed.).<br>K. Kerameus, G. Kremlis & H. Tagaras, *The Brussels Convention on International Jurisdiction and Enforcement of Judgments, as* in *Force*, in Greece, Interpretation per Article (1989).<br>Nikolaos K. Klamaris, *Enforcement of Court Orders and Judgments: Greece*, in Recognition and Enforcement of Foreign Judgments Outside the Scope of the Brussels and Lugano Conventions (The Hague, Kluwer Law Int'l., 2002).<br>G. Maridakis, The Enforceability of Foreign Judgments (3d ed., 1970). |

| | |
|---|---|
| | MARTINDALE-HUBBELL, MARTINDALE-HUBBELL INTERNATIONAL LAW DIGEST, GREECE LAW DIGEST (2004). |
| Jersey | MARTINDALE-HUBBELL, MARTINDALE-HUBBELL INTERNATIONAL LAW DIGEST, CHANNEL ISLANDS (JERSEY) LAW DIGEST (2004). |
| Hong Kong | MARTINDALE-HUBBELL, MARTINDALE-HUBBELL INTERNATIONAL LAW DIGEST, HONG KONG LAW DIGEST (2004). |
| Hungary | Miklos Kengyel, *Die Anerkennung und Vollstreckung der gerichtlichen Entscheidungen ausserhalb des Geltungsbereiches des Bruesseler und Lugano-Uebereinkoommens in Ungarn*, in RECOGNITION AND ENFORCEMENT OF FOREIGN JUDGMENTS OUTSIDE THE SCOPE OF THE BRUSSELS AND LUGANO CONVENTIONS (The Hague, Kluwer Law Int'l 2002). |
| India | MARTINDALE-HUBBELL, MARTINDALE-HUBBELL INTERNATIONAL LAW DIGEST, INDIA LAW DIGEST (2004).<br>M. SUBRAYA PAI, LAW OF EXECUTION 314 (Bangalore, Indian Law House, 1984). |
| Indonesia | J. BALL, INDONESIAN LEGAL HISTORY 1602–1848 (Sydney, Oughtershaw Press, 1982).<br>R. SOEPONO, LAW IN CIVIL PROCEDURE BEFORE DISTRICT COURTS (Jakarta, Pradnya Paramita, 1972).<br>THE SUPREME COURT OF THE REPUBLIC OF INDONESIA, COMPILATION OF QUESTIONS AND ANSWERS ON CIVIL LAWS (Jakarta, 1984). |
| Iran | Lawrence W. Newman & Michael Burrows, *Enforcement of Foreign Judgments – Iran*, in THE PRACTICE OF INTERNATIONAL LITIGATION (2d ed., 1983).<br>MATT PELLONPAEAE & DAVID B. CARON, UNCITRAL ARBITRATION UNCITRAL ARBITRATION RULES AS INTERPRETED AND APPLIED: SELECTED PROBLEMS IN LIGHT OF THE PRACTICE OF THE IRAN-UNITED STATES CLAIMS TRIBUNAL (Helsinki, Finnish Lawyers' Pub., 1994). |
| Ireland | J. BRADY & T. KERR, THE LIMITATION OF ACTIONS IN THE REPUBLIC OF IRELAND CH. 4, at 58.<br>J.KELLY, THE IRISH CONSTITUTION (2d ed., 1984).<br>J. WYLIE, A CASE BOOK OF IRISH LAW CH. 9, at 473. |
| Israel | MARTINDALE-HUBBELL, MARTINDALE-HUBBELL INTERNATIONAL LAW DIGEST, ISRAEL LAW DIGEST (2004).<br>A. Shapira, *Recognition and Enforcement of Foreign Money Judgments in Civil and Commercial Matters*, in ISRAELI REPORTS TO THE XII INTERNATIONAL CONGRESS OF COMPARATIVE LAW 132 (1986). |
| Italy | M. CAPPELLETTI ET AL., THE ITALIAN LEGAL SYATEM: AN INTRODUCTION 156 (1967).<br>G. CERTOMA, THE ITALIAN LEGAL SYSTEM 214 (1985).<br>Michele Angelo Lupoi, *The Recognition and Enforcement of Judgments Outside the Scope of the Application of the Brussels and Lugano Conventions: Italy*, in RECOGNITION AND |

| | |
|---|---|
| | ENFORCEMENT OF FOREIGN JUDGMENTS OUTSIDE THE SCOPE OF THE BRUSSELS AND LUGANO CONVENTIONS (The Hague, Kluwer Law Int'l., 2002).<br>2 R. MYRICK, WORLD LITIGATION AND PRACTICE UNIT B: EUROPE: ITALY §§ 9.01–.03 (1986). |
| Japan | Alexander D. Calhoun, *Enforcing U.S. Judgments in Japan*, in INTERNATIONAL LITIGATION 503 (ABA Section of International Law and Practice, 1989).<br>ALBERT EHRENZWEIG, SUEO IKEHARA, & NORMA JENSEN, AMERICAN-JAPANESE PRIVATE INTERNATIONAL LAW 30 (Bilateral Studies in Private International Law No. 12, published for the Parker School of Foreign and Comparative Law, Columbia University, New York, Oceana Publications, 1964).<br>Yasuhiro Fujita, *Recognition and Enforcement of Foreign Judgments and Arbitration Awards*, in DOING BUSINESS IN JAPAN, PT. 15, CH. 5 (Matthew Bender, 1980).<br>ELLIOT J. HAHN, JAPANESE BUSINESS LAW AND THE LEGAL SYSTEM (1984).<br>TAKAAKI HATTORI & DAN F. HENDERSON, CIVIL PROCEDURE IN JAPAN § 11.02 (New York, Matthew Bender, 1985).<br>THE JAPANESE LEGAL SYSTEM (Hideo Tanaka ed., Tokyo, University of Tokyo Press, 1976). |
| Korea | DAI KWON CHOI, EXECUTION OF FOREIGN JUDGMENTS IN KOREA (1977).<br>MARTINDALE-HUBBELL, MARTINDALE-HUBBELL INTERNATIONAL LAW DIGEST, REPUBLIC OF KOREA LAW DIGEST (2004). |
| Luxembourg | MARTINDALE-HUBBELL, MARTINDALE-HUBBELL INTERNATIONAL LAW DIGEST, LUXEMBOURG LAW DIGEST (2004). |
| Malaysia | MARTINDALE-HUBBELL, MARTINDALE-HUBBELL INTERNATIONAL LAW DIGEST, MALAYSIA LAW DIGEST (2004). |
| Mexico | S. A. BAYITCH & JOSE L. SIQUEIROS, CONFLICT OF LAWS: MEXICO AND THE UNITED STATES: A BILATERAL STUDY 233–40 (Coral Gables, University of Miami Press, 1968) [general enforcement of judgments, divorce decrees, and commercial arbitration].<br>Mark N. Bravin, *Suing Private Companies or Individuals from Mexico in American Courts*, in DOING BUSINESS IN MEXICO § 89.05[2] (M. W. Gordon ed., 1992). |
| Netherlands | R. KOLLEWIGN, AMERICAN-DUTCH PRIVATE INTERNATIONAL LAW (Bilateral Studies in Private International Law No. 3, published for the Parker School of Foreign and Comparative Law, Columbia University, New York, Oceana Publications, 1968).<br>P. Kokkini-Iatridou & J. P. Verheul, *Recognition and Enforcement of Foreign Judgments in Civil and Commercial Matters*, in NETHERLANDS REPORTS TO THE TWELFTH INTERNTAIONAL CONGRESS OF COMPARATIVE LAW 189 (1987). |

MARTINDALE-HUBBELL, MARTINDALE-HUBBELL INTERNATIONAL LAW DIGEST, NETHERLANDS LAW DIGEST (2004).
Stein, *Civil Procedure*, in INTRODUCTION TO DUTCH LAW FOR FOREIGN LAWYERS 258 (D. C. Fokkema et al. eds., 1978).
Rene Ch. Vershuur, *Recognition and Enforcement of Foreign Judgments in the Netherlands*, in RECOGNITION AND ENFORCEMENT OF FOREIGN JUDGMENTS OUTSIDE THE SCOPE OF THE BRUSSELS AND LUGANO CONVENTIONS (The Hague, Kluwer Law Int'l., 2002).

New Zealand

ALBERT V. DICEY, DICEY AND MORRIS ON THE CONFLICT OF LAWS (J. H. C. Morris ed., London, Lawrence, Stevens & Sons Limited, 10th ed., 1980).
8 HALSBURY'S LAW OF ENGLAND paras. 715–68 (London, Butterworth's, 4th ed., 1984).
MARTINDALE-HUBBELL, MARTINDALE-HUBBELL INTERNATIONAL LAW DIGEST, NEW ZEALAND LAW DIGEST (2004).
SIM & CRAIN, PRACTICE AND PROCEDURE (12th ed., 1987).
EDUARD I. SYKES & MICHAEL C. PRYLES, AUSTRALIAN PRIVATE INTERNTAIONAL LAW (2d ed., 1987).

Nigeria

MARTINDALE-HUBBELL, MARTINDALE-HUBBELL INTERNATIONAL LAW DIGEST, NIGERIA LAW DIGEST (2004).

Northern Ireland

MARTINDALE-HUBBELL, MARTINDALE-HUBBELL INTERNATIONAL LAW DIGEST, NORTHERN IRELAND LAW DIGEST (2004).

Norway

Henrik Bull, *The Recognition and Enforcement of Judgments Outside the Scope of the Application of the Brussels and Lugano Conventions: Norway*, in RECOGNITION AND ENFORCEMENT OF FOREIGN JUDGMENTS OUTSIDE THE SCOPE OF THE BRUSSELS AND LUGANO CONVENTIONS (The Hague, Kluwer Law Int'l., 2002).

Panama

MARTINDALE-HUBBELL, MARTINDALE-HUBBELL INTERNATIONAL LAW DIGEST, PANAMA LAW DIGEST (2004).

Peru

MARTINDALE-HUBBELL, MARTINDALE-HUBBELL INTERNATIONAL LAW DIGEST, PERU LAW DIGEST (2004).

Philippines

A. F. Santos, *Enforcement of Judgments and Auxiliary Remedies in Aid of Execution*, in INSTITUTE ON REMEDIAL LAW REVISITED. . . . TRENDS IN REMEDIAL LAW (Quezon City, 1978).

Poland

Mieczyslaw Sawczuk, *The Recognition and Enforcement of Judgments Outside the Scope of the Application of the Brussels and Lugano Conventions: Poland*, in RECOGNITION AND ENFORCEMENT OF FOREIGN JUDGMENTS OUTSIDE THE SCOPE OF THE BRUSSELS AND LUGANO CONVENTIONS (The Hague, Kluwer Law Int'l., 2002).

Russia

F. FELDBRUGGE, G. VAN DEN BERG, & W. SIMONS, ENCYCLOPEDIA OF SOCIET LAW 617 (2d ed., 1985).

| | |
|---|---|
| | MARTINDALE-HUBBELL, MARTINDALE-HUBBELL INTERNATIONAL LAW DIGEST, RUSSIAN FEDERATION LAW DIGEST (2004). |
| South Africa | C. FORSYTH, PRIVATE INTERNATIONAL LAW (Juta, 1981).<br>H. R. HAHLO & ELLISON KAHN, THE UNION OF SOUTH AFRICA: THE DEVELOPMENT OF ITS LAWS AND CONSTITUTION (London: Stevens, 1960).<br>L. D. VAN WINSEN, A. C. CILLIERS, C. LOTZ & N. DEND, THE CIVIL PRACTICE OF THE SUPERIOR COURTS IN SOUTH AFRICA (Juta, 4th ed., 1997).<br>JONES & BUCKLE, THE CIVIL PRACTICE OF THE MAGISTRATES COURTS IN SOUTH AFRICA (I Baker, Erasmus, & Farlam, Juta 2d, 3d ed., 1980); (II Baker, Erasmus, & Farlam, Juta, 7th ed., 1979).<br>W. POLLAK, THE SOUTH AFRICAN LAW ON JURISDICTION (Juta, 1937) [Second edition published as POLLAK ON JURISDICTION [2d ed., 1993].<br>H. SILBERBERG, THE RECOGNITION AND ENFORCEMENT OF FOREIGN JUDGMENTS IN SOUTH AFRICA (Ifcol Publication, UNISA, 1977). |
| Scotland | MARTINDALE-HUBBELL, MARTINDALE-HUBBELL INTERNATIONAL LAW DIGEST, SCOTLAND LAW DIGEST (2004). |
| Singapore | MARTINDALE-HUBBELL, MARTINDALE-HUBBELL INTERNATIONAL LAW DIGEST, SINGAPORE LAW DIGEST (2004). |
| Spain | MARTINDALE-HUBBELL, MARTINDALE-HUBBELL INTERNATIONAL LAW DIGEST, SPAIN LAW DIGEST (2004).<br>Francisco Ramos Mendez, *Derecho Processual Civil Internacional* (J. M. Bosh ed., 2001). |
| Sweden | Mikael Berglund, *Recognition of Foreign Judgments in Sweden*, in RECOGNITION AND ENFORCEMENT OF FOREIGN JUDGMENTS OUTSIDE THE SCOPE OF THE BRUSSELS AND LUGANO CONVENTIONS (The Hague, Kluwer Law Int'l., 2002).<br>MARTINDALE-HUBBELL, MARTINDALE-HUBBELL INTERNATIONAL LAW DIGEST, SWEDEN LAW DIGEST (2004).<br>HAKAN NIAL, AMERICAN-SWEDISH PRIVATE INTERNATIONAL LAW 108 (Bilateral Studies in Private International Law No. 13, published for the Parker School of Foreign and Comparative Law, Columbia University, New York, Oceana Publications, 1965). |
| Switzerland | ARTHUR NUSSBAUM, AMERICAN-SWISS PRIVATE INTERNATIONAL LAW 90 (Bilateral Studies in Private International Law No. 3, published for the Parker School of Foreign and Comparative Law, Columbia University, New York, Oceana Publications, 1968).<br>Fridolin M. R. Walther, *Die Anerkennung und Vollstreckung der gerichtlichen Entscheidungen ausserhalb des Geltungsbereiches des Bruesseler und Lugano-Uebereinkommens in der Schweiz*, in RECOGNITION AND ENFORCEMENT OF FOREIGN JUDGMENTS OUTSIDE THE SCOPE OF THE BRUSSELS AND LUGANO CONVENTIONS (The Hague, Kluwer Law Int'l., 2002). |

| | |
|---|---|
| Thailand | MARTINDALE-HUBBELL, MARTINDALE-HUBBELL INTERNATIONAL LAW DIGEST, THAILAND LAW DIGEST (2004). |
| Turkey | TUGRUL ANSAY, AMERICAN-TURKISH PRIVATE INTERNATIONAL LAW 99 (Bilateral Studies in Private International Law No. 16, published for the Parker School of Foreign and Comparative Law, Columbia University, New York, Oceana Publications, 1966). |
| Venezuela | RICHARD S. LOMBARD, AMERICAN-VENEZUELAN PRIVATE INTERNATIONAL LAW 119 (Bilateral Studies in Private International Law No. 14, published for the Parker School of Foreign and Comparative Law, Columbia University, New York, Oceana Publications, 1965). |
| Vietnam | MARTINDALE-HUBBELL, MARTINDALE-HUBBELL INTERNATIONAL LAW DIGEST, VIETNAM LAW DIGEST (2004). |

## 5. Specialized Areas

### *a. Admiralty*

WILLIAM TETLEY, MARITIME LIENS AND CLAIMS 470–476 (London, Business Law Communications, 1985).

### *b. Antitrust*

ALAN D. NEALE & M. L. STEPHENS, INTERNATIONAL BUSINESS AND NATIONAL JURISDICTION 151 (New York, Oxford University Press, 1988).

### *c. Arbitration Awards/NewYork Convention*

GEOFFREY C.C. CHESHIRE, PRIVATE INTERNATIONAL LAW 435 (P. M. North ed., London, Butterworth's, 11th ed., 1987).

David K. Schollenberger, *International Commercial Arbitration in Europe*, in 1 A THE LAW OF TRANSNATIONAL BUSINESS TRANSACTIONS CH. 19 (Ved P. Nanada ed., New York, Clark Boardman Callaghan, 1992).

M. SORNARAJAH, INTERNATIONAL COMMERCIAL ARBITRATION: THE PROBLEM OF STATE CONTRACTS 198–246 (Singapore, Longmann, 1990).

### *d. Bankruptcy and Creditors' Rights*

JAN H. DALHUISEN, DALHUISEN ON INTERNATIONAL INSOLVENCY AND BANKRUPTCY §§ 1.03 1.04, 2.01–.06 (New York, Matthew Bender, 1986).

CARL FELSENFELD, FESENFELD ON INTERNATIONAL INSOLVENCY (Juris Publishing, 2003).

Toshiyuki Kono, *The Recognition of Foreign Insolvency Proceedings and Private International Law*, in LEGAL ASPECTS OF GLOBALIZATION: CONFLICT OF LAWS, INTERNET, CAPITAL MARKETS AND INSOLVENCY IN THE GLOBAL ECONOMY (The Hague, Kluwer Int'l., 2000).

Lowell, *Conflict of Laws as Applied to Assignments for Creditors*, 1 HARVARD LAW REV. 259 (1888).

Alexander Trunk, *German International Insolvency Law Under the New Insolvency Code: Continuity and Evolution*, in LEGAL ASPECTS OF GLOBALIZATION: CONFLICT OF LAWS, INTERNET, CAPITAL MARKETS AND INSOLVENCY IN THE GLOBAL ECONOMY (The Hague, Kluwer Law Int'l., 2000).

Philip R. Wood, *Principles of International Insolvency*, in LAW AND PRACTICE OF INTERNATIONAL FINANCE (LONDON, SWEET & MAXWELL, 1995).

### *e. Domestic Relations*

INTERNATIONAL CHILD ABDUCTIONS: A GUIDE TO APPLYING THE 1988 HAGUE CONVENTION, WITH FORMS (Gloria F. DeHart ed., ABA Section of Family Law, 1989).

JOHN DAVID MCCLEAN, RECOGNITION OF FAMILY JUDGMENTS IN THE COMMONWEALTH 209 (1983).

PHILLIP SCHWARTZ, INTERNATIONAL SUPPORT REMEDIES, IN INTERSTATE CHILD SUPPORT REMEDIES 243 (M. Haynes & G. Dodson eds., ABA Center on Children and the Law, 1990).

### *f. Nonmonetary Judgments (Equitable Remedies)*

TRENDS IN THE ENFORCEMENT OF NON-MONEY JUDGMENTS AND ORDERS (Ulla Jocobsson & Jack Jacobs eds., Norwell, MA, Kluwer Law and Taxation Publishers, 1988).

## C. JOURNALS

### 1. General

Winston Anderson, *Enforcement of Foreign Judgments Founded upon a Cause of Action Unknown in the Forum*, 42 INT'L & COMP. L.Q. 697 (1993).

Anne-Marie S. Burley, *International Law and International Relations Theory: A Dual Agenda*, 87 AM. J. INT'L L. 205 (1993).

Kevin M. Clermont, *Jurisdictional Salvation and the Hague Treaty*, 85 CORNELL L. REV. 89 (1999).

Committee on Foreign and Comparative Law, Assn. of Bar, City of N.Y., *Survey on Foreign Recognition of U.S. Money Judgments* (July 2001).

Joseph W. Dellapenna, *Suing Foreign Governments and Their Corporations*, 22 VAND. J. TRANSNAT'L L. 1029 (1989).

P. Eeckhout, *[WTO, 1995] Judicial Enforcement of WTO Law in the European Union – Some Further Reflections*, J. INT'L ECON. L. 91 (2002).

Alan Golomb, *Recognition of Foreign Money Judgments: A Goal-Oriented Approach*, 43 ST. JOHN'S L. REV. 604 (1969).

Joaquim-J. Forner, *Special Jurisdiction in Commercial Contracts: From the 1968 Brussels Convention to "Brussels-One Regulation,"* 13 INT'L COMP. COM. L. REV. 131 (2002).

H. L. Ho, *Policies Underlying the Enforcement of Foreign Commercial Judgments*, 46 INT'L & COMP. L.Q. 443 (1997).

Friedrich K. Juenger, *The Recognition of Money Judgments in Civil and Commercial Matters*, 36 AM. J. COMP. L. 1 (1988).

P. Kalbe, *The Award of Contracts and the Enforcement of Claims in the Context of EC External Aid and Development Cooperation*, 38 COMMON MARKET L. REV. 1217 (2001).

Andreas Lowenfeld, *International Litigation and the Quest for Reasonableness*, 245 RECEUIL DES COURS (1994) [general course on private international law, The Hague Academy of International Law].

Andreas F. Lowenfeld, *Forum Shopping, Anti-suit Injunctions, Negative Declarations, and Related Tools of International Litigation*, 91 AM. J. INT'L L. 314 (1997).

Andreas F. Lowenfeld, *Nationalizing International Law: Essay in Honor of Louis Henkin*, 36 COLUM. J. TRANSNAT'L L. 121, 128 (1997).

Kurt H. Nadelmann, *Non-Recognition of American Money Judgments Abroad and What to Do About It*, 42 IOWA L. REV. 236 (1957).

Helen Scott & N. W. Barber, *State liability Under Francovich for Decisions of National Courts*, 120 L.Q. REV. 403 (2004).

Koji Takahashi, *External Competence Implications of the EC Regulation on Jurisdiction and Judgments*, 52 INT'L COM. L.Q. 529 (2003).

Marta B. Varela, *Arbitration and the Doctrine of Manifest Disregard*, 49 DISP. RESOL. J. 64 (1994).

Mark A. A. Warner, *Decisions of Foreign Courts*, 88 AM. J. INT'L L. 532 (1994).

Phillip R. Weems, *How to Enforce U.S. Money Judgments Abroad*, TRIAL, July 1988, at 72.

## 2. Conventions

### *a. Brussels Convention and EEC [EU]*

Lee S. Bartlett, *Full Faith and Credit Comes to the Common Market: An Analysis of the Provisions of the Convention on Jurisdiction and Enforcement of Judgments in Civil and Commercial Matters*, 24 INT'L & COMP. L.Q. 44 (1975).

Gulum Bayraktaroglu, *Forum Contractus and Article 5(1) of the Brussels I Regulation*, 2 J. INT'L COM. L. 401 (2004).

Paul R. Beaumont, *Current Developments: European Community Law, European Court of Justice and Jurisdiction and Enforcement of Judgments on Civil and Commercial Matters*, 41 INT'L & COMP. L.Q. 206 (1992).

J. Beraudo, *The Arbitration Exception of the Brussels and Lugano Conventions: Jurisdiction, Recognition and Enforcement of Judgments*, 18 J. INT'L ARB. 13 (2001).

N. J. Byrne & Rosa Greaves, *The Brussels Convention on Jurisdiction and Judgments*, 131 NEW L.J. 395 (1981).

Beverly M. Carl, *The Common Market Judgments Convention – Its Threat and Challenges to Americans*, 8 INT'L LAW. 446 (1974).

Lawrence Collins, *Provisional Measures, the Conflict of Laws and Brussels Convention*, 1 Y.B. EUR. L. 249 (1981).

John D. Denson, *Recent Developments, Enforcement of Judgments – Interpretation of EEC Convention on Jurisdiction and Enforcement of Judgments in Civil and Commercial Matters Does Not Cover Provisional Ex Parte Measures*, 17 TEX. INT'L L.J. 252 (1982).

Adair Dyer, *Synthesis of the Recognition and Enforcement of Judgments Under the Hague Conventions and the EEC Conventions*, 7(1) INT'L LEGAL PRAC. 23 (1982).

Elizabeth Freeman, *The EEC Convention on Jurisdiction and Enforcement of Civil and Commercial Judgments*, 3 NW. J. INT'L L. & BUS. 496 (1981).

Andrea Giardina, *The European Court and the Brussels Convention on Jurisdiction and Judgments*, 27 INT'L & COMP. L.Q. 263 (1978).

Joseph P. Griffin, *EC and U.S. Extra-Territoriality: Activism and Cooperation*, 17 FORDHAM INT'L L.J. 353 (1994).

Peter Hay, *The Common Market Preliminary Draft Convention on the Recognition and Enforcement of Judgments – Some Considerations of Policy and Interpretation*, 16 A.J. COMP. L. 149 (1968).

Neville M. Hunnings, *Default Judgments in the EEC*, J. BUS. L. 303 (1985).

Peter Kaye, *The EEC Judgments Convention and the Outer World: Goodbye to Forum Non Conveniens?*, J. BUS. L. 47 (1992).

Michael Kerr, *The EEC Judgments Convention: Some Repercussions Beyond the EEC*, 15 EUROPARECHTXS 353 (1980).

Christian Kohler, *Practical Experience of the Brussels Jurisdiction and Judgments Convention in the Six Original Contracting States*, 34 INT'L & COMP. L.Q. 563 (1985).

Suriyakumari Lane, *Free Movement of Judgments Within the EEC*, 35 INT'L & COMP. L.Q. 629 (1986).

Alexander Layton, *The Interpretation of the Brussels Convention by the European Court and English Courts*, 11 CIV. JUST. Q. 28 (1992).

K. Lipstein, *Enforcement of Judgments Under the Jurisdiction and Judgments Convention: Safeguards*, 36 INT'L & COMP. L.Q. 873 (1987).

Errol P. Mendes, *The Troublesome Workings of the Judgments Convention of the European Economic Community*, 13 VAND. J. TRANSNAT'L L. 75 (1980).

Kurt H. Nadelmann, *Jurisdictionally Improper Fora in Treaties on Recognition of Judgments: The Common Market Draft*, 67 COLUM. L. REV. 995 (1967).

Maria O'Neill, *The Brussels Convention: A Stillborn Child?*, 50 N. IR. LEGAL Q. 243 (1999).

Robert C. Reuland, *The Recognition of Judgments in the European Community: The Twenty-Fifth Anniversary of the Brussels Convention*, 14 MICH. J. INT'L L. 559 (1993).

Phillip Rocher, *Jurisdiction and Enforcement of Judgments in Europe*, 5 INT'L L. PRACTICUM 15 (1992).

B. J. Rodger, *The Communitarianism of International Private Law: Reform of the Brussels Convention by Regulation*, 2001 JURID. REV. 59 (2001).

Kathryn A. Russell, *Exorbitant Jurisdiction and Enforcement of Judgments: The Brussels System as an Impetus for United States Action*, 19 SYRACUSE INT'L L. COMM. 57 (1993).

Cynthia B. Schultz, *Selected Bibliography of the European Economic Community*, 5 AM. U.J. INT'L L. REV. 161 (1986).

Kate Sedman, *European Aspects of Security for Costs*, 141 NEW L.J. 313 (1991).

P. L. C. Torremans, *The Uniform Interpretation of the Brussels and Lugano Conventions*, 28 EUR. L. REV. 752 (2003).

K. Vasiljeva, 1968 *Brussels Convention and EU Council Regulation* No. 44/2001: *Jurisdiction in Consumer Contracts Concluded Online*, 10 EUR. L.J. 123 (2004).

P. Vlas, *The Protocol on Interpretation of the EEC Convention of Jurisdiction and Enforcement of Judgments: Over Ten Years in Legal Practice* (1975–1985), 33 NETH. INT'L L. REV. 84 (1986).

Arthur T. von Mehren, *Recognition and Enforcement of Sister-State Judgments: Reflections on General Theory and Current Practice in the European Economic Community and the United States*, 81 COLUM. L. REV. 1044 (1981).

Horatia Muir Watt, *Evidence of an Emergent European Legal Culture: Public Policy Requirements of Procedural Fairness under the Brussels and Lugano Conventions* (Symposium on Teaching and Practicing Law in the 21st Century), 36 TEX. INT'L L.J. 539 (2001).

Donald L. Woodward, *Reciprocal Recognition and Enforcement of Civil Judgments in the United States, the United Kingdom and the European Economic Community*, 8 N.C. J. INT'L L. & COM. REG. 299 (1983).

### *b. Lugano and San Sebastian Conventions*

John Fitzpatrick, *The Lugano Convention and Western European Integration: A Comparative Analysis of Jurisdiction and Judgments in Europe and the United States*, 8 CONN. J. INT'L L. 695 (1993).

Horace Gautier & Eva Stormann, *Lugano Convention on Jurisdiction and on the Enforcement of Judgments*, 19 INTL BUS. LAW. 410 (1991).

Hans Jung, *The Brussels and Lugano Conventions: The European Court's Jurisdiction, Its Procedures and Methods*, 11 CIV. JUST. Q. 38 (1992).

Elizabeth M. McCaffrey, *The Lugano and San Sebastian Conventions: General Effects*, 11 CIV. JUST. Q. 12 (1992).

Jacqueline Moinor, *The Lugano Convention: Some Problems of Interpretation*, 27 COMMON MKT. L. REV. 507 (1990).

### *c. Hague Conventions*

Ronald A. Brand, *Intellectual Property, Electronic Commerce, and the Preliminary Hague Jurisdiction and Judgments Convention*, 62 U. PITT. L. REV. 581 (2001).

Patrick J. Borchers, *The Incredible Shrinking Hague Evidence Convention*, 38 TEX. INT'L L.J. 73 (2003).

Stephen B. Burbank, *Jurisdictional Equilibration, the Proposed Hague Convention and Progress in National Law*, 49 Am. J. Comp. L. 203 (2001).

Kristen Hudson Clayton, *The Draft Hague Convention on Jurisdiction and Enforcement of Judgments and the Internet – A New Jurisdictional Framework*, 36 J. MARSHALL L. REV. 223 (2002).

George A. L. Droz & Adair Dyer, *The Hague Conference and the Main Issues of Private International Law for the Eighties*, 3, No. 1 NW. J. INT'L L. & BUS. 155 (1981).

Benjamin Elacqua, *The Hague Runs into B2B: Why Restructuring the Hague Convention on Foreign Judgments in Civil and Commercial Matters to Deal with B2B Contracts Is Long Overdue*, 3 J. HIGH TECH. L. 93 (2004).

Johnathan Franklin and Roberta Morris, *International Jurisdiction and Enforcement of Judgments in the Era of Global Networks: Irrelevance of, Goals for, and Comments on Current Proposals*, 77 CHI.-KENT L. REV. 1213 (2002).

Peter Hay, *The United States and International Unification of Law: The Tenth Session of the Hague Conference*, 1965 U. ILL. L.F. 820.

*Information Concerning the Hague Conventions on Private International Law*, 36 INT'L L. REV. 185 (1989).

Harold G. Maier, *A Hague Conference Judgments Convention and United States Courts: A Problem and a Possibility*, 61 ALB. L. REV. 1207 (1998).

Kurt H. Nadelmann, *The United States Joins the Hague Conference on Private International Law*, 30 LAW. & CONTEMP. PROBS. 291 (1965).

William E. O'Brian, *The Hague Convention on Jurisdiction and Judgments: The Way Forward*, 66 MOD. L. REV. 491 (2003).

Arthur T. von Mehren, *Enforcing Judgments Abroad: Reflections on the Design of Recognition Conventions*, 24 BROOKLYN J. INT'L L. 17 (1998).

Arhur T. von Mehren, *Drafting a Convention on International Jurisdiction and the Effects of Foreign Judgments Acceptable World-Wide: Can the Hague Convention Project Succeed?*, 49 AM. J. COMP. L. 191 (2001).

Svetozara Petkova, *The Potential Impact of the Draft Hague Convention on International Jurisdiction and Foreign Judgments in Civil and Commercial Matters on Internet-Related Disputes with Particular Reference to Copyright*, INTELLECTUAL PROP. Q. 173 (Spring 2004).

Linda Silberman, *Comparative Jurisdiction in the International Context: Will the Proposed Hague Judgments Convention Be Stalled?* (Symposium: Export/Import; American Civil Justice in a Global Context), 52 DEPAUL L. REV. 319 (2002).

Jason Webb Yackee, *A Matter of Good Form: The (Downsized) Hague Judgments Convention and Conditions of Formal Validity for the Enforcement of Forum Selection Agreements*, 53 DUKE L.J. 1179 (2003).

Russel J. Weintraub, *How Substantial Is Our Need for a Judgments Recognition Convention and What Should We Bargain Away to Get It?*, 24 BROOKLYN J. INT'L L. 167 (1998).

Joachim Zekoll, *The Role and Status of American Law in the Hague Judgments Convention Project*, 61 ALB. L. REV. 1283, 1305–1306 (1998).

### d. *Inter-American Conventions*

Lucinda A. Low, *International Judicial Assistance Among the American States – the Inter-American Conventions*, 18 INT'L LAW. 705 (1984).

Kurt H. Nadelmann, *The Need for Revision of the Bustamante Code on Private International Law*, 65 AM. J. INT'L L. 782 (1971).

### e. *New York Convention*

Abdul H. El-Ahdab, *Saudi Arabia Accedes to the New York Convention*, 11, NO. 3 J. INT'L ARB. 87 (1994).

Fraser P. Davidson, *Where Is an Arbitral Award Made? Hiscox v. Outhwaite*, 41 INT'L & COMP. L.Q. 637 (1992).

Moon S. Lee and Elli Yum, *Recognition and Enforcement of Foreign Arbitral Awards in the Republic of Korea under the New York Convention*, 7 INT'L L.Q. 31 (1995).

Kristin T. Roy, *The New York Convention and Saudi Arabia: Can A Country Use the Public Policy Defense to Refuse Enforcement of Non-Domestic Arbitral Awards?*, 18 FORDHAM INT'L L.J. 920 (1995).

Eric A. Schwartz, *Resolution of International Construction Disputes*, 23 INT'L BUS. LAW. 149 (1995).

## 3. Regional

### *Africa*

Samson L. Semposa, *Obstacles to International Commercial Arbitration in African Countries*, 41 INT'L & COMP. L.Q. 387 (1992).

### *Asia*

Banlue Kongchan, *Recognition and Enforcement of Foreign Judgments Among Law Asia Group*, LAW JOURNAL, 3d year, ed. 12, B.E. 2535 (1992).

### *Eastern Europe*

Clare Ambrose, *Can Anti-Suit Injunctions Survive European Community Law?*, 52.2 INT'L & COMP. L.Q. 401 (2003).

*A Bibliograhy of Transnational Litigation in Socialist Countries: Discovery, Evidence, and Enforcement of Foreign Judgments*, 21 TEX. INT'L L.J. 383 (1986).

V. Shaleva, *The "Public Policy" Exception to the Recognition and Enforcement of Arbitral Awards in the Theory and Jurisprudence of the Central and East European States and Russia*, 19 ARB. INT'L 67 (2003).

### *Latin America*

Jose Daniel Amado, *Recognition and Enforcement of Foreign Judgments in Latin American Countries: An Overview and Update*, 31 VA. J. INT'L L. 99 (1990).

Jeff Larsen, Note, *Enforcement of Foreign Judgments in Latin America: Trends and Individual Differences*, 17 TEX. INT'L L.J. 213 (1982).

*Middle East*

Al Mulla, *Conventions of Enforcement of Foreign Judgments in the Arab States*, 14 ARAB L.Q. 33 (1999).

*Western Europe*

Paul R. Beaumont, *European Court of Justice and Jurisdiction and Enforcement of Judgments*, 42 INT'L & COMP. L.Q. 728 (1993).

Rudolph Graupner, *Some Recent Aspects of Recognition and Enforcement of Foreign Judgments in Western Europe*, 12 INT'L & COMP. L.Q. 367 (1963).

Peter Kaye, *Product Liability in Europe: Jurisdiction of Courts and Enforcement of Foreign Judgments*, 132 SOLIC. J. 1334 (1988).

Brian Pearce, *The Comity Doctrine as a Barrier to Judicial Jurisdiction: A U.S. – E.U. Comparison*, 30 STAN. J. INT'L L. 525 (1994) [county-by-county].

*Australia*

Okezie Chukwumerije, *Enforcement of Foreign Awards in Australia: The Implications of Resort Condominiums*, 5 AUSTRALIAN DISP. L.J. 237 (1994).

Martin Davies & Kate Lewins, *Foreign Maritime Liens: Should They Be Recognised in Australian Courts?* 76 AUSTL. L.J. 775 (2002).

Phillip K. Eure, *Extraterritoriality: Australian Limitations on Foreign Judgments and Discovery*, 26 HARV. INT'L L.J. 578 (1982).

J. Evans, *Registration of Foreign Judgments in Victoria*, 74 L. INST. J., vol. 4, 66 (2000).

J. David Fine, *Defenses Against Recognition of Enforcement of Interstate or Foreign Judgments*, 61 AUSTL. L.J. 350 (1987).

Richard Garnett, *Dow Jones & Company Inc. v. Gutnick: An Adequate Response to Transnational Internet Defamation?*, 4 MELBOURNE J. INT'L L. 196 (2003).

Leslie Glek, *Foreign Civil Judgments: Direct Enforcement Legislation In Australia*, 48 AUSTL. L.J. 538 (1974).

P. E. Nych, *The Enforcement of United States Anti-Trust Judgments in Australia*, 16 GONZ. L. REV. 1 (1980).

*Austria*

F. Matscher, *Grundfragen der Anerkennung und Vollstreckung auslaendischer Entscheidungen in Zivilsachen (aus oesterreichischer Sicht)*, 103 ZEITSCHRIFT FUER ZIVILPROZESSRECHT (Z.Z.P.) 294 (1990).

*Belgium*

W. Kennet, *Enforcement of Judgments*, 5 EUR. REV. PRIVATE L. 321 (1997).

### *Bermuda*

Jan Woloniecki, *Commentary Pre-Answer Security and Public Policy in Bermuda – A Commentary on Muhl V. Ardra Insurance Co. Ltd.*, 2, No. 21 Andrews Int'l Reinsurance Disp. Rep. 3 (1998).

### *Brazil*

J. Dolinger, *Brazilian Confirmation of Foreign Judgments*, 19 Int'l Law. 853 (1985).

Keith Rosen, *Enforcement of Foreign Arbitral Awards in Brazil*, 28 Am. J. Comp. L. 498 (1980).

K. S. Rosenn, *Civil Procedure in Brazil*, 34 Am. J. Comp. L. 487, 496 (1986).

Brian L. Zimbler, *Debtor State Law and Default: Enforcement of Foreign Loan Agreements in Brazilian Courts*, 17 U. Miami Inter-Am. L. Rev. 509 (1986).

### *Bulgaria*

T. Cipev, *Die Anerkennung und Vollstreckung ausländischer Zivilurteile in Bulgarien*, 33 Monatshefte für osteuropäisches recht 109 (1991).

### *Canada*

Marvin G. Baer, *Conflict of Laws – Recognition of Foreign Judgments – Fraud – Finality – Public Policy – Proof of Foreign Law*, 52 Can. B. Rev. 118 (1974).

Jost Blom, *The Enforcement of Judgments in Canada*, 57 Or. L. Rev. 399 (1978).

John Caher, *Quebec Court's Default Ruling Binds U.S. Firm (Wimmer Canada, Inc. v. Abele Tractor)(New York)*, 228 N.Y.L.J. 1 (2002).

J. G. Castel, *Reciprocal Enforcement of Judgments in the Province of Quebec*, 21 R. De B. 128 (1961).

J. G. Castel, *Recognition and Enforcement of Foreign Judgments In Personum and In Rem in the Common Law Provinces of Canada*, 17 McGill L.J. 11 (1971).

J.G. Castel, *Proof of Foreign Law*, 22 U. Toronto L.J. 33 (1972).

Kenneth O. Eikenberry, et al., *Enforcing Washington Judgments in British Columbia: "Reciprocating State" Status for Washington Will Make Enforcement Easier*, 13 Puget Sound L. Rev. 491 (1990).

Kenneth O. Eikenberry, et al., *Enforcing Washington Judgments in Canadian Courts: Taking the Dams Out of the Stream of Commerce*, Wash. St. B. News, Jan. 1991, at 10.

Ivan R. Feldman, *Reciprocal Enforcement of Judgments Act*, 1 U.B.C.L. Rev. 229 (1959).

H. Patrick Glenn, *Foreign Judgments, the Common Law and the Constitution; De Savoye v. Morguard Investments, Ltd.*, 37 McGill L.J. 537 (1992).

Joy Goodman & Jeffrey A. Talpis, *Beals v. Saldanha and the Enforcement of Foreign Judgments in Canada*, 40 Can. Bus. L.J. 227 (2004).

D. M. Gordon, *Judgments – Reciprocal Enforcement – Foreign Judgments for Costs*, 32 Can. B. Rev. 1146 (1954).

G. F. Henderson, *Foreign Court and the National Interest, the Effect of Foreign Judgments on Activities in Canada*, 3 INT'L BUS. L. 133 (1975).

Michael Hertz, *The Constitution and the Conflict of Laws: Approaches in Canadian and American Law*, 27 U. TORONTO L.J. 1 (1977).

William G. Horton, *The Recognition and Enforcement of Foreign Judgments in Ontario*, 10 ADVOC. Q. 89 (1988).

Walter S. Johnson, *Foreign Judgments in Quebec*, 35 CAN. B. REV. 911 (1957).

Gilbert D. Kennedy, *"Reciprocity" in the Recognition of Foreign Judgments*, 32 CAN. B. REV. 359 (1954).

Donald J. A. Lange, *Conflict of Laws – Recognition and Enforcement of Foreign Judgments In Personum – Jurisdiction*, 61 CAN. B. REV. 637 (1983).

Phillip J. Loree, Jr., Note, *The Recognition and Enforcement of United States Judgments in the Canadian Common Law Provinces: The Problem of In Personum Jurisdiction*, 15 BROOKLYN J. INT'L L. 317 (1989) [helpful as a procedural guide].

Kurt H. Nadelman, *Enforcement of Foreign Judgments in Canada*, 38 CAN. B. REV. 68 (1960).

Stephen G. A. Pitel, *Enforcement of Foreign Judgments: Where Morguard Stands after Beals*, 40 CAN. BUS. L.J. 189 (2004).

Eric D. Ram, Note, *Reciprocal Recognition of Foreign Country Money Judgments: The Canada-United States Position*, 45 FORDHAM L. REV. 1456 (1977), reprinted in 8 Man. L.J. 473 (1977).

Genevieve Saumier, *The Recognition of Foreign Judgments in Quebec – The Mirror Crack'd?*, 81 CAN. BAR REV. 677 (2002).

Gerald Stotland, *Recognition of Foreign Support and Property Orders in Canada*, 17 AM. J. FAMILY L. 230 (2004).

*Strangers in a Strange Land – Transnational Litigation, Foreign Judgment Recognition, and Enforcement in Ontario*, 13 J. TRANSNT'L L. & POL'Y 347 (Spring 2004).

John Sullivan, *The Enforcement of Foreign Judgments in B.C. – Ten Years After Morguard*, 59 THE ADVOCATE 399 (2001).

John Swan, *Uniform Enforcement of Canadian Judgments Act*, 22 CAN. BUS. L.J. NO. 1, 87 (1993).

Dierk Ullrich, *Money Is Not Everything: Recent Developments in the Recognition and Enforcement of Foreign Non-Monetary Judgments*, 63 THE ADVOCATE 53 (2005).

Janet Walker, *The Great Canadian Comity Experiment Continues*, 120 LAW Q. REV. 365 (2004).

J. S. Ziegel, *Enforcement of Foreign Judgments in Canada, Unlevel Playing Fields, and Beals v. Saldanha: A Consumer Perspective*, 38 CAN. BUS. L.J. 294 (April 2003).

### *China*

P. Gilligan & J. Bannister, *Recovering Assets in China*, 21 INT'L FIN. L. REV. 52 (2002).

Andrew Kui-Nung Cheung, *Enforcement of Foreign Arbitral Awards in the People's Republic of China*, 34 AM. J. COMP. L. 295 (1986).

Pat Chew-LaFitte, *The Resolution of Transnational Commercial Disputes in the People's Republic of China: A Guide for U.S. Practitioners*, 8 YALE J. WORLD PUB. ORD. 236 (1982).

Donald C. Clarke, *Power and Politics in the Chinese Court System: The Enforcement of Civil Judgments*, 10 COLUM. J. ASIAN L. 1 (1996).

Sally Lord Ellis & Laura Shea, *Foreign Commercial Dispute Settlement in the People's Republic of China*, 6 INT'L TRADE L.J. 155 (1981).

R. E. J. Reyes, *The Enforcement of Foreign Court Judgments in the People's Republic of China: What the American Lawyer Needs to Know*, 23 BROOKLYN J. INT'L L. 241 (1997).

Hu Zhenjie, *Recognition and Enforcement of Foreign Judgments in China: Rules, Interpretation and Practice*, 46 NETH. INT'L. L. REV. 291 (1999).

### *Colombia*

Gabriela Mancero, *Foreigners Entering into Contracts with the Colombian Government Can Submit Their Differences to International Arbitration*, 32 INT'L BUS. LAW. 299 (2004).

### *Czechoslovakia*

Josef Macur, *Execution Proceedings*, 15 BULL. CZECHOSLOVAK L. 49 (1976).

H.Steiner, *The Recognition of Money Judgments in Civil and Commercial Matters*, 7 TRAVAUX DE DROIT COMPARÉ 99 (1986).

### *Cyprus*

S. Nathanael, *An Overview of Civil Litigation as Practiced in Cyprus and Enforcement of Foreign Judgments*, 1989 EPITHEORESE KYPRIAKOU DIKAIOU (CYPRUS L. REV.) 4034.

### *England and the Common Wealth of Nations*

Adrian Briggs, *Which Foreign Judgments Should We Recognize Today?*, 36 INT'L & COMP. L.Q. 240 (1987).

Bradford A. Caffrey, *Recognition and Enforcements of Foreign Civil Judgments in New Zealand*, AUSTRALIAN AND ENGLISH LAW, 1 COMP. L.Y.B. 265 (1977).

Bradford A. Caffrey, *Invoking an Enforcement Statute to a Common Law Application for Enforcement*, 29 INT'L & COMP. L.Q. 766 (1980).

Fraser P. Davidson, *Where Is an Arbitral Award Made? Hiscox v. Outhwaite*, 41 INT'L COMP. L.Q. 637 (1992).

Neil Fagan, *Enforcement of Gaming Debts in Britain*, 8 N.Y. L. SCH. J. INT'L & COMP. L. 7 (1986).

Tina J. Kahn, Comment, *The Protection of Trading Interests Act of 1980: Britain's Response to U.S. Extraterritorial Antitrust Enforcement*, 2 NW. J. INT'L L. & BUS. 476 (1980).

K. Lipstein, *The Evidence (Proceedings in Other Jurisdictions) Act 1975: An Interpretation*, 39 INT'L & COMP. L.Q. 120 (1990).

A. V. Lowe, *Blocking Extraterritorial Jurisdiction: The British Protection of Interests Act, 1980*, 75 AM. J. INT'L L. 257 (1981).

Catherine V. Manick, *Recent Developments, Anti-Trust: British Restrictions on Enforcement of Foreign Judgments*, 21 HARV. INT'L L.J. 727 (1980).

Joseph E. Neuhaus, *Power to Reserve Foreign Judgments: The British Clawback Statute Under International Law*, 81 COLUM. L. REV. 1097 (1981).

P. M. North, *Insurance and Foreign Judgments*, 128 NEW L.J. 315 (1978).

Courtland H. Peterson, *Choice of Law and Forum Clauses and the Recognition of Foreign Country Judgments Revisited Through Lloyd's of London Cases*, 60 LA. L. REV. 1259 (2000).

Recent Developments, *International Enforcement of Judgments: Evasion of a Garnishee Order – Deutsche Schachtbau-und-Tiefbohrgesellschaft mbH v. Shell International Petroleum Co., Ltd.*, 30 HARV. INT'L L.J. 256 (1989).

Thomas B. Stoel, Jr., *The Enforcement of Foreign Non-Criminal Penal and Revenue Judgments in England and the United States*, 16 INT'L & COMP. L.Q. 663 (1983).

P. A. Stone, *The Civil Jurisdiction and Judgments Act of 1982: Some Comments*, 32 INT'L & COMP. L.Q. 477 (1983).

P. A. Stone, *The Recognition and Enforcement in England of Foreign Personal and Property Judgments*, 1983 LLOYDS'S MAR. & COM. L.Q. 1 (1983).

Gregory T. Walters, *Bachchan v. India Abroad Publications, Inc.: The Clash Between Protection of Free Speech in the United States and Great Britain*, 16 FORDHAM INT'L L.J. 895 (1993).

David Westin, *Enforcing Foreign Commercial Judgments and Arbitral Awards in the United States, West Germany, and England*, 19 LAW & POL'Y INT'L BUS. 325 (1987).

David L. Woodward, *Reciprocal Recognition and Enforcement of Civil Judgments in the United States, the United Kingdom and the European Economic Community*, 8 N.C.J. INT'L L. & COM. REG. 299 (1983).

Barbara Simpson, *The Perils of REMO (Recognition in Enforcement of Maintenance Orders) (United Kingdom)*, 33 FAMILY LAW 121 (2003).

### *Ethiopia*

S. Teshale, *Reciprocity with Respect to Enforcement of Foreign Judgments in Ethiopia: A Critique of the Supreme Court's Decision in the Paulos Papassinous Case*, 12 AFR. J. INT'L & COMP. L. 569 (2000).

### *Finland*

Tom Brandt, *Prospective Measures for Recovering Commercial Debts in Finland*, 2 INT'L CONT. 519 (1981).

### *France*

D. F. Martin, *A Comparative Study of Enforcement in England and France*, 1 CIV. JUST. Q. 219 (1982).

Kurt H. Nadelman, *Recognition of Foreign Money Judgments in France*, 5 AM. COMP. L. 248 (1956).

Kurt H. Nadelman, *French Courts Recognize Foreign Money Judgments: One Down and More to Go*, 13 AM. COMP. L. 72 (1964).

James C. Regan, *The Enforcement of Foreign Judgments in France Under the Nouveau Code de Procedure Civile*, 4 B.C. INT'L & COMP. L. REV. 149 (1981).

G. T. Yates III, *Substantive Law Aspects of Foreign Judgments Between Foreigners in France: The Competence Question*, 9 INT'L LAW. 251 (1975).

### *Germany*

Volker Behr, *Symposium on U.S.-E.C. Legal Relations: Enforcement of United States Money Judgments in Germany*, 13 J. L. & COM. 211 (1994).

Klaus Beucher & John Byron Sandage, *United States Punitive Damage Awards in German Courts: The Evolving German Position on Service and Enforcement*, 23 VAND. J. TRANSNAT'L L. 967 (1991).

M. N. Brenscheidt, *The Recognition and Enforcement of Foreign Money Judgments in the Federal Republic of Germany*, 11 INT'L LAW. 261 (1977).

Brice Dickson, *The Reform of Private International Law in the Federal Republic of Germany*, 34 INT'L & COMP. L.Q. 231 (1985).

Gerfried Fischer, *Recognition and Enforcement of American Tort Judgments in Germany*, 68 ST. JOHN'S L. REV. 199 (1994).

Peter Hay, *The Recognition and Enforcement of American Money-Judgments in Germany – The 1992 Decision of the German Supreme Court*, 40 AM J. COMP. L. 729 (1992).

Heidenberger, *Similarities and Differences in the Enforcement of Foreign Decrees and Judgments in the Federal Republic of Germany and the United States*, 33 D.C. B.J. 433 (1966).

Burkhard, Hess, *Die Anerkennung eines Class Action Settlement in Deutschland*, 55 JURISTEN ZEITUNG 373 (2000).

Hans-Michael Kraus, *Enforcement of Foreign Money Judgments in the Federal Republic of Germany*, 17 TEX. INT'L L.J. 195 (1982).

Dieter Martiny, *Recognition and Enforcement of Foreign Money Judgments in the Federal Republic of Germnay*, 35 AM. J. COMP. L. 721 (1987).

Hans-Bertram Nothnagel, *Enforcement of Foreign Judgments and Arbitral Awards in West Germany*, 17 VA. J. INT'L LAW. 385 (1977).

Otto Sandrock & Matthias K. Hentzen, *Enforcing Foreign Arbitral Awards in the Federal Republic of Germany: The Example of the United States Award*, 2 TRANSNAT'L L. 49 (1989).

Rolf A. Schutze, *The Recognition and Enforcement of American Civil Judgments Containing Punitive Damages in the Federal Republic of Germany*, 11 U. PA. J. INT'L BUS. L. 581 (1990).

John R. Schmertz & Mike Meier, *Supreme Court of German Land Denies Enforcement of Wisconsin Judgment Because, According to German Rules, Wisconsin Federal Court Lacked Jurisdiction Over Any Assets Belonging to German Defendant. Citation: OLG Hamm, Urteil vom 4.6.1997 – 1 U 2/96*, 1997 RIW, HEFT 12, INTERNATIONALES, 4 INT'L UPDATE 29 (March 1998).

Ernst C. Stiefel et al., *The Enforceability of Excessive U.S. Punitive Damage Awards in Germany*, 39 AM. J. COMP. L. 779 (1991).

David Westin, *Enforcing Foreign Commercial Judgments and Arbitral Awards in the United States, West Germany, and England*, 19 L. & POL'Y INT'L BUS. 325 (1987).

James Young, *Extending the Free Movement of Judgments in Western Europe*, LLOYD'S MAR. & COM. L.Q. (Feb. 1992), at 109.

Yoachim Zekoll, *Recognition and Enforcement of American Products Liability in the Federal Republic of Germany*, 37 AM. J. COMP. L. 301 (1989).

Yoachim Zekoll, *The Enforceability of American Money Judgments Abroad: A Landmark Decision by the German Federal Court of Justice*, 30 COLUM. J. TRANSNAT'L L. 641 (1992).

***Hungary***

Gyula Gayer, *Amendment to Law Concerning Jurisdiction, Recognition and Execution of Foreign Decisions in Hungary*, 29 INT'L BUS. LAW. 207 (2001).

***India***

Tony Khindria, *Enforcement of Arbitration Awards in India*, 23 INT'L BUS. LAW. 11 (1995).

***Indonesia***

Robert N. Hornick, *The Recognition and Enforcement of Foreign Judgments in Indonesia*, 18 HARVARD INT'L L.J. 97 (1977).

Robert N. Hornick, *Foreign Arbitral Awards Are Not Enforceable*, E. ASIAN EXEC. REP. (Nov. 15, 1985), at 11.

***Iran***

G. R. Delaume, *Enforcement of State Contract Awards: Jurisdictional Pitfalls and Remedies*, 8 FOREIGN INV. L.J. 29 (1993).

John A. Westberg, *Applicable Law, Expropriatory Takings and Compensation in Cases of Expropriation: ICSID and Iran-United States Claims Tribunal Case Law Compared*, 8 FOREIGN INV. L.J. 1 (1993).

***Ireland***

A. V. Gill, *Jurisdiction and Enforcement of Foreign Judgments in Ireland*, 1980 J. IRISH SOC'Y FOR EUR. L. 3.

***Israel***

Chaim L. Goldwater, *Amendments to the Foreign Judgments Enforcement Law*, 10 ISR. L. REV. 247 (1975).

Chaim L. Goldwater, *Issue Estoppel by Foreign Judgment in Israeli Law*, 25 INT'L & COMP. L.Q. 868 (1976).

D. Kapeliuk, *Enforcement of Foreign Arbitration Agreements: The Israeli Experience*, 17 J. INT'L ARB. 109 (2000).

David M. Klaristenfeld, *Old Wine in Recycled Bottles: An Overview of Israeli Commercial and Insolvency Law*, 1994 A.B.I.J., *Available in* LEXIS 2621 (Mar. 1994).

A. V. Levontin, *Two Paradoxes in the Recognition of Foreign Judgments*, 2 ISR. L. REV. 197 (1967).

Amos Shapira, *Recognition and Enforcement of Foreign Judgments in Personam in Israel*, 3 TEL AVIV UNIV. STUD. L. 171 (1978).

### *Italy*

Arturo Barone, *Reciprocal Enforcement of Judgments in the United Kingdom and Italy*, 131 NEW L.J. 572 (1981).

Vicenzo Vigoriti, *Recent Developments in the Recognition and Execution of Foreign Judgments and Arbitral Awards in Italy*, 6 CIV. JUST. Q. ANN. 248 (1987).

### *Japan*

Yasuhori Fujita, *Service of American Process on Japanese Nationals by Registered Airmail and Enforceability of Resulting American Judgments in Japan*, 12 LAW IN JAPAN 69 (1979).

Akira Ishikawa, *Civil Execution Procedure in Japan: Basic Ideas of the Law of Civil Execution and an Outline of Execution Procedure Against Immovable*, 5 KEIO L. REV. 47 (1985).

G. Kajitani, *Computation of Damages and Enforcement of Foreign Judgments in Japan*, 23 INT'L LEGAL PRAC. 18 (1998).

John Kakinuki, *Dispute Resolution in Japan: Choosing the Right Alternative*, E. ASIAN EXEC. REP., Nov. 15, 1987, at 7 [arbitration].

Takao Sawaki, *Recognition and Enforcement of Foreign Judgments in Japan*, 23 INT'L LAW. 29 (1989) [brief but useful for practice].

Hoken Seki, *Effective Dispute Resolution in United States-Japan Commercial Transactions*, 6 NW. J. INT'L L. & BUS. 979 (1984–85).

M. Takeshita, *The Recognition of Foreign Judgments by the Japanese Courts*, 39 JAPAN ANN. INT'L L. 55 (1996).

*Requirements for the Recognition of a Foreign Judgment – Tokyo District – September 17, 1979*, 25 JAPAN ANN. INT'L L. (1982).

### *Korea*

Younggap Kim, *The Recognition and Enforcement of Foreign Judgments in Korea: With Particular Reference to United States Judgments*, LL.M. Thesis, Georgetown University, 1994.

Moon S. Lee & Elli Yum, *Recognition and Enforcement of Foreign Arbitral Awards in the Republic of Korea Under the New York Convention*, 7 INT'L Q. 31 (1995).

### *Malaysia*

Marasighe, *The Recognition and Enforcement of Foreign Judgments*, J. MALAYSIAN & COMP. L. 197 (1985).

A. H. Mohamed, *Reciprocal Enforcement of Judgments and Service of Process in Malaysia*, 1981(II) MALAYSIAN L.J. (1982).

*Mexico*

R. R. Evans, *Enforcement of U.S. Judgments in* Mexico: *Illusion or Reality?*, 64 TEX. B.J. 138 (2001).

Dale B. Furnish, *Foreign Judgments in Mexico and the United States*, 1985 ARIZ. J. INT'L & COMP. L. 173.

Francisco Acuna Griego, *Execution of Foreign Judgments in the State of Sonora*, 1985 ARIZ. J. INT'L & COMP. L. 162.

Friedrich K. Juenger, *The Recognition of Money Judgments in Civil and Commercial Matters*, 36 AM. J. COMP. L. 1 (1988).

Jeffrey J. Mayer, *Recent Mexican Arbitration Reform: The Continued Influence of the "Pubilcistas,"* 47 U. MIAMI L. REV. 913 (1993).

Fernando Alejandro Vazquez Pando, *New Trends in Mexican Private International Law*, 23 INT'L LAW. 995 (1989).

Jose Luis Siqueiros, *Enforcement of Foreign Civil and Commercial Judgments in the Mexican Republic*, 1986 ARIZ. J. INT'L & COMP. L. 149 (1986).

Jose Luis Siqueiros, *Enforcement of Foreign Civil and Commercial Judgments in the Mexican Republic*, 2 HOUS. J. INT'L L. 375 (1980).

Jorge A. Vargas, *Enforcement of Judgments in Mexico: The 1988 Rules of the Federal Code of Civil Procedure*, 14 J. INT'L L. BUS. 376 (1994).

Jorge A. Vargas, *Mexican Law on the Web: The Ultimate Research Guide*, 32 INT'L J. LEGAL INFO. 34 (2004).

***New Zealand***

Laurette Barnard, *Enforcement of Foreign Judgments*, 1996 N.Z. L.J. 227.

***Oman***

Terence Lane & William Morton, *Enforcement of a Foreign Award in Oman*, 2 ARB. INT'L 75 (1986).

***Pakistan***

Anees Jillani, *Recognition and Enforcement of Foreign Arbitral Awards in Pakistan*, 37 INT'L & COMP. L.Q. 926 (1988).

***Saudi Arabia***

Jeanne Ashereman, *Doing Business in Saudi Arabia: The Contemporary Application of Islamic Law*, 16 INT'L LAW. 321, 324 (1982).

Abdul H. El-Ahdab, *Saudi Arabia Accedes to the New York Convention*, 11 J. INT'L ARB. 87 (1994).

David J. Karl, *Islamic Law in Saudi Arabia: What Foreign Attorneys Should Know*, 25 GEO. WASH. J. INT'L L. & ECON. 131 (1992).

Kristin T. Roy, *The New York Convention and Saudi Arabia: Can A Country Use the Public Policy Defense to Refuse Enforcement of Non-Domestic Arbitral Awards?* 18 FORDHAM INT'L L.J. 920 (1995).

Nancy Truck, *Saudi Board of Grievances Enforces Foreign Judgment*, MIDDLE E. EXEC. REP., (May 1990), at 9.

### *Scotland*

G. Maher, *Community Law: Enforcing EEC Convention Judgments in Scotland*, 34 J.L. SOC'Y SCOT. 130 (1989).

G. Maher, *The Enforcement of Judgments in Scots Law*, 2 CIV. JUST. Q. 244 (1983).

### *Singapore*

Mark Gross, *Foreign Creditor Rights: Recognition of Foreign Bankruptcy Adjudications in the United States and the Republic of Singapore*, 12 U. PA. J. INT'L BUS. L. 125 (1991).

R. Martin, *Reciprocal Enforcement of Judgments and Service of Processes in Singapore*, MALAYSIAN L.J. (Aug. 1981) at xlii.

### *South Africa*

P. S. G. Leon, *Roma Non Mocuta Est: The Recognition nad Enforcement of Foreign Judgments in South Africa*, 16 COMP. & INT'L L.J. S. AFR. 325 (1983).

R. D. Leslie, *The Non-Enforcement of Foreign Revenue Laws*, 93 S. AFR. L.J. 46 (1976).

### *South Korea*

J. M. Hwang, *Recognition and Enforcement of Foreign Judgments in South Korea*, 10 CAL. INT'L PRAC. 31 (2000).

### *Spain*

J. T. Clare, *Enforcement of Foreign Judgments in Spain*, 9 INT'L LAW. 509 (1975).

Enrique Dahl, *Enforcement of American Judgments in Spain*, 5 B.U. INT'L L.J. 29 (1987).

Marta Requejo Isidro, *Medidas Antiprocesso: Turner v. Grovit, Final Discutible de un Debate*, LA LEY. 6051 (June 2004).

### *Switzerland*

Martin Bernet & Nicotas C. Ulmer, *Recognition and Enforcement of Foreign Civil Judgments in Switzerland*, 27 INT'L LAW 317 (1993).

M. Bernet, *Recognition and Enforcement in Switzerland of U.S. Judgments Containing an Award of Punitive Damages*, 22 INT'L BUS. LAW. 272 (1994).

Yves P. Piantino, *Review Essay, Switzerland's Treatment of U.S. Money Judgments*, 46 AM J. COMP. L. 181 (Winter 1998).

Francisco Ramos Romeu, *Litigation Under the Shadow of an Exequatur: The Spanish Recognition of U.S. Judgments*, 38 INT'L LAW. 945 (2004).

Markus H. Wirth, *Attachment of Swiss Bank Accounts: International Debt Collection*, 36 Bus. Law. 1029 (1981).

### *Taiwan*

K. C. Fan, *Commercial Litigation, Arbitration and Enforcement of Foreign Judgments in Taiwan*, 12 Comp. L.Y.B. Int'l Bus. 119 (1990).

J. V. Uchima, *Recognition and Enforcement of U.S. Judgments in Taiwan*, 3 Cal. Int'l Prac. 17 (1991/1992).

### *Thailand*

Panthip Karnchanachitra Saisonthorn, *The Procedure for Introducing Foreign Judgments to the Thai Courts*, Law Journal, 20th year, ed. 3, B.E. 2533 (1990).

### *United Arab Emirates*

Giles Dixon & Priscilla Wood, *Arbitration Law, Practice and Enforcement of Awards in the United Arab Emirates*, Middle E. Exec. Rep. (Nov. 1988), at 24.

### *Vietnam*

David Howell, A *Realistic Look at Vietnam: Can Disputes Be Resolved and Awards Enforced?*, E. Asian Exec. Rep. (Mar. 15), 1992, at 9.

### *Yugoslavia (former)*

Peter Ŝarĉević, *The New Yugolav Private International Law Act*, 33 Am. J. Comp. L. 283 (1985).

## 5. Specialized Areas

### *a. Admiralty*

J. Kodwo Bentil, *Enforcement of Judgments in Foreign Admiralty Courts*, 128 Solic. J. 375 (1984).

H. Ringbom, *EU Regulation 44/2001 and Its Implications for the International Maritime Liability Conventions*, 35 J. Mar. L. & Com. 1 (2004).

### *b. Antitrust*

Jeffrey L. Cotter, *Extraterritorial Jurisdiction; The Application of U.S. Antitrust Laws to Acts Outside the United States*, 20 Wm. Mitchell L. Rev. 1109 (1994).

Catherine Mannick, *Recent Developments, Antitrust: British Restrictions on Enforcement of Foreign Judgments*, 21 Harv. Int'l L.J. 727 (1980).

Spencer W. Walter, *Neo-Realism and the International Harmonization of Law: Lessons from Antitrust*, 42 Kan L. Rev. 557 (1994).

### *c. Bankruptcy and Creditors' Rights*

John S. Diaconis, *Corcoran v. Ardra: The Impact of Insolvency on International Reinsurance Arbitration*, 28 Tort & Ins. L.J. 109 (1992).

Roland Montfort, *European Law on Cross-Border Insolvencies*, 23 AM. BANKR. INST. J. 28 (2004).

### d. Domestic Relations

Annotation, *Injunction Against Suit in Another State or Country for Divorce or Separation*, 54 A.L.R.3d 1240 (1992 & Supp. 2004).

Robert A. Arenstein, *Interjurisdictional Enforcement of Matrimonial Orders*, AM. J. FAM. L. (Spring 1988), at 7.

David F. Cavers, *International Enforcement of Family Support*, 81 COLUM. L. REV. 994 (1981).

Dorothy C. Daigle, *Due Process Rights of Parents and Children in International Child Abductions: An Examination of the Hague Convention and Its Exceptions*, 26 VAND J. TRANSNAT'L L. 865 (1993).

Michael M. O'Hear, *"Some of the Most Embarrassing Questions": Extraterritorial Divorces and the Problem of Jurisdiction Before Pennoyer*, 104 YALE L.J. 1507 (1995).

Phillip Schwartz, *How to Collect Support from Overseas*, FAIRSHARE (Mar. 1988), at 8.

Sheldon R. Shapiro, *Annotation, Extraterritorial Effect of Valid Award of Custody of Child of Divorced Parents, in Absence of Substantial Change in Circumstances*, 35 A.L.R.3d 520 (1991 & SUPP. 2004).

### e. Sovereign Immunity

M. P. A. Kindall, *Immunity of States for Non-Commercial Torts: A Comparative Analysis of the International Law Commission's Draft*, 75 CAL. L. REV. 1849 (1987).

Robert A. Klotz, *Enforcement of Judgments Against Foreign States in Canada*, NEWSL. ON INT'L LITIG. ABA SEC. ON INT'L L. & PRAC. (Apr. 1990), at 13.

Andreas Zimmermann, *Sovereign Immunity and Violations of International Jus Cogens – Some Critical Remarks*, 16 MICH. J. INT'L L. 433 (1995).

### f. Defamation and First Amendment Issues

Mark D. Rosen, *Exporting the Constitution*, 53 EMORY L.J. 171 (2004).

Jeff Sanders, *Extraterritorial Application of the First Amendment to Defamation Claims Against American Media*, 19 N.C.J. INT'L L. & COM. REG. 515 (1994).

### g. Hazardous Waste

Sean D. Murphy, *Prospective Liability Regimes for the Transboundary Movement of Hazardous Wastes*, 88 AM. J. INT'L L. 24 (1994).

### h. Construction

Eric A. Schwartz, *Resolution of International Construction Disputes*, 23 INT'L BUS. LAW. 149 (1995).

### i. U.S. Securities Law

Darrell Hall, *No Way Out: An Argument Against Permitting Parties to Opt Out of U.S. Securities Laws in International Transactions*, 97 COLUM. L. REV. 57 (1997).

### *j. Intellectual Property*

Rochelle C. Dreyfuss & Jane C. Ginsburg, *Draft Convention on Jurisdiction and Recognition of Judgments in Intellectual Property Matters* (Symposium on Constructing International Intellectual Property Law: The Role of National Courts), 77 CHI.-KENT L. REV. 1065 (2002).

Paul Goldstein, Lawrence Hadley, David Kendall, & Carl Oppedahl, *Copyright's Long Arm: Enforcing U.S. Copyrights Abroad*, 24. LOY. L.A. ENT. L. REV. 45 (2004).

E. Jooris, *Infringement of Foreign Copyright and the Jurisdiction of English Courts*, 18 EUR. INTELL. PROP. REV. 127 (1996).

### *k. Internet (E-Commerce)*

Marc H. Greenberg, *A Return to Lilliput: the LICRA v. Yahoo! Case and the Regulation of Online Content in the World Market*, 18 BERKELEY TECH. L.J. 1191 (2003).

Stratton Shartel, *Hague Delegates Revise Choice of Court Convention, but Some Concerns Remain*, 8 ELEC. COM. & L. REP. 1134 (December 17, 2003).

Stratton Shartel, *Hague Delegates Find Consensus, Narrow Disputes, as Diplomatic Conference Nears*, 9 ELEC. COM. & L. REP. 450 (May 12, 2004).

### *l. Intellectual Property*

Rochelle C. Dreyfuss & Jane C. Ginsburg, *Draft Convention on Jurisdiction and Recognition of Judgments in Intellectual Property Matters* (Symposium on Constructing International Intellectual Property Law: The Role of National Courts), 77 CHI.-KENT L. REV. 1065 (2002).

## D. SELECTED CASES

### Australia

*Dow Jones & Co. v. Gutnick*, [2002] HCA 56 (2002) [First Amendment issues].

*Lewis v. Beck*, unreported, Bench J of Supreme Court of Victoria, May 12, 1998 [conversion of damages and registration issues].

### Brazil

*Kappel Indust. Cal. & Equipt. Co. v. Banco de Recife*, SE No. 4811, 85 Rev. de Direito 481 (1927) [denying enforcement of New York judgment based on jurisdiction].

### Canada

*Beals v. Saldanha*, [2003] S.C.C. 72 WL No. 28829 (Can. Dec. 18, 2003). [Florida judgment enforced; jurisdiction based on "real and substantial connection" test for presence-based jurisdiction; for synopsis and analysis *see* 13 J. TRANSNAT'L L. & POL'Y 347, 364 (2003)].

*Bangoura v. Washington Post*, O.J. No. 284 (S.C.) (2004), available at www.canlii.org/on/cas/onsc/2004/2004onsc10181.html [defamation, First Amendment issues].

*European Community*

*Krombach v. Bamberski*, [2000] E.C.R. I-1935 (Case C-7/98).

*Germany*

*Einstweilige Anordnung vom 25. Juli 2003*, BVerfG 2.Senat [temporary court order of July 25, 2003, denying recognition of service of a New York class action judgment].

*Beschluss vom 13. Februar 2001*, OLG Frankfurt 20.Zivilsenat [decision of February 13, 2001 denying recognition of American judgment based on German public policy].

*Urteil vom 24. November 1999*, LG Stuttgart 24.Zivilkammer [judgment of November 24, 1999 on the effect of a pending U.S. class action suit].

*South Korea*

*Judgment of 14 April 1987*, Supreme Court, 86 Mu 57, 58 [New York judgment enforced].

*Judgment of 12 September 1984*, Seoul District Court, 84 Kaha 364 [Massachusetts judgment enforced].

*Switzerland*

*M.P. v. A, SA & D Est.*, ATF 122 III 439 (Federal Tribunal 1996) [enforced Southern District of New York award, dealt with forum selection clause].

*G v. B Laboratories, X & Y Corp.*, ATF 120 II 83, SJ 1994 470 (Federal Tribunal 1994) [enforcement of California judgment despite defect that would have rendered the judgment unenforceable in the United States].

*Rostuca Holdings v. Polo and Cour de Justice du Canton de Geneve*, ATF 116 II 25, JT 1992 II 182 (Federal Tribunal 1990) [enforced New York default judgment; for synopsis, see 46 Am. J. Comp. L. 181, 186].

*Trade Center Services AG v. Security Forwarders*, ATF 116 II 376, JT 1990 I 616 (Federal Tribunal 1990) [California judgment enforced].

*United Kingdom*

*Smith Kline & French Labs. Ltd. v. Bloch*, [1983] 1 W.L.R. 730 (C.A. 1982) (Lord Denning, MR).

*Turner v. Grovit*, [2002] 1 W.L.R. 107 (H.L. 2001).


## D. HARMONIZATION AND OTHER TYPES OF REFORM

### 1. Treatises and Books


Jurgen Basedow, et al., Private Law in The International Arena: From National Conflict Rules Towards Harmonization and Unification (Jurgen Basedow, et al., eds., Cambridge, MA, Kluwer Law International, 2000).

Rene David, The Legal Systems of the World, Their Comparison and Unification, in 2 International Encyclopedia of Comparative Law ch. 5 (Rene David ed., New York, Oceana Publications, 1969).

COLIN ONG, CROSS-BORDER LITIGATION WITHIN ASEAN: THE PROSPECTS FOR HARMONIZATION OF CIVIL AND COMMERCIAL LITIGATION (Cambridge, MA, Kluwer Law International, 1997).

## 2. Journals

Ronald S. Brand, *Enforcement of Foreign Money Judgments in the United States: In Search of Uniformity and International Acceptance*, 67 NOTRE DAME L. REV. 253 (1991).

Bernardo M. Cremades & Stephen L. Plehn, *The New Lex Mercatoria and the Harmonization of the Laws of International Commercial Transactions*, 2 B.U. INT'L L.J. 317 (1984).

Jenny S. Martinez, *Towards an International Judicial System*, 56 STAN. L. REV. 429 (2003).

Jeffrey J. Mayer, *Recent Mexican Arbitration Reform: The Continued Influence of the "Publicistas,"* 47 U. MIAMI L. REV. 913 (1993).

Kurt H. Nadelmann, *The United States of America and Agreements on Reciprocal Enforcement of Foreign Judgments*, 1 NETH. INT'L L. REV. 156 (1953).

Kurt H. Nadelmann, *Ignored State Interest: The Federal Government and International Effort to Unify Rules of Private Law*, 102 PA. L. REV. 323 (1954).

Peter H. Pfund, *United States Participation in International Unification of Private Law*, 19 INT'L LAW. 505 (1985).

Peter H. Pfund, *International Unification of Private Law: A Report on United States Participation, 1985–86*, 20 INT'L LAW. 623 (1986).

Peter H. Pfund, *International Unification of Private Law: A Report on United States Participation, 1986–87*, 21 INT'L LAW. 1245 (1986).

Peter H. Pfund, *International Unification of Private Law: A Report on United States Participation, 1987–88*, 22 INT'L LAW. 1157 (1988).

Peter H. Pfund, *Overview of the Codification Process*, 15 BROOKLYN. J. INT'L L. 8 (1989).

Peter Pfund & George Taft, *Congress' Role in the International Unification of Private Law*, 16 GA. J. INT'L & COMP. L. 671 (1986).

Spencer W. Wailer, *Neo-Realism and the International Harmonization of Law: Lessons from Antitrust*, 42 KAN. L. REV. 557 (1994).

# Instruments, Laws, and Other Materials – Part Two

## 1. International Treaties and Related Documents Available in Part One – Instruments, Laws, and Other Materials

a. 9 U.S.C.A. § 201, *et seq.*

   http://www.gpoaccess.gov/uscode/index.html

b. New York Convention – United Nations Convention on the Recognition and Enforcement of Foreign Arbitral Awards, June 10, 1958. 21 U.S.T. 2517, 330 U.N.T.S. 38 (1959)

   http://www.jus.uio.no/lm/un.arbitration.recognition.and.enforcement.convention.new.york.1958/doc.html#2

c. Ratification/Accession List for the New York Convention

   http://www.adr.org/sp.asp?id=22096

d. Convention on the Service Abroad of Judicial and Extrajudicial Documents in Civil and Commercial Matters (Hague Service Convention) 20 U.S.T. 361, 658 U.N.T.S. 163, 4 I.L.M. 341 (1965),
   Nov. 15, 1965

   http://www.hcch.net/index_en.php?act=conventions.text&cid=17

e. Conclusions and Recommendations Adopted by the Special Commission on the Practical Operation of the Hague Apostille, Evidence and Service Conventions, Oct. 28–Nov. 4, 2003

   http://www.hcch.net/index_en.php?act=publications.details&pid=3121&dtid=2

f. Status Table for the Hague Service Convention

   http://www.hcch.net/index_en.php?act=conventions.status&cid=17

g. Request for Service Abroad of Judicial or Extrajudicial Documents [Annex to Service Convention] – USM-94

   http://www.hcch.net/index_en.php?act=conventions.text&cid=17

h. Convention on the Choice of Court – 4 I.L.M. 348, Receueil de Conventions Hague [RCH] 96 – November 25, 1965

   http://www.hcch.net/index_en.php?act=conventions.text&cid=77

i. Convention on the Recognition and Enforcement of Foreign Judgments in Civil and Commercial Matters – 4 I.L.M. 350 – February 1, 1991

   http://www.hcch.net/index_en.php?act=conventions.text&cid=78

j. Convention on the Taking of Evidence Abroad in Civil or Commercial Matters (Hague Evidence Convention). 23 U.S.T. 2555, 8 I.L.M. 37, March 18, 1970

http://www.hcch.net/index_en.php?act=conventions.text&cid=82

k. Member States of the Hague Conference for Private International Law as of April 7, 2005

http://www.hcch.net/index_en.php?act=states.listing [For list of Conventions each Member State has signed or ratified, go to this Web page and click on the icon of the particular country.]

l. Hague Jurisdiction and Foreign Judgments/Choice of Court Convention Documents

i. Convention on Choice of Court Agreements, Concluded June 2005

http://hcch.e-vision.nl/index_en.php?act=conventions.pdf&cid=98

ii. Draft Report on the Preliminary Draft Convention on Exclusive Choice of Court Agreements. December 2004

http://www.hcch.net/upload/wop/jdgm_pd26e.pdf

m. Convention Abolishing the Requirement of Legalization for Foreign Public Documents (Hague Apostille Convention). 527 U.N.T.S. 189, 20 I.L.M. 1405, Oct. 5, 1961

http://www.hcch.net/index_en.php?act=conventions.text&cid=41

n. Model of Service Certificate

http://hcch.e-vision.nl/upload/apostille.pdf

o. Hague Service Convention: How to Serve Process in a Foreign Nation, Addresses of Domestic and Foreign Central Authorities, and Reference Material

www.travel.state.gov/law/hague_service.html

p. Hague Apostille Convention: Reference and Instructional Material on Legalization of Foreign Public Documents, Addresses of Domestic and Foreign Central Authorities

www.travel.state.gov/family/hague_foreign_docs.html

q. Hague Evidence Convention: Reference and Instructional Material on Taking of Evidence Abroad, Addresses of Domestic and Foreign Central Authorities

www.travel.state.gov/law/hague_evidence.html

## 2. International Conventions Related to Part Two

EC Convention on Jurisdiction and the Enforcement of Judgments in Civil and Commercial Matters, Brussels 1968
(Full Faith and Credit Convention)

Preamble

[Preamble]

The High Contracting Parties to the Treaty establishing the European Economic Community, Desiring to implement the provisions of Article 220 of that Treaty by virtue of which they undertook to secure the simplification of formalities governing the reciprocal recognition and enforcement of judgments of courts or tribunals;

Anxious to strengthen in the Community the legal protection of persons therein established; Considering that it is necessary for this purpose to determine the international jurisdiction of their courts, to facilitate recognition and to introduce an expeditious procedure for securing the enforcement of judgments, authentic instruments and court settlements;

Have decided to conclude this Convention and to this end have designated as their Plenipotentiaries: [____________________]

Who, meeting within the Council, having exchanged their Full Powers, found in good and due form,

Have agreed as follows:

Title I - Scope

Article 1

This Convention shall apply in civil and commercial matters whatever the nature of the court or tribunal. It shall not extend, in particular, to revenue, customs or administrative matters.

This Convention shall not apply to:

1. the status or legal capacity of natural persons, rights in property arising out of a matrimonial relationship, wills and succession;

2. bankruptcy, proceedings relating to the windingup of insolvent companies or other legal persons, judicial arrangements, compositions and analogous proceedings;

3. social security;

4. arbitration.

## Title II - Jurisdiction

### Section 1. - General provisions

#### Article 2

Subject to the provisions of this Convention, persons domiciled in a Contracting State shall, whatever their nationality, be sued in the courts of that State. Persons who are not nationals of the State in which they are domiciled shall be governed by the rules of jurisdiction applicable to nationals of that State.

#### Article 3

Persons domiciled in a Contracting State may be sued in the courts of another Contracting State only by virtue of the rules set out in Sections 2 to 6 of this Title. In particular the following provisions shall not be applicable as against them:

- in Belgium: Article 15 of the civil code (Code civil Burgerlijk Wetboek) and Article 638 of the judicial code (Code judiciaire Gerechtelijk Wetboek),
- in Denmark: Article 248 (2) of the law on civil procedure (Lov om rettens pleje) and Chapter 3. Article 3 of the Greenland law on civil procedure (Lov for Gr?nland om rettens pleje),

- in the Federal Republic of Germany: Article 23 of the code of civil procedure (Zivilproze□dnung),
- in France: Articles 14 and 15 of the civil code (Code civil),

- in Ireland: the rules which enable jurisdiction to be founded on the document instituting the proceedings having been served on the defendant during his temporary presence in Ireland,

- in Italy: Articles 2 and 4, Nos 1 and 2 of the code of civil procedure (Codice di procedura civile),
- in Luxembourg: Articles 14 and 15 of the civil code (Code civil),

- in the Netherlands: Articles 126 (3) and 127 of the code of civil procedure (Wetboek van Burgerlijke Rechtsvordering),

- in the United Kingdom: the rules which enable jurisdiction to be founded on:

(a) the document instituting the proceedings having been served on the defendant during his temporary presence in the United Kingdom; or

(b) the presence within the United Kingdom of property belonging to the defendant; or

(c) the seizure by the plaintiff of property situated in the United Kingdom.

Article 4

If the defendant is not domiciled in a Contracting State, the jurisdiction of the courts of each Contracting State shall, subject to the provisions of Article 16, be determined by the law of that State.

As against such a defendant, any person domiciled in a Contracting State may, whatever his nationality, avail himself in that State of the rules of jurisdiction there in force, and in particular those specified in the second paragraph of Article 3, in the same way as the nationals of that State.
Section 2. - Special jurisdiction

Article 5

A person domiciled in a Contracting State may, in another Contracting State, be sued:

1. in matters relating to a contract, in the courts for the place of performance of the obligation in question;

2. in matters relating to maintenance, in the courts for the place where the maintenance creditor is domiciled or habitually resident or, if the matter is ancillary to proceedings concerning the status of a person, in the court which, according to its own law, has jurisdiction to entertain those proceedings, unless that jurisdiction is based solely on the nationality of one of the parties;

3. in matters relating to tort, delict or quasidelict, in the courts for the place where the harmful event occurred;

4. as regards a civil claim for damages or restitution which is based on an act giving rise to criminal proceedings, in the court seised of those proceedings, to the extent that that court has jurisdiction under its own law to entertain civil proceedings;

5. as regards a dispute arising out of the operations of a branch, agency or other establishment, in the courts for the place in which the branch, agency or other establishment is situated;

6. as settlor, trustee or beneficiary of a trust created by the operation of a statute, or by a written instrument, or created orally and evidenced in writing, in the courts of the Contracting State in which the trust is domiciled;

7. as regards a dispute concerning the payment of remuneration claimed in respect of the salvage of a cargo or freight, in the court under the authority of which the cargo or freight in question:

(a) has been arrested to secure such payment, or

(b) could have been so arrested, but bail or other security has been given; provided that this provision shall apply only if it is claimed that the defendant has an interest in the cargo or freight or had such an interest at the time of salvage;

Article 6

A person domiciled in a Contracting State may also be sued:

1. where he is one of a number of defendants, in the courts for the place where any one of them is domiciled;

2. as a third party in an action on a warranty or guarantee or in any other third party proceedings, in the court seised of the original proceedings, unless these were instituted solely with the object of removing him from the jurisdiction of the court which would be competent in his case;

3. on a counterclaim arising from the same contract or facts on which the original claim was based, in the court in which the original claim is pending.

Article 6a

Where by virtue of this Convention a court of a Contracting State has jurisdiction in actions relating to liability arising from the use or operation of a ship, that court, or any

other court substituted for this purpose by the internal law of that State, shall also have jurisdiction over claims for limitation of such liability.
Section 3. - Jurisdiction in matters relating to insurance

Article 7

In matters relating to insurance, jurisdiction shall be determined by this Section, without prejudice to the provisions of Articles 4 and 5 (5).

Article 8

An insurer domiciled in a Contracting State may be sued:

1. in the courts of the State where he is domiciled, or

2. in another Contracting State, in the courts for the place where the policyholder is domiciled, or

3. if he is a coinsurer, in the courts of a Contracting State in which proceedings are brought against the leading insurer.

An insurer who is not domiciled in a Contracting State. but has a branch, agency or other establishment in one of the Contracting States shall, in disputes arising out of the operations of the branch, agency or establishment, be deemed to be domiciled in that State.

Article 9

In respect of liability insurance of immovable property, the insurer may in addition be sued in the courts for the place where the harmful event occurred. The same applies if movable and immovable property are covered by the same insurance policy and both are adversely affected by the same contingency.

Article 10

In respect of liability insurance, the insurer may also, if the law of the court permits it, be joined in proceedings which the injured party has brought against the insured. The provisions of Articles 7, 8 and 9 shall apply to actions brought by the injured party directly against the insurer, where such direct actions are permitted. If the law governing such direct actions provides that the policyholder or the insured may be joined as a party to the action, the same court shall have jurisdiction over them.

Article 11

Without prejudice to the provisions of the third paragraph of Article 10, an insurer may bring proceedings only in the courts of the Contracting State in which the defendant is domiciled, irrespective of whether he is the policyholder, the insured or a beneficiary. The provisions of this Section shall not affect the right to bring a counterclaim in the court in which, in accordance with this Section, the original claim is pending.

Article 12

The provisions of this Section may be departed from only by an agreement on jurisdiction:

1. which is entered into after the dispute has arisen, or

2. which allows the policyholder, the insured or a beneficiary to bring proceedings in courts other than those indicated in this Section, or

3. which is concluded between a policyholder and an insurer, both of whom are at the time of conclusion of the contract domiciled or habitually resident in the same Contracting State, and which has the effect of conferring jurisdiction on the courts of that State even if the harmful event were to occur abroad, provided that such an agreement is not contrary to the law of that State, or

4. which is concluded with a policyholder who is not domiciled in a Contracting State, except in so far as the insurance is compulsory or relates to immovable property in a Contracting State, or

5. which relates to a contract of insurance in so far as it covers one or more of the risks set out in Article 12a.

Article 12a

The following are the risks referred to in Article 12 (5):

1. Any loss of or damage to (a) seagoing ships, installations situated offshore or on the high seas, or aircraft, arising from perils which relate to their use for commercial

purposes, (b) goods in transit other than passengers' baggage where the transit consists of or includes carriage by such ships or aircraft;

2. Any liability, other than for bodily injury to passengers or loss of or damage to their baggage,

(a) arising out of the use or operation of ships, installations or aircraft as referred to in (1) (a) above in so far as the law of the Contracting State in which such aircraft are registered does not prohibit agreements on jurisdiction regarding insurance of such risks,

(b) for loss or damage caused by goods in transit as described in (1)

(b) above;

3. Any financial loss connected with the use or operation of ships, installations or aircraft as referred to in (1) (a) above, in particular loss of freight or charterhire;

4. Any risk or interest connected with any of those referred to in (1) to (3) above.

Section 4. - Jurisdiction over consumer contract

Article 13

In proceedings concerning a contract concluded by a person for a purpose which can be regarded as being outside his trade or profession, hereinafter called "the consumer", jurisdiction shall be determined by this Section, without prejudice to the provisions of Articles 4 and 5 (5), if it is:

1. a contract for the sale of goods on instalment credit terms, or

2. a contract for a loan repayable by instalments, or for any other form of credit, made to finance the sale of goods, or

3. any other contract for the supply of goods or a contract for the supply of services, and

(a) in the State of the consumer's domicile the conclusion of the contract was preceded by a specific invitation addressed to him or by advertising, and

(b) the consumer took in that State the steps necessary for the conclusion of the contract.

Where the consumer enters into a contract with a party who is not domiciled in a Contracting State but has a branch, agency or other establishment in one of the Contracting States, that party shall, in disputes arising out of the operations of the branch, agency or establishment, be deemed to be domiciled in that State.

This Section shall not apply to contracts of transport.

Article 14

A consumer may bring proceedings against the other party to a contract either in the courts of the Contracting State in which that party is domiciled or in the courts of the Contracting State in which he is himself domiciled.

Proceedings may be brought against a consumer by the other party to the contract only in the courts of the Contracting State in which the consumer is domiciled.

These provisions shall not affect the right to bring a counterclaim in the court in which, in accordance with this Section, the original claim is pending.

Article 15

The provisions of this Section may be departed from only by an agreement:

1. which is entered into after the dispute has arisen, or

2. which allows the consumer to bring proceedings in courts other than those indicated in this Section, or

3. which is entered into by the consumer and the other party to the contract, both of whom are at the time of conclusion of the contract domiciled or habitually resident in the same Contracting State, and which confers jurisdiction on the courts of that State, provided that such an agreement is not contrary to the law of that State.

Section 5. - Exclusive jurisdiction

Article 16

The following courts shall have exclusive jurisdiction, regardless of domicile:

1. in proceedings which have as their object rights in rem in, or tenancies of, immovable property, the courts of the Contracting State in which the property is situated;

2. in proceedings which have as their object the validity of the constitution, the nullity or the dissolution of companies or other legal persons or associations of natural or legal

persons, or the decisions of their organs, the courts of the Contracting State in which the company, legal person or association has its seat;

3. in proceedings which have as their object the validity of entries in public registers, the courts of the Contracting State in which the register is kept;

4. in proceedings concerned with the registration or validity of patents, trade marks, designs, or other similar rights required to be deposited or registered, the courts of the Contracting State in which the deposit or registration has been applied for, has taken place or is under the terms of an international convention deemed to have taken place;

5. in proceedings concerned with the enforcement of judgments, the courts of the Contracting States in which the judgment has been or is to be enforced.

Section 6. - Prorogation of jurisdiction

Article 17

If the parties, one or more of whom is domiciled in a Contracting State, have agreed that a court or the courts of a Contracting State are to have jurisdiction to settle any disputes which have arisen or which may arise in connection with a particular legal relationship, that court or those courts shall have exclusive jurisdiction. Such an agreement conferring jurisdiction shall be either in writing or evidenced in writing or, in international trade or commerce, in a form which accords with practice in that trade or commerce of which the parties are or ought to have been aware. Where such an agreement is concluded by parties, none of whom is domiciled in a Contracting State, the courts of other Contracting States shall have no jurisdiction over their disputes unless the court or courts chosen have declined jurisdiction. The court or courts of a Contracting State on which a trust instrument has conferred jurisdiction shall have exclusive jurisdiction in any proceedings brought against a settlor, trustee or beneficiary, if relations between these persons or their rights or obligations under the trust are involved.

Agreements or provisions of a trust instrument conferring jurisdiction shall have no legal force if they are contrary to the provisions of Article 12 or 15, or if the courts whose jurisdiction they purport to exclude have exclusive jurisdiction by virtue of Article 16.

If an agreement conferring jurisdiction was concluded for the benefit of only one of the parties, that party shall retain the right to bring proceedings in any other court which has jurisdiction by virtue of this Convention.

Article 18

Apart from jurisdiction derived from other provisions of this Convention, a court of a Contracting State before whom a defendant enters an appearance shall have jurisdiction. This rule shall not apply where appearance was entered solely to contest the jurisdiction, or where another court has exclusive jurisdiction by virtue of Article 16.

Section 7. - Examination as to jurisdiction and admissibility

Article 19

Where a court of a Contracting State is seised of a claim which is principally concerned with a matter over which the courts of another Contracting State have exclusive jurisdiction by virtue of Article 16, it shall declare of its own motion that it has no jurisdiction.

Article 20

Where a defendant domiciled in one Contracting State is sued in a court of another Contracting State and does not enter an appearance, the court shall declare of its own motion that it has no jurisdiction unless its jurisdiction is derived from the provisions of this Convention.

The court shall stay the proceedings so long as it is not shown that the defendant has been able to receive the document instituting the proceedings or an equivalent document in sufficient time to enable him to arrange for his defence, or that all necessary steps have been taken to this end.

The provisions of the foregoing paragraph shall be replaced by those of Article 15 of the Hague Convention of 15 November 1965 on the service abroad of judicial and extrajudicial documents in civil or commercial matters, if the document instituting the proceedings or notice thereof had to be transmitted abroad in accordance with that Convention.

Section 8. - Lis Pendens related actions

Article 21

Where proceedings involving the same cause of action and between the same parties are brought in the courts of different Contracting States, any court other than the court first seised shall of its own motion decline jurisdiction in favour of that court.

A court which would be required to decline jurisdiction may stay its proceedings if the jurisdiction of the other court is contested.

Article 22

Where related actions are brought in the courts of different Contracting States, any court other than the court first seised may, while the actions are pending at first instance, stay its proceedings.

A court other than the court first seised may also, on the application of one of the parties, decline jurisdiction if the law of that court permits the consolidation of related actions and the court first seised has jurisdiction over both actions.

For the purposes of this Article, actions are deemed to be related where they are so closely connected that it is expedient to hear and determine them together to avoid the risk of irreconcilable judgments resulting from separate proceedings.

23

Where actions come within the exclusive jurisdiction of several courts, any court other the court first seised shall decline jurisdiction in favour of that court.

Section 9. - Provisional, including protective, measures

Article 24

Application may be made to the courts of a Contracting State for such provisional, including protective, measures as may be available under the law of that State, even if, under this Convention, the courts of another Contracting State have jurisdiction as to the substance of the matter.

Title III - Recognition and enforcement

Article 25

For the purposes of this Convention, "judgment" means any judgment given by a court or tribunal of a Contracting State, whatever the judgment may be called, including a decree, order, decision or writ of execution, as well as the determination of costs or expenses by an officer of the court.

Section 1. - Recognition

Article 26

A judgment given in a Contracting State shall be recognized in the other Contracting States without any special procedure being required.

Any interested party who raises the recognition of a judgment as the principal issue in a dispute may, in accordance with the procedures provided for in Sections 2 and 3 of this Title, apply for a decision, that the judgment be recognized.

If the outcome of proceedings in a court of a Contracting State depends on he determination of an incidental question of recognition that court shall have jurisdiction over that question.

Article 27

A judgment shall not be recognized:

1. if such recognition is contrary to public policy in the State in which recognition is sought;

2. where it was given in default of appearance, if the defendant was not duly served with the document which instituted the proceedings or with an equivalent document in sufficient time to enable him to arrange for his defence;

3. if the judgment is irreconcilable with a judgment given in a dispute between the same parties in the State in which recognition is sought;

4. if the court of the State in which the judgment was given, in order to arrive at its judgment, has decided a preliminary question concerning the status or legal capacity of natural persons, rights in property arising out of a matrimonial relationship, wills or succession in a way that conflicts with a rule of the private international law of the State in which the recognition is sought, unless the same result would have been reached by the application of the rules of private international law of that State;

5. if the judgment is irreconcilable with an earlier judgment given in a nonContracting State involving the same cause of action and between the same parties, provided that this latter jugdment fulfils the conditions necessary for its recognition in the State addresses.

Article 28

Moreover, a judgment shall not be recognized if it conflicts with the provisions of Section 3, 4 or 5 of Title II, or in a case provided for in Article 59.

In its examination of the grounds of jurisdiction referred to in the foregoing paragraph, the court or authority applied to shall be bound by the findings of fact on which the court of the State in which the judgment was given based its jurisdiction .

Subject to the provisions of the first paragraph, the jurisdiction of the court of the State in which the judgment was given may not be reviewed; the test of public policy referred to in Article 27 (1) may not be applied to the rules relating to jurisdiction.

Article 29

Under no circumstances may a foreign judgment be reviewed as to its substance.

Article 30

A court of a Contracting State in which recognition is sought of a judgment given in another Contracting State may stay the proceedings if an ordinary appeal against the judgment has been lodged.

A court of a Contracting State in which recognition is sought of a judgment given in Ireland or the United Kingdom may stay the proceedings if enforcement is suspended in the State in which the judgment was given by reason of an appeal.

Section 2. - Enforcement

Article 31

A judgment given in a Contracting State and enforceable in that State shall be enforced in another Contracting State when, on the application of any interested party, the order for its enforcement has been issued there.

However, in the United Kingdom, such a judgment shall be enforced in England and Wales, in Scotland, or in Northern Ireland when, on the application of any interested party, it has been registered for enforcement in that part of the United Kingdom.

Article 32

The application shall be submitted:

- in Belgium, to the tribunal de premiere instance or rechtbank van eerste aan leg.

- in Denmark, to the underret,

- in the Federal Republic of Germany, to the presiding judge of a chamber of the Landgericht,

- in France, to the presiding judge of the tribunal de grande instance, in Ireland, to the High Court,

- in Italy, to the corte d'appello,

- in Luxembourg, to the presiding judge of the tribunal d'arrondissement,

- in the Netherlands, to the presiding judge of the arrondissementsrechtbank, - in the United Kingdom:

1. in England and Wales, to the High Court of Justice or in the case of a maintenance judgment to the Magistrates' Court on transmission by the Secretary of State;

2. in Scotland, to the Court of Session, or in the case of a maintenance judgment to the Sheriff Court on transmission by the Secretary of State;

3. in Northern Ireland, to the High Court of Justice, or in the case of a maintenance judgment to the Magistrates' Court on transmission by the Secretary of State.

The jurisdiction of local courts shall be determined by reference to the place of domicile of the party against whom enforcement is sought. If he is not domiciled in the State in which enforcement is sought, it shall be determined by reference to the place of enforcement.

Article 33

The procedure for making the application shall be governed by the law of the State in which enforcement is sought.

The applicant must give an address for service of process within the area of jurisdiction of the court applied to. However, if the law of the State in which enforcement is sought does not provide for the furnishing of such an address, the applicant shall appoint a representative ad litem.

The documents referred to in Articles 46 and 47 shall be attached to the application.

Article 34

The court applied to shall give its decision without delay; the party against whom enforcement is sought shall not at this stage of the proceedings be entitled to make any submissions on the application.

The application may be refused only for one of the reasons specified in Articles 27 and 28. Under no circumstances may the foreign judgment be reviewed as to its substance.

Article 35

The appropriate officer of the court shall without delay bring the decision given on the application to the notice of the applicant in accordance with the procedure laid down by the law of the State in which enforcement is sought.

Article 36

If enforcement is authorized, the party against whom enforcement is sought may appeal against the decision within one month of service thereof.
If that party is domiciled in a Contracting State other than that in which the decision authorizing enforcement was given, the time for appealing shall be two months and shall run from the date of service, either on him in person or at his residence. No extension of time may be granted on account of distance.

Article 37

An appeal against the decision authorizing enforcement shall be lodged in accordance with the rules governing procedure in contentious matters:

- in Belgium, with the tribunal de premiere instance or rechtbank van eersteaanleg.

- in Denmark, with the landsret,

- in the Federal Republic of Germany, with the Oberlandesgericht,

- in France, with the cour d'appel,

- in Ireland, with the High Court,

- in Italy, with the corte d'appello,

- in Luxembourg, with the Court superieure de justice sitting as a court of civil appeal,

- the Netherlands, with the arrondissementsrechtbank,

- in the United Kingdom:

1. in England and Wales, with the High Court of Justice, or in the case of a maintenance judgment with the Magistrates' Court;

2. in Scotland, with the Court of Session, or in the case of a maintenance judgment with the Sheriff Court;

3. in Northern Ireland, with the High Court of Justice, or in the case of a maintenance judgment with the Magistrates' Court.

The judgment given on the appeal may be contested only:

- in Belgium, France, Italy, Luxembourg and the Netherlands, by an appeal in cassation,

- in Denmark, by an appeal to the h?eret, with the leave of the Minister of Justice,

- in the Federal Republic of Germany, by a Rechtsbeschwerde,

- in Ireland, by an appeal on a point of law to the Supreme Court,

- in the United Kingdom, by a single further appeal on a point of law.

Article 38

The court with which the appeal under the first paragraph of Article 37 is lodged may, on the application of the appellant, stay the proceedings if an ordinary appeal has been lodged against the judgment in the State in which that judgment was given or if the time for such an appeal has not yet expired; in the latter case, the court may specify the time within which such an appeal is to be lodged.

Where the judgment was given in Ireland or the United Kingdom, any form of appeal available in the State in which it was given shall be treated as an ordinary appeal for the purposes of the first paragraph.

The court may also make enforcement conditional on the provision of such security as it shall determine.

Article 39

During the time specified for an appeal pursuant to Article 36 and until any such appeal has been determined, no measures of enforcement may be taken other than protective measures taken against the property of the party against whom enforcement is sought.

The decision authorizing enforcement shall carry with it the power to proceed to any such protective measures.

Article 40

If the application for enforcement is refused, the applicant may appeal:

- in Belgium, to the cour d'appel or hof van beroep,

- in Denmark, to the landsret,

- in the Federal Republic of Germany, to the Oberlandesgericht,

- in France, to the cour d'appel,

- in Ireland, to the High Court,

- in Italy, to the corte d'appello,

- in Luxembourg, to the Court superieure de justice sitting as a court of civil appeal.

- in the Netherlands, to the arrondissementsrechtbank,

- in the United Kingdom:

1. in England and Wales, to the High Court of Justice, or in the case of a maintenance judgment to the Magistrates' Court;

2. in Scotland, to the Court of Session, or in the case of a maintenance judgment to the Sheriff Court;

3. in Northern Ireland, to the High Court of Justice, or in the case of a maintenance judgment to the Magistrates' Court.

The party against whom enforcement is sought shall be summoned to appear before the appellate court. If he fails to appear, the provisions of the second and third paragraphs of Article 20 shall apply even where he is not domiciled in any of the Contracting States.

Article 41

A judgment given on an appeal provided for in Article 40 may be contested only:

- in Belgium, France, Italy, Luxembourg and the Netherlands, by an appeal in cassation,

- in Denmark, by an appeal to the h0jesteret, with the leave of the Minister of Justice.

- in the Federal Republic of Germany, by a Rechtsbeschwerde,

- in the United Kingdom, by a single further appeal on a point of law.

Article 42

Where a foreign judgment has been given in respect of several matters and enforcement cannot be authorized for all of them, the court shall authorize enforcement for one or more of them.

An applicant may request partial enforcement of a judgment.

Article 43

A foreign judgment which orders a periodic payment by way of a penalty shall be enforceable in the State in which enforcement is sought only if the amount of the payment has been finally determined by the courts of the State in which the judgment was given.

Article 44

An applicant who, in the State in which the judgment was given, has benefited from complete or partial legal aid or exemption from costs or expenses, shall be entitled, in the procedures provided for in Articles 32 to 35, to benefit from the most favourable legal aid or the most extensive exemption from costs or expenses provided for by the law of the State addressed. However, an applicant who requests the enforcement of a decision given by an administrative authority in Denmark in respect of a maintenance order may, in the State addressed, claim the benefits referred to in the first paragraph if the presents a statement from the Danish Ministry of Justice to the effect that he fulfils the economic requirements to qualify for the grant of complete or partial legal aid or exemption from costs or expenses.

Article 45

No security, bond or deposit, however described, shall be required of a party who in one Contracting State applies for enforcement of a judgment given in another Contracting State on the ground that he is a foreign national or that he is not domiciled or resident in the State in which enforcement is sought.

Section 3. - Common provisions

Article 46

A party seeking recognition or applying for enforcement of a judgment shall produce:

1. a copy of the judgment which satisfies the conditions necessary to establish its authenticity;

2. in the case of a judgment given in default, the original or a certified true copy of the document which establishes that the party in default was served with the document instituting the proceedings or with an equivalent document.

Article 47

A party applying for enforcement shall also produce:

1. documents which establish that, according to the law of the State in which it has been given, the judgment is enforceable and has been served;

2. where appropriate, a document showing that the applicant is in receipt of legal aid in the State in which the judgment was given.

Article 48

If the document specified in Articles 46 (2) and 47 (2) are not produced, the court may specify a time for their production, accept equivalent documents or, if it considers that it has sufficient information before it, dispense with their production.

If the court so requires, a translation of the documents shall be produced; the translation shall be certified by a person qualified to do so in one of the Contracting States.

Article 49

No legalization or other similar formality shall be required in respect of the documents referred to in Article 46 or 47 or the second paragraph of Article 48, or in respect of a document appointing a representative ad litem.

Title IV - Authentic Instruments and Court Settlements

Article 50

A document which has been formally drawn up or registered as an authentic instrument and is enforceable in one Contracting State shall, in another Contracting State, have an order for its enforcement issued there, on application made in accordance with the procedures provided for in Article 31 et seq. The application may be refused only if enforcement of the instrument is contrary to public policy in the State in which enforcement is sought.

The instrument produced must satisfy the conditions necessary to establish its authenticity in the State of origin.

The provisions of Section 3 of Title III shall apply as appropriate.

Article 51

A settlement which has been approved by a court in the course of proceedings and is enforceable in the State in which it was concluded shall be enforceable in the State in which enforcement is sought under the same conditions as authentic instruments.

Title V - General Provisions

Article 52

In order to determine whether a party is domiciled in the Contracting State whose courts are seised of a matter, the Court shall apply its internal law.

If a party is not domiciled in the State whose courts are seised of the matter, then, in order to determine whether the party is domiciled in another Contracting State, the court shall apply the law of that State.

The domicile of a party shall, however, be determined in accordance with his national law if, by that law, his domicile depends on that of another person or on the seat of an authority.

Article 53

For the purposes of this Convention, the seat of a company or other legal person or association of natural or legal persons shall be treated as its domicile. However, in order to determine that seat, the court shall apply its rules of private international law.

In order to determine whether a trust is domiciled in the Contracting State whose courts are seised of the matter, the court shall apply its rules of private international law.

Title VI - Transitional Provisions

Article 54

The provisions of this Convention shall apply only to legal proceedings instituted and to documents formally drawn up or registered as authentic instruments after its entry into force. However, judgments given after the date of entry into force of this Convention in proceedings instituted before that date shall be recognized and enforced in accordance with the provisions of Title III if jurisdiction was founded upon rules which accorded with those provided for either in Title II of this Convention or in a convention concluded between the State of origin and the State addressed which was in force when the proceedings were instituted.

Title VII - Relationship to other Conventions

Article 55

Subject to the provisions of the second paragraph of Article 54, and of Article 56, this Convention shall, for the States which are parties to it, supersede the following conventions concluded between two or more of them:

- the Convention between Belgium and France on jurisdiction and the validity and enforcement of judgments, arbitration awards and authentic instruments, signed at Paris on 8 July 1899,

- the Convention between Belgium and the Netherlands on jurisdiction, bankruptcy, and the validity and enforcement of judgments, arbitration awards and authentic instruments, signed at Brussels on 28 March 1925,

- the Convention between France and Italy on the enforcement of judgments in civil and commercial matters, signed at Rome on 3 June 1930,

- the Convention between the United Kingdom and the French Republic providing for the reciprocal enforcement of judgments in civil and commercial matters, with Protocol, signed at Paris on 18 January 1934,

- the Convention between the United Kingdom and the Kingdom of Belgium providing for the reciprocal enforcement of judgments in civil and commercial matters, with Protocol, signed at Brussels on 2 May 1934,

- the Convention between Germany and Italy on the recognition and enforcement of judgments in civil and commercial matters, signed at Rome on 9 March 1936,

- the Convention between the Federal Republic of Germany and the Kingdom of Belgium on the mutual recognition and enforcement of judgments, arbitration awards and authentic instruments in civil and commercial matters, signed at Bonn on 30 June 1958,

- the Convention between the Kingdom of the Netherlands and the Italian Republic on the recognition and enforcement of judgments in civil and commercial matters, signed at Rome on 17 April 1959,

- the Convention between the United Kingdom and the Federal Republic of Germany for the reciprocal recognition and enforcement of judgments in civil and commercial matters, signed at Bonn on 14 July 1960,

- the Convention between the Kingdom of Belgium and the Italian Republic on the recognition and enforcement of judgments and other enforceable instruments in civil and commercial matters, signed at Rome on 6 April 1962,

- the Convention between the Kingdom of the Netherlands and the Federal Republic of Germany on the mutual recognition and enforcement of judgments and other enforceable instruments in civil and commercial matters, signed at The Hague on 30 August 1962,

- the Convention between the United Kingdom and the Republic of Italy for the reciprocal recognition and enforcement of judgments in civil and commercial matters, signed at Rome on 7 February 1964, with amending Protocol signed at Rome on 14 July 1970,

- the Convention between the United Kingdom and the Kingdom of the Netherlands providing for the reciprocal recognition and enforcement of judgments in civil matters, signed at The Hague on 17 November 1967,

and, in so far as it is in force:

- the Treaty between Belgium, the Netherlands and Luxembourg on jurisdiction, bankruptcy, and the validity and enforcement of judgments, arbitration awards and authentic instruments, signed at Brussels on 24 November 1961.

Article 56

The Treaty and the conventions referred to in Article 55 shall continue to have effect in relation to matters to which this Convention does not apply.

They shall continue to have effect in respect of judgments given and documents formally drawn up or registered as authentic instruments before the entry into force of this Convention.

Article 57

This Convention shall not affect any conventions to which the Contracting States are or will be parties and which, in relation to particular matters, govern jurisdiction or the recognition or enforcement of judgments.

This Convention shall not affect the application of provisions which, in relation to particular matters, govern jurisdiction or the recognition or enforcement of judgments and which are or will be contained in acts of the institutions of the European Communities or in national laws harmonized in implementation of such acts.

Article 58

This Convention shall not affect the rights granted to Swiss nationals by the Convention concluded on 15 June 1869 between France and the Swiss Confederation on Jurisdiction and the enforcement of judgments in civil matters.

Article 59

This Convention shall not prevent a Contracting State from assuming, in a convention on recognition and enforcement of judgments, an obligation towards a third State not to recognize judgments given in other Contracting States against defendants domiciled or habitually resident in the third State where, in cases provided for in Article 4, the judgment could only be founded on a ground of jurisdiction specified in the second paragraph of Article 3.

However, a Contracting State may not assume an obligation towards a third State not to recognize a judgment given in another Contracting State by a court basing its jurisdiction on the presence within that State of property belonging to the defendant, or the seizure by the plaintiff of property situated there:

1. if the action is brought to assert or declare proprietary or possessory rights in that property, seeks to obtain authority to dispose of it, or arises from another issue relating to such property, or,

2. if the property constitutes the security for a debt which is the subject matter of the action.

Title VIII - Final Provisions

Article 60

This Convention shall apply to the European territories of the Contracting States, including Greenland, to the French overseas departments and territories, and to Mayotte. The Kingdom of the Netherlands may declare at the time of signing or ratifying this Convention or at any later time, by notifying the SecretaryGeneral of the Council of the European Communities, that this Convention shall be applicable to the Netherlands Antilles. In the absence of such declaration, proceedings taking place in the European territory of the Kingdom as a result of an appeal in cassation from the judgment of a court in the Netherlands Antilles shall be deemed to be proceedings taking place in the latter court.

Notwithstanding the first paragraph, this Convention shall not apply to:

1. The Faroe islands, unless the Kingdom of Denmark makes a declaration to the contrary;

2. any European territory situated outside the United Kingdom for the international relations of which the United Kingdom is responsible, unless the United Kingdom makes a declaration to the contrary in respect of any such territory.

Such declaration may be made at any time by notifying the SecretaryGeneral of the Council of the European Communities.

Proceedings brought in the United Kingdom on appeal from courts in one of the territories referred to in subparagraph 2 of the third paragraph shall be deemed to be proceedings taking place in those courts.

Proceedings which in the Kingdom of Denmark are dealt with under the law on civil procedure for the Faroe Islands (lov for F?roerne om rettens pleje) shall be deemed to be proceedings taking place in the courts of the Faroe Islands.

Article 61

This Convention shall be ratified by the signatory States. The instruments of ratification shall be deposited with the Secretary General on the Council of the European Communities.

Article 62

This Convention shall enter into force on the first day of the third month following the deposit of the instrument of ratification by the last signatory State to take this step.

Article 63

The Contracting States recognize that any State which becomes a member of the European Economic Community shall be required to accept this Convention as a basis for the negotiations between the Contracting States and that State necessary to ensure the implementation of the last paragraph of Article 220 of the Treaty establishing the European Economic Community.

The necessary adjustments may be the subject of a special convention between the Contracting States of the one part and the new Member States of the other part.

Article 64

The SecretaryGeneral of the Council of the European Communities shall notify the signatory States of:

(a) the deposit of each instrument of ratification;

(b) the date of entry into force of this Convention;

(c) any declaration received pursuant to Article 60;

(d) any declaration received pursuant to Article IV of the Protocol;

(e) any communication made pursuant to Article VI of the Protocol.

Article 65

The Protocol annexed to this Convention by common accord of the Contracting States shall form an integral part thereof.

Article 66

This Convention is concluded for an unlimited period.

Article 67

Any Contracting State may request the revision of this Convention. In this event, a revision conference shall be convened by the President of the Council of the European Communities.

Article 68

This Convention, drawn up in a single original in the Dutch, French, German and Italian languages, all four texts being equally authentic, shall be deposited in the archives of the Secretariat of the Council of the European Communities. The SecretaryGeneral shall transmit a certified copy to the Government of each signatorv State.

Endnotes

# CONVENTION

## on jurisdiction and the enforcement of judgments

## in civil and commercial matters**

*Done at Lugano on 16 September 1988*

## PREAMBLE

*THE HIGH CONTRACTING PARTIES TO THIS CONVENTION,*

*ANXIOUS to strengthen in their territories the legal protection of persons therein established,*

*CONSIDERING that it is necessary for this purpose to determine the international jurisdiction of their courts, to facilitate recognition and to introduce an expeditious procedure for securing the enforcement of judgments, authentic instruments and court settlements,*

*AWARE of the links between them, which have been sanctioned in the economic field by the free trade agreements concluded between the European Economic Community and the States members of the European Free Trade Association,*

*TAKING INTO ACCOUNT the Brussels Convention of 27 September 1968 on jurisdiction and the enforcement of judgments in civil and commercial matters, as amended by the Accession Conventions under the successive enlargements of the European Communities,*

*PERSUADED that the extension of the principles of that Convention to the States parties to this instrument will strengthen legal and economic cooperation in Europe,*

*DESIRING to ensure as uniform an interpretation as possible of this instrument,*

*HAVE in this spirit DECIDED to conclude this Convention and*

*HAVE AGREED AS FOLLOWS:*

## TITLE I

## SCOPE

### *Article 1*

[omissis]

## TITLE II

# JURISDICTION

### Section 1

## General provisions

### *Article 2*

[omissis]

### *Article 3*

Persons domiciled in a Contracting State may be sued in the courts of another Contracting State only by virtue of the rules set out in Sections 2 to 6 of this Title.

In particular the following provisions shall not be applicable as against them:

- in Belgium: Article 15 of the civil code (Code civil - Burgerlijk Wetboek) and Article 638 of the judicial code (Code judiciaire - Gerechtelijk Wetboek),

- in Denmark: Article 246 (2) and (3) of the law on civil procedure (Lov om rettens pleje),

- in the Federal Republic of Germany: Article 23 of the code of civil procedure (Zivilprozeßordnung),

- in Greece: Article 40 of the code of civil procedure ( Κώδικας Πολιτικής Δικονομίας ),

- in France: Articles 14 and 15 of the civil code (Code civil),

- in Ireland: the rules which enable jurisdiction to be founded on the document instituting the proceedings having been served on the defendant during his temporary presence in Ireland,

*- in Iceland: Article 77 of the Civil Proceedings Act (lög um meðferð einkamála í héraði),*

- in Italy: Articles 2 and 4, Nos 1 and 2 of the code of civil procedure (Codice di procedura civile),

- in Luxembourg: Articles 14 and 15 of the civil code (Code civil),

- in the Netherlands: Articles 126 (3) and 127 of the code of civil procedure (Wetboek van Burgerlijke Rechtsvordering),

*- in Norway: Section 32 of the Civil Proceedings Act (tvistemålsloven),*

*- in Austria: Article 99 of the Law on Court Jurisdiction (Jurisdiktionsnorm),*

- in Portugal: Articles 65 (1) (c), 65 (2) and 65A (c) of the code of civil procedure (Código de Processo Civil) and Article 11 of the code of labour procedure (Código de Processo de Trabalho),

*- in Switzerland: le for du lieu du séquestre /Gerichtsstand des Arrestortes / foro del luogo del sequestro within the meaning of Article 4 of the loi fédérale sur le droit international privé / Bundesgesetz über das internationale Privatrecht / legge federale sul diritto internazionale privato,*

*- in Finland: the second, third and fourth sentences of Section 1 of Chapter 10 of the Code of Judicial Procedure (oikeudenkäymiskaari / rättegångsbalken),*

*- in Sweden: the first sentence of Section 3 of Chapter 10 of the Code of Judicial Procedure (Rättegångsbalken),*

- in the United Kingdom: the rules which enable jurisdiction to be founded on:

(a) the document instituting the proceedings having been served on the defendant during his temporary presence in the United Kingdom; or

(b) the presence within the United Kingdom of property belonging to the defendant; or

(c) the seizure by the plaintiff of property situated in the United Kingdom.

### *Article 4*

[omissis]

## Section 2

# Special jurisdiction

### *Article 5*

A person domiciled in a Contracting State may, in another Contracting State, be sued:

*1. in matters relating to a contract, in the courts for the place of performance of the obligationin question; in matters relating to individual contracts of employment, this place is that where the employee habitually carries out his work, or if the employee does not habitually carry out his work in any one country, this place shall be the place of business through which he was engaged;*

2. in matters relating to maintenance, in the courts for the place where the maintenance creditor is domiciled or habitually resident or, if the matter is ancillary to proceedings concerning the status of a person, in the court which, according to its own law, has jurisdiction to entertain those proceedings, unless that jurisdiction is based solely on the nationality of one of the parties;

3. in matters relating to tort, delict or quasi-delict, in the courts for the place where the harmful event occurred;

4. as regards a civil claim for damages or restitution which is based on an act giving rise to criminal proceedings, in the court seised of those proceedings, to the extent that that court has jurisdiction under its own law to entertain civil proceedings;

5. as regards a dispute arising out of the operations of a branch, agency or other establishment, in the courts for the place in which the branch, agency or other establishment is situated;

6. in his capacity as settlor, trustee or beneficiary of a trust created by the operation of a statute, or by a written instrument, or created orally and evidenced in writing, in the courts of the Contracting State in which the trust is domiciled;

7. as regards a dispute concerning the payment of remuneration claimed in respect of the salvage of a cargo or freight, in the court under the authority of which the cargo or freight in question:

(a) has been arrested to secure such payment,

or

(b) could have been so arrested, but bail or other security has been given; provided that this provision shall apply only if it is claimed that the defendant has an interest in the cargo or freight or had such an interest at the time of salvage.

*Article 6 - Article 6A*

[omissis]

**Section 3**

# Jurisdiction in matters relating to insurance

*Article 7 - Article 12A*

[omissis]

**Section 4**

# Jurisdiction over consumer contracts

*Article 13 - Article 15*

[omissis]

**Section 5**

# Exclusive jurisdiction

*Article 16*

The following courts shall have exclusive jurisdiction, regardless of domicile:

1. (a) in proceedings which have as their object rights *in rem* in immovable property or tenancies of immovable property, the courts of the Contracting State in which the property is situated;

> *(b) however, in proceedings which have as their object tenancies of immovable property concluded for temporary private use for a maximum period of six consecutive months, the courts of the Contracting State in which the defendant is domiciled shall also have jurisdiction, provided that the tenant is a natural person and neither party is domiciled in the Contracting State in which the property is situated;*

2. in proceedings which have as their object the validity of the constitution, the nullity or the dissolution of companies or other legal persons or associations of natural or legal persons, or the decisions of their organs, the courts of the Contracting State in which the company, legal person or association has its seat;

3. in proceedings which have as their object the validity of entries in public registers, the courts of the Contracting State in which the register is kept;

4. in proceedings concerned with the registration or validity of patents, trade marks, designs, or other similar rights required to be deposited or registered, the courts of the Contracting State in which the deposit or registration has been applied for, has taken place or is under the terms of an international convention deemed to have taken place;

5. in proceedings concerned with the enforcement of judgments, the courts of the Contracting State in which the judgment has been or is to be enforced.

### Section 6

## Prorogation of jurisdiction

### *Article 17*

1. If the parties, one or more of whom is domiciled in a Contracting State, have agreed that a court or the courts of a Contracting State are to have jurisdiction to settle any disputes which have arisen or which may arise in connection with a particular legal relationship, that court or those courts shall have exclusive jurisdiction. Such an agreement conferring jurisdiction shall be either:

(a) in writing or evidenced in writing, or

(b) in a form which accords with practices which the parties have established between themselves, or

(c) in international trade or commerce, in a form which accords with a usage of which the parties are or ought to have been aware and which in such trade or commerce is widely known to, and regularly observed by, partiesto contracts of the type involved in the particular trade or commerce concerned.

Where such an agreement is concluded by parties, none of whom is domiciled in a Contracting State, the courts of other Contracting States shall have no jurisdiction over their disputes unless the court or courts chosen have declined jurisdiction.

2. The court or courts of a Contracting State on which a trust instrument has conferred jurisdiction shall have exclusive jurisdiction in any proceedings brought against a settlor, trustee or beneficiary, if relations between these persons or their rights or obligations under the trust are involved.

3. Agreements or provisions of a trust instrument conferring jurisdiction shall have no legal force if they are contrary to the provisions of Article 12 or 15, or if the courts whose jurisdiction they purport to exclude have exclusive jurisdiction by virtue of Article 16.

4. If an agreement conferring jurisdiction was concluded for the benefit of only one of the parties, that party shall retain the right to bring proceedings in any other court which has jurisdiction by virtue of this Convention.

*5. In matters relating to individual contracts of employment an agreement conferring jurisdiction shall have legal force only if it is entered into after the dispute has arisen.*

### *Article 18*

[omissis]

### Section 7

## Examination as to jurisdiction and admissibility

### *Article 19 - Article 20*

[omissis]

### Section 8

## *Lis Pendens* - related actions

### *Article 21 - Article 23*

[omissis]

### Section 9

## Provisional, including protective, measures

### *Article 24*

[omissis]

### TITLE III

## RECOGNITION AND ENFORCEMENT

### *Article 25*

[omissis]

## Section 1

# Recognition

### *Article 26 - Article 27*

[omissis]

### *Article 28*

Moreover, a judgment shall not be recognized if it conflicts with the provisions of Sections 3, 4 or 5 of Title II or in a case provided for in Article 59.

*A judgment may furthermore be refused recognition in any case provided for in Article 54B (3) or 57 (4).*

In its examination of the grounds of jurisdiction referred to in the foregoing paragraphs, the court or authority applied to shall be bound by the findings of fact on which the court of the State of origin based its jurisdiction.

Subject to the provisions of the first and second paragraphs, the jurisdiction of the court of the State of origin may not be reviewed; the test of public policy referred to in Article 27 (1) may not be applied to the rules relating to jurisdiction.

### *Article 29 - Article 30*

[omissis]

## Section 2

# Enforcement

### *Article 31*

[omissis]

### *Article 32*

1. The application shall be submitted:

- in Belgium, to the tribunal de première instance or rechtbank van eerste aanleg,

- in Denmark, to the byret,

- in the Federal Republic of Germany, to the presiding judge of a chamber of the Landgericht,

- in Greece, to the μονομελές πρωτοδικείο,

- in Spain, to the Juzgado de Primera Instancia,

- in France, to the presiding judge of the tribunal de grande instance,

- in Ireland, to the High Court,

*- in Iceland, to the héraðsdómari,*

- in Italy, to the corte d'appello,

- in Luxembourg, to the presiding judge of the tribunal d'arrondissement,

- in the Netherlands, to the presiding judge of the arrondissementsrechtbank,

*- in Norway, to the herredsrett or byrett as namsrett,*

*- in Austria, to the Landesgericht or the Kreisgericht,*

- in Portugal, to the Tribunal Judicial de Círculo,

*- in Switzerland:*

> *(a) in respect of judgments ordering the payment of a sum of money, to the juge de la mainlevée / Rechtsöffnungsrichter / giudice competente a pronunciare sul rigetto dell'opposizione, within the framework of the procedure governed by Articles 80 and 81 of the loi fédérale sur la poursuite pour dettes et la faillite / Bundesgesetz über Schuldbetreibung und Konkurs / legge federale sulla esecuzione e sul fallimento;*
>
> *(b) in respect of judgments ordering a performance other than the payment of a sum of money, to the juge cantonal d'exequatur compétent / zuständiger kantonaler Vollstreckungsrichter /giudice cantonale competente a pronunciare l'exequatur,*

*- in Finland, to the ulosotonhaltija /överexekutor,*

*- in Sweden, to the Svea hovrätt,*

- in the United Kingdom:

(a) in England and Wales, to the High Court of Justice, or in the case of a maintenance judgment to the Magistrates' Court on transmission by the Secretary of State;

(b) in Scotland, to the Court of Session, or in the case of a maintenance judgment to the Sheriff Court on transmission by the Secretary of State;

(c) in Northern Ireland, to the High Court of Justice, or in the case of a maintenance judgment to the Magistrates' Court on transmission by the Secretary of State.

2. The jurisdiction of local courts shall be determined by reference to the place of domicile of the party against whom enforcement is sought. If he is not domiciled in the State in which enforcement is sought, it shall be determined by reference to the place of enforcement.

## *Article 33 - Article 36*

[omissis]

## *Article 37*

1. An appeal against the decision authorizing enforcement shall be lodged in accordance with the rules governing procedure in contentious matters:

- in Belgium, with the tribunal de première instance or rechtsbank van eerste aanleg,

- in Denmark, with the landsret,

- in the Federal Republic of Germany, with the Oberlandesgericht,

- in Greece, with the , εφετείο

- in Spain, with the Audiencia Provincial,

- in France, with the cour d'appel,

- in Ireland, with the High Court,

*- in Iceland, with the héraðsdómari,*

- in Italy, with the corte d'appello,

- in Luxembourg, with the Cour supérieure de justice sitting as a court of civil appeal,

- in the Netherlands, with the arrondissementsrechtbank,

*- in Norway, with the lagmannsrett,*

*- in Austria, with the Landesgericht or the Kreisgericht,*

- in Portugal, with the Tribunal da Relação,

*- in Switzerland, with the tribunal cantonal /Kantonsgericht / tribunale cantonale,*

*- in Finland, with the hovioikeus / hovrätt,*

*- in Sweden, with the Svea hovrätt,*

- in the United Kingdom:

(a) in England and Wales, with the High Court of Justice, or in the case of amaintenance judgment with the Magistrates' Court;

(b) in Scotland, with the Court of Session, or in the case of a maintenance judgment with the Sheriff Court;

(c) in Northern Ireland, with the High Court of Justice, or in the case of a maintenance judgment with the Magistrates' Court.

2. The judgment given on the appeal may be contested only:

- in Belgium, Greece, Spain, France, Italy, Luxembourg and in the Netherlands, by an appeal in cassation,

- in Denmark, by an appeal to the højesteret, with the leave of the Minister of Justice,

- in the Federal Republic of Germany, by a Rechtsbeschwerde,

- in Ireland, by an appeal on a point of law to the Supreme Court,

*- in Iceland, by an appeal to the Hœstiréttur,*

*- in Norway, by an appeal (kjæremål or anke) to the Hoyesteretts Kjæremålsutvalg or Hoyesterett,*

*- in Austria, in the case of an appeal, by a Revisionsrekurs and, in the case of opposition proceedings, by a Berufung with the possibility of a Revision,*

- in Portugal, by an appeal on a point of law,

*- in Switzerland, by a recours de droit public devant le tribunal fédéral / staatsrechtliche Beschwerde beim Bundesgericht / ricorso di diritto pubblico davanti al tribunale federale,*

*- in Finland, by an appeal to the korkein oikeus / högsta domstolen,*

*- in Sweden, by an appeal to the högsta domstolen,*

- in the United Kingdom, by a single further appeal on a point of law.

## *Article 38 - Article 39*

[omissis]

## *Article 40*

1. If the application for enforcement is refused, the applicant may appeal:

- in Belgium, to the cour d'appel or hof van beroep,

- in Denmark, to the landsret,

- in the Federal Republic of Germany, to the Oberlandesgericht,

- in Greece, to the εφετείο,

- in Spain, to the Audiencia Provincial,

- in France, to the cour d'appel,

- in Ireland, to the High Court,

*- in Iceland, to the héraðsdómari,*

- in Italy, to the corte d'appello,

- in Luxembourg, to the Cour supérieure de justice sitting as a court of civil appeal,

- in the Netherlands, to the gerechtshof,

*- in Norway, to the lagmannsrett,*

*- in Austria, to the Landesgericht or the Kreisgericht,*

- in Portugal, to the Tribunal da Relação,

*- in Switzerland, to the tribunal cantonal /Kantonsgericht / tribunale cantonale,*

*- in Finland, to the hovioikeus / hovrätt,*

*- in Sweden, to the Svea hovrätt,*

- in the United Kingdom:

(a) in England and Wales, to the High Court of Justice, or in the case of a maintenance judgment to the Magistrates' Court;

(b) in Scotland, to the Court of Session, or in the case of a maintenance judgment to the Sheriff Court;

(c) in Northern Ireland, to the High Court of Justice, or in the case of a maintenance judgment to the Magistrates' Court.

2. The party against whom enforcement is sought shall be summoned to appear before the appellate court. If he fails to appear, the provisions of the second and third paragraphs of Article 20 shall apply even where he is not domiciled in any of the Contracting States.

## *Article 41*

A judgment given on an appeal provided for in Article 40 may be contested only:

- in Belgium, Greece, Spain, France, Italy, Luxembourg and in the Netherlands, by an appeal in cassation,

- in Denmark, by an appeal to the højesteret, with the leave of the Minister of Justice,

- in the Federal Republic of Germany, by a Rechtsbeschwerde,

- in Ireland, by an appeal on a point of law to the Supreme Court,

*- in Iceland, by an appeal to the Hæstiréttur,*

*- in Norway, by an appeal (kjæremål or anke) to the Hoyesteretts kjæremålsutvalg or Hoyesterett,*

*- in Austria, by a Revisionsrekurs,*

- in Portugal, by an appeal on a point of law,

*- in Switzerland, by a recours de droit public devant le tribunal fédéral / staatsrechtliche Beschwerde beim Bundesgericht / ricorso di diritto pubblico davanti al tribunale federale,*

- *in Finland, by an appeal to the korkein oikeus / högsta domstolen,*

- *in Sweden, by an appeal to the högsta domstolen,*

- in the United Kingdom, by a single further appeal on a point of law.

***Article 42 - Article 45***

[omissis]

**Section 3**

## Common provisions

***Article 46 - Article 49***

[omissis]

**TITLE IV**

## AUTHENTIC INSTRUMENTS AND COURT SETTLEMENTS

***Article 50 - Article 51***

[omissis]

**TITLE V**

## GENERAL PROVISIONS

***Article 52 - Article 53***

[omissis]

**TITLE VI**

## TRANSITIONAL PROVISIONS

***Article 54***

The provisions of this Convention shall apply only to legal proceedings instituted and to documents formally drawn up or registered as authentic instruments after its entry into force in the State of origin and, where recognition or enforcement of a judgment or authentic instrument is sought, in the State addressed.

However, judgments given after the date of entry into force of this Convention between the State of origin and the State addressed in proceedings instituted before that date shall be recognized and enforced in accordance with the provisions of TitleIII if jurisdiction was founded upon rules which accorded with those provided for either in Title II of this Convention or in a convention concluded between the State of origin and the State addressed which was in force when the proceedings were instituted.

*If the parties to a dispute concerning a contract had agreed in writing before the entry into force of this Convention that the contract was to be governed by the law of Ireland or of a part of the United Kingdom, the courts of Ireland or of that part of the United Kingdom shall retain the right to exercise jurisdiction in the dispute.*

## *Article 54A*

For a period of three years from the entry into force of this Convention for Denmark, Greece, Ireland, Iceland, Norway, Finland and Sweden, respectively, jurisdiction in maritime matters shall be determined in these States not only in accordance with the provisions of Title II, but also in accordance with the provisions of paragraphs 1 to 7 following. However, upon the entry into force of the International Convention relating to the arrest of sea-going ships, signed at Brussels on 10 May 1952, for one of these States, these provisions shall cease to have effect for that State.

1. A person who is domiciled in a Contracting State may be sued in the courts of one of the States mentioned above in respect of a maritime claim if the ship to which the claim relates or any other ship owned by him has been arrested by judicial process within the territory of the latter State to secure the claim, or could have been so arrested there but bail or other security has been given, and either:

(a) the claimant is domiciled in the latter State; or

(b) the claim arose in the latter State; or

(c) the claim concerns the voyage during which the arrest was made or could have been made; or

(d) the claim arises out of a collision or out of damage caused by a ship to another ship or to goods or persons on board either ship, either by the execution or non-execution of amanoeuvre or by the non-observance of regulations; or

(e) the claim is for salvage; or

(f) the claim is in respect of a mortgage or hypothecation of the ship arrested.

2. A claimant may arrest either the particular ship to which the maritime claim relates, or any other ship which is owned by the person who was, at the time when the maritime claim arose, the owner of the particular ship. However, only the particular ship to which the maritime claim relates may be arrested in respect of the maritime claims set out under 5. (o), (p) or (q) of this Article.

3. Ships shall be deemed to be in the same ownership when all the shares therein are owned by the same person or persons.

4. When in the case of a charter by demise of a ship the charterer alone is liable in respect of a maritime claim relating to that ship, the claimant may arrest that ship or any other ship owned by the charterer, but no other ship owned by the owner may be arrested in respect of such claim. The same shall apply to any case in which a person other than the owner of a ship is liable in respect of a maritime claim relating to that ship.

5. The expression `maritime claim' means a claim arising out of one or more of the following:

(a) damage caused by any ship either in collision or otherwise;

(b) loss of life or personal injury caused by any ship or occurring in connection with the operation of any ship;

(c) salvage;

(d) agreement relating to the use or hire of any ship whether by charterparty or otherwise;

(e) agreement relating to the carriage of goods in any ship whether by charterparty or otherwise;

(f) loss of or damage to goods including baggage carried in any ship;

(g) general average;

(h) bottomry;

(i) towage;

(j) pilotage;

(k) goods or materials wherever supplied to a ship for her operation or maintenance;

(l) construction, repair or equipment of any ship or dock charges and dues;

(m) wages of masters, officers or crew;

(n) master's disbursements, including disbursements made by shippers, charterers or agents on behalf of a ship or her owner;

(o) dispute as to the title to or ownership of any ship;

(p) disputes between co-owners of any ship as to the ownership, possession, employment or earnings of that ship;

(q) the mortgage or hypothecation of any ship.

6. In Denmark, the expression `arrest' shall be deemed as regards the maritime claims referred to under 5. (o) and (p) of this Article, to include a `forbud', where that is the only procedure allowed in respect of such a claim under Articles 646 to 653 of the law on civil procedure (lov om rettens pleje).

*7. In Iceland, the expression `arrest' shall be deemed, as regards the maritime claims referred to under 5. (o) and (p) of this Article, to include a `lögbann', where that is the only procedure allowed in respect of such a claim under Chapter III of the law on arrest and injunction (lög um kyrrsetningu og lögbann).*

## TITLE VII

# RELATIONSHIP TO THE BRUSSELS CONVENTION AND TO OTHER CONVENTIONS

### *Article 54B*

*1. This Convention shall not prejudice the application by the Member States of the European Communities of the Convention on Jurisdiction and the Enforcement of Judgments in Civil and Commercial Matters, signed at Brussels on 27 September 1968 and of the Protocol on interpretation of that Convention by the Court of Justice, signed at Luxembourg on 3 June 1971, as amended by the Conventions of Accession to the said Convention and the said Protocol by the States acceding to the European Communities, all of these Conventions and the Protocol being hereinafter referred to as the `Brussels Convention'.*

*2. However, this Convention shall in any event be applied:*

*(a) in matters of jurisdiction, where the defendant is domiciled in the territory of a Contracting State which is not a member of the European Communities, or where Article 16 or 17 of this Convention confer a jurisdiction on the courts of such a Contracting State;*

*(b) in relation to a lis pendens or to related actions as provided for in Articles 21 and 22, when proceedings are instituted in a Contracting State which is not a member of the European Communities and in a Contracting State which is a member of the European Communities;*

*(c) in matters of recognition and enforcement, where either the State of origin or the State addressed is not a member of the European Communities.*

*3. In addition to the grounds provided for in Title III recognition or enforcement may be refused if the ground of jurisdiction on which the judgment has been based differs from that resulting from this Convention and recognition or enforcement is sought against a party who is domiciled in a Contracting State which is not a member of the EuropeanCommunities, unless the judgment may otherwise be recognized or enforced under any rule of law in the State addressed.*

## *Article 55*

Subject to the provisions of Articles 54 (2) and 56, this Convention shall, for the States which are parties to it, supersede the following conventions concluded between two or more of them:

*- the Convention between the Swiss Confederation and France on jurisdiction and enforcement of judgments in civil matters, signed at Paris on 15 June 1869,*

*- the Treaty between the Swiss Confederation and Spain on the mutual enforcement of judgments in civil or commercial matters, signed at Madrid on 19 November 1896,*

*- the Convention between the Swiss Confederation and the German Reich on the recognition and enforcement of judgments and arbitration awards, signed at Berne on 2 November 1929,*

*- the Convention between Denmark, Finland, Iceland, Norway and Sweden on the recognition and enforcement of judgments, signed at Copenhagen on 16 March 1932,*

*- the Convention between the Swiss Confederation and Italy on the recognition and enforcement of judgments, signed at Rome on 3 January 1933,*

*- the Convention between Sweden and the Swiss Confederation on the recognition and enforcement of judgments and arbitral awards, signed at Stockholm on 15 January 1936,*

*- the Convention between the Kingdom of Belgium and Austria on the reciprocal recognition and enforcement of judgments and authentic instruments relating to maintenance obligations, signed at Vienna on 25 October 1957,*

*- the Convention between the Swiss Confederation and Belgium on the recognition and enforcement of judgments and arbitration awards, signed at Berne on 29 April 1959,*

*- the Convention between the Federal Republic of Germany and Austria on the reciprocal recognition and enforcement of judgments, settlements and authentic instruments in civil and commercial matters, signed at Vienna on 6 June 1959,*

*- the Convention between the Kingdom of Belgium and Austria on the reciprocal recognition and enforcement of judgments, arbitral awards and authentic instruments in civil and commercial matters, signed at Vienna on 16 June 1959,*

*- the Convention between Austria and the Swiss Confederation on the recognition and enforcement of judgments, signed at Berne on 16 December 1960,*

*- the Convention between Norway and the United Kingdom providing for the reciprocal recognition and enforcement of judgments in civil matters, signed at London on 12 June 1961,*

*- the Convention between the United Kingdom and Austria providing for the reciprocal recognition and enforcement of judgments in civil and commercial matters, signed at Vienna on 14 July 1961, with amending Protocol signed at London on 6 March 1970,*

*- the Convention between the Kingdom of the Netherlands and Austria on the reciprocal recognition and enforcement of judgments and authentic instruments in civil and commercial matters, signed at The Hague on 6 February 1963,*

*- the Convention between France and Austria on the recognition and enforcement of judgments and authentic instruments in civil and commercial matters, signed at Vienna on 15 July 1966,*

*- the Convention between Luxembourg and Austria on the recognition and enforcement of judgements and authentic instruments in civil and commercial matters, signed at Luxembourg on 29 July 1971,*

*- the Convention between Italy and Austria on the recognition and enforcement of judgments in civil and commercial matters, of judicial settlements and of authentic instruments, signed at Rome on 16 November 1971,*

*- the Convention between Norway and the Federal Republic of Germany on the recognition and enforcement of judgments and enforceable documents, in civil and commercial matters, signed at Oslo on 17 June 1977,*

*- the Convention between Denmark, Finland, Iceland, Norway and Sweden on the recognition and enforcement of judgments in civil matters, signed at Copenhagen on 11 October 1977,*

*- the Convention between Austria and Sweden on the recognition and enforcement of judgments in civil matters, signed at Stockholm on 16 September 1982,*

*- the Convention between Austria and Spain on the recognition and enforcement of judgments, settlements and enforceable authentic instruments in civil and commercial matters, signed at Vienna on 17 February 1984,*

*- the Convention between Norway and Austria on the recognition and enforcement of judgments in civil matters, signed at Vienna on 21 May 1984, and*

*- the Convention between Finland and Austria on the recognition and enforcement of judgments in civil matters, signed at Vienna on 17 November 1986.*

### *Article 56*

[omissis]

### *Article 57*

1. This Convention shall not affect any conventions to which the Contracting States are or will be parties and which in relation to particular matters, govern jurisdiction or the recognition or enforcement of judgments.

2. This Convention shall not prevent a court of a Contracting State which is party to a convention referred to in the first paragraph from assuming jurisdiction in accordance with that convention, even where the defendant is domiciled in a Contracting State which is not a party to that convention. The court hearing the action shall, in any event, apply Article 20 of this Convention.

*3. Judgments given in a Contracting State by a court in the exercise of jurisdiction provided for in a convention referred to in the first paragraph shall be recognized and enforced in the other Contracting States in accordance with Title III of this Convention.*

*4. In addition to the grounds provided for in Title III, recognition or enforcement may be refused if the State addressed is not a contracting party to a convention referred to in the first paragraph and the person against whom recognition or enforcement is sought is domiciled in that State, unless the judgment may otherwise be recognized or enforced under any rule of law in the State addressed.*

5. Where a convention referred to in the first paragraph to which both the State of origin and the State addressed are parties lays down conditions for the recognition or enforcement of judgments, those conditions shall apply. In any event, the provisions of this Convention which concern the procedures for recognition and enforcement of judgments may be applied.

### *Article 58*

***(None)***

### *Article 59*

[omissis]

## TITLE VIII

# FINAL PROVISIONS

### *Article 60*

*The following may be parties to this Convention:*

*(a) States which, at the time of the opening of this Convention for signature, are members of the European Communities or of the European Free Trade Association;*

*(b) States which, after the opening of this Convention for signature, become members of the European Communities or of the European Free Trade Association;*

*(c) States invited to accede in accordance with Article 62 (1) (b).*

### *Article 61*

*1. This Convention shall be opened for signature by the States members of the European Communities or of the European Free Trade Association.*

*2. The Convention shall be submitted for ratification by the signatory States. The instruments of ratification shall be deposited with the Swiss Federal Council.*

*3. The Convention shall enter into force on the first day of the third month following the date on which two States, of which one is a member of the European Communities and the other a member of the European Free Trade Association, deposit their instruments of ratification.*

*4. The Convention shall take effect in relation to any other signatory State on the first day of the third month following the deposit of its instrument of ratification.*

### *Article 62*

*1. After entering into force this Convention shall be open to accession by:*

*(a) the States referred to in Article 60 (b);*

*(b) other States which have been invited to accede upon a request made by one of the Contracting States to the depositary State. The depositary State shall invite the State concerned to accede only if, after having communicated the contents of the*

*communications that this State intends to make in accordance with Article 63, it has obtained the unanimous agreement of the signatory States and the Contracting States referred to in Article 60 (a) and (b).*

*2. If an acceding State wishes to furnish details for the purposes of Protocol 1, negotiations shall be entered into to that end. A negotiating conference shall be convened by the Swiss Federal Council.*

*3. In respect of an acceding State, the Convention shall take effect on the first day of the third month following the deposit of its instrument of accession.*

*4. However, in respect of an acceding State referred to in paragraph 1 (a) or (b), the Convention shall take effect only in relations between the acceding State and the Contracting States which have not madeany objections to the accession before the first day of the third month following the deposit of the instrument of acce□sion.*

## *Article 63*

*Each acceding State shall, when depositing its instrument of accession, communicate the information required for the application of Articles 3, 32, 37, 40, 41 and 55 of this Convention and furnish, if need be, the details prescribed during the negotiations for the purposes of Protocol 1.*

## *Article 64*

*1. This Convention is concluded for an initial period of five years from the date of its entry into force in accordance with Article 61 (3), even in the case of States which ratify it or accede to it after that date.*

*2. At the end of the initial five-year period, the Convention shall be automatically renewed from year to year.*

*3. Upon the expiry of the initial five-year period, any contracting State may, at any time, denounce the Convention by sending a notification to the Swiss Federal Council.*

*4. The denunciation shall take effect at the end of the calendar year following the expiry of a period of six months from the date of receipt by the Swiss Federal Council of the notification of denunciation.*

## *Article 65*

*The following are annexed to this Convention:*

*- a Protocol 1, on certain questions of jurisdiction, procedure and enforcement,*

*- a Protocol 2, on the uniform interpretation of the Convention,*

*- a Protocol 3, on the application of Article 57.*

*These Protocols shall form an integral part of the Convention.*

## *Article 66*

*Any Contracting State may request the revision of this Convention. To that end, the Swiss Federal Council shall issue invitations to a revision conference within a period of six months from the date of the request for revision.*

## *Article 67*

*The Swiss Federal Council shall notify the States represented at the Diplomatic Conference of Lugano and the States who have later acceded to the Convention of:*

*(a) the deposit of each instrument of ratification or accession;*

*(b) the dates of entry into force of this Convention in respect of the Contracting States;*

*(c) any denunciation received pursuant to Article 64;*

*(d) any declaration received pursuant to Article Ia of Protocol 1;*

*(e) any declaration received pursuant to Article Ib of Protocol 1;*

*(f) any declaration received pursuant to Article IV of Protocol 1;*

*(g) any communication made pursuant to Article VI of Protocol 1.*

## *Article 68*

*This Convention, drawn up in a single original in the Danish, Dutch, English, Finnish, French, German, Greek, Icelandic, Irish, Italian, Norwegian, Portuguese, Spanish and Swedish languages, all fourteen texts being equally authentic, shall be deposited in the archives of the Swiss Federal Council. The Swiss Federal Council shall transmit a certified copy to the Government of each State represented at the Diplomatic Conference of Lugano and to the Government of each acceding State.*

In witness whereof, the undersigned Plenipotentiaries have signed this Convention.

*Done at Lugano on the sixteenth day of September in the year one thousand nine hundred and eighty-eight.*

## Brussels Regulation, Council Regulation (EC) No. 44/2001

Council Regulation (EC) No 44/2001 of 22 December 2000 on jurisdiction and the recognition and enforcement of judgments in civil and commercial matters THE COUNCIL OF THE EUROPEAN UNION,

* * * *

Whereas:

(1) The Community has set itself the objective of maintaining and developing an area of freedom, security and justice, in which the free movement of persons is ensured. In order to establish progressively such an area, the Community should adopt, amongst other things, the measures relating to judicial cooperation in civil matters which are necessary for the sound operation of the internal market.

(2) Certain differences between national rules governing jurisdiction and recognition of judgments hamper the sound operation of the internal market. Provisions to unify the rules of conflict of jurisdiction in civil and commercial matters and to simplify the formalities with a view to rapid and simple recognition and enforcement of judgments from Member States bound by this Regulation are essential.

* * * *

HAS ADOPTED THIS REGULATION:

### Chapter I
### Scope

**Article 1**

1. This Regulation shall apply in civil and commercial matters whatever the nature of the court or tribunal. It shall not extend, in particular, to revenue, customs or administrative matters.

2. The Regulation shall not apply to:

(a) the status or legal capacity of natural persons, rights in property arising out of a matrimonial relationship, wills and succession;

(b) bankruptcy, proceedings relating to the winding-up of insolvent companies or other legal persons, judicial arrangements, compositions and analogous proceedings;

(c) social security;

(d) arbitration.

3. In this Regulation, the term "Member State" shall mean Member States with the exception of Denmark.

### Chapter II
### Jurisdiction

#### Section 1
#### General Provisions

**Article 2**

1. Subject to this Regulation, persons domiciled in a Member State shall, whatever their nationality, be sued in the courts of that Member State.

2. Persons who are not nationals of the Member State in which they are domiciled shall be governed by the rules of jurisdiction applicable to nationals of that State.

**Article 3**

1. Persons domiciled in a Member State may be sued in the courts of another Member State only by virtue of the rules set out in Sections 2 to 7 of this Chapter.

2. In particular the rules of national jurisdiction set out in Annex I shall not be applicable as against them.

**Article 4**

1. If the defendant is not domiciled in a Member State, the jurisdiction of the courts of each Member State shall, subject to Articles 22 and 23, be determined by the law of that Member State.

2. As against such a defendant, any person domiciled in a Member State may, whatever his nationality, avail himself in that State of the rules of jurisdiction there in force, and in particular those specified in Annex I, in the same way as the nationals of that State.

**Section 2**
**Special jurisdiction**

**Article 5**

A person domiciled in a Member State may, in another Member State, be sued:

1. (a) in matters relating to a contract, in the courts for the place of performance of the obligation in question;

(b) for the purpose of this provision and unless otherwise agreed, the place of performance of the obligation in question shall be:

- in the case of the sale of goods, the place in a Member State where, under the contract, the goods were delivered or should have been delivered,

- in the case of the provision of services, the place in a Member State where, under the contract, the services were provided or should have been provided,

(c) if subparagraph (b) does not apply then subparagraph (a) applies;

2. in matters relating to maintenance, in the courts for the place where the maintenance creditor is domiciled or habitually resident or, if the matter is ancillary to proceedings concerning the status of a person, in the court which, according to its own law, has jurisdiction to entertain those proceedings, unless that jurisdiction is based solely on the nationality of one of the parties;

3. in matters relating to tort, delict or quasi-delict, in the courts for the place where the harmful event occurred or may occur;

4. as regards a civil claim for damages or restitution which is based on an act giving rise to criminal proceedings, in the court seised of those proceedings, to the extent that that court has jurisdiction under its own law to entertain civil proceedings;

5. as regards a dispute arising out of the operations of a branch, agency or other establishment, in the courts for the place in which the branch, agency or other establishment is situated;

6. as settlor, trustee or beneficiary of a trust created by the operation of a statute, or by a written instrument, or created orally and evidenced in writing, in the courts of the Member State in which the trust is domiciled;

7. as regards a dispute concerning the payment of remuneration claimed in respect of the salvage of a cargo or freight, in the court under the authority of which the cargo or freight in question:

(a) has been arrested to secure such payment, or

(b) could have been so arrested, but bail or other security has been given; provided that this provision shall apply only if it is claimed that the defendant has an interest in the cargo or freight or had such an interest at the time of salvage.

**Article 6**

A person domiciled in a Member State may also be sued:

1. where he is one of a number of defendants, in the courts for the place where any one of them is domiciled, provided the claims are so closely connected that it is expedient to hear and determine them together to avoid the risk of irreconcilable judgments resulting from separate proceedings;

2. as a third party in an action on a warranty or guarantee or in any other third party proceedings, in the court seised of the original proceedings, unless these were instituted solely with the object of removing him from the jurisdiction of the court which would be Competent in his case;

3. on a counter-claim arising from the same contract or facts on which the original claim was based, in the court in which the original claim is pending;

4. in matters relating to a contract, if the action may be combined with an action against the same defendant in matters relating to rights In rem in immovable property, in the court of the Member State in which the property is situated.

**Article 7**

Where by virtue of this Regulation a court of a Member State has jurisdiction in actions relating to liability from the use or operation of a ship, that court, or any other court substituted for this purpose by the internal law of that Member State, shall also have jurisdiction over claims for limitation of such liability.

## Section 3
## Jurisdiction in matters relating to insurance

**Article 8**

In matters relating to insurance, jurisdiction shall be determined by this Section, without prejudice to Article 4 and point 5 of Article 5.

**Article 9**

1. An insurer domiciled in a Member State may be sued:

(a) in the courts of the Member State where he is domiciled, or

(b) in another Member State, in the case of actions brought by the policyholder, the insured or a beneficiary, in the courts for the place where the plaintiff is domiciled,

(c) if he is a co-insurer, in the courts of a Member State in which proceedings are brought against the leading insurer.

2. An insurer who is not domiciled in a Member State but has a branch, agency or other establishment in one of the Member States shall, in disputes arising out of the operations of the branch, agency or establishment, be deemed to be domiciled in that Member State.

**Article 10**

In respect of liability insurance or insurance of immovable property, the insurer may in addition be sued in the courts for the place where the harmful event occurred. The same applies if movable and immovable property are covered by the same insurance policy and both are adversely affected by the same contingency.

**Article 11**

1. In respect of liability insurance, the insurer may also, if the law of the court permits it, be joined in proceedings which the injured party has brought against the insured.

2. Articles 8, 9 and 10 shall apply to actions brought by the injured party directly against the insurer, where such direct actions are permitted.

3. If the law governing such direct actions provides that the policyholder or the insured may be joined as a party to the action, the same court shall have jurisdiction over them.

**Article 12**

1. Without prejudice to Article 11(3), an insurer may bring proceedings only in the courts of the Member State in which the defendant is domiciled, irrespective of whether he is the policyholder, the insured or a beneficiary.

2. The provisions of this Section shall not affect the right to bring a counter-claim in the court in which, in accordance with this Section, the original claim is pending.

**Article 13**

The provisions of this Section may be departed from only by an agreement:

1. which is entered into after the dispute has arisen, or

2. which allows the policyholder, the insured or a beneficiary to bring proceedings in courts other than those indicated in this Section, or

3. which is concluded between a policyholder and an insurer, both of whom are at the time of conclusion of the contract domiciled or habitually resident in the same Member State, and which has the effect of conferring jurisdiction on the courts of that State even if the harmful event were to occur abroad, provided that such an agreement is not contrary to the law of that State, or

4. which is concluded with a policyholder who is not domiciled in a Member State, except in so far as the insurance is compulsory or relates to immovable property in a Member State, or

5. which relates to a contract of insurance in so far as it covers one or more of the risks set out in Article 14.

**Article 14**

The following are the risks referred to in Article 13(5):

1. any loss of or damage to:

(a) seagoing ships, installations situated offshore or on the high seas, or aircraft, arising from perils which relate to their use for commercial purposes;

(b) goods in transit other than passengers' baggage where the transit consists of or includes carriage by such ships or aircraft;

2. any liability, other than for bodily injury to passengers or loss of or damage to their baggage:

(a) arising out of the use or operation of ships, installations or aircraft as referred to in point 1(a) in so far as, in respect of the latter, the law of the Member State in which such aircraft are registered does not prohibit agreements on jurisdiction regarding insurance of such risks;

(b) for loss or damage caused by goods in transit as described in point 1(b);

3. any financial loss connected with the use or operation of ships, installations or aircraft as referred to in point 1(a), in particular loss of freight or charter-hire;

4. any risk or interest connected with any of those referred to in points 1 to 3;

5. notwithstanding points 1 to 4, all "large risks" as defined in Council Directive 73/239/EEC(7), as amended by Council Directives 88/357/EEC(8) and 90/618/EEC(9), as they may be amended.

**Section 4**
**Jurisdiction over consumer contracts**

**Article 15**

1. In matters relating to a contract concluded by a person, the consumer, for a purpose which can be regarded as being outside his trade or profession, jurisdiction shall be determined by this Section, without prejudice to Article 4 and point 5 of Article 5, if:

(a) it is a contract for the sale of goods on instalment credit terms; or

(b) it is a contract for a loan repayable by instalments, or for any other form of credit, made to finance the sale of goods; or

(c) in all other cases, the contract has been concluded with a person who pursues commercial or professional activities in the Member
State of the consumer's domicile or, by any means, directs such activities to that Member State or to several States including that Member State, and the contract falls within the scope of such activities.

2. Where a consumer enters into a contract with a party who is not domiciled in the Member State but has a branch, agency or other establishment in one of the Member States, that party shall, in disputes arising out of the operations of the branch, agency or establishment, be deemed to be domiciled in that State.

3. This Section shall not apply to a contract of transport other than a contract which, for an inclusive price, provides for a combination of travel and accommodation.

**Article 16**

1. A consumer may bring proceedings against the other party to a contract either in the courts of the Member State in which that party is domiciled or in the courts for the place where the consumer is domiciled.

2. Proceedings may be brought against a consumer by the other party to the contract only in the courts of the Member State in which the consumer is domiciled.

3. This Article shall not affect the right to bring a counter-claim in the court in which, in accordance with this Section, the original claim is pending.

**Article 17**

The provisions of this Section may be departed from only by an agreement:

1. which is entered into after the dispute has arisen; or

2. which allows the consumer to bring proceedings in courts other than those indicated in this Section; or

3 . which is entered into by the consumer and the other party to the contract, both of whom are at the time of conclusion of the contract domiciled or habitually resident in the same Member State, and which confers jurisdiction on the courts of that Member State, provided that such an agreement is not contrary to the law of that Member State.

## Section 5
## Jurisdiction over individual contracts of employment

**Article 18**

1. In matters relating to individual contracts of employment, jurisdiction shall be determined by this Section, without prejudice to Article 4 and point 5 of Article 5.

2. Where an employee enters into an individual contract of employment with an employer who is not domiciled in a Member State but has a branch, agency or other establishment in one of the Member States, the employer shall, in disputes arising out of the operations of the branch, agency or establishment, be deemed to be domiciled in that Member State.

**Article 19**

An employer domiciled in a Member State may be sued:

1. in the courts of the Member State where he is domiciled; or

2. in another Member State:

(a) in the courts for the place where the employee habitually carries out his work or in the courts for the last place where he did so, or

(b) if the employee does not or did not habitually carry out his work in any one country, in the courts for the place where the business which engaged the employee is or was situated.

**Article 20**

1. An employer may bring proceedings only in the courts of the Member State in which the employee is domiciled.

2. The provisions of this Section shall not affect the right to bring a counter-claim in the court in which, in accordance with this Section, the original claim is pending.

**Article 21**

The provisions of this Section may be departed from only by an agreement on jurisdiction:

1. which is entered into after the dispute has arisen; or

2. which allows the employee to bring proceedings in courts other than those indicated in this Section.

## Section 6
## Exclusive jurisdiction

**Article 22**

The following courts shall have exclusive jurisdiction, regardless of domicile:

1. in proceedings which have as their object rights in rem in immovable property or tenancies of immovable property, the courts of the Member State in which the property is situated. However, in proceedings which have as their object tenancies of immovable property concluded for temporary private use for a maximum period of six consecutive months, the courts of the Member State in which the defendant is domiciled shall also have jurisdiction, provided that the tenant is a natural person and that the landlord and the tenant are domiciled in the same Member State;

2. in proceedings which have as their object the validity of the constitution, the nullity or the dissolution of companies or other legal persons or associations of natural or legal persons, or of the validity of the decisions of their organs, the courts of the Member State in which the company, legal person or association has its seat. In order to determine that seat, the court shall apply its rules of private international law;

3. in proceedings which have as their object the validity of entries in public registers, the courts of the Member State in which the register is kept;

4. in proceedings concerned with the registration or validity of patents, trade marks, designs, or other similar rights required to be deposited or registered, the courts of the Member State in which the deposit or registration has been applied for, has taken place or is under the terms of a Community instrument or an international convention deemed to have taken place. Without prejudice to the jurisdiction of the European Patent Office under the Convention on the Grant of European Patents, signed at Munich on 5 October 1973, the courts of each Member State shall have exclusive jurisdiction, regardless of domicile, in proceedings concerned with the registration or validity of any European patent granted for that State;

5. in proceedings concerned with the enforcement of judgments, the courts of the Member State in which the judgment has been or is to be enforced.

**Section 7**
**Prorogation of jurisdiction**

**Article 23**

1. If the parties, one or more of whom is domiciled in a Member State, have agreed that a court or the courts of a Member State are to have jurisdiction to settle any disputes which have arisen or which may arise in connection with a particular legal relationship, that court or those courts shall have jurisdiction. Such jurisdiction shall be exclusive unless the parties have agreed otherwise. Such an agreement conferring jurisdiction shall be either:

(a) in writing or evidenced in writing; or

(b) in a form which accords with practices which the parties have established between themselves; or

(c) in international trade or commerce, in a form which accords with a usage of which the parties are or ought to have been aware and which in such trade or commerce is widely known to, and regularly observed by, parties to contracts of the type involved in the particular trade or commerce concerned.

2. Any communication by electronic means which provides a durable record of the agreement shall be equivalent to "writing".

3. Where such an agreement is concluded by parties, none of whom is domiciled in a Member State, the courts of other Member States shall have no jurisdiction over their disputes unless the court or courts chosen have declined jurisdiction.

4. The court or courts of a Member State on which a trust instrument has conferred jurisdiction shall have exclusive jurisdiction in any proceedings brought against a settlor, trustee or beneficiary, if relations between these persons or their rights or obligations under the trust are involved.

5. Agreements or provisions of a trust instrument conferring jurisdiction shall have no legal force if they are contrary to Articles 13, 17 or 21, or if the courts whose jurisdiction they purport to exclude have exclusive jurisdiction by virtue of Article 22.

**Article 24**

Apart from jurisdiction derived from other provisions of this Regulation, a court of a Member State before which a defendant enters an appearance shall have jurisdiction. This rule shall not apply where appearance was entered to contest the jurisdiction, or where another court has exclusive jurisdiction by virtue of Article 22.

**Section 8**
**Examination as to jurisdiction and admissibility**

**Article 25**

Where a court of a Member State is seised of a claim which is principally concerned with a matter over which the courts of another Member State have exclusive jurisdiction by virtue of Article 22, it shall declare of its own motion that it has no jurisdiction.

**Article 26**

1. Where a defendant domiciled in one Member State is sued in a court of another Member State and does not enter an appearance, the court shall declare of its own motion that it has no jurisdiction unless its jurisdiction is derived from the provisions of this Regulation.

2. The court shall stay the proceedings so long as it is not shown that the defendant has been able to receive the document instituting the proceedings or an equivalent document in sufficient time to enable him to arrange for his defence, or that all necessary steps have been taken to this end.

3. Article 19 of Council Regulation (EC) No 1348/2000 of 29 May 2000 on the service in the Member States of judicial and extrajudicial documents in civil or commercial matters(10) shall apply instead of the provisions of paragraph 2 if the document instituting the proceedings or an equivalent document had to be transmitted from one Member State to another pursuant to this Regulation.

4. Where the provisions of Regulation (EC) No 1348/2000 are not applicable, Article 15 of the Hague Convention of 15 November 1965 on the Service Abroad of Judicial and Extrajudicial Documents in Civil or Commercial Matters shall apply if the document instituting the proceedings or an equivalent document had to be transmitted pursuant to that Convention.

## Section 9
## Lis pendens - related actions

**Article 27**

1. Where the proceedings involving the same cause of action and between the same parties are brought in the courts of different Member States, any court other than the court first seised shall of its own motion stay its proceedings until such time as the jurisdiction of the court first seised is established.

2. Where the jurisdiction of the court first seised is established, any court other than the court first seised shall decline jurisdiction in favour of that court.

**Article 28**

1. Where related actions are pending in the courts of different Member States, any court other than the court first seised may stay its proceedings.

2. Where these actions are pending at first instance, any court other than the court first seised may also, on the application of one of the parties, decline jurisdiction if the court first seised has jurisdiction over the actions in question and its law permits the consolidation thereof.

3. For the purposes of this Article, actions are deemed to be related where they are so closely connected that it is expedient to hear and determine them together to avoid the risk of irreconcilable judgments resulting from separate proceedings.

**Article 29**

Where actions come within the exclusive jurisdiction of several courts, any court other than the court first seised shall decline jurisdiction in favour of that court.

**Article 30**

For the purposes of this Section, a court shall be deemed to be seised:

1. at the time when the document instituting the proceedings or an equivalent document is lodged with the court, provided that the plaintiff has not subsequently failed to take the steps he was required to take to have service effected on the defendant, or

2. if the document has to be served before being lodged with the court, at the time when it is received by the authority responsible for service, provided that the plaintiff has not subsequently failed to take the steps he was required to take to have the document lodged with the court.

## Section 10
## Provisional, including protective, measures

**Article 31**

Application may be made to the courts of a Member State for such provisional, including protective, measures as may be available under the law of that State, even if, under this Regulation, the courts of another Member State have jurisdiction as to the substance of the matter.

## CHAPTER III
## RECOGNITION AND ENFORCEMENT

**Article 32**

For the purposes of this Regulation, "judgment" means any judgment given by a court or tribunal of a Member State, whatever the judgment may be called, including a decree, order, decision or writ of execution, as well as the determination of costs or expenses by an officer of the court.

### Section 1
### Recognition

**Article 33**

1. A judgment given in a Member State shall be recognised in the other Member States without any special procedure being required.

2. Any interested party who raises the recognition of a judgment as the principal issue in a dispute may, in accordance with the procedures provided for in Sections 2 and 3 of this Chapter, apply for a decision that the judgment be recognised.

3. If the outcome of proceedings in a court of a Member State depends on the determination of an incidental question of recognition that court shall have jurisdiction over that question.

**Article 34**

A judgment shall not be recognised:

1. if such recognition is manifestly contrary to public policy in the Member State in which recognition is sought;

2. where it was given in default of appearance, if the defendant was not served with the document which instituted the proceedings or with an equivalent document in sufficient time and in such a way as to enable him to arrange for his defence, unless the defendant failed to commence proceedings to challenge the judgment when it was possible for him to do so;

3. if it is irreconcilable with a judgment given in a dispute between the same parties in the Member State in which recognition is sought;

4. if it is irreconcilable with an earlier judgment given in another Member State or in a third State involving the same cause of action and between the same parties, provided that the earlier judgment fulfils the conditions necessary for its recognition in the Member State addressed.

**Article 35**

1. Moreover, a judgment shall not be recognised if it conflicts with Sections 3, 4 or 6 of Chapter II, or in a case provided for in Article 72.

2. In its examination of the grounds of jurisdiction referred to in the foregoing paragraph, the court or authority applied to shall be bound by the findings of fact on which the court of the Member State of origin based its jurisdiction.

3. Subject to the paragraph 1, the jurisdiction of the court of the Member State of origin may not be reviewed. The test of public policy referred to in point 1 of Article 34 may not be applied to the rules relating to jurisdiction.

**Article 36**

Under no circumstances may a foreign judgment be reviewed as to its substance.

**Article 37**

1. A court of a Member State in which recognition is sought of a judgment given in another Member State may stay the proceedings if an ordinary appeal against the judgment has been lodged.

2. A court of a Member State in which recognition is sought of a judgment given in Ireland or the United Kingdom may stay the proceedings if enforcement is suspended in the State of origin, by reason of an appeal.

## Section 2
## Enforcement

**Article 38**

1. A judgment given in a Member State and enforceable in that State shall be enforced in another Member State when, on the application of any interested party, it has been declared enforceable there.

2. However, in the United Kingdom, such a judgment shall be enforced in England and Wales, in Scotland, or in Northern Ireland when, on the application of any interested party, it has been registered for enforcement in that part of the United Kingdom.

**Article 39**

1. The application shall be submitted to the court or competent authority indicated in the list in Annex II.

2. The local jurisdiction shall be determined by reference to the place of domicile of the party against whom enforcement is sought, or to the place of enforcement.

**Article 40**

1. The procedure for making the application shall be governed by the law of the Member State in which enforcement is sought.

2. The applicant must give an address for service of process within the area of jurisdiction of the court applied to. However, if the law of the Member State in which enforcement is sought does not provide for the furnishing of such an address, the applicant shall appoint a representative ad litem.

3. The documents referred to in Article 53 shall be attached to the application.

**Article 41**

The judgment shall be declared enforceable immediately on completion of the formalities in Article 53 without any review under Articles 34 and 35. The party against whom enforcement is sought shall not at this stage of the proceedings be entitled to make any submissions on the application.

**Article 42**

1. The decision on the application for a declaration of enforceability shall forthwith be brought to the notice of the applicant in accordance with the procedure laid down by the law of the Member State in which enforcement is sought.

2. The declaration of enforceability shall be served on the party against whom enforcement is sought, accompanied by the judgment, if not already served on that party.

**Article 43**

1. The decision on the application for a declaration of enforceability may be appealed against by either party.

2. The appeal is to be lodged with the court indicated in the list in Annex III.

3. The appeal shall be dealt with in accordance with the rules governing procedure in contradictory matters.

4. If the party against whom enforcement is sought fails to appear before the appellate court in proceedings concerning an appeal brought by the applicant, Article 26(2) to (4) shall apply even where the party against whom enforcement is sought is not domiciled in any of the Member States.

5. An appeal against the declaration of enforceability is to be lodged within one month of service thereof. If the party against whom enforcement is sought is domiciled in a Member State other than that in which the declaration of enforceability was given, the time for appealing shall be two months and shall run from the date of service, either on him in person or at his residence. No extension of time may be granted on account of distance.

**Article 44**

The judgment given on the appeal may be contested only by the appeal referred to in Annex IV.

**Article 45**

1. The court with which an appeal is lodged under Article 43 or Article 44 shall refuse or revoke a declaration of enforceability only on one of the grounds specified in Articles 34 and 35. It shall give its decision without delay.

2. Under no circumstances may the foreign judgment be reviewed as to its substance.

**Article 46**

1. The court with which an appeal is lodged under Article 43 or Article 44 may, on the application of the party against whom enforcement is sought, stay the proceedings if an ordinary appeal has been lodged against the judgment in the Member State of origin or if the time for such an appeal has not yet expired; in the latter case, the court may specify the time within which such an appeal is to be lodged.

2. Where the judgment was given in Ireland or the United Kingdom, any form of appeal available in the Member State of origin shall be treated as an ordinary appeal for the purposes of paragraph 1.

3. The court may also make enforcement conditional on the provision of such security as it shall determine.

**Article 47**

1. When a judgment must be recognised in accordance with this Regulation, nothing shall prevent the applicant from availing himself of provisional, including protective, measures in accordance with the law of the Member State requested without a declaration of enforceability under Article 41 being required.

2. The declaration of enforceability shall carry with it the power to proceed to any protective measures.

3. During the time specified for an appeal pursuant to Article 43(5) against the declaration of enforceability and until any such appeal has been determined, no measures of enforcement may be taken other than protective measures against the property of the party against whom enforcement is sought.

**Article 48**

1. Where a foreign judgment has been given in respect of several matters and the declaration of enforceability cannot be given for all of them, the court or competent authority shall give it for one or more of them.

2. An applicant may request a declaration of enforceability limited to parts of a judgment.

**Article 49**

A foreign judgment which orders a periodic payment by way of a penalty shall be enforceable in the Member State in which enforcement is sought only if the amount of the payment has been finally determined by the courts of the Member State of origin.

**Article 50**

An applicant who, in the Member State of origin has benefited from complete or partial legal aid or exemption from costs or expenses, shall be entitled, in the procedure provided for in this Section, to benefit from the most favourable legal aid or the most extensive exemption from costs or expenses provided for by the law of the Member State addressed.

**Article 51**

No security, bond or deposit, however described, shall be required of a party who in one Member State applies for enforcement of a judgment given in another Member State on the ground that he is a foreign national or that he is not domiciled or resident in the State in which enforcement is sought.

**Article 52**

In proceedings for the issue of a declaration of enforceability, no charge, duty or fee calculated by reference to the value of the matter at issue may be levied in the Member State in which enforcement is sought.

**Section 3**
**Common provisions**

**Article 53**

1. A party seeking recognition or applying for a declaration of enforceability shall produce a copy of the judgment which satisfies the conditions necessary to establish its authenticity.

2. A party applying for a declaration of enforceability shall also produce the certificate referred to in Article 54, without prejudice to Article 55.

**Article 54**

The court or competent authority of a Member State where a judgment was given shall issue, at the request of any interested party, a certificate using the standard form in Annex V to this Regulation.

**Article 55**

1. If the certificate referred to in Article 54 is not produced, the court or competent authority may specify a time for its production or accept an equivalent document or, if it considers that it has sufficient information before it, dispense with its production.

2. If the court or competent authority so requires, a translation of the documents shall be produced. The translation shall be certified by a person qualified to do so in one of the Member States.

**Article 56**

No legalisation or other similar formality shall be required in respect of the documents referred to in Article 53 or Article 55(2), or in respect of a document appointing a representative ad litem.

## CHAPTER IV
## AUTHENTIC INSTRUMENTS AND COURT SETTLEMENTS

**Article 57**

1. A document which has been formally drawn up or registered as an authentic instrument and is enforceable in one Member State shall, in another Member State, be declared enforceable there, on application made in accordance with the procedures provided for in Articles 38, et seq. The court with which an appeal is lodged under Article 43 or Article 44 shall refuse or revoke a declaration of enforceability only if enforcement of the instrument is manifestly contrary to public policy in the Member State addressed.

2. Arrangements relating to maintenance obligations concluded with administrative authorities or authenticated by them shall also be regarded as authentic instruments within the meaning of paragraph 1.

3. The instrument produced must satisfy the conditions necessary to establish its authenticity in the Member State of origin.

4. Section 3 of Chapter III shall apply as appropriate. The competent authority of a Member State where an authentic instrument was drawn up or registered shall issue, at the request of any interested party, a certificate using the standard form in Annex VI to this Regulation.

**Article 58**

A settlement which has been approved by a court in the course of proceedings and is enforceable in the Member State in which it was concluded shall be enforceable in the State addressed under the same conditions as authentic instruments. The court or competent authority of a Member State where a court settlement was approved shall issue, at the request of any interested party, a certificate using the standard form in Annex V to this Regulation.

## CHAPTER V
## GENERAL PROVISIONS

**Article 59**

1. In order to determine whether a party is domiciled in the Member State whose courts are seised of a matter, the court shall apply its internal law.

2. If a party is not domiciled in the Member State whose courts are seised of the matter, then, in order to determine whether the party is domiciled in another Member State, the court shall apply the law of that Member State.

**Article 60**

1. For the purposes of this Regulation, a company or other legal person or association of natural or legal persons is domiciled at the place where it has its:

(a) statutory seat, or

(b) central administration, or

(c) principal place of business.

2. For the purposes of the United Kingdom and Ireland "statutory seat" means the registered office or, where there is no such office anywhere, the place of incorporation or, where there is no such place anywhere, the place under the law of which the formation took place.

3. In order to determine whether a trust is domiciled in the Member State whose courts are seised of the matter, the court shall apply its rules of private international law.

**Article 61**

Without prejudice to any more favourable provisions of national laws, persons domiciled in a Member State who are being prosecuted in the criminal courts of another Member State of which they are not nationals for an offence which was not intentionally committed may be defended by persons qualified to do so, even if they do not appear in person. However, the court seised of the matter may order appearance in person; in the case of failure to appear, a judgment given in the civil action without the person concerned having had the opportunity to arrange for his defence need not be recognised or enforced in the other Member States.

**Article 62**

In Sweden, in summary proceedings concerning orders to pay (betalningsföreläggande) and assistance (handräckning), the expression "court" includes the "Swedish enforcement service" (kronofogdemyndighet).

**Article 63**

1. A person domiciled in the territory of the Grand Duchy of Luxembourg and sued in the court of another Member State pursuant to Article 5(1) may refuse to submit to the jurisdiction of that court if the final place of delivery of the goods or provision of the services is in Luxembourg.

2. Where, under paragraph 1, the final place of delivery of the goods or provision of the services is in Luxembourg, any agreement conferring jurisdiction must, in order to be valid, be accepted in writing or evidenced in writing within the meaning of Article 23(1)(a).

3. The provisions of this Article shall not apply to contracts for the provision of financial services.

4. The provisions of this Article shall apply for a period of six years from entry into force of this Regulation.

**Article 64**

1. In proceedings involving a dispute between the master and a member of the crew of a seagoing ship registered in Greece or in Portugal, concerning remuneration or other conditions of service, a court in a Member State shall establish whether the diplomatic or consular officer responsible for the ship has been notified of the dispute. It may act as soon as that officer has been notified.

2. The provisions of this Article shall apply for a period of six years from entry into force of this Regulation.

**Article 65**

1. The jurisdiction specified in Article 6(2), and Article 11 in actions on a warranty of guarantee or in any other third party proceedings may not be resorted to in Germany and Austria. Any person domiciled in another Member State may be sued in the courts:

(a) of Germany, pursuant to Articles 68 and 72 to 74 of the Code of Civil Procedure (Zivilprozessordnung) concerning third-party notices,

(b) of Austria, pursuant to Article 21 of the Code of Civil Procedure (Zivilprozessordnung) concerning third-party notices.

2. Judgments given in other Member States by virtue of Article 6(2), or Article 11 shall be recognised and enforced in Germany and Austria in accordance with Chapter III. Any effects which judgments given in these States may have on third parties by application of the provisions in paragraph 1 shall also be recognised in the other Member States.

## CHAPTER VI
## TRANSITIONAL PROVISIONS

**Article 66**

1. This Regulation shall apply only to legal proceedings instituted and to documents formally drawn up or registered as authentic instruments after the entry into force thereof.

2. However, if the proceedings in the Member State of origin were instituted before the entry into force of this Regulation, judgments given after that date shall be recognised and enforced in accordance with Chapter III,

(a) if the proceedings in the Member State of origin were instituted after the entry into force of the Brussels or the Lugano Convention both in the Member State or origin and in the Member State addressed;

(b) in all other cases, if jurisdiction was founded upon rules which accorded with those provided for either in Chapter II or in a convention concluded between the Member State of origin and the Member State addressed which was in force when the proceedings were instituted.

## CHAPTER VII
## RELATIONS WITH OTHER INSTRUMENTS

**Article 67**

This Regulation shall not prejudice the application of provisions governing jurisdiction and the recognition and enforcement of judgments in specific matters which are contained in Community instruments or in national legislation harmonised pursuant to such instruments.

**Article 68**

1. This Regulation shall, as between the Member States, supersede the Brussels Convention, except as regards the territories of the Member States which fall within the territorial scope of that Convention and which are excluded from this Regulation pursuant to Article 299 of the Treaty.

2. In so far as this Regulation replaces the provisions of the Brussels Convention between Member States, any reference to the Convention shall be understood as a reference to this Regulation.

* * * *

CONVENTION BETWEEN THE UNITED KINGDOM OF GREAT BRITAIN AND NORTHERN IRELAND AND THE UNITED STATES OF AMERICA PROVIDING FOR THE RECIPROCAL RECOGNITION AND ENFORCEMENT OF JUDGMENTS IN CIVIL MATTERS

The United Kingdom of Great Britain and Northern Ireland and the United States of America;

Desiring to provide on the basis of reciprocity for the recognition and enforcement of judgments in civil matters;

Have agreed as follows:

CHAPTER I: USE OF TERMS

Article 1

In this Convention:

(a) "counterclaim" includes a cross action;

(b) "court addressed" includes any authority to which application is made for recognition or enforcement of a judgment under this Convention;

(c) "court of a Contracting State" means any court exercising jurisdiction for a "territory" of a Contracting State, but does not include any international court;

(d) "court of origin" means the court which gave a judgment for which recognition or enforcement is sought under this Convention;

(e) "defendant" means the defendant in the original proceedings including, where appropriate, a defendant to a counterclaim;

(f) "plaintiff" means the plaintiff in the original proceedings including, where appropriate, a counterclaimant;

(g) "respondent" means the person against whom recognition or enforcement is sought;

(h) "review" includes appeal;

(i) "territory" means, as may be appropriate, the United Kingdom, a constituent part thereof, or the area adjacent to the United Kingdom over which its courts exercise jurisdiction, the United States, a constituent part thereof, the area adjacent to the Unites States over which its courts exercise jurisdiction, the area in or adjacent to the United States over which a federal court of the United States exercises jurisdiction, or any territory to which this Convention shall have been extended under Article 23; and

(j) "territory of origin" means the "territory" for which the court of origin was exercising jurisdiction.

CHAPTER II: SCOPE OF THE CONVENTION

Article 2

(1) This Convention shall apply to judgments given after this Convention enters into force, by courts of the Contracting States in the exercise of their civil or commercial jurisdiction and, for the purposes of Article 18, to civil or commercial judgments given by courts of third States. Such application shall be irrespective of the name given to the proceedings which gave rise to the judgment or of the name given to the judgment, such as order or decree.

(2) Except for the purposes of Article 18, this Convention shall not apply to judgments:

(a) for customs duties, taxes and other charges of a like nature;

(b) to the extent that they are for punitive or multiple damages;

(c) which are interlocutory;

(d) for disclosure of evidence;

(e) given by or on appeal from administrative tribunals;

(f) against States, including their constituent units;

(g) determining the existence or constitution of legal persons or the powers of their officers or directors; or

(h) determining questions relating to damage or injury resulting from a nuclear incident.

(3) This Convention shall not apply to judgments which determine:

(a) the status or legal capacity of natural persons;

(b) matters of family law, including marital rights in property;

(c) maintenance claims, obligations assumed in whole or in part to satisfy a legal obligation to support another, or claims seeking to recover all or part of amounts paid by another for maintenance;

(d) matters of succession to, or the administration of, estates of deceased persons;

(e) issues in bankruptcy proceedings, in proceedings for the reorganisation or winding-up of companies or other legal persons, or in proceedings for judicial arrangements, compositions and analogous matters;

(f) matters of social security or public assistance to the extent that the claim lies against a public fund or authority;

(g) matters concerning the judicial supervision of the administration of the property or affairs of a person who is incompetent or incapable of managing and administering his property and affairs.

(4) This Convention shall apply to a judgment where the court of origin, in order to determine an issue not falling under paragraph (2)(g) or (h) or paragraph (3) of this Article, had to determine a matter falling within these provisions as a preliminary issue.

(5) Severable parts of a judgment in respect of different matters shall be entitled to recognition or enforcement under this Convention if such parts would have been so entitled had they taken the form of separate judgments.

Article 3

The provisions of this Convention shall not prevent the recognition or enforcement of a judgment of a court of a Contracting State if that judgment would be recognizable or enforceable in accordance with the law otherwise applicable in the court addressed.

CHAPTER III: CONDITIONS OF RECOGNITION AND ENFORCEMENT

Article 4

(1) A judgment given by a court of a Contracting State shall, subject to the provisions of this Convention, be recognized in the territory of the other Contracting State if:

(a) it was given by a court having jurisdiction under Articles 10 or 11; and

(b) it has binding effects within the territory of origin, notwithstanding that an application for review may be pending against it, or that it may still be subject to review, in that territory.

(2) A judgment entitled to recognition under paragraph (1) shall, subject to the provisions of this Convention, be enforced in the territory of the other Contracting State if it is entitled to enforcement in the territory of origin.

(3) To the extent that judgments given by courts of a Contracting State are inconsistent, priority shall be determined for the purposes of paragraphs (1) and (2) as follows:

(a) where the judgments were given in more than one territory of the Contracting State, any priority accorded by the law of that State shall be recognised; and

(b) where the judgments were given in a single territory of the Contracting State, any priority accorded by the law applicable in the courts of that territory shall be recognized.

Article 5

(1) Where a judgment is subject to any form of review under the law applicable in the court of origin, and the respondent satisfies the court addressed that review has been or will be sought the court addressed may grant or defer recognition or enforcement in accordance with the law applicable in that court.

(2) Where recognition is sought in proceedings respecting a different cause of action, binding effects shall not be accorded to the judgment until all ordinary forms of review have been exhausted. However, the court may suspend the proceedings.

Article 6

Recognition or enforcement of a judgment is not required by this Convention if:

(a) by reason of the subject-matter of the action, exclusive jurisdiction over the claim adjudicated lies, under the law applicable in the court addressed, in courts or authorities other than those of the territory of origin; or

(b) the judgment was given in proceedings brought in violation of an agreement between the parties to the original proceedings giving exclusive jurisdiction to a court or other authority, or to an arbitral tribunal; or

(c) the judgment relates to an issue, arising under a trust instrument, in respect of which, by virtue of the terms of that instrument, exclusive jurisdiction lies in courts or authorities other than those of the territory of origin.

Article 7

Recognition or enforcement of a judgment is not required by this Convention:

(a) where recognition or enforcement of the judgment would be manifestly repugnant to public policy;

(b) where the judgment was obtained by fraud;

(c) if proceedings based on the same transaction or occurrence:

(i) have resulted in an irreconcilable judgment by a court or authority of the Contracting State of the court addressed;

(ii) are pending before a court or authority of the Contracting State of the court addressed, were the first to be instituted, and may result in such an irreconcilable judgment; or

(iii) have resulted in an irreconcilable judgment by a court or authority of a third State that qualifies for recognition or enforcement under the law applicable in the court addressed;

(d) if, in the view of the court addressed, either the respondent enjoys immunity from the jurisdiction of that court or the defendant should have enjoys immunity in the original proceedings; or

(e) where, to give its judgment, the court of origin had to decide a question relating to a matter specified in paragraph 2(g) or (h) or paragraph (3) of Article 2, and the decision differs from that which would have followed from the application to that question of the rules of private international law applicable in the court addressed.

Article 8

If the defendant or his successor in interest so requests recognition or enforcement of a judgment is not required by this Convention:

(a) where the defendant did not receive either actual notice of the proceedings in sufficient time to enable him to present his case or constructive notice substantially equivalent to that accepted by the law applicable in the court addressed;

(b) where jurisdiction for the purposes of paragraph (1) of Article 4 is based on the agreement of the parties, the defendant did not appear, and in the view of the court addressed the agreement is invalid;

(c) to the extent that recognition or enforcement would afford a recovery exceeding monetary limits upon liability fixed by a statute of the territory of the court addressed which applies under that court's rules of private international law;

(d) where, under the rules of private international law of the court addressed, its own law would have been applicable to the case if it had been brought in that court and the judgment disregards provisions of that law which would have been applied by that court even if the parties had chosen another system of law;

(e) where the judgment is one recognizing or enforcing another judgment; or

(f) to the extent that the judgment gave relief directly against a person, natural or legal, whose liability results from an obligation of indemnification and that liability does not, under the law selected in accordance with the rules of private international law applicable in the court addressed, arise until liability has been established on the part of the person entitled to indemnification.

Article 9

Except as permitted by this Convention, there shall be no review of the judgment given by the court of origin, and recognition or enforcement shall not be refused for the reason that the court of origin reached a result different from that which would have been reached by application of the law selected in accordance with the rules of private international law applicable in the court addressed.

Article 10

A judgment is given by a court having jurisdiction for the purposes of paragraph (1) of Article 4 where one of the following can be established:

(a) the respondent or his predecessor in interest brought the original proceedings;

(b) the defendant had, at the time when the proceedings were instituted, a place of habitual residence within the territory of origin, or, if the defendant is not a natural person, had a principal place of business there, or was incorporated, or if unincorporated had its headquarters, there;

(c) the defendant had a branch or other establishment (other than a subsidiary corporation) within the territory of origin and the proceedings were in respect of a transaction or occurrence arising from business done by or through that establishment;

(d) the defendant, not acting pursuant to a statutory requirement, by an agreement in writing or by an oral agreement confirmed in writing had agreed expressly in respect of disputes which had arisen or might arise regarding a specified legal relationship, to submit to the jurisdiction of the court of origin, or of the courts of the territory of origin;

(e) the defendant had been conducting business on a continuing basis within the territory of origin otherwise than through a subsidiary corporation, had appointed, or been under a legal duty to appoint, an agent to receive service of process there in respect of such business, and the proceedings were in respect of a transaction or occurrence arising from such business;

(f) in the case of a contract to supply goods or services the conclusion of the contract was preceded by an invitation to treat made by advertisement or otherwise either in or specifically directed to the territory of origin and the use of the goods or the performance of the services was in the contemplation of the parties to the contract to occur in whole or in substantial part within that territory;

(g) in the case of contractual claim the parties to the contract resided or, if not natural persons, had a place of business in the territory of origin at the time the contract was concluded and the obligation in issue was to be wholly or mainly performed there;

(h) in the case of an action whose object was to determine rights of ownership, use, possession or security in immovable or tangible movable property, that property was situated within the territory of origin when the action was instituted;

(i) in the case of an action whose object was to decide upon the validity, construction, interpretation, variation or implementation of a trust instrument or to determine disputes under that instrument between or among trustees and beneficiaries, the trust's principal place of administration was within the territory of origin, or the trust instrument provided expressly or by implication that the courts of that territory should have jurisdiction in such actions; or

(j) in the case of an action to recover damages for physical injuries to the person or for damage to tangible property, the acts or omissions that occasioned the injury or damage substantially occurred, and the injury or damage was suffered, in the Contracting State in which the court of origin was exercising jurisdiction, and either those acts or omissions substantially occurred or that injury or damage was suffered in the territory of origin.

Article 11

A judgment on a counterclaim is given by a court having jurisdiction for the purposes of paragraph (1) of Article 4 where one of the following conditions is satisfied:

(a) the respondent or his predecessor in interest voluntarily brought the counterclaim;

(b) the court of origin would have had jurisdiction to try the counterclaim as a principal claim under sub-paragraphs (b) - (j) of Article 10; or

(c) the court of origin had jurisdiction under Article 10 to try the principal claim and the counterclaim arose out of the transaction or occurrence on which the principal claim was based.

Article 12

In determining whether jurisdiction for the purposes of paragraph (1) of Article 4 is established under Articles 10 and 11, the court addressed shall not be bound by any conclusions reached by the court of origin relevant to the application of these Articles The court addressed shall, however, be bound by findings of fact made by the court of origin unless the respondent establishes that they are incorrect. The respondent may not dispute such findings where the defendant appeared in the court of origin and failed to challenge its jurisdiction.

CHAPTER IV: EXTENT OF RECOGNITION

Article 13

(1) A judgment entitled to recognition under this Convention shall, in any proceedings in the other Contracting State between the same parties, be given the same binding effects as if it were a judgment of the court addressed. However, the court addressed may, if the interests of justice so require, and shall, if the respondent so requests, give the judgment such binding effects as it would be given under the law of the territory of origin.

(2) For the purpose of this Article, parties shall include all persons who were represented by parties in the original proceedings and the successors and assigns of such persons or parties.

CHAPTER V: PROCEDURES FOR RECOGNITION AND ENFORCEMENT

Article 14

Recognition under this Convention shall be accorded upon presentation of such of the documents specified in Article 15 as the court addressed considers requisite.

Article 15

(1) A judgment for the payment of money which is entitled to enforcement under this Convention shall, to the extent that it has not been fully satisfied or carried out, be enforced by the court addressed. To the extent that a judgment orders forms of relief other than the payment of money, the court addressed may refuse enforcement or may order any measures of enforcement which the law of the court addressed permits for similar domestic judgments. The procedures for enforcement shall, except as otherwise provided in this Convention, be governed by the law applicable in the court addressed.

(2) The court addressed may require:

(a) a copy of the judgment authenticated by the court of origin;

(b) unless the required information is set forth in the judgment, documentary evidence as to the form and modalities of the notice given to the defendant and as to the grounds upon which jurisdiction was assumed;

(c) a statement of the grounds relied upon to establish the jurisdiction of the court of origin under Articles 10 and 11; and

(d) an affidavit of such other facts as may be required by the rules of the court addressed.

Article 16

(1) A judgment given in the United Kingdom shall be enforced in the United States by that procedure which provides for a form of notice to the respondent and is the simplest and most rapid provided by the law applicable in the court addressed for the enforcement of non-local judgments. Application for enforcement may be made to any court which exercises jurisdiction for the territory where enforcement is sought and which is competent to afford the relief requested.

(2) A judgment given in the United States shall be registered for enforcement in the United Kingdom upon application made to a court of competent jurisdiction.

Article 17

(1) A period of six years from the date of the original judgment if review has not been sought in a court of the territory of origin, or from the date of the most recent judgment, if review has been sought, shall be allowed for applications for enforcement under Article 16. However, no application shall be entertained where the judgment is no longer entitled to enforcement in the territory of origin.

(2) No security for costs may be required of any person applying for enforcement of a judgment entitled to recognition under this Convention except where enforcement is granted of a judgment still subject to review.

(3) Interest recoverable on a judgment enforced under this Convention shall, in respect of the period preceding the date on which enforcement is granted under paragraph (1) of Article 16 or registration for enforcement is effected under paragraph (2) of Article 16, be at such rate, if any, as may be specified in the judgment or in a certificate given by the court of origin.

(4) From the date on which enforcement is granted under paragraph (1) of Article 16 or registration for enforcement is effected under paragraph (2) of Article 16, the judgment shall, for enforcement purposes, including prescriptive time limits and interest charges, be treated as a judgment given on that date by the court addressed.

(5) Money judgments entitled to enforcement under this Convention may be enforced by the court addressed either in the currency specified in the judgment or in the local currency at the buying rate in the place where and on the date when enforcement is granted under paragraph (1) of Article 16 or registration for enforcement is effected under paragraph (2) of Article 16.

CHAPTER VI: RECOGNITION AND ENFORCEMENT OF THIRD STATE JUDGMENTS

Article 18

(1) Subject to any obligations under a treaty existing at the date of entry into force of this Convention or arising as the result of the accession of further States to such a treaty, a judgment given by a court or other authority of a third State against a person who is a national of a Contracting State or who has a domicile, a place of residence or a place of business, or which is incorporated or has its registered office, in a Contracting State shall be refused recognition or enforcement by the courts of the other Contracting State at the request of the respondent.

(a) where, pursuant to a treaty obligation, the courts of the third State would be precluded from exercising jurisdiction in proceedings against a person having the same connection with the State of the court addressed as the person sued had with the other Contracting State, or

(b) where the judgment would, if it had been given against a person having the same connection with the State of the court addressed, be denied recognition or enforcement on jurisdictional grounds or because proper notice was not given.

(2) The provisions of paragraph (1) shall also be subject to any new treaty obligations assumed by a Contracting State where the consent of the other Contracting State has been obtained.

CHAPTER VII: FINAL PROVISIONS

Article 19

This Convention shall not prevail over other treaties in special fields to which both Contracting States are or shall have become Parties.

Article 20

A Contracting State may, on the exchange of instruments of ratification or at any time thereafter, declare that it will not apply the Convention to judgments given by courts of the other Contracting State in respect of cultural objects which, having been determined by the competent authorities of the declaring Contracting State to be of cultural significance, are imported into the State for temporary display or exhibition pursuant to an agreement entered into between the object's foreign owner or custodian and that State or one or more cultural institutions therein.

Article 21

Either Contracting State may, on the exchange of instruments of ratification or at any time thereafter, declare that it will not apply the Convention to a judgment that imposes a liability which that State is under a treaty obligation toward any other State not to recognize or enforce. Any such declaration shall specify the treaties containing the said obligations.

Article 22

The Contracting States may, by an exchange of notes, define the meaning of the term "habitual residence" as used in this Convention.

Article 23

(1) Either Contracting State may, on the exchange of instruments of ratification or at any time thereafter, declare that this Convention shall extend to any territory for the international relations of which it is responsible. Any extension of the Convention under this Article shall enter into force three months after the date of the notification, and may be terminated by six months' notice of termination.

(2) Termination of the Convention in accordance with Article 25 shall, unless otherwise expressly agreed by both Contracting States, terminate it in respect of any territory to which it has been extended in accordance with paragraph (1) of this Article.

Article 24

Any difficulties which may arise in connection with the interpretation or application of this Convention shall be settled through the diplomatic channel or through any other means agreed by the Contracting States. Any such difficulty which is not settled by agreement may be submitted by either Contracting State to the International Court of Justice for decision upon three months' notice to the other Contracting State.

Article 25

This Convention shall be subject to ratification. Instruments of ratification shall be exchanged at The Convention shall enter into force three months after the date on which the instruments of ratification are exchanged and shall remain in force for three years. If neither of the Contracting States gives notice to the other, not less than six months before the expiration of the said period of three years, of intention to terminate the Convention, it shall remain in force until the expiration of six months from the date on which either of the Contracting States gives notice of termination.

Article 26

This Convention shall be known as the "United Kingdom/United States Civil Judgments Convention 197..."

IN WITNESS WHEREOF the undersigned, being duly authorised thereto, have signed this Convention.

Done in duplicate at this day of 19

For the United Kingdom of Great Britain and Northern Ireland:

For the United States of America:

**INTER-AMERICAN CONVENTION ON EXTRATERRITORIAL VALIDITY OF FOREIGN JUDGMENTS AND ARBITRAL AWARDS**

The Governments of the Member States of the Organization of American States,

CONSIDERING that the administration of justice in the American States requires their mutual cooperation for the purpose of ensuring the extraterritorial validity of judgments and arbitral awards rendered in their respective territorial jurisdictions, have agreed as follows:

Article 1

This Convention shall apply to judgments and arbitral awards rendered in civil, commercial or labor proceedings in one of the States Parties, unless at the time of ratification it makes an express reservation to limit the Convention to compensatory judgments (sentencias de condena) involving property. In addition, any one of them may declare, when ratifying the Convention, that it also applies to rulings that end proceedings, to the decisions of authorities that exercise some jurisdictional function and to judgments in penal proceedings ordering compensation for damages resulting from an offense.

The rules of this Convention shall apply to arbitral awards in a11 matters not covered by the Inter-American Convention on International Commercial Arbitration, signed in Panama on January 30, 1975.

Article 2

The foreign judgments, awards and decisions referred to in Article 1 shall have extraterritorial validity in the States Parties if they meet the following conditions:

a. They fulfill all the formal requirements necessary for them to be deemed authentic in the State of origin;
b. The judgment, award or decision and the documents attached thereto that are required under this Convention are duly translated into the official language of the State where they are to take effect;
c. They are presented duly legalized in accordance with the law of the State in which they are to take effect;
d. The judge or tribunal rendering the judgment is competent in the international sphere to try the matter and to pass judgment on it in accordance with the law of the State in which the judgment, award or decision is to take effect;
e. The ptantiff has been summoned or subpoenaed in due legal form substantially equivalent to that accepted by the law of the State where the judgment, award or decision is to take effect;
f. The parties had an opportunity to present their defense;
g. They are final or, where appropriate, have the force of res judicata in the State in which they were rendered;
h. They are not manifestly contrary to the principles and laws of the public policy (ordre public) of the State in which recognition or execution is sought.

Article 3

The documents of proof required to request execution of judgments, awards an< decisions are as follows:

a. A certified copy of the judgment, award or decision;

b. A certified copy of the documents proving that the provisions of items (( and (f) of the foregoing article have been complied with; and
c. A certified copy of the document stating that the judgment, award or decision is final or has the force of res judicata.

Article 4

If a foreign judgment, award or decision cannot be executed in its entirety, the judge or tribunal may agree to its partial execution at the request of an interested party.

Article 5

A declaration in forma pauperis recognized in the State of origin of the judgment shall be recognized in the State of destination.

Article 6

The procedures for ensuring the validity of foreign judgments, awards and decisions, including the jurisdiction of the respective judges and tribunals, shall be governed by the law of the State in which execution is sought.

Article 7

This Convention shall be open for signature by the Member States of the Organization of American States.

Article 8

This Convention is subject to ratification. The instruments of ratification shall be deposited with the General Secretariat of the Organization of American States.

Article 9

This Convention shall remain open for accession by any other State. The instrument of accession shall be deposited with the General Secretariat of the Organization of American States.

Article 10

Each State may, at the time of signature, ratification or accession, make reservations to this Convention, provided that each reservation concerns one or more specific provisions and is not incompatible with the object and purpose of the Convention.

Article 11

This Convention shall enter into force on the thirtieth day following the date of deposit of the second instrument of ratification.

For each State ratifying or acceding to the Convention after the deposit of the second instrument of ratification, the Convention shall enter into force on the thirtieth day after deposit by such State of its instrument of ratification or accession.

Article 12

If a State Party has two or more territorial units in which different systems of law apply in relation to the matters dealt with in this Convention, it may, at the time of signature, ratification or accession, declare that this Convention shall extend to all its territorial units or only to one or more of them.

Such declaration may be modified by subsequent declarations, which shall expressly indicate the territorial unit or units to which this Convention applies. Such subsequent declarations shall be transmitted to the General Secretariat of the Organization of American States and shall become effective thirty days after the date of their receipt.

Article 13

This Convention shall remain in force indefinitely, but any of the States Parties may denounce it. The instrument of denunciation shall be deposited with the General Secretariat of the Organization of American States. After one year from the date of deposit of the instrument of denunciation, the Convention shall no longer be in effect for the denouncing State, but shall remain in effect for the other States Parties.

Article 14

The original instrument of this Convention, the English, French, Portuguese and Spanish texts of which are equally authentic, shall be deposited with the General Secretariat of the Organization of American States, which will forward an authenticated copy of its text to the Secretariat of the United Nations for registration and publication in accordance with Article 102 of its Charter. The General Secretariat of the Organization of American States shall notify the Member States of that Organization and the States that have acceded to the Convention of the signatures, deposits of instruments of ratification, accession and denunciation as well as of reservations, if any. It shall also transmit the declarations referred to in Article 12 of this Convention.

IN WITNESS WHEREOF the undersigned Plenipotentiaries, being duly authorized thereto by their respective Governments, have signed this Convention.

DONE AT MONTEVIDEO, Republic of Uruguay, this eighth day of May, one thousand nine hundred and seventy-nine.

**INTER-AMERICAN CONVENTION ON JURISDICTION IN THE INTERNATIONAL SPHERE FOR THE EXTRATERRITORIAL VALIDITY OF FOREIGN JUDGMENTS**

The Governments of the Member States of the Organization of American States,

DESIROUS of improving the administration of justice through greater judicial cooperation among the American States, and

CONSIDERING that, for the effective application of Article 2 (d) of the Inter-American Convention on Extraterritorial Validity of Foreign Judgments and Arbitral Awards signed at Montevideo on May 8, 1979, provisions are necessary to prevent jurisdictional disputes among the States Parties,

HAVE AGREED to sign the following

Article 1

For the purposes of the extraterritorial validity of foreign judgments, the requirement of jurisdiction in the international sphere is deemed to be satisfied when the judicial or other adjudicatory authority of the State Party that rendered the judgment would have had jurisdiction in accordance with any of the following provisions:

A. In an action in persona for a money judgment, any of the following bases or, if applicable, that provided for in section D of this article shall be satisfied:

1. At the time the action was initiated, the defendant, if a natural person, had his domicile or habitual residence in the territory of the State Party in which judgment was rendered or, if a juridical person, had its principal place of business in that territory;

2. In an action against a private non-commercial or business enterprise, the defendant had its principal place of business at the time the action was initiated in the State Party in which judgment was rendered or was organized in that State Party;

3. In an action against a branch, agency, or affiliate of a private non-commercial or business enterprise, the activities that gave rise to such action took place in the State Party in which judgment was rendered, or

4. In the case of non-exclusive fora permitting submission to other fora, the defendant either consented in writing to the jurisdiction of the judicial or other adjudicatory authority that rendered the judgment or, despite making an appearance, failed to submit a timely challenge to the jurisdiction of that authority.

B. In an action involving rights relating to tangible movable property, either of the following bases shall be satisfied:

1. The property was located, at the time the action was initiated, in the territory of the State Party in which the judgment was rendered, or

2. Any of the bases provided for in section A of this article is satisfied.

C. In an action involving property rights relating to immovable property, the property was located, at the time the action was initiated, in the territory of the State Party in which the judgment was rendered.

D. In an action arising from an international business contract, the parties agreed in writing to submit to the jurisdiction of the State Party in which the judgment was rendered, provided that such jurisdiction was not established in an abusive manner and had a reasonable connection with the subject matter of the action.

Article 2

The requirements for jurisdiction in the international sphere shall also be deemed to be satisfied if, in the opinion of the judicial or other adjudicatory authority of the State Party in which the judgment is to be given effect, the judicial or other adjudicatory authority that rendered the judgment assumed jurisdiction in order to avoid a denial of justice because of the absence of a competent judicial or other adjudicatory authority.

Article 3

In case of a judgment made on a counterclaim, the requirement of jurisdiction in the international sphere shall be deemed to be satisfied if:

1. One of the foregoing provisions would have been satisfied, had the counterclaim been brought as an independent action;

2. The principal claim satisfied one of the foregoing provisions and the counterclaim arose out of the transaction or occurrence on which the principal claim was based.

Article 4

The extraterritorial validity of the judgment may be denied if the judgment has infringed the exclusive jurisdiction of the State Party in which it is being invoked.

Article 5

Foreign judgments shall not have extraterritorial validity unless, in addition to being final and non-appealable, they are entitled to recognition and execution throughout the territory of the State Party in which they were rendered.

Article 6

This Convention shall apply only to the cases governed by the foregoing articles and shall not apply to the following subjects:

a. Personal status and capacity of natural persons;
b. Divorce, annulment, and marital property;
c. Child support and alimony;
d. Decedents' estates (testate or intestate);
e. Bankruptcy, insolvency proceedings, composition with creditors, or other similar proceedings;
f. Liquidation of business enterprises;
g. Labor matters;
h. Social security;
i. Arbitration;
j. Torts, and
k. Maritime and aviation matters.

Article 7

The States Parties may declare that they will also apply this Convention to interlocutory rulings that discontinue proceedings, to the decisions of non-adjudicatory authorities that perform some adjudicatory function, and to judgments in penal proceedings ordering compensation for damages for wrongful action.

Article 8

The rules contained in this Convention shall not limit any broader provisions contained in bilateral or multilateral conventions among the States Parties regarding jurisdiction in the international sphere or more favorable practices in regard to the extraterritorial validity of foreign judgments.

Article 9

This Convention shall be open for signature by the Member States of the Organization of American States.

Article 10

This Convention is subject to ratification. The instruments of ratification shall be deposited with the General Secretariat of the Organization of American States.

Article 11

This Convention shall remain open for accession by any other State. The instruments of accession shall be deposited with the General Secretariat of the Organization of American States.

Article 12

A signatory State of the Inter-American Convention on Extraterritorial Validity of Foreign Judgments and Arbitral Awards, signed in Montevideo on May 8, 1979, may, in addition, declare at any time that this Convention shall be applied to determine the jurisdiction in the international sphere referred to in Article 2 (d) of the aforesaid Convention.

If not made at the time of the signing of this Convention, and if not contained in the instrument of ratification of or accession to this Convention, such declarations shall be transmitted to the General Secretariat of the Organization of American States, which shall notify the signatory States of the content of such declarations.

Article 13

This Convention shall enter into force on the thirtieth day following the date of deposit of the second instrument of ratification.

For each State ratifying or acceding to the Convention after the deposit of the second instrument of ratification, the Convention shall enter into force on the thirtieth day after deposit by such State of its instrument of ratification or accession.

Article 14

If a State Party has two or more territorial units in which different systems of law apply in relation to the matters dealt with in this Convention, it may, at the time of signature, ratification or accession, declare that this Convention shall extend to all its territorial units or only to one or more of them.

Such declaration may be modified by subsequent declarations, which shall expressly indicate the territorial unit or units to which this Convention applies. Such subsequent declarations shall be transmitted to the General Secretariat of the Organization of American States, and shall become effective thirty days after the date of their receipt.

Article 15

This Convention shall remain in force indefinitely, but any of the States Parties may denounce it. The instrument of denunciation shall be deposited with the General Secretariat of the Organization of American States. After one year from the date of deposit of the instrument of denunciation, the Convention shall no longer be in effect for the denouncing State, but shall remain in effect for the other States Parties.

Article 16

The original instrument of this Convention, the English, French, Portuguese and Spanish texts of which are equally authentic, shall be deposited with the General Secretariat of the Organization of American States, which shall forward an authenticated copy of its text to the Secretariat of the United Nations for registration and publication in accordance with Article 102 of its Charter. The General Secretariat of the Organization of American States shall notify the Member States of the Organization and the States that have acceded to the Convention of the signatures, deposits of instruments of ratification, accession and denunciation as well as of reservations, if any. It shall also transmit the declarations referred to in Articles 7, 12 and 14 of this Convention.

IN WITNESS WHEREOF, the undersigned Plenipotentiaries, duly authorized thereto by their respective Governments, have signed this Convention.

DONE AT LA PAZ, Republic of Bolivia, on the twenty-fourth day of May, one thousand nine hundred and eighty-four.

**PART THREE**

# The Future of Enforcing Foreign Judgments

## I. INTRODUCTION

The enforcement of foreign judgments has always posed problems for transnational commerce, which depends on dispute resolution that is efficient, certain, and final. Countries' varying systems of jurisdiction, public policies, and diverse concepts of civil law often clash with and complicate the ultimate goal of having an effective and even-handed enforcement of judgments regime. In the hopes of facilitating future processes for the recognition and enforcement of foreign judgments, a number of efforts have been made to negotiate multi- or bilateral treaties. Failed U.S. efforts in the late 1970s to achieve some sort of a bilateral treaty[1] were refocused in the early 1990s into negotiating a convention under the auspices of the Hague Conference on Private International Law.[2] Emerging from the Hague Conference was the Hague Convention on Jurisdiction and the Enforcement of Judgments [hereinafter Jurisdiction and Judgments Convention], which was eventually narrowed in scope to the Hague Convention on Exclusive Choice of Court Agreements [hereinafter Choice of Court Convention].[3] The Choice of Court Convention was finalized on June 30, 2005 at the Hague Conference on Private International Law.[4] This third part of the handbook will track the tortuous development of the Choice of Court Convention, from early U.S. efforts to achieve a similar U.S.-U.K. treaty to the final convention. It will also discuss the difficulties that were encountered while drafting and negotiating the Choice of Court Convention.

Related to, but still separate from the Choice of Court Convention, is the effort of the American Law Institute (ALI)[5] to draft a U.S. federal law on the enforcement of foreign judgments. In 1998, the ALI began work on a model statute to help implement at the federal level in the United States what was to have been a final version of a judgment enforcement convention being negotiated under the auspices of the Hague Conference, as mentioned earlier.[6] As the prospects of successfully completing negotiations for a judgment enforcement convention waned, however, the ALI project switched focus to devising domestic legislation that might assist the future improvement of this area of law. Since the ALI project will likely influence the direction and nature of developments in this legal area, this part also discusses the 2005 final draft of the ALI project, as well as the problems presented in connection with it.[7]

[1] *See* Part Two, Instruments, Laws, and Other Materials, item 4e.

[2] Formed in 1893, the Hague Conference on Private International Law is an organization that provides a forum for negotiating conventions to respond to global legal issues, primarily in the commercial, business, and family law areas, where various forms of harmonization are needed. *See* http://www.hcch.net/index_en.php (last visited August 22, 2005).

[3] Other Hague conventions important to this area are, of course, the Hague Convention on the Taking of Evidence Abroad in Civil or Commercial Matters (Mar. 18, 1970), the Hague Convention on the Service Abroad of Judicial and Extrajudicial Documents in Civil and Commercial Matters (Nov. 15, 1965), and the Hague Convention on the Service Abroad of Judicial and Extrajudicial Documents in Civil and Commercial Matters (Nov. 15, 1965), which were reviewed in 2003 by a Conference Special Committee.

[4] See http://www.hcch.net/index_en.php?act=conventions.text&cid=98 (last accessed Aug. 22, 2005).

[5] The American Law Institute (ALI) was founded in 1923 with the stated goal of clarifying the law by proposing Restatements, Model Codes, and other proposals for beneficial legal reform. *See* http://ali.org/ (last accessed Aug. 22, 2005).

[6] Foreword, American Law Inst., International Jurisdiction and Judgments Project, at xi (Discussion Draft, Mar. 29, 2002) [hereinafter ALI March 2002 Discussion Draft].

[7] Recognition and Enforcement of Foreign Judgments: Analysis and Proposed Federal Statute (ALI Proposed Final Draft, April 11, 2005) [hereinafter ALI Proposed Final Draft]. ALI membership has approved the proposed final draft; however it is still pending final approval by the ALI Council. *See* http://ali.org/.

Another organization that has attempted to promote statutory uniformity in the United States regarding foreign country money judgments is the National Conference of Commissioners on Uniform State Laws (NCCUSL), the organization that provided the Uniform Foreign-Country Judgment Recognition Act that today is adopted in 30 U.S. states. The NCCUSL develops uniform state laws by drafting and promulgating acts for adoption by state legislatures.[8]

In 1962, the NCCUSL first proposed the Uniform Foreign Money-Judgments Recognition Act, a model statute for individual state adoption to provide a means by which foreign judgments would be recognized and/or enforced.[9] The Act (now called the Uniform Foreign-Country Money Judgments Recognition Act) was revised in 2005 to clarify interpretive issues arising in the common law and the implementation of 1962 Uniform Law. Part Three, IV will present a discussion of those issues.

Yet another force shaping future development of processes for the recognition and enforcement of foreign judgments manifests itself in international trade agreements. The trade agreements to which the United States is a party reflect a new flexibility and openness to other countries' manners of doing business. Thus, having yet failed to find a more streamlined future for an enforcement of foreign judgment regime in either model legislation or international treaties, perhaps the future of the enforcement of foreign judgments will build on a framework of emerging trade flexibility, which is intended to facilitate aspects of doing business in foreign countries such as private commercial dispute-settlement. A brief discussion of using this vehicle of transnational commercial law-making to advance agreement on mutual judgment enforcement procedures concludes Part Three.

[8] *See* http://nccusl.org (last accessed Aug. 22, 2005).

[9] Reporters' Notes in Redline Draft of Uniform Foreign-Country Money Judgments Recognition Act (200_) (March, 2005) [hereinafter Redline Draft] at 6.

## II. HAGUE CONVENTION ON EXCLUSIVE CHOICE OF COURT AGREEMENTS

### A. MOVING TOWARD A CONVENTION ON JURISDICTION AND JUDGMENT ENFORCEMENT

The current state of enforcing foreign judgments is imbalanced with regard to the United States.[1] As noted in Parts One and Two, the United States is not (and never has been) a party to any treaty requiring the enforcement of foreign judgments, and U.S. judgments are often not enforced abroad due to opposition to American bases for jurisdiction[2] or clashes of substantive law (e.g., the availability of punitive damages). Moreover, although a federal law on the subject would be possible as in the case of foreign arbitral awards and would preempt the many different state laws,[3] U.S. state law today still determines the inbound enforcement process for foreign judgments.[4]

#### 1. The U.S.-U.K. Convention Draft

The U.S.-U.K. Convention on the Reciprocal Recognition and Enforcement of Judgments in Civil Matters,[5] initiated on October 26, 1976, represents the first American effort to increase recognition of U.S. judgments overseas.[6] Although rather narrow in scope, the treaty strove toward uniform treatment of U.K. judgments in U.S. state and federal courts and non-discriminatory enforcement of American judgments in the United Kingdom.[7] In addition, the treaty allowed either State to refuse recognition of "discriminatory judgments."[8] Nevertheless, negotiations for the project failed due to the U.K. manufacturers' and insurers' concerns about high U.S. jury awards.[9]

#### 2. The Hague Convention

Thereafter, development in this area took more than a 10-year break, resuming in 1992 when the United States proposed the creation of a multilateral treaty on the recognition and enforcement of civil judgments to the Secretary General of the Hague Conference on

[1] *See* Jonathan A. Franklin & Roberta J. Morris, *International Jurisdiction and Enforcement of Judgments in the Era of Global Networks: Irrelevance of, Goals for, and Comments on the Current Proposals*, 77 CHI.-KENT L. REV. 1213, 1237–8 (2002).

[2] *See id.* at 1294 n.55.

[3] Convention on the Recognition and Enforcement of Foreign Arbitral Awards [hereinafter New York Convention], 9 U.S.C.A. §201, 21 U.S.T. 2517, 330 U.N.T.S. 38 (1959).

[4] *See supra*, Part One, III.C.

[5] 16 I.L.M. 71 (1977), revised in 1979, reprinted in 8 N.C.J. INT'L & COMM. REG. 322 (1983); *see* Parts Two, Instruments, Laws, and Other Materials.

[6] *The Effect of the Proposed U.S.-U.K. Reciprocal Recognition and Enforcement of Civil Judgments Treaty on Current Recognition Practices in the U.S*, 18 COLUM. J. TRANSNAT'L L. 119, 120 (1979).

[7] *Id.* at 139, 119–20.

[8] *Id.* at 121.

[9] *See* Internet and Federal Courts: Issues and Obstacles: Hearing Before the Subcomm. on Courts and Intellectual Property of the Comm. on the Judiciary of the House of Representatives, 106th Cong. 2 (2000) (witness Testimony of Jeffrey Kovar, Assistant Legal Advisor for Private International Law, U.S. Department of State) [hereinafter Kovar Testimony], at 22.

Private International Law.[10] The perceived reluctance of most countries to enforce U.S. judgments was a large motivating factor in U.S. efforts.[11] Such a convention would unify the procedure of recognizing and enforcing foreign judgments, setting out requirements, which, if met, would ensure the enforcement of the judgment of any signatory country in any other signatory country. This would ideally avoid duplication of proceedings, prevent debtors from avoiding legitimate debts, and soothe countries' concerns about the domestic effects of overbroad jurisdiction in other countries. Moreover, it could serve to remedy the imbalanced preference for arbitration of private commercial disputes resulting from the recognition and enforcement process under the widely adopted New York Convention. After adding jurisdiction to the scope of the convention at the behest of the reluctant European participants,[12] it was decided in 1993 that the Conference would "undertake work on a convention dealing with the recognition and enforcement of foreign judgments."[13]

The form of the convention was the first of many conflicts among the negotiating parties. Whereas the majority of the states sought a "double convention," the United States sought a "mixed convention."[14] A mixed convention had the advantage that it would not interfere with jurisdictional traditions the United States wanted to maintain[15] and still gave it the freedom not to recognize judgments based on certain disfavored "gray area" concepts of jurisdiction.[16] Although a 1994 Special Commission[17] expressed serious doubts as to the possibility of successfully negotiating a mixed convention,[18] it was nevertheless agreed

[10] Ronald A. Brand, *Intellectual Property, Electronic Commerce and the Preliminary Hague Jurisdiction and Judgments Convention*, 62 U. PITT. L. REV. 581, 582 (2001).

[11] Katherine R. Miller, *Playground Politics: Assessing the Wisdom of Writing a Reciprocity Requirement into U.S. International Recognition and Enforcement Law*, 35 GEORGETOWN J. INT'L L. 239, 257 (2004); *see also* Sarah Hudleston, Note, *Preserving Free Speech in a Global Courtroom: The Proposed Hague Convention and the First Amendment*, 10 MINN. J. GLOBAL TRADE 403, 417 (2001).

[12] European countries were reluctant to enter into such a treaty with the United States because judgments of their courts were already generally recognized by American courts via common law or the Uniform Foreign Money-Judgments Recognition Act, 13-II U.L.A. 39 (2002 & Supp. 2003) [hereinafter Recognition Act] (*see supra*, Part One, III.C.). Moreover, the European nations found U.S. jurisdictional law confusing and "excessive" jury verdicts problematic. *See* Kristen Hudson Clayton, *The Draft Hague Convention on Jurisdiction and Enforcement of Judgments and the Internet – A New Jurisdictional Framework*, 36 J. MARSHALL L. REV. 223, 227–8 (2002); *see also* Catherine Kessedjian, Remarks, *Proceedings of the 76th Annual Meeting of the American Law Institute*, 76 A.L.I. PROC. 465 at 457 (1999).

[13] Permanent Bureau of Haugue Conference on Private International Law, *Conclusions of the Working Group Meeting on Enforcement of Judgments in the Hague Conference on Private International Law, Proceedings of the Seventeenth Session 10 to 29 May 29, 1993*, TOME I, 17 H.C.P.I.L. PROC. 257 (1995).

[14] A "double convention" deals with both jurisdictional issues and enforcement of judgments. Both a double convention and "mixed convention" establish a "white list" of permissible jurisdictional bases and a "black list" of prohibited jurisdictional bases. A double convention requires that a country recognize and enforce judgments made on white list bases, whereas a mixed convention does not. Bases not mentioned on either list are on the "gray list" and need not be enforced.

[15] Brandon Danford, *The Enforcement of Foreign Money Judgments in the United States and Europe: How Can We Achieve A Comprehensive Treaty?*, 23 REV. LITIG. 381, 403 (2004).

[16] Catherine Kessedjian, *International Jurisdiction and Foreign Judgments in Civil and Commercial Matters* 12 (Hague Conference on Private Int'l Law, Prel. Doc. No. 7, 1997) [hereinafter Kessedjian Report] at 88, *cited in* Russell J. Weintraub, *How Substantial Is Our Need For a Judgments Recognition Convention and What Should We Bargain Away to Get it?*, 24 BROOKLYN J. INT'L L. 167, 186 (1998).

[17] The 1994 Special Commission was called to meet by the Conference Secretary General from June 20–24, 1994, to discuss the nature of the future of the convention, its substantive scope, and several other key issues.

[18] *Id.*

that the convention would take a mixed form. Still, the 1999 and 2001 drafts both strongly resembled double conventions.[19]

## B. THE 1999 DRAFT CONVENTION ON JURISDICTION AND JUDGMENTS

The first draft of this mixed convention did not appear until October of 1999.[20] Oddly enough, the 1999 Preliminary Draft Convention enjoyed the support of virtually all negotiating countries except the United States. The main American qualm was that the draft generally did not represent "a worldwide compromise among extremely different legal systems" with respect to jurisdiction.[21] The United States felt the draft too strongly resembled the European approach to jurisdiction[22] and did not make enough concessions to the U.S. system of jurisdiction.[23] U.S. constitutional due process guarantees also presented a problem with respect to the European approach to jurisdiction, since these guarantees limit the exercise of jurisdiction considerably and render the United States "unable to accept certain grounds of jurisdiction as they are applied in Europe."[24]

Although jurisdictional issues were clearly in the foreground,[25] the United States also noted the draft's lack of clarity and failure to deal definitively with certain intellectual property rights and electronic commerce issues.[26] Additionally, the United States took issue with the draft's bar on so-called doing business jurisdiction.[27]

[19] *See* William H. Theis, *Admiralty Proceedings and the Proposed Hague Convention on Jurisdiction and Judgments*, 32 J. MARSHALL L. & COM. 59, 61–2 (2001). For further discussion of the positive and negative aspects of a mixed convention, *see* Harold G. Meier, *A Hague Conference Judgments Convention and United States Courts: A Problem and a Possibility*, 61 ALB. L. REV. 1207 (1998); *see also* Arthur von Mehren, *Enforcing Judgments Abroad: Reflections on the Design of Recognition Conventions*, 24 BROOKLYN J. INT'L L. 17 (1998).

[20] *See generally* Preliminary Draft Convention, October 1999 [hereinafter PDC].

[21] Letter from Jeffrey D. Kovar, Assistant Legal Adviser for Private International Law, U.S. Department of State, to J.H.A. van Loon, Secretary General, Hague Conference on Private International Law (Feb. 22, 2000) [hereinafter February Kovar Letter].

[22] Letter from Jeffrey Kovar, Assistant Legal Advisor for Private International Law, U.S. Department of State, to Alasdair Wallace, Head of International and Common Law Services Division, England, (Sept. 10, 2000) (noting that the regional success of the Brussels Convention does not indicate success when used on an international level) [hereinafter September Kovar letter].

[23] *Id.* ("the October 1999 draft presents a deal on jurisdiction that is heavily weighted against U.S. jurisdictional practices"); for further discussion, *see generally* William E. O'Brien, *The Hague Convention on Jurisdiction and Judgments: The Way Forward*, 66 MOD. L. REV. 491(2003); for a view on the conflict as a result of varying views on the role of adjudication, *see* Arthur von Mehren, *Drafting a Convention on International Jurisdiction and the Effects of Foreign Judgments Acceptable World-Wide: Can the Hague Convention Project Succeed?*, 49 AM. J. COMP. L. 191, 194 (2001).

[24] Kovar Testimony, *supra* note 9 at 23 (e.g., tort jurisdiction based on place of injury and contract jurisdiction based on place of performance).

[25] For more on problems of the U.S. jurisdictional framework in an international context, *see* Fredriech K. Juenger, *A Shoe Unfit for Globetrotting, IV. Impediments to International Accommodation*, 28 U.C. DAVIS L. REV. 1027, 1050 (1995) [hereinafter Juenger].

[26] September Kovar letter, *supra* note 22 at 5 (noting that establishing bases of exclusive jurisdiction would likely be problematic due to "wide disparity" in approaches to exclusive jurisdiction, especially in areas such as intellectual property); von Mehren, *supra* note 23 at 192 (noting draft's failure to properly address these issues).

[27] For further discussion *see* M. Twitchell, *Why We Keep Doing Business with Doing-Business Jurisdiction*, 171 U. CHI. LEGAL F. 202 (2001); Paul R. Dubinsky, *The Reach of Doing Business Jurisdiction and Transacting Business Jurisdiction Over Non-U.S. Individuals and Entities*, New York Law School, (March 1998), available at: http://www.state.gov/www/global/legal_affairs/dubinsky.html, (last accessed June 14 2004).

Although based on the European Economic Communities (EEC) Convention on Jurisdiction and Enforcement of Judgments in Civil and Commercial Matters (otherwise known as the "Brussels Convention" and the precursor of Brussels Regulation),[28] which served as the uniform European law on recognition and enforcement of judgments within the European states until 2001, the 1999 Draft did incorporate some American and common law concepts of jurisdiction. General jurisdiction under the draft convention was premised mainly on defendant's forum, as in the Brussels Convention.[29] However, the draft extended the limits of general jurisdiction through the definition of "habitual residence" to include corporations, albeit not as generously as they are included under U.S. jurisdictional law.[30] The 1999 Draft adopted the Brussels approach to specific jurisdiction, requiring a close connection between the forum and the dispute, as well as the Brussels approach to torts, immovable property, intellectual property, and consumer employment contracts.[31] The recognition and enforcement provisions were also similar to those of the Brussels Convention, although the European and American approaches prove to be quite similar in this area.[32]

The limited forms of the doctrines of *lis pendens* and *forum non conveniens* in the 1999 draft represented a significant departure from the Brussels model. The draft set out an exception to the rule of *lis pendens* in the case of a potential defendant seeking a declaration of non-liability.[33] The 1999 Draft also included a restricted form of *forum non conveniens.*[34] Finally, the draft convention included the option to decline to enforce judgments for punitive, non-compensatory or excessive damages, but it set a minimum for damages at the amount the recognizing court itself would have awarded.[35]

## C. THE 2001 DRAFT CONVENTION

In 2001, a Special Committee drafted "what can only be characterized as a summary of options for the Convention," a maze of bracketed provisions and areas of disagreement.[36] The 2001 Draft convention is the result of a general attempt to achieve more clarity and consensus, and includes some key changes and many lingering areas of non-consensus. For example, it eliminated jurisdiction over multiple defendants and third party claims and excluded (in brackets) anti-trust, nuclear liability, immovable property, and legal persons

[28] 28 I.L.M. 620 (1989) [hereinafter Brussels Convention]. *See generally* P.L.C. Torremans, *The Uniform Interpretation of the Brussels and Lugano Conventions*, 28 EUR. L. REV. 752 (2003); *see also* Part Two, Bibliography.

[29] PDC, *supra* note 20 at Art. 1.

[30] O'Brien, *supra* note 23 at 499; *see* P. Nygh and F. Pocar, *Report of the Special Commission*, available at the Hague Conference Web site, www.hcch.net.

[31] O'Brien, *supra* note 23 at 500; for U.S. responses to this, *see* September Kovar Letter, *supra* note 22.

[32] O'Brien, *supra* note 23 at 502 (with the exception that the recognizing court is allowed to examine the jurisdiction of the rendering court).

[33] *Id.* at 501; PDC, *supra* note 20 at Art. 21; *see generally* Martin Stueckelberg, *Lis Pendens and Forum Non Conveniens at the Hague Conference*, 26 BROOKLYN J. INT'L L. 949 (2001).

[34] PDC, *supra* note 20 at Art. 22; *see generally* Note of Question of *Forum Non-Conveniens* in the Perspective of the Double Convention on Judicial Jurisdiction and the Enforcement of Decisions, Prel. Doc No. 3, (1996) available at: http://www.state.gov/www/global/legal_affairs/forum.html (last accessed Aug. 22, 2005).

[35] PDC, *supra* note 20 at Art. 33; this issue preoccupied the 1994 and 1996 Special Commissions as well, *see* Kessedjian Report, *supra* note 16 at 106.

[36] Danford, *supra* note 15 at 403; *see generally* Summary of the Outcome of the Discussion in Commission II of the First Part of the Diplomatic Conference of 6–20 June 2001, available at www.hcch.net, [hereinafter 2001 Draft].

issues from the scope of the convention.[37] Most bases of permitted and prohibited jurisdiction remained in brackets, and the compromises in the areas of *lis pendens* and punitive damages remained substantively the same.[38]

More unresolved areas expanded – such as intellectual property and e-commerce – despite negotiation efforts.[39] The 2001 Draft could not reach an agreement as to whether or not intellectual property issues should even be included within the scope, and wrestled with other issues, such as whether to treat patents and copyrights differently, the relationship between anti-trust and intellectual property provisions, and exclusive jurisdiction.[40] Disagreements regarding e-commerce seemed to stem from varying approaches to consumer protection, since some nations viewed jurisdiction as a powerful tool of consumer protection.[41] In stark contrast with the jurisdictional debate, the United States sought to take an "extremely careful and deliberate approach" to this area and consulted with "concerned private sector interests in the business and consumer communities."[42] The 2001 Draft presented alternatives that would allow states to continue their policies on the enforcement of choice of forum clauses against e-consumers. Other issues raised with regard to e-commerce included defamation and copyright infringement issues.

Similarly, the main jurisdictional issues remained unresolved, since the United States sought to permit jurisdiction on bases considered exorbitant abroad, and it yet declined to approve the "white list" bases of the Brussels Convention.[43] One of the main issues for the United States was thus attempting to keep the touchstones of its jurisdictional framework, for example transacting business jurisdiction, off the "black list." Other areas of contention for the United States in the debate over jurisdiction included specific jurisdiction in libel cases,[44] the form of tort and contract long arm statutes,[45] quasi *in rem* jurisdiction, and class actions.[46] Issues regarding e-commerce and the Internet served only to further complicate the jurisdictional discussion, since the already conflicting jurisdictional frameworks are all territory-based, a concept that the Internet betrays.[47]

### D. DOWNSCALING THE SCOPE OF THE JURISDICTION AND JUDGMENTS CONVENTION

Unresolved areas of contention led to a decision in June 2001 to postpone further negotiations under the convention.[48] In April 2002, the Hague Conference's Commission I on General Affairs and Policy decided that further work on the convention would have to focus solely on "core issues," such as choice of court agreements in business-to-business (B2B) cases, submission, defendant's forum, counterclaims, trusts and physical torts.[49] This

[37] *Id.* at Art. 1, 14 and 16, pp. 2, 15, and 16.
[38] *Id.* at Art. 21 and 33, pp. 19 and 26.
[39] *Id.* at 13.
[40] Brand, *supra* note 10 at 600.
[41] *Id.* at 602.
[42] Kovar Testimony, *supra* note 9 at 24.
[43] Juenger, *supra* note 25 at 1045.
[44] *See* Weintraub, *supra* note 16 at 195.
[45] *See id.* at 199.
[46] *See generally* Edward F. Sherman, *American Class Actions: Significant Features and Developing Alternatives in Foreign Legal Systems*, 215 F.R.D.130 (2003).
[47] *See* Brand, *supra* note 10 at 596–8.
[48] Reflection Paper to Assist in Preparation of a Convention on Jurisdiction and Recognition and Enforcement of Foreign Judgments in Civil and Commercial Matters, Prel. Doc. No. 19, Aug. 2002, p. 6.
[49] Masato Dogauchi and Trevor Hartley, Draft Report on Preliminary Draft Convention on Exclusive Choice of Court Agreements, Prel. Doc. No. 25 (March 2004) at 6–7. [hereinafter March Draft Report].

decision was generally accepted, with Japan and Australia urging to return to the 1999 Draft.[50] The scope of the convention was later scaled down even further to a Convention on Exclusive Choice of Court Agreements, which appeared as a first draft in 2003.[51] The convention's main goal was efficiency and uniformity, seeking to be the litigation equivalent of the New York Convention[52] that is applicable to the recognition and enforcement of foreign *arbitral awards*. A Special Commission produced another draft in April 2004,[53] which contained some additions and lingering areas of non-consensus.[54] A diplomatic conference was convened in June 2005 to resolve the pending issues, and the member states present at it signed the final draft on June 30.[55]

## E. CURRENT STATUS: MAIN PROVISIONS AND MAJOR ISSUES OF THE 2005 FINAL CONVENTION

### 1. Main Obligations and Exceptions of the 2005 Final Convention

The final Convention on Exclusive Choice of Court Agreements, concluded on June 30, 2005,[56] set out three major obligations for signatory countries.[57] These are:

1. The obligation of the chosen court to utilize the jurisdiction granted it under the Convention;
2. The obligation of all other courts to abstain from exercising jurisdiction;
3. The obligation of all courts to enforce and recognize the judgment made by a properly chosen court.[58]

As to the first obligation, Article 5 grants the chosen court jurisdiction unless the agreement is found null and void under the laws of the state of the chosen court.[59] As to the second obligation, Article 6 requires that all courts not designated in the agreement dismiss or suspend any proceeding regarding the dispute over which the chosen court was granted jurisdiction. This obligation is subject to enumerated exceptions, such as incapacity and injustice.[60] The third obligation – and for the purposes of this text the most pertinent – is

[50] O'Brien, *supra* note 23 at 507.

[51] Draft on Exclusive Choice of Court Agreements, Work. Doc. No. 49 E, Revised, December 2003. [hereinafter 2003 Draft].

[52] *See* United Nations Convention on the Recognition and Enforcement of Foreign Arbitral Awards [hereinafter New York Convention], 9 U.S.C. §§201–208. *See also* March Draft Report, *supra* note 49 at 6.

[53] Draft on Exclusive Choice of Court Agreements, Work. Doc. No. 110 E, Revised, April 2004. [hereinafter 2004 Draft].

[54] Another Draft Report on the Preliminary Draft of the Exclusive Choice of Court Convention was drawn up in August 2004. *See* Preliminary Draft Convention on Exclusive Choice of Court Agreement, Draft Report, Prel. Doc. No. 26, August 2004 [hereinafter August Draft Report]. This report further explained the intended meaning of the 2004 Draft and provided clarifying examples and a handful of further suggested changes. For the most part, these changes did not depart in any significant way from the areas of consensus and of indecision apparent in the March Draft Report, *supra* note 49.

[55] Final Draft Convention on Exclusive Choice of Court Agreements, Doc. No. 37 (June 30, 2005) [hereinafter Final Draft].

[56] *Id.*

[57] The Convention encompasses: (1) international cases (2) based on business-to-business contracts (3) regarding commercial or civil matters (4) that include an exclusive choice of court agreement.

[58] Final Draft, *supra* note 55 at Art. 6.

[59] *See* Final Draft, *supra* note 55 at Art. 5.

[60] *Id.* at Art. 6.

the requirement in Article 8 that a judgment of a chosen court be recognized and enforced by all signatory countries.[61] Article 9 does, however, list exceptions to this obligation.[62] A receiving court need not enforce the foreign judgment of a chosen court if its choice of court agreement is null and void under the laws of the receiving court, was entered into by an incapacitated party,[63] or was obtained by fraud.

A receiving court may also refuse enforcement if service on the defendant did not allow sufficient time to prepare a defense or was given in a way that violates the public policy of the receiving state.[64] The second part of this exception represents a change from the 2003 Draft. Under the 2003 Draft, a receiving court could deny enforcement if the defendant had not been properly notified of the suit under the laws of the state in which he was notified. The focus of the improper service exception thus shifted in the 2004 Draft to the due process standards of the court asked to enforce.

This shift is in accordance with another exception that a judgment need not be enforced or recognized if doing so would be manifestly incompatible with the public policy of the requested state.[65] This exception focuses on concepts of procedural fairness, for example the U.S. constitutional guarantee of due process of law, or the European Commission on Human Rights' guarantee of a fair trial.

The final draft also contains two additional exceptions to the Article 9 requirement, both of which helped resolve the indecision in the 2003 Draft on estoppel and incidental questions. The estoppel exception is permissive and provides that a court is not required to enforce a judgment if doing so would be inconsistent with a prior judgment in the same dispute between the same two parties, on the condition that the receiving court recognizes the prior judgment.[66] This is a more direct version than that of the 2003 Draft, which denied enforcement to judgments that could not be enforced in their state of origin.

The incidental question exception is divided into two categories: incidental questions regarding the excepted subject areas listed in Article 2 and certain intellectual property questions.[67] The language of the former category is proscriptive and requires a court to refuse enforcement of the judgment if it involved preliminary questions regarding any of the subject matter listed as outside the scope of the Convention in Article 2 (e.g., family law, insolvency, etc.). The latter contained complicated permissive exceptions to the enforcement requirement. The general effect of these is to prevent a judgment based on the validity of an intellectual property right (other than copyright) from contradicting the intellectual property law of the requested state or any pending proceedings on the validity of that right. The addition of these exceptions was likely the result of scholarly commentary on the inadequacy of the 2001 Draft with regard to intellectual property issues.[68]

The last pertinent provision is Article 11, which deals with the enforcement of damage awards. The Convention indicates that a foreign judgment may be refused recognition and enforcement where the damages awarded are not for actual loss or harm suffered.[69]

[61] *See id*, at Art. 8.

[62] *Id.* at Art. 9.

[63] There was some discussion in both the 2003 and 2004 drafts as to whether or not incapacity should be stricken as already included under "null and void."

[64] *See* Final Draft, *supra* note 55 at Art. 9 (c)(ii).

[65] *Id.* at Art. 9(e).

[66] *See* Final Draft, *supra* note 55 at Art. 9(f), (g).

[67] *Id.* at Art. 10.

[68] *See, e.g.*, Franklin & Morris, *supra* note 1 at 1220–1.

[69] Final Draft, *supra* note 55, at Art. 11.

## 2. Problems and Issues That Emerged from the Draft Convention

A 2003 survey showed that the majority of international businesses specify a certain court, or courts, in the contracts that govern their businesses.[70] Thus, if the United States becomes a party to this Convention, its enforcement obligation with respect to choice of court agreements could have a widespread impact on the enforcement of foreign judgments. Whether or not the Convention will ultimately be acceptable to all affected parties depends on several issues that emerged from the earlier negotiations that spanned almost 15 years, including issues related to the Internet, the arbitration and public policy exceptions, and the effect of omitting the fundamental issue of jurisdiction from the Convention.

Advanced information technology is a key issue framing the potential effects of the Convention. Generally speaking, this issue embodies very basic questions as to the usefulness and necessity of the Convention. On the one hand, the Internet and the expansion of e-commerce could be viewed as encouraging the ratification of the convention. As the World Wide Web melts away many physical borders, the need for harmonizing procedural devices seems acute in order to prevent calamitous clashes of substantive law.[71] On the other hand, the nature of the information displayed and the business done on the Internet defies, to a certain extent, the rules of any such convention. Technology exists to prevent access to Internet sites based on where the user's computer is located, thereby at least potentially reinstating a type of border. These programs, known as digital rights management systems,[72] are already widely used and seem to put a dent in the view of the Internet as fluidly internationalizing the world. Furthermore, such technology could transform the Convention into a threat to the free flow of the online market, should online businesses seek to isolate themselves from the large potential coverage created by the Convention.[73] Whether working for or against the efficiency of the Convention, the Internet is a major force influencing the practical future of both the Convention and the enforcement of foreign judgments.

The Internet also presents the more specific issue of click-wrap agreements.[74] Click-wrap agreements are the agreements resulting from Internet users clicking the "I agree" icons at the end of seldom-read contract terms. Although the scope of the Convention clearly excludes unilateral choices of court, it does not exclude non-negotiated agreements such as click-wrap contracts.[75] Thus, assuming that a contract meets all other requirements of Articles 1, 2 and 3, a forum selection clause in a click-wrap agreement could be enforceable under the Convention. That forum selection clauses will appear in click-wrap agreements seems likely, since online businesses will inevitably seek to shield themselves from being sued all over the world. It may thus be necessary for the Convention to deal more specifically

[70] *See Survey Regarding Business Practices on Jurisdictional Issues*, Int'l Chamber of Comm. (Mar. 2003).

[71] *See, e.g., Yahoo! Inc. v. La Ligue Contre Le Racisme et L'Antisemitisme*, 169 F. Supp. 2d 1181 (2001).

[72] Franklin & Morris, *supra* note 1 at 1227.

[73] For a general discussion of this, see Franklin & Morris, supra note 1; see also Weintraub, supra note 25; *contra* Clayton, supra note 12.

[74] For a general discussion, *see* Benjamin C. Elacqua, *The Hague Runs Into B2B: Why Restructuring the Hague Convention of Foreign Judgments in Civil and Commercial Matters to Deal with B2B Contracts Is Long Overdue*, 3J. High Tech. L. 93 (2004).

[75] Earlier drafts stressed that an exclusive choice of court agreement could not be made unilaterally, but they did not suggest changes in language to prevent such click-wrap agreement from falling under the scope of the Convention.

with such mass-marketed, non-negotiated agreements. The issue of click-wrap agreements leads to the more general issue of forum shopping. Since the court chosen need not have any connection with either contracting party, a business could choose a forum based solely on its favorable law or strategic location.

The public policy and arbitration exceptions were also points of contention among member countries. One of the main goals of the United States in seeking the original form of this Convention was to achieve uniformity in the enforcement of foreign judgments. The public policy exception could possibly defy this goal – overuse would lead to the Convention losing its "teeth." On the other hand, since the public policies of various countries are known and fairly static, failures to enforce based on the public policy exception will fall into a pattern that, if not uniform, could uniformly be anticipated. The arbitration exception could likewise be seen as placing a practical damper on the Convention's goal of efficiency, since it provides an opportunity for businesses to effectively skirt the requirements of the Convention by designating arbitration as the chosen mode of dispute resolution.

Finally, the successful negotiation of a convention on enforcing foreign judgments hinged on the ability to harmonize several dramatically different legal systems and concepts of jurisdiction without explicit jurisdictional provisions. The major differences in jurisdictional frameworks of the signatory countries led to the shrinking of the Convention.[76] These differences ended up being the underlying reason for difficulties resulting from the drafting and implementation of the Convention as well. Issues relating to the public policy, service, and "manifestly unjust" exceptions all seem to trail back to differences between the bases of jurisdiction in the respective member countries. This emerged as the major factor hindering negotiations toward a convention that addressed the other knotty transnational legal issues of enforcement of foreign judgments. However, given the disparities of practice and legal approach to these issues, a choice of court agreement was all that could be achieved at that time, and it may over time be the foundation upon which a true enforcement of foreign judgment regime can be built.

[76] *See* Hague Conference [Andrea Schulz], *The Future Convention on Exclusive Choice of Court Agreements and Arbitration*, Prel. Doc. No. 32 of June 2005, available at: http://www.hcch.net.

## III. INTERNATIONAL JURISDICTION AND JUDGMENTS PROJECT OF THE AMERICAN LAW INSTITUTE

### A. INTRODUCTION

A force more likely to shape the future of the enforcement of foreign judgments in the United States than the Hague Convention on Choice of Court Agreements is the American Law Institute's (ALI)[1] recent drafting of a model federal statute called the International Jurisdiction and Judgments Project. In 1998, "in anticipation of conclusion and ratification of the Hague Convention,"[2] this project commenced to draft implementing federal legislation for executing in the United States the then-proposed Hague Convention of Recognition and Enforcement of Foreign Judgments, which was in negotiation at the time.[3] When both the scope and success of the Convention became doubtful in 2000,[4] the ALI switched focus to drafting federal legislation without relationship to any outside convention.[5] The project that was originally motivated by a need to increase support for the Hague Convention[6] took on the new goal of creating a "federal standard" for the enforcement and recognition of foreign judgments in the United States.[7]

The project incorporates the principle that foreign judgments should not be reviewed on the merits by enforcing courts, and it proposes a framework of recognition designed to simplify and unify the process.[8] The success of the project depended on the ability of the drafters to reach a consensus as to two major issues: reciprocity and public policy as grounds for non-recognition. In 2004, the Council submitted a redlined version recommending changes to be included in the Proposed Final Draft.[9] A version containing those revisions was published April 11, 2005.[10] At the Eighty-second Annual ALI Meeting in May, the membership approved the proposed final draft with some minor revisions, and it is pending approval of the ALI Council.[11]

[1] Incorporated in 1923, the ALI's object is "promotion, clarification and simplification of the law and its better adaptation to social needs, to secure the better administration of justice and to encourage and carry on scholarly and scientific work." *See* ALI Certificate of Incorporation, available at: www.ali.org under "Charter, Bylaws and Rules."

[2] Miller, *supra* Part Three, II, note 11 at 261; ALI March 2002 Discussion Draft, *supra* Part Three, I, note 6 at xi.

[3] *See supra* at Part Three, II.

[4] Linda J. Silberman, *Can the Hague Project Be Saved? A Perspective from the United States*, in A GLOBAL LAW OF JURISDICTION AND JUDGMENTS: LESSONS FROM THE HAGUE 159, 182 (John J. Barcelo III & Kevin M. Clermont eds., 2002).

[5] Reporter's Memorandum in ALI March 2002 Discussion Draft, *supra* Part Three, I, note 6 at xvii; *see also* Andreas F. Lowenfeld, Remarks, *Proceedings of the 79th Annual Meeting of the American Law Institute*, 79 A.L.I. PROC. 329 (2002).

[6] ALI March 2002 Discussion Draft, *supra* Part Three, I, note 6 at xi.

[7] Comment in AMERICAN LAW INST., INTERNATIONAL JURISDICTION AND JUDGMENTS PROJECT at 31 (Tentative Draft No. 2, April 14, 2004) [hereinafter 2004 ALI DRAFT]; Miller, Part Three, II, *supra* note 11 at 270.

[8] Comment in 2004 ALI Draft, *supra* note 7 at 30.

[9] *See* http://www.ali.org/ali/IJJ2Redline.pdf (last accused Aug. 22, 2005).

[10] *See* ALI Proposed Final Draft, *supra* Part Three, I, note 7.

[11] *Id.* The title of the ALI project officially changed to "Recognition and Enforcement of Foreign Judgments: Analysis and Proposed Federal Statute." As a member of ALI, the author participated in many of the discussions involved in this project.

## B. GENERAL PROVISIONS OF THE AMERICAN LAW INSTITUTE PROJECT

The major provisions of the proposed final draft set out prerequisites that dictate treatment of a foreign judgment comparable to that required for sister-state judgments under the U.S. Constitution's Full Faith and Credit Clause.[12] In an effort to achieve the most uniformity possible, the scope of the project was quite broad.[13] Although it encompasses many areas that current state law explicitly excludes – for example, domestic and tax judgments – it does so within a scheme of mandatory and permissive grounds of recognition.[14] It lists exclusive grounds for non-recognition, and the burden of proof is on the party resisting the enforcement of the judgment, except in the case of forum selection clauses.[15] The 2005 proposed final draft contains a black list of jurisdictional bases, on which a foreign judgment will be considered invalid for lack of jurisdiction unless it falls into one of the excepted categories.[16] As a response to the problem of parallel litigation, the draft project also suggested a rule of *lis pendens* and a registration process, both of which were aimed at avoiding double adjudication of the enforceability of foreign judgments.[17] Finally, in an effort to encourage enforcement of American judgments abroad, the project contained a reciprocity requirement.[18]

## C. THE MANDATORY AND PERMISSIVE BASES OF NON-RECOGNITION AND THE BLACK LIST OF JURISDICTIONAL BASES

The mandatory bases for non-recognition are set forth in Section 5(a):

- The rendering court was not an impartial tribunal;
- There is substantial and justifiable doubt as to the integrity of the rendering court;
- Jurisdiction on which judgment was based is unacceptable under the Section 6 black list;
- No proper notice in original proceeding;
- Extrinsic (but not intrinsic) fraud; and
- Public policy.[19]

These bases were mostly recycled from various enforcement statutes with a few removed to or from the mandatory category. However, one noteworthy new basis is section 5(a)(ii), which provides that judgments "rendered in circumstances . . . rais[ing] substantial and justifiable doubt about the integrity of the rendering court with respect to the judgment in question" are not entitled to recognition. This standard is quite high, however, since it requires that the corruption in question be shown to have existed in the specific case and that it

[12] ALI Proposed Final Draft, *supra* Part Three, I, note 7 at 38.
[13] Reporter's Notes in 2004 ALI Draft, *supra* note 7 at 33–4.
[14] *Id.*
[15] ALI Proposed Final Draft, *supra* Part Three, I, note 7 at § 5.
[16] *Id.* at § 6.
[17] *Id.* at §§ 10 and 11(Reporter's Notes).
[18] *Id.* at § 7.
[19] ALI Proposed Final Draft, *supra* Part Three, I, note 7 at § 5.(a).

had a probable impact on the judgment.[20] After the court has ruled not to enforce on this ground, it is required to explain why as well.[21]

It is also notable that the threshold for the public policy basis "remains high," requiring that either the claim or the judgment be contrary to public policy.[22] Additionally, as noted in Section 5(b), a foreign judgment shall not be recognized if it proceeded in a forum contrary to an agreement, and the party raised the defense of the forum-selection agreement and was improperly rejected by the foreign court.[23]

The permissive bases for non-recognition are set forth in Section 5(c):

- Lack of jurisdiction of rendering court;
- Judgment conflicts with another judgment;
- Judgment conflicts with pending case in the United States (parallel litigation);
- Judgment results from an anti-suit injunction; and
- Lack of subject matter jurisdiction.[24]

These bases again do not represent anything new, save the categorization of some bases as permissive rather than mandatory. It is also important to note that the subject matter jurisdiction basis refers to a situation in which "the matter would be better decided by U.S. or other country's law."[25]

The black list of jurisdictional bases listed in Section 6 includes several bases already generally rejected in the United States, as well as bases rejected based on basic principles of fairness and international law. These bases are: seizure of property, the nationality or domicile of the plaintiff, and tag jurisdiction (unless the defendant is considered a fugitive of a human rights violation).[26]

## D. MAJOR ISSUES AND PROBLEM AREAS IN THE INTERNATIONAL JURISDICTION AND JUDGMENTS PROJECT

In the discussions leading up to the adoption by the ALI membership of the proposed final draft, the issue most threatening to the success of the project was undoubtedly the reciprocity requirement. Under the proposed final draft, a foreign judgment need not be enforced in the United States if a comparable U.S. judgment would not be enforceable in the country of origin.[27] The party resisting enforcement may plead a lack of reciprocity as an affirmative defense to enforcing a foreign judgment, and the project sets forth considerations in reviewing the evidence of such a defense.[28] The goal of the requirement is to "create an incentive to foreign countries to commit to the recognition and enforcement of judgments rendered in the U.S."[29] and to encourage other countries and the United States to enter into agreements "recording their commitment to recognizing and enforcing

[20] *Id.* at § 5 (Comment d).
[21] *Id.*
[22] *Id.* at § 5 (Comment h).
[23] *Id.* at § 5(b).
[24] *Id.* at § 5(c).
[25] *Id.* at § 5 (Comments).
[26] *Id.* at § 6 (Comments and Reporter's Notes); *see also* Beth Van Shaak, *In Defense of Civil Redress: The Domestic Enforcement of Civil Rights Norms in the Context of the Proposed Hague Judgments Convention*, 42 HARV. INT'L L.J. 141 (2001).
[27] ALI Proposed Final Draft, *supra*, Part Three, I, note 7 at § 7.
[28] *Id.* at § 7(b), and 7(c).
[29] *Id.* at § 7 (Comment b).

judgments rendered in the United States."[30] With this goal in mind, Section 7 also allows for the negotiation of agreements between the United States and other countries to establish reciprocity between them as a rule.[31]

Although there was certainly debate over what constitutes a "comparable" judgment[32] and which party should bear the burden of proof, the main point of contention was the inclusion of the reciprocity requirement at all. This had been the subject of several documents submitted by members for consideration and debate, and it was certainly a key issue in the final stages of the project's development.

There are several valid arguments both for and against the reciprocity requirement. On the one hand, there is no reciprocity requirement in most state enforcement statutes,[33] thus the inclusion of such a requirement would go against many years of precedent.[34] In addition, many critics disagree that the requirement will function as an incentive to foreign nations because the inability to enforce judgments in the United States is not a strong enough bargaining tool.[35] The uniformity goal is also arguably ill-served, since varying federal and state law will only lead to forum-shopping and state enforcement laws are already relatively uniform.[36] It has also been questioned whether shifting the statutory focus to the federal level would be an over-extension of federal power and a waste of state expertise in the area.[37] Furthermore, the original motivation for including the requirement – namely as a bargaining compromise to encourage adoption of the Hague Convention – no longer exists because the enforcement of foreign judgment aspects of the proposed convention was abandoned in favor of the more limited choice of court convention.[38] Finally, the reciprocity requirement could complicate enforcement adjudication and merely "fuel collateral litigation."[39]

On the other hand, a number of state enforcement statutes already allow non-recognition based on a lack of reciprocity, so the concept is by no means foreign to current statutes or to current practice in the area.[40] A reciprocity requirement also appears quite often in other areas of federal law, for example, 42 U.S.C. Section 659a, dealing with duties of support owed to residents of the United States, and 46 U.S.C. Section 785, which requires reciprocity in order for foreign nationals to receive the right to sue the U.S.government for damages caused by U.S. vessels.[41] Such a prerequisite for the enforcement of a foreign

[30] *Id.* at § 7 (Reporter's Notes 1).

[31] *Id.* at § 7(e).

[32] *E.g.*, *see id.* at § 7 (Reporter's Note 7).

[33] Nine U.S. states have included reciprocity provisions in their Enforcement Acts. Florida, Idaho, Maine, North Carolina, Ohio, and Texas authorize the consideration of reciprocity when deciding to enforce a foreign judgment. Only Massachusetts and Georgia require reciprocity, and New Hampshire demands it with respect to Canadian judgments only. *See* ALI Proposed Final Draft, *supra* Part Three, I, note 7, at § 7 (Reporter's Note 3).

[34] *See* Richard W. Hulbert, *Statement in Support of Motion to Delete the Requirement of Reciprocity*, submitted to the Executive Office of the American Law Institute at the Eighty-First Annual Meeting on May 17, 18, and 19, 2004. [hereinafter Hulbert Statement].

[35] *See* K. King Burnett, *Memorandum in Support of the Motion by Guy Miller Struve, et al, Concerning Proposed Federal Statute on Recognition and Enforcement of Foreign Country Judgments*, submitted to the Executive Office of the American Law Institute at the Eighty-First Annual Meeting on May 17, 18, and 19, 2004.

[36] *Id.*

[37] *Id.*

[38] *See* Hulbert Statement, *supra* note 34.

[39] *Id.*

[40] ALI Proposed Final Draft, *supra* Part Three, I, note 7, at § 7 (Reporter's Note 3).

[41] *Id.* at § 7 (Reporter's Note 5).

judgment is also common in other countries, for example, in France, Germany, the European Union, Canada, and Australia.[42]

Another major issue in the drafting of the project was the public policy basis for non-recognition as it pertains to the First Amendment. Due to several recently decided libel and defamation cases,[43] some critics feel that the approach taken by the reporters on this issue[44] is not conclusive enough, and that the project should clearly and explicitly include libel judgments violative of the First Amendment in the public policy exception.[45] The Internet is obviously a major topic in such discussion as well: Some maintain that its expansion will further threaten the First Amendment, while others claim that this area of law must and will develop its own system of regulation.[46] While the membership of the ALI voted its acceptance of the Final Draft in May 2005, final adoption awaits approval of the ALI Council, which has the final word on such matters. Every indication is that, with a few if any changes, the Proposed Final Draft reviewed here will receive the Council's enthusiastic approval.

Given the ALI International Jurisdiction and Judgments Project's broad and thorough examination of U.S. law and policy with respect to the enforcement of foreign judgments, there is every reason to believe that it will play an important role in the future development of the law of enforcing foreign judgments.

[42] *Id.* at § 7 (Reporters' Note 7).

[43] *See, e.g., Matusevitch v. Telkinoff*, 159 F.3d 636 (1998); *Bachchan v. Indian Abroad Publications*, 154 Misc.2d 228, 585 N.Y.S.2d 661 (1992); *Yahoo! v. La Ligue Contre le Racisme et L'Antisemitisme*, 169 F. Supp. 2d 1181(2001).

[44] *See generally* ALI Proposed Final Draft, *supra* Part Three, I, note 7, at § 5 (Reporter's Note 5(d)).

[45] Eric M. Freedman, *Memorandum to ALI Membership and Council, Re: International Jurisdiction and Judgments Project Public Policy Exception – First Amendment*, May 17, 2004.

[46] *See id.*; *see* ALI Proposed Final Draft, *supra* Part Three, I, note 7, at § 5 (Reporter's Note 5(d)).

## IV. REVISION OF THE UNIFORM FOREIGN-MONEY JUDGMENT RECOGNITION AND ENFORCEMENT ACT

### A. THE UNIFORM ACT EXPERIENCE

In the 1960s, when the United States did not accede to any international agreements for the recognition and enforcement of civil judgments, the laws of the several states governed recognition and enforcement of civil judgments rendered abroad. This lack of national uniformity posed a problem in terms of having the judgments of the several states recognized in foreign countries, since the United States as a whole did not have reciprocal agreements with the other countries. The National Conference of Commissioners on Uniform State Laws (NCCUSL), an organization that develops uniform state laws by drafting and promulgating model/uniform acts, sought to remedy this problem for the individual states.[1] Thus, in 1962, the NCCUSL drafted the Uniform Foreign Money-Judgments Recognition Act (UFJRA).[2] The Act strove to codify the most prevalent common law rules regarding the recognition of foreign-country money judgments to satisfy reciprocity concerns of foreign courts, thus making it more likely that money judgments rendered in the states would be recognized in other countries.[3]

The (UFJRA) details the circumstances under which the courts in states adopting the Act must recognize foreign country money judgments. Although under the UFJRA, foreign country judgments rendered according to its provisions must be recognized by the courts of adopting states, courts also have discretion under the Act with respect to recognizing foreign country judgments that do not meet certain requirements.[4] The Act sets standards for recognition and enforcement of foreign judgments, but it does not establish specific court procedures; that is left to the specific court jurisdiction.

In June, 2003, a Study Committee was authorized by NCCUSL to consider possible revision of the 1962 Act.[5] The Committee's report concluded that there were several interpretative issues raised by the Act, and a revision was necessary to clarify those issues.[6] The Drafting Committee, appointed in January 2004, was responsible for the current draft of the revised Act.[7] The Study Report identified the following issues that needed to be addressed in the revision:

1. Clarification of the definitions section;
2. Allocation of the burden of proof in application of the Act;

[1] *See* http://nccusl.org

[2] National Conference of Commissioners on Uniform State Laws, Uniform Foreign Money-Judgments Recognition Act, 13 UNIFORM LAWS ANNOTATED 263 (1986) [hereinafter 1962 UFMJRA]. *See* Part One of this guide for additional information about the UFMJRA.

[3] *Id.*

[4] *Id.*

[5] Reporters' Notes in Redline Draft of Uniform Foreign-Country Money Judgments Recognition Act (200_) (July 22–29, 2005) at 7 [hereinafter Redlined UFCMJRA]. To avoid confusion with the Uniform Enforcement of Foreign Judgments Act (*see* Enforcement Act, *supra* Part One, Introduction, Note 1, the revised version of the Uniform Foreign-Money Judgment Recognition Act (UFMJRA) added the word "country" to the title. The Act is now entitled Uniform Foreign-Country Money Judgment Recognition Act (UFCMJRA).

[6] *Id.*

[7] In July 2005, the Drafting Committee approved the Uniform Foreign-Country Money Judgments Recognition Act (2005) [hereinafter UFCMJRA 2005] (the final text is still subject to revision by the Committee on Style of the NCCUSL), available at: http://www.law.upenn.edu/bll/ulc/ufmjra/2005AMAppText.htm (last accessed

3. The provision of specific procedures to achieve recognition of a foreign country money judgment;
4. Clarification of the grounds for denying recognition, considering the conflicting interpretations of provisions in the case law;
5. The express allocation of the burden of proof regarding grounds for denying recognition;
6. Whether there should be a statute of limitations for certain recognition actions; and
7. Re-analysis of whether a reciprocity requirement should be included in the Act in light of non-uniform state enactments that included such a requirement.[8]

These issues and the proposed revisions to the Act were discussed at a March 2005 Committee meeting.[9] Further discussion of the Act was on the agenda at the July 2005 annual meeting of the NCCUSL,[10] and the revisions were finally approved at that meeting.[11]

## B. PROPOSED REVISIONS

An amendment to the definitions of the Section 2 of the current Act changed the terms "foreign state" and "foreign judgment" to "foreign country" and "foreign-country judgment" to clarify that the Act does not merely apply to decisions between sister states but to foreign country judgments.[12] The additional commentary states that the judgment in question need not be between two private parties, as a governmental entity can be a party to an enforceable judgment.[13] Additionally, with respect to Section 2 of the Act, there is discussion of the Full Faith and Credit Clause regarding the states' recognition of judgments made by governmental units. Essentially, the courts are given the discretion to determine which courts or judicial bodies are considered "governmental units" that may issue recognizable money judgments. There are, however, limitations – for example, arbitral awards are excluded from this Act.[14] Moreover, judgments that are not made by adjudicative bodies of a foreign country will not be entitled to recognition and enforcement.[15]

In the amended draft, there is discussion of the issue of which party has the burden of proof to establish whether a foreign country judgment is within the scope of the Act.[16] The burden of proof is generally on the party seeking recognition of an enforceable judgment, and this is supported by the case law.[17] In October 2004, the Drafting Committee ultimately agreed with the case law and concluded that the party seeking recognition of a foreign judgment shall bear the burden of proof.[18]

In Section 4 of the Act, a revision proposes clarifications to the discretionary circumstances in which a court need not recognize a foreign judgment. The amendment to the

Aug. 22, 2005). This review is based on the approved text, as well as the commentary to a July 2005 draft prepared in advance of the July meeting. *See* Meeting Draft of Uniform Foreign-Country Money Judgments Recognition Act (200_), available at: http://www.law.upenn.edu/bll/ulc/ufmjra/2005annmtgdraft.htm [hereinafter July 2005 Draft Revisions].

8 *See* July 2005 Draft Revisions, *supra* note 7.

9 *See* http://nccusl.org/Update/CommitteeSearchResults.aspx?committee=92.

10 *See* http://nccusl.org/Update/Annual_Meeting_2005/AnnMtg05_Drafts.htm.

11 UFCMJRA 2005, *supra* note 7.

12 July, 2005 Draft Revisions, *supra* note 7, at § 2 (Comment 1).

13 *Id.* at § 2 (Comment 4).

14 *Id.* at § 2 (Comment 3).

15 *Id.*

16 *Id.* at § 3 (Comment 6).

17 *Id.*

18 *See* UFCMJRA 2005, *supra* note 7, at § 3.

1962 Act is consistent with the courts' interpretation of what type of "fraud" is required for a court to deny recognition. Section 4 (c)(2) indicates "fraud that deprived the losing party of an adequate opportunity to present its case," and the commentary accompanying the Act clarifies that extrinsic (as opposed to intrinsic) fraudulent conduct is what is covered.[19] Section 4 (c)(3) also provides grounds for denying recognition if the "cause of action" is "repugnant to public policy."[20] The revision and commentary indicates that the scope of this public policy exception clause pertains to the cause of action and the judgment itself, and also notes that the "public policy" in question may either be that of the State "or of the United States."[21] Finally, in Section 4 (c)(7), the Act creates a new provision – apparently inspired by Section 5(a)(ii) of the ALI Project[22] – stating that a court may deny recognition if the foreign judgment was rendered "in circumstances that raise substantial doubt about the integrity of the rendering court."[23]

With the registration procedure set forth in the Uniform Enforcement of Foreign Judgments Act[24] and adopted in most states, there is little difficulty in enforcing foreign judgments in other U.S. states once they have been recognized by a U.S. court. However, several issues remain regarding the specific procedures for recognizing a foreign country judgment, as the current Act does not provide clear procedural directions in these areas. Thus, courts have been divided as to whether recognition of a foreign judgment under the Enforcement Act could only occur after the foreign judgment is recognized in a separate proceeding. Other courts have ruled that its registration procedure can be utilized without distinction as to whether the foreign country judgment is entitled to recognition under the Enforcement Act. Ultimately, the Draft Revision did not create any new procedure for recognition, but rather left procedural requirements to the states.

A final and quite important issue that remains to be settled by the revisionists is whether the amended Act should contain a reciprocity requirement, either as a mandatory or discretionary ground for denying judgment recognition. While the current draft revision of the Uniform Foreign-Country Money Judgments Recognition Act does not include a reciprocity requirement, it is noteworthy that the collateral ALI project – and, arguably more broadly proscribed proposal[25] – does include such a provision.[26]

[19] July 2005 Draft Revisions, *supra* note 7, at § 4 (Comment 7).

[20] *Id.* at § 4 (c)(3).

[21] *Id.* at § 4 (Comment 8).

[22] ALI Proposed Final Draft, *supra* Part Three, I, note 7 at §7.

[23] UFCMJRA 2005, *supra* note 7, at § 4 (c)(7).

[24] Uniform Enforcement of Foreign Judgments Act (1964). For discussion about how this Act operates with respect to inbound foreign judgments (i.e., those foreign judgments sought to be enforced in the U.S.), *see supra* Part One.

[25] *See supra* Part Three, III, notes 1–46 and accompanying text.

[26] *See* ALI Proposed Final Draft, *supra* Part Three, I, note 7, at § 7.

## V. INTERNATIONAL TRADE FLEXIBILITY AND ENFORCING FOREIGN JUDGMENTS

The United States has employed bilateral and multilateral trade agreements to enlarge the scope and liberalize the rules affecting its trading markets. In recent years, it has signed such free trade agreements with Canada and Mexico,[1] Israel,[2] Bahrain,[3] Jordan,[4] Chile,[5] Singapore,[6] Morocco,[7] Australia,[8] and Central America (the countries of Guatemala, El Salvador, Honduras, Nicaragua, Costa Rica, Panama, and the Dominican Republic).[9] The United States is negotiating free trade agreements with New Zealand,[10] Thailand, the United Arab Emirates, with the five member countries of the Southern African Customs Union (SACU) – Botswana, Lesotho, Namibia, South Africa, and Swaziland[11] – Oman, Panama, Peru (trade promotion agreement), and a free trade agreement with the Andean countries of Colombia, Peru, Ecuador, and Bolivia.[12] Discussions have also commenced recently with Korea and Malaysia.[13] These agreements demonstrate U.S. acceptability of other countries' business cultures and suggest an acceptance of a variety of legal cultures for administering justice. Most of these agreements lack provisions for monetary judgment recognition and enforcement, and they do not state a means for resolving disagreements between private commercial parties engaged in transnational transactions.

However, at least one of the more recent bilateral trade agreements in which the United States has entered – with Australia – contains specific language regarding narrow areas of the recognition and enforcement of monetary judgments.[14] The Australian agreement states at Article 14:7 that a monetary judgment should be recognized and enforced, whether it is penal or revenue in nature or based on foreign public law.[15] The purpose of this provision is to recognize civil proceedings by each country's governmental agencies, such as the U.S. Securities and Exchange Commission and the Australian Securities and Investments

[1] *See* http://ustr.gov/Trade_Agreements/Regional/NAFTA/Section_Index.html.

[2] *See* http://ustr.gov/Trade_Agreements/Bilateral/Israel/Section_Index.html.

[3] *See* http://ustr.gov/Trade_Agreements/Bilateral/Bahrain_FTA/Section_Index.html.

[4] *See* http://ustr.gov/Trade_Agreements/Bilateral/Jordan/Section_Index.html.

[5] *See* http://ustr.gov/Trade_Agreements/Bilateral/Chile_FTA/Section_Index.html.

[6] *See* http://ustr.gov/Trade_Agreements/Bilateral/Singapore_FTA/Section_Index.html.

[7] *See* http://ustr.gov/Trade_Agreements/Bilateral/Morocco_FTA/Section_Index.html.

[8] *See* http://ustr.gov/Trade_Agreements/Bilateral/Australia_FTA/Section_Index.html.

[9] *See* http://ustr.gov/Trade_Agreements/Bilateral/CAFTA/Section_Index.html.

[10] *See* www.ustr.gov.

[11] *See* http://ustr.gov/Trade_Agreements/Bilateral/Southern_Africa_FTA/Background_Information_on_the_U.S.-SACU_FTA.html.

[12] *See* http://ustr.gov/Trade_Agreements/Bilateral/Andean_FTA/Section_Index.html.

[13] *See* http://ustr.gov/Trade_Agreements/Bilateral/Section_Index.html.

[14] *Id.*

[15] "When an agency listed in paragraph 1 obtains a civil monetary judgment from a judicial authority of a Party for the purpose of providing monetary restitution to consumers, investors, or customers who have suffered economic harm as a result of being deceived, defrauded, or misled, a judicial authority of the other Party generally should not disqualify such a monetary judgment from recognition or enforcement on the ground that it is penal or revenue in nature or based on other foreign public law, including where such judgment contains provisions for recovery of monies or other disposition in the event that restitution is impractical or for payment of expenses related to the collection or distribution of such a monetary judgment." Article 14:7, Paragraph 2. *See* http://ustr.gov/assets/Trade_Agreements/Bilateral/Australia_FTA/Final_Text/asset_upload_file148_5168.pdf.

Commission, in order to provide monetary restitution to consumers, investors, or customers who may be deceived, defrauded, or misled.[16]

Thus, including such foreign judgment recognition provisions in bilateral and regional trade agreements may be the most effective means of developing acceptability of U.S. judgments abroad and the best method of building consistency and uniformity of procedures in the U.S. Recalling that the ALI Project also recommended that the U.S. Secretary of State negotiate agreements with foreign countries for the reciprocal recognition and enforcement of judgments as a way to satisfy reciprocity concerns,[17] the use of trade agreements to achieve these goals may be the preferable strategy.

## VI. CONCLUSION

The trends in the legal area of recognition and enforcement of foreign judgments are reflected in the four recent developments described in this Part. Despite what was for many private law internationalists a great disappointment when the Hague Conference failed to negotiate an enforcement convention, there seems to be a new interest and focus in the United States to improve the operation of our very disparate, but functioning, system of enforcement of foreign judgments. The completion of the ALI project and the Uniform Law revision effort, coupled with new advances via trade agreements, signal that this legal area is ripe for review and adjustment, and that having a workable procedure in the United States is essential to being an active participant in the ever-growing globalization of business and the rule of law.

[16] "The Parties recognize the importance of civil proceedings by the FTC, U.S. Securities and Exchange Commission, U.S. Commodity Futures Trading Commission, Australian Securities and Investments Commission, and the ACCC to provide monetary restitution to consumers, investors, or customers who have suffered economic harm as a result of being deceived, defrauded, or misled. The Parties further recognize the importance of facilitating cross-border recognition and enforcement of monetary judgments obtained for such purposes." Article 14:7, Paragraph 1. *See* http://ustr.gov/assets/Trade_Agreements/Bilateral/Australia_FTA/Final_Text/asset_upload_file148_5168.pdf.

[17] Section 7(e) states: "The Secretary of State is authorized to negotiate agreements with foreign states or groups of states setting forth reciprocal practices concerning recognition and enforcement of judgments rendered in the United States. The existence of such an agreement between a foreign state or group of foreign states and the United States establishes that the requirement of reciprocity has been met as to judgments covered by the agreement." *See* Final Draft, *supra* note 55, at §7 (e).

# Bibliography

## A. HAGUE CONVENTION

### 1. Background

Matthew H. Adler, *If We Build It, Will They Come? The Need for a Multilateral Convention on the Recognition and Enforcement of Civil Monetary Judgments*, 26 LAW & POL'Y INT'L BUS. 79 (1989).

Paul R. Beaumont, *A United Kingdom Perspective on the Proposed Hague Judgments Convention*, 24 BROOKLYN J. INT'L L. 75, 100 (1998).

Christophe Bernasconi, *Provisional Version of the New Practical Handbook on the Operation of the 1965 Hague Service Convention*. July, 2003. Available at: http://hcch.e-vision.nl/upload/wop/lse_pd01e.pdf (last visited Aug. 15, 2005).

Richard Birke & Louise Ellen Teitz, *American Law in a Time of Global Interdependence: U.S. National Reports to the 26th International Congress of Comparative Law: Section II, U.S. Mediation in 2001: The Path that Brought America to Uniform Laws and Mediation in Cyberspace*. 50 AM. J. COMP. L. 181 (Fall 2002).

Carol S. Bruch, *The 1989 Inter-American Convention on Support Obligations*, 40 AM. J. COMP. L. 817 (1992).

GARY B. BORN, INTERNATIONAL CIVIL LITIGATION IN UNITED STATES COURTS 298 (3d ed., Kluwer Law Int'l., 1996).

H. Patrick Glenn, *Foreign Judgments, the Common Law and the Constitution: De Savoye v. Morguard Investments Ltd*, 37 MCGILL L.J. 537 (1992).

Hague Conference on Private International Law, Recognition and Enforcement of Foreign Judgments, Prel. Docs. Nos. 2–6 (Dec. 1995–Aug. 1996).

Hague Conference on Private International Law, Conclusions of the Special Commission of May 2000 on General Affairs and Policy of the Conference, Prel. Doc. No. 10 (June 2000).

Internet and Federal Courts: Issues and Obstacles: Hearing before the Subcomm. on Courts and Intellectual Property of the Comm. on the Judiciary of the House of Representatives, 106th Cong. 2 (2000) (witness testimony of Jeffrey Kovar, Assistant Legal Advisor for Private International Law, U.S. Department of State), at 22.

Fredriech K. Juenger, *A Shoe Unfit for Globetrotting, IV. Impediments to International Accommodation*, 28 U.C. Davis L. Rev. 1027, 1050 (1995).

Kurt Lipstein, *One Hundred Years of the Hague Conference on Private International Law*, 42 Int'l Comp. L.Q. 554 (1993).

Katherine Lynch, The Forces of Economic Globalization: Challenges to the Regime of International Commercial Arbitration (The Hague: Kluwer Law Int'l., 2003).

Harold G. Maier, *A Hague Conference Judgments Convention and United States Courts: A Problem and a Possibility*, 61 Alb. L. Rev. 1207 (1998).

Peter Nygh, *Arthur's Baby: The Hague Negotiations for a World-Wide Judgments Convention* in Law and Justice in a Multistate World: Essays in Honor of Arthur T. von Mehren 151 (J. Nafziger & S. Symeonides, eds., 2002, Transnational Publishers, Inc,).

Gonzalo Parra-Aranguren, *The Centenary of the Hague Conference on Private International Law* in Etudes de Droit International en L'Honneur de Pierre Lalive (Christian Dominice, Robert Patry, & Claude Reymond eds., 1993).

Peter H. Pfund, *International Unification of Private Law: A Report on United States Participation, 1985–1986*, 20 Int'l Law. 623 (1986).

Peter H. Pfund, *The Hague Conference Celebrates Its 100th Anniversary*, 28 *Tex.* Int'l L.J. 531 (1993).

Peter H. Pfund, *United States Participation in International Unification of Private Law*, 19 Int'l Law. 505 (1985).

W. Reese & V. Johnson, *The Scope of the Full Faith and Credit to Judgments*, 49 Colum. L. Rev. 153, 161 (1949) (quoting *Sherrer v. Sherrer*, 334 U.S. 343, 355 (1948)).

Andrea Schultz, Reflection Paper to Assist in Preparation of a Convention on Jurisdiction and Recognition and Enforcement of Foreign Judgments in Civil and Commercial Matters, Prel. Doc. No. 19, p. 6 (Aug. 2002), Hague Conference on Private International Law, available at: http://www.hcch.net/upload/wop/jdgm_pdlge.pdf (last accessed Mar. 22, 2006) .

U. Schneider, *The Uniform Rules for International Credit Transfers Under the UNCITRAL Model Law* in Legal Issues in International Credit Transfers 451 (W. Hadding & U. Schneider eds., Berlin, 1993).

Edward F. Sherman, *American Class Actions: Significant Features and Developing Alternatives in Foreign Legal Systems*, 215 F.R.D.130 (2003).

*Survey Regarding Business Practices on Jurisdictional Issues*, Int'l Chamber of Commerce (Mar. 2003).

*Symposium: New Directions in Comparative Law*, 46 Am. J. Comp. L. 597 (1998).

*Symposium: New Approaches to Comparative Law*, 1997 Utah L. Rev. 255 (1997).

Farrow, Trevor C. W., *Globalization, International Human Rights, and Civil Procedure*, 41 Alberta L. Rev. 671 (Dec. 2003).

U.S. Department of State Authentication Office, available at: http://www.state.gov/m/a/auth/ (last visited Aug. 15, 2005).

Varady, J. Barcelo III, & A. von Mehren, International Commercial Arbitration (3d ed., Thomson-West 2006).

Arthur von Mehren & Donald T. Trautman, *Recognition of Foreign Adjudications: A Survey and a Suggested Approach*, 81 Harv. L. Rev. 1601, 1610 (1968).

Arthur von Mehren, *Recognition and Enforcement of Foreign Judgments: a New Approach for the Hague Conference?*, 57 Law & Contemp. Prob. 271 (1994).

G. Walter & S. Baumgartner, *General Report – The Recognition and Enforcement of Judgments Outside the Scope of the Brussels and Lugano Conventions* in 3 Civil Procedure in Europe – the Recognition and Enforcement of Judgments Outside the Scope of the Brussels and Lugano Conventions (G. Walter & S. Baumgartner eds. Klewer Law Int'l., 2000).

Russell J. Weintraub, *How Substantial Is Our Need for a Judgments Recognition Convention and What Should We Bargain Away to Get It?* 24 Brooklyn J. Int'l. 174 (1998).

Joachim Zekoll, *The Role and Status of American Law in the Hague Judgments Convention Project*, 61 Albany L. Rev. 1283, 1297–1306 (1998).

## 2. Relevant Statutes and Principles

Congress Approving the United States as a Member of the Hague Conference. 22 U.S.C. 269(g) (1988).

Restatement (Third) of the Foreign Relations Law of the United States 421, Reporters' Note 4 (1987).

Uncitral Model Law on International Credit Transfers, adopted by the United Nations Commission on International Law on May 15, 1992.

## 3. General

### *a. Relevant Case Law*

*Schlunk v. Volkswagenwerk A. G., 486 U.S. 694 (1988)* [Service of Process].

*Yahoo! Inc. v. La Ligue Contre Le Racisme et L'Antisemitisme*, 169 F. Supp. 2d 1181 (2001) [Comity].

*Delbruek v. Manufacturers Hanover Trust Company, 464 F. Supp. 989 (S.D.N.Y. 1979)*, at 993 [Choice of Law].

*Evra Corporation v. Swiss Bank Corporation, 522 F. Supp. 820 (N.D. Ill. 1981)*, at 826 [Choice of Law].

*Smith Kline & French Laboratories Ltd. v. Bloch*, [1983] 1 W.L.R. 730, 733 (Eng. C.A. 1982).

### *b. Drafts*

Draft on Exclusive Choice of Court Agreements, Work. Doc. No. 110 E, Revised, April 2004.

Draft on Exclusive Choice of Court Agreements, Work. Doc. No. 49 E, Revised, December 2003.

Final Draft Convention on Exclusive Choice of Court Agreements, Doc. No. 37 (June 30, 2005).

Masato Dogauchi and Trevor Hartley, Draft Report on Preliminary Draft Convention on Exclusive Choice of Court Agreements, Prel. Doc. No. 25 (March 2004), at 6–7.

### c. *Reports, Conventions, and Committee Actions*

Brussels Convention for most EC Member States, 348 final of July 14, 1999.

Collection of Hague Conference Conventions (1951–2003). HCCH Publications, 2003.

Comment, The United States and the Hague Conferences on Private International Law, 1 Am. J. Comp. L. 268 (1952).

Comments on IPR Aspects of Hague Convention on Jurisdiction and Foreign Judgment in Civil and Commercial Matters (Consumer Project on Technology, Washington, D.C.), Jan. 12, 2001, available at: http://www.cptech.org/ecom/hague/CPT-Hague-IPR-Jan12-USPTO.html (last accessed Aug. 15, 2005).

Comments to the USPTO on Hague Convention (Jurisdiction/Judgments) (A.I.P.L.A. Arlington, VA), Dec. 8, 2000, available at: http://www.aipla.org/Content/ContentGroups/Issues_and_Advocacy/Comments2/Hague_Convention/HagueConvention.pdf (last accessed Aug. 15, 2005).

Commission of the European Communities, Proposal for a Council Regulation (EC) on Jurisdiction and the Recognition and Enforcement of Judgments in Civil and Commercial Matters 19 (1999) (on file with author).

Communication of 9 August 2000 from the Permanent Bureau of the Hague Conference to the National Organs of the Member States, L.C. ON No. 44 (00), 2 (2000).

Convention of 15 November 1965 on the Service Abroad of Judicial and Extrajudicial Documents in Civil or Commercial Matters, available at: http://www.hcch.net/index_en.php?act=conventions.text&cid=17 (last accessed Aug. 15, 2005)

Convention of 25 October 1980 on the Civil Aspects of International Child Abduction, available at: http://www.hcch.net/index_en.php?act=conventions.text&cid=24 (last accessed Aug. 15, 2005).

Convention of 5 October 1961 Abolishing the Requirement of Legalization for Foreign Public Documents, available at: http://www.hcch.net/index_en.php?act=conventions.text&cid=41 (last accessed Aug. 15, 2005).

Convention on the Grant of European Patents, Oct. 5, 1973, 1065 U.N.T.S. 255, 13 I.L.M. 270 [hereinafter EPC].

Convention on the Recognition and Enforcement of Foreign Arbitral Awards [New York Convention], 9 U.S.C.A. §201, 21 U.S.T. 2517, 330 U.N.T.S. 38 (1959).

European Communities, Convention on Jurisdiction and the Enforcement of Judgments in Civil and Commercial Matters, 1972 O.J. (L299) 32, reprinted as amended in 29 I.L.M. 1413 (1990).

Explanatory Report on the 1965 Hague Choice of Court Convention; L. Welamson; 1965.

Explanatory Report on the 1965 Hague Service Convention; V. Taborda Ferreira; 1965.

Explanatory Report on the 1971 Hague Judgments Convention; C.N. Fragistas & G. Droz; 1969.

Hague Conference on Private International Law. Proceedings of the Special Commission with a Diplomatic Character of September–October 1999, at 461.

Hague Convention on the Law Applicable to Certain Rights in respect of Securities held with an Intermediary, 13 December 2002.

Hague Conference on Private International Law, available at: http://www.hcch.net/index_en.php?act=conventions.text&cid=98.

Inter-American Convention on Support Obligations, July 15, 1989, Art. 8, 29 I.L.M. 73 (1990).

International Criminal Court (ICC): Report of the Prosecutor of the International Criminal Court on Sudan (June 29, 2005).

International Law Commission, Draft Code of Crimes Against the Peace and Security of Mankind, 1996, art. 18, at http://www.un.org/law/ilc/texts/dcodefra.htm (last accessed Aug. 15, 2005).

International Tribunal for the Law of the Sea (ITLOS): Election of Seven Members (June 22, 2005).

Catherine Kessedjian, Synthesis of the Work of the Special Commission of March 1998 on International Jurisdiction and the Effects of Foreign Judgments in Civil and Commercial Matters, Hague Conf. Prelim. Doc. No. 9 (July 1998).

Catherine Kessedjian, Synthesis of the Work of the Special Commission of March 1998 on International Jurisdiction and the Effects of Foreign Judgments in Civil and Commercial Matters, Preliminary Document No. 9, at 40–44 (1998).

Letter from Edwin D. Williamson, Legal Adviser, U.S. Department of State, to Georges Droz, Secretary General, The Hague Conference on Private International Law (May 5, 1992) (Hague Conference document L.C. ON No. 15 (92)).

Letter from Jeffrey D. Kovar, Assistant Legal Adviser for Private International Law, U.S. Dept. of State, to J. H. A. van Loon, Secretary General, Hague Conference on Private International Law (Feb. 22, 2000).

Letter from Jeffrey D. Kovar, Assistant Legal Advisor for Private International Law, United States Department of State, to J. H. A. van Loon, Secretary General, Hague Conference on Private International Law (Feb. 22, 2000) (on file with author).

Letter from Jeffrey Kovar, Assistant Legal Advisor for Private International Law, U.S. Department of State, to Alasdair Wallace, Head of International and Common Law Services Division, England, (Sept. 10, 2000).

Note of Question of "Forum Non-Conveniens" in the Perspective of the Double Convention on Judicial Jurisdiction and the Enforcement of Decisions, Prel. Doc. No. 3 (1996), available at: http://www.state.gov/www/global/legal_affairs/forum.html (last accessed Aug. 15, 2005).

P. Nygh & F. Pocar, Report of the Special Commission, available at the Hague Conference Web site, http://www.hcch.net (last accessed Aug. 15, 2005).

Permanent Bureau, Conclusions of the Working Group Meeting on Enforcement of Judgments in the Hague Conference on Private International Law, Proceedings of the Seventeenth Session 10 to 29 May 29, 1993, Tome I, 17 H.C.P.I.L. Proc. 257 (1995).

Resolution adopted by the Seventeenth Session of the Hague Conference on Private International Law, 19 May 1993, available at: www.hcch.net/e/resolution.html.

Statute of the Hague Conference on Private International Law, July 1955.

Statute of The Hague Conference on Private International Law, available at: http://www.hcch.net/index_en.php?act=conventions.text&cid=29 (last accessed Aug. 15, 2005).

Summary of the Outcome of the Discussion in Commission II of the First Part of the Diplomatic Conference of 6–20 June 2001, available at: www.hcch.net, (2001 Draft).

Supplementary Protocol to The Hague Convention on the Recognition and Enforcement of Foreign Judgments in Civil and Commercial Matters, 1 February 1971.

Supplementary Protocol to the Hague Convention on the Recognition and Enforcement of Foreign Judgments in Civil and Commercial Matters, 1971 Hague Convention.

The Hague Conference on Private International Law. *See* http://www.hcch.net/index_en.php (last accessed Aug. 15, 2005).

The Hague Convention Concerning the International Administration of the Estates of Deceased Persons, 2 October 1973.

The Hague Convention Concerning the Recognition of the Legal Personality of Foreign Companies, Associations and Institutions, 1 June 1956.

The Hague Convention listing of Member States. *See* http://www.hcch.net/index_en.php?act=states.listing (last accessed Aug. 15, 2005).

The Hague Convention on International Access to Justice, 25 October 1980.

The Hague Convention on Jurisdiction, Applicable Law and Recognition of Decrees Relating to Adoptions, 15 November 1965.

The Hague Convention on Jurisdiction, Applicable Law, Recognition, Enforcement and Co-Operation in Respect of Parental Responsibility and Measures for the Protection of Children, 19 October 1996.

The Hague Convention on Protection of Children and Co-Operation in Respect of Intercountry Adoption, 29 May 1993.

The Hague Convention on the Choice of Court, 25 November 1965.

The Hague Convention on the International Protection of Adults, 13 January 2000.

The Hague Convention on the Jurisdiction of the Selected Forum in the Case of International Sales of Goods, 15 April 1958.

The Hague Convention on the Law Applicable to Agency, 14 March 1978.

The Hague Convention on the Law Applicable to Contracts for the International Sale of Goods, 22 December 1986.

The Hague Convention on the Law Applicable to International Sales of Goods, 15 June 1955.

The Hague Convention on the Law Applicable to Maintenance Obligations, 2 October 1973.

The Hague Convention on the Law Applicable to Trusts and on Their Recognition, 1 July 1985.

The Hague Convention on the Law Governing Transfer of Title in International Sales of Goods, 15 April 1958.

The Hague Convention on the Recognition and Enforcement of Decisions Relating to Maintenance Obligations, 2 October 1973.

The Hague Convention on the Recognition and Enforcement of Foreign Judgments in Civil and Commercial Matters, 1 February 1971.

The Hague Convention on the Service Abroad of Judicial and Extrajudicial Documents in Civil and Commercial Matters (Nov. 15, 1965).

The Hague Convention on the Service Abroad of Judicial and Extrajudicial Documents in Civil and Commercial Matters (Nov. 15, 1965), which were reviewed in 2003 by a Conference Special Committee.

The Hague Convention on the Taking of Evidence Abroad in Civil or Commercial Matters (Mar. 18, 1970).

The Hague Convention Relating to Civil Procedure, 1 March 1954.

The Hague Convention Relating to the Settlement of the Conflicts Between the Law of Nationality and the Law of Domicile, 15 June 1955.

U.S.-U.K. Convention on the Reciprocal Recognition and Enforcement of Judgments in Civil Matters. 16 I.L.M. 71 (1977), revised in 1979, reprinted in 8 N.C.J. INT'L. & COMM. REG. 322 (1983).

UNCC Governing Council: Report and Recommendations Made by the Panel of Commissioners Concerning the Fifth Installment of F4 Claims (June 30, 2005).

UNCITRAL: Adoption of Draft Convention on the Use of Electronic Communications in International Contracting (July 15, 2005).

United Nations Convention on the Recognition and Enforcement of Foreign Arbitral Awards, June 10, 1958, 21 U.S.T. 2517, T.I.A.S. No. 6997, 330 U.N.T.S. 38.

U.S. participation in the Hague Conference on Private International Law was authorized by Congress in 1963. H.R.J. Res. 778, 88th Cong., 77 Stat. 775 (1963), codified as amended at 22 U.S.C. § 269g (1988).

U.S. Participation in the Hague Conference and the Rome Institute: Hearing Before the Subcomm. on International Organizations and Movements of the House Comm. on Foreign Affairs, 88th Cong., 1st Sess. 732 (1963).

Arthur von Mehren, Minutes No. 3, Commission I, Seventeenth Session, Hague Conference on Private International Law, Meeting of 20 May 1993, at 1 (on file with the Cornell International Law Journal).

### 4. Specific Issues

#### *a. Choice of Law Concerns*

Ronald A. Brand, *Foreign Judgments in U.S. Courts* 2 CAN. INT'L LAW. 10 (1996).

M. J. Coffino & M. T. Wolff, *Choice of Law and Forum Clauses*, INT'L COMM. LIT. 37. (Dec. 1995–Jan. 1996).

W. Kennett, *Forum Non Conveniens in Europe*, 54 CAMBRIDGE L.J. 552 (1995).

Burckhardt Lober, *Forum Shopping, Forum non Conveniens oder Schlicht: Justizgewahrungsanspruch*, 6 IPRAX 283 (1986).

Andreas F. Lowenfeld, *Thoughts About a Multinational Judgments Convention: A Reaction to the von Mehren Report*, 57 LAW & CONTEMP. PROBS. 289 (1994).

Arthur R. Miller & David Crump, *Jurisdiction and Choice of Law in Multistate Class Actions After Phillips Petroleum Co. v. Shutts*, 96 YALE L.J. 1, 16 (1986).

M. Paul Mitchell, *Forum Selection Clauses and Fundamental Breach: Z.I. Pompey Industrie v. Ecu-Line N.V., The Canmar Fortune*, 36 CAN. BUS. L.J. 453 (2002).

ERNST RABEL, THE CONFLICT OF LAWS – A COMPARATIVE STUDY (4 vols., 1945–1954). Martin Stueckelberg, *Lis Pendens and Forum Non Conveniens at the Hague Conference*, 26 BROOKLYN J. INT'L L. 949 (2001).

Mathias Reimann, *Parochialism in American Conflicts Law*. 49 AM. J. COMP. L. 369 (Summer 2001).

Robertson, *The Federal Doctrine of Forum Non Conveniens: "An Object Lesson in Uncontrolled Discretion,"* 29 TEX. INT'L L.J. 353, 370, n.139 (1994).

Symeon C. Symeonides, Wendy Collins Perdue, & Arthur T. von Mehren, CASES AND MATERIALS ON CONFLICT OF LAWS: AMERICAN, COMPARATIVE, INTERNATIONAL 820–21 (2d ed., Thomson-West, 2003).

Arthur T. von Mehren & Donald T. Trautman, *Recognition of Foreign Adjudications: A Survey and a Suggested Approach*, 81 HARV. L. REV. 1601, 1606–07 (1968).

Arthur T. von Mehren, *Drafting A Convention on International Jurisdiction and the Effects of Foreign Judgments Acceptable Worldwide: Can the Hague Conference Project Succeed?* 49 AM. J. COMP. L. 191 (2001).

### *b. Intellectual Property Issues*

Ronald A. Brand, *Intellectual Property, Electronic Commerce and the Preliminary Hague Jurisdiction and Judgments Convention*, 62 U. PITT. L. REV. 581, 582 (2001).

Ronald A. Brand, *Intellectual Property, Electronic Commerce and the Preliminary Draft Hague Convention on Jurisdiction and Foreign Judgments in Civil and Commercial Matters*, 62 U. PITT. L. REV. 581, 587 (2001).

Jan J. Brinkhof, *Could the President of the District Court of the Hague Take Measures Concerning the Infringement of Foreign Patents?* 16 EUR. INTELL. PROP. REV. 360, 361 (1994).

Christopher D. DeCluitt, *International Patent Prosecution, Litigation and Enforcement*, 5 TULSA J. COMP. & INT'L L. 135 (1997).

Rochelle C. Dreyfuss, *Symposium: Intellectual Property Challenges in the Next Century – An Alert to the Intellectual Property Bar: The Hague Judgments Convention*, U. ILL. L. REV. 421, 427 (2001), citing Draft Hague Convention art. 17.

Benjamin C. Elacqua, *The Hague Runs into B2B: Why Restructuring the Hague Convention of Foreign Judgments in Civil and Commercial Matters to Deal With B2B Contracts Is Long Overdue*, 3 J. HIGH TECH. L. 93 (2004).

Dick C. J. A. Van Engelen, *Intellectual Property Issues in Cross-Border Transactions*, 5 TULSA J. COMP. & INT'L L. 135 (1997).

### c. Anti-Suit Injunctions

George A. Bermann, *The Use of Anti-Suit Injunctions in International Litigation*, 28 COLUM. J. TRANSNAT'L L. 589, 594–5 (1990).

Trevor C. Hartley, *Antisuit Injunctions and the Brussels Jurisdiction and Judgments Convention*, 49 INT'L & COMP. L.Q. 166 (2000).

Andreas F. Lowenfeld, *Forum Shopping, Antisuit Injunctions, Negative Declarations and Related Tools of International Litigation*, 91 AM. J. INT'L L. 314 (1997).

### d. Civil Rights and Freedoms Issues

Sarah Hudleston, Note, *Preserving Free Speech in a Global Courtroom: The Proposed Hague Convention and the First Amendment*, 10 MINN. J. GLOBAL TRADE 403, 427–28 (2001).

Karen E. Minehan, *The Public Policy Exception to the Enforcement of Foreign Judgments: Necessary or Nemesis?*, 18 LOY. L.A. INT'L & COMP. L.J. 795, 798 (1996).

Beth Van Shaak, *In Defense of Civil Redress: The Domestic Enforcement of Civil Rights Norms in the Context of the Proposed Hague Judgments Convention*, 42 HARV. INT'L L.J. 141 (2001).

### e. Recognition and Enforcement Issues

Mary Anne Alford, *The Effect of the Proposed U.S.-U.K. Reciprocal Recognition and Enforcement of Civil Judgments Treaty on Current Recognition Practices in the U.S*, 18 COLUM. J. TRANSNAT'L L. 119, 120 (1979).

Brandon Danford, *The Enforcement of Foreign Money Judgments in the United States and Europe: How Can We Achieve A Comprehensive Treaty?*, 23 REV. LITIG. 381, 403 (2004).

Genevieve Saumier, *The Recognition of Foreign Judgments in Quebec – The Mirror Crack'd* 81 CAN. BAR REV. 677 at 704–09, 713–15 (2002).

Giovanoli, Paiements et obligations Monetaires internationales, in COLLECTED COURSES OF THE HAGUE ACADEMY OF INTERNATIONAL LAW (1997).

H. Scott Fairley, *Enforcement of Foreign Judgments by Canadian Courts: A New Age of Uncertainty* 2 CAN. INT'L LAW. 1 (1996).

Johnathan A. Franklin & Roberta J. Morris, *International Jurisdiction and Enforcement of Judgments in the Era of Global Networks: Irrelevance of, Goals for, and Comments on the Current Proposals*, 77 CHI.-KENT L. REV. 1213, 1237–8 (2002).

Katherine R. Miller, *Playground Politics: Assessing the Wisdom of Writing a Reciprocity Requirement into U.S. International Recognition and Enforcement Law*, 35 GEORGETOWN J. INT'L L. 239, 257 (2004).

Arthur von Mehren, *Enforcing Judgments Abroad: Reflections on the Design of Recognition Conventions*, 24 BROOKLYN J. INT'L L. 17 (1998).

*f. Jurisdiction Issues*

Debra Lyn Bassett, *U.S. Class Actions Go Global: Transnational Class Actions and Personal Jurisdiction*, 72 FORDHAM L. REV. 41, 72–3, 91 (2003).

Patrick J. Borchers, *Comparing Personal Jurisdiction in the United States and European Community: Lessons for American Reform*, 40 AM. J. COMP. L. 121, 143–6 (1992).

Patrick J. Borchers, *Could a Treaty Trump Supreme Court Jurisdictional Doctrine? Judgments Conventions and Minimum Contacts*, 61 ALB. L. REV. 1161. (1998).

G. Born, *Forum Selection Clauses Anatomized*, INT'L COMM. LIT. 26 (May 1999).

Brand, *Due Process, Jurisdiction and a Hague Judgments Convention*, 60 U. PITT. L. REV. 661 (1999).

Stephan B. Burbank, *Interjurisdictional Preclusion, Full Faith and Credit and Federal Common Law: A General Approach*, 71 CORNELL L. REV. 733, 744 (1986).

Stephan B. Burbank, *Jurisdiction to Adjudicate: End of the Century or Beginning of the Millennium?*, 7 TUL. J. INT'L COMP. L. 111, AT 119 (1999).

Stephan B. Burbank, *The Reluctant Partner: Making Procedural Law for International Civil Litigation*, 57 LAW & CONTEMP. PROBS. 103, 131–5 (1994).

Catherine Kessedjian, International Jurisdiction and Foreign Judgments in Civil and Commercial Matters 12, Hague Conference on Private Int'l Law, Prel. Doc. No.7, 1997 (Kessedjian Report), at 88, cited in Russell J. Weintraub, *How Substantial Is Our Need For a Judgments Recognition Convention and What Should We Bargain Away to Get it?*, 24 BROOKLYN J. INT'L L. 167, 186 (1998).

Kristen Hudson Clayton, *The Draft Hague Convention on Jurisdiction and Enforcement of Judgments and the Internet – A New Jurisdictional Framework*, 36 J. MARSHALL L. REV. 223, 227–8 (2002).

Kevin M. Clermont, *Jurisdictional Salvation and the Hague Treaty*, 85 CORNELL L. REV. 89 (1999).

PAUL R. DUBINSKY, THE REACH OF DOING BUSINESS JURISDICTION AND TRANSACTING BUSINESS JURISDICTION OVER NON-U.S. INDIVIDUALS AND ENTITIES (New York Law School, March 1998), available at: http://www.state.gov/www/global/legal_affairs/dubinsky.html.

Eric B. Fastiff, *The Proposed Hague Convention on the Recognition and Enforcement of Civil and Commercial Judgments: A Solution to Butch Reynold's Jurisdiction and Enforcement Problems*, 28 CORNELL INT'L L.J. 469, 470 (1995).

J. J. Fawcett, *General Report*, in DECLINING JURISDICTION IN PRIVATE INTERNATIONAL LAW 10 (J. J. Fawcett ed., Oxford University Press, New York, 1995).

Trevor C. Hartley, *Introduction to the Brussels Jurisdiction and Judgments Convention*, in 1994/vol. v COLLECTED COURSES OF THE ACADEMY OF EUROPEAN LAW, BOOK 1, 229 (Aspen Publishers, 1996).

P. KAYE, CIVIL JURISDICTION AND THE ENFORCEMENT OF FOREIGN JUDGMENTS (1987).

William E. O'Brian, *The Hague Convention on Jurisdiction and Judgments: The Way Forward*, 66 MOD. L. REV. 491 (2003).

Kenneth C. Randall, *Universal Jurisdiction Under International Law*, 66 TEX. L. REV. 785, 789 (1988).

Linda J. Silberman, *Can the Hague Project Be Saved? A Perspective from the United States*, in A GLOBAL LAW OF JURISDICTION AND JUDGMENTS: LESSONS FROM THE HAGUE 159, 182 (John J. Barcelo III & Kevin M. Clermont eds., The Hague/New York: Klewer Law Int'l., 2002).

William H. Theis, *Admiralty Proceedings and the Proposed Hague Convention on Jurisdiction and Judgments*, 32 J. MARSHALL L. & COM. 59, 61–2 (2001).

Peter D. Trooboff, *Proposed Hague Conference General Convention on Jurisdiction and the Recognition and Enforcement of Judgments – Some Thoughts on Finding Solutions to Tough Issues*, in, E PLURIBUS UNUM – LIBER AMICORUM GEORGES A. L. DROZ (Barras et al., eds. 1996) 461, at 464–5.

M. Twitchell, *Why We Keep Doing Business with Doing-Business Jurisdiction*, 171 U. CHI. LEGAL F. 202 (2001).

Arthur von Mehren & Donald Trautman, *Jurisdiction to Adjudicate: A Suggested Analysis*, 79 HARV. L. REV. 1131 (1966).

Arthur von Mehren, *Drafting a Convention on International Jurisdiction and the Effects of Foreign Judgments Acceptable World-Wide: Can the Hague Convention Project Succeed?*, 49 AM. J. COMP. L. 191, 194 (2001).

Arthur von Mehren, *Recognition and Enforcement of Foreign Judgments – General Theory and the Role of Jurisdictional Requirements*, in ACADEMY OF INTERNATIONAL LAW, 167 RECEUIL DES COURS (1980-II) 9–112 (1981).

Horatia Muir Watt, *New Perspectives for Jurisdiction and Judgements in Europe: A Critical View* (on file with author).

James Weinstein, *The Early American Origins of Territoriality in Judicial Jurisdiction*, 37 ST. LOUIS U. L.J. 1 (1992).

## B. AMERICAN LAW INSTITUTE (ALI)

### 1. Background

Matthew H. Adler, *If We Build It, Will They Come? – The Need for a Multilateral Convention on the Recognition and Enforcement of Civil Monetary Judgments*, Law & Pol'y INT'L BUS., 79, 91 (Fall 1994).

Jennifer M. Anglim, *Crossroads in the Great Race: Moving Beyond the International Race to Judgment in Disputes Over Artwork and Other Chattels*, 45 HARV. INT'L L.J. 239 (2004).

American Law Institute Certificate of Incorporation, available at: http://www.ali.org, under "Charter, Bylaws and Rules."

American Law Institute (ALI). *See* http://ali.org (last accessed Aug. 15, 2005).

A. B. Conant, Jr., *The Act of State Doctrine and Its Exceptions: An Introduction*, 12 VAND. J. TRANSNAT'L L. 259, 259 (1979).

Debra Lyn Bassett, *U.S. Class Actions Go Global: Transnational Class Actions and Personal Jurisdiction*, 72 FORDHAM L. REV. 41, 72–3, 91 (2003).

Samuel P. Baumgartner, *Is Transnational Litigation Different?* 25 U. PA. J. INT'L ECON. L. 1297 (2004).

Kathryn L. Boyd, *Collective Rights Adjudication in U.S. Courts: Enforcing Human Rights at the Corporate Level*, 1999 B.Y.U L. Rev. 1139, 1208.

Stephen B. Burbank, *Jurisdictional Conflict and Jurisdictional Equilibration: Paths to a Via Media?* 26 HOUS. J. INT'L L. 385 (2004).

Anne Marie Burley, *Law Among Liberal States: Liberal Internationalities and the Act of State Doctrine*, 92 COLUM. L. REV. 1907, 1948 (1992).

P. B. Carter, *Transnational Recognition and Enforcement of Public Foreign Laws*, 48 CAMBRIDGE L.J. 417 (1989).

J. G. Castel, *Foreign Tax Claims and Judgments in Canadian Courts*, 42 CAN. B. REV. 277 (1964).

Brandon B. Danford, *The Enforcement of Foreign Money Judgments in the United States and Europe: How Can We Achieve a Comprehensive Treaty?* 23 REV. LITIG. 381 (2004).

Benjamin C. Elacqua, *The Hague Runs into B2B: Why Restructuring the Hague Convention of Foreign Judgments in Civil and Commercial Matters to Deal with B2B Contracts is Long Overdue*, 3 J. HIGH TECH. L. 93 (2004).

Ruth Bader Ginsburg, *Recognition and Enforcement of Foreign Civil Judgments: A Summary View of the Situation in the United States*, 4 INT'L LAW. 720 (1970).

Adolf Homburger, *Recognition and Enforcement of Foreign Judgments*, 18 AM. J. COMP. L. 367, 384–85 (1970).

INTERNATIONAL BAR ASSOCIATION, ENFORCEMENT OF FOREIGN JUDGMENTS WORLDWIDE (Charles Platto and William G. Horton eds., 2d ed., 1993).

Mark W. Janis, *The Recognition and Enforcement of Foreign Law: The Antelope's Penal Law Exception*, 20 INT'L LAW. 303 (1986).

Andreas F. Lowenfeld, *Public Law in the International Arena: Conflict of Laws, International Law, and Some Suggestions for Their Interaction*, 163 RECUEIL DES COURS 311, 322–6 (1979-II).

F. A. Mann, *The International Enforcement of Public Rights*, 19 N.Y.U. J. INT'L L. & POL. 603 (1987).

Raymond P. Marks, Note, *Alternative Theories for Establishing a Federal Common Law of Foreign Judgments in Commercial Cases: The Foreign Affairs Power and the Dormant Foreign Commerce Clause*, 16 VA. J. INT'L L. 635, 642 (1976).

Philip J. McConnaughay, *Reviving the "Public Law Taboo" in International Conflict of Laws*, 35 STAN. J. INT'L L. 255, 283 (1999).

Antonio F. Perez, *The International Recognition of Judgments: The Debate Between Private and Public Law Solutions*, 19 BERKELEY J. INT'L L. 44, 44 (2001).

Willis L. Reese, *The Status in This Country of Judgments Rendered Abroad*, 50 COLO. LAW. 783, 790–93 (1950).

Dr. George J. Roman, Recognition and Enforcement of Foreign Judgments in Various Foreign Countries, 36 (Washington, D.C.: Law Library of Congress, 1984).

Linda J. Silberman, *The Impact of Jurisdictional Rules and Recognition Practice on International Business Transactions: The U.S. Regime*, 26 Hous. J. Int'l L. 327 (2004).

Arthur T. von Mehren & Donald T. Trautman, *Recognition of Foreign Adjudications: A Survey and a Suggested Approach*, 81 Harv. L. Rev. 1601, 1670 (1968).

Jay Lawrence Westbrook, *Choice of Avoidance Law in Global Insolvencies*, 17 Brooklyn J. Int'l L. 499, 520 (1991).

## 2. Relevant Statutes and Principles

Full Faith and Credit Clause of the Constitution and the implementing statute, 28 U.S.C. § 1738.

U.S. Arbitration Act, 9 U.S.C. §§ 201–08, ch. 2, implementing the United Nations Convention on the Recognition and Enforcement of Foreign Arbitral Awards (the New York Convention).

Fla. Stat. Ann. § 55.605(2)(g).

N.H. Rev. Stat. Ann. § 524:11.

Restatement (Third), The Foreign Relations Law of the United States § 481, Comment c.

Restatement (Third), The Foreign Relations Law of the United States §§ 402, 403, 415, 416.

Restatement (Third), The Foreign Relations Law of the United States § 482 (1987).

Unif. Foreign Money-Judgments Recognition Act 2, U.L.A. 3 (1962).

Unif. Foreign Money-Judgments Recognition Act, 13 (pt. 2) U.L.A. 43 (2002).

EU Regulation on Jurisdiction and the Recognition and Enforcement of Judgments, Council Reg. 44/2001, OJ L 12/1 (2000) Art. 34(1).

## 3. General

### *a. Enforcement*

A. R. Albrecht, *The Enforcement of Taxation Under International Law*, 1953 Brit. Y.B. Int'l L. 454.

Hamid G. Gharavi, The International Effectiveness of the Annulment of an Arbitral Award (Kluwer Law Int'l., 2002).

William J. Kovatch, Jr., *Recognizing Foreign Tax Judgments: An Argument for the Revocation of the Revenue Rule*, 22 Hous. J. Int'l L. 265 (2000).

L. Silberman & A. Lowenfeld, A *Different Challenge for the ALI: Herein of Foreign Country Judgments, an International Treaty, and an American Statute*, 75 Ind. L.J. 635 (2000).

Andreas F. Lowenfeld & Linda J. Silberman, *U.S. of America*, in Enforcement of Foreign Judgments Worldwide 123 (Charles Platto & William G. Horton eds., 2nd ed., Graham & Trotman, London; 1993).

Mark D. Rosen, *Exporting the Constitution: The Grave Misconception Concerning "Un-American" Foreign Judgments*, 53 Emory L.J. (2004).

Eugene F. Scoles, et al., Conflict of Laws 24.45, at 1211 n.12 (3d ed., Thomsons-West St. Paul: 2000).

Linda J. Silberman & Andreas F. Lowenfeld, *A Different Challenge for the ALI: Herein of Foreign Country Judgments, an International Treaty, and an American* Statute, 75 Ind. L.J. 635, 635 (2000).

Barbara A. Silver, *Modernizing the Revenue Rule: The Enforcement of Foreign Tax Judgments,* 22 Ga. J. Int'l & Comp. L. 609 (1992).

Felix D. Strebel, *The Enforcement of Foreign Judgments and Foreign Public Law,* 21 Loy. L.A. Int'l & Comp. L. Rev. 55, 55 (1999).

### *b. Drafts*

American Law Institute, Recognition and Enforcement of Foreign Judgments: Analysis and Proposed Federal Statute. ALI Proposed Final Draft, April 11, 2005.

American Law Institute, Reporter's Memorandum in 2002 ALI Draft.

American Law Institute, Transnational Rules of Civil Procedure (Preliminary Draft No. 2, March 17, 2000).

American Law Institute /UNIDROIT, Principles and Rules of Transnational Civil Procedure, Proposed Final Draft (2004).

Comment in American Law Institute, International Jurisdiction and Judgments Project at 31 (Tentative Draft No. 2, April 14, 2004).

Foreword, American Law Institute, International Jurisdiction and Judgments Project, at xi (Discussion Draft, Mar. 29, 2002).

K. King Burnett, Memorandum in Support of the Motion by Guy Miller Struve, et al, Concerning Proposed Federal Statute on Recognition and Enforcement of Foreign Country Judgments, submitted to the Executive Office of the American Law Institute at the Eighty-First Annual Meeting on May 17, 18, and 19, 2004.

### *c. Reports, Hearings, and Committee Actions*

Assn. of the Bar, City of N.Y., Committee on Foreign and Comparative Law, Survey on Foreign Recognition of U.S. Money Judgments (July 2001).

Effect of the Japanese Patent System on American Business: Hearing Before the Subcomm. on Foreign Commerce and Tourism of the Senate Comm. on Commerce, Science and Transportation, $100^{th}$ Cong., 2d Sess. 39 (1988).

Eric M. Freedman, Memorandum to ALI Membership and Council, Re: International Jurisdiction and Judgments Project Public Policy Exception – First Amendment, May 17, 2004.

Richard W. Hulbert, Statement in Support of Motion to Delete the Requirement of Reciprocity, submitted to the Executive Office of the American Law Institute at the Eighty-First Annual Meeting on May 17, 18, and 19, 2004.

International Law Association, Report of International Committee on Transnational Recognition and Enforcement of Foreign Public Laws, in Report of the Sixty-Third Conference 719 (1988).

Catherine Kessedjian, *Remarks, Proceedings of the 76th Annual Meeting of the American Law Institute*, 76 A.L.I. PROC. 465, at 457 (1999).

Andreas F. Lowenfeld, *Remarks, Proceedings of the 79th Annual Meeting of the American Law Institute*, 79 A.L.I. PROC. 329 (2002).

United Nations Convention 53 on the Recognition and Enforcement of Foreign Arbitral Awards (the New York Convention), Article V(2)(b).

Gerhard Walter & Samuel P. Baumgartner, CIVIL PROCEDURE IN EUROPE – THE RECOGNITION AND ENFORCEMENT OF FOREIGN JUDGMENTS OUTSIDE THE SCOPE OF THE BRUSSELS AND LUGANO CONVENTIONS, 1–45 (G. Walter & S. Baumgartner, eds., Kluwer Law Int'l, 2000).

## 4. Specific Issues

### *a. The Public Policy Exception and the First Amendment*

Derek Devgun, *United States Enforcement of English Defamation Judgments: Exporting the First Amendment?*, 23 ANGLO-AM. L. REV. 195, 203 (1994).

Eric P. Enson, *Comment, A Roadblock on the Detour Around the First Amendment: Is the Enforcement of English Libel Judgments in the United States Unconstitutional?*, 21 LOY. L.A. INT'L & COMP. L. REV. 159, 160 (1999).

Jeremy Maltby, Note, *Juggling Comity and Self-Government: The Enforcement of Foreign Libel Judgments in U.S. Courts*, 94 Colum. L. Rev. 1978, 1995–6 (1994).

Craig A. Stern, *Foreign Judgments and the Freedom of Speech: Look Who's Talking*, 60 BROOKLYN L. REV. 999, 1033–34 (1994).

Kyu Ho Youm, *Suing American Media in Foreign Courts: Doing an End-Run Around U.S. Libel Law?*, 16 HASTINGS COMM. & ENT. L.J. 235, 256–62 (1994).

### *b. Intellectual Property Law*

Brian P. Biddinger, Note: *Limiting the Business Method Patents: A Comparative and Proposed Alignment of European, Japanese, and United States Patent Law*, 69 FORDHAM L. REV. 2523, 2543 (2001).

Curtis A. Bradley, *Extraterritorial Application of U.S. Intellectual Property Law – Principal Paper: Territorial Intellectual Property Rights in an Age of Globalism*, 37 VA. J. INT'L L. 505 (1997).

Kevin Cuenot, *Perilous Potholes in the Path Toward Patent Law Harmonization*, 11 J. LAW. & PUB. POL'Y 101 (1999).

Christopher D. DeCluitt, *International Patent Prosecution, Litigation and Enforcement*, 5 TULSA J. COMP. & INT'L L. 135 (1997).

Rochelle C. Dreyfuss & Jane C. Ginsburg, A Standalone Treaty on Jurisdiction and Recognition of Judgments in Intellectual Property Matters, presented at Chicago-Kent Symposium on Constructing International Intellectual Property Law: The Role of National Courts, October 19, 2001 [hereinafter Draft IP Treaty], available at: http://www.kentlaw.edu/depts/ipp/intl-courts/materials.html (last visited Aug. 15, 2005).

Martin Kalikow , *Multi-Country Patent Litigation: Strategy and Administration of Multi-Country Patent Litigation*, in INTERNATIONAL PATENT LITIGATION: A COUNTRY-BY-COUNTRY ANALYSIS (Michael N. Meller ed., BNA Books, 1994).

John R. Thomas, *Litigation Beyond the Technological Frontier: Comparative Approaches to Multinational Patent Enforcement*, 27 LAW & POL'Y INT'L BUS. 277, 277 (1996).

Dick C. J. A. Van Engelen, *Intellectual Property Issues in Cross-Border Transactions*, 5 TULSA J. COMP. & INT'L L. 135 (1997).

### c. Forum Non Conveniens and Forum Clauses

Paul Schiff Berman, *The Globalization of Jurisdiction*, 151 U. PA. L. REV. 311, 389 n.305, 519–21 (2002).

Martin Davies, *Time to Change the Federal Forum Non Conveniens Analysis*, 77 TUL. L. REV. 309, 381 (2002).

Michael M. Karayanni, *The Myth and Reality of a Controversy: "Public Factors" and the Forum Non Conveniens Doctrine*, 21 WIS. INT'L L.J. 327, 330, 379 (2003).

Courtland H. Peterson, *Choice of Law and Forum Clauses and the Recognition of Foreign Judgments Revisited Through Lloyd's of London Cases*, 60 LA. L. REV. 1259 (2000).

Courtland H. Peterson, *Limits on the Enforcement of Foreign Country Judgments and Choice of Law and Forum Clauses, Law and Justice in a Multistate World* (James A. R. Nafziger & Symeon C. Symeonides eds., Transnational, 2002).

Megan Waples, Note, *The Adequate Alternative Forum Analysis in Forum Non Conveniens: A Case for Reform*, 36 CONN. L. REV. 1475, 1484–5 (2004).

John R. Wilson, Note, *Coming to America to File Suit: Foreign Plaintiffs and the Forum Non Conveniens Barrier in Transnational Litigation*, 65 OHIO ST. L.J. 659, 684–90 (2004).

### d. Preclusion and Final Judgments

Robert C. Casad, *Intersystem Issue Preclusion and the Restatement (Second) of Judgments*, 66 CORNELL L. REV. 510, 513–14 (1981).

Robert C. Casad, *Issue Preclusion and Foreign Country Judgments Whose Law?*, 70 IOWA L. REV. 53, 79 (1984).

Professor Peterson, *Res Judicata and Foreign Country Judgments*, 24 OHIO ST. L.J. 291 (1963).

Hans Smit, *International Res Judicata and Collateral Estoppel in the United States*, 9 UCLA L. REV. 44 (1962).

Allan D. Vestal, *Preclusion/Res Judicata Variables: Adjudicating Bodies*, 54 GEO. L.J. 857, 869–73 (1966).

### e. Reciprocity

Katherine R. Miller, *Playground Politics: Assessiing the Wisdom of Writing a Reciprocity Requirement into U.S. International Recognition and Enforcement Law*, 35 GEO. J. INT'L L. 239 (2004).

#### *f. Concurrent or Parallel Proceedings*

Louise Ellen Teitz, *Developments in Parallel Proceedings: The Globalization of Procedural Responses*, 38 INT'L LAW. 303 (2004).

### 5. Relevant Case Law

*Sosa v. Alvarez-Machain*, 124 S. Ct. 2739, 2754, 2762 *(2004)* [Sources of Law].

*Semtek International, Inc. v. Lockheed Martin Corporation*, 531 U.S. 497 (2001) [Full Faith & Credit; *Res Judicata*].

*Missouri v. Holland*, *252 U.S. 416 (1920)*. [Supremacy Clause].

*The Antelope*, *23 U.S. (10 Wheat.)* 66, *123 (1825)* [Conflicts of Law].

*Matusevitch v. Telnikoff*, 159 F.3d 636 (D.C. 1998) [Public Policy].

*Baker Marine (Nigeria) Ltd. v. Chevron (Nigeria) Ltd.*, 191 F.3d 194 (2d Cir. 1999) [Enforcement of Arbitration Awards].

*Success Motivation Inst. of Japan, Ltd. v. Success Motivation Inst. Inc.*, 966 F.2d 1007, 1008 (5th Cir. 1992) [Choice of Law].

*Banque Libanaise Pour Le Commerce v. Khreich*, 915 F.2d 1000, 1003 (5th Cir. 1990) [Choice of Law].

*Zorgias v. SS Hellenic Star and Hellenic Lines Ltd.*, 487 F.2d 519, 519 (5th Cir. 1973) [Res Judicata].

*Spinozzi v. ITT Sheraton Corp.*, 174 F.3d 842 (7th Cir. 1999) [Choice of Law].

*Posner v. Essex Insurance Company, Ltd.*, 178 F.3d 1209, 1222 (11th Cir. 1999) [Comity Doctrine; International Abstention].

*Turner Entertainment Co. v. Degeto Films GmbH*, 25 F.3d 1512, 1519 (11th Cir. 1994) [Comity Doctrine].

*Yahoo! v. La Ligue Contre le Racisme et L'Antisemitisme*, 169 F. Supp. 2d 1181 (N.D. Cal. 2001) [Comity Doctrine].

*Films by Jove, Inc. v. Berov*, 250 F. Supp. 2d 158 (E.D.N.Y. 2003) [Comity Doctrine].

*S. C. Chimexim S. A. v. Velco Enterprises Ltd.*, 36 F. Supp. 2d 206, 212 (S.D.N.Y. 1999) [Comity Doctrine].

*Voreep v. Tarom Romanian Air Transport*, 1999 WL 311811 (S.D.N.Y. May 18, 1999) [Comity Doctrine; *Res Judicata*].

*Hilton v. Guyot*, 159 U.S. 113 (1894) [Comity Doctrine].

*Philips Electronics, N.V. v. New Hampshire Insurance Co.*, 692 N.E.2d 1268 (Ill. App. 1998) [Choice of Law].

*Manches & Co. v. Gilbey*, 646 N.E.2d 86 (Mass. 1995) [Currency of Award].

*Kam-Tech Systems Limited v. Yardeni*, 340 N.J. Super. 414, 774 A.2d 644 (2001) [Full Faith & Credit].

*Neporany v. Kir*, 5 A.D.2d 438 (N.Y. App. Div. 1958) [Comity Doctrine].

*Bachchan v. Indian Abroad Publications*, 154 Misc.2d 228, 585 N.Y.S.2d 661 (1992) [Due Process; Public Policy; Choice of Law].

*CIBC Mellon Trust Co. v. Mora Hotel*, 100 N.Y.2d 215, 792 N.E.2d 155 (N.Y. 2003) [Comity Doctrine].

*Watts v. Swiss Bank Corporation*, 27 N.Y.2d 270, 317 N.Y.S.2d 315, 265 N.E.2d 739 (1970) [Comity Doctrine; Res Judicata].

*Red Fox v. Hatttich*, 494 N.W.2d 638, 641 (S.D. 1993) [Comity Doctrine regarding Indian Tribes].

*Mori v. Mori*, 896 P.2d 1237, 1240 (Utah Ct. App. 1995) [Full Faith & Credit].

## C. UNIFORM STATE LAW

### 1. Background

Full Faith and Credit Clause, Art. IV, Section 1, The U.S. Constitution.

Interstate Family Support Act and the federal International Child Support Enforcement Act, 42 U.S.C. § 659a (1996).

Martindale-Hubbell Massachusetts Law Digest Civil Action & Procedure (1999).

Martindale-Hubbell North Carolina Law Digest Civil Actions & Procedures (1999).

Martindale-Hubbell Ohio Law Digest Civil Actions & Procedures (1999).

Restatement (Third) of the Foreign Relations Law of the United States § 481 (1986).

Restatement (Third) of the Foreign Relations Law of the United States, § 482(2)(d) (1986).

Restatement Third of the Foreign Relations Law of the United States § 483 (1986).

The National Conference of Commissioners on Uniform State Laws (NCCUSL). *See* http://nccusl.org (last visited Aug. 15, 2005).

The National Conference of Commissioners on Uniform State Laws (NCCUSL). Annual Meeting information, available at: http://nccusl.org/Update/Annual_Meeting_2005/AnnMtg05_Drafts.htm (last visited Aug. 15, 2005).

The National Conference of Commissioners on Uniform State Laws (NCCUSL). Drafting Committee update, available at: http://nccusl.org/Update/CommitteeSearchResults.aspx?committee=92 (last visited Aug. 15, 2005).

The National Conference of Commissioners on Uniform State Laws Legislative Fact Sheet, available at: http://www.nccusl.org/nccusl/DesktopDefault.aspx?tabindex=0&tabid=1

U.S. Arbitration Act, 9 U.S.C. §§ 201–08, ch. 2, implementing the United Nations Convention on the Recognition and Enforcement of Foreign Arbitral Awards.

U.S. Arbitration Act, 9 U.S.C. §§ 301–07, ch. 3, implementing the Inter-American Convention on International Commercial Arbitration.

### 2. Drafts

Comment to §4, Uniform Foreign Money-Judgment Recognition Act (1962).

Harvard Draft Convention on the International Responsibility of States for Injuries to Aliens, Art. 10(3), reprinted in R. R. Baxter & Louis B. Sohn, *Responsibility of States for Injuries to the Economic Interests of Aliens*, 55 AJIL 545, 553 (1961).

Meeting Draft of Uniform Foreign-Country Money Judgments Recognition Act (200_) (March, 2005). *See* http://www.law.upenn.edu/bll/ulc/ufmjra/2005annmtgdraft.htm (last visited Aug. 15, 2005).

Meeting Draft of Uniform Foreign-Country Money Judgments Recognition Act (200_) (July 22–29, 2005).

Reporters' Notes in Redline Draft of Uniform Foreign-Country Money Judgments Recognition Act (200_) (March, 2005).

Reporters' Notes in Redline Draft of Uniform Foreign-Country Money Judgments Recognition Act (200_) (July 22–29, 2005).

Uniform Enforcement of Foreign Judgments Act, § 1 (1964).

### 3. Recognition Issues

Ronald A. Brand, *Enforcement of Foreign Money-Judgments in the United States: In Search of Uniformity and International Acceptance*, 67 NOTRE DAME L. REV. 253, 275 (1991).

Carl B. *Recognition of Texas Judgments in Courts of Foreign Nations – and Vice Versa*, 13 HOUS. L. REV. 680 (1976).

Barbara Kulzer, *Recognition of Foreign Country Judgment in New York: The Uniform Foreign Money-Judgments Recognition Act*, 18 BUFFALO L. REV. 1, 32 (1968).

Leo Panitch, *Rethinking the Role of the State*, in GLOBALIZATION: CRITICAL REFLECTIONS 83, 96–7 (James H. Mittelman ed., Lynne Reinner-Publishers, 1996).

Eugene F. Scoles & Laila E. Aarnas, *The Recognition and Enforcement of Foreign Nation Judgments: California, Oregon, and Washington*, 57 OR. L. REV. 377 (1978).

Arthur T. von Mehren & Michael E. Patterson, *Recognition and Enforcement of Foreign-Country Judgments in the United States*, 6 LAW & POL'Y INT'L BUS. 37 (1974).

Arthur T. von Mehren & Donald Trautman, *Recognition of Foreign Adjudications: A Survey and a Suggested Approach*, 81 HARV. L. REV. 1601 (1968).

Wanda Ellen Wakefield, *Annotation, Judgment of Court of Foreign Country as Entitled to Enforcement or Extraterritorial Effect in State Court*, 13 A.L.R. 4th 1109 (1998).

### 4. Choice of Law Concerns

Comment, Conflict of Laws – *Recognition of Judgments – Federal Courts Are to Apply State Laws on Recognition of Foreign Judgments*, 8 TEX. INT'L L.J. 247, 253 (1973).

Hart Ely, *Choice of Law and the State's Interest in Protecting its Own*, 23 WM. & MARY L. REV. 173 (1981).

Professor Peterson, *Foreign Country Judgments and the Second Restatement of Conflict of Laws*, 72 COLUM. L. REV. 220 (1972).

Eugene F. Scoles, *Interstate and International Distinctions in the Conflict of Laws in the United States*, 54 CALIF. L. REV. 1599, 1605–07 (1966).

Donald P. Troutman, *Toward Federalizing Choice of Law*, 70 TEX. L. REV. 1715, 1736 n.95 (1992).

### 5. Relevant Case Law

*Society of Lloyd's v. Ashenden*, 233 F.3d 473 (7th Cir. 2000) [Due Process].

*Society of Lloyd's v. Turner*, 303 F.3d 325 (5th Cir. 2002) [Public Policy].

*Southwest Livestock & Trucking Co., Inc. v. Ramon*, 169 F.3d 317 (5th Cir. 1999) [Public Policy].

*Chase Manhattan Bank, N.A. v. Hoffman*, 665 F. Supp 73 (D. Mass. 1987) [Choice of Law].

*Bridgeway Corp. v. Citibank*, 45 F. Supp. 2d 276, 285 (S.D.N.Y. 1999) [Due Process].

*S. C. Chimexim S. A. v. Velco Enterprises, Ltd.*, 36 F. Supp. 2d 206, 212 (S.D.N.Y. 1999) [Comity Doctrine].

*Eagle Leasing v. Amandus*, 476 N.W.2d 35 (S.Ct. Iowa 1991) [Personal Jurisdiction].

Wolff v. Wolff, 389 A.2d 413 (My. App. 1978) [Personal Jurisdiction].

*Day v. Montana Dept. of Social & Rehab. Servs.*, 900 P.2d 296 (Mont. 1995) [Full Faith & Credit for Child Support Orders].

*Kam-Tech Systems, Ltd. v. Yardeni*, 74 A.2d 644, 649 (N.J. App. 2001) [Full Faith & Credit].

*CIBC Mellon Trust Co. v. Mora Hotel Corp., N.V.*, 743 N.Y.S.2d 408, 415 (N.Y. App. 2002) [Comity Doctrine].

*Bachchan v. India Abroad Publications, Inc.*, 585 N.Y.S.2d 661 (N.Y. Sup. Ct. 1992) [Due Process, Public Policy; Choice of Law].

*Johnston v. Compagnie Generale Transatlantique*, 242 N.Y. 381 (1926) [Reciprocity – Full Faith and Credit].

*Fredericks v. Eide-Kirschmann Ford*, 462 N.W.2d 164, 170 (N.D. 1990) [Comity on Tribal Court Judgment].

*Hunt v. BP Exploration Co. (Libya) Ltd.*, 492 F. Supp. 885, 901 (N.D. Tex. 1980) [*Res Judicata* & Collateral Estoppel].

*The Courage Co. LLC v. The ChemShare Corp.*, 93 S.W.3d 323, 331 (Tex. App. 2002) [Arbitration Contractual Provision].

*Mayekawa Mfg. Co. Ltd. v. Sasaki*, 888 P.2d 183, 189 (Wash. App. 1995) [Comity Doctrine].

## D. FREE TRADE AGREEMENTS

### 1. Background

Administration Works on Investment Position for Singapore FTA, *Inside U.S. Trade*, Dec. 15, 2000.

Chandler P. Anderson, *The Extent and Limitations of the Treaty-Making Power Under the Constitution*, 1 A.J.I.L. 636, 648 (1907).

Mark S. Bergmann, Bilateral Investment Protection Treaties: An Examination of the Evolution and Significance of the U.S. Prototype Treaty, 16 N.Y.U. J. INT'L L. & POL. 1 (1983).

Raj Bhala, *The Myth About Stare Decisis and International Trade Law*, 14 AM. U. INT'L L. REV. 845, 849 (1999).

Stewart C. Boyd, *Interest for the Late Payment of Money*, 1 ARB. INT'L 153 (1985).

David J. Branson & Richard E. Wallace, Jr., *Awarding Interest in International Commercial Arbitration: Establishing a Uniform Approach*, 28 VA. J. INT'L L. 919 (1988).

Paolo Cerina, *Interest as Damages in International Commercial Arbitration*, 4 AM. REV. INT'L ARB. 255 (1993).

Sungjoon Cho, *A Bridge Too Far: The Fall of the Fifth WTO Ministerial Conference in Cancun and the Future of Trade Constitution*, 7 J. INT'L ECON. L. 219 (2004).

Mark Clodfelter, *U.S. State Department Participation in International Economic Dispute Resolution*, 42 S. TEX. L. REV. 1273, 1283 (2001).

Compare Trade in Services and E-Commerce: Hearing Before the Subcommittee on Commerce, Trade and Consumer Protection of the House Energy and Commerce Comm., 108th Cong. 3 (2003).

Mark Friedman & Gaetan Verhoosel, *Arbitrating over BIT Claims; Under Bilateral Investment Treaties, More Investors Are Taking Action Against Foreign States*, 26 NAT'L L.J. 15, 17 (2003).

John Y. Gotanda, *Awarding Interest in International Arbitration*, 90 AM. J. INT'L L. 40 (1996).

Don Henry, Editorial, "Free-Trade Clause Would Be a Dangerous Weakening of the Law," *Sydney Morning Herald*, Oct. 27, 2003, at 2003 WL 66059983.

Robert E. Hudec, *Circumventing Democracy: The Political Morality of Trade Negotiations*, 25 *N.Y.U.J.* INT'L L. & POL. 311 (1993).

Martin Hunter & Volker Triebel, *Awarding Interest in International Arbitration – Some Observations Based on a Comparative Study of the Laws of England and Germany*, 6(1) J. INT'L ARB. 7 (1989).

John H. Jackson, The Effect of Treaties in Domestic Law in the United States, in THE JURISPRUDENCE OF GATT & THE WTO 297 (2000).

Kathleen Kunzer, Developing a Model Bilateral Investment Treaty, 15 *L. & POL'Y INT'L BUS.* 273 (1983).

Julian D. M. Lew, *Interest on Money Awards in International Arbitration*, in MAKING COMMERCIAL LAW: ESSAYS IN HONOUR OF ROY GOODE 543 (Ross Cranston ed., 1997).

F. A. MANN, FURTHER STUDIES IN INTERNATIONAL LAW 234, 238 (1990).

Pierre Mayer, *Mandatory Rules of Law in International Arbitration* 2 ARB. INT'L 274, 281 (1986).

Margaret L. Moses, *Vacatur or Non-enforcement of International Commercial Arbitration: A Dual System of Judicial Control* (unpublished manuscript, on file with author).

Permanent Court of Arbitration (PCA), available at: http://www.pca-cpa.org (last visited Aug. 15, 2005).

David Schneiderman, *Investment Rules and the New Constitutionalism*, 25 LAW & SOC. INQUIRY 757, 771 (2000).

Hans Smit, *Substance and Procedure in International Arbitration: The Development of a New Legal Order*, 65 TULANE L. REV. 1309, 1310–11 (1991).

M. SORNARAJAH, THE INTERNATIONAL LAW ON FOREIGN INVESTMENT 299 (1994).

USTR Information on U.S. Trade Agreements, available at http://ustr.gov/Trade_Agreements/Bilateral/Section_Index.html (last visited Aug. 15, 2005).

USTR Web site, available at http://www.ustr.gov (last visited Aug. 15, 2005).

Nathalie Voser, *Mandatory Rules of Law as a Limitation on the Law Applicable in International Commercial Arbitration*, 7 AM. REV. INT'L ARB. 319 (1997).

Laura L. Wright, *Trade Promotion Authority: Fast Track for the Twenty-First Century?* 12 WM. & MARY BILL RTS. J. 979 (2004).

Quincy Wright, *The United States and International Agreements*, 38 A.J.I.L. 341, 348, 355 (1944).

Robert B. Zoellick, "Our Credo: Free Trade and Competition," *Wall Street Journal* July 10, 2003.

## 2. Reports, Conventions, and Committee Actions

134 Cong. Rec. H6611–02 (daily ed. Aug. 9, 1988).

139 Cong. Rec. H9875–01 (daily ed. Nov. 17, 1993).

Article 1 of the Organization for Economic Cooperation and Development Draft Convention on the Protection of Foreign Property, 7 I.L.M. 117, 119 (1968).

Convention on the Recognition and Enforcement of Foreign Arbitral Awards, June 10, 1958, 21 U.S.T. 2517, 330 U.N.T.S. 3.

Convention on the Settlement of Investment Disputes Between States and Nationals of Other States, Mar. 18, 1965, 17 U.S.T. 1270, 575 U.N.T.S. 159.

Letter from Benjamin A. Gilman, Chairman, House Committee on International Relations, to Sir Leon Brittan, Vice President, The European Commission (Jan. 8, 1999) in Inside U.S. Trade (Jan. 22, 1999).

The Convention on the Settlement of Investment Disputes Between States and Nationals of Other States, opened for signature, 17 U.S.T. 1270, 575 U.N.T.S. 159 (Mar. 18, 1965).

The International Centre for Settlement of Investment Disputes also maintains documentation on the cases arbitrated under its auspices, at http://www.worldbank.org/icsid/ (last visited Aug. 15, 2005).

U.S. Bilateral Investment Treaties, available at: http://www.tcc.mac.doc.gov/cgi-bin/doit.cgi?219:64:d5c333fdc357d3df07e119f1bf7aa0a6f42c164ff5d2bf29e8e65dde9058144b:0:TOVR!-!Bilateral%20Investment%20Treaties!-!QuickLink!-!BILATERAL (last visited Aug. 15, 2005).

U.S. Dep't of State Advisory Comm. on International Economic Policy (ACIEP), Report Regarding the Draft Model Bilateral Investment Treaty 2–3 (Jan. 30, 2004), available at http://www.ciel.org/ (last visited Aug. 15, 2005).

U.S. Dep't of State Press Release on U.S. Bilateral Investment Treaty Program (July 1, 2003), available at http://www.state.gov/e/eb/rls/fs/22422.htm (last visited Aug. 15, 2005).

United Nations Centre on Transnational Corporations, Bilateral Investment Treaties, 41–4 (1988).

UN Commission on International Trade Law (UNCITRAL), available at http://www.uncitral.org (last visited Aug. 15, 2005).

Vienna Convention on the Law of Treaties, May 23, 1969, 1155 U.N.T.S. 331, reprinted in 8 I.L.M. 679 (1969).

### 3. Relevant Rules and Acts

American Arbitration Association (AAA) Rules, Art. 29(2).

Bipartisan Trade Promotion Authority Act, 19 U.S.C. § 3802(b)(3) (Supp. 2002).

Bipartisan Trade Promotion Authority Act of 2002. Compare 19 U.S.C.S. § 2903(b) (2004) with 19 U.S.C.S. § 3803 (2004).

Final Act Embodying the Results of the Uruguay Round of Multilateral Trade Negotiations, Apr. 15, 1994, Legal Instruments – Results of the Uruguay Round; 33 I.L.M. 1140 (1994).

General Agreement on Tariffs and Trade, Oct. 30, 1947, 61 Stat. A-11, T.I.A.S. No. 1700, 55 U.N.T.S. 187.

Hong Kong International Arbitration Centre Rules, Art. 33.

ICC Rules, Art. 17(1) (1998).

Int'l Centre for Settlement of Investment Disputes, ICSID Additional Facility Rules art. 53(3) (2003), available at: http://www.worldbank.org/icsid/facility/facility.htm (last visited Aug. 15, 2005).

Restatement (Third) of Foreign Relations Law § 712, cmt. g (1987).

Trade Act of 1974, Section 301, 19 U.S.C. §§ 2411–2420 (1994).

Senate Report on the Bipartisan Trade Promotion Act of 2002, Feb. 28, 2002, at 107 Cong., 2d Sess.

Statute of the International Court of Justice, June 26, 1945, Art. 38, 59 Stat. 1055, 1058.

Super 301 of the Omnibus Trade and Competitiveness Act of 1988, 19 U.S.C. § 2420 (A)(1)(a)-(b) (1994).

U.N. Commission on Int'l Trade Law, UNCITRAL Arbitration Rules, Art. 32(5) (1976), available at: http://www.jus.uio.no/lm/un.arbitration.rules.1976/32 (last visited Aug 15, 2005).

UNCITRAL Arbitration Rules, Art. 33; UNCITRAL Model Law, Art. 28; International Chamber of Commerce (ICC) Rules, Art. 13(5).

UNCITRAL Model Law (U.N. Doc A/40.17 Annex 1 as Adopted by the UN Commission on International Trade Law on June 21, 1985).

Understanding on Rules and Procedures Governing the Settlement of Disputes, April 15, 1994, Art. 17(6), Marrakesh Agreement Establishing the World Trade Organization, Annex 2, The Results of the Uruguay Round of Multilateral Trade Negotiations: The Legal Texts 404, 418 (1994), reprinted in 33 I.L.M. 1226, 1236 (1994).

United Nations Charter of Economic Rights and Duties of States, Art. 2, 14 I.L.M. 254 (1975).

### 4. U.S. Free Trade Agreements

#### *a.* NAFTA

Frederick M. Abbott, *NAFTA and the Legalization of World Politics: A Case Study*, in LEGALIZATION AND WORLD POLITICS 135, 149, 158 (Judith L. Goldstein et al., eds., Cambridge, MA, MIT Press, 2001).

Frederick M. Abbott, *Integration Without Institutions: The NAFTA Mutation of the EC Model and the Future of the GATT Regime*, 40 AM. J. COMP. L. 917 (1992).

Frederick M. Abbott, *The North American Free Trade Agreement and Its Implications for the European Union*, 4 TRANSNAT'L L. & CONTEMP. PROBS. 119 (1994).

Frederick M. Abbott, *The North American Integration Regime and Its Implications for the World Trading System*, in THE EU, THE WTO, AND THE NAFTA: TOWARDS A COMMON LAW OF INTERNATIONAL TRADE? 169, 170 (J. H. H. Weiler ed., 2000).

BRUCE ACKERMAN & DAVID GOLOVE, IS NAFTA CONSTITUTIONAL? (1995).

Edward Alden, "Canada Seeks Tighter NAFTA rules to Limit Compensation", *Fin. Times* (London), Jan. 22, 1999.

BARRY APPLETON, NAVIGATING NAFTA: A CONCISE USER'S GUIDE TO THE NORTH AMERICAN FREE TRADE AGREEMENT 169 (Carswell Legal Publications, 1994).

Stefan Baumgarten, "Canadian Group to Fight Methanex on NAFTA MTBE Spat," *Chem. News & Intelligence*, Feb. 4, 2004.

Vicki Been & Joel C. Beauvais, *The Global Fifth Amendment? NAFTA's Investment Protections and the Misguided Quest for an International "Regulatory Takings" Doctrine*, 78 N.Y.U. L. REV. 30, 88–100 (2003).

Charles N. Brower & Lee A. Steven, *Who Then Should Judge?: Developing the International Rule of Law Under NAFTA Chapter 11*, 2 CHI. J. INT'L L. 193 (2001).

*Canada Appeals NAFTA Chapter 11 Case, Arguing That Panel Exceeded Its Jurisdiction*, 18 INT'L TRADE REP. 273 (BNA, Feb. 15, 2001).

*Canada Seeks NAFTA Chapter 11, Improvements, Trade Minister Marchi Says*, 16 INT'L TRADE REP. 1634 (BNA, Oct. 13, 1999).

Canada-United States: Free-Trade Agreement, Jan. 2, 1988, 27 I.L.M. 281 (1988).

Canadian Department of Foreign Affairs and International Trade, available at: http://www.dfait-maeci.gc.ca/tna-nac/gov-en.asp (last accessed Aug. 15, 2005).

JAMES R. CANNON, JR., RESOLVING DISPUTES UNDER NAFTA CHAPTER 19 (Shepard's McGraw-Hill, 1994).

Michael J. Chrush, Note, *The North American Free Trade Agreement: Reasons for Passage and Requirements to Be a Foreign Legal Consultant in a NAFTA Country*, 3 I.L.S.A. J. INT'L COMP. L. 177, 178 (1996).

Dep't of External Affairs, "North American Free Trade Agreement: Canadian Statement on Implementation," *Canada Gazette*, Jan. 1, 1994.

William S. Dodge, *Case Report: Waste Management, Inc. v. Mexico*, 95 A.J.I.L. 186, 191–92 (2001).

John P. Fitzpatrick, *The Future of the North American Free Trade Agreement: A Comparative Analysis of the Role of Regional Economic Institutions and the Harmonizaton of Law in North America and Western Europe*, 19 HOUS. J. INT'L L. 1 (1996).

Free Trade Commission Clarifications Related to NAFTA Chapter 11 (July 31, 2001), available at: http://www.ustr.gov/regions/whemisphere/.

Free Trade Commission, Statement of the Free Trade Commission on Non-Disputing Party Participation, available at: http://www.ustr.gov/regions/whemisphere/nafta2003/statement-nondisputingparties.pdf.

"Full Slate of Negotiations Underway on Chile's Entry to NAFTA," *Inside U.S. Trade*, Jul. 28, 1995.

Noemi Gal-Or, *Private Party Direct Access: A Comparison of the NAFTA and the EU Disciplines*, 21 B.C. INT'L & COMP. L. REV. 1, 6–7 (1998).

Lauren E. Godshall, Student Article, In the Cold Shadow of Metalclad: The Potential for Change to NAFTA's Chapter Eleven, 11 N.Y.U. ENVTL. L.J. 264 (2002).

PIERRE MARC JOHNSON & ANDRE BEAULIEU, THE ENVIRONMENT AND NAFTA: UNDERSTANDING AND IMPLEMENTING THE NEW CONTINENTAL LAW 117–18 (Island Press, 1996).

Barton Legum, The Innovation of Investor-State Arbitration Under NAFTA, 43 HARV. INT'L L.J. 531, 538–9 (2002).

*Loewen Group v. United States*, Decision on Hearing of Respondent's Objection to Competence and Jurisdiction, paras. 25–6, 28 (NAFTA Ch. 11 Arb. Trib. Jan. 9, 2001) (discussing the tribunal's September 1999 and June 2000 orders on confidentiality).

David Lopez, *Dispute Resolution Under NAFTA: Lessons from the Early Experience*, 32 TEX. INT'L L.J. 163 (1997).

Daniel Magraw, *NAFTA & the Environment: Substance & Process*, in NAFTA & THE ENVIRONMENT: SUBSTANCE & PROCESS 1, 23 (Daniel Magraw ed., 1995).

Howard Mann, First North American Symposium on Understanding the Linkage Between Trade and the Environment: Assessing the Impact of NAFTA on Environmental Law and Management Processes 25 (2000), available at: http://www.iisd.org/pdf/2001/trade mann final.pdf.

Peter Manyasz, *Regulatory Chill of NAFTA Chapter 11 to Be Avoided in FTAA, Lawyer Warns*, 18 INT'L TRADE REP. 626 (2001).

Demetrios G. Metropoulos, *Constitutional Dimensions of the North American Free Trade Agreement*, 27 CORNELL INT'L L.J. 141, 145–6 (1994).

NAFTA Free Trade Commission, Notes of Interpretation of Certain Chapter 11 Provisions, Part B (July 31, 2001), available at: http://www.dfait-maeci.gc.ca/tna-nac/gov-en.asp.

NAFTA Implementation Act, Pub. L. No. 103–82, 401–08, 411, 107 Stat. 2057, 2129 (codified as amended at 19 U.S.C. 3431-3438, 1516a (1994)).

NAFTA claims, available at: http://www.naftalaw.org (last visited Aug. 15, 2005).

News Release, Methanex Corp., Methanex Seeks Damages Under NAFTA for California MTBE Ban (June 15, 1999), available at: http://www.methanex.com/investorcentre/newsreleases/nafta.pdf.

North American Agreement on Environmental Cooperation, Sept. 8, 9, 12, & 14, 1993, Can.-Mex.-U.S., 32 I.L.M. 1480.

North American Free Trade Agreement, Annex 1901.2, Dec. 17, 1992, U.S.-Can.-Mex., 32 I.L.M. 605 (1993).

North American Free Trade Agreement Implementation Act, Pub. L. No. 103–82, 107 Stat. 2057 (1993).

Daniel Q. Posin, *The Multi-Faceted Investment Arbitration Rules of* NAFTA, 13 World Arb. & Mediation Rep. 13, 15 (2002).

Press Release, Int'l Centre for Settlement of Investment Disputes, *United Parcel Service of American, Inc. v. Government of Canada* NAFTA/UNCITRAL Arbitration Rules Proceeding (Jul. 25, 2002).

Daniel M. Price & P. Bryan Christy, III, *An Overview of the NAFTA Investment Chapter: Substantive Rules and Investor-State Dispute Settlement*, in The North American Free Trade Agreement: A New Frontier in International Trade and Investment in the Americas 174 (Judith H. Bello et al., eds., ABA Section of International Laws, 1994).

Response of Respondent United States of America to Methanex's Submission Concerning the NAFTA Free Trade Commission's July 31, 2001 Interpretation, Oct. 26, 2001, available at: http://www.state.gov/documents/organization/6028.pdf.

Joseph A. Strazzeri, Note, *A Lucas Analysis of Regulatory Expropriations Under* NAFTA *Chapter Eleven*, 14 Geo. Int'l Envtl. L. Rev. 837, 846 (2002).

Alan C. Swan, *Case Report:* Ethyl Corporation v. Canada: *Award on Jurisdiction (Under NAFTA/UNCITRAL)*, 94 A.J.I.L. 159 (2000).

J. C. Thomas & Sergio Lopez Ayllon, NAFTA *Dispute Settlement and Mexico: Interpreting Treaties and Reconciling Common and Civil Law Systems in a Free Trade Area*, 33 Can. Y.B. Int'l L. 75 (1995).

Chris Tollefson, Metalclad v. United Mexican States *Revisited: Judicial Oversight of* NAFTA*'s Chapter Eleven Investor-State Claim Process*, 11 Minn. J. Global Trade 183, 226–7 (2002).

Uruguay Round Agreements Act, Pub. L. No. 103–465, 108 Stat. 4809 (1994).

USTR NAFTA information, available at: http://ustr.gov/Trade_Agreements/Regional/NAFTA/Section_Index.html (last visited Mar. 23, 2005).

Michael S. Valihora, NAFTA *Chapter 19 or the WTO's Dispute Settlement Body: A Hobson's Choice for Canada?*, 30 Case W. Res. J. Int'l L. 447 (1998).

Marisa Yee, *The Future of Environmental Regulation After Article 1110 of* NAFTA*: A Look at the Methanex and Metalclad Cases*, 9 Hastings W.-NW. J. Envtl. L. & Pol'y 85, 89 (2002).

Stephen Zamora, *NAFTA and the Harmonization of Domestic Legal Systems: The Side Effects of Free Trade*, 12 ARIZ. J. INT'L & COMP. L. 401, 406–08 (1995).

### *b. Australian FTA*

Exchange of Letters on Implementation of the U.S.-Australia Free Trade Agreement, available at: http://ustr.gov/Trade_Agreements/Bilateral/Australia_FTA/Implementation/Section_Index.html (last visited Aug. 15, 2005).

Final Text of the Australian FTA, available at: http://ustr.gov/assets/Trade_Agreements/Bilateral/Australia_FTA/Final_Text/asset_upload_file148_5168.pdf (last visited Aug. 15, 2005).

Transcript of U.S.-Australia FTA Signing, U.S. Trade Representative Robert B. Zoellick, May 18, 2004, available at: http://ustr.gov/assets/Document_Library/Transcripts/2004/May/asset_upload_file697_3379.pdf (last visited Aug. 15, 2005).

United States-Australia Free Trade Agreement Implementation Act, Pub. L. No. 108–286, § 2, 118 Stat. 919 (2004) Jul. 15, 2004 (to be codified at 19 U.S.C. § 3805 note).

U.S.-Australia FTA Quotes of Support, Jul. 15, 2004, available at: http://ustr.gov/Trade_Agreements/Bilateral/Australia_FTA/U.S.-Australia_FTA_Quotes_of_Support.html.

USDA Fact Sheet on the United States and Australian Free Trade Agreement, available at: http://www.fas.usda.gov/itp/Australia/us-auscommodityfactsheets.html (last visited Aug. 15, 2005).

USTR Australian FTA information, available at: http://ustr.gov/Trade_Agreements/Bilateral/Australia_FTA/Section_Index.html (last visited Aug. 15, 2005).

### *c. Andean*

Andean FTA Federal Register Notices, available at: http://ustr.gov/Trade_Agreements/Bilateral/Andean_FTA/Andean_FTA_Federal_Register_Notices/Section_Index.html (last visited Aug. 15, 2005).

Interim Environmental Review U.S.-Andean Free Trade Agreement, February 2005, available at: http://ustr.gov/assets/Trade_Agreements/Bilateral/Andean_FTA/asset_upload_file27_7305.pdf (last visited Aug. 15, 2005).

Press Release, USTR Notifies Congress of Intent to Initiate Free Trade Talks with Andean Countries. 11/18/2003. Available at: http://ustr.gov/Document_Library/Press_Releases/2003/November/USTR_Notifies_Congress_of_Intent_to_Initiate_Free_Trade_Talks_with_Andean_Countries.html (last visited Aug. 15, 2005).

Treaty with Argentina Concerning the Reciprocal Encouragement and Protection of Investment, Nov. 14, 1991, U.S.-Arg., Art. IV(1), S. Treaty Doc. No. 103–2.

USTR Andean FTA information, available at: http://ustr.gov/Trade_Agreements/Bilateral/Andean_FTA/Section_Index.html (last visited Mar. 23, 2006).

### *d. Chile*

Center for International Environmental Law, Comments on the Chile and Singapore Free Trade Agreements (2003), available at: http://www.citizenstrade.org/pdf/chile-sing_ciel.pdf (last vistited Mar. 23, 2006).

"Chile FTA Labor, Environment Measures in Doubt with Bush Administration Bilateral Negotiations – Chile and U.S. Officially Launch Negotiations on Free Trade Pact," *Inside U.S. Trade*, Dec. 15, 2000.

"Chilean Minister Presses Pre-Fast Track Bilateral U.S. Trade Talks," *Inside U.S. Trade*, Aug. 13, 1999.

Final Text of the Chile FTA, available at: http://ustr.gov/Trade_Agreements/Bilateral/Chile_FTA/Final_Texts/Section_Index.html.

James Langman, *Chilean Lawmaker Says Free Trade Accord with U.S. Unconstitutional, Plans Challenge*, 26 INT'L ENV'T REP. 1100 (2003).

Melissa Ann Miller, Note, *Will the Circle Be Unbroken? Chile's Accession to the NAFTA and the Fast-Track Debate*, 31 VAL. U. L. REV. 153, 178–9 (1996).

Press Release, Office of the United States Trade Representative, U.S. and Chile Conclude Historic Free Trade Agreement (Dec. 11, 2002).

Christopher S. Rugaber, Chile, Singapore Draft Legislation Approved by House, Senate Panels, *Daily Rep. for Executives* (BNA), July 11, 2003.

Tratado de Libre Comercio entre el Gobierno de la Republica de Chile y el Gobierno de los Estados Unidos Mexicanos, Oct. 1, 1998.

United States-Chile Free Trade Agreement Implementation Act, H.R. Rep. No. 108–224, pt. I, at 2 (2003).

USTR Chile FTA information, available at: http://ustr.gov/Trade_Agreements/Bilateral/Chile_FTA/Section_Index.html (last visited Mar. 23, 2006).

### *e. Singapore*

Center for International Environmental Law, Comments on the Chile and Singapore Free Trade Agreements (2003), available at http://www.citizenstrade.org/pdf/chile sing ciel.pdf (last visited Aug. 15, 2005).

Christopher S. Rugaber, Chile, Singapore Draft Legislation Approved by House, Senate Panels, *Daily Rep. for Executives* (BNA), July 11, 2003.

"Congress, Business Surprised by Singapore FTA Announcement," *Inside U.S. Trade*, Nov. 24, 2000.

Final Text of the Singapore FTA, available at: http://ustr.gov/Trade_Agreements/Bilateral/Singapore_FTA/Final_Texts/Section_Index.html (last visited Mar. 23, 2006).

Press Release, President Signed U.S.-Singapore Free Trade Agreement, May, 2003, available at: http://www.whitehouse.gov/news/releases/2003/05/20030506–11.html (last visited Mar. 23, 2006).

TPA and Advisor Reports for the Singapore FTA, available at: http://ustr.gov/Trade_Agreements/Bilateral/Singapore_FTA/Reports/Section_Index.html (last visited Mar. 23, 2006).

"U.S. Completes Deal with Singapore on Capital Controls, Freeing FTA," *Inside U.S. Trade*, Jan. 17, 2003.

U.S. Dept. of State, Background Note: Singapore (detailing how Singapore has acted as a beneficial trade partner and political ally to the United States), available at: http://www.state.gov/r/pa/ei/bgn/2798htm (last visited Mar. 23, 2006).

USTR Singapore FTA information, available at: http://ustr.gov/Trade_Agreements/Bilateral/Singapore_FTA/Section_Index.html (last visited Mar. 23, 2006).

*f. Free Trade Area of the Americas*

Free Trade Area of the Americas, First Summit of the Americas Declaration of Miami, December 19–21, 1994, available at: http://www.ftaa-alca.org/Summits/Miami/declara e.asp (last visited Mar. 24, 2006).

Free Trade Area of the Americas, Ministerials, available at: http://ustr.gov/Trade_Agreements/Regional/FTAA/FTAA_Ministerials/Section_Index.html (last visited Mar. 24, 2006).

Free Trade Area of the Americas, Negotiating Team, available at: http://ustr.gov/assets/Trade_Agreements/Regional/FTAA/asset_upload_file791_3678.pdf (last visited Mar. 24, 2006).

Free Trade Area of the Americas, Official Reports, available at: http://www.ftaa-alca.org/SPCOMM/COMMCS_E.ASP#pubs (last visited Mar. 24, 2006).

Free Trade Area of the Americas, Second Draft Agreement, available at: http://www.ftaa-alca.org/ftaadraft02/draft e.asp (last visited Mar. 24, 2006).

Free Trade Area of the Americas, Third Draft Agreement, available at: http://www.ftaa-alca.org/FTAADraft03/Index e.asp (last visited Mar. 24, 2006).

Opinion of the Inter-America Juridical Committee on Resolution AG/DOC. 3375/96 Freedom of Trade and Investment in the Hemisphere, OEA/ser. G/CP, doc. 2803/96, paras. 5, 6 (Aug. 23, 1996), available in 35 I.L.M. 1322 (1996).

Press Release, Office of the U.S. Trade Representative, USTR Zoellick Says Publication of Free Trade Area of the Americas (FTAA) Text Will Help Explain Trade Benefits (July, 3, 2001).

*g. Jordan*

Final Environmental Review of the Agreement on the Establishment of a Free Trade Area Between the Government of the United States and the Government of the Hashemite Kingdom of Jordan, November 18, 1999, available at: http://ustr.gov/assets/Trade_Agreements/Bilateral/Jordan/asset_upload_file64_5111.pdf (last visited Mar. 24, 2006).

Final Text of the Jordan FTA, available at: http://ustr.gov/assets/Trade_Agreements/Bilateral/Jordan/asset_upload_file250_5112.pdf (last visited Mar. 24, 2006).

USTR Jordan FTA information, available at: http://ustr.gov/Trade_Agreements/Bilateral/Jordan/Section_Index.html (last visited Mar. 24, 2006).

*h. Israel*

Background Information on the United States-Israel Free Trade Area (FTA) Agreement, available at: http://www.itds.treas.gov/us-israel.html (last visited Mar. 24, 2006).

Final Text of the Israel FTA, available at: http://www.mac.doc.gov/tcc/data/commerce_html/TCC_Documents/IsraelFreeTrade.html (last visited Mar. 24, 2006).

USTR Israel FTA information, available at: http://ustr.gov/Trade_Agreements/Bilateral/Israel/Section_Index.html (last visited Mar. 24, 2006).

### *i. Southern African Customs Union*

Letter from the USTR, USTR Notifies Congress Administration Intends to Initiate Free Trade Negotiations with Sub-Saharan Nations, 11/05/2, available at: http://ustr.gov/Document_Library/Letters_to_Congress/2002/USTR_Notifies_Congress_Administration_Intends_to_Initiate_Free_Trade_Negotiations_with_Sub-Saharan_Nations.html (last visited Mar. 24, 2006).

Letter from the USTR, USTR Notifies Congress Administration Intends to Initiate Free Trade Negotiations with Sub-Saharan Nations – House Letter, 11/05/02, available at: http://ustr.gov/Document_Library/Letters_to_Congress/2002/USTR_Notifies_Congress_Administration_Intends_to_Initiate_Free_Trade_Negotiations_with_Sub-Saharan_Nations_–_House_Letter.html (last visited Mar. 24, 2006).

Press Release, U.S. and Southern African Nations Plan for Upcoming FTA Negotiations, 1/13/03, available at: http://ustr.gov/Document_Library/Press_Releases/2003/January/U.S._Southern_African_Nations_Plan_for_Upcoming_FTA_Negotiations.html?ht= (last visited Mar. 24, 2006).

USTR Southern Africa FTA information, available at: http://ustr.gov/Trade_Agreements/Bilateral/Southern_Africa_FTA/Background_Information_on_the_U.S.-SACU_FTA.html (last visited Mar. 24, 2006).

### *j. Morocco*

Final text of the Morocco FTA, available at: http://ustr.gov/Trade_Agreements/Bilateral/Morocco_FTA/FInal_Text/Section_Index.html (last visited Mar. 24, 2006).

Informational Web site on the United States and Morocco Free Trade Agreement, available at: http://www.moroccousafta.com/index_ang.htm (last visited Mar. 24, 2006).

Press Releases for the Morocco FTA, available at: http://ustr.gov/Trade_Agreements/Bilateral/Morocco_FTA/Press_Releases/Section_Index.html (last visited Mar. 24, 2006).

Transcripts of the Morocco FTA, available at: http://ustr.gov/Trade_Agreements/Bilateral/Morocco_FTA/Transcripts/Section_Index.html (last visited Aug. 15, 2005).

United States-Morocco Free Trade Agreement Implementation Act, Pub. L. No. 108–302, 118 Stat. 1103 (2004) (to be codified at 19 U.S.C. § 3805 note).

USTR Morocco FTA information, available at: http://ustr.gov/Trade_Agreements/Bilateral/Morocco_FTA/Section_Index.html (last visited Aug. 15, 2005).

USTR Morocco FTA Quotes of Support, available at: http://ustr.gov/Trade_Agreements/Bilateral/Morocco_FTA/Morocco_FTA.html (last visited Aug. 15, 2005).

### *k. Bahrain*

USTR Bahrain FTA information, available at: http://ustr.gov/Trade_Agreements/Bilateral/Bahrain_FTA/Section_Index.html (last visited Aug. 15, 2005).

*l. Panama*

Federal Register seeking Comments on the Panama FTA Negotiations, available at: http://a257.g.akamaitech.net/7/257/2422/14mar20010800/edocket.access.gpo.gov/2004/pdf/04-3872.pdf (last visited Mar. 23, 2006).

Joint Statement by Panama and the United States on the Second Round of U.S.-Panama Free Trade Negotiations, June 11, 2004, available at: http://ustr.gov/Document_Library/Press_Releases/2004/June/Joint_Statement_by_Panama_the_United_States_on_the_Second_Round_of_U.S.-Panama_Free_Trade_Negotiations.html?ht= (last visited Mar. 24, 2006).

Press Release, U.S. and Panama to Begin FTA Negotiations on April 26, 2004, issued on 3/26/04, available at: http://ustr.gov/Document_Library/Press_Releases/2004/March/U.S._Panama_to_Begin_FTA_Negotiations_on_April_26.html (last visited Mar. 24, 2006).

USTR Panama FTA information, available at: http://ustr.gov/Trade_Agreements/Bilateral/Panama_FTA/Section_Index.html (last visited on Mar. 24, 2006).

*m. CAFTA*

CAFTA-DR Final Text, available at: http://ustr.gov/Trade_Agreements/Bilateral/CAFTA/CAFTA-DR_Final_Texts/Section_Index.html (last visited on Mar. 24, 2006).

CAFTA-DR Final Text en espanol (from El Salvador's Ministry of Economy), available at: http://www.minec.gob.sv/default.asp?id=84&mnu=70 (last visited Mar. 23, 2006).

Final Environmental Review of the Dominican Republic – Central America – United States Free Trade Agreement, available at: http://ustr.gov/assets/Trade_Agreements/Bilateral/CAFTA/asset_upload_file953_7901.pdf (last visited Mar. 24, 2006).

Statement of USTR Rob Portman on Signing of U.S.-Central American-Dominican Republic Free Trade Agreement. August 2, 2005, available at: http://ustr.gov/Document_Library/Press_Releases/2005/August/Statement_of_USTR_Rob_Portman_on_Signing_of_U.S.-Central_American-Dominican_Republic_Free_Trade_Agreement.html?ht= (last visited on Mar. 23, 2006).

USTR CAFTA information, available at: http://ustr.gov/Trade_Agreements/Bilateral/CAFTA/Section_Index.html (last visited Mar. 24, 2006).

**5. Other Countries**

Free Trade Agreement Between the Government of Canada and the Government of the Republic of Chile, Dec. 5, 1996, available at: http://www.sice.oas.org/trade/chican_e/chca07ae.asp (last visited Mar. 24, 2006).

London Court of International Arbitration (LCIA) Rules, Art. 26.6 (1998).

F. A. Mann, *British Treaties for the Promotion and Protection of Investments*, 52 Brit. Y.B. Int'l L. 241, 244 (1981).

The Treaty of Rome Establishing the European Economic Community, Mar. 25, 1957, 298 U.N.T.S. 3. Article 63 of the Brussels Convention.

***a. Relevant Case Law***

*American Coalition for Competitive Trade v. Clinton*, 128 F.3d 761, 765 (D.C. Cir. 1997) (citing 19 U.S.C. 1516a (g)(4)(A) (1994)) [Standing/Interested Party – Due Process].

*Barcelona Traction, Light & Power Co. (Belgium v. Spain)*, Second Phase, 1970 I.C.J. REP. 3 (Feb. 5) [Standing].

*Pope & Talbot, Inc. v. Canada*, Damages (May 31, 2002), 41 I.L.M. 1347 (2002) [NAFTA Chapter 11 – National Treatment/Expropriation].

*United States (L.F. Neer) v. United Mexican States* (U.S.-Mex. General Claims Comm'n Oct. 15, 1926), 4 R.I.A.A. 60, 3 ILR 213 (1927).

*Mondev Int'l Ltd. v. United States* (NAFTA Ch. 11 Arb. Trib. Oct. 11, 2002), 42 I.L.M. 85 (2003) [State Agency Statutory Immunity].

*Feldman Karpa v. United Mexican States* (NAFTA Ch. 11 Arb. Trib. Dec. 16, 2002) [Expropriation / National Treatment].

S. D. *Myers v. Canada*, Second Partial Award (NAFTA Ch. 11 Arb. Trib. Oct. 21, 2002) [Parties – Indirect Control].

*Pope & Talbot, Inc. v. Canada*, Interim Award (NAFTA Ch. 11 Arb. Trib. June 26, 2000), para. 99, 23 HASTINGS INT'L & COMP. L. REV. 455, 480 (2000), available at: http://www.dfait-maeci.gc.ca/tna-nac/NAFTA-e.asp (last visited Aug. 15, 2005).

# Index